DEVELOPING SKILLS FOR BUSINESS LEADERSHIP

Edited by Gillian Watson and Stefanie C. Reissner

The Chartered Institute of Personnel and Development is the leading publisher of books and reports for personnel and training professionals, students, and all those concerned with the effective management and development of people at work. For details of all our titles, please contact the publishing department:

tel: 020-8612 6204

e-mail publish@cipd.co.uk

The catalogue of all CIPD titles can be viewed on the CIPD website:

www.cipd.co.uk/bookstore

DEVELOPING SKILLS FOR BUSINESS LEADERSHIP

Edited by Gillian Watson and Stefanie C. Reissner

Chartered Institute for Personnel and Development

Published by the Chartered Institute of Personnel and Development,
151, The Broadway, London, SW19 1JQ

First published 2010

Typeset by Curran Publishing Services
Printed and bound in Malta b y Gutenberg Press Ltd

British Library Cataloguing in Publication Data
A catalogue of this publication is available from the British Library

ISBN 9781843982609

Chartered Institute of Personnel and Development, CIPD House,

151, The Broadway, London, SW19 1JQ

Tel: 020 8612 6200

E-mail: cipd@cipd.co.uk

Website: www.cipd.co.uk

Incorporated by Royal Charter. Registered Charity No. 1079797.

Summary table of contents

Detailed table of contents

Figures

Tables

Activities

Case studies

Author biographies

Gillian Watson is currently a principal lecturer in the Faculty of Business and Law at the University of Sunderland, responsible for partnerships and recruitment and also Chair of the Applied Management, FdA and HND Board. Her previous role was as Chair of the PG Board in the faculty, where she led several key initiatives to enhance the learning experience for postgraduate students. Her current role allows her to foster co-operation and share good practice with the faculty's partner institutions. She has co-authored *Managing for results* for CIPD with Kevin Gallagher.

Stefanie C. Reissner is a senior lecturer at Sunderland Business School. She conducted her doctoral research, a cross-cultural study of organisational change and learning, at the University of Durham and has received ESRC funding for her current project on managerial storytelling. Stefanie has a keen interest in helping people to learn – both in a university context and through advanced development methods like coaching; this is reflected in her recently completed studies for an MA in teaching and learning in higher education and an MA in coaching for organisational excellence. She teaches mainly at research methods postgraduate level.

Ivana Adamson built her academic career on her background as a manager in industry. She taught management, entrepreneurship and strategy at British universities and abroad. Her research interests and her PhD research were on evaluating the effectiveness of management consultants in SMEs. She is currently a freelance management consultant and corporate trainer.

Mike Ashwell, BSc (Hons), FCMA, FHEA, is a senior lecturer in accounting at Teesside University Business School. Mike's wide experience prior to joining the university encompassed varied roles within the finance profession, as a management accountant, finance manager, and systems implementation manager in a number of organisations, including major multinationals. He currently teaches on a range of courses, from first-year undergraduate to MBA levels, and delivers introductory finance sessions for non-finance staff from local organisations. His key research area is the role of business simulation activities in the enhancement of overall business awareness and knowledge.

Julie Beardwell, BA, MA, is Head of Corporate Development at Leicester Business School, De Montfort University. She is also currently the Chief Standards Moderator for the Chartered Institute of Personnel and Development. Julie is joint editor with Tim Claydon of *HRM: a contemporary approach*, now in its sixth edition, and has also contributed to other textbooks on HRM and HRD. Her current interests include talent management and management development.

Jeffrey Evans is a senior lecturer at the Business School of the University of Sunderland and teaches quantitative and statistical analysis. His professional interests include decision analysis and research into company insolvency (currently using Bayesian statistical techniques).

Kevin Gallagher is a senior lecturer at Sunderland Business School. After graduation Kevin worked on civil engineering projects both in the UK and overseas. Developing his qualifications in management he then changed career direction, taking a business development manager's role in a major UK paper company. Further part-time study followed which enabled him to successfully apply to teach management at the University of Sunderland. Kevin has since been a teaching fellow at the university and is the author of a number of management and skills textbooks, including co-authorship with Gillian Watson on a previous CIPD textbook *Managing for results*.

Donglin Pei, BSc, MBA, PhD, is a senior lecturer in accounting in the Faculty of Business and Law, University of Sunderland. His research focuses on market efficiency theory with particular emphasis on how investors respond to stock market announcements. Donglin has been teaching accounting and financial management at both undergraduate and postgraduate level on courses such as international financial reporting and financial management for the last seven years.

Gail Sanders is Principal Lecturer responsible for learning and teaching development at Sunderland Business School. She has a special interest in work-based and professional learning, and for many years has been involved in the development and delivery of work-based learning programmes for her institution, including most recently the professional doctorate. Other recent work has included leading a university-wide project on research-informed teaching, and the development of a professional identity model to support the Business School's vision of graduates for the twenty-first century.

Sue Stirk is currently Associate Dean (Recruitment and Development) in the Faculty of Business and Law at the University of Sunderland. Prior to this she was a principal lecturer in computing where she taught information systems, databases and security engineering amongst other things. She is the co-author of a number of journal articles and conference papers in the database field. Sue has previously worked as a systems analyst and programmer in both the public and private sectors for a number of years.

Fred A. Yamoah is an academic, a management consultant and public speaker. Fred holds a BSc, Dip.Ed, PgDMS, MBA and DBA. He has extensive experience in management practice and consultancy, decision-making, team facilitation and problem-solving through performing-leading and team membership roles within corporate and academic institutions, committees and boards in Britain and Ghana. Fred has addressed issues such as strategic management and decision-making, personal development, and presentational skills at various conferences, including the postgraduate conference at Sunderland Business School, UK, in 2006. He was a select committee member for the Ford Foundation's International Fellowships Programme (IFP) for West Africa 2008.

Permissions and acknowledgements

This book has been a truly collective endeavour and the editors wish to thank:

- All contributors, without whose expertise and hard work this book would not have been possible. Special thanks to those contributors who agreed to come on board at a very late stage and whose efforts in making this book a reality have been tremendous.

- The following companies and individuals for giving their help, support, time and information:

  - Barrie Watson, member of Belbin Associates and Managing Director of CERT Consultancy and Training (www.belbin.com and www.belbin.info).

  - Belbin Associates for use of Belbin materials (www.belbin.com and www.belbin.info).

  - Craig Smith, consultant at Flint Consulting, for allowing us insights into his exciting work, resulting in the Case Study 'Leading bold change™'.

  - Paul Andrew, Debbee Forster, Andrew Hambler and Gabi Greiner for supplying us with case studies and raw materials for original case studies.

  - Diane Klose for permission to use the sample assignment 'HR in Russia'.

- The anonymous reviewers who helped us to improve earlier versions of this book. Special thanks to other colleagues who have helped us out with informal reviews, including Candice Watson, Andrew Hambler, Ian Carr and Seema Bhate.

- Andrea Barber, who helped us to format, organise and manage the manuscript – a very special thank you to you.

- All at CIPD Publishing for their support throughout this endeavour, particularly Kirsty Smy and Ruth Anderson.

- Our long-suffering families for their patience and support.

We also wish to thank for the following individuals, organisations and publishers for giving us their kind permission to use their material as acknowledged in the text where appropriate. Among these, we would like to express our particular gratitude to:

- The CIPD for extracts from *People Management*, materials from their website and case studies from their case studies club as well as materials from other publications.

- Barrie Watson, member of Belbin Associates and Managing Director of CERT Consultancy and Training (www.belbin.com and www.belbin.info).

- Belbin Associates for use of Belbin materials (www.belbin.com and www.belbin.info).

- McGraw-Hill for permission to reproduce Figure 7.3, the Johari Window, from J. Luft (1984), *Group process: an introduction to group dynamics*, 3rd edn., Fig. 7.4, p60. Palo Alto, CA: Mayfield.

- Fenman Ltd for permission to use material adapted from material originally published in *Training Journal*.

- ACCA for permission to use material from the official study text on *Financial reporting*.

- Peter Cook, Managing Director Human Dynamics for permission to reproduce material from his books *Best practice creativity* and *Sex, leadership and rock'n'roll* (Box 14.1, page 427, reproduced by permission of Crown House Publishing Ltd). .

- Harper and Row for permission to reproduce material from Edward De Bono's book *Lateral thinking*.

- Penguin for permission to reproduce material from Edward De Bono's book *Six thinking hats*.

- Educational Publishers Ltd for permission to reproduce material from Tony Buzan's *Mind map* book.

- Debbee Forster and Susan Doyle (Area HRD Manager) Intercontinental Hotels Group for case study material.

- Oxford University Press for permission to reproduce material from Murray and Richardson's book *Organisational change in 100 days*.

- Kogan Page for permission to reproduce material from Cameron and Green's book *Making sense of change management*.

- Craig Smith, consultant at Flint Consulting for case study material.

Walkthrough of textbook features and online resources

OVERVIEWS

Brief chapter overviews outline the focus and aims of each chapter.

LEARNING OUTCOMES

By the end of this chapter, provided you engage with the activities, you should be able to:

- understand the characteristics and techniques of effective writing
- apply critical thinking skills to the writing of reports, essays, reviews, projects and dissertations
- reference other authors' work correctly

LEARNING OUTCOMES

At the beginning of each chapter, a set of learning outcomes summarises what you can expect to learn from the chapter, helping you to track your progress.

ACTIVITY 3.2

WRITING A PROPOSAL

Take any task – for instance a project or dissertation topic, an assignment brief or a project brief from work – and identify the key stages and elements. Map out what needs to be done at the different stages, what support you will need and how long you will need to complete each of them. You may also want to refer to Chapter 5 of this book for other skills that will help you in this process.

ACTIVITIES

Designed to support your learning, a number of activities in each chapter require you to identify, analyse and reflect on particular issues, skills or management practice.

TONY

CASE STUDY 4.1

Tony had spent nine years in the army, the only job he had done since leaving school at the age of 16. Although he loved the job and was proud that he had done well, he decided to leave because he had a young family and no longer wanted to spend long periods away from them. He had gained a lot of experience and developed many skills in his army career so he felt fairly confident of securing a good job in civilian life. However, this proved to be more difficult than he expected, and after many months of searching he eventually found a position as a supervisor of a production line in a food processing factory, which was rather less than he had been hoping

discussing and sharing their experiences and interpretation of the theory. This was not what he expected at all. He did not consider his fellow students to be sufficiently expert to be able to offer him the right answers. Despite his misgivings Tony attended all classes and group discussion sessions, but he rarely spoke up and contributed. He managed to pass all of the assignments he was given, but achieved poor marks, the feedback indicating that his work was too descriptive and insufficiently analytical.

Six months after joining his degree programme Tony was at work late one

CASE STUDIES

A range of case studies illustrate important skills, so that you can practice them in a real-life context and gain second-hand experience about a management situation.

3.6 CONCLUSION

The essential skill of writing may be an art, but there are rules that you can learn and follow to improve your writing for assignments and examinations. Effective writing is effective communication of your skills and knowledge, and professional writers have a box of tools from which you can benefit for your postgraduate study, your continuing professional development and overall career. You may wonder how you can find the time to learn the tricks of the writer's trade and practise your writing, but doing so may make more efficient use of your precious

CONCLUSIONS

At the end of each chapter, we draw conclusions from the issues raised in the chapter.

KEY LEARNING POINTS

- Recognise and manage the stages in team development.
- Harness the techniques of team development and evaluate which method suits a particular situation.
- Take an enlightened view of team roles and an individual's self-worth within the team.
- Be sensitive to the nuances of co-ordinating a virtual team successfully.
- Having developed a deeper knowledge and understanding of the vital role communication has when building a team show the skills necessary to give quality feedback and reflect on the outcome.

KEY LEARNING POINTS

Bulleted lists of key learning points are designed to consolidate your learning and pull out key points for you to remember.

PAUSE FOR THOUGHT

Identify at least three things that you have learned by studying this chapter and engaging with the activities. How will your newly acquired knowledge and skills support your continuing professional development? What value do you expect your learning to have for your daily routines and your further career? In what area have you identified a need for further development and how are you planning to fill that gap? Address these issues in your learning journal and/or CPD log. You may also wish to discuss them with a peer, colleague, mentor or coach to aid your further development.

PAUSE FOR THOUGHT

The reflective questions in these sections are designed to get you thinking about what you have learnt and how you can apply your learning in practice.

Belbin Associates: http://www.belbin.com or http://www.belbin.info [accessed 30 May2010].

BELBIN, R.M. (2007) *Management teams: why they succeed or fail*. London: Elsevier Butterworth Heinemann.

CANNALL, M. (2009) *CIPD Fact sheet: team working*. Revised August 2009. London: CIPD.

STRACHAN, A. (2004) Lights, camera, interaction. *People Management Magazine*. 16 September, p44. Available online at: http://www.peoplemanagement.co.uk/pm/articles/2004/09/LightsCameraInteraction.htm [accessed 26 May 2010].

STEVENS, M. (2010) Public sector 'intellectually but not emotionally engaged'. *People Management*, 26 January. Available online at: http://www.peoplemanagement.co.uk/pm/ar ticles/2010/01/public-sector-intellectually-but-not-emotionally-engaged.htm [accessed 26 May 2010].

EXPLORE FURTHER

Explore further boxes contain suggestions for further reading and useful websites, encouraging you to delve further into areas of particular interest.

ONLINE RESOURCES FOR STUDENTS

- Examples of reflective practice and log book development
- Video clips illustrating good and poor practice

Visit **www.cipd.co.uk/sss**

ONLINE RESOURCES FOR TUTORS

- Lecturer's Guide – including tools to help tutors carry out assessment
- PowerPoint slides – ready-made lectures linking to each chapter
- Longer activities – these can be used in a workshop context

Visit **www.cipd.co.uk/tss**

Developing Skills for Business Leadership

The content of this CIPD module is covered as follows:

Developing Skills for Business Leadership learning outcome	*Developing Skills for Business Leadership* chapters
Understand, analyse and critically evaluate:	
1 Manage themselves more effectively at work or in another professional context.	Chapter 4: Developing your professional identity Chapter 5: Concepts of self and self management skills
2 Manage interpersonal relationships at work more effectively.	Chapter 6: Effective team-building and communication Chapter 7: Negotiating and liaising within the political organisation
3 Make sound and justifiable decisions and solve problems more effectively.	Chapter 14: Decision-making and problem-solving at the workplace Chapter 15: Decision-making and problem-solving in practice
4 Lead and influence others more effectively.	Chapter 16: Leadership and team dynamics Chapter 17: Leading change and development in organisations
5 Interpret financial information and manage financial resources.	Chapter 10: Interpreting financial information Chapter 11: Managing financial resources
6 Demonstrate enhanced IT proficiency.	Chapter 12: Handling statistical data using IT Chapter 13: Integrated IT skills
7 Demonstrate an essential people management skill-set.	Chapter 8: Interviewing and managing performance Chapter 9: Effective training
8 Demonstrate competence in postgraduate study skills.	Chapter 2: Essential postgraduate study skills Chapter 3: Practical aspects of postgraduate study skills

PART 1
Introduction

CHAPTER 1

Skills for continuing professional development and practice

Stefanie C. Reissner *and* Gillian Watson

1.1 INTRODUCTION

Knowledge, skills and continuing professional development are at the top of the twenty-first-century human resources agenda. Skills are 'the capabilities and expertise in a particular occupation or activity' (Leitch Review of Skills 2006, p6) which enhance a person's employability and contribute significantly to business success, national prosperity and personal fulfilment (DFES 2003, 2005). Managers across the globe are increasingly required to demonstrate in what way they make a difference to their organisation's operations through their knowledge and skills (Routledge and Carmichael 2007), particularly in managing complex projects. The focus is on transferable skills, ie on skills that are required for a wide variety of roles regardless of the organisation and industry in which they are being employed (Bennett 2002). Such transferable skills include the ability to manage oneself and others effectively at the workplace, to analyse and resolve problems, to negotiate, lead and manage change (Rankin 2003). They need to be continually developed in line with advances in knowledge, training and learning to equip managers with everything that they need to make a difference at the workplace (Routledge and Carmichael 2007).

This is where continuing professional development (CPD) comes in, which is fruitfully defined as 'the maintenance and enhancement of the knowledge, expertise and competence of professionals throughout their careers according to a plan formulated with regard to the needs of the professional, the employer, the profession and society' (Madden and Mitchell as cited in Jones and Fear 1994, p50). It involves 'a combination of approaches, ideas and techniques' that will enable professionals to manage their learning, growth and development (CIPD 2010a), and it includes training, learning, mentoring, coaching, networking and reflective practice.

Building and developing skills is a joint effort between employers and employees, and other stakeholders like government, employer organisations, professional bodies and education institutions also have a role in this process (Leitch Review of Skills 2006). Skill-building is a lifelong effort in which professionals are required to demonstrate that they keep on top of their knowledge and skills through a wide range of CPD measures, and that they apply any newly acquired knowledge and skills into their daily routines for the benefit of the organisation (CIPD 2007a). This book has been compiled in response to these vital issues. This chapter consists of two sections. Section 1, which follows this introduction, outlines the rationale, approach and structure of this book as it seeks to support your skill-building and continuing professional development. Section 2 expands on many of the issues raised in the introduction and in Section 1, focusing on the skills required for continuing professional development in an increasingly diverse work environment. It discusses issues pertinent to the debate about skill-building and continuing professional development from both an individual and an organisational perspective, such as competence, diversity, career development, succession planning, talent management and human capital.

SECTION 1: RATIONALE, PHILOSOPHY AND APPROACH OF THIS BOOK

1.2 WHY WE WROTE THIS BOOK: WHAT YOU NEED TO KNOW

As university lecturers, we have experienced the importance of skills in three key areas. Firstly, the British government has made universities one pillar of their skill-building agenda (Leitch Review of Skills 2006), and there is increasing pressure to make skill-building more explicit in the curriculum, which comes also from employers (Bennett 2002). Hence, we are encouraged to reflect on the provision of skill-building measures and identify new opportunities to help our students to build new skills and to hone existing ones. While some explicit skill-building will be integrated in existing modules, new specialist skills modules are being developed to meet the need for systematic and focused skill-building.

Secondly, employers are increasingly looking for staff – both graduate and postgraduate – who can think independently, analyse and evaluate complex situations, and resolve challenging problems (Targett 1995). An increasing number of employers expect potential applicants to master these skills prior to employment (Bennett 2002). As university lecturers we are required to provide our students with the opportunities to build these skills and to hone them as part of their studies so as to allow them to 'hit the ground running' after graduation. This also includes creating an awareness of the skills that they possess and the ability to identify any skills gaps as well as any development measures to fill such gaps.

Thirdly and most importantly, as university lecturers we work with you, the student, on a daily basis and know how much easier studying becomes with the right skills. All the ambition and hard work of this world will only get you so far if you do not possess the right skills to study and work smartly. It may be useful to think of skills as tools which, if applied correctly, will make any task much easier. The trick, it seems, is to help you to learn how to learn, which will allow you to adapt to constantly changing circumstances in a rapidly changing world (Rawson 2000). The key to this is to become aware of the skills that you already possess and those that you need to build or hone so that you can employ them more effectively in your daily work and to change and adapt as required.

As university lecturers we are also aware that skill-building is often regarded by students as an add-on to a programme of study, particularly at present, when skill-building has become more explicit. Many of you will wonder when you will have the time to engage in skill-building with other commitments that you may be juggling. These concerns are very valid, with many of you having to work whilst studying (or study whilst working) and many of you will also have family and other commitments competing for your time. However, skill-building has always been an essential part of higher education and students have always built and honed skills as part of their studies, albeit often unawares. In twenty-first-century education, skill-building has become more prominent over subject knowledge, and skill-building initiatives – whether as part of a module or a specialist skills module – are designed to complement your studies and to help you to study and work smarter. We therefore regard it as essential that you engage with any skill-building initiative that is part of your programme of study to become smarter students and more competent professionals. Skill-building does not end with your time at university as there is increasing emphasis on work-based learning and employer training as well as continuing professional development (DIUS 2008). CPD is designed to help professionals to stay in touch with the latest developments in their profession, and it is your chance to hone the skills that you will have built at university and at the workplace and to develop as an individual and professional. A positive correlation between the level of skills that a professional possesses and their employability in higher positions has already been established (DFES 2005; DIUS 2007b), so if you are striving up the career ladder, you had better start building and honing the skills that you need. This book is designed to help you on your journey.

The objective of this book is to help postgraduate students and those studying for continuing professional development to develop and hone skills that are essential for the management of their talent and the progression of their career. It covers skills that are regarded as vital for human resource professionals, such as communication, teamworking, information technology (IT) and organisation (see Bennett 2002) as well as self-management, people management, training, financial, decision-making and problem-solving, leadership, change management and postgraduate study skills. However, it seeks to go beyond mere skill-building and to help you to integrate any newly developed skills into your work and career, which we regard as vital at postgraduate level and beyond. This is done through reflection, which is an integral part of experiential learning (Mezirow 1991), sensemaking (Weick 1995) and competent practice (Schön 1983). Reflective learning comes naturally to some of you (even though you may not be aware of it), whereas it is more difficult for others. However, reflective learning has proven an effective means of learning and continuing professional development, and we encourage you to give it a go with the numerous reflective activities provided throughout this book.

This book is rooted in the Anglo-Saxon tradition of business, management, leadership and education, and is targeted at individuals and groups studying in such a context. We have used many elements of the content and processes on which this book draws successfully with diverse and multicultural student groups in human-resource-specific and more generic postgraduate programmes. Despite initial scepticism, the vast majority of our students have found them invaluable for their studies and further career development. If this book is adopted in a different cultural and educational context, lecturers and other teaching staff are encouraged to explore with their students how they can adapt the skills, theories and models presented in this book to their respective context. We put particular emphasis on reflective and experiential learning, as in our experience skill-building as such is not enough. For best results, students and professionals alike must identify how newly developed skills can be applied in their daily routines and how they can foster a future career path. Hence, many of the activities in this book require students to reflect on their learning as well as their professional practice, and we appreciate that to some students this may be both unfamiliar and at first glance ineffective. However, we encourage all of you to give it a try to make most of your learning with this book.

1.3 STRUCTURE AND CONTENT OF THIS BOOK

This book consists of 18 chapters in 10 parts. With the exception of Part 1 and Part 10, there are two chapters in each part which relate to a particular theme. You may find that the approach and style adopted in some chapters differ considerably from the approach and style adopted in others, as the conventions in different disciplines vary. We hope that this variety of approaches and styles will enrich your learning experience with this book rather than hamper it. In particular, this book covers the themes outlined below.

Part 2 focuses on postgraduate study skills to support your studies. It will give you insights into what is expected from students at postgraduate level and beyond, and it will provide you with useful tips and tricks to help you to study smarter. Chapter 2 is designed to help you to hone skills like critical thinking, critical reading and critical writing, which you may have built up in your undergraduate studies or at the workplace. It provides background information as well as activities and practical advice. Chapter 3 focuses on conventions of academic writing (including referencing), effective writing practice and effective exam preparation. This part seeks to make explicit some of the expectations that your tutors may have but never spell out. This is particularly important if you have not studied formally for some time or if you are unfamiliar with the Anglo-Saxon university system. We recommend that you study this part before any of the others as the skills covered here will help you with your studies and beyond.

Part 3 focuses on concepts of self and self-management, including self-awareness, professionalism, time and stress management as well as organising skills. Chapter 4 introduces the notion of professional identity that integrates expert knowledge, skills and professional behaviours. The approach taken in this chapter, which has proven successful with many of our students, encourages you to reflect on your personality, values, emotions and norms, and the way they affect your behaviour at work as well as your professional success. Chapter 5 creates a contemporary view of time management, procrastination, personal organisation skills and managing stress. Its reflective approach will allow you to identify your constructive and also your less helpful behaviours in your daily routine so that you can address them if you wish. The techniques discussed in this chapter will also help you to manage yourself and your career more effectively and to keep stress to a healthy level.

Part 4 focuses on the management of interpersonal relationships at work, including teambuilding, communication, negotiation and the management of conflict. Chapter 6 introduces you to the theory and practice of effective teambuilding and communication within teams. It discusses different types of teams and different team roles to aid your analysis at the workplace. You are encouraged in the various activities to analyse and reflect upon your own experiences as a team player and perhaps also leader. Chapter 7 focuses on the political nature of organisations, particularly the role of power in liaising and negotiating within and outside an organisation. It seeks to make you more aware of political forces within organisations and the different ways in which power is played out in interaction between individuals, teams and organisations. It also discusses different forms of negotiation and identifies situations when they may be most appropriate. You are introduced to different types of power and invited to identify which types of power you have in different situations at the workplace.

Part 5 focuses on people management, including interviewing, performance management and training. Chapter 8 introduces different types of interviews commonly used by HR professionals and their use in managing employee performance. It identifies the core interviewing skills that can maximise the effectiveness of an interview and discusses different types of questions commonly used in different types of interviews. Various activities encourage you to engage critically with interviewing practice and to discover new ways of approaching interviews in a HR context. Chapter 9 focuses on training, which continues to have a vital role in staff and continuing professional development. It discusses the current context in which training, learning and staff development are taking place, identifying opportunities and constraints. This chapter examines in more detail the different roles a learning professional or trainer can take, and the skills required for each role.

Part 6 focuses on financial issues, including the interpretation of basic financial information and the management of financial resources. Chapter 10 emphasises corporate governance and financial statements, arguing the case for solid corporate governance procedures and introducing agency theory and creative accounting, as well as the regulatory framework of international financial reporting. It also discusses how financial statements, particularly balance sheets and income statements, are presented and interpreted. Detailed case examples show the mathematics behind the statements and make financial information straightforward to understand. Chapter 11 examines the role of financial information in decision-making and business performance. It discusses in detail the business plan and its role and content, followed by an introduction to budgets. This chapter also considers different types of cost (including calculation of the break-even point), cash management, performance monitoring, environmental accounting and the evaluation of capital expenditure. In addition, it considers the key attributes of management accountants and other professionals involved in the management of financial resources.

Part 7 focuses on information technology (IT), particularly the handling of statistical data and IT systems. Chapter 12 introduces statistical analysis to non-specialists with emphasis on frequency distribution, hypothesis testing, correlation and regression. Reference is made to several statistical software packages and detailed workings of statistical analysis in Microsoft Excel are provided. This chapter contains activities and case studies to allow you to practise your analytical and statistical skills. Chapter 13 focuses on the integrated nature of IT skills. It discusses in detail the benefits and potential risks associated with the use of information technology for private, professional and developmental purposes. A series of reflective activities will allow you to become more aware of your use of information technology in your private and professional life and to identify any development issues. This chapter also considers how information technology can support training, learning and development in organisations. It discusses how the IT requirements of an organisation can be analysed and by whom, and how the human resources function in particular can benefit from IT systems.

Part 8 focuses on decision-making and problem-solving, including evidence-based, ethical, creative and team-based approaches as well as finding and evaluating appropriate evidence. Chapter 14 introduces you to a range of techniques that can support managers' creative decision-making and problem-solving. It focuses on techniques that can help managers to look at a decision or problem from different perspectives and that can lead to new and potentially fruitful solutions. It also considers the role of groups in the decision-making and problem-solving process as well as ethical issues, and discusses how decisions can be fruitfully communicated to others. Chapter 15 contains a series of case studies that relate to more than one chapter of this book, giving you a prime opportunity to employ your newly acquired knowledge and practise your newly gained skills in a safe environment. The case studies have been specifically written for this book and cover a range of issues that not only feature in this book but in contemporary managerial practice. They are about real organisations and real people, although the names of some of them have been disguised to respect their anonymity.

Part 9 focuses on issues of leadership and change, including supervision, delegation and conflict resolution as well as managing change, coaching and consultancy. Chapter 16 focuses on leadership in a team environment, looking at different leadership theories and how they have evolved over time. There are activities that encourage you to decide how you would react in a particular situation and to reflect on your own style of leadership. Chapter 17 introduces you to theories of organisational change and to a wide range of skills that are required to manage organisational change successfully. It also discusses consulting and coaching as means to facilitate organisational change in the context of increasing competitive pressures and a need to develop staff.

Part 10 brings together the themes and skills discussed throughout this book. Chapter 18 consists of two sections. Section 1 focuses on project management and discusses in detail the different phases in a project, along with stakeholders, organisational structure, project control, project team, learning, training and change. It explores these issues through a case study that illustrates how transferable and interpersonal skills can be applied in the context of a project. Section 2 draws a close to this book with its emphasis on talent management, career enhancement and continuing professional development. We invite you to reflect upon how you will continue your journey of professional development and career enhancement.

Each chapter contains specifically designed activities to support your learning, many of which require you to identify, analyse and reflect on a particular issue, skill or management practice. Most chapters also include case studies to illustrate a particular skill, to give you the opportunity to practise a particular skill in a real-life context and to gain second-hand experience about a management situation. There is much more material – case studies, readings, activities, guides – on the companion website, so please do follow up any links in the respective chapters. Towards the end of each chapter you will find a section called 'Pause for thought', in which you are invited to identify your learning and to reflect on how you can include it in your daily practice in true CPD style (for details, please refer to Section 1.6 below). You will find that some of the key skills, such as communication, teamwork, leadership and change management skills, feature in more than one chapter and we encourage you to explore them in more detail as you go along, alone or with your peers.

SECTION 2: SKILLS FOR CONTINUING PROFESSIONAL DEVELOPMENT

1.4 CONTINUING SKILLS DEVELOPMENT

Research indicates that building and developing skills – whether transferable or specific to an industry or organisation – remains underdeveloped in many organisations because managers themselves lack vital interpersonal, people-management and leadership skills to deal effectively with the increasing pressures in their daily routines (CIPD 2010b). This suggests a need for the development of managers in the first instance so that they can support the continuing professional development of their subordinates by providing appropriate opportunities for their development (Grugulis 2003). Skill-building has therefore become a vital element of managerial training, including postgraduate qualifications and other continuing professional development measures. Effective support of learning, training and development in organisations, which includes a focused and continuing development of skills, depends on the three factors (CIPD 2008a) graphically represented in Figure 1.1 below.

Figure 1.1 suggests that it is not enough for managers to develop particular skills: they need to integrate their knowledge and skills with a wider understanding of their identity as professionals as well as their roles and relationships at work. While training initiatives, mentoring and coaching will help managers to develop

Figure 1.1 Continuing skills development

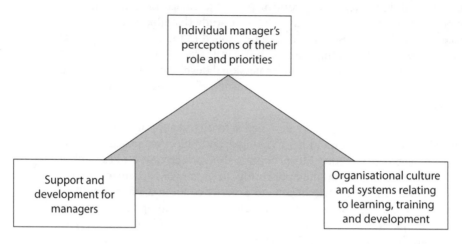

Source: adapted from CIPD (2008), *Diversity: an overview*, p5.

and hone their skills, they need to engage in continuous reflective practice to make these skills part of their daily routines in order to make a difference to their immediate team and wider organisation. Any learning, training and development must also be seen in the context in which an organisation operates, including its culture and any systems that support or hinder the professional development of managers and staff, such as opportunities for networking and knowledge sharing. Hence, there is no 'one-size-fits-all' approach to skill-building and continuing professional development. Critical thinking, analysis and reflective practice can help managers to determine the approach that is right for their organisation. This organisation may be a culturally diverse place, so let us now consider how different learning and cultural traditions can impact on working or learning together.

1.5 DIFFERING LEARNING AND CULTURAL TRADITIONS

Business, trade and education are becoming increasingly culturally diverse, bringing together people from different learning and cultural traditions. Hence, we must consider the cultural diversity of our fellow students and work colleagues, who may be from many different nationalities and a wide array of cultural backgrounds. In other words, they amount to a mix of cultures common in a globalised (Hall 1992) business community. Indeed, managing and leading a diverse workforce is becoming more the norm than a rarity, and therefore learning to work together and to embrace cultural diversity is of great consequence to individuals and organisations.

Browaeys and Price (2008, p9) suggest that 'culture is a structure that gives form to behaviour and fixes the framework of exchange between the people of this group ... [through] adaption, integration, communication and expression.' It is therefore a way of organising a group, such as work colleagues or fellow learners on a programme of study. In many instances such a group is not homogeneous but very diverse, as individuals from different nationalities are brought together by working for the same organisation or by enrolling on the same programme of study. Consequently, working and learning together can be difficult and at times confusing for those involved. There are new rules to master and stereotypic assumptions to cast aside, but there is also the opportunity to communicate and express your identity and the prospect of forming a coherent working or learning alliance.

But again it is culture that forms these alliances and enables them to function. Schein (2004, p14) defines culture as: 'a set of basic assumptions – shared solutions to universal problems of external adaption (how to survive) and internal integration (how to stay together) – which have evolved over time and are handed down from one generation to the next'. Hence, the prospect of survival and staying together as a group is a form of enlightened self-interest in which working and learning together for common goals are the foundation, particularly in organisations with an international focus.

From a learning perspective, there are many factors hidden under the surface (DFES 2007b) that are not always immediately recognisable to those familiar with the system. The system of learning and educating in Britain, for instance in university education, differs significantly from other systems, particularly in some Asian, African and Middle Eastern countries. Individuals from other countries often face a number of barriers, ranging from language difficulties to reticence to enter into discussion or a reluctance to deal with conflict. However, this creates challenges for the learning group, particularly as in the learner-centred view adopted in British higher education group members need to interact with each other as active and engaged learners. Many educational environments would advocate diversity as instilling respect for all (Leicester 1996), which can be seen as promoting difference. This, in turn, includes being a member of a group that has a mix of ethnicities and/or genders. The authors of this edited book reflect this concept of diversity with their gender mix of five women and six men whose ethnic backgrounds include British, German, Irish, African, Czech and Chinese. Acknowledging and exploring cultural difference is therefore essential as we continue to learn and work in multicultural groups at universities and at the workplace. The following case study from our own experience of teaching multicultural postgraduate student groups seeks to illuminate some cultural misunderstandings as it offers elements for debate that encourage us to understand those under the surface issues.

Engaging in discussion about diversity or difference can mitigate disadvantage and discrimination. As a learner/individual involved in such a debate you might also opt to consider the following.

EVERYONE'S ENTITLED TO AN OPINION

CASE STUDY 1.1

The subjects of this case study are a group of students new to the university (which is located in the north of England) studying on a postgraduate programme in international management. The cohort group consists of 20 students with 11 different nationalities and a plethora of religious backgrounds and cultures. They had undergone development in appreciating each others' cultures, which included food, religion, cultural dress, tolerance of different societal norms and so on. This had all helped to encourage camaraderie and sense of working together for a common goal. The students had been tasked to complete a project in set groups of five. This type of cultural inclusivity as a learning process had worked very well in previous years.

A new student arrived who joined one of the established groups. This particular group, now six, was made up of two British women (Jennifer and Sylvia), one Canadian male (John), two Chinese – one man and one woman (Tie and Ping), the newcomer was male and came from the United Arab Emirates (Ali).

Not long after the introduction Ali announced to the group how he liked all things American and intended to go and live there one day. John offered a view of the United States from his perspective, which included the advantages and disadvantages of having a porous border and a powerful neighbour. Ping identified Canada as a great place to live as some of her relatives had moved to Toronto and really liked it. Ali was somewhat dismissive and reacted as if he was being challenged, and disagreement grew. Tie had said he should not speak to Ping in such a way. The tutor responded immediately, realising that there was some tension. He sat with the group for about 10 minutes, calming down the confused Ping and the equally confused Ali. The tutor reminded them that

everyone was entitled to an opinion.

The next day the students were to continue developing their project and had arranged to meet in the coffee bar. Previously the group had split the task up into several parts so that the accumulated research could be analysed and evaluated when the group re-convened the following Monday.

Jennifer asked Ali if he wouldn't mind researching a particular topic over the weekend as he had not contributed to the project thus far. It was the last piece of work before the report writing commenced. Ali declined, saying he was going out to a restaurant at the weekend with his uncle. Sylvia, somewhat annoyed, said: 'Well I'm going to the "Bigg Market" with some friends but it doesn't stop me doing my work for Uni.' She continued 'Why should we do your work for you "flash-Harry"?' She was referring to Ali's two-carat diamond earring, designer clothes and the like. Some cultural issues like the Bigg Market (an area in Newcastle upon Tyne noted for having several bars, restaurants and similar establishments) and 'flash Harry' (flaunting your possessions) had been explained, and the fact that Ali's uncle lived in London had to be clarified. Again, Ali reacted to the challenge with the view that women should not drink liquor and go out at night on their own. The two British women attacked him verbally in a way that he had not encountered. He was shocked and upset saying that he was only thinking of their safety. Jennifer and Sylvia were furious at being told what they should and should not do. Ping and Tie thought the atmosphere was bad and said they were going to ask the tutor if they could move to another group as they did not want to fail in the project assignment. John tried to calm them all down and started taking some control of the situation.

Questions

1. Consider the cultural issues from each participant's perspective.

2. If you were John what would you do now?

3. Should the tutor have seen this coming?

4. What role should the tutor take in this scenario?

5. What social and cultural issues can you identify from this case?

6. What about your current and potential future workplace?

 ACTIVITY 1.1

REFLECTING ON YOUR BACKGROUND

Think about your life journey to date in a holistic sense, focusing on your family and cultural background, who you are, your route to university and/or employment, and where you believe life will take you in the future.

Although somewhat philosophical and related to intuitive ways of thinking, this exercise focuses on yourself and your beliefs. Now focus in a much deeper way on the following questions and issues.

- Describe your cultural background – what does it mean to you?

- Has this impacted on your life choices in any way?

- What were the implications for your learning choices?

- Consider how many culturally diverse backgrounds are represented in your workplace and/or student group?

- How much do you actually know about many of those diverse cultures in your work or student group, and how do you investigate this issue?

Discuss the questions posed above in multicultural groups where possible; you might be surprised by what you discover.

Harnessing the diversity in groups can create a vibrant learning and working environment where difference is celebrated and individuals are respected. To clarify: diversity 'consists of visible and non-visible factors, which include personal characteristics such as background, culture, personality and work-style' (CIPD 2008b, p1) and other features consist of gender, race, disability, age, religion and belief, and sexual orientation. Canas and Sondak take this a step further by identifying the following five principles for an improved definition of diversity:

- 'Diversity is expansive but not without boundaries.

- Diversity is fluid and dynamic.

- Diversity is based on both differences and similarities.

- Diversity is rooted in non-essentialist thought.

- Diversity is directly related to how one approaches work [learning]' (Canas and Sondak (2008, p11).

Let us discuss these principles in more detail (see Table 1.1 overleaf).

Table 1.1 Evaluating the five principles of diversity

Diversity is:	Evaluating five principles of defining diversity
Expansive but has boundaries	Not limited to demographic identities such as skin colour and gender; it can embrace single parenthood and different levels of spirituality. Definitions can become over-extended to include someone's work location and functional area. Boundaries also need to be set because if diversity included every characteristic of each individual in every work or learning-related situation, it would become useless. The goal is to be able to distinguish between what constitutes diversity and what does not.
Fluid and dynamic	Diversity affiliation is not absolute but continuously being redefined; for example some individuals may suggest they do not belong to a particular grouping and others may belong to two. Litvin (1997, p202) states: 'The categories constructed through the discourse of workplace diversity as natural and obvious are hard pressed to accommodate the complexity of real people.' In reality many people may associate themselves with a range of social category diversity dimensions: for example, a disabled, Nigerian, Christian woman. People can move in and out of categories: able-bodied to disabled, single parent to married, someone assumed to be straight to gay.
Based on differences as well as similarities	People may see themselves as having similar qualities; potential disadvantages can be eliminated. Multiple demographic characteristics influence group dynamics; they can create divisions when people align to a particular person or take sides. These fault lines may have a detrimental effect on morale and performance as well as make conflict more probable.
Rooted in nonessentialist thought	This element is related to making assumptions about 'human nature', in other words stereotyping because of the group or individual's diversity category; for example, assuming all women want to have children. Conceptually this segment requires nonessentialist thinking to go beyond generalisations and encourage celebration of individuals and their fundamental characteristics.
Directly related to how one approaches work (learning)	This concerns taking into account how people perceive and perform in their job as well as their capacity to learn. It also allows us to reflect on their interaction with others both in and outside their organisational work group or learning group. Organisations that believe in managing through diversity would integrate people's point of view in relation to diversity into the main stream and continually re-evaluate their culture, mission, strategies and business practices to maintain a positive approach.

Source: drawing on Canas and Sondak (2008, p11), Litvin (1997) and CIPD (2008b).

The characteristics outlined in Table 1.1 may help and encourage learners, leaders and managers to recognise the intricacies that managing diversity promotes, and it highlights the need for all participants to formulate their own approaches to managing or being part of a diverse group. Continuing professional development and reflective practice in particular, which we will discuss under the next heading, will help you with this.

1.6 CONTINUING PROFESSIONAL DEVELOPMENT AND REFLECTIVE LEARNING

Continuing professional development focuses on an individual's learning and growth in their current role and future career path. It is an investment in yourself that will make a positive difference to your professional practice and career development (CIPD 2007a). Continuing professional development is a self-managed process in which you will manage your development on an ongoing basis using appropriate measures (CIPD 2009a). These include formal study, vocational training courses, mentoring and coaching, membership in professional bodies like the Chartered Institute of Personnel and Development (CIPD), lectures, workshops, seminars, professional conferences and many more. Any event, activity or encounter from which you have learned something can count as continuing professional development (CIPD 2007a), and this is reflected in the CIPD's CPD template which, among other aspects, focuses on three areas of learning that you can identify and any tangible outcomes resulting from this learning, as well as its value to the organisation and other stakeholders. CPD also requires you to reflect on and learn from your daily work and other professional experience resulting from both formal and informal opportunities (CIPD 2009a), and reflective techniques will help you to apply theoretical learning to your practice (Schön 1983). Reflection, although rarely encouraged at the workplace, is therefore an integral part of managerial development and practice.

While the focus of CPD is on the individual, it has long been recognised that it should also reflect the needs of the employing organisation (Jones and Fear 1994). Many twenty-first century organisations support their employees' professional development through organising training courses, operating mentoring schemes, allowing time off for formal study or networking, and supporting their employees' formal studies or coaching financially – all of which is costly to them. It is therefore not surprising that they expect a return on their investment beyond improved staff satisfaction, morale and productivity. Table 1.2 lists the potential benefits of continuing professional development for both individuals and organisations, which, of course, are inter-related.

While the benefits of CPD for the individual focus on career development, the benefits for the organisation emphasise increased productivity, efficiency and effectiveness of staff. The knowledge, experience and expertise created through continuing professional development are invaluable to an organisation because they are contextual and practical – organisations can make use of them instantly without reinterpretation. Through professional associations (like the CIPD) and trade unions, employees can create standards for professional practice and market their skills more flexibly by passing on their knowledge and skills to a wider range of organisations (Grugulis, 2003). Hence, organisations need to adjust reward systems to support the development of their employees in order to retain them and reap the biggest rewards in terms of increased productivity, efficiency and effectiveness.

The key to successful continuing professional development is reflective practice, which is closely linked to the notion of experiential learning. The CIPD (2010d)

Table 1.2 Benefits of CPD

Benefits of CPD to individual	Benefits of CPD to organisations
Build confidence and credibility as a professional	Helps maximise staff potential by linking learning to actions and theory to practice
Earn more by showcasing your abilities and achievements	Helps HR professionals to link objectives more closely to business needs
Achieve your career goals by focusing your training and development where it is most effective	Promotes staff development, improves morale and motivation
Cope positively with change by constantly updating your skills	Adds value to the organisation as staff will consciously apply their learning to their routines
Be more productive and efficient through reflection on your learning and identification of any gaps in your knowledge, skills and experience	Supports performance appraisals

Source: based on CIPD 2010c.

stresses that reflective learning encourages professionals to take responsibility for their growth and development, to identify the benefits of any professional development measures, to see the value in different learning experiences and to help them to learn how to learn. The trick is to turn everyday experiences into formal learning on which you can draw in the future (which Boud, Keogh and Walker 1985 and Kolb 1984 call 'experiential learning') and you can do that by asking yourself a simple question: 'what did I get out of this event or experience?' (CIPD 2010d). Following Schön's (1983) theory of the *Reflective Practitioner,* you will observe the processes and benefits of your learning, formulate small-scale hypotheses, test these hypotheses through further observation (and perhaps even experimentation), and in that way create new knowledge about your daily routines and develop your identity as a professional. Continuing professional development is therefore learning in action through action and reflection. The reflective element of this process will foster your critical thinking and emancipate you as an individual and professional (see Chapters 2 and 4 for details).

Such learning is a both a great opportunity and a great challenge for twenty-first-century postgraduate students and professionals like you. On the one hand, experiential learning through reflection will provide you with a valuable opportunity to pause and focus on your skills and further career development. It will allow you to change your thinking and behaviour and in that way improve your professional practice (Hartog 2002). By engaging in reflective practice, you will realise what skills you possess and at what level, and what your strengths and weaknesses are. You can compile evidence for these skills from assignments from university or the workplace and in that way strengthen a job application, performance appraisal or promotion request. In short, reflection will give you the opportunity to get to know yourself better and take a strategic position towards your further career development. The CIPD (2010d) suggests that it is possible to make reflection an intrinsic part of your job and to take up further development opportunities as they become apparent, making your experiences at work richer and more stimulating.

Becoming a reflective practitioner involves the development and integration of the following values into daily practice (drawing on Hartog 2002):

- the ability to listen and learning to hear what colleagues and subordinates are saying
- caring for subordinates and peers, perceiving them as whole individuals and supporting their learning and development
- integrating reflective practice into our daily routines in a way that allows us to interpret what is going on at the present moment in a thoughtful manner
- adopting a critical stance to challenge the status quo and develop professional and managerial practice.

On the other hand, reflection is often considered to be a waste of time and something that people can do when they have no better use for their time. This is a great shame for it loses the benefits outlined above. The reasons for this perception, however, are simple: on the one hand, the benefits of reflective learning are often difficult to assess without a mindset that is tuned into the subtleties of human learning, and on the other hand the absence of reflective learning is often not obvious. In order to encourage you to engage in reflective learning to a greater degree, many postgraduate programmes of study will require you to keep a reflective journal (Hubbs and Brand 2005, Moon 2006). Even if your programme of study does not, we strongly recommend that you keep a learning journal to give you the opportunity to internalise what you are learning in your studies and at work and to connect theory and practice.

Learning journals (or learning logs), learning plans and personal development plans – all of which serve to make you more aware of your learning and development, to help you to track your learning and to help you to develop – come in a number of formats. They can be structured (as shown in Example 1.1 below and in the templates provided on the companion website) or make use of more creative means such as diary entries, letters and blogs. For professional purposes – that is, to demonstrate to your current or a future employer what you have learned as part of your postgraduate studies – you may want to choose a more structured (and therefore professional-looking) format in the style of the following example.

Example 1.1: Individual development plan

A development plan or log can be quite simple and to the point; it therefore does not have to be a daunting task to fill it in. The example shown in the figure below is related to a particular concern or behaviour the individual wants to develop or/ and change. In this instance, it relates to feelings of pressure or stress at work (for further reading on this subject, see Chapter 5).

This type of development plan can be accumulative; it can help you to assess your progress over a period of time as well as being an adequate document to add to a portfolio in the style of a development log. People often make plans to achieve their goals, but as we have seen above, they must have a purpose, contain objectives and have a mechanism for prioritising and reviewing. If a plan proves unrealistic and does not match your preferred way of working, a review of the plan may be necessary. The following activity gives some suggestions for such a review process.

Development log 1

Date	Purpose	Action required	Review
Record the instances of adding to your log. You will be able to assess how long it took to change or learn a new skill or behaviour.	*What aspects of stress or pressure would you be interested in managing more successfully?* This section will change depending on the behaviour you wish to alter.	What action will you take? Set out your criteria for development. Use CSMART objectives (see Chapter 9)	State the progress you are making at timely intervals. Do you need to make changes or adjustments to your plan?
Evaluate your development. Produce a summary of your main achievements			

This example focused on planning individual learning; you may also have to keep a group learning log to plan and record any collective learning. Personal development plans are quite similar in style and purpose to development plans and logs, and are a versatile tool in an individual's appraisal. They can be

ACTIVITY 1.2

REVIEW YOUR LEARNING PLAN

Drawing on the example provided above, draw up a learning plan and scrutinise it by answering the following questions:

- Do you have goals that you wish to achieve next week/month/year?
- Do you have an unambiguous view of the priorities?
- Do you have specific objectives?
- Does your plan need adjustment or are you on course to achieve your stated goals?
- When will you revisit your plan?

Such a strategic and thoughtful approach to your learning – whether in formal study or at the workplace – can help you to focus your continuing professional development and career management on what really matters to you.

included as an assessment for a postgraduate programme of study or form part of your CPD process. An example that can be adapted to the purpose for which it is being used is available on the companion website.

We recommend that all of you keep track of your learning throughout your course of study in some form of learning journal or log as this will help you to provide evidence of your learning, thus helping you to make a strong case for promotion or employment. At the end of each chapter there is a section called 'Pause for thought', in which you are encouraged to identify what you have learned from studying the respective chapter and to consider the potential impact that this learning is likely to have on your studies and career. In this section, we will refer to your learning log and hope that you will have learned enough about such logs to find a way of keeping track of your learning in a way that works for you.

Those of you who are in work may be encouraged (or perhaps even required by your employer) to keep a CPD log that captures your learning and development needs arising from your studies or work. An effective CPD log consists of two parts (CIPD 2010e): first, the CPD record, which is a review of your learning in the past review period (usually one year), and second, a plan of further CPD activities for the following review period (usually one year). In a good CPD log, these two parts will complement each other. There are many formats that a CPD log can take and we have provided some examples on the companion website to give you an idea of what an effective CPD log looks like.

You may want to adapt the development plans and logs which are available on the companion website to a format that works for you to help you to plan your learning and professional development, to keep a record of it as well as to evaluate your current and to plan further learning and professional development. The complexity of these plans dictates that they must be well thought through to be successful. Therefore, each aspect will be discussed and explained in the following section so that you can use this development tool to its best effect.

1.7 PRACTICAL ADVICE IN DEVELOPING EVIDENCE OF COMPETENCE FOR PERSONAL DEVELOPMENT

Development plans and learning logs require evidence for your learning and this is not always easy to gather. Before we embark on giving you practical advice on how to develop and gather evidence for personal and professional development purposes, let us make explicit the assumptions that we have made when writing this section. We have assumed:

- that you have embarked on a postgraduate programme of study or another formal CPD measure
- that you are reading this book to develop your current managerial skills
- that you have had some discussion with your line manager, a tutor or/and had a developmental appraisal
- that you have considered your current level of competence and achievement in specific areas of your current or future work

- that you will have the need to produce a learning diary or log and possibly conduct a developmental portfolio
- that you will be engaged in CPD.

Tracking your learning will require you to provide evidence. In this section we will draw your attention to what counts as evidence in your line of work, how you can gather it and how it can provide proof that the learning activity has been undertaken and achieved in a way that meets any assessment criteria. This record of your learning can then be used in a workplace context and/or for CPD purposes, which implies that your goal should be to display a range of knowledge and skills that demonstrate that you are able to meet the required level of competence. Acceptable evidence usually includes:

- documentary evidence of your work
- your own (reflective) account of your learning
- an independent authentication of your ability from mentors/peers or others involved in or affected by your actions.

It is useful to break down evidence into two categories: inherent and exclusive. Inherent evidence originates in the work that you will already be involved in. For example, the learning log which we encourage you to keep while studying for this module is a powerful example of your accounts of your learning. In contrast, exclusive evidence is specific to you and has some special meaning. It refers, for instance, to an event or development measure in which you have taken part and in which you have exhibited a particular competence.

One key purpose of keeping a learning or development log is to achieve competence as well as to demonstrate this achievement. Sometimes you will find that a distinction is drawn between competence and competency. The CIPD (2009b, p1) puts this as follows: '"Competency" is more precisely defined as the behaviours that employees must have, or must acquire, to input into a situation in order to achieve high levels of performance, while "competence" relates to a system of minimum standards or is demonstrated by performance and outputs.' Therefore achieving competence is a transitional process toward competency. Both, however, are outcome-based approaches. Organisations use competencies to indicate to an employee the performance level they require. They offer a marker to the individual of the behaviours and skills that are valued, appreciated or even rewarded in the organisation. The CIPD (2009b, p1) maintains: 'Competencies can be understood to represent the language of performance in an organisation, articulating both the expected outcomes of an individual's efforts and the manner in which these activities are carried out.' Therefore, accumulating competence in a range of skills will enhance your overall development. Evidence of competence is gathered through personal reflections, products such as letters, e-mails and reports that you have created, and statements confirming your competence from independent sources. Let us look at these in more detail.

As outlined in Section 1.3 above, reflection plays a key role in learning and gathering evidence for competence and competency. This includes personal reflections about the things that you have done, whether they worked or whether further action is required, and consequently to demonstrate what you would do differently, if anything. It can also establish your understanding and knowledge as opposed to your ability to perform effectively in any given situation. Hence, personal reflection in an ongoing learning diary can be useful source of evidence, particularly for the types of learning for which there is little or no documentary evidence.

Evidence can also include letters, e-mails, reports, budgets, surveys, plans, notes, very brief and well-chosen audio and visual recordings of you in operation, minutes of meetings and so on. The main points to remember are that items of evidence must be of your own work and must be chosen selectively to demonstrate that the learning outcomes or criteria have been met.

Finally, evidence can be provided by a third party, such as through a testimony or personal report from a line manager or client. Such evidence should reinforce that what you have done is experienced by others exactly as you have claimed. This information should come from someone who is able to comment critically and directly on your skill or behaviour. This may be your line manager, colleagues in your own and other departments, staff you work with or managers in other departments. From a student's perspective it could be a tutor, peer or students of another discipline. In any case, witness testimony needs to be written and explicit: 'I have always found Carla Conrad to be a very efficient manager' may be gratifying to hear but does not provide much in the way of evidence. 'I can confirm that Carla Conrad led the successful negotiation with ABZ Direct' does.

A cautionary note if you need witnesses to write a statement: they will do this task in any way they want. To assure what they have written is agreeable (and to minimise the effort they are making on your behalf), it may be sensible to produce a standard letter or questionnaire that can be easily completed; this also allows them to insert whatever comment/s they wish (the companion website has an example which you may want to adapt). A brief note, a signature and a date on each item of evidence is advisable.

To be really effective, however – that is, to present a convincing case – you will need to provide different types of evidence. For example, evidence for chairing meetings might include the following:

- an e-mail inviting participants to a meeting
- a briefing paper sent out to participants prior to the meeting and any papers to which you spoke during the meeting
- points copied on to a memory stick produced during the meeting as aide-memoire or summaries of discussions (you may need to arrange for a colleague to conduct this activity)
- minutes and a letter of thanks to participants
- an e-mail to your line manager amplifying the minutes and outlining the next steps
- witness testimony from those who participated in the meeting.

This list is not exhaustive, and it is often a good idea to add a personal reflection to explain and analyse the background to the activity, the selection of participants, what you did to ensure that everyone was encouraged to contribute to the process by which a decision was reached, and how you handled any potential or actual unhelpful arguments or digressions. This is only one example and not necessarily a suitable for your unique circumstances. In addition, evidence of your learning should meet certain criteria (see online resources for more details).

Compiling evidence of knowledge, learning, skill and competence needs to be a deliberate and systematic process, and this requires a particular attitude of mind. It can be very frustrating to know, for instance, that you are leading a team that pioneered a new initiative last year but that the detail of what you did and how you did it has long since been forgotten. We therefore repeat our encouragement to keep track of your learning and development both in your studies and at the workplace.

The bulk of your evidence will have originated from your current studies or employment. Product evidence is obtainable from documentation that you will generate during the course of your job, such as letters, reports, proposals, budgets or performance appraisals. It is highly unlikely that every competency can be encompassed by means of inherent evidence from your current job. It is more likely that you will need to show some exclusive evidence to accomplish all your confirmation of competencies. Whatever the situation, gathering evidence of competence is a particular feature of verifying our current and continuing professional development; it is essential therefore, for your career aspirations.

ACTIVITY 1.3

REFLECTION ON EVIDENCE

Referring to a recent learning or development situation and any evidence for it, answer the following questions:

- Does the evidence show that you understand the principles and concepts as well as that you acted appropriately? Again it is best to use a personal report. This allows reflection upon what you did, or the inclusion of activities from the workbooks or an assignment to demonstrate your knowledge and understanding.

- Have you included too little or too much?

- Do you need to highlight parts of documents or to provide extracts or summaries to ensure that everything presented is directly relevant to demonstrating competence?

1.8 CAREER DEVELOPMENT

1.8.1 CAREER DEVELOPMENT

Careers are important to individuals, organisations and society as they define us, give us status, enable us to achieve personal fulfilment or simply to earn enough for a comfortable lifestyle for ourselves and our family. The goal for many of us therefore is to develop and enhance our career in the medium and long term. Career development is the pursuit of improving the disposition of our working lives so that the best use is made of our intrinsic knowledge, skills and attributes. It is connected with the individual's capability and the environment that supports their continuing learning and development. It does not always imply promotional opportunities, however. Career development can make an individual's current job become more interesting or even satisfying and can be enabling to the extent that the person becomes more effective in their employment, thus benefiting organisations, too. The resources necessary to aid career development can be viewed from an organisational and individual point of view; Table 1.3 below depicts this.

Table 1.3 is not exhaustive but gives an insight into many factors that need to be in place to allow career enhancement to succeed. The following activity allows you the opportunity to reflect on your career development.

Activity 1.4 may bring to light circumstances beyond our control that may support or hinder our career development; this can be a challenge for each of us. While some people are in the right place at the right time by chance, or happen to know the right people to help them progress, others plan to be there and others again may never make it. Nevertheless, a strategic and thoughtful approach to your career development that includes development planning and keeping track of your learning and development greatly enhances your chances of fulfilling your goals and developing your career.

Table 1.3 Career development: a resource perspective

Individual	Organisational
Own talent skills and abilities	The overall national education system • The facility to develop from one level to the next
Own personality and professionalism	Human resource/development professionals
Personal motivation	The organisation's employee development and talent management process
Opportunity to take up learning initiatives	Consultants and other types of training and coaching initiatives
Learning aids • Books, journals etc • Attending university/college etc • In house training and development	Financial resources to pay for development plans
The individuals' professional institution, eg CIPD, ACCA, CMI, CIM	A well-thought-through personal/ professional development planning system for each employee
Support of peer group family and friends	Managers in the organisation securing training and development for their staff

ACTIVITY 1.4

CRITICAL REFLECTION ON YOUR CAREER DEVELOPMENT

- Consider your career from the first time you entered employment. Analyse the periods or events of critical importance for representing one of the following:
  - worst growth period
  - best growth period
  - static period (how did this change?)
  - working for a particular company or individual
  - meeting a specific individual
  - participating in a particular training or development event
  - being at the right place at the right time!
- How much of this was planned or happened by chance?
- Discuss your finding within a group and share your experiences.
- In the future do you intend that your career development should be left to chance?

We need to bear in mind, though, that the opportunity to enhance our career is dependent on achieving success in the job market, and on the individual gaining access to organisational resources and proving worthy of their investment in developing their staff. (The link between skills and employability has been demonstrated by the Leitch Review of Skills 2006.) Career enhancement is not altruistic on the part of the organisation, it is just good business sense. If the purpose of the organisation is to gain in market share and to maintain or enhance profitability, then it will need the best-developed people. In turn, this should realise the most profit or at least ensure survival of the organisation. People give of their best when appreciated by being placed in the right role and given the relevant development opportunities with suitable chances for growth. Let us consider the labour market now.

1.8.2 LABOUR MARKET

The *Barometer of HR trends and prospects* (CIPD 2010f, p5) suggests that 'employers' recruitment intentions decreased, with four out of ten organisations saying they would be recruiting fewer people in 2009 than in 2008.' In the current economic climate characterised by little economic growth and financial constraints, this is perhaps no surprise. It is, however, a cause of concern to those who are seeking to enter or change their employment. Critically, the same report affirms that 81 per cent of organisations have encountered recruitment problems because of a lack of necessary skills (73 per cent) and insufficient experience (39 per cent). The upshot of this dilemma was that organisations relied on appointing people who they believed had the potential to grow. Consequently, if increasing a starting salary or the overall employment package is not an option for a business, then it will have to consider other ways of tackling skills shortages and lack of experience in recruits.

Options include the provision of further training to internal staff, taking into account personal attributes linked to a realistic job profile rather than relying on qualifications alone so that the recruitment pool expands.

So, what lessons can we learn from this? We suggest that:

- The labour market will continue to be volatile for some time to come.
- There will be fewer jobs available in the near future.
- There is the potential for organisations to exploit more internal promotional places.
- More internal staff development will therefore be required.
- Individuals seeking employment must show they have the ability to learn, develop and grow in their role or profession.

Crucially, the main lesson for those seeking advancement is that they will have to demonstrate an array of skills and attributes that shows that they have either potential or the requisite abilities that businesses require. This makes the acquisition of skills and a vehicle for evidencing those skills all the more important when seeking employment or promotion in the contemporary labour market. Let us now consider the organisational perspective.

1.9 ORGANISATIONAL CONTEXT

1.9.1 SUCCESSION PLANNING

Every organisation will need to attract people with the requisite skills to encompass and ensure that their key positions are filled. The salient dilemma for managers is whether to grow the skills and talent from within or recruit from outside. Succession planning is seen as the method by which organisations ensure a supply of internal talent to climb up the career ladder. The CIPD (2009c, p1) suggests that 'this process needs to be managed, and traditionally, large blue-chip companies ran highly-structured, mechanistic, secretive and top-down schemes aimed at identifying internal successors for key posts and planning their career paths to provide the necessary range of experience.' The development of those employees regarded as heirs to senior management positions would be assured.

This approach to succession planning is appropriate in a constant environment in which careers are expected to be long term. However, it is problematic in turbulent times in which businesses are uncertain of growth and perhaps even survival. Consequently, businesses tend to plan for types of jobs that are required for their future development. Succession planning will focus on retaining talented individuals by ensuring that they have the relevant career development so that the organisation keeps the human capital it needs to fulfil its current and anticipated future requirements. Therefore, in contemporary business terms, succession planning is defined by Hirsh (2002 as cited in CIPD 2009c, p1) as: 'a process by which one or more successors are identified for key posts (or groups of similar key posts), and career moves and/or development activities are planned for these successors. Successors may be fairly ready to do the job (short-term successors) or seen as having longer-term potential (long-term successors).'

Another option is sideways or lateral development in which a person moves on to another job at the same level in the organisation (eg a move from training manager to recruitment manager). Indeed, organisations are increasingly likely to develop people in this way. This may also be part of your personal career management choices, as it may fit in with your life style and offer a broadening of your portfolio. You may also wish to take a secondment or manage a new project in a different area, thus opening up opportunities that will not have fitted into the classic upward progression of the past. Although broadening their experience may well be what further leaders are required to do!

1.9.2 TALENT MANAGEMENT

Talent management, as defined by the CIPD, is: 'Identification, development. Engagement/retention and deployment of those employees who are particularly valuable to the organisation – either in view of their high potential for the future or because they are fulfilling business/operational-critical roles' (CIPD 2009d).

The role of the talent manager is to seek out talent, to nurture it and to develop individuals to engage with the current and future skill requirements and needs of the organisation. Therefore, talent managers are involved in recruitment, selection, performance enhancement, succession planning and development, and it is these individuals that will engage our future business leaders. In other words organisations recognise the importance of having a strategy for managing talent that will also develop their investment in human capital and harness their abilities (CIPD 2007b). Organisations will usually develop their specific concepts of what constitutes talent; CIPD research (2007b, p3) upholds this by suggesting that it is:

- organisationally specific
- highly influenced by the type of industry and the nature of the work
- dynamic, and so likely to change over time according to organisational priorities.

Organisations seek to incorporate ongoing, flexible and tangible arrangements that take into consideration a range of strategic objectives, such as:

- building a high-performance workplace or a learning organisation
- adding value to the employer of choice and branding agenda
- contributing to diversity management (CIPD 2007b, p3).

Talent and skills therefore will continue to remain high on the organisational and particularly the human resources agenda so as to enable business to build a sustainable future for all their stakeholders. We will come back to this issue in Chapter 18, but let us explore the concept of human capital now.

1.9.3 HUMAN CAPITAL

Organisations are increasingly concerned that they have the requisite 'human capital' to survive and ensure success continues; Whetton and Cameron (2007, p568) advise that to make certain that 'positive change continues is to have capable people in place'. In order to build human capital, organisations need to provide development opportunities for their employees, which means that individuals have greater opportunity to strengthen and improve their own skills sets. The organisation therefore would be investing in its people and in so doing concentrate on long-term goals and developments rather than just seeking immediate short-term gain. The following quote by Butler (2010, p1) endorses that view that organisations need to prioritise the growth of talent and thus human capital:

> For whatever reason the critical, quantitative evaluation of pivotal skills – the foundation of any organisation's future success and that of the economy – remains too shaky in too many places. But the war for talent has too often provided a neat get-out clause. It externalises and avoids the problem. The focus narrows to short-term recruitment – gap-plugging – and away from proper planning of skills.

From a HR perspective, human capital can be viewed as 'people and their collective skills, abilities, experience and potential' (CIPD 2009e, p1), a positive connotation linked to what the organisation can gain from its employees as well as what development the employees can expect from their employer. In contrast, some might suggest that using the term 'capital' in relation to people rather than inanimate objects is degrading (Whetton and Cameron 2007). The CIPD factsheet on human capital (2009e) suggests that the term should be used in a wider context as it is only one factor in what represents a more collective view of intellectual capital:

- **Human capital**: the knowledge, skills, abilities and capacity to develop and innovate possessed by people in an organisation.
- **Social capital**: the structures, networks and procedures that enable those people to acquire and develop intellectual capital represented by the stocks and flows of knowledge derived from relationships within and outside the organisation.
- **Organisational capital**: the institutionalised knowledge possessed by an organisation which is stored in databases, manuals etc. This would also include HR policies and processes used to manage people (CIPD 2009e, p1).

Intellectual capital is therefore 'the knowledge assets that are available to the organisation and is a large part of intangible value' (CIPD 2009e, p1). It is in the best interest of organisations to genuinely comprehend the connection that lies within these discrete characteristics of 'capital'. Essentially, although more emphasis may be placed on human capital, in itself it does not create value. Instead, it is the development and experiences of the individuals concerned that gives them a worth or value to the organisation. The workforce must be managed, motivated, given opportunity for development and an outlet for their talent to enable organisations to perform and succeed. The skills, knowledge and attributes which the human capital possesses must be entrenched in the products and services that the customer requirements necessitate in order to be of value to the business.

1.10 CONCLUSION

Knowledge, skills and continuing professional development are at the top of the twenty-first-century human resources agenda for a good reason: they are the future for professionals and organisations alike to secure survival and success. This chapter has demonstrated the wide-reaching implications of skill-building and continuing professional development in an increasingly diverse environment. It has discussed the need of professionals and organisations alike to engage in skill-building and continuing professional development to manage their careers, plan the succession of today's executives, and manage talent and human capital.

While there is a range of stakeholders in skill-building and continuing professional development – including employers and professional bodies like the CIPD – there is much emphasis on the individual. We encourage each of you to take responsibility for your own learning, professional development and employability by engaging in a wide variety of CPD measures on a regular basis, by reflecting on your learning and by keeping track of how you develop your knowledge, skills and competences in an often challenging work environment.

PAUSE FOR THOUGHT

Identify at least three things that you have learned by studying this chapter and engaging with the activities. How will your newly acquired knowledge and skills support your continuing professional development? What value do you expect your learning to have for your daily routines and your further career? In what area have you identified a need for further development and how are you planning to fill that gap? Address these issues in your learning journal and/or CPD log. You may also wish to discuss them with a peer, colleague, mentor or coach to aid your further development.

- There is a need to build transferable skills like communication, teambuilding, negotiation, decision-making, problem-solving, leadership and change management among professionals and managers in order to increase the workforce's skills base.

- Skill-building and continuing professional development increase an individual's employability and help to develop his/her career. This involves reflective and experiential learning, which can be planned and tracked using development plans and logs.

- An increasingly international, and therefore culturally diverse, work environment provides new opportunities and challenges for learning and development of individuals and groups in organisations.

- Organisations are increasingly looking after their human capital by growing talent from inside and by planning succession of their executives from their own talent pool. This requires them to develop their workforce rigorously and to identify talent and foster its development.

EXPLORE FURTHER

CIPD website, http://www.cipd.co.uk

MOON, J. (1999) *Learning journals: a handbook for academics, students and professional development*. London: Kogan Page.

1.11 REFERENCES

BENNETT, R. (2002) Employers' demands for personal transferable skills in graduates. *Journal of Vocational Education and Training*. Vol. 54, No. 4. pp457–475.

BOUD, D., KEOGH, R. and WALKER, D. (eds). (1985) *Reflection: turning experience into learning*. London: Kogan Page.

BROWAEYS, M.J. and PRICE, R. (2008) *Understanding cross-cultural management*. London: Pearson Education Ltd.

BUTLER, M. (2010) The talent of the future. *People Management*. Available online at: http://www.peoplemanagement.co.uk/pm/articles2010 [accessed 30 March 2010].

CANAS, K.A. and SONDAK, H. (2008) *Opportunities and challenges of workplace diversity*. 2nd ed. New Jersey: Prentice Hall.

CIPD. (2007a) *Continuing professional development (CPD). Student guide No. 8*, revised September 2007. Available online at: http://www.cipd.co.uk/NR/rdonlyres/3F6D3423–3463–4638–A590–7C1A99FDD418/0/student_guide_8_cpd.pdf [accessed 12 March 2010].

CIPD. (2007b) *Talent management: research insight*, revised August 2008. Available online at: http://www.cipd.co.uk/subjects/recruitmen/general/_tlntmgnt.htm [accessed 26 May 2010].

CIPD. (2008a) *Learning and the line*. Available online at: http://www.cipd.co.uk/NR/rdonlyres/D34E7BC5–2CE5–4CC8–87DD–3F7141C2D477/0/learningandtheline.pdf, [accessed 15 February 2010].

CIPD. (2008b) *Diversity: an overview*, revised November 2008. Available online at: http://www.cipd.co.uk/subject/dvsequl/general/divover?NRMOD [accessed 6 January 2010].

CIPD. (2009a) *Continuing professional development (CPD): practitioner-level standards*. Policy, revised September 2009. Available online at: http://www.cipd.co.uk/cpd/aboutcpd/cpd-policy.htm [accessed 12 March 2010].

CIPD. (2009b) *Competency and competency frameworks*. Fact sheet, revised June 2009. Available online at: http://www.cipd.co.uk/subjects/perfmangmt/competnces/comptfrmwk.htm?IsSrchRes=1 [accessed 26 May 2010].

CIPD. (2009c) *Succession planning*. Factsheet, revised November 2009. Available online at: http://www.cipd.co.uk/subjects/hrpract/general/successplan.htm?issrchres=1 [accessed 26 May 2010].

CIPD. (2009d) *The war on talent*. Survey report, revised February 2009. Available online at: http://www.cipd.co.uk/subjects/recruitmen/general/_war-on-talent.htm [accessed 26 May 2010].

CIPD. (2009e) *Human capital*. Factsheet, revised November 2009. Available online at: http://www.cipd.co.uk/subjects/corpstrtgy/hmncapital/humancap.htm?IsSrchRes=1 [accessed 26 May 2010].

CIPD. (2010a) *What is CPD?* Available online at: http://www.cipd.co.uk/cpd/aboutcpd/whatiscpd.htm [accessed 12 March 2010].

CIPD. (2010b) *The skills agenda in the UK*. Factsheet, revised February 2010. Available online at: http://www.cipd.co.uk/subjects/lrnanddev/general/ukskillsagenda.htm [accessed 15 February 2010].

CIPD. (2010c) *Benefits of CPD*. Available online at: http://www.cipd.co.uk/cpd/benefitscpd.htm [accessed 12 March 2010].

CIPD. (2010d) *What is reflective learning?* Available online at: http://www.cipd.co.uk/cpd/aboutcpd/reflectlearn.htm [accessed 12 March 2010].

CIPD. (2010e). *Download a CPD template*. Available online at: http://www.cipd.co.uk/cpd/guidance/CPDrecordandplan.htm [accessed 12 March 2010].

CIPD. (2010f) *A barometer of HR trends and prospects*. Available online at: http://www.cipd.co.uk/subjects/hrpract/general/overofsurvs.htm?IsSrchRes=1 [accessed 26 May 2010].

DFES. (2003) *21st century skills: realising our potential*. Department for Education and Skills. Norwich: HMSO.

DFES. (2005) *Skills: getting on in business, getting on at work*. Department for Education and Skills. Norwich: HMSO.

DFES. (2007a). *Curriculum diversity guide in collaboration with NIACE*. Norwich: HMSO.

DIUS. (2007b) *World class skills: implementing the Leitch review of skills in England*.

Department for Innovation, Universities and Skills. Norwich: HMSO.

DIUS. (2008) *Higher education at work: high skills, high value*. Consultation Document, Department for Innovation, Universities and Skills. Available online at: http://www.dius. gov.uk/consultations/con_0408_hlss.html [accessed 15 July 2008].

GRUGULIS, I. (2003) Putting skills to work. *Human Resource Management Journal*. Vol. 13, No. 2. pp3–12.

HALL, S. (1992) The question of cultural identity. In S. Hall and T. McGrew (eds), *Modernity and its futures*. Cambridge: Polity Press.

HARTOG, M. (2002) Becoming a reflective practitioner. *Business Ethics: A European Review*. Vol. 11, No. 3. pp233–243.

HUBBS, D.L. and BRAND, C.F. (2005) The paper mirror: understanding reflective journaling. *Journal of Experiential Education*. Vol. 28, No. 1. pp60–71.

JONES, N. and FEAR, N. (1994) Continuing professional development: Perspectives for human resource professionals. *Personnel Review*. Vol. 23, No. 8. pp49–60.

KOLB, D. (1984) *Experiential learning*. Englewood Cliffs, CA: Prentice Hall.

LEICESTER, M. (1996) Equal opportunities in education. *Journal of Philosophy in Education*. Vol. 30, No. 2. pp278–287.

LEITCH REVIEW OF SKILLS. (2006) *Prosperity for all in the global economy*. Final Report, December 2006. Norwich: HMSO.

LITVIN, D.R. (1997) The discourse of diversity. *Discourse and Organisations*. Vol. 4, No, 2. pp202.

MEZIROW, J. (1991) *Transformative learning dimensions of adult learning*. San Francisco, CA: Jossey-Bass.

MOON, J.A. (2006) *Learning journals: a handbook for reflective practice and professional development*. 2nd ed. London: Routledge.

RANKIN, N. (2003) Hard as nails? The skills that employers really want. *Competency and Emotional Intelligence*. Vol. 10, No. 2. pp25–28.

RAWSON, M. (2000) Learning to learn: more than a skill set. *Studies in Higher Education*. Vol. 25, No. 2. pp225–238.

ROUTLEDGE, C. and CARMICHAEL, J. (2007) *Personal development and management skills*. London: CIPD.

SCHEIN, E.H. (2004) *Organisational culture and leadership*. 3rd ed. San Fransisco, CA: Jossey-Bass.

SCHÖN, D.A. (1983) *The reflective practitioner*. London: Temple Smith.

TARGETT, S. (1995) CBI calls for skills passport boost. *Times Higher Education*, 8 December. Available online at: http://www.timeshighereducation.co.uk/story.asp?storyCode=961 37&sectioncode=26 [accessed 22 July 2008].

WEICK, K.E. (1995) *Sensemaking in organisations*. Thousand Oaks, CA: Sage.

WHETTON, D.A. and CAMERON, K.S. (2007) *Developing management skills*. New Jersey: Pearson.

CHAPTER 2

Essential postgraduate study skills

Stefanie C. Reissner

OVERVIEW

Critical thinking, reading and writing are the pillars of postgraduate study, managerial work and continuing professional development (CPD). While this is critical in other domains of our life, many of us find it difficult to critique teachers, scholars and other experts at university or at the workplace. In this chapter, you will learn to understand critical methods in an educational context and to apply them to your work at university and beyond. In particular, you will learn the characteristics of an argument so that you can read and write critically, which is the basis for independent thinking, the creation of knowledge and the improvement of professional and managerial practice.

Moreover, you will get useful background information on how to study smartly by following a structured process for approaching tasks during your postgraduate study and other CPD measures. You will also learn why your university tutors expect certain things from you and what the rationale behind these seemingly strange expectations is. The information, activities and checklists provided in this chapter will help you to build a strong foundation for your postgraduate study, managerial work and continuing professional development.

LEARNING OUTCOMES

By the end of this chapter, provided you engage with the activities, you should be able to:

- understand the qualitative difference between undergraduate and postgraduate study skills
- understand the importance of critical thinking for postgraduate study and CPD
- apply critical thinking to your studies and work
- access high-quality information for study tasks
- analyse and evaluate written and oral materials
- develop and justify original arguments
- apply strategies to improve your writing.

2.1 INTRODUCTION

If you are about to skip this chapter, thinking that you have done all of this before, stop! Yes, the content of this section will sound very familiar to you. Yes, you will have had plenty of practice (and perhaps even study skills training) while studying for your degree (eg a British Bachelor's degree which corresponds to Level 6 of the European Qualifications Framework, QAA 2008). And yes, you may wonder what the point of doing it again is. Let me assure you that this chapter is not a repetition of what you may already know, even though its content may look very similar. Postgraduate study (eg a British Master's degree which corresponds to Level 7 of the European Qualifications Framework, QAA 2008) and continuing professional development (CPD) differ *qualitatively* from undergraduate study, and in order to be successful you will need to hone the skills that you already possess and develop another, crucial skill: critical thinking. Critical thinking is a meta-skill – that is, a skill that subsumes and enhances many other skills that competent professionals possess. Metaphorically speaking, if postgraduate study and CPD is a house, critical thinking is its foundation. The application of critical thinking to other aspects of postgraduate study and CPD, such as reading and writing, are the walls of this house (see Figure 2.1 below). Your aim as a postgraduate student and smart professional should be to build a strong foundation and solid walls, and this chapter seeks to help you with that.

Figure 2.1 Critical thinking in postgraduate study and CPD

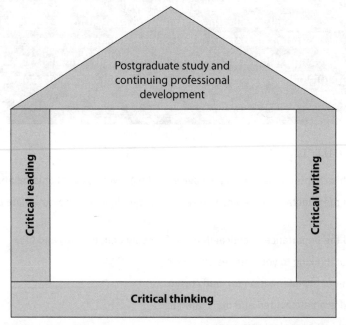

You may not be convinced about this yet, perhaps recalling your undergraduate student days in which critical thinking may have featured strongly. Indeed, critical thinking, analysis and synthesis are key skills of any business and management student (QAA 2007), but they are even more important at postgraduate level and beyond (QAA 2002). The Quality Assurance Agency for Higher Education in the UK (QAA) puts it at the forefront of their official subject benchmark statement for Masters Awards in Business and Management:

> Critical thinking and creativity: managing creative processes in self and others; *organising thoughts*, analysis, synthesis, *critical appraisal*. This includes the capability to identify assumptions, evaluate statements in terms of evidence, detect false logic or reasoning, identify implicit values, define terms adequately and generalise appropriately. (QAA 2002, emphasis added)

So critical thinking and appraisal as well as self-management and the organisation of thought are the official minimum requirements for postgraduate study (QAA 2002). Hence, as a postgraduate student you are expected to work at a more advanced and independent level than as an undergraduate. You will not only manage yourself and your studies more independently and professionally, but you will also gain deeper understanding of the subject matter by scrutinising any materials that you are working with through a more critical approach. In addition, by becoming a postgraduate student, you will also become a member of a community of knowledge and scholarly activity in your chosen field. You are expected to think independently and contribute to the knowledge of your field of study by engaging in research and other thought experiments (Hart 1998). You may wonder what this actually means for you as a postgraduate student, so let me try to illustrate this qualitative difference with the following example.

Imagine that you have been given an assignment asking you to analyse the human resource function in a country of your choice. Such an assignment may feature both in undergraduate and postgraduate courses, but your tutor would expect a different, more advanced approach at postgraduate level, which is summarised in Table 2.1 (overleaf).

Sounds difficult? Well, it may not be easy at first to approach such a seemingly simple task critically. With the necessary skills and some practice, however, you should be able to make good progress (Hughes 2000). This chapter will provide you with exercises, activities, tips and tricks to support your learning journey towards becoming a more critical student and competent professional. Practice is famously the first step to mastery, so we will start off with an activity.

 ACTIVITY 2.1

NEW APPROACHES TO PREVIOUS STUDENT WORK

If you have kept any previous assignments from your undergraduate student days, look at them again and analyse your approach in the light of what you have been reading so far. (Those of you who have not kept any assignments, please use the sample assignment 'HRM in Russia' provided on the companion website.) Read through the assignment and ask yourself the following questions:

1. What is the main argument of this assignment?

2. What does the reader learn about the topic under investigation?

3. What kind of sources does this assignment draw on?

4. How much detail is provided about the topic under investigation?

5. How is this assignment structured and what kind of language is used?

6. How sensible and original are the conclusions and recommendations?

I recommend you write down your answers and discuss them with a peer or in a small group, if possible. Asking such questions about a written piece of work, particularly if it is your own, is the first step to a more critical approach to your studies (Wallace and Wray, 2006). Exercises like this allow you to view your work with the eyes of a third party, so I expect this to be an eye-opening exercise for you. Just a few hints with regard to your answers to these questions:

1. If you cannot identify a main argument, there probably is none. Any assignment should have something to say and it is your task to work it out before you start writing. There is a range of techniques that can help you to identify your argument and present it in an effective manner; see Sections 2.3 and 2.4 below for details.

2. If you cannot answer the second question, then there is probably not much new or original in your assignment. Again, any assignment should have something in it that the reader can take away – and that does not have to be groundbreaking new knowledge! A well-developed argument can help you to elicit the key learning points of your assignment; see Sections 2.3 and 2.4 below for details.

3. If you have used academic journal articles, conference papers, research monographs – well done and keep up the good work! If you have relied heavily on websites and textbooks, then Section 2.3.1 will be of utmost importance to you. Postgraduate students are expected to draw on high-quality sources for their work and your reading should reflect this.

4. The fourth question really is whether you are looking at the topic under investigation in a superficial manner or whether the analysis digs deeper into what is going on. A superficial assignment will lack numbers and figures as well as specific examples to illustrate the main argument.

5. A good assignment has a clear structure that builds the main argument. It uses formal yet simple language and provides clear definitions of the key terms and issues. See also Chapter 3, Section 3.2 for the characteristics of effective writing.

6. The answer to this question will tell you a lot about the quality of your assignment and is closely linked to points 1, 2 and 4. It is not difficult to conclude that 'organisation A needs to improve its employment practices', but more so to specify what that improvement could look like, how it might be achieved and how much it may cost.

I do encourage you to engage with Activity 2.1 and identify any areas of the assignment that you are either particularly happy or unhappy with. If you are working with a peer or in a small group, you may want to compare your notes and discuss any discrepancies of opinion. In that way, you will find out what other ways this piece of work can be approached, which will enhance your understanding.

While Activity 2.1 provided you with an opportunity to learn about your own writing (or my early student writing if you used the sample assignment 'HRM in Russia'), you may now want to look ahead to your postgraduate study with Activity 2.2.

Table 2.1 Undergraduate and postgraduate approaches to study

Undergraduate approach	Postgraduate approach
• Collecting information about the country (probably from the Internet) • Using theory to understand the different aspects of the human resource function • Describing your understanding of the human resource function employment practices in the country in question • Identifying good and bad practice, possibly followed by some basic recommendations	• Collecting information about the country from more than one source and scrutinising it for quality and veracity • Using (and possibly integrating) different theories to understand the different aspects of the human resource function, looking at the situation from different angles and evaluating the theories for their suitability • Describing your understanding of the human resource function in the country with the help of theory and with a clear argument and concise language, eliciting the meaning of the situation • Identifying and evaluating practices, taking the country's wider context into account, possibly offering some thoughtful recommendations with consideration to the consequences

ACTIVITY 2.2

REFLECT ON AND ANALYSE POSTGRADUATE STUDYING

Now consider alternative approaches to tackling the assignment that you have analysed in Activity 2.1. Again, it will be beneficial if you do this with a peer or in a small group and if you make a note of your thoughts and ideas. Here are some questions that may help you with this and there are no answers apart from the ones that you come up with:

- What could be done differently?
- What other points could be raised?
- What other sources could the assignment draw upon and of what quality are they? (See also Section 2.3.1 below.)
- What level of detail could be added to the text?
- How could the assignment be structured differently?
- What other conclusions could be added?

This exercise will allow you to step back from your own knowledge and understanding, to question it and to see it differently. It will also tell you much about your approach and your way of working and will highlight any areas for development. By knowing both your strengths and weaknesses, you can target any intervention to where it is needed most, thus helping you to study more effectively and efficiently and to enhance your capacity as a competent professional.

The remainder of this chapter will elaborate on many of the issues raised so far. In more detail, Section 2.2 will examine critical methods with a focus on critical thinking in an educational and work context. It will provide questions commonly used to scrutinise written and oral materials in order to understand the argument comprehensively. Section 2.3 will apply critical thinking skills to reading, including the analysis of texts such as research reports and other academic literature. It will also distinguish between different sources of literature and outline how to access them. Section 2.4 will apply critical thinking skills to writing with a focus on the development and justification of original arguments. The activities and exercises will help you to hone your current study skills for postgraduate study and beyond, and checklists will help you along the way.

2.2 BEING CRITICAL: THE MOTHER OF POSTGRADUATE SKILLS

Before delving into critical methods in more detail, I would like you to consider the following (somewhat fictional) excerpt from an advert of a promise of extra income. Ask yourself if you would respond to it or what might prevent you from responding:

> Is your monthly income really enough? Supplement your income by £250–£500+ immediately and develop a passive stream of income of £2,000+ every month with no boss, full control over the hours you work, no targets, no fuss and no hassle. We are looking for motivated people aged 18 or over who want freedom and control of their life to take up this fantastic opportunity.

So, what would your reaction be? Would you respond straightaway? My guess is that you would not. You would probably either discard this advert straightaway, thinking that this offer sounds too good to be true or you would scrutinise it using questions like 'What kind of work is this?', 'What is the risk?', 'Who is behind this?', 'What is in it for them?', 'Is this legal?', 'Where is the catch?', 'Do I have to put funds into this?' to find out more about it. So, if you would be cautious, you already have a critical mindset. Your experiences in life will have taught you that a healthy level of scepticism will protect you from people who want to take advantage of you. Unfortunately, this will not be enough to turn you into a critical student and professional. It does not come naturally to most of us to critique our teachers and other people whom we consider to be experts (Cottrell 2005), probably because most of us were brought up to respect (meaning: not to question) them. After all, academic authors mean to be honest and present truthful accounts (Wallace and Wray 2006) and many of them are experts in their field, knowing more about a particular subject than most other people. Moreover, academic sources usually have to pass stringent quality tests by other academics in a process called 'peer review' before they are published

(UNC University Libraries 2007). However, despite the authors' expert status and stringent quality checks, educational and academic materials may contain untrue assumptions, flawed reasoning and conflicting information, and may even use evidence selectively to highlight a particular point (Wallace and Wray 2006). Hence, we ought to be equally sceptical in educational and academic matters as we are in other domains of our life, asking more critical questions such as:

- Why?
- To what extent?
- For what reasons?
- How do we know this is true?
- Is there sufficient evidence for the claim?
- Does the evidence add up?
- What do we not know about the topic?
- Is there any bias?
- How reliable is the source of evidence?
- What are the authors' credentials?
- Is there a hidden agenda?
- What are the implications?

This means that as a postgraduate student you are not only allowed but *expected* to think independently, which includes scrutinising the materials that you are exposed to or working with, such as lecture and seminar content, case studies, papers and presentations – both other people's and your own (Cottrell 2005). This also includes asking critical questions about the content of the material, the key terms and definitions, the underlying assumptions, the methods used to gather information, the process and approach of writing as well as the credentials of the author(s). It means identifying the key elements of the argument, the key learning points, benefits and advantages, but also omissions, pitfalls and disadvantages. Hence, a critical mindset does not mean taking materials at face value and accepting every point that is being made. A critical mindset does not mean either rejecting everything that you are presented with or being negative, bitter and disgruntled. It means being open to accept the valuable points the author makes while being sceptical about content and approach; it is about a reasonable balance between 'uncritical acceptance' and 'overcritical rejection' (Wallace and Wray 2006, p5), which Paul and Elder (2002) describe as 'fair-mindedness'. 'What a task,' you may think. 'How am I ever going to finish reading or writing anything at all?' Yes, it will take you some time to get into the habit of thinking critically, scrutinising and questioning what you are hearing, reading or writing, but it will be worth it for your postgraduate studies and your further professional development as the quality of your work with improve considerably. The following activity will help you to apply critical thinking to a short text, using the critical questions above.

ACTIVITY 2.3

CRITICAL DISCUSSION OF ASSIGNMENT

Print a copy of the sample assignment 'Is knowledge the only source of competitive advantage today' provided on the companion website and approach it critically using the questions listed above. You may find it useful to discuss your findings with a peer or in a small group.

Let us delve more deeply into critical methods now, beginning with critical thinking. The term 'critical thinking' has become a buzzword in higher education over recent years, but has actually been around for more than a century (Fisher 2001). It is sometimes seen as one of the pillars of the educational trinity of knowledge, intelligence and thinking (De Bono 1976). Critical thinking is a way of interacting with others (Cottrell 2005) and is fruitfully defined as 'that mode of thinking – about any subject, content or problem – in which the thinker improves the quality of his or her thinking by skilfully taking charge of the structures inherent in thinking and imposing intellectual standards upon them' (Paul et al 1993, quoted in Fisher 2001, pp4–5). Hence, critical thinking is a very deep, reflective and independent form of thinking that seeks to understand the assumptions and thought structures behind a statement or argument and that integrates the following three skills (Hughes 2000):

- *interpretive skills* to identify the *meaning* of a statement

- *verification skills* to determine the *veracity* of a statement

- *reasoning skills* to analyse the *inferences* made in an argument.

Through the integration of these skills, critical thinking leads to informed and thoughtful decision-making by constantly challenging the status quo; this can even modify practice (Brookfield 1987), for instance in management. Critical thinking will give you a more independent mind that is able to appreciate both sides of an argument (Wallace and Wray 2006) and that can engage in thought experiments to create new knowledge. Critical thinking will also help you to approach tasks in your studies or at work in a more strategic fashion (Moon 2007). As such, it permeates many other fundamental skills that you will need as a postgraduate student and competent professional, such as advanced reading, writing, evaluation and analysis. The process of critical thinking contains the following elements (drawing on Brookfield 1987, Fisher 2001, Cottrell 2005, and Wallace and Wray 2006):

- identifying and challenging assumptions, arguments and conclusions

- evaluating evidence that supports any points made and identifying any unsupported claims

- weighing up opposing arguments and taking supporting evidence into account

- reading between the lines and understanding deeper meaning

- recognising any flaws, hidden agendas or mismatch with other authors' arguments

- taking context, purpose and values into account

- matching authors' claims with your own knowledge and experiences

- reflecting on issues in a structured, logical and insightful way

- drawing conclusions based on evidence and reasonable assumptions

- clarifying expressions, claims and meanings

- producing logical arguments

- presenting a viewpoint clearly and with good reasoning

- exploring alternatives in a creative and reflective manner.

So, what does this mean for postgraduate study and continuing professional development? It means being more sceptical about what you hear, read, say and write in the classroom, in independent study and in the workplace. It means stepping back from taken-for-granted knowledge, questioning it and reflecting on it, both in your own work and in the work of others. While it may not come naturally to you to be critical in such contexts, you will be able to hone your critical skills and apply them if you follow the guidance in this chapter and follow up other, specialist resources. Critical thinking will emancipate you (Paul and Elder 2002) as a learner and professional and it will improve your work for postgraduate study and other continuing professional development.

2.3 APPLYING CRITICAL THINKING (1): READING

Reading is an integral part of postgraduate study, but you will not have time to read everything that sounds interesting or relevant to a particular task or project. Instead, you will need to select appropriate materials for your study, access them strategically through your library, read them critically and evaluate them in the light of any claims made and any evidence presented. This process requires some thought and preparation every time you approach a new task, but it will not be a waste of time. Thorough preparation is famously half the work, and reading for academic purposes is no different. I propose the following six-stage process (see Figure 2.2), through which the remainder of this section will guide you.

Critical reading can be time-consuming (Cottrell 2003), particularly if you do not have the necessary knowledge and skills to do it effectively and efficiently. The following headings will guide you through this process, giving you background knowledge and introducing you to smart strategies for critical reading as well as the evaluation and analysis of texts.

2.3.1 KNOWING WHY YOU READ

Before opening a book or accessing any other written source, you need to establish your motivation for wanting to read that item. Do you want to find out

Figure 2.2 The process of critical reading

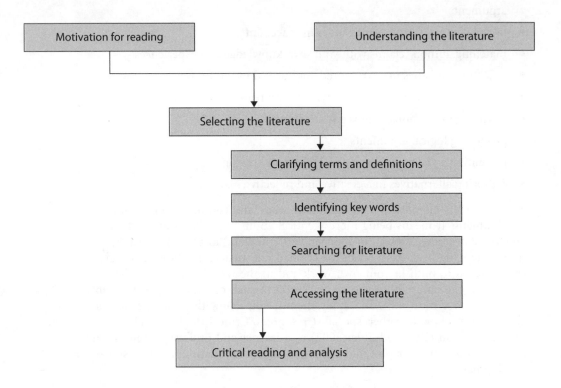

more about a new subject area? Are you more interested in methods and approaches? Or are you searching for the practical application of knowledge? So the very first question should be: 'What do I want to get out of reading this item?'. Then bear this question in mind when reading (Cameron 2007). Knowing in what way a text will inform your understanding will determine what sources will be most appropriate, and it is useful to distinguish between the following types of literature:

- *reference literature*, which provides definitions and explanations of terms and concepts

- *theoretical literature*, which develops and reports theoretical advances in a field

- *research literature*, which reports original research to deepen the understanding of a topic of interest or to test theory

- *review literature*, which reviews current theory and research in a field of study

- *methodological literature*, which suggests advances in methods of study

- *practice literature*, which focuses on practical aspects (for example of managerial work)

- *policy literature*, which reviews policies and suggest amendments.

So, if you seek to learn more about a topic, the theoretical, research and review literature is likely to provide you with the necessary information. If you seek to learn more about current practice in your field of study, the practice or perhaps policy literature will be more appropriate. If you seek to learn more about approaches to gathering and analysing data, the methodological literature will be the place to start. Hence, knowing your motivation for reading will help you to search specifically for a particular type of literature. It is smart to target your reading and read different types of literature for different purposes and at different stages of your studies. For instance, an assignment in the early stages of your studies may draw on a limited number of types, while your project or dissertation is likely to draw on most if not all of them. The difficulty is that not all sources belong in only one category; a good research paper, for example, will contain sections on theory, methods and original data. A better understanding of different types of literature may help you to judge what category an item may belong in and which elements of the item will be most suitable for your purposes.

2.3.2 UNDERSTANDING DIFFERENT SOURCES OF LITERATURE

You will need to know your literature to make most of your literature search for your postgraduate studies and beyond. You may have worked with many sources of literature before, but what you know from your undergraduate student days or work experience does not necessarily apply to postgraduate study and continuing professional development. Table 2.2 below outlines the nine most common sources of literature which you will draw on for your studies to find out what is already known in a subject area. Not all sources are of appropriate quality, however, which means that you will have to make an informed judgement about which materials to select for your work.

You need to be aware of the limitations of free materials available on the Internet, which can be accessed through search engines such as Google. As a postgraduate student, you are expected to access high-quality sources that are recognised by the experts in your field of study because they have been published following peer review, which is a rigorous quality assessment by fellow academics (UNC University Libraries 2007). These are usually sources that draw on original research and the content of which can be trusted; examples include reference materials, journal articles and specialist books. You should always be able to identify the author and/or editor of a source as well as their affiliation, and ensure that the information is still up-to-date (Fink 2005); this is a great challenge for web-based materials that do not come from a university's or other trustworthy organisation's website (Wallace and Wray 2006). You also need to bear in mind that all sources will, to a greater or lesser extent, reflect the personal choice of the author(s) or editor(s) of what is important enough to be included in that particular item. Nothing that you will read in the social sciences will represent a universal truth or a complete account, and as a postgraduate student you will be encouraged to look for different viewpoints and alternative interpretations and juxtapose them. Your critical thinking skills will help you in this process.

The ability to develop and share knowledge within your community of scholars or practitioners depends on organised collections of knowledge – a library. Hence,

Table 2.2 Common sources of literature, their use and quality

Type	Definition and examples	Use in postgraduate study	Quality of information	Accessibility	Category
Reference materials	Dictionaries, encyclopaedias.	Good starting point to learn more about a new subject area and its language.	Print and licensed online versions are usually very reliable. Beware of free web-based dictionaries and encyclopaedias (such as Wikipedia) as entries can contain false information.	Reference section of your library or online portals. Also available for purchase in hard copy or on CD/DVD.	Reference literature
Skills textbooks	Focus on building transferable skills, usually practical and process-oriented.	Valuable resource for any student and professional to complement their studies and work.	Contents can usually be trusted, but level of detail may vary considerably.	Hardcopies in library, increasingly also as e-books.	
Subject textbooks	Introduction to a field of study through summary of prevalent knowledge in that field.	Useful support for course or module, good starting point for research because of detailed reference list. Not suitable for assignments or projects.	Contents can usually be trusted but is only an abbreviated interpretation of knowledge. Level of detail may vary.	Hardcopies in library, increasingly also available as e-books.	
Journal articles	Academic papers reporting on current research and academic debates.	Peer-reviewed journal articles should be the staple diet of your reading. Special issues offer debates on a particular topic.	Up-to-date information published after scrutiny by review panels.	Hardcopies in library, increasingly also available as e-journals.	Theoretical, research, review, methodological or practice literature

Table 2.2 continued

Readers	Edited book containing research reports about a particular subject area.	Focused reading of sources that the editors regard as classic sources. Some chapters may have been published as journal articles in their own right.	Content can usually be trusted but is only a selection of knowledge in a particular area.	Hardcopies in library.	Theoretical, research, review, methodological or practice literature
Research monographs	Report on original research with great detail about results and interpretations provided.	Detailed information about a research project.	Content is usually reliable because of peer review procedures.	Hardcopies in library.	Research literature
Conference and working papers	Report on original research at a preliminary stage of development.	Up-to-date knowledge in concise format and easily accessible.	Content tends to be assessed through peer review before publication.	Through university websites or specialist databases.	Theoretical or research literature
Government and other reports	Report on policy or other relevant issues.	Useful for background and contextual knowledge.	Content is usually reliable but may represent a particular political ideology.	Through government departments or the Internet.	Practice literature
Internet	Websites, often commercial.	Use Google Scholar (http://scholar.google.com) to search for academic sources. Otherwise, use websites sparingly, eg for company or industry information. Avoid sites that provide basic subject information and also free encyclopaedias.	Content is freely publishable without any quality procedure, hence it requires careful scrutiny. There are subject gateways which can help you find suitable online sources; ask your librarian.	Everywhere and at any time.	

your university's library (nowadays sometimes called 'information services') will be your closest ally in your studies as a portal from which to access a wide range of high-quality sources. If you have not been to a university library for some time and think about dusty volumes stacked high on shelves – think again. Although the concept of the library remains unchanged, the way in which libraries operate has changed significantly over recent years and continues to change in accordance with technical advances. Modern libraries provide a range of services that are invaluable to twenty-first-century students, particularly at postgraduate level. In addition to the traditional hard-copy books and academic journals, you will find a wide variety of audio-visual, digital and online resources to support your study, and your library is the portal from which to access these increasingly virtual resources that are not accessible through other means. The best thing you can do at the beginning of your studies is to attend the library tour that your institution is likely to offer and spend some time in the library to familiarise yourself with the facilities and what is on offer. Moreover, Easterby-Smith et al (2002) recommend that you build a good relationship with your subject librarian, who is a highly trained specialist who will select the materials provided in the library on the recommendation of teaching staff. Librarians will be able to advise you on the availability of sources and help you to get materials from other libraries through a system called 'inter-library loans' (ILL). The following activity will help you to get to know your library at bit better.

ACTIVITY 2.4

LIBRARY CHECKLIST

Download the library checklist from the companion website and complete it if you have not done so yet as part of your university's induction programme.

In addition to your university library, your local library may stock relevant materials and is worth checking, too. If there is another university nearby, you may want to enquire what level of access is offered to visitors. There are different arrangements; some will only allow you to study on site while others will allow you to take out a limited number of sources (online materials are usually exempt from any arrangement, though). If you are a member (whether full or associate) of a professional body such as the CIPD, you may also want to check what materials are available through them. Working in and with libraries and other collections will give you access to a wide range of print sources and will keep down your expenses on books.

2.3.3 SELECTING AND ACCESSING ACADEMIC LITERATURE

Once you know your motivation to read and which type of literature will be most appropriate for your purposes, you can start searching for materials. 'What?' you may ask, 'I am still not reading yet? I really cannot afford to waste more time!' I know how tempting it is to roll up your sleeves, get stuck in and play things by ear. But after studying successfully for six degrees, I also know that it is more effective and efficient in the long term to be strategic and follow a logical process. Thorough preparation is the key to success in postgraduate study and beyond.

You may find it useful to focus your selection of literature early on. Currie (2005), for instance, suggests you look at the research field (eg human resource management), followed by the parent discipline (eg human resource planning), sub-discipline (eg recruitment) and research subject (eg interviewing). While in some instances you will be able to identify them relatively easily, you may have to be creative in others and use brainstorming and associated techniques (see also Chapters 14 and 16). Do ask your tutor or librarian for help if you are stuck.

2.3.3.1 Clarifying terms and definitions

If you are new to a field of study (or if you are a non-native speaker exposed to subject vocabulary for the first time), you may want to start browsing the reference literature. You may find that a specialist dictionary and a subject textbook in a particular area are a good starting point for getting to know the subject-specific language of your field of study (this is often called 'jargon'). The dictionary will provide you with key definitions and the textbook will give you a broad overview of the subject, indicating how different aspects of a field of study are related. Both sources will introduce you to the prevalent terminology of the field of study, which is the basis for the identification of key words and a focused search for literature.

2.3.3.2 Identifying key words

Key words describe your area of interest and may even reflect the title of an assignment, project or dissertation (Cottrell 2003) and they are sometimes called 'descriptors' or 'identifiers' (Fink 2005). Key words are the terms that you will type in the library catalogue or online database to identify which sources will be most relevant for your purposes. According to Easterby-Smith et al (2002), a good set of key words is the greatest asset for your literature search, but you need to be aware that a term may refer to different things in databases originating in other (English-speaking) countries and also in different subject areas. If your search is unsuccessful, remember alternative spellings and identify synonyms of the terms you are searching for; a thesaurus will be of great help (Fink 2005). Some search engines allow you to search for more than one term using the AND function or for alternative terms using the OR function to make your search more specific to your needs. Some search engines also allow you to search for subject areas and to exclude a term using the NOT function. So check with the search engine that you are using how to improve your searches, and consult your librarian if in any doubt. Key words can feature in the title of a book or paper, in the list of key words provided in most journal articles, in the table of contents of a book or in the text as such. As a rule, if the key words feature in the title or list of key words, the source tends to be more relevant.

Hart (2002) suggests that you also think about the boundaries of your topic: that is, what is relevant and needs to be included in a particular piece and what is not. Considerations like this may be the last thing on your mind when starting a project, but it is something to be aware of. Any assignment or project will have a word limit and will therefore be limited in scope, yet, a characteristic of postgraduate assignments is their open-endedness. Many of my students complain that the word count of an assignment or project is insufficient, but in my experience even 100,000 words would not be enough for everything that you may want to say. Hence, you will not be able to include everything that might be relevant and you will have to choose carefully what to include and what to leave out. Let me illustrate this.

Imagine you have been given a 2,000 word assignment asking you to discuss theories of motivation that are relevant to explain employee behaviour in twenty-first-century organisations. On the one hand, there is a myriad of theories that seek to explain motivation in employees (the earliest are Maslow and Herzberg), and on the other hand, there is a wide range of behaviours in modern-day organisations, both desired and unacceptable. It is beyond the scope of any piece of work, let alone a 2,000 word assignment, to deal with all of that. It makes sense to focus on a small number of behaviours (for example the recent phenomenon of employees engaging in social networking during working hours) and a small number of theories to explain why this may be the case. This will allow you not only to focus your literature search and reading, but also to deal with the theories and behaviours in sufficient depth to create a critical, discursive argument in your writing and in that way contribute to the knowledge in your field of study.

2.3.4 SEARCHING FOR LITERATURE

Once you have identified the key words of your assignment or project, you can start searching for relevant materials. Wallace and Wray (2006) recommend that you draw up a long list of possible sources, comprising items from reading lists past and present, one or two key textbooks and the names of a few journals that publish relevant papers. It is a good idea to do an initial appraisal of each item before adding it to your long list. Your long list should include both the seminal works by the key authors of your subject area and more recent work that builds on them. The question will be, however, what constitutes a seminal work and how to recognise it. As a rule, the more often you hear about an author or a book or journal article, the more importantly this item is regarded in the subject area. For instance, Herzberg and Maslow are widely recognised as the key authors on motivation and therefore their names will be frequently mentioned in that context. Another clue can be found in the library catalogue: the more copies of a particular book that are available and the more editions of a particular book that have been published, the more important it is regarded as being by those teaching the subject.

When producing your long list of potential sources, make sure you note down the full reference (ie author, date of publication, title of book or journal article, publisher or name of journal plus volume, issue and page numbers; for details

ACTIVITY 2.5

SEARCHING THE LIBRARY CATALOGUE

Search your library catalogue for human resource management textbooks. How many different titles are available? How many copies of a particular title are being provided? Which textbook do you think is the most popular (and possibly the most relevant) among teaching staff?

on referencing please refer to Chapter 3) together with information on how to access it. The latter includes the name of the library or library site if you access more than one, the floor and the shelf mark. You may want to check the availability of these items using the library catalogue and big databases with journal articles and conference proceedings (in business and management, these are currently Business Source Premier, Emerald, JStor, Science Direct and Web of Knowledge). Keeping track of your library search is vital: we all think that we can do without it but never quite manage. There is nothing more stressful than hunting for references in the last few hours before an assignment or project is due!

Currie (2005) proposes eight criteria which can be used to determine the relevance of any source you may wish to include in your written work (see Table 2.3).

2.3.5 ACCESSING THE LITERATURE

Once you have identified how to access what sound like the most appropriate sources, you can access them through your library or any other information portal that it may provide. If you can, scan an item before taking it out (in the case of a hardcopy book or journal article) or before printing it (in the case of an e-book or online journal article) to ensure that the item is indeed what you are looking for. It can be frustrating to locate an item that sounds exactly what you were looking for, just to find that the title is misleading and that the item is not suitable after all. The earlier you come to realise this, however, the better.

One common myth among my students is that you need to start reading at the beginning of a book or paper and finish at the end. Well, it *really* is just a myth. The key to postgraduate study and CPD is strategic and selective reading (Cottrell 2003), always bearing in mind your motivation for reading a particular item. So, when accessing a written source for the first time, start with the **summary information**. In the case of a book, this will be the back flap, table of contents, index and list of figures. In the case of a journal article or other paper, it will be the abstract or executive summary and the list of key words. If the information there sounds promising, progress to the **introduction** and **conclusion** to learn more. You may find that you have already got enough information or that the item is not as relevant or useful as expected; if this is the case, discard it. It is a good idea to make a note of it, though, as it is frustrating to take out an unsuitable item more than once simply because you have lost track.

Table 2.3 Evaluating the relevance of literature

Question	Guidance
1. How recent is the item?	This question does not mean that all of your data should be recent. In fact, many tutors like you to draw on seminal work in the area, which can be 20, 30 or 40 years old and still valid, relevant and important. However, you are expected to demonstrate your awareness of up-to-date thinking.
2. Is the item likely to have been superseded?	To find out, compare the item with other similar items of data, note the dates and assess the degree to which they all match up. If the item is the oldest, does not match up and other theories may be taken as modern alternatives to those in the item, then the likelihood is that it has been superseded.
3. How relevant is the item for the purpose of reading?	Evaluate the degree to which the item is central to your motivation for reading. If it is only marginally relevant, hold on to it and decide later whether to include it.
4. Have you seen references to this item (or its author) in other items that were useful?	If you have, then study those other items to see if this one should be integrated with them. How does it relate to them? Is the item relevant enough to justify inclusion? At the early stages of your literature search, it is not advisable to discard marginal material.
5. Does the item support or contradict your arguments?	If the item supports your argument and is central to what you have to say, it will serve as evidence for your case. If it is contrary, you may still decide to use it when you are comparing and contrasting what others have said.
6. Does the item appear to be biased? Even if it does, it may still be relevant.	While not all published material provides a balanced view of the subject, what is said may be relevant to the questions you are answering. You have to decide whether it fits into your argument and, if so, where. Depending on your task, you may have to justify why you included this item despite its bias.
7. What are the methodological omissions from the work? Even if there are any, it may still be relevant.	Does the item include sufficient evidence to support what is being said? Should the researcher have used different research methods and, perhaps, further methods so that the data could be cross-checked? How valuable is it to your task? Depending on your task, you may have to justify why you included this item despite its methodological omissions.
8. Is the precision sufficient? Even if it is imprecise, it may be the only item that you can find, and so may still be relevant.	Lack of precision may have occurred in the application of the data gathering and analytic techniques. Before you use imprecise data, you have to check their validity. If you decide to use something you should point out where you think the imprecision lies. If it is the only item you could find when you did the search, try searching further for other items that support the claim. Depending on your task, you may have to justify why you included in this item despite its imprecision.

Source: adapted from D. Currie (2005), *Developing and applying study skills,* CIPD, London, p78.

If the source is relevant and suitable, you will need to select the most relevant **parts, headings and subheadings** of the book or paper. Buzan (1977) suggests that scanning the item with a focus on headings and anything that is highlighted (with figures, colour, bullet points, bigger font, bold or italic print etc) will give you the gist of the text. Once you have selected the most relevant parts, read the **first paragraph of a section** (Cottrell 2003) as well as the last, which should contain the most important information (Buzan 1977). Bearing in mind your motivation for reading that particular item, you need to decide how you can use what you are reading and how much detail you need; this may vary from source to source. More often than not, you will read for content of a particular theory or research project. Sometimes, it will be enough to briefly mention a particular fact, but sometimes you will have to discuss large parts of it in great depth. However, you may also wish to adopt a particular research approach used in your source or borrow elements of style that are particularly effective. Once you have decided which elements of a source to read, you can start to read critically and in depth. But what does this mean, you may wonder?

2.3.6 CRITICAL READING AND ANALYSIS

Critical reading means applying your critical thinking skills when selecting, reading and analysing written materials. This means identifying and evaluating the main argument of the text, asking questions like 'What is this text about?', 'What is the purpose of this text?', 'What is the author trying to say?' (Wallace and Wray 2006). It will be useful to bear in mind the different types of literature here. As the names suggest, a theoretical piece will be written to advance theory, while a practical piece will focus on practice. Hence, you cannot expect a theoretical piece to tell you much about practice and vice versa, and you will need to bear this in mind when analysing that piece. Critical reading is a slow process (Cottrell 2003) because you will need to read, scrutinise what you have read using the questions listed in Section 2.2 above, think over what you have read, make notes of both content and your thoughts, and maybe go back to the text to re-read a particular passage and go through the above steps again. However, only such a thorough process will give you the in-depth understanding that is required for many tasks that you will encounter during your postgraduate studies and beyond.

Critical reading focuses on the main argument of a text and you will therefore need to understand the components of an argument and how to analyse it. It is widely recognised that an argument consists of a claim and a justification and that an unjustified claim is nothing but an opinion (eg Fisher 2001, Wallace and Wray 2006, Lapakko 2009). Let us take the following sentence, which I have seen in many student assignments: 'Organisation A is an innovative organisation.' This is an opinion. If we add a justification, such as 'because it has adopted the latest management thinking for their human resource processes', then we have created a very basic argument. So, an argument is essentially a causal relationship between two pieces of information (the claim and the justification), and this causal relationship is often highlighted by the use of the following language indicators (Fisher 2001, Wallace and Wray 2006):

because, since, for, so, hence, thus, consequently, therefore

it follows that, x demonstrates that, it must be concluded that.

This list is not exhaustive, of course, but intended to serve as a starting point for your critical analysis of text. You may want to look out for such language indicators when reading and analysing a text, but you may find that the causal relationship that you are looking for is simply implied (Lapakko 2009). The logical strength of an argument depends not only on the extent to which the claim is justified (Hughes 2000), but also on the way this is done – whether by facts, data or other evidence, by definitions or principles, or by causal explanations, recommendations and value judgements (Fisher 2001). Claims justified by facts, data or evidence tend to be strong (Lapakko 2009), so be aware of value judgements and unfounded recommendations, particularly if they are well presented. Your prime task will be to determine how convincing the argument is by evaluating the claim, the accompanying justification and any evidence presented against the background of its purpose. It will be useful to identify which evidence is essential to prove a point (necessary conditions) and whether there is a range of conditions that must be met if a point is to be proven (sufficient conditions). Cottrell (2005) distinguishes the two as follows: a necessary condition can be identified through the statement 'without this, then not that ...' (p109) and a sufficient condition can be identified through the statement 'if this, then that' (p110). For instance, a university degree is a sufficient condition for access to postgraduate study, while a particular degree classification, a relevant degree, finance and work experience may be necessary conditions to be admitted to the programme of your choice.

It is also the reader's task to identify the critical assumption behind an argument and to determine whether it is reasonable (Lapakko 2009, drawing on Toulmin 1958). So, in the example above about the innovative organisation, the critical assumption (ie the assumption on which the causal relationship between claim and justification depends) is that an organisation that has adopted the latest management thinking for its human resource processes is innovative. As the term 'innovative' is defined as 'featuring new methods' (*Oxford dictionary thesaurus and wordpower guide* 2001, p669), the argument that 'Organisation A is an innovative organisation because it has adopted the latest management thinking for their human resource processes' is probably reasonable. The absence of such a critical assumption is often called a non-sequitur, which is Latin for 'does not follow' and which suggests that the assumptions do not support the claim of the argument. You can see that scrutinising a text in that way answers many of the questions outlined in Section 2.2 above. You may want to track the claim and justification(s) of an argument graphically through an **argument map** (Cameron 2007). An argument map identifies the claim, justifications and evidence as well as any supporting or opposing links, as illustrated by Figure 2.3.

An argument map can also help you to identify any flaws in the argument, of which there are many different types. Firstly, if you are left with questions like 'Why?' or 'So what?' while reading a text in detail (Wallace and Wray 2006), there is likely to be something missing. So, if you are left asking 'Why?', then the justification is weak or missing. If in the earlier example the argument consisted only of the claim, ie that 'Organisation A is an innovative organisation', then you

Figure 2.3 Argument map for 'HRM in Russia'

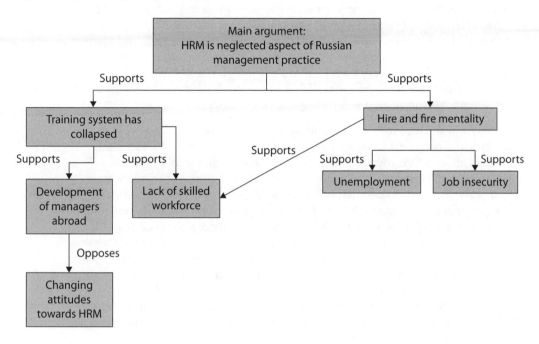

would quite rightly ask why that was allegedly the case. If you are left asking 'So what?', then the claim is weak or missing. If in that example the argument consisted only of the justification, ie that 'Organisation A has adopted the latest management thinking for their human resource processes,' you might rightly wonder why this is important or relevant. In addition, it will be beneficial to examine the evidence that is provided for the justification (Lapakko 2009). In the above example, you may want to determine whether the management thinking that has been adopted by Organisation A is indeed as recent as claimed, or whether these allegedly new ideas have indeed been applied to their human resource processes.

Other flaws in the argument are more difficult to detect, and some authors can be very good at masking a flaw in the argument through the use of deflective language (Cottrell 2005). On the one hand, deflective language includes words that suggest that a claim is so obvious that it does not need to be proved, such as 'naturally, of course, clearly, obviously'. On the other hand, deflective language also includes attempts by the author(s) to collude with the audience through phrases like 'everybody knows/believes, as we all know, anyone with any sense' and so on. Critical reading will help you to identify such tactics.

It is crucial that you take detailed notes about what you are reading as well as your thoughts about the text. Cameron (2007) suggests that note-taking enhances both your concentration and understanding, helps you to retain what you have read and is useful when revising content. Perhaps more importantly, writing supports your thinking (Huff 2002) and allows you to create new knowledge. To support your reading and note-taking, you may want to photocopy or print relevant sections of a book or journal article so that you can code, highlight, cross-reference and comment on the most important parts of the text (this is also called annotation, Cameron 2007) or use a voice recorder to record your thoughts. It may be a good idea to start a small database of what you have read and what you learned from each item to keep you on track (Hart 2002). Specialist software packages are available, but a simple database on record cards or a computer spreadsheet will usually do the trick (see also Chapter 13).

In order to enhance your understanding of what you have read, you may find it particularly beneficial to create a **knowledge web** (Birkenbihl 2007) for each subject about which you are reading. A knowledge web is a collection of information that you already know about the field of study (or maybe even a particular aspect of it) and that helps you to 'trap' other pieces of information like a spider's web. A good starting point for a knowledge web is the creation of an **alphabetical list** (Birkenbihl 2007) at the beginning of your project and this is how to do it. Divide a plain sheet of paper into two columns. Write the alphabet from top to bottom in the first column. Then take a minute or two to fill in the second column with relevant words, terms and concepts that you already know about the subject in question. It is important to write anything down in the order you think of it rather than alphabetically to get as full an account of your previous knowledge as possible. Feel free to write down more than one word per letter if necessary. Why not give it a try?

ACTIVITY 2.6

ABC LISTS

Take a plain sheet of paper, fold it in half to create two columns and write the alphabet from the top down in the first column. Then allow yourself 90 seconds to jot down anything you know about 'coaching' or a subject that is closer to your heart. Your time starts now.

What does your list look like? How many terms and concepts have you come up with? How many blanks are there? You may want to compare results with a peer or in a small group and fill in any more terms and concepts that you are learning in this process. You will be surprised at how quickly your alphabetical list will fill up and how easy it is to add any other terms. Once you have built a framework of terms and concepts with your alphabetical list, you can start mapping your knowledge web graphically and add any links in the style of a **MindMap** (Buzan 2000). If you prefer, you can apply the **post-it note technique**, in which you write each key term and concept of your subject of study on an individual post-it note and then use a big sheet of paper to determine the relationship between the different elements. The advantage is that you can move things around, either on your own or in a small group, until you are happy with how they relate to each other. In that way, you can build up your understanding about the subject in question and link anything you read to information that you already know. Do not worry if the techniques outlined above are not for you, there are many more and I would encourage you to experiment with different techniques to find out what suits you best.

In conclusion, critical reading is an in-depth way of engaging with written materials that helps you to enhance your understanding of a subject and your ability to make informed decisions. Critical reading will enable you to analyse both written and oral materials for their quality and their relevance, allowing you to make informed judgements about which sources to draw on and to what extent. This will have a major impact on your studies, particularly the way in which you approach any new task, access written texts and select materials to include in your writing. Critical reading is also the foundation for critical writing in postgraduate study and beyond. It is a somewhat time-consuming process, but what counts in postgraduate study is the depth of your analysis. Engaging with the process of critical reading will enable you to work more efficiently and effectively as you will be more thoughtful about the decisions you make and more careful in approaching your work. As a result, you will waste less time on unproductive ad hoc reading and writing.

2.4 APPLYING CRITICAL THINKING (2): WRITING

2.4.1 CRITICAL WRITING

Critical writing means applying your critical thinking skills to your writing, which is a vital process for the creation and communication of knowledge in the social sciences. Critical writing is best perceived as the continuation of the critical reading process outlined in the previous section as you will be drawing on the understanding of argumentation that you will have built there. Critical writing is about carefully crafting the argument of your writing by determining the claim, justification and any supporting evidence in the light of the intended audience (Wallace and Wray 2006). The deconstruction of ideas as well as the analysis and evaluation of arguments are at the heart of critical writing (Moon 2007), which also involves asking questions such as:

- What is the critical assumption I am making? How reasonable is it?
- Are all claims I am making supported by evidence? How credible and appropriate is the evidence supporting my argument?
- Are my conclusions based on evidence and reasonable assumptions?
- Have I clarified expressions, claims and the meaning of key terms and concepts?
- Does my argument follow a logical line of thought?
- Have I considered alternative arguments?

You can see from the above questions that critical writing is a well-planned process that will enhance the quality of your work in various ways. Firstly, it will allow you to develop what Moon (2007) calls 'academic assertiveness', a concept which comprises notions of challenging other authors' work, acknowledging alternative viewpoints, finding your voice and developing confidence in your writing. Secondly, your writing will be more logical and convincing because the claim and justification of your argument can be clearly identified and supported by high-quality evidence. Thirdly, your writing will be more concise if you approach it in a critical fashion because you will be more thoughtful in the way you work (see also Chapter 3, Section 3.2). Remember that as a postgraduate student you are expected to contribute to the knowledge of your subject area through research and independent thought experiments. Only if you know your subject, will you be able to do so with confidence, and this is what examiners tend to look for in postgraduate students' work. You are unlikely to receive good grades without it.

2.4.2 DEVELOPING ORIGINAL ARGUMENTS

One of the biggest let-downs I encounter in student work is a lack of argument: it is not clear what the student wants to say (lack of claim) and/or why this is worth saying (lack of justification). Hence, it is fundamental that you establish the claim and justification of your argument at the outset of a new writing project. This is often easier said than done but the analysis of text through critical reading will have given you a sound understanding of your subject, and the development of a knowledge web or other techniques will have supported this. You may also wish to map out your argument using an argument map (Cameron 2007), which is useful both for critical reading and writing. Wallace and Wray (2006) recommend the creation of a **subject map**, which brings together the key elements of a topic under investigation as well as their causal relationships; an example can be found on the companion website.

Most of us will go through an unstructured thought process looking at different observations, experiences, theories and models that will lead us to the conclusion. This conclusion will then constitute the claim of our argument. For instance, in the example of the presentation on HRM in Russia (Klose and Reissner 2000), my colleague and I will have drawn on what fellow students (Russian managers studying for a British MBA) will have told us about their work and organisation. We will have looked at the literature on human resource management in different countries to see if our fellow students' experiences have been validated by other sources. We will have developed our argument by discussing our observations and our understanding from the literature. According to Fisher (2001) there are two approaches for the structure of reasoning, which allow you to check whether your argument is logical. The first approach is about the development of a chain of reasoning, which consists of at least four elements that are linked by the words 'so – thus – therefore': firstly, a statement which leads to claim 1 ('so'), which is the justification for claim 2 ('thus'), which leads to the overall conclusion or claim ('therefore'). Going back to the above example, this chain of reasoning could look as follows: increasing globalisation requires an effective HR function in Russian firms, so Russian firms need to adapt and build an HR function; thus attitudes of Russian managers towards HR need to change; therefore, there is a need for HR training and reform in Russian firms. This chain of reasoning can be graphically presented as shown in Figure 2.4.

Figure 2.4 Arguing through a chain of reasoning

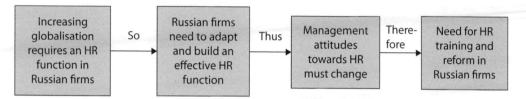

The second approach is to list a series of side-by-side justifications, which lead to the overall claim and which are linked by 'also – furthermore – for all these reasons'. Again, going back to the example of HRM in Russia, the argument could be structured as follows: globalisation requires an effective HR function in Russian firms; also the previous training system has collapsed; furthermore the workforce needs new skills; so for all these reasons, there is a need for HR training and reform in Russian firms. This structure of reasoning is graphically represented in Figure 2.5 below.

Figure 2.5 Arguing through side-by-side justification

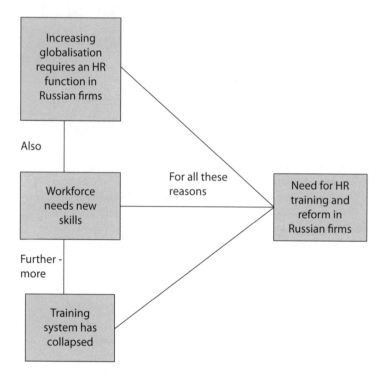

An alternative approach to developing your argument and structuring it logically is the use of pyramids (Minto 2002). Every piece of writing should have one key thought (claim), which summarises other ideas (justification and evidence). Each idea will receive its own box and all boxes will be structured to form a pyramid, in which the claim is at the top. The pyramid can consist of an indefinite number of layers, which are linked by the question 'Why?'. Find it difficult to picture? Again going back to the example of HRM in Russia, our argument pyramid could look like Figure 2.6 below.

Figure 2.6 Example of an argument pyramid

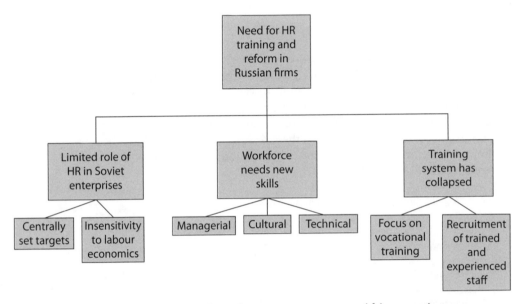

Do bear in mind that the creation of your argument pyramid is a creative process in which the different elements, groupings and links are likely to change. You can build your pyramid from the top down or from the bottom up. Minto (2002) suggests that the former is usually more effective if you already know what you want to say as you can map out your claim, justifications and supporting evidence to keep you on track. The latter is usually more effective if you are unsure of your argument because you can list all the points that should feature in your writing, establish the relationship between them and draw conclusions from that. You may find it useful to build a skeleton pyramid and fill in any gaps as you go along. If you feel restricted by writing down your pyramid on paper, try the post-it note technique again or use a computer programme that allows you to shift any boxes (most graphical software will allow you to do that, although this can be cumbersome). If you find it difficult to determine the top of your pyramid, the central idea of your text, ask yourself what it is that you want the reader to learn from your writing. It is often useful to write this down and simplify it until you have reached a basic sentence or question; this will be the claim of your argument. In addition, you may want to consider how much the reader is likely to know and may want to learn as well as how much you know and may want to tell (Kaye 1989). It may also make sense to check your plan against the assignment title to make sure that you answer all the elements of the assignment question.

2.4.3 STRATEGIES FOR SMART WRITING

The act of writing is an integral part of logical thinking and creativity, and it is therefore a smart move to make writing a regular habit as a postgraduate student (Huff 1999). You may wonder how you can write for what seems like the sake of writing when you have many other balls to juggle? Writing has been used for centuries to explore ideas and search for answers, so disciplined writing will enhance the quality of your thinking and therefore the quality of your written work. Writing will help you to express what you are thinking, deconstruct your ideas on paper and confront your own ideas in small thought experiments. Clear writing reflects clear thinking and this is what examiners are looking for in postgraduate work, and it will also support any other CPD measures that you are undertaking. Admittedly, this sometimes is easier said than done and there are a number of techniques that you can employ to start thinking and writing.

The **bubble technique** is a good tool to think (and write) about the relationship between different aspects of a field of study, or elements of an argument or theory, in a structured and logical manner. Once you have identified the key aspects or elements of what you are going to write about, put each of them into a bubble and let the bubbles overlap. Then assign a number to each bubble and each area of overlap, as graphically presented in Figure 2.7.

Now you can think about the different areas and relationships (there are 13 in this example) in a structured and logical manner, writing down your thoughts as well as any evidence that you may wish to provide for support. For example, Number Four will help you to take stock of what you know about training in the context of your studies in general, a particular module or even task. Number

Figure 2.7 The bubble technique applied to HRM in Russia

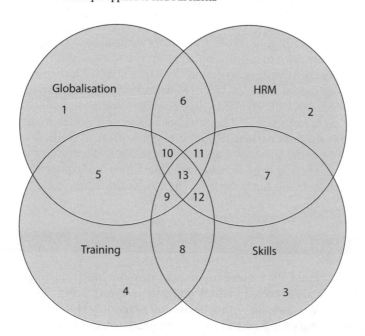

Eight will help you to think about the relationship between training and skills, and you may want to explore what skills can be built effectively through training and what the limitations of training as a means of skills-building are. Number Thirteen will help you to explore training and skills development in the wider context of human resource management and a trend towards globalisation. Exploratory writing in such a structured manner can be most beneficial and I encourage you to give it a go – it may well work for you! Often, you will be able to use large parts of what you have written in such an exploratory fashion for your final piece with only minor rephrasing required, and it is in these instances that thorough preparation pays off.

I find it also useful to check my writing prior to submission using the **PowerPoint technique**. If you are familiar with PowerPoint or a similar computer package, this may well work for you. I put the claim of my argument on the first slide and then map the key points (justification) on to other slides as they appear in the text. A few words for each slide are usually enough, so this exercise can be done quickly. This allows me to check for structure, causal links, repetitions and omissions, and gives me the confidence to submit a piece of writing that is the best that I can master at a particular point in time.

ACTIVITY 2.7

USING MAPPING TECHNIQUES

Experiment with the different techniques discussed in this section to see which ones work best for you. You may want to use an assignment as part of your study, a report for work or anything else that you are working on at present to practise critical reading and writing.

Following the critical reading and writing processes outlined above and checking your work thoroughly prior to submission will help you to avoid the most common faults in student writing as outlined by Barrass (2002): lack of knowledge and understanding, lack of evidence, lack of logic, lack of relevance, lack of balance, lack of order, lack of originality, bias, repetition and poor organisation. These faults are more easily detected in other people's writing, which makes scrutinising your own work particularly important. If you are in doubt that you can do it entirely by yourself, why not ask a peer, a colleague, a friend or a relative to help you? There is bound to be somebody in your network of contacts who is both critical and honest and can help you to improve your written work.

2.5 CONCLUSION

Postgraduate study and CPD require you to become more independent as a learner, because you are expected to think critically and work independently to create and share new knowledge with scholars and practitioners in your field of study. While your tutors will give you guidance and advice, much of your learning will come from the level of engagement in the tasks and the quality of the processes and techniques that you employ in your studies. The one skill that will allow you to do this is critical thinking, the foundation of postgraduate study and CPD. It will allow you to approach any task or project in a structured and thoughtful manner, to make decisions as to which sources to consult and which content to include, to analyse and evaluate arguments and to develop and justify your own. I encourage you to keep honing your ability to be critical when studying the other chapters in this book as your ability as a learner will improve. I also encourage you, in true postgraduate fashion, to delve more deeply into any areas that you feel may benefit from more theoretical understanding or practical application.

PAUSE FOR THOUGHT

Identify at least three things that you have learned by studying this chapter and engaging with the activities. How will your newly acquired knowledge and skills support your continuing professional development? What value do you expect your learning to have for your daily routines and your further career? In what area have you identified a need for further development and how are you planning to fill that gap? Address these issues in your learning journal and/or CPD log. You may also wish to discuss them with a peer, colleague, mentor or coach to aid your further development.

KEY LEARNING POINTS

- Postgraduate study and CPD are more advanced than undergraduate study, and previously built skills will need to be honed to achieve mastery at the required level.

- Critical thinking is a meta-skill that subsumes and enhances other skills. It is the foundation for successful postgraduate study and CPD.

- As a postgraduate student, you are expected to think independently, critique the experts and develop knowledge for the community of scholarly activity in your chosen field.

EXPLORE FURTHER

FISHER, A. (2001) *Critical thinking: an introduction*. Cambridge: Cambridge University Press.

FOUNDATION FOR CRITICAL THINKING [website]: http://www.criticalthinking.org/.

VAN DEN BRINK-BUDGEN, R. (2000) *Critical thinking for students*. 3rd ed. Oxford: How To Books.

2.6 REFERENCES

BARRASS, R. (2002) *Study! A guide to effective learning, revision and examination techniques*. 2nd ed. London: Routledge.

BIRKENBIHL, V.F. (2007) *ABC Kreativ: Techniken zur kreativen Problemlösung*. 4th expanded ed. Munich: Hugendubel (Ariston).

BROOKFIELD, S. (1987) *Developing critical thinkers*. Milton Keynes: Open University Press.

BUZAN, T. (1977) *Speed reading*. Newton Abbot: David & Charles.

BUZAN, T. (2000) *The MindMap book*. With Barry Buzan. Millennium ed. London: BBC Books.

CAMERON, S. (2007) *The business student's handbook*. 4th ed. Harlow: Pearson.

COTTRELL, S. (2003) *The study skills handbook*. 2nd ed. Basingstoke: Palgrave Macmillan.

COTTRELL, S. (2005) *Critical thinking skills*. Basingstoke: Palgrave Macmillan.

CURRIE, D. (2005) *Developing and applying study skills*. London: CIPD.

DE BONO, E. (1976) *Teaching thinking*. Harmondsworth: Penguin.

EASTERBY-SMITH, M., THORPE, R. and LOWE, A. (2002) *Management research: an introduction*. 2nd ed. London: Sage.

FINK, A. (2005) *Conducting research literature reviews*. Thousand Oaks, CA: Sage.

FISHER, A. (2001) *Critical thinking: an introduction*. Cambridge: Cambridge University Press.

HART, C. (1998) *Doing a literature review*. London: Sage.

HART, C. (2002) *Doing a literature search*. London: Sage.

HUFF, A. (1999) *Writing for scholarly publication*. London: Sage.

HUFF, A. (2002) Learning to be a successful writer. In D. Partington (ed), *Essential skills for management research*. London: Sage, pp72–83.

HUGHES, W. (2000) *Critical thinking: an introduction to the basic skills*. 3rd ed. Toronto: Broadview Press.

KAYE, S. (1989) *Writing under pressure*. New York and Oxford: Oxford University Press.

KLOSE, D. and REISSNER, S.C. (2000) HRM in Russia: stepchild of management practices? Presentation for module International Human Resource Management, MA International

Business Administration, Newcastle Business School, University of Northumbria at Newcastle, 7th December.

LAPAKKO, D. (2009) *Argumentation: critical thinking in action*. 2nd ed. New York: iUniverse.

MINTO, B. (2002) *The pyramid principle*, 3rd ed. Harlow: Pearson.

MOON, J. (2007) *Critical thinking: an exploration of theory and practice*. London: Routledge.

Oxford dictionary thesaurus and wordpower guide. (2001) Oxford: Oxford University Press.

PAUL, R.W. and ELDER, L. (2002) *Critical thinking: tools for taking charge of your professional and personal life*. Harlow: Pearson.

QAA. (2002) *Subject benchmark statements: Masters awards in business and management*. Available online at: http://www.qaa.ac.uk/academicinfrastructure/benchmark/masters/mba.pdf [accessed 13 October 2009].

QAA. (2007) *Subject benchmark statements: General business and management*. Available online at: http://www.qaa.ac.uk/academicinfrastructure/benchmark/statements/GeneralBusinessManagement.pdf [accessed 13 October 2009].

QAA. (2008) *The framework for higher education qualifications in England, Wales and Northern Ireland*. Available online at: http://www.qaa.ac.uk/academicinfrastructure/FHEQ/EWNI08/FHEQ08.pdf [accessed 2 December 2009].

UNC UNIVERSITY LIBRARIES. (2007) Library terms glossary. Available online at: http://www.lib.unc.edu/instruct/international/glossary/#p [accessed 13 November 2009].

WALLACE, M. and WRAY, A. (2006) *Critical reading and writing for postgraduates*. London: Sage.

CHAPTER 3

Practical aspects of postgraduate study skills

Stefanie C. Reissner

OVERVIEW

Writing is a crucial means of communication for postgraduate students and competent professionals, and it is vital that you master this skill with confidence. Building on the critical thinking skills developed in the previous chapter, this chapter explores the characteristics of effective writing. You will learn about what makes an effective report, essay, review, project and dissertation, as well as tips and tricks from the writer's toolbox. You will also learn the basic rules of academic referencing (including the rationale for it) and how you can avoid the academic sin of sins – plagiarism. Finally, you will learn how to revise and prepare for examinations the smart way with the exam revision guide available on the companion website.

LEARNING OUTCOMES

By the end of this chapter, provided you engage with the activities, you should be able to:

- understand the characteristics and techniques of effective writing
- apply critical thinking skills to the writing of reports, essays, reviews, projects and dissertations
- reference other authors' work correctly
- revise subject knowledge for examinations.

3.1 INTRODUCTION

Writing is the main means of communicating new knowledge and ideas to others and is therefore a crucial skill for postgraduate students and competent professionals. Writing is both an art and a science, which means that although having a talent for writing is beneficial, there are techniques that you can learn in order to make your writing more effective (Peck and Coyle 2005a). There are widely recognised norms of formal writing that are relevant to postgraduate students and those studying for continuing professional development, and in addition there are specific norms that ought to be adhered to in an academic and educational setting. That is what this chapter is about: helping you to understand what effective writing in a university context looks like and providing advice on how to improve your writing for academic and professional purposes. Academic writing will also help you to compile an effective CPD log as required by your employer and professional associations like the CIPD.

This chapter builds on the previous one by explaining the specific norms of different types of writing which you will encounter during your postgraduate studies and beyond. They are specific to the Anglo-Saxon tradition of education, and if you use this book in a different context, please ask your tutor about the relevant conventions. Issues of critical writing, argumentation and the structuring of thought as discussed in Chapter 2 apply to this chapter. In the following sections, we will discuss generic characteristics of effective texts before moving on to effective reports, essays and reviews as well as effective projects and dissertations. In addition, we will cover the basic rules of referencing and how to avoid plagiarism. There is also a detailed exam revision guide available on the companion website.

3.2 EFFECTIVE WRITING IN AN ACADEMIC AND PROFESSIONAL CONTEXT

Effective writing means communicating knowledge, understanding and skills to others in a clear and concise manner. It is a transferable skill that will enhance both formal studies and career progression (Cameron 2007). Effective writing requires understanding of arguments (see Chapter 2), structure and language as well as practice of how to construct a text. It has been compared to building a house (Cottrell 2003, Peck and Coyle 2005a), which requires careful planning, a logical structure, building blocks (ie sections and paragraphs) as well as cement to stick the building blocks together (ie language indicators). We have attended to the planning aspects in the previous chapter. This section will focus on the structure and language of effective writing in an academic and professional context. Like building a house, however, effective writing requires hard work and patience, and you are encouraged to take every opportunity to hone your writing skills at university and at work.

3.2.1 THE STRUCTURE OF EFFECTIVE WRITING

The structure of a text is the framework in which the argument is placed and according to which it is organised. It should follow a logical line of thought and leave the reader with no further questions. A clear structure will enhance the content of a text as it makes it easier for the reader to understand and assess what is being communicated. Some students make a big mistake by copying the structure of an effective text and adding some mediocre content to it, thinking that they have produced a great piece of work. A good structure will only enhance good content, but it will not improve the content as such. The smart writing techniques outlined in Chapter 2 may help you to determine what structure would be most appropriate to communicate an argument. An effective piece of writing has the following three main parts, which you are probably familiar with:

1. Introduction.

2. Main body, which comprises reporting and evaluating content (Wallace and Wray 2006).

3. Conclusion.

The introduction states the claim of an argument, ie what the text is about. In a short text, such as a 2,000-word assignment, one or two paragraphs are usually enough (Peck and Coyle 2005b), and it is good practice to start with a simple and straightforward **opening statement**. This will encompass the argument and awaken the readers' interest (Peck and Coyle 2005a). You can even be controversial here, for instance starting a critical discussion of organisational change with a statement like 'change is good'. This will make the reader suspicious yet curious to learn more about what you have to say. The opening statement should be a simple sentence consisting of subject, verb and object (Cameron 2007). Alternatively, for a longer piece, such as a 20,000-word dissertation, the **narrative technique** may be employed, which outlines a situation, introduces a complication and ends with a question (Minto 2002); the answer is given in the main body of the text. The advantage of such a direct opening is that it establishes a point of reference that will help the reader to follow the argument more easily (Peck and Coyle 2005a).

The claim of an argument is justified in the main body of the text and supported by appropriate evidence (see Chapter 2). By the time the reader has finished with the introduction, he/she should want to learn more about the justification of the claim and any supporting evidence, particularly if the text started with a controversial opening statement. It is a good idea to limit the number of points that build the argument and deal with them in turn and in depth, employing different argumentation techniques (Fisher 2001), as discussed in the previous chapter.

The conclusion summarises the argument and highlights any key points, such as what you want the reader to learn or take away for further thought or discussion. It is sometimes appropriate to include general learning points or practical recommendations, so please check your assignment brief or ask your tutor if in doubt.

It is often beneficial to reinforce the structure of a text as different paragraphs will represent different thoughts (Minto 2002). While it is not untypical to use the heading 'Introduction' for the introduction and 'Conclusion' for the conclusion, it is bad practice to label the main body of the text as 'main body'. The main body of the text represents the justification of the claim presented in the introduction and its heading should reflect this. It may be useful to provide a sub-heading for each point of justification and its evidence. Other highlighting techniques include the use of numbering or bullet points in the text, the use of underlined or bold font, indentation, frames, shades and figures. Some of these may not be appropriate in a short assignment, but may be useful for longer projects or dissertations if used strategically and sparingly.

3.2.2 THE LANGUAGE OF EFFECTIVE WRITING

Language is symbolic and does not have intrinsic meaning, and this complicates any act of communication (Lapakko 2009); there are also cultural differences in the way language is used. Hence, to be effective, the language of formal writing should be:

- concise
- unambiguous, and
- professional.

Concise means 'giving a lot of information clearly and in few words' (*Oxford dictionary thesaurus and wordpower guide* 2001, p244) and is about using specific terminology and cutting out unnecessary words. Firstly, this is about avoiding unfounded generalisations and vague terminology. For instance, 'Organisation A makes huge profits' could be replaced by 'Organisation A has made profits in excess of £100,000 over the last five years' to make it more precise. Secondly, words that do not add to the meaning of a sentence should be avoided. For instance, the sentence 'A psychologist called Abraham Maslow developed a theory of motivation' could be made more concise by leaving out 'a psychologist called'. Concise also means avoiding tautology, ie expressing the same thing in different words in the same sentence (Cottrell 2005), for example 'visual image'.

Language in formal writing should be unambiguous, which means that a term should have only one meaning and that this meaning is clearly defined. For instance, you may have to refer to different types of employees in a text. You may want to call those with management responsibility 'managers', those in administrative positions 'staff' and those in a production environment 'workers'. The reader will then be able to follow the argument without wondering what the different terms mean.

Finally, effective writing uses professional language, ie formal and objective language in which abbreviations are used sparingly (Cottrell 2003) and only after introduction. Formal and objective language avoids terminology such as 'huge', 'wonderful' or 'great' and instead provides specific details to produce the desired effect (see earlier example about profits in Organisation A). It is considered bad form to use contractions, such as wasn't, didn't, couldn't, as this is colloquial rather than formal or professional use of language (Peck and Coyle 2005b). Moreover, Orwell (1962) warns of the use of extensively used metaphors and clichés in a text. Simple language and simple sentences are widely regarded as the most effective communication tool as they allow the communication of complex thoughts in a concise and therefore effective manner. American or British spelling should be used consistently throughout a text (with the exception of direct quotations from other sources, which need to be left in their original spelling); please be aware that your tutor may prefer British or American spelling, so do check with him or her if in doubt.

There are two more pitfalls in academic writing which you should be aware of. Firstly, it is considered bad form to use absolute terms, such as 'always', 'never', 'all/every' because such a clear relationship can rarely be established in the social sciences, and academic writing is expected to reflect this, particularly at postgraduate level. It is much more effective to substitute these terms with 'in most instances', 'in most cases', 'generally', 'typically', 'usually', 'often', 'tend to', 'unlikely', 'rarely', 'some', 'many', 'most' and the like. (Cottrell 2005). Secondly, it is also considered bad form to use linguistic tricks to persuade your audience, such as to provoke an emotional response, to attack a person or group of persons, or to suggest that something is appropriate because somebody else has done it that way (Cottrell 2005). The language in academic writing should be more objective than in other forms of writing so that knowledge can be shared and developed further within a community of scholars and practitioners, for instance for CPD purposes.

3.2.3 THE INTERPLAY OF STRUCTURE AND LANGUAGE

Structure and language in a text are interdependent. Sentences are independent units in their own right, which consist of subject, verb and object and at the same time depend on the other sentences in a text to create a logical argument. Often the relationship between sentences is implicit in the text, but sometimes it is effective to use language indicators to clarify the relationship between sentences. Table 3.1 below summarises the most common ones.

The use of language indicators will also make the relationship between sentences, sections and possibly chapters explicit. They signpost the structure of the text to the audience and thus help the reader to follow the argument more easily, which is vital for long texts such as projects and dissertations.

3.2.4 TIPS AND TRICKS OF EFFECTIVE WRITING

Effective writing is writing with a *purpose* and with an *audience* in mind (Peck and Coyle 2005b). The purpose of writing may be exploratory or, probably more commonly, to convince the audience of one's knowledge and understanding of a subject as well as the mastery of relevant skills. Hence, the language should be objective, formal and professional as discussed above. It also good practice to avoid any tendency, however, innocent, of sexism (Peck and Coyle 2005b), for instance any stereotypes that managers are male and secretaries female. The pronouns 'he' and 'she' can often be replaced by the plural 'they' or the sentence can be rephrased so that it does not require a pronoun. Another pitfall is certain professions or roles, such as spokesman or chairman, which are more appropriately called 'spokesperson' or 'chairperson'.

Effective writing is about striving to achieve high standards (Peck and Coyle 2005b), and a few simple steps can ensure marked improvement. It should be

Table 3.1 Language indicators

Purpose	Examples
Opening a phrase	first of all, firstly, to begin with, at the outset
Adding a point	furthermore, moreover, in addition
Emphasising a point	however, nevertheless, indeed, not only … but also
Reinforcing a point	similarly, likewise, also, besides, in addition, as well as, furthermore, moreover, indeed
Providing examples	for instance, for example, namely, particularly, notably, including
Listing different points	firstly, secondly, thirdly, finally, in conclusion
Presenting alternatives	it might be argued that, on the one hand … on the other hand, by contrast, alternatively, despite, even though
Dealing with contrast	although, in fact, by contrast
Expressing a consequence	hence, thus, therefore, as a result, consequently
Concluding	in conclusion, thus we can see

Source: based on Cottrell (2003, 2005).

second nature for postgraduate students and competent professionals to use the **grammar and spell checker** of their word processor before submitting any piece. If spelling and grammar are not your strengths or English is not your first language, ask somebody to proofread your piece for you. An occasional mistake will be readily excused, but too many typos, unfinished sentences or grammatical errors will create an unfavourable impression in the reader's mind.

It is a great though somewhat eccentric idea to **read out loud** what you have written (Peck and Coyle 2005a), which I use regularly. By reading out loud, you will get a better idea of how clear the argument is, how well the sentences hang together, how well the language works and whether there are any repetitions or omissions. If you struggle to read to yourself what you have written without pausing or changing emphasis, then something is not quite right. Take the opportunity to restructure sentences, use different words and introduce language indicators and headings to make the text clearer; this can be the difference between a decent and a good grade.

3.3 WRITING EFFECTIVE REPORTS, ESSAYS AND CRITICAL REVIEWS

3.3.1 WRITING EFFECTIVE REPORTS AND ESSAYS

The characteristics of effective writing outlined in the previous section will apply to writing effective reports and essays and will not be repeated here. The report is one of the most common formats of writing in postgraduate studies in business and management and continuing professional development. It seeks, as its name suggests, to report on something, such as a fresh look at the literature or research into management practice. A good report is informative and concise and uses a formal structure with headings. While, according to Cottrell (2003), it is customary to provide acknowledgements, an abstract and a table of contents for longer reports (such as projects or dissertations, see Section 3.4 below), an average 2,000-word assignment does not normally require these elements; if in doubt, please ask your tutor.

Another common format of academic writing is the essay, a formal type of writing that responds to a question or proposition 'in a logical, reasoned and evidenced manner' (Horn 2009, p292). It can help you to explore a question in depth (Cottrell 2003) and to develop your thinking through writing (Huff 1999). You need to ensure that you understand the essay question (which may not be phrased as a question) as it is easy to overlook one crucial word and write an essay about something that is only marginally relevant. So your first task is to analyse the question in detail; words like *interpret, discuss, to what extent* and so on suggest that you need to analyse and provide evidence for other materials (Peck and Coyle 2005b).

There is widespread agreement that each paragraph in an essay has a clearly specified role. Cottrell (2003) suggests that the introduction should take up no more than 10 per cent of the total word limit with 80 per cent devoted to the argument and 10 per cent to the conclusion. As essays usually do not contain headings, each paragraph is linked to the previous one by appropriate language indicators (see Table 3.1 above) to create a coherent narrative. Ideally there are clear links between the essay question, the introduction and the conclusion (Cottrell 2003). Most essays will also include a list of references (see Section 3.5). Peck and Coyle (2005a) argue for a rigid structure with eight paragraphs (one for the introduction, six for the main body and one for the conclusion), but this is controversial among many tutors. Please be also aware that some tutors use the terms 'essay' and 'report' interchangeably. If you are in doubt about the correct format of an assignment, please ask your tutor for advice.

3.3.2 WRITING AN EFFECTIVE CRITICAL REVIEW

A critical literature review is an integral part of a project or dissertation (see Section 3.4) and has become a popular assignment task in its own right. It is best defined as a systematic method for identifying, evaluating and synthesising existing literature in a topic area (drawing on Fink 2005, p3). Hence, a critical review of the literature is an original assessment of previously published research

(Jesson and Lacey 2006), in which different theories are analysed and the link between them established. It will allow you to demonstrate your understanding of the main theories and debates in your subject area (Hart 1998) as well as your understanding of the different perspectives (or paradigms) from which the topic has been approached (Jesson and Lacey 2006). Writing a literature review is not particularly difficult, but writing a *critical* literature review is not easy at first. Writing a *good* critical literature review requires you to engage in depth with the literature in the chosen topic area, and the skills of critical reading outlined in the previous chapter will help you with this.

Many students do not understand why a critical literature review is such an important part of a project or dissertation or even an assignment task in its own right. However, there are compelling reasons for this. Firstly, knowing the literature of your field of study on which you are building your project or dissertation (and to which your project or dissertation will contribute in turn) is crucial to avoid repetition and a waste of resources (Hart 1998). Since postgraduate students are expected to contribute to the knowledge in their field of study, they need to create new knowledge and therefore need to know what is already known in their subject area. Secondly, a literature review can help you to identify current practice or effective methods that in turn can influence your own or those of your organisation (Fink 2005). While studies of the (academic) literature may be regarded as too abstract, they often have implications for management practice, and how better to learn about that than through the first-hand study of the literature? Thirdly, a literature review can help you to build expert knowledge about a subject for your studies or professional purposes (Hart 1998). As many of you are certainly aware, employers increasingly expect their staff to have expertise in a particular field, and the research literature is an integral part of this.

A critical literature review tells the story of what is known in a field of study by describing current knowledge, synthesising its key aspects and analysing the context of research (Jesson and Lacey 2006). In order to be of appropriate quality for postgraduate study, a critical literature review has the following characteristics (Hart 1998):

- breadth (ie the number of theories and debates discussed)
- depth (ie the level of detail in which the theories and debates are discussed),
- rigour (ie the extent to which all sources were treated the same)
- clarity
- conciseness
- effective analysis and synthesis of ideas.

The last of these is crucial. Your synthesis of ideas is expected to bring new insights into the current knowledge in your subject area (Horn 2009) and to identify a gap in the current knowledge base. The foundation of a good critical literature review is your knowledge and understanding of the literature, and you will need to read critically and refer to the original sources wherever possible (Jesson and Lacey 2006).

Another area of confusion among many students is what they are adding. To them, it seems, doing a critical literature review is merely reporting on what is known in their field of study without any input of their own and, not surprisingly, this is considered boring. However, a good critical literature review is very much about *your* interpretations of the current literature. You will strategically select and critically read what you consider the most appropriate sources, analyse and interpret them as well as synthesise their content. In addition, your critical literature review will have an argument, ie a claim and a justification, which you create, structure and defend. A critical literature review is therefore a challenging yet exciting piece of writing. The critical reading and writing skills outlined in the previous chapter will help you to find your way in the information jungle and make good use of your time.

Jesson and Lacey (2006) provide some worthwhile tips for writing critical literature reviews, which complement Section 2.3 of the previous chapter. Firstly, a critical literature review needs to feature opposing views, and your task is to identify which schools of thoughts are the most common in your subject area and how they differ. Secondly, try to read as much of a source as possible as it can be a risky strategy to read summary information (eg abstract, book flap, table of contents) only. Thirdly, scan the shelves in your library, as sometimes a valuable source may be in an unexpected place. Finally, identify the theories used in a source, the conceptual variations or different schools of thought, empirical research findings, methodological issues and implications for practice (if applicable). You may want to use some of the graphical tools outlined in Chapter 2 to create a subject map (Wallace and Wray 2006) or similar framework for the topic.

A good critical literature review is structured according to themes (Jesson and

ACTIVITY 3.1

ANALYSING CRITICAL LITERATURE REVIEWS

Writing a critical literature review cannot be taught in a classroom setting, it is something that you will need to teach yourself. A good starting point is the study of good literature reviews: that is, literature reviews that have been published in academic journals. The British Academy of Management publishes a journal that is dedicated to literature reviews written by academics; it is called the *International Journal of Management Reviews*. Check with your library if you have access to this journal either in print or through the online provision, and browse through a few articles that interest you. If you cannot access this particular journal, identify relevant articles in the top-quality journals of your field of study (your tutor will be able to suggest a few if you are stuck). Some will publish dedicated literature reviews, but if you cannot find one use the literature review section of a research paper instead. Analyse the articles, noting the structure, language, stylistic means, references and other devices that the authors use, with particular emphasis on the synthesis of different paradigms, theories and models. Identify what works and what does not and learn the lesson. You may want to work with a peer or in a small group again so as to get different views on the matter.

Lacey 2006) rather than authors (which would be more like an annotated bibliography, according to Hart 1998). It has an introduction, which may outline the rationale for the review and any procedure employed. In the main body of the review, discuss each theme in turn. Within each theme, compare and contrast the prevailing schools of thought, the key authors or the most important theories. Identify any gaps in the knowledge base which need to be filled with new original research to enhance the understanding of the field of study. Each paragraph in your critical review should build on the previous one and link in with the following one, thus creating a coherent argument. You should make good use of the language indicators (see Table 3.1) to demonstrate how issues within a theme are linked as well as how the themes themselves relate to each other. The conclusion of your review should be balanced and you may want to highlight any gap in the knowledge base again. All sources cited need to be referenced; for details please refer to Section 3.5 below.

3.4 WRITING EFFECTIVE PROJECTS AND DISSERTATIONS

The project or dissertation will be the most important single piece of work of your postgraduate studies, bringing together knowledge and skills that you will have acquired through the taught elements of your course. The project or dissertation will account for a considerable part of your degree and will enable you to build specialist knowledge in your field of study which you can communicate to your current or any potential employer for promotion purposes. Hence, while it will be primarily an academic piece of work, it has real 'street value'. It will be a rare opportunity to design, carry out, manage and write up research into a topic of interest and make a contribution to the knowledge and debates in your subject area. This is undoubtedly a big task, with many pitfalls along the way. Many skills discussed in this book, however, will allow you to approach your project or dissertation more confidently and professionally.

A project is 'a piece of research work by a ... student' (*Oxford dictionary thesaurus and wordpower guide* 2001, p1024) that is unique, focused on in-depth knowledge and based on research (Cottrell 2003). A dissertation is simply a somewhat bigger project. In postgraduate study, a project usually completes the diploma stage for those students who do not continue to the dissertation stage, while the dissertation usually leads to a Master's degree. Both project and dissertation require good planning (White 2000) and a systematic approach (Cottrell 2003). It may be useful to divide a project or dissertation into the stages shown in Figure 3.1.

The design stage is about deciding on a topic and devising the questions which the project or dissertation seeks to answer ('research questions'). At this stage, you will be writing your project or dissertation proposal, which is a planning document for your research (see Section 3.4.1 for details). The research stage involves the collection of background data through secondary research ('desk research') as well as first-hand data in real organisations ('primary research'). The analysis stage involves the analysis and interpretation of the data collected in

Figure 3.1 Stages in a project or dissertation

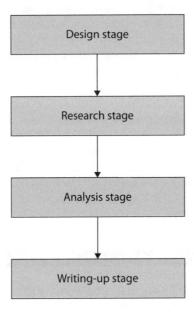

the research stage, and may involve the creation of a tentative theory to advance the knowledge in your subject area. A detailed discussion of the research and analysis stages is beyond the scope of this chapter, but a research methods course or book will give you the necessary information. The final stage of a project or dissertation is the writing-up stage, in which the work will be presented in written and sometimes also in oral format (the latter is called 'viva voce examination' or 'viva', which comes from Latin meaning 'living voice'); aspects of writing will be discussed in Section 3.4.2.

3.4.1 THE PROJECT OR DISSERTATION PROPOSAL

Thorough planning is vital for a successful project or dissertation, particularly at the design stage. It may be tempting to skip any preparatory work, which may not reap many immediate rewards, but you will be paying the price at the end of your research if you cut corners here. The first step in the project or dissertation journey is the choice of topic. Some of you may have little choice in the matter as your employer may have asked you to look into a particular issue at work. Others, however, may wonder how to come up with a topic. Here are some ideas. Firstly, think about what interests you at work, at university or in your leisure. Is there anything that annoys or fascinates you? You may want to ask your employer or colleagues if there is anything that they regard as worth looking into. You may want to browse newspapers, journals or listen to news programmes for inspiration and ideas. You may want to look at previous dissertations to get an idea of what other students have done; most university libraries will have copies available for reference purposes. You may also want to consider your future career path: what kind of specialist knowledge would be most beneficial for you?

If you are in the privileged yet difficult position of deciding what to write about, there are a number of techniques that can help you with this process. Try **brainstorming** by putting all ideas, no matter how strange they seem at first, onto a big sheet of paper. Then scrutinise all ideas and discard the ones that are unsuitable (see also Chapters 14 and 16). You may want to do this in a group with your peers as different people will have different ideas and take on different roles in the discussion process, which will benefit all of you. A variation of brainstorming is the **post-it note technique** (White 2000), in which you put your ideas down on post-it notes. You can then arrange and rearrange them according to themes. Do not forget to write up your discussion on a sheet of paper or take a photograph so that you can go back to it later.

Currie (2005) recommends the **Delphi technique**, which enlists the help of groups to tackle problems in an interactive way. It is best if the group is made up of no more than six people who ideally are seated around a table. They are asked *not* to communicate with each other throughout the process. Each group member receives an A4 notepad with the problem stated on the top of the first sheet and a set of instructions (eg the criteria that your research topic must fulfil). Group members are given time to study the problem, think about it and write down a solution. After the allocated time has passed, group members are asked to pass their written solutions to the person on their right. Each reads the solution, tries to improve it and in turn passes it on. The trick is to improve on an existing solution rather than imposing one's own answer on others. The process is repeated until each solution has reached its originator. This is done in silence. At the end of this process, all final solutions (ie improved solutions) are collated and discussed, ideally ending in consensus. You may also want to keep a **notebook** with ideas to which you can refer when writing your proposal or final piece of work. Do not be put off by any limiting thoughts, which we all experience from time to time. There is a dissertation topic in any field of interest if you frame it correctly.

If you come up with more than one potential topic, you will need to decide which one to go for. It is a good idea to map out the key criteria which your project or dissertation topic will need to fulfil and then rate every topic accordingly to reveal the best option. Issues you may want to consider include your level of interest, ease of access to the research setting, the amount of work already existing in this area, the timeliness of your work, resources and support required, and so on. (A checklist is provided on the companion website.) It is always a good idea to discuss possible topics with a third person, for example peers, a course tutor, family members or friends, employer or work colleagues, as they may give you new ideas or refine what you already know. You may want to employ the Delphi technique again at this stage. But remember: unless your employer has decided it for you, the topic of your project or dissertation will be your decision and nobody else's. You may also want to bear in mind that the best topic for your project or dissertation is not necessarily the one that you feel most attached to but the one that you will be able to do to a sufficient level of detail within the time frame available to you.

Currie (2005) has identified the following seven criteria that a suitable research topic must fulfil:

- **Relevance to the discipline of study**: If you are studying for a human resources management degree, for example, your project or dissertation must cover an aspect of human resources management.

- **Topic of interest**: Writing a project or dissertation can be a long and time-consuming process, so a genuine interest in the topic will help you to deal with any problems or difficulties.

- **Prior knowledge and expertise**: Ideally, you are already familiar with the topic through your daily work or your programme of study. This will allow you to focus more readily on what your research is about and potentially make use of personal contacts.

- **Researchable**: Any potential research topic must relate to the academic literature in your field of study, to which your work will contribute in turn.

- **Level of study**: Your topic must allow you to achieve the standards required by your programme of study. A bachelor's dissertation differs qualitatively from a master's dissertation. If in doubt about whether your potential topic is of sufficient standard, please ask your tutor for advice.

- **Research capability**: You need the skills to complete the project or dissertation, including communicating, networking, problem-solving and decision-making.

- **Feasibility**: You need to be able to do the research within the allocated time frame and with the resources that you have available.

Once you have a topic for your project or dissertation, you will need to focus your attention on some specific research questions which your research seeks to answer. Research questions must be very specific to allow you to examine a particular aspect of your topic in great detail. You may be disappointed at how seemingly little you may be able to achieve as part of your research, but it is depth that your examiners will be looking for (White 2000), and in order to achieve depth within a limited time frame, you will have to limit the scope of your investigation. So do not be disheartened if your tutor suggests that the proposed research is too big – that is quite normal. Follow your tutor's guidance and advice; he or she will be more experienced than you and well qualified to advise.

The culmination of the design stage is writing a **research proposal** (sometimes called a project or dissertation proposal), in which you will determine the topic, scope and methods of your research. Your proposal is the map for your project or dissertation journey and its purpose is planning. Most universities will require you to produce a research proposal, but even if this is not common practice at your institution, I strongly recommend you do it anyway. Careful planning at this stage will prevent many problems later on. Your project or dissertation proposal will answer three key questions:

- What will your research be about ('what question')?

- How will you go about answering your research questions ('how question')?

- Why will this be important ('why question')?

Table 3.2 Elements of a project or dissertation proposal

Section	Content	Question addressed
Introduction	Outlines what the research will be about. Details the research questions to be answered in the project or dissertation.	What
Literature review	Identifies the areas of literature informing the research. Critical and analytical. Identifies gaps in knowledge base.	Why
Methods	Identifies and justifies methods of data collection. Identifies and justifies methods of data analysis. Identifies ethical issues and potential problems. Identifies how you will get access to the research setting. Outlines what the limitations of the research will be.	How
Conclusion	Summarises the key issues raised in the proposal.	
References	Provides a list of references cited in the proposal.	
Timescale	Schedules key tasks of the project.	

It is not as difficult as it may sound. The 'what question' is about your topic and research questions. The 'how question' deals with the methods of data collection and analysis you plan to employ, and the 'why question' addresses whether your research is worthwhile. Your research proposal will address these three questions, often in a format similar to the one outlined in Table 3.2. Check with your tutor whether there is a particular format in use at your institution and how long your proposal should be – this can range from a few hundred words to a few thousand.

A project or dissertation proposal usually follows a report format (see Section 3.3.1) and is written in the future tense as its purpose is planning. You should provide a preliminary title, your name, student number and name of your tutor if you have already been assigned one (White 2000). Your proposal should begin with a brief introduction, which answers the 'what' question of your proposed research. It is customary to state the research question(s) and a few sentences about the research setting.

The second section of your research proposal is usually a critical literature review (see Section 3.3.2) covering your research topic. It should focus on academic theories and models, and you will be expected to actually identify the key strands of literature informing your project as well as the key authors in each field and their main propositions. In order to identify the key authors in your field of study, you will have to use the skills and processes discussed in Chapter 2. Ideally, the literature review will identify gaps in the knowledge base of your field of study, which will allow you to justify why your research is worthwhile, thus addressing the 'why' question.

The third section of your research dissertation proposal is usually about method and methodology, outlining how you will approach your research so as to answer your research questions (the 'how' question). The term 'method' refers to methods of data collection and analysis, whereas the term 'methodology' refers to the intellectual traditions which your research follows, answering broad philosophical questions like what constitutes reliable knowledge and how we come to know what we know (Bryman and Bell 2007). Your methods, methodology and research questions should dovetail and the language you use should reflect this. Methodological issues can be quite difficult to understand at first, so make sure that you have access to a good research methods book at all times during your project or dissertation journey, and do not hesitate to ask your tutor for clarification. In the methods section of your research proposal, you will be expected to outline your methodological stance and identify the methods you propose to use to collect and analyse data. Try to be as specific as possible, for instance detailing the number of research participants (or subjects) and type and number of data collection and analysis vehicles. This will require careful planning, so take your time over your proposal. You should also plan how you will gain access to the research setting, which may be difficult if you do not work or run a business of your own. You will also have to consider any ethical issues, which is always a concern when conducting research in real-life organisations (Bryman and Bell 2007). Another element that some tutors like to see is the limitations of your project: that is, what your project will not be able to find out with the methods you are proposing. Nothing may be further from your mind at the very outset of your project or dissertation journey, but these details will allow your tutor to judge the potential of your proposal and anticipate any problems along the way.

A good research proposal will then provide a brief conclusion, all references and a timescale. The latter is sometimes called 'plan of work' (see White 2000) and is an essential element of a research proposal as you will find it difficult to judge what is feasible for you to do within the available time frame and you will require your tutor's guidance. Most students do not allow enough time for data analysis, for revising drafts, for proofreading and for any unforeseen problems (like computers crashing or printer queues). In most instances, universities are not very sympathetic if you get your timing wrong, so make sure that you are realistic from the outset and follow your tutor's advice. Conventions at your institution may require you to include other items, so do check with your tutor. It is extremely beneficial to discuss your proposal and other ideas with your peers, tutor, employer, colleagues, family members, friends and others to be able to refine your plans. The most important thing is to be realistic. One of my students, for example, wanted to do research in the local Premier League football club even though he did not know anybody there. It may not be impossible to be granted access to such an organisation, but it will be extremely difficult without the necessary contacts. Another of my students highlighted in her proposal that she did not have much money but proposed to send out thousands of questionnaires by mail including a self-addressed envelope. How she expected to finance this endeavour remains unclear. But you should get the idea. So in short, if you get your proposal right (ie a detailed plan with realistic timing and a 'Plan B' in case something goes wrong), you have good chances of achieving good marks in your project or dissertation. Going back to my previous metaphor, if you have a good map, your chances of arriving at your destination on time are good too.

You may find it useful to apply a similar planning process to an assignment at university or a project at work. Mapping out the key stages, any resources and other vital details will help you to focus your attention on the essentials of any task.

 ACTIVITY 3.2

WRITING A PROPOSAL

Take any task – for instance a project or dissertation topic, an assignment brief or a project brief from work – and identify the key stages and elements. Map out what needs to be done at the different stages, what support you will need and how long you will need to complete each of them. You may also want to refer to Chapter 5 of this book for other skills that will help you in this process.

3.4.2 WRITING A RESEARCH PROJECT OR DISSERTATION

The culmination of the fourth stage in the project or dissertation process will be your finished piece of work, and this is what this section is about. Successful students start writing at the beginning of their project or dissertation journey, as writing aids thinking (Huff 2002). The structure of your project or dissertation will be very similar to that of your proposal and will answer the same three questions – what, why and how – in a report format (see Section 3.3.1). However, the purpose of your project or dissertation is different. While your proposal was about planning your research, your project or dissertation is about reporting research and is therefore usually written in the past tense. Table 3.3 outlines the typical elements of a project or dissertation, but bear in mind that the way your project or dissertation is structured does not necessarily reflect the way in which you approached the different tasks (the introduction is usually best written last).

The introduction of your project or dissertation will introduce the reader to your work by providing basic information, such as what the research was about (research questions) and where it was conducted (research setting). You may also want to provide other contextual information (eg socio-economic changes, industry changes) if that is relevant to your topic. It is customary to tell the reader how the project or dissertation is structured and what its conclusion is. The latter may sound strange but examiners (the prime audience of your project

Table 3.3 Basic elements of a project or dissertation

Chapter	Content	Question addressed
Introduction	Outlines what the research was about. Details the research questions that were answered in the project or dissertation.	What
Literature review	Critically discusses the key authors and their arguments. Best structured according to themes that are relevant to your research. Identifies gaps in knowledge base.	Why
Methods	Details and justifies methods of data collection. Details and justifies methods of data analysis. Details ethical issues and the limitations of your research.	How
Findings	Details the key findings of your research. Best structured according to themes raised in the literature review.	What
Conclusion	Summarises the key issues raised in the project or dissertation. Determines the extent to which the research questions have been answered. Suggests areas of further research. May include recommendations or a reflective comment on your project or dissertation journey.	What, why, how
References	Provides a list of references cited in the proposal.	
Appendices (if applicable)	It is customary to provide a copy of the questionnaire or an interview schedule. Check with your tutor what he/she expects to be included in the appendices.	

or dissertation) like to know what to expect. By knowing from the outset what your project or dissertation is about, what you found out and by which methods, they are in a much better position to judge the journey that you have taken. You may also want to bear in mind that the examiners are unlikely to read your project or dissertation from beginning to end. The introduction and conclusion and/or the reference list are popular starting points, and many sections of your project or dissertation may only be skimmed and scanned by the examiner. It is therefore crucial that you make clear what you have done, why you have done it and how. This is usually done by 'sign-posting': that is, telling the reader what they can expect, telling them the content and then drawing out the key points of the argument. This will help the reader to stay in touch with what you have written (Peck and Coyle 2005a).

The literature review of your project or dissertation is a substantial chapter and a good opportunity to demonstrate that you can work critically and analytically. As highlighted above, a good literature review will outline a gap in the knowledge base that can be (tentatively) filled by your work. This contribution may seem insignificant to you but is worthwhile in the wider context of the research and practitioner community in your field of study. If many people studied a topic in different organisations, their work would go a long way towards good theory! Be aware, however, that not every item of written text ('literature') belongs in the literature review. The literature review focuses on academic theories, which are used to analyse the data of your research project; these are published in academic journal articles and research-oriented books. Methodological literature on how to do research belongs in the methods chapter. In contrast, government publications, company information, industry information, newspaper articles and similar texts usually constitute secondary data, which you can use to create a context for your study or as evidence to strengthen your argument. A sound understanding of different types of literature (see Chapter 2) is therefore vital for your project or dissertation.

The methods chapter (including methodology) will cover the same elements as your proposal, but in more detail. You will be expected to cover methodological issues in more depth than in your proposal and you will also need to specify what you actually did rather than what you planned to do (although it may be appropriate in some projects or dissertations to contrast the two). It is customary to reflect on any ethical issues, particularly anything that has come up unexpectedly (eg an interviewee breaking down in tears) and how you handled the situation. You will also be in a much better position to judge what your research has achieved and what was beyond its scope (ie the limitations of your research).

The findings chapter is probably the most exciting part of your project or dissertation because it is truly yours. You will be presenting findings that are unique to your study, even though they can be generalised or repeated. But it may also be one of the most difficult chapters that you write because you will have to put a lot of thinking into it. One common (and very understandable) mistake among students is that they take the data created by an analysis tool as analytical. However, any data analysis protocol will provide you with a set of *descriptive* data, which you will need to interpret in order to turn them into analytical data. This process of interpretation, which is usually aided by linking your data to the theories and models discussed in your literature review, is time-consuming and little is known about how you actually do it. It may be helpful to write up your results and then scrutinise what you have written with the question 'So what?' This will give you some insights into what this actually means, why it is important and how this newly created knowledge may be used by scholars and practitioners in your field of study.

The conclusion chapter will identify the extent to which the objectives of the research have been met. It will also outline the key points of your project or dissertation; it is the answer to the question of what you want your readers to learn from reading it. You may feel that your work is too insignificant to ask such a question, but it will help you to structure your thinking and present your project or dissertation in a focused and professional manner. As I explained above, your examiners are unlikely to read your project or dissertation in full as they do not have the time to do so, so you will have to make clear what the key points are and what you want them to learn from it. The better you do that, the better are your chances of a good grade (provided you have a strong argument of course). Some tutors expect you to outline areas of further research, ie questions that your present study have raised and that are important to follow up. You may also be expected to include recommendations or a reflective account of your learning journey. Please check with your tutor what the norms in your institution are.

The list of references should contain all sources that you have cited in the main body of your project or dissertation and in the appendices. Details on referencing and compiling a reference list will be provided in the following section. In addition to your list of references, you may be expected to provide a bibliography, which details all sources used for preparing your project or dissertation that you did not cite (Pears and Shields 2008). Check with your tutor what the position in your institution is.

Most projects or dissertations will contain one or more appendices, but it is by no means compulsory to include them. Appendices are commonly used as 'dumping grounds' for material that provides too much detail in the text or that does not fit anywhere. This is not the purpose of an appendix, however, and most examiners will see through such tactics. As a rule, it is customary to provide a copy of a questionnaire, a list of interview questions, an observation structure and maybe even an interview transcript. Some projects may produce large sets of statistical data or other supporting literature, which may be appropriately put in the appendix. Use appendices sparingly and appropriately; your tutor can advise on what to include and what to leave out.

It is a good exercise to spend some time in the library to browse previous projects and dissertations to get a better idea of how they can be approached. Although the structure outlined above looks somewhat rigid, there are endless possibilities for structuring a project or dissertation. It will be down to you to analyse previous projects or dissertations and find out what effective practice is and what works for you and your research. Using the strategies for critical reading outlined in the previous chapter will help you. However, bear in mind that each project or dissertation is a unique piece of work that will require a unique approach which is appropriate for the type of work that you have done. Your tutor can advise you, particularly once you are past the early stages of the writing-up process.

It is important that you look at more than one dissertation to get the best overview. You will soon find out what may be effective for your particular study and what your style and preferences are.

A project or dissertation will also contain a number of elements that do not belong to the main part of the text; these are called 'preliminary materials' (or 'prelims' to use publishing jargon) and include, usually in this order:

- title page, stating the title of your project or dissertation, your name and student number, the title of the degree for which you are submitting and the name of your tutor

- any declaration of your authorship that may be required by your institution
- abstract/executive summary (if required)
- acknowledgements of people who helped you with your project or dissertation (such as supervisor, research participants, proofreader and family members and friends who supported you)
- table of contents
- table of figures, table of tables or glossary (if applicable).

It is customary to number the pages of the prelims in Roman numerals (i, ii, iii, etc) and the main body of the text and any appendices with Arabic numbers (1, 2, 3, etc). You may be required to add your name, student number, the title of your project or dissertation or any other information to each page, so please read the project or dissertation brief carefully and follow your tutor's advice.

 ACTIVITY 3.3

ANALYSING DISSERTATIONS

Identify a small number of previous dissertations, ideally from your programme of study. Analyse them using the following questions:

- What are the research questions? How focused and detailed are they?
- What methods were used? How were they justified?
- What findings did the research reveal? How were they presented and justified?
- How analytical and critical is the presentation and justification of research results?
- Are there any recommendations? How sensible and thoughtful are they?
- What is the structure of the dissertation?
- How is the dissertation presented?
- What language is being used?
- How easy is it to follow the argument?
- How many and what kind of sources did the author cite?
- Are there any appendices? If so, how many and what has been included?
- What do I like or dislike about the dissertation?

It is absolutely essential that you allow plenty of time to prepare your project or dissertation for submission. This involves not only the revision of your draft manuscript, but also further editing. Even though it may sound counter-intuitive, it is usually a good idea to write what you want to write without worrying too much about the word limit. Huff (1999) suggests that text can be reduced by 30 per cent to 50 per cent without serious loss of content. However, such revision of drafts and further editing takes time and is best done in stages. It is also good practice to have your project or dissertation proofread prior to submission. You do not have to enlist the services of a professional proofreader, a family member or friend may do this for you. Your project or dissertation is such a large piece of work that you will lose track of what you have done. Although there are strategies to help you to see your work with a new pair of eyes (see Chapter 2), a third party will bring a completely new view to the project or dissertation, particularly if they are unfamiliar with the topic of study. They may be able to comment on any omissions or repetitions, point out any ambiguities, correct common typos and grammatical mistakes, and check for consistency of spelling (eg British or American English); as a matter of courtesy you should mention them in the acknowledgement section of your project or dissertation. Remember that your project or dissertation should be a professional piece of work that you can be proud of, and getting these seemingly insignificant things right is part of that. Please be aware that not all tutors are happy for you to have your work proofread if it goes beyond checking spelling and grammar.

3.5 REFERENCING THE WORK OF OTHERS

3.5.1 THE PURPOSE OF REFERENCING

Referencing is about identifying and acknowledging other authors' work on which you are drawing as evidence of your argument (Pears and Shields 2008) – a skill that every university student needs to master. Although primarily an academic skill, referencing has wider implications for employment and continuing professional development because essentially it means being truthful about the ownership of ideas. Acknowledging any ideas taken from other authors' work is a sign of respect and is regarded as good practice in the Anglo-Saxon and Germanic university systems. Not doing so is passing off somebody else's ideas as your own, which constitutes fraud and is a serious academic offence called plagiarism (Carroll 2002). Hence, by not referencing correctly, you do pass off somebody else's work as your own, whether intended or not, and commit plagiarism. You can expect to be penalised for incorrect referencing – even if it is by mistake – and in an extreme case you may even be expelled from your programme of study. Plagiarism is so serious an offence that a professor at one of Britain's top universities lost his job following evidence that he had committed it. The dean of Durham Business School was suspended years after the offence took place (MacLeod 2007) and has since resigned (Shepherd 2007). Hence, accusations of plagiarism can haunt you for years to come, so do it avoid it – it is not worth it. If you come from a different education system into the Anglo-Saxon or Germanic tradition, you may have to learn more about the acceptable norms and standards. Your tutor will be able to advise.

In practice, the source will be identified in the text (this is called 'in-text referencing' or 'citation'), and a list of all sources cited in the text will be compiled (this is called a 'reference list'). Many students find referencing arduous and confusing, but it actually follows a logical and structured process. Several referencing systems (or referencing styles) have been developed, but the most common one in business and management studies is the Harvard system. It identifies a source with the surname(s) of the author(s) and the year of publication in the text, regardless of what kind of source it is. At the end of the text, there should be a reference list which identifies each source unambiguously and in alphabetical order starting with the surname(s) of the author(s) and year of publication.

ACTIVITY 3.4

IDENTIFYING REFERENCE SOURCES

We have used the Harvard system in this book, so do take a look through the chapters and consult the reference lists for details. How many different sources have the authors drawn on? What kinds of sources are represented? How many different types of sources can you identify?

As a rule, you should reference every piece of information (including theories, models, data) that is not your own. There is only one exception to this rule, and that is common knowledge or knowledge that most people in a particular field of study will know. The difficulty is, however, to distinguish between common knowledge and specialist knowledge that needs to be referenced, particularly if you are new to a field of study. Pears and Shields (2008) suggest that you need to answer the following two questions in the affirmative to make it common knowledge: firstly, that a particular piece of information was known to you before your course of study, and secondly, that a particular idea has originated in your own mind. If you cannot answer these two questions in the affirmative (or if you are in any doubt), provide a reference. Many students get confused about what is their own work and what is somebody else's, as a good assignment, project or dissertation will integrate other people's work in their own. Your understanding of the elements of an argument will help you to distinguish the two: the claim of your argument tends to be your own ideas and the justification of the claim tends to come from already published ideas, theories, models and data in the form of evidence (a key exception of the latter is your dissertation, in which most of the justification will originate in your own research).

3.5.2 THE BASIC RULES OF REFERENCING

The practice of referencing can be confusing, particularly if a source does not conform to the norm. There are rules to govern every possibility and a good referencing guide (eg Pears and Shields 2008) will cover them all. It will be easy to memorise the rules for sources that you use regularly, and for all others consult the referencing guide, which will be an indispensable companion for your studies.

Under the headings below, I will outline how to reference the most common sources and exceptions used in postgraduate study and formal CPD. This is list is only a brief summary; please consult your referencing guide for anything not listed here.

ACTIVITY 3.5

AVAILABILITY OF A REFERENCING GUIDE

Check with your library if there are hard copies and/or electronic versions of a good referencing guide available. At some universities, these are provided on the virtual learning environment (such as Blackboard). If you cannot access a referencing guide when you need it, you may want to purchase your own copy.

3.5.2.1 In-text referencing (1): paraphrased items

The most commonly used references in an academic piece should be paraphrased items. Particularly at postgraduate level, you should aim to integrate other authors' ideas with your own and this involves putting these ideas in your own words (this is called paraphrasing). In the Harvard system, an in-text reference consists of the author's surname/the name of the authoring organisation, the year of publication and sometimes a page number (eg Huff 1999, QAA 2002). If the item has been authored by two people, the surnames are separated by the word 'and' (eg Pears and Shields 2008) and there are three or more authors, it is customary to use the surname of the first author followed by et al to reduce the number of words (eg Easterby-Smith et al 2002). (Please be aware, however, that different publishers have different styles and guidelines therefore may vary).

There are three slight variations of presentation depending on where in the text the reference appears:

- If you want to attribute a sentence or parts of it to an author:

  Management research is being conducted by both scholars and practitioners (Easterby-Smith et al 2002).

  Critical thinking is a minimum requirement for postgraduate study (QAA 2002).

- If you want to include the reference as part of your writing:

  Easterby-Smith et al (2002) argue that management research is being conducted by both scholars and practitioners.

  (The verb 'argue' is commonly used in this context, but other verbs that you may want to use are: suggest, contend, outline, highlight, point out, demonstrate, explain and the like. Never use 'write', 'say', 'think', 'feel' or 'believe' as they tend to be weak and unprofessional.)

- If you need to include more than one item to justify your claim:

  If you need to refer to more than one item, it is customary to list the items in chronological order by year of publication. If there is a long list of authors, which you do not want to quote, you may wish to add 'eg' before the first. For example:

  Learning can be defined as a process of sensemaking, in which the learner can gain new perspectives, new ways of thinking and a new identity through interaction with others (eg Bruner 1990, Wenger 1998).

If you cannot identify the author of an item (this can happen for reports and surveys, for newspaper articles or more commonly for Internet resources) or if you are referring to a dictionary, it is customary to use the title of the item followed by the year of publication. If the year of publication is unknown, you should put 'ND' for 'no date' in lieu of the year of publication. For example:

> *'Creativity enriches the life of the learner' (Qualifications and Curriculum Authority, ND).*

Another common source of confusion is two or more items authored by the same person(s) in one year. In these cases, it is customary to add the letters a, b, c, etc after the year of publication, both in the text and in the list of references to make each reference unambiguous. This could look like this:

> *Coaching may facilitate organisational change (Reissner 2008a).*

> *Reissner (2008b) argues that the context has to be taken account when studying organisational change.*

3.5.2.2 In-text referencing (2): direct and secondary quotations

There may be instances when you may wish to quote another author word by word; this is called direct quotation. In this case, you will need to provide the number(s) of the page on which it is written.

Short direct quotations (usually a sentence or two) will be put in inverted commas, for instance:

> *Reissner (2004, p106) argues that 'stories are not only told, but lived as they become visible and real in symbols'.*

Direct quotations longer than a sentence or two will be formatted as a paragraph of their own, usually indented and without the use of inverted commas, for example:

> *Reissner explains the implications of narrative research on the researcher:*

> > *In most cases, though, fragmented experience is turned into a coherent explanation through story-telling, but conflictual and corrosive stories remain nevertheless. To increase the veracity and validity of the stories and their interpretations, it is crucial for the researcher/observer, as demonstrated here, to give back the stories to the story-tellers so that they can comment on them. In this way researchers can become confident about the validity of their interpretations of narratives (Reissner 2004, p110).*

If you need to modify a direct quotation, you need to make this explicit. In particular, if you need to omit parts of a direct quotation because not every word is relevant for your purposes, use '...' to substitute the omitted text. For instance:

> *Reissner (2004, p106) argues that 'stories are ... lived as they become visible and real in symbols'.*

If you need to add to a direct quotation, put any added text in [ ] and the reader will know that these are your words and do not belong to the quotation. For example:

> 'The methodological problem is to discover the most appropriate ways to record, explain and report these complex shifts in understanding [as a result of organisational change]' (Reissner 2004, p110).

If you want to emphasise part of a quotation, put the respective words in bold or italic print or underline it and add 'emphasis added' or something similar to the reference. For instance:

> Reissner (2004, p106) argues that 'stories are not only told, but lived as they become visible and real in symbols' (emphasis added).

In contrast, if you want to show that the quotation contains highlighted text, add 'emphasis original' or something similar to the reference. For example:

> Transformational learning 'is the process of effecting change in a **frame of reference**' (Mezirow 1997, p5, emphasis original).

If you need to make it clear that a direct quotation contains a mistake, leave the text and put [sic.] (Latin for 'like that') after the mistake to demonstrate that it is an original mistake. For instance:

> 'Increasing global competitive pressures on companies are universal, but the ways in which different organisations react on [sic.] them reflects the diversity of different local contexts' (Reissner 2004, p101).

Referring to an item that has been quoted by another author is called secondary referencing. It should be used sparingly and only if you cannot get access to the item in question. It is customary to add 'cited in' or 'quoted by' followed by the reference of the item where you read about it (ie the author's surname, year of publication and page number). For example:

> Allan et al (2002, as cited in Reissner 2004, p100) suggest that the analysis of stories is a powerful tool for workplace learning.

3.5.2.3 Reference list and bibliography

All references quoted in the text, including any in the appendices (but with the exception of secondary references) need to be provided in a list of references at the end of your text. The reference list is firstly in alphabetical and secondly in chronological order beginning with the oldest item, and follows a similar process to in-text referencing. The first item provided is the surname(s) of author(s) plus initials (or the title of the item if the author has not been identified) and the year of publication (or 'ND' if this has not been identified). Any further information required depends on the type of source and will be dealt with in the following sections.

In addition to the surnames of the author(s), initials and year of publication, you will need to provide the title of the article in inverted commas, the title of the journal in italics or underlined, volume, issue number and page numbers. All these details are usually printed on the source or listed in an electronic database. For a newspaper article, you need to add the date of publication (day and month) and for a conference paper, put the name of the conference in lieu of the journal title and add the date of the conference (day and month) as well as any page numbers (if published in conference proceedings) at the end. For example:

Jesson, J. and Lacey, F. (2006) 'How to do (or not to do) a critical literature review', *Pharmacy Education*, Vol. 6, No. 2, pp. 139–148.

Reissner, S. C. (2006) 'Making sense of sudden change', *22nd EGOS Colloquium*, Grieg Hallen, Bergen, Norway, 6–8 July.

Thompson, L. (2010) 'Mixed bag for small businesses', *The Times*, 27 March, p. 86.

In addition to the surnames of the author(s), initials and year of publication, you will need to provide the title of the book/dissertation/thesis, usually capitalised and in italics or underlined, the edition if it is not the first, followed by the place of publication (or 'unpublished') and the publisher's name (or the name of the degree-awarding institution). For example:

Easterby-Smith, M., Thorpe, R. and Lowe, A. (2002) *Management Research: An Introduction*. 3rd ed. London: Sage.

External Examiner Report (2008) University of Sunderland, School of Business, Law and Psychology, unpublished.

Reissner, S.C. (2009) *Theory and Practice of Narrative and Storytelling in Coaching*. Unpublished MA dissertation. University of Sunderland.

In addition to the surnames of the author(s), initials and year of publication, you will need to provide information on the chapter as well as the book itself. Start with the author(s) of the chapter (rather than the editors), their initials, year of publication, title of the chapter in inverted commas, followed by 'in', surnames and initials of the editor(s) followed by '(ed.)' if there is one editor or '(eds.)' if there is more than one, the title of the book in italics, the place of publication, the publisher's name and the relevant page numbers. For example:

Huff, A. (2002) 'Learning to be a successful writer', in Partington, D. (ed.) *Essential Skills for Management Research*, London: Sage, pp. 72–83.

For digital sources it is customary to put [online] after the title or issue number, followed by 'Available at:' and the URL. As digital content can change unexpectedly, you will also have to add the date on which you accessed it. For instance:

Reissner, S.C. (2008a). 'Narrative and story: New perspectives on coaching'. *International Mentoring and Coaching Journal*, Vol. 6, No. 3 [online]. Available at: www.emccouncil.org, accessed 26 February 2009.

Shepherd, J. (2007). 'When plagiarism is academic'. *The Guardian*, 30 October [Online]. Available at http://www.guardian.co.uk/education/2007/oct/30/highereducation.uk, accessed 2 November 2009.

There are separate rules for many more items and media, which will be included in a good referencing guide. It is important that you use one referencing system (such as the Harvard system) consistently and correctly. You also need to be aware that there are variations in presenting references in the text and in the list of references, largely depending on a publisher's house style. Please check with your tutors what their preferences are if in doubt.

ACTIVITY 3.6

EXAM REVISION

Download and study the detailed exam revision and preparation guide available on the companion website.

3.6 CONCLUSION

The essential skill of writing may be an art, but there are rules that you can learn and follow to improve your writing for assignments and examinations. Effective writing is effective communication of your skills and knowledge, and professional writers have a box of tools from which you can benefit for your postgraduate study, your continuing professional development and overall career. You may wonder how you can find the time to learn the tricks of the writer's trade and practise your writing, but doing so may make more efficient use of your precious time at later stages of your studies. Why produce a mediocre piece of work when you can produce a good one with minimal extra effort? You may even discover that writing is fun and that it gives deep satisfaction to communicate effectively through the written word, both at university and the workplace.

PAUSE FOR THOUGHT

Identify at least three things that you have learned by studying this chapter and engaging with the activities. How will your newly acquired knowledge and skills support your continuing professional development? What value do you expect your learning to have for your daily routines and your further career? In what area have you identified a need for further development and how are you planning to fill that gap? Address these issues in your learning journal and/or CPD log. You may also wish to discuss them with a peer, colleague, mentor or coach to aid your further development.

KEY LEARNING POINTS

- Effective formal writing is about applying simple rules to your written work.

- Effective writing makes explicit the relationship between different sentences, paragraphs, sections and chapters, and communicates to the readers what they can expect at any point in time.

- Referencing is a crucial academic skill that needs to be mastered confidently by postgraduate students. The norms and rules are logical and easy to follow if you are disciplined.

- Examinations do not have to be stressful events as their success depends on three factors: revision, preparation and performance on the day.

EXPLORE FURTHER

PEARS, A. and SHIELDS, G. (2008) *Cite them right: the essential guide to referencing and plagiarism*. Newcastle-upon-Tyne: Pear Tree Books..

3.7 REFERENCES

BRYMAN, A. and BELL, E. (2007) *Business research methods*. 2nd ed. Oxford: Oxford University Press.

CAMERON, S. (2007) *The business student's handbook: learning skills for study and employment*. 4th ed. Harlow: Pearson.

CARROLL, J. (2002) *A handbook for deterring plagiarism in higher education*. Oxford: Oxford Centre for Staff and Learning Development.

COTTRELL, S. (2003) *The study skills handbook*. 2nd ed. Basingstoke: Palgrave Macmillan.

COTTRELL, S. (2005) *Critical thinking skills: developing effective analysis and argument*. Basingstoke: Palgrave Macmillan.

CURRIE, D. (2005) *Developing and applying study skills*. London: CIPD.

FINK, A. (2005) *Conducting research literature reviews: from the Internet to paper*. Thousand Oaks, CA: Sage.

FISHER, A. (2001) *Critical thinking: an introduction*. Cambridge: Cambridge University Press.

HART, C. (1998) *Doing a literature review*. London: Sage.

HORN, R. (2009) *Researching and writing dissertations: a complete guide for business and management students*. London: CIPD.

HUFF, A. (1999) *Writing for scholarly publication*. London: Sage.

HUFF, A. (2002) Learning to be a successful writer. In D. Partington (ed), *Essential skills for management research*. London: Sage, pp72–83.

JESSON, J. and LACEY, F. (2006) How to do (or not to do) a critical literature review. *Pharmacy Education*. Vol. 6, No. 2, pp139–148.

LAPAKKO, D. (2009) *Argumentation: critical thinking in action*. 2nd ed. New York: iUniverse.

MACLEOD, D. (2007) Durham dean suspended for plagiarism. *Guardian*. 30 October. Available online at: http://www.guardian.co.uk/education/2007/oct/30/highereducation.news [accessed 2 November 2009].

MINTO, B. (2002) *The pyramid principle*. 3rd ed. Harlow: Pearson.

ORWELL, G. (1962) *Inside the whale and other essays*. Harmondsworth: Penguin.

Oxford dictionary thesaurus and wordpower guide. (2001) Oxford: Oxford University Press.

PEARS, A. and SHIELDS, G. (2008) *Cite them right: the essential guide to referencing and plagiarism*. Reprint. Newcastle-upon-Tyne: Pear Tree Books.

PECK, J. and COYLE, M. (2005a) *Write it right: a handbook for students*. London: Palgrave.

PECK, J. and COYLE, M. (2005b) *The student's guide to writing: grammar, punctuation and spelling*. 2nd ed. London: Palgrave.

REISSNER, S.C. (2008) *Narratives of organisational change and learning: making sense of testing times*. Cheltenham: Edward Elgar.

SHEPHERD, J. (2007) When plagiarism is academic. *Guardian*. 30 October. Available online at: http://www.guardian.co.uk/education/2007/oct/30/highereducation.uk [accessed 2 November 2009].

WALLACE, M. and WRAY, A. (2006) *Critical reading and writing for postgraduates*. London: Sage.

WHITE, B. (2000) *Dissertation skills for business and management students*. London: Cassell.

PART 3

Effective Self-Management in the Workplace

CHAPTER 4

Developing your professional identity

Gail Sanders

OVERVIEW

As you engage with your postgraduate programme you will no doubt be looking forward to a rewarding professional career in your chosen field and you will be working hard to acquire the specialist knowledge that you will need to make you successful in your dream job. But already you will be aware that simply having specialist knowledge is not enough to convince employers that you are the right person for that job. In a very competitive world, employers are now looking for people who can demonstrate a broad repertoire of professional attributes that can make them effective as soon as they join the organisation. This book has been designed to help you to develop those attributes by enhancing skills such as teamwork and communication. However, the acquisition of skills is only one part of the equation, and this chapter aims to set the context for that development by looking at how you can become adept at knowing how and when to use those skills in the best way in professional situations, thus developing the behaviours that are expected of a professional in your chosen field – what we call here your professional identity.

LEARNING OUTCOMES

By the end of this chapter, provided you engage with the activities, you should be able to:

- understand the concept of professional identity and how it relates to effectiveness in the workplace
- use a simple conceptualisation of professional identity to practise the skill of self-awareness
- understand how different organisations communicate the professional behaviours that they expect from their employees, and how individuals learn to conform
- apply the skill of self-awareness in a practical way to critically evaluate your own professional behaviours and those of others.

4.1 INTRODUCTION

The term 'professional' is often associated with highly esteemed jobs such as doctor or lawyer, or associated with particular 'professional standards' (CIPD standards are an example here). However, being professional is important to success in any working role, irrespective of whether that role is defined or regulated by explicit standards of professionalism. We can explore what this means by taking an everyday example with which most of us will be familiar – a carpenter. Every carpenter will have a toolkit – perhaps a selection of saws, a plane, hammers, pliers, chisels and so on. All carpenters will have a similar selection of tools that they use in basically the same way. Why, then, are there some carpenters that we would be happy to invite into our homes to do work for us, whilst there are others that we would never want to employ?

 ACTIVITY 4.1

THE CARPENTER

Note down the things that would make someone a bad carpenter.
Now list some of the things that would make someone a good carpenter.

Your 'bad' list may include some of the following:

- uses tools clumsily so that the work is not perfect
- makes a mess and does not clear up
- does not do the job that was asked for
- makes changes to the work without checking with you
- makes mistakes
- takes too long and spends lots of time drinking cups of tea
- is unreliable and does not turn up when agreed
- charges more for the completed job than was agreed.

Your 'good' list may include:

- takes time to discuss the job with you so that it is clear what is required
- arrives promptly at the time you agreed
- completes the job exactly as specified
- uses tools expertly so that the work is perfect
- works cleanly and tidily
- completes on time
- charges exactly what was agreed on the work estimate.

So what does this show? The difference between these two is not in their expert knowledge or their tools, but in the way they do their work – in the behaviours of the two individuals. This applies to anyone, in any job or profession, from those that require no formal qualification to those that are very highly qualified through years of education and training. For example, in Canada it has been recognised that medical undergraduates need more than medical knowledge and expert clinical skills to make them good doctors, and so the *CanMEDS physician competency framework* (Frank 2005, p23) has been introduced to inculcate in undergraduates 'ethical practice, profession-led regulation, and *high personal standards of behaviour*' (my italics). Some of the elements included in this framework are altruism, integrity, honesty, compassion, morality, self-awareness and self-assessment, and these may be relevant to other professions, too.

You can see from these examples that professionalism depends not only on those things for which you can be trained or educated, but also on personal attributes that are unique to you as an individual. When you complete your postgraduate studies you will have been assessed to have the same level of expert knowledge and toolkit of skills as the rest of your cohort (as defined by the learning outcomes of your programme), but how good a professional you become, whatever field you choose to work in, will depend upon how those things interact with your behaviours. Of course this interaction is very personal and unique to you, such that it defines your identity as a professional. It is what makes you an individual, and although you can be taught about the elements that make up this identity, no one can teach you how to successfully interact all those elements together. That really is a job for you in your personal and continuing professional development. What we aim to do is make you more aware of them and of how they can impact upon your professional life. We will do this in three stages: firstly we will consider how to develop an understanding of the components of professional identity through the skill of self-awareness. For this we will use a straightforward conceptualisation of professional identity. Then we will take a look at how different organisations communicate the professional standards that they expect from their employees, and how individuals learn to conform. Finally we will consider how you can apply the skill of self-awareness in a practical way to your career.

4.2 A MODEL OF PROFESSIONAL IDENTITY

The study of identity has its roots in psychology but it has been usefully adopted by researchers in organisational behaviour to understand how individuals adapt and operate within organisational settings. The various aspects that contribute towards an individual's identity are very complex. McAdams (1996), for example, talks about contributions from personality traits, motives, values, defence mechanisms, attachment styles and strategies that people might use, which may differ according to time, place and context (in this way these elements differ from traits). Another feature of McAdams's view of identity is that it is constructed through experience – it combines a reconstructed past, perceived present and anticipated future. This means that one's identity is not 'set in stone' – it evolves and adapts to the situations we find ourselves in. We will see later in this chapter that this is important in terms of our ability to adapt to different work environments.

In the work setting, Schein (1978 as cited in Ibarra 1999) defines *professional identity* as 'the relatively stable and enduring constellation of attributes, beliefs, values, motives and experiences in terms of which people define themselves in a professional role'. Ibarra (1999) argues that an understanding of our own professional identity is important because it defines how we see ourselves and how others perceive us within our professional role. Any incongruence between what the role demands and what we see as our (professional) identity can lead to problems with fulfilling that role. In essence, then, understanding your professional identity means questioning who you are in a professional context, and understanding also who your organisation wants you to be. Do the two match, and if not, are you able (and willing) to change to make sure that you meets the needs of your employer?

As a newly qualified professional your task is to start developing self-awareness about who you are in your professional role, so that you can begin to understand your professional identity and learn how to appreciate what your organisation or profession demands of you. This chapter aims to help you start that process by introducing you to a straightforward model of professional identity that you can use as a framework for self-awareness and self-development. As you move through your career you should build on this framework to include additional features of professional identity that you will find in the suggested readings (see 'Explore further' section at the end of this chapter).

We have already discussed how professional identity is determined by the interaction between your expert knowledge, your skills and your personal behaviours. We know that a good professional will seek to ensure that all three elements work in harmony together to fulfil his or her professional role. It is relatively easy to ensure that we have the appropriate skills and knowledge for any given job – but what about behaviour? How do we know what sort of behaviour is appropriate? How do we control it and change it as required? To be able to do these things we first of all need to understand what determines our behaviour.

ACTIVITY 4.2

REFLECTION ON BEHAVIOUR

Think about an incident when someone's behaviour has either shocked or surprised you. (You could use yourself as the example.) Note down the circumstances of the incident and what the person did. Then reflect on why they might have behaved in that way. List anything that you think may have helped to determine their behaviour.

Many things can affect an individual's behaviour in different situations, but some that you may have noted are:

- **Personality**: For example, someone with a very assertive personality may surprise you by behaving in an aggressive way when there is a dispute.

- **Values**: Someone with moral or religious values that differ from your own may make decisions that you might feel are difficult to understand. An example here may be someone refusing a potentially life-saving blood transfusion because of their religious beliefs.

- **Emotions:** We all act in different ways according to the emotional state we are in at the time. When we are angry, upset or distressed we can say or do things that we might later regret. Understanding our emotions and being able to step back from them is one of the fundamental skills of reflective learning, which was covered in Chapter 1.

These three elements are a good place to start when we construct our basic conceptualisation of professional identity because most of us will be able to recognise the potential they have to affect behaviour. However, I would like to include one further element that may not have occurred to you when you were thinking about the last question, and that is norms. By this I mean the accepted standards of behaviour within a given profession or organisation (Ibarra 1999, Sanders 2010). It is an important determinant of professional identity because of the potential problem of incongruence, as we saw earlier. In the rest of this chapter we will explore how each of these features affects our use of expert knowledge and skills, and determine how effective we are as professionals. We can visualise them as part of the DNA that determines our identity, forming the bonds that link our skills and knowledge (Figure 4.1).

We are going to examine each of the four binding elements in this model in turn, but first (overleaf) is a real-life case study about one of my students.

Figure 4.1 Six key elements of professional identity

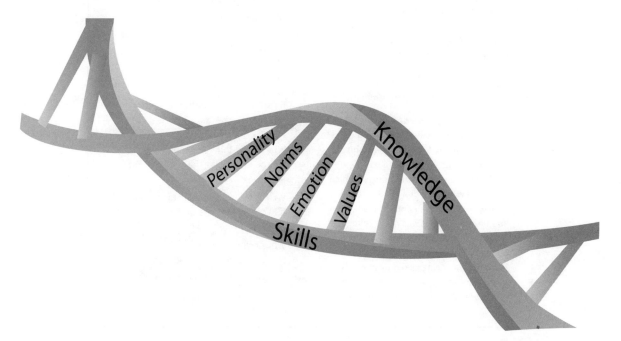

TONY

Tony had spent nine years in the army, the only job he had done since leaving school at the age of 16. Although he loved the job and was proud that he had done well, he decided to leave because he had a young family and no longer wanted to spend long periods away from them. He had gained a lot of experience and developed many skills in his army career so he felt fairly confident of securing a good job in civilian life. However, this proved to be more difficult than he expected, and after many months of searching he eventually found a position as a supervisor of a production line in a food processing factory, which was rather less than he had been hoping for.

Most of the people that Tony had to manage were immigrant workers with a very limited grasp of the English language, and Tony found it frustrating when he asked them to do something and they did not respond in the way he wanted them to. When they did not do what he had asked he tended to shout at them until they eventually 'got the message'.

Tony's production line did not always meet company targets, and as a result he was frequently subjected to questions and criticism from his manager. Tony usually responded to these sessions in the same way as he did with his staff – by shouting – which resulted in target reviews becoming regular weekly confrontations.

By this stage Tony was desperate to find another job and realised that he needed to do something that might increase his chances, so he enrolled on a part-time business and management degree which he hoped would tell him all he needed to know about management. However, he soon realised that it was not meeting his expectations at all. Instead of lecturers telling him all the theory he needed to know, he was being asked to spend some of the time with a group of peers (who, like him, were all in junior management jobs),

discussing and sharing their experiences and interpretation of the theory. This was not what he expected at all. He did not consider his fellow students to be sufficiently expert to be able to offer him the right answers. Despite his misgivings Tony attended all classes and group discussion sessions, but he rarely spoke up and contributed. He managed to pass all of the assignments he was given, but achieved poor marks, the feedback indicating that his work was too descriptive and insufficiently analytical.

Six months after joining his degree programme Tony was at work late one Friday afternoon, engaged in one of his regular shouting matches with his manager. He got so angry that he stormed out, slamming the door behind him, determined to go home. Then, halfway to the car park he stopped as his colleagues in his learning group at university came into his mind. Recently they had been discussing conflicts in the workplace, and he began thinking about the things they had said. He realised then that his way of handling difficult situations was probably wrong, and that he had to do something about his behaviour if he was ever going to do well. He returned to his manager's office and apologised (much to the manager's astonishment) and asked if they could start afresh. From that day he worked to change his behaviour, and within six months he was promoted.

Questions

- Why do you think Tony behaved the way he did when he started his new job?
- What effect do you think his behaviour had on his staff and on his performance in the job?
- Why do you think he initially behaved the way he did during his studies?
- What was it that changed Tony's behaviour?

In our conceptualisation of professional identity we are considering how behaviour can be affected by personality, values, emotions and norms, so we can look at each of these to see if they offer an explanation of Tony's behaviours. Let us start with norms. Tony had been in the army for nine years, and this was the only job he had ever had. The army norms that he was used to meant that when he asked his staff to do something he would have expected them to obey his 'orders' without question. When they did not do so (albeit because they did not understand) he became angry and frustrated, and responded by shouting. Tony's mistake was to assume that what had worked very well for him in the past would work just as well in this new situation. What he did not appreciate was that in assuming new roles people must also adopt the social norms and rules that govern how they should conduct themselves (Van Maanen and Schein 1979). New roles require new skills, behaviours, attitudes and patterns of interactions (Ibarra 1999). Tony was unable to change the norms of the factory, so to be effective he would have to change. Identity changes often accompany career transitions (Ibarra 1999), a fact that Tony took some time to realise, and he held on to his 'soldier' identity even though it was no longer congruent with his new work situation.

Tony's reaction to this situation leads us to the next factor – that of emotions. Tony was clearly disappointed with the job, and so he may already have been feeling some underlying frustrations. When staff did not respond to his requests, this increased and emerged as anger. However, in reacting in this way it was likely that Tony was merely exacerbating the problem. The emotional behaviour of a manager has an important effect on any organisational climate (Momeni 2009). Research has shown that failure of managers to empathise and manage their own emotions can create costs within the organisation through a range of productivity issues (Kiel and Watson 2009). For this reason the study of emotions in the workplace, particularly emotional intelligence (EI) and emotional labour, have become important issues in business and management. Many effective leadership programmes place emphasis on emotional awareness, control and management. We will look at these later in this chapter to help you avoid making the same mistake as Tony.

What does the case tell us about Tony's *personality*? The anger response would indicate that he was quite an aggressive person, but could also point to some other features. He clearly was not a natural 'people person', and he perhaps was suffering from lack of confidence and low self-esteem because of his job disappointments. So is there anything that Tony could do? You may have heard of the 'nature vs nurture' debate about whether our personality and behaviour are determined by our genes (and therefore fixed and unchangeable) or by our upbringing and environment. The good news is that, whilst research is still going on in this field, the general consensus is that only around 50 per cent of our personality is determined by our genes, while the other 50 per cent is formed through our interaction with our environment (Atkinson et al 1993). So, whilst there are some aspects of our personality that we cannot change, we do have the opportunity to modify or to manifest our personality in different ways if we find that it has a detrimental effect on our work effectiveness.

We know little of Tony's *values*, but we do know that he gave up a job he loved for the sake of his family, so we can assume that family values meant a great deal to him. If he felt that he had made a mistake in leaving the army because he could not find a job that enabled him to support his family in the way he wanted, then that may have exacerbated his feelings of frustration, and consequently affected his behaviour.

Tony's behaviour was clearly adversely affecting both his staff and the job performance. We can imagine how those staff were feeling – working in a strange country and different culture, for a boss who shouted and seemed angry all the time. They undoubtedly were feeling a range of very negative emotions, such as misery, fear, uncertainty, unhappiness. No wonder their performance was poor and Tony had to explain low production figures to his manager each week.

The same features again acted to affect his performance adversely when Tony joined his university programme. Having been used to authority figures in the army telling junior ranks exactly what to do, he found it difficult to accept when the 'authority figures' at the university – the lecturers – did not behave in this way. This time his anger and frustration were not manifested in shouting because here he was not in a position to tell others what to do, and his low self-confidence in this strange situation made him reluctant to speak out. Instead, he responded by withdrawing and refusing to co-operate. Despite this being a less aggressive response than he showed at work, it nevertheless upset his group colleagues and affected how they worked together.

So, what was it that made Tony finally decide that his behaviour needed to change? Although he had not been actively engaging in class discussions when he attended university, he clearly had been listening to the different viewpoints offered by others, and eventually he began to realise that there were different ways of doing things. He started to become aware of the detrimental effect that his own behaviour was having on himself and others. Most importantly, he resolved to do something about it. The change did not happen overnight, but Tony began to reflect regularly on his own behaviour and performance, and proactively addressed anything that he felt was standing in the way of him doing a good job. He started to become more expert in the skills of reflective learning, which were covered in Chapter 1. This helped him to make the shift from being a professional soldier to a professional manager; in other words, he fundamentally changed his professional identity.

Tony's story shows how the features of our professional identity model interact in a complex way to determine our professional behaviour, and what can happen when that interaction goes wrong. The real key to Tony's making the changes that made such a difference to his career was self-awareness. We will come back to Tony later, but next we are going to look at what self-awareness means and how we can refine our skills of self-awareness to make positive changes to our professional behaviours if and as required.

4.3 SELF-AWARENESS: DEFINING YOUR PROFESSIONAL IDENTITY

Self-awareness is about understanding our personal characteristics and how our actions affect both ourselves and other people. Becoming self-aware can help us to improve our professional behaviours – allowing us to make better decisions and improving our judgement. It is a crucial element in making our expert knowledge and professional skills work together effectively to maximise our performance. Of course as individuals we are all very complex and it would be impossible to look at all aspects of self-awareness here. Instead, we are going to concentrate on the four elements that we have already identified in our professional identity model: personality, values, emotions and norms.

4.3.1 PERSONALITY

ACTIVITY 4.3

REFLECTION ON PERSONALITY

'Julia has a great personality.'

'Ummar doesn't have the right personality for a sales job.'

We often hear people saying something like this, but what does it mean? Think about the statements and note down what you would understand from them about these two individuals.

Personality is one of those concepts, like 'quality' and 'faith', that can be very difficult to define, and yet we use the term regularly when talking about different individuals. The problem is that it can be very subjective – our interpretation of Julia's personality will depend on what we consider to be 'great'. For example, we may be drawn to people who are quiet and thoughtful or we may prefer people who are gregarious, outgoing and fun. It may be easier to interpret Ummar's personality from the statement made about him because here we are using an external reference to a particular type of job. This makes it less subjective. Most of us would agree on some common traits that would be appropriate to a sales job, for example being outgoing, assertive, confident and communicative. We might then assume from our statement that Ummar does not display these traits. If then we return to Julia, we may understand a little more about her personality if we knew the circumstances in which the statement was made. If it was made by a member of an interview panel who was selecting someone to lead a holiday tour to Ibiza, then the gregarious, fun Julia might be what we consider to be 'great'. However, if the statement was made in the context of looking for someone to manage a care home, then we may be more inclined to favour the quiet, thoughtful Julia.

Cultural perspectives may also affect our judgement on these individuals. For example, most Western, industrialised nations value individuals who are independent, self-assertive and motivated to achieve, whilst in contrast most non-Western cultures place much less value on these characteristics, particularly for females (Atkinson et al 1993).

Herein lies the value in considering personality as one of our elements of our professional identity model. Although personality is complex and difficult to define, and can be difficult to change, an understanding of our personality can help us to find positions in which we can thrive and avoid situations to which we are unsuited and which may make us feel unhappy and stressed. We may also be able to identify which parts of our personality we can modify to improve our organisational effectiveness. Thinking back to Tony, his assertive personality was just right for his position in the army; we would not expect someone with a shy or nervous personality to feel comfortable with an active military role. When it became a problem in his new job, however, he could take steps to express his assertiveness in a different, less aggressive way that was more suited to that role. The fundamentals of his personality did not change, but the way he behaved did.

The importance that personality plays in personal well-being and effectiveness has long been recognised, and as such has been the subject of much research, particularly in the field of psychology. As a result there are many different views of what constitutes personality, but all generally agree that it is what makes an individual unique. We will use the following definition: 'Personality is the distinctive and characteristic patterns of thought, emotion and behaviour that define an individual's personal style and influence his or her interactions with the environment. In addition to mental abilities, personality includes variables like sociability, emotional stability, impulsiveness, conscientiousness and many others' (Atkinson et al 1993, p489).

Much of the research on personality has focused on personality traits. This is useful to us because usually if we were asked to describe someone's personality we would list traits that we associate with them – for example being aggressive, friendly, talkative, outgoing. Researchers largely agree that there are five core traits that interact to form human personality, now known commonly as 'The Big Five' (McCrae and Costa 1987, 1997). Although there is some disagreement on what these factors should be called, the most commonly used terms are shown in Table 4.1 opposite.

It is important to remember that these are very broad definitions and personality is very complex, so although we may be able to identify an individual as predominantly agreeable, such a person is also likely to demonstrate traits across the other dimensions, too. Nevertheless, this characterisation offers us an opportunity to become more aware of our personality characteristics and therefore gives us some insight into how we might behave in different environments.

ACTIVITY 4.4

EXPLORING THE BIG FIVE

Access the Big Five questionnaire on the companion website. Give yourself a score of 1–5 for each of the personality traits, where 1 means 'not much like me' and 5 means 'very much like me'. Which of the Big Five best describes your personality?

Next, ask at least three people who know you well to complete the same assessment for you. You may find it informative to ask people who know you in different environments, such as family members, friends, work colleagues, associates in sports or leisure teams and so on.

Table 4.1 'Big Five' dimensions of personality

Dimension	Typical personality traits
Extraversion	• Sociable • Talkative • Assertive • Gregarious • Excitable • Emotionally expressive
Neuroticism	• Anxious • Moody • Irritable • Self-conscious • Angry • Impulsive
Conscientiousness	• Thoughtful • Organised • Self-disciplined • Attentive to details • Competent • Goal-directed
Openness	• Imaginative • Insightful • Interested • Broad-minded • Daring • Feeling
Agreeableness	• Kind • Trusting • Altruistic • Modest • Straightforward • Selfless

Source: adapted from McCrae and Costa (1987, 1997).

 ACTIVITY 4.5

REFLECTION ON THE BIG FIVE

Reflect on what the results tell you about your own perception of your personality characteristics and how you appear to others. Are the results similar or are there significant differences? Is there anything that surprises you? Reflect on any differences and analyse why different aspects of your personality emerge in different situations.

To conclude this discussion on personality it is worth taking a little time to consider just how important personality factors can be to our professional success. You may already be familiar the work of Abraham Maslow and his theories of motivation. If so, you will remember that Maslow proposed that there is a hierarchy of needs that drives humans towards achievement, with physiological needs at the bottom of the hierarchy and something that Maslow called 'self-actualisation' at the top. Self-actualisation can be defined as the need for self-fulfilment and to realise one's true potential. Maslow made a study of famous self-actualisers, people who he judged to have made extraordinary use of their potential such as Abraham Lincoln and Albert Einstein. From this study Maslow was able to compile a list of personality characteristics common to these high-achieving individuals, which included creativity, spontaneity, toleration of uncertainty, objectivity and a good sense of humour amongst others (Maslow 1967).

Does this mean that those of us who do not posses these personality characteristics have no chance of ever realising out full potential? Well, Maslow followed up his work with subjects from the normal population and found that whilst most people do not achieve the sustained self-actualisation of his famous subjects, many people experienced transient periods of self-actualisation, and he was able to identify behaviours that could lead to this sort of achievement. These are summarised in Box 4.1 below.

BOX 4.1: BEHAVIOURS LEADING TO SELF-ACTUALISATION

Experience life as a child does, with full absorption and concentration.

Try something new rather than sticking to secure and safe ways.

Listen to your own feelings in evaluating experiences rather than to the voice of tradition or authority to the majority.

Be honest; avoid pretences or 'game playing'.

Be prepared to be unpopular if your views do not coincide with those of most people.

Assume responsibility.

Work hard at whatever you decide to do.

Try to identify your defences and have the courage to give them up.

(Atkinson et al 1993, after Maslow 1967)

To summarise, personality can be a crucial factor in our professional identity because it can determine what job role we may be most comfortable with (identifying which of the 'Big Five' we most resemble can help with this); it can affect our health, stress levels and relationships with our professional colleagues (and knowing if we are more Type A or B can help us to address these issues: see online resource) and it can affect how much fulfilment we can achieve in our

ACTIVITY 4.6

REFLECTION ON PERSONALITY AND BEHAVIOUR

Which of these behaviours, if any, do you routinely display?

Choose one item from the list that you do not usually display and reflect on how you can practise and develop that behaviour so that it becomes part of the way you work.

Examples you could try are:

- Next time you are discussing something with a group, make an effort to present a different point of view from the others'.
- Give yourself some 'clear time' to complete a task. Do not allow yourself to be distracted by all the other things you have to do; commit yourself fully to the task in hand.
- Next time you have group task, volunteer to take responsibility for team leadership.
- Volunteer to get involved in something you have never done before, for example abseiling for charity or giving a presentation to local schools about the benefits of higher education.

lives and careers (Maslow's tips on behaviours point us towards useful avenues of self-development).

4.3.2 VALUES

ETHAN'S DILEMMA

CASE STUDY 4.2

Ethan was taking a short break from preparing an important tender for his design company. It had been intensive work – the contract was worth £2 million, and his boss was relying on him to do a good job. He was almost done. By the end of the afternoon he should have the tender document completed and ready to show to his boss. He was quite pleased to have it completed two days ahead of schedule, and he felt justified in taking an hour out of the office to relax and unwind in the nearby gym. The gym was quiet at that time in the morning, and he was the only person in the changing room after he had showered. He noticed a plain leather folio lying on the bench. Clearly someone must have left it behind, but there was nothing on the outside of the folio to indicate who that might be, and so he opened it to see it offered any clues. To a mixture of horror and delight he realised that it contained a

rival bid for the same contract that he had been working on. The bid belonged to a small design company nearby. He knew a couple of the guys there and spoke to them occasionally in the gym, but he had had no idea that they were building a competitive bid for this tender. He could not remember if he had ever spoken to them about his own tender. He started to feel a little bit angry. What if he had inadvertently mentioned something to these guys from the other company that had helped them to put together their tender? He racked his brains to try to remember anything he had said, but he just could not recall. He had been so stressed recently that he found he was forgetful about lots of things – the tender was the only thing on his mind. There was only one thing to do – he had to read their document to see if was similar to his own.

Ethan read the document with growing

dismay. He realised that it was considerably superior to his, and there was one particularly inventive idea in there that was bound to secure this company the contract. If he let this go ahead, all his hard work would have been for nothing. What was he to do? He mulled over the options in his mind. He guessed the easiest thing would be to leave the folio where it was and forget he had ever seen it. But then, he knew that this other company would win the tender. What would his boss say to him if he failed? And what if someone else came into the gym and read the document as he had done, but then they took it away and used it prepare another rival bid – there were still two days to go, so it could be done. What would happen if his boss ever suspected that he had known of this rival bid and had done nothing about it? When this company was awarded the bid, the tale of them nearly losing it because someone had left it in the gym would inevitably get out and become an industry legend. He could smuggle the folio out of the gym and dispose of it discreetly so that the other firm could not submit, but then they probably had copies anyway.

Then another thought occurred to Ethan. He felt guilty at first, but then the idea started to grow on him. He could leave the folio where it was, but he could go back to amend his own tender. He could use this other company's idea but improve on it so that his own company was almost certain to win. Who would know that it had not been his idea in the first place? His boss would be so

pleased that he might even be awarded a junior partnership, something he had aspired to for years. His wife would be really proud. The bigger salary would come in really handy too – his daughter was due to go off to university soon and it would be so good to know that he could provide for her and not have to worry about money. No one would ever find out that he had stolen the idea, would they? And anyway, how can ideas be 'stolen'? Everyone was free to have their own thoughts, and he was just as likely to have a good idea as the next man. What if someone did find out though? The gym has a swipe card system, so there would be a record of him being there at the same time as the folio. His boss would not mind – he would probably slap him on the back and say 'well done!' But what would his wife and daughter think of him?

Ethan then remembered something else. He had heard a rumour that this other firm was not doing too well, and that there were likely to be redundancies unless they secured a good contract in the near future. If he used their idea and they did not win this tender, would he be responsible for some of their staff losing their jobs? But honestly, if they were stupid enough to leave their ideas lying around did they deserve to be in this business anyway?

Oh, this was such a difficult one! Ethan wished he had never left the office that morning!

What should Ethan do?

ACTIVITY 4.7

EXPLORING ETHAN'S DILEMMA

Discuss this case study with a group of colleagues.

Does everyone in the group reach a consensus on what Ethan should do?

If there are differences of opinion, why?

What do you think are the conflicting values that are creating Ethan's dilemma?

Ethan's dilemma results from a conflict between his personal values. Values are our personal beliefs or rules that help us to decide what is right or wrong and what course we choose to take in life. They act to determine our behaviour in complex situations (see for example University of Kent Career Advisory Service ND). We all have a set of values that derive largely from our background, upbringing and moral education. Personality also has a role to play, which we will discuss later. Very often the values that we hold will conflict with one another, and in such circumstances it will be the values that we hold most dear that will determine what we do.

In this scenario Ethan is struggling with a number of conflicting values:

- **Honesty**: He knows that passing off the other company's idea as his own is not honest, despite the fact that he is trying to convince himself otherwise.

- **Loyalty**: Having worked for his company for some time, Ethan feels that he should do all he can to help them to be successful.

- **Accomplishment/success**: He has worked really hard on this tender and naturally wants it to succeed.

- **Status**: Using the other firm's ideas is very likely to help Ethan achieve the partnership status that he has long coveted.

- **Money**: Promotion would give him a much bigger salary.

- **Security**: As a junior partner he would be much less susceptible to the vagaries of the economy. If the firm had to downsize more junior staff would go before him.

- **Family**: Not all of Ethan's values are self-centred. The approval of his wife and daughter are clearly important to him, and he wants them to be proud of him. He also wants to provide for them both financially.

- **Concern for others**: Ethan is worried that his actions could mean that a number of people may lose their jobs.

Whatever Ethan finally decides to do will depend upon which of these values are most important to him. What would you do? Understanding your personal values is important because they are an indicator of your underlying motivations. They can be a crucial point of reference when you are making important decisions.

 ACTIVITY 4.8

EXPLORING VALUES

Can you think of any examples of when values might affect life-changing decisions? List all examples that you can think of. You may want to discuss this with a peer or in a small group.

There are many examples from the world of politics where personal values have dictated the actions of individuals. Of course, people join and serve a political party because their values align with that of their chosen party. Someone with strong socialist values is unlikely to seek employment as a researcher for the Conservative party in the UK. However, sometimes the policies of the party conflict so strongly with the values of an individual that that person is driven to resign.

There are also many examples of individuals who feel so strongly about their values that they are willing to give up their life or their freedom to defend them. Examples here include very famous personalities such as Nelson Mandela, Benazir Bhutto and Martin Luther King who devoted their whole lives to defending their values, but also people who, up until their moment of sacrifice or notoriety, were just like us, such as Neda Agha-Soltan, the young Iranian shot on the streets of Teheran during the election protests in 2009.

Personal values can drive individuals to extraordinary acts of achievement: Barack Obama defying all predictions to become the first black president of the United States of America; Lance Armstrong surviving cancer to compete successfully in the Tour de France; or Bill Gates, who has dedicated his career to his vision of 'a computer on every desk in every home' – a vision which seemed incomprehensible when he first expressed it in 1977 but is now the accepted norm for many of us.

Of course, values do not just affect the motivations of high-profile individuals – they drive us all. We may decide to take a job that is less well paid because it offers more freedom to take time with our family or to play a sport that is important to us. Our values may change as our life circumstances change, and that can affect our choice of friends or where we want to live. For example, some young people may value career success and socialising above other things, and so may choose to live in a city apartment close to work and clubs. Later family values may become more important, so they then may choose to live in the suburbs close to good schools and open areas where children can play, even if it means a long commute to work for them. The friends they choose now are unlikely to be the same as those they had in their city days – the difference in their values now will mean that they no longer have much in common.

ACTIVITY 4.9

REFLECTION ON VALUES

Can you think of any examples where your personal values have affected decisions you have made?

It is not only individuals that are guided and motivated by values. Organisations too can have values that give them a distinct identity. Very often they will use these values as a promotional aid. For example, the UK retailer John Lewis strongly promotes its values of corporate social responsibility, and also uses the catchphrase 'never knowingly undersold' on all of its advertising (John Lewis 2009). A less commercial example is provided by the British army which promotes values such as loyalty, trust and service (British Army 2010).

Values are the second element in our conceptualisation of professional identity – we will see later how personal values can interact with the other elements to make us unique individuals and with organisational values to determine our professional behaviours.

ACTIVITY 4.10

PERSONAL VALUES

Make a list of the things that you value most. Write down as many as you can. (You may need to come back to your list several times as different things occur to you.) Once you think you have got a complete list, try to rank them in order of importance. Keep this list for future reference.

4.3.3 EMOTIONS

ACTIVITY 4.11

REFLECTING ON EMOTIONS

Think back to a time when you have had a very heated argument with someone you care about, for example a partner, parent or good friend. Have there been any times when you have said or done something that you have later regretted? What were they? What did you do next? How did the other person react? What were the consequences?

Chances are that your answer to the first question is 'yes'. We all do irrational things and make inappropriate decisions when emotions are high. In the middle of an argument it is difficult, if not impossible, to see the other person's point of view; if we are convinced that we are right, we tend to get more and more angry if they will not accept our argument. Later, when we have calmed down and had time to reflect, we can often then start to accept some of the points they were making. What we do next is all-important. Do we stubbornly refuse to admit that we might have been wrong, or do we apologise and then talk through the issue in a more even-tempered way? Sometimes the things we do or say when we are very emotional may have irreversible effects. For example, we might say such hurtful things to our partner that they decide that they no longer want a relationship with us; we may be so excited by a new idea that has been presented at a meeting that we volunteer to be part of a team that implements it, only to realise later that we do not really have the necessary skills or the time to do the job well. Has something like that happened to you?

One of the most important aims of developing self-awareness is to be able to avoid such situations happening in a professional context. We need to be able to control our emotional reactions so that we are able to make rational judgements and do not lose control, and we need to understand how the emotional state of others might affect their behaviour so that we can respond in an appropriate way. This is by no means an easy task because we rarely plan to be emotional and our emotions often take us by surprise. Emotional self-awareness is something we have to practise until it becomes natural to us. The steps are (drawing on Goleman 2005; Ashkanasy and Daus 2002; Momeni 2009):

1. **Recognising emotions**: Few of us regularly devote any time to thinking about how we are feeling, and throughout the day we may go through a range of emotions without ever noticing or appreciating how they are affecting our behaviour. But how can we ever hope to control our emotions if we do not know what they are? The first step, then, must be to actively think about what we are feeling in different situations.

2. **Understanding emotions**: Once we have learnt to recognise the different emotions we experience, we then need to know what triggers them: that is, what make us angry, excited, jealous, unhappy and so on. How do we respond when we are feeling that way and what are the consequences? How do our emotions affect our behaviour towards those around us and how do they respond?

3. **Controlling emotions**: We are now well on the way towards having control over our emotions because we have started to understand the processes of emotional reactions. Now it is important to develop personal strategies for emotional self-control. The skill of reflection is very important here. Reflection requires us to take a step back from a situation and try to see it from multiple perspectives. Our view of situations can change over time, and as emotions subside, so we need to

ACTIVITY 4.12

EXPLORING EMOTIONAL CONTROL STRATEGIES

As a first step towards constructing your own emotional control strategies keep a 'critical incident' log (Goodwin 1995) for a month to develop your emotional self-awareness. Whenever something non-routine or unexpected happens (it may be something that involves you directly or you may be just a close observer) note down in your log:

- At this moment I am feeling …
- I feel this way because …
- Because I feel this way, I did …
- Because of the way I behaved, this happened: …

Remember that you can have mixed emotions; try to capture everything you are feeling when you make your entries in your log.

At the end of the month review your entries. Are there any surprises or revelations? Is there anything you would do differently now that you have had time to reflect? Can you identify what situations trigger an emotional response that may not be constructive at the workplace or help your career?

consider not only how we felt about a situation at the time, but also later on. It is also useful to seek the opinions of others who have been involved to compare their opinion with ours. Only then are we likely to be able to construct a considered strategy for dealing with given types of emotional response.

Emotional self-awareness has been the subject of much attention in the field of professional development in recent years. The term 'emotional intelligence' (EI) has been introduced to refer to individuals' ability to recognise and manage their own emotions, use those emotions as a self-motivator, recognise emotions in others and handle relationships. Research has shown that having high EI can be more important than high IQ in determining professional success (Goleman 2005). So, for example, some managers with a relatively low IQ but a high EI have been more successful than those with a high IQ but an inferior EI. However, EI and IQ are not opposites. Everyone has a mix of both, but unlike IQ there are no questionnaire-based measures that can score an individual on an EI scale, and aspects of emotional intelligence tend to be measured by observation within given situations. One of the aspects of emotional intelligence that can be observed in this way is an individual's sensitivity to the emotions of others. Try Activity 4.12 to test your own ability:

 KAREN

CASE STUDY 3.3

Karen has worked for a medium-sized haulage company for the last 10 years and was promoted to supervisor three years ago when the company was doing well. However, over the last two years business has declined because of a downturn in the economy, and for the last six months there have been rumours of redundancies. This reached a head two months ago when a new director was appointed at head office. The new man is known to have a reputation for turning ailing companies around by cutting costs and streamlining operations. An announcement has been made that the new director will visit the site at which Karen works the following week and will be requesting meetings with individual staff. On Friday afternoon Karen receives an e-mail instructing her to go to the director's office at 11 am next Wednesday.

How do you think Karen will feel?

On Monday the director commences a series of meetings with a number of staff. News quickly gets round that some have been told that they will lose their jobs whilst others are told that they are being reassigned. Some are keeping their jobs without change. There seems to be no pattern to the decisions.

How will Karen feel now? What effect do you think this situation will have on her job performance?

At 10.30 am on Wednesday morning Karen receives am e-mail to say that her meeting is delayed for one hour, without any explanation.

How will she feel now?

When Karen finally meets the director he tells her that he is delighted to inform her that she will be keeping her job. In fact, he wants her to take over from one of the senior supervisors who is being 'let go'. He seems surprised that Karen doesn't seem more pleased.

How is Karen feeling now?

Karen would undoubtedly have been feeling a great deal of **anxiety** when she first heard of the planned meeting with the boss. She may have feared the worst and assumed that if the boss wanted to speak to her it would mean bad news about her job. This anxiety may or may not have increased after news spread on Monday about the first meetings, and she realised that some people were being given good news. This would depend largely upon her personality: if she tended towards optimism she may have been hoping that her job would be safe; if she tended towards pessimism she would assume that she was going to lose her job. Whatever the case, the **uncertainty** of the situation was likely to be affecting her job performance; she would be preoccupied with thinking about what was going to happen – after all, she had six days to worry about it. Her attention to detail would decline and she would be prone to making mistakes. She may also be **upset** about what is happening to her colleagues; chances are that some of the people who are losing their jobs are her friends.

When the day of her meeting finally arrives and she then finds that it is inexplicably delayed, another emotion may emerge; this sort of treatment is disrespectful and inconsiderate and the least she could expect is an explanation for the delay, and better still an apology. She is likely to feel **anger**, and in an angry state is much less likely to be accepting of anything that is proposed to her. This could explain why she does not react in the way that the boss expects when he tells her that her job is safe; so, although she will surely feel **relief** that her job is safe, she may already have misgivings about staying to work for someone who has so little regard for the employees' feelings. In addition, if she is being asked to take over from someone who is being dismissed she may feel **guilt** – this is a common emotion of 'survivors' of redundancy situations.

You will probably agree that this situation was not handled well. Although any situation such as this is going to be painful, the director could have shown more consideration for his employees' feelings and dealt with it more sensitively. Keeping people waiting for news in a state of anxiety or stress was unlikely to smooth the way to effective organisational change. How would you have handled it if you were the director?

Personality and emotions are interrelated, and indeed all three factors that we have looked at so far – personality, values and emotions – are interdependent. For example, emotional intelligence has been shown to be related to personality types of males and females in the way shown in Table 4.2 opposite. (These characterisations are 'pure' types, which are relatively rare. Most people of either gender display a mix of IQ and EI characteristics.)

The interrelationship between emotions, values, personality and behaviour can be further demonstrated by returning to Ethan and his dilemma. We looked in detail at how his values might affect the decision he made, but what emotions might we guess he was feeling at the time? Perhaps guilt, excitement, anticipation, fear, uncertainty were all part of what he was feeling. And what of his personality?

Ethan's behaviour in his difficult situation would be dependent on a complex interaction between his personality, his emotions and his values. We all have a

Table 4.2 Emotional intelligence and personality types

	Male personality	Female personality
High emotional intelligence	Socially poised Outgoing Cheerful Not prone to fearfulness or worry Commitment to people or causes Responsible Ethical outlook Caring in relationships	Assertive Express feelings directly Feel positive about themselves Outgoing Gregarious Adapt well to stress Playful Spontaneous Rarely anxious or guilty
High intelligence quotient	Has a wide range of intellectual interests Ambitious Productive Predictable Dogged Critical Condescending Fastidious Inhibited Inexpressive Detached Emotionally bland and cold	Intellectually confident Fluent in expressing thoughts Value intellectual matters Has a wide range of intellectual and aesthetic interests Introspective Anxious Prone to feelings of guilt Hesitate to express anger openly

Source: drawing on Goleman (2005).

ACTIVITY 4.13

EXPLORING PERSONALITY AND VALUES

How do you think Ethan is likely to react if his personality is most like the Big Five dimension of 'Openness'?

Would his response be different if he was more typical of the Big Five dimension 'Conscientious'?

unique mix of these factors, making us the individuals we are and thus defining our professional identity. By being aware of what these factors are and how they interact with each other as well as our expert knowledge and skills we can develop strategies to maximise our professional capabilities.

However, there is one further factor that is less under our control than the others but nevertheless just as important in determining our professional behaviour. Understanding of professional and organisational **norms** is the final step in our definition of professional identity.

4.3.4 NORMS

ACTIVITY 4.14

PROFESSIONS

Write down three words that come immediately to mind to describe each of the following individuals:

- police officer
- teacher
- journalist
- doctor.

Whenever I ask groups of students to complete this activity the same words appear to describe each of these individuals:

- Police officers are typically described as: authoritarian, firm, trustworthy, honest, safe, judgemental.
- Teachers are most often described as: caring, educated, interested, fair, nurturing.
- Journalists tend to be described as: inquisitive, creative, ruthless, biased, relentless, 'selective with the truth'.
- Doctors are usually considered to be: intelligent, educated, caring, trustworthy, honest, dependable.

Were any of your words included here?

There are two interesting points to note here. Firstly, the fact that many different individuals come up with the same words to describe a profession suggests that there is some kind of externally recognised identity to that profession. People broadly know what it means to be a doctor or police officer. There are generally recognised norms for those professions. Secondly, many of the words used describe behaviours.

These points raise some important questions. If certain professions have recognisable identities defined by behavioural norms, does that mean that only those people with an individual professional identity to match can do well in that profession, or does it mean that the individual's professional identity is somehow shaped by the profession they have entered? Then if we join a profession, how do we know what behaviours are appropriate? Job descriptions will list the knowledge and skills required for specific roles but do not describe behaviour.

Let us consider the first question. All of us will have a tendency to select a job or profession that we believe suits us, but because there are many external variables that affect our choice of career mistakes can be made, and these often do not become evident until someone has been in a profession for some time. For example, our parents may have particular ambitions for us and so we choose a career path that makes them happy. We may receive inaccurate or incomplete career advice that gives us the wrong impression of what it is like to work in our chosen profession, or we may select a profession because we know someone who enjoys it and is doing well in it, but do not take into account that this person may be very different to us. Whatever the influences on our career choice, sometimes by the time we have realised that the career is not for us we have invested so much effort into it that we feel that we cannot change. However, in this section we will focus on helping you to avoid such problems by understanding how to match your individual professional identity with that of your chosen profession.

This leads us to the second point: through developing the skills of self-awareness we can have a much better understanding of our own professional identity. But how do we develop an understanding of the organisation or profession? We will look at two strategies: first, identifying behaviours that are explicitly defined, and second, learning the tacit behaviours that act as norms within the profession.

Explicit norms: Despite that fact that behavioural norms are unlikely to be defined in any job description or role profile, organisations and professions very often express them in other formats.

ACTIVITY 4.15

EXPLORING PROFESSIONAL NORMS

Can you think of any ways in which behavioural norms might be presented by organisations or professions?

You should have thought of 'professional standards' (CIPD is a good example), but you could also have mentioned 'professional ethics', 'professional codes of practice' or 'professional competency statements'. These are common ways in which professions communicate their expected standards of behaviour explicitly. At an organisational level companies will often publish value statements that they expect all employees to adhere to.

Ethics are similar to values, but whereas values tend to be personal and implicit, ethics are more formally defined, explicit and apply to a profession rather than an individual. Professional ethics and codes of practice are designed to prevent the abuse of power that members of a profession possess by virtue of their specialist knowledge and training. So, for example, medical ethics demand that doctors act solely to benefit the patient. It would not be acceptable for a doctor to perform a procedure on a patient simply for the sake of research or to try out a new technique. Although patients are commonly used in research studies, these practices are tightly controlled by being subject to ethical review and formal permissions, both from members of the profession and from the patient him/herself.

ACTIVITY 4.16

EXPLORING PROFESSIONAL ETHICS AND PERSONAL VALUES

Sometimes there are occasions when professional ethics and personal values can conflict. Can you think of any examples?

The medical profession can offer many examples here; a doctor may be asked to perform an operation to terminate a pregnancy although it is in conflict with his beliefs; a paramedic may decide to perform a blood transfusion on an accident victim to save her life even though she indicates that she does not want the transfusion because of her religious beliefs; a doctor may covertly offer a terminally ill patient medication to end his life because she strongly believes in the right to die with dignity, despite the fact that she knows that this contravenes ethical practice.

There are, of course, high profile examples from other professions, too. The world financial crisis during 2009 was often blamed on unethical practice in the financial sector, although many working in the sector maintained that it was their job to make money and protect the banks rather than to consider the customers. Can you think of any example from your own experience?

So, ethical standards, where they exist, are a first step in identifying the behaviours that are expected in any given profession. Competency frameworks or standards administered by professional bodies (eg CIPD 2009), although less formal than ethical standards, are another valuable source of information. These are often supported by a monitored system of continuing professional development as a requirement of entry to the professional body, and this provides a way of maintaining and monitoring the sustained professional behaviour of its members. Although these standards are not legally binding, adherence to them is often crucial simply because some organisations will make membership of the relevant professional body a prerequisite for a job. Codes of ethical practice and professional competency frameworks often coexist. For example, the Royal College of Physicians and Surgeons of Canada employs a competency framework called CanMEDS in the training of doctors, which we mentioned early in this chapter. This is designed to ensure that doctors not only have the prerequisite medical knowledge and skills to do their job effectively, but that they also adopt appropriate behaviours to support patient care. Their framework covers six different dimensions of behaviour, one of which is 'professional', which includes values such as (Frank 2005):

- altruism
- integrity and honesty
- compassion and caring
- self-awareness

- disclosure of error or adverse events
- responsibility to society.

Doctors in Canada are therefore prepared before they graduate for the appropriate behaviours demanded by their chosen profession. Unfortunately there are no comparable frameworks for the business and management profession. Currently the guidelines for higher education in this field concentrate only on knowledge and skills. This may perhaps be because students of business and management are likely to go into a very diverse range of jobs, all of which will have their own varied standards of behaviour. It is therefore important that as an individual you become astute at identifying behavioural requirements in your chosen field or organisation.

In our search for professional norms, the next step is to discover if a particular organisation in which we are interested has defined a statement of expected behaviours. This would most commonly be published as a vision or value statement, which is often found on company websites or in publicity material. Very often you will be supplied with a copy of this when you apply for a job with a company. It is important to familiarise yourself with this information – firstly, it will help you decide if this organisation is right for you, and then, if you are invited for interview, you will be able to demonstrate how your own values and behaviours fit those of the organisation.

So now we have seen that there are a number of ways that we can start to identify the norms of behaviour within any given profession, and we have briefly discussed the fact that sometimes these might conflict with our own professional identity. However, there are still many rules of behaviour that are not specified in any written form. How might we understand these?

ACTIVITY 4.17

LEARNING THE RULES

Think back to a time when you have joined a new group or organisation. It may be a new school or college, a new club, a new job, or being introduced to a new group of friends. At first it is normal to feel like an outsider, that we do not really fit in. Then, over time, we begin to feel that we belong and any awkwardness, uncertainty or shyness disappears. How does this happen in your experience?

We start to feel part of a new group when we start to learn its language and culture. Any group tends to have its own jargon, insider knowledge or 'in jokes'. Newcomers at first do not understand, and need to learn through observation and experience. Similarly, the newcomers will gradually learn through experience about the informal hierarchy in the group – who is the most powerful member, who is respected, who can and cannot be trusted and so on. None of these things are written down anywhere – they are tacit. Tacit knowledge is knowledge that cannot be easily articulated.

ACTIVITY4.18

LEARNING TO RIDE A BIKE

Think about how you ride a bike. Could you explain to someone exactly how you do it?

This is a very simple example; yet you probably found it very difficult to explain in words all that is entailed in riding a bike properly. It is a complex skill, much of which is tacit. We learn through trial and error how to maintain balance, make different manoeuvres and so on. In the same way, learning how an organisation operates is largely tacit. There may be lots of procedures written down, but finding out how the organisation really works. through things such as the organisational politics, the underlying culture and working norms, is tacit. Nevertheless, if we are to be effective professionals in that organisation we need to learn these things. So how do we do this if the knowledge is not written down and cannot be articulated to us by those that are already 'in the know'? We absorb this organisational know-how in the same way that we learn to ride a bike – through observation, experimentation, reflection and trial and error (Schön 1983 refers to the person doing this as the *Reflective Practitioner*).

Tacit knowledge in organisations has been widely researched and has been found to be a key factor in organisational performance. Consider for a moment the fact that it is not uncommon for people who are highly successful in their occupations to have unremarkable academic records or, on the other hand, for those who were highly successful in school to be only moderately successful in their career (Wagner 1987). The British entrepreneurs Richard Branson or Alan Sugar are good examples of this. Researchers have found little correlation between IQ tests, which measure academic intelligence, and actual job performance (Neisser 1976). You will remember that we have already discussed how emotional intelligence can be just as influential, if not more so, than IQ. Now we can consider an alternative form of intelligence that has been postulated as a major contributor to professional success – practical intelligence, which may be defined as 'a person's ability to apply components of intelligence to everyday life' (Sternberg 1993, p518). This is the intelligence gained not through formal teaching in academic settings, but through informal processes in complex situations; the knowledge of experience; 'soft knowledge' as opposed to 'hard knowledge.

Researchers have argued that the acquisition of tacit knowledge is fundamental to the development of practical intelligence (Polanyi 1962), although there is still a lot of argument about how tacit knowledge can be defined. Despite this, most researchers tend to agree that tacit knowledge is acquired through intensive personal experience and observation in the absence of direct instruction, and that its acquisition is highly correlated with career success (Insch et al 2008). Of course, sharing and transferring tacit knowledge is not going to be simple; we have seen that by its very nature it cannot easily be articulated. However, by considering how tacit knowledge develops and transfers, it is possible to construct a model that we can use to expedite that process of our acquisition of organisational 'know-how' and norms that help us to integrate more quickly. There are three processes of knowledge transfer that we are going to consider here (Nonaka 1990):

- **Tacit to tacit**: Development of tacit knowledge is a social process. Individuals acquire tacit knowledge from one another without the use of language (Baumard 1999). It requires intense personal experience and happens most effectively when the learner is immersed in action and using as many senses as possible (McNett, Wallace and Athanassiou 2004). Transfer occurs not through dialogue but through action, observation and reflection. Ibarra (1999) describes the process of socialisation as the newcomer learning 'display rules' such as appropriate mannerisms, attitudes and social rituals.

- **Tacit to explicit**: The conversion of tacit knowledge into explicit knowledge is effected through articulation. For example, discussion about the way a problem should be tackled will gradually tease out tacit knowledge to form a strategy or plan of action.

- **Explicit to tacit**: The knowledge transfer loop is only complete when individuals can take newly acquired explicit knowledge and internalise it in order to broaden, extend and reframe their own tacit knowledge (Nonaka 2007). Only when the knowledge becomes internalised will the individual be able to access it without conscious thought and reference to codified explicit knowledge – it simply becomes part or the toolkit with which they are able to do their job. Internalisation can be encouraged through a process of reflection on action (Schön 1983).

So, socialisation, articulation and internalisation are the three essential elements in our efforts to harness the power of tacit knowledge. But what do these processes mean to us in practical terms?

ACTIVITY 4.19

KNOWLEDGE CREATION IN PRACTICE

Think about the processes of socialisation, articulation and internalisation. Can you think of practical ways that you could apply these processes to your own work?

Socialisation might be achieved by engaging collaboratively with others. Remember that we talked earlier about only being able to understand group norms through a process of observation and experience. Working collaboratively with a group allows us to observe how the members do things and who is who in the group.

Articulation can occur by talking through problems and issues. Sometimes, even if we cannot think how to explain something in an explicit way we can gradually tease out an understanding of if by talking it over. Think back to our earlier example. Although we may find it very difficult to write a manual to explain to a novice how to ride a bike, most of us could help her to learn whilst watching her try, correcting her mistakes as we observe them and answering her questions as they arise.

Internalisation occurs through a process of reflection, which has already been discussed in Chapter 1. It is important that we internalise the things we learn so that we can use the knowledge almost instinctively. It would be very inefficient if we always had to consciously think about how to tackle things or refer to a manual every time we had a problem to solve. Our knowledge must become part of our individual 'know-how' that provides the toolkit with which we operate on a day-to-day basis. Using a model (see Figure 4.2 below) can help us to visualise these processes as a continuing process of learning that supports our acquisition and understanding of professional/organisation norms.

Figure 4.2 Learning processes for tacit knowledge acquisition

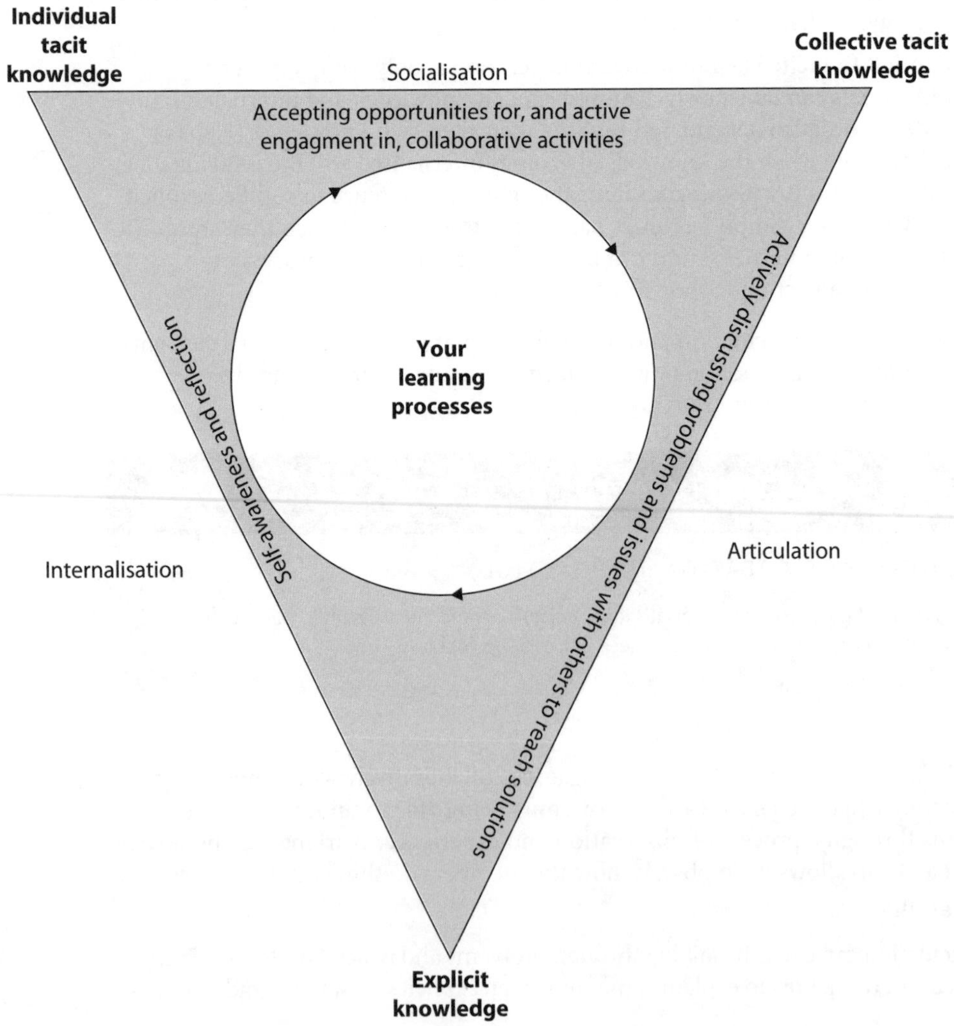

This model demonstrates that we need to take positive action to ensure that organisational knowledge becomes *our* knowledge. Those of us who prefer to work individually or for whom debate and dialogue does not come naturally need to make an extra effort to engage – and here we see another link with personality.

We have now considered the four elements that link our expert knowledge and skills to determine our professional behaviours – the elements that combine to define our professional identity. However, we have seen that these elements are not as easy to capture and define as knowledge or skills, and that they are unique to each of us, and so we have discussed how self-awareness underpins our ability to understand these elements and utilise them in a way that supports our continued professional success.

4.4 CONCLUSION

Clarity of professional identity is important to career success (Hall 2002, Ibarra, 1999). It is not something that can be taught or acquired through a training programme; it is up to each of you to understand how your identity affects your professional behaviours and 'fits' with your chosen profession. By actively practising the skills of self-awareness throughout your career, you can ensure that your professional identity is developing and evolving in a way that supports your performance and development in your professional role.

PAUSE FOR THOUGHT

Identify at least three things that you have learned by studying this chapter and by engaging with the exercises and activities. How will your newly acquired knowledge and skills support your continuing professional development? What value do you expect your learning to have for your daily routines and your further career? In what area have you identified a need for further development and how are you planning to fill that gap? Address these issues in your learning journal and/or CPD log. You may also wish to discuss them with a peer, colleague, mentor or coach to aid your further development.

- Professional identity determines who we are as professionals and how we behave in our professional role.

- It is determined by a mix of factors unique to each of us, including personality, values and emotions.

- Professional identity can also be affected by the norms of the organisation or profession within which we work. These are communicated through explicit means (for example, professional standards) and by implicit means (the 'politics' of the workplace, see also Chapter 7).

- Having a clear understanding of our professional identity can help us to be more effective in the workplace by understanding why we feel and behave in the way we do, thereby offering us the chance to change behaviour if necessary or, alternatively, seek a different form of employment that is a better fit with our identity.

- Developing the skills of self-awareness and reflection helps us to explore and understand the unique mix of attributes that make up our professional identity, and, because professional identity evolves as we go through our careers, actively practising these skills on an ongoing basis can help to ensure enduring success.

EXPLORE FURTHER

UNIVERSITY OF KENT CAREER ADVISORY SERVICE, *Analysing your career values*, http://www.kent.ac.uk/careers/Choosing/values.htm

IBARRA, H. (2004) *Working identity: Unconventional strategies for reinventing your career*. Boston, MA: Harvard Business School Press.

4.5 REFERENCES

ASHKANASY, N.M. and DAUS, C.S. (2002) Emotion in the workplace: the new challenge for managers. *Academy of Management Executive*. Vol. 16, No. 1, pp76–86.

ATKINSON, R.L., ATKINSON, R.C., SMITH, E.E. and BEM, D.J. (1993) *Introduction to psychology*. Fort Worth: Harcourt Brace.

BAUMARD, P. (1999) *Tacit knowledge in organisations*. London: Sage.

BRITISH ARMY. (2010) *Discipline, values and standards*. Crown Copyright. Available online at: http://www.army.mod.uk/join/terms/standards.aspx [accessed 23 April 2010].

CIPD. (2009) *Competency and competency framework*. Factsheet. Available online at: http://www.cipd.co.uk/subjects/perfmangmt/competnces/comptfrmwk.htm [accessed on 23 April 2010].

FRANK, J.R. (ed). (2005) *The CanMEDS 2005 physician competency framework: better standards; better physicians; better care*. Ottawa: The Royal College of Physicians and Surgeons of Canada.

GOLEMAN, D. (2005) *Emotional intelligence: why it can matter more than IQ*. New York: Bantam.

GOODWIN, C.J. (1995) *Research in psychology: methods and design*. New York: Wiley.

HALL, D.T. (2002) *Careers in and out of organisations*. Thousand Oaks, CA: Sage.

IBARRA, H. (1999) Provisional selves: experimenting with image and identity in professional adaptation. *Administrative Science Quarterly*. Vol. 44, No. 4, pp746–791.

INSCH, G.S., MCINTYRE, N. and DAWLEY, D. (2008) Tacit knowledge: a refinement and empirical test of the academic tacit knowledge scale. *The Journal of Psychology*. Vol. 142, No. 6, pp561–579.

JOHN LEWIS. (2009). *Never knowingly undersold*. Available online at: https://johnlewis.co.uk/jl_assets/pdf/nku_leaflet_november_2009.pdf [accessed 23 April 2010].

KIEL, L.D. and WATSON, D.J. (2009) Affective leadership and emotional labour: a view from the local level. *Public Administration Review*. Vol. 69, No. 1, pp21–24.

MASLOW, A.H. (1967) Self-actualisation and beyond. In L. Atkinson, R.C. Atkinson, E.E. Smith and D.J. Bem (eds), *Introduction to Psychology*. Fort Worth: Harcourt Brace, p547.

MCADAMS, D. (1996) Personality, modernity, and the storied self: a contemporary framework for studying persons. In M. Tennant (ed) (2006), *Psychology and adult learning*. Abingdon: Routledge, pp53–57.

MCCRAE, R.R. and COSTA, P.T. (1987) Validation of a five-factor model of personality across instruments and observers. *Journal of Personality and Social Psychology*. Vol. 52, No. 1, pp81–90.

MCCRAE, R.R. and COSTA, P.T. (1997) Personality trait structure as a human universal. *American Psychologist*. Vol. 52, No. 5, pp509–516.

MCNETT, J.M., WALLACE, R.M. and ATHANASSIOU, N. (2004) *Tacit knowledge in the classroom: a strategy for learning*. Paper presented at 29th Improving University Teaching Conference, 12–15 July. Bern, Switzerland.

MOMENI, N. (2009) The relation between managers' emotional intelligence and the organisational climate they create. *Public Personnel Management*. Vol. 38, No. 2, pp35–48.

NEISSER, U. (1976) General, academic and artificial intelligence. In I. Resnick (ed). *The nature of intelligence*. Hillsdale, NJ: Erlbaum, pp307–337.

NONAKA, I. (1990) Managing innovation as a knowledge creation process. In P. Baumard (ed), *Tacit knowledge in organisations*. London: Sage, p24.

NONAKA, I. (2007) The knowledge creating company. *Harvard Business Review*. Vol. 85, No. 7/8, pp162–171.

POLANYI, M. (1962) *Personal knowledge*. London: Harper.

SANDERS, G. (2010) *Building communities of learners through development of professional identity*. Improving University Teaching (IUT) 35th International Conference, 1–3 July. Washington DC, USA.

SCHEIN, E.H. (1978) *Career dynamics: matching individual and organisational needs*. Reading, MA: Addison-Wesley.

SCHÖN, D.A. (1983) *The reflective practitioner: how professionals think in action*. London: Temple Smith.

STERNBERG, R.J. (1993) Would you rather take orders from Kirk or Spock? The relation between rational thinking and intelligence. *Journal of Learning Disabilities*. Vol. 26, No. 8, pp516–519.

UNIVERSITY OF KENT CAREER ADVISORY SERVICE (ND) *Analysing your career values*. Available online at: http://www.kent.ac.uk/careers/Choosing/values.htm, accessed 7 May 2010.

VAN MAANEN, J. and SCHEIN, E.H. (1979) Toward a theory of organisational socialisation. In B.M. Straw (ed), *Research in Organisational Behaviour*, Vol. 1. London: JAI Press, pp209–264.

WAGNER, R.K. (1987) Tacit Knowledge in Everyday Intelligent Behaviour. *Journal of Personality and Social Psychology*. Vol. 52, No. 6, pp1236–1247.

CHAPTER 5

Concepts of self and self-management skills

Kevin Gallagher

OVERVIEW

To be effective as a team member or a team leader you need to manage yourself. At work you will be expected to take responsibility for keeping some sense of order about your own organisation of tasks and responsibilities. You will be expected to turn up on time to meetings and to hit deadlines. If you have a managerial role your job will often include making decisions, sometimes in tough circumstances, and handling 'disturbances'. Being in control of yourself within the workplace is an ongoing process as your work environment is often in a state of flux, which means that you too have to be dynamic in your responses. It is quite normal to feel at times that you are under pressure, but it is not good if you are constantly feeling overwhelmed by everything that is happening to you (and this includes your so-called 'work–life balance'). This chapter is written with the purpose of outlining a number of self-management strategies for you to consider, perhaps try, and then reflect upon. It uses a range of methods, some of which you may already be aware of and using, while others may be new to you.

LEARNING OUTCOMES

By the end of this chapter, provided you engage with the activities, you should be able to:

- audit your time at work in terms of your technical, managerial and personal activities
- identify time-wasting activities
- recognise occasions when you tend to procrastinate
- apply strategies to improve your personal time management
- use plans, diaries and other personal organisation skills
- recognise the symptoms of micro-managing
- analyse work and personal stressors
- understand how stress management techniques can help you
- apply some of these techniques to your own situation.

5.1 INTRODUCTION

Within this chapter we will consider three broad areas of self-management: time management, personal organisation and stress management. These areas often overlap. In some respects, time management and personal organisation may be regarded as aspects of an all-encompassing stress management. However, as time management and personal organisation are often considered in their own right as managerial skills, the distinction is used within this chapter to allow focus on specific techniques. These three areas are shown in Figure 5.1, overlapping in the 'doughnut' shape. What Figure 5.1 also shows is differing levels of sophistication which may be adopted, from 'quick fix' to 'longer-term' strategies. For instance, a quick fix approach for personal organisation may mean that you tidy your desk and attend to filing; a longer-term approach may mean that you analyse which items you need to file and which ones you can ignore or give to someone else. You should note that, although we are considering self-management skills, there may well be an element of personal development linked to your staff appraisal and to organisational strategies and policies. These may be linked to personal effectiveness and/or well-being.

It is worth spending a little more time on Figure 5.1 with regard to the merits and limitations of the 'quick fix' and the 'longer-term strategies'. Quick fix strategies as discussed in this chapter should not be seen as somehow inferior to the more sophisticated 'longer-term' strategies. The term 'sticking plaster' has sometimes been used to describe an approach that helps the obvious symptoms but not the underlying cause of a problem, the inference being that this is a poor strategy. The view taken here is that strategies should be judged in the light of what is appropriate for a particular set of circumstances, and that often it is not a case of 'either/or' but a mix of strategies. For instance, performing some simple breathing exercises before a presentation is an example of a quick fix, but this

Figure 5.1 Self-management skills approaches in the workplace

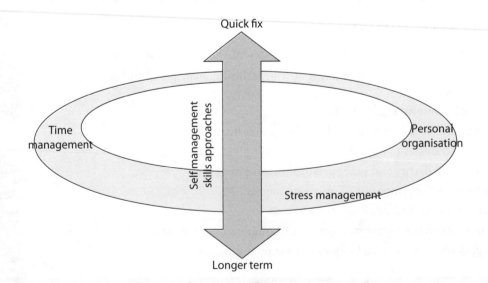

should be coupled with arranging a long-term series of presentational opportunities designed to gradually build confidence.

The chapter begins with a section on time management, followed by a section on personal organisation. It is aimed at those who currently have to juggle a whole range of operational and/or managerial tasks and responsibilities. Both of these sections are relatively brief, focusing on one or two techniques but providing an overview for further reading. We will be spending most of our time in this chapter on stress management. There is an overwhelming mass of information on stress – which is indicative of its prevalence and negative impact. However, there have been a number of recent advances in our understanding of how stress is best tackled in the workplace, linked to ongoing government-funded/university-led research in the UK. We shall consider these as they have implications for both individual well-being and associated corporate welfare strategies.

5.2 TIME MANAGEMENT SKILLS

Why is time management so important for managers? The answer is twofold: in the short term it allows tasks to be accomplished more effectively (doing the right things) and efficiently (optimal use of time); in the longer term it enables managers to feel some sense of control in an often turbulent environment and thus helps them to avoid burn-out through stress.

Consider a day in the life of a typical manager; this is probably most easily explored through reference to influential studies carried out by Henry Mintzberg, who put forward the concept of managerial roles. He argued that in a typical day's work, a manager had to adopt a range of different managerial personas, grouped into what he described as 'interpersonal', 'informational' and 'decisional'. These could, for instance include acting as a 'leader' (for example, directing staff – an interpersonal role), a 'disseminator' (for example, briefing staff members – an informational role), or a 'disturbance handler' (for example, resolving a problem situation – a decisional role). In this managerial world managers did not spend significant amounts of time on any one task but, rather, they were involved throughout the day in a series of activities which sometimes demanded the ability to be extremely mentally agile. Pedler et al (2007, p251) refer to this as the 'helicopter' ability. This scenario would seem to reflect reality for many managers. In itself it presents a challenge. However, you will be well aware that on those days when you feel under pressure, other factors will also impact upon how you feel and how you cope with the work situation. If you have outside work commitments or pressures, these have a habit of adding to your level of pressure (notice we have not yet used the term 'stress' as we shall see that the point at which pressure becomes stress varies amongst individuals).

5.2.1 EAT YOUR FROG!

If you find the image of eating a live frog repulsive then this phrase is likely to be memorable and effective! I first came across it in a personal development presentation by one of my part-time management students working for a major

continues on p134

ACTIVITY 5.1

PERSONAL TIME AUDIT

To manage your time you first of all need to be aware of how you spend it. One way to do this is simply to keep a work diary and note the time you spend on various activities. In the light of what we have just discussed you are asked to go a stage further than this and complete the daily chart shown in Figure 5.2 over several days. You will notice that you have been asked to categorise your activities under various headings, including Mintzberg's '10 managerial roles' (Mintzberg 1990). When Mintzberg first published this concept in the *Harvard Business Review* (August 1975) it heralded a new realism about what it was really like to be a manager. In a sense it was the equivalent of 'a day in the life of a typical manager', and it was far from the cosy traditional model of managerial functions (for example, planning, organising, leading and controlling). The 10 roles, sub-divided into the three broad categories of interpersonal roles, informational roles and decision roles, are briefly listed below and should be sufficient to allow you to categorise your managerial activities. Mintzberg's original article, as given in the references, is recommended further reading.

- **Figurehead**: for example, as the head of your department, representing your company at ceremonies etc.
- **Leader**: giving direction to others in your organisation (includes delegating and developing others).
- **Liaison**: acting as a communication link with others outside of the vertical chain of command.
- **Monitor**: keeping an eye open for relevant information – an active scanning approach.
- **Disseminator**: giving relevant information to staff, for instance in staff briefings and e-mails.
- **Spokesperson**: speaking on behalf of the organisation to outsiders.
- **Entrepreneur**: making things happen, using initiative to get things done.
- **Disturbance handler**: resolving issues which have not gone to plan, handling arguments.
- **Resource allocator**: deciding how to apportion limited resources (staff time, budgets, equipment, materials).
- **Negotiator**: formal and informal bargaining (for instance with own staff, with customers).

You may be carrying out some of these roles simultaneously, so do not expect your total time for activities in the day to tally with your actual working day. Also, do not think, because you do not have the title of manager, that you do not carry our some or all of the managerial roles that Mintzberg describes (for instance, as a lecturer in a university I lead a module team of other tutors but at other times I am engaged purely with teaching).

After you have completed your time management audit, take a moment to reflect upon where you spend your time. Here are a few typical questions that you may wish to ask yourself:

- Where am I spending my time? Is this consistent with my job role?
- Are there any obvious time wasters?
- As a manager, am I spending too much time on non-managerial tasks that someone else could do?
- Do I seem to be spending a lot of time in peripheral meetings?

Figure 5.2 Time management audit

Date	Activity description	Time start	Time finish	Activity duration	Categorise activity (may use more than one)												Comment
					Managerial roles (mark X)										Own operational/technical task	Social/break	
					Figurehead	Leader	Liaison	Monitor	Disseminator	Spokesperson	Entrepreneur	Disturbance Handler	Resource Allocator	Negotiator			

insurance company. She had been introduced to this technique during in-house training delivered by time management consultants and it seemed to be working very well for her. The phrase is used by a prodigious writer of self-help books, Brian Tracy, in the book of the same name *Eat that frog* (Tracy 2007). The message is simple but effective: tackle your biggest, most important jobs first. The idea is that once you have done this the rest of the day will seem relatively easy. It suggests that we sometimes put off doing important but unpleasant or difficult tasks and keep ourselves busy on lesser but more pleasant ones.

5.2.2 DON'T WAIT FOR INSPIRATION!

In a similar pragmatic vein to the previous advice, Rowena Murray (2005) advises writers at university 'not to wait for the mood'. Waiting for inspiration will not get that report written! She suggests setting aside time on a regular basis, preferably in a comfortable environment, and then committing to put pen to paper. Usually, ideas will start to flow after a while. However, you should note that researching and planning for the report also count as activities in the writing process. The important thing is to do something on most days.

5.2.3 POINTERS TO A DEEPER APPROACH?

You may note that the 'Eat that frog' and 'Don't wait for inspiration' techniques may work for you as 'quick fix', pragmatic solutions. You will see that both are, in essence, psychological approaches; in the case of 'Eat that frog' this is demonstrated by the way it hooks your imagination with the image of the frog and the resultant 'buzz' of achieving a big, important task; with the 'Don't wait for inspiration' technique the effect is to lessen the overall fear of starting a large task by taking it in small chunks and of pushing through your initial reluctance to start a task. So it may not be too much of a surprise to learn that recent psychological research has been shedding further light on our motivation to engage with our work, under the general heading of 'procrastination' studies. In the following section we will outline some of this recent research and its links with time management, personal organisation and stress.

5.3 PROCRASTINATION – OR 'I'LL DO IT IN THE MORNING'

If you look in the *Oxford English dictionary* (Oxford University Press 2006, p811) you will find the following definition:

> **Procrastinate:** *verb*: delay or postpone action.

> Original Latin *procastinare* 'defer until the morning'.

It would be simplistic to think that effective time management and personal organisation are achieved solely through knowing what to do, though ignorance of proven techniques may certainly act as barriers to our success. It is rather like living a healthy lifestyle: most of us know what to do – it is the doing that is the problem! Much of this is down to our psychological approach; for instance, Seo (2009, p911) refers to Lay and Schouwenburg's (1993) definition of procrastination as 'unnecessarily delaying activities that one ultimately intends to complete, especially when done to the point of creating emotional discomfort'.

Nor do we necessarily grow out of this tendency. In one series of studies some 70 per cent of American college students experienced frequent delays in starting and/or completing tasks, but as many as 20 per cent of 'normal adult men and women in everyday life' also suffered from this (Ferrari, O'Callaghan and Newbigin 2005, p1). This prompted the writers to suggest that procrastination could be related to particular circumstances (for example, completing college coursework on time) but they were more concerned with 'persons who ... chronically engage in task delays as a maladaptive lifestyle' (ibid, p2). As though to add insult to injury the same writers go on to tell us that 'chronic procrastination is a complex phenomenon involving more than time management difficulty.' It all sounds rather drastic, doesn't it, you can almost hear yourself saying 'What – me, leading a maladaptive lifestyle? Sounds almost criminal!' Yet, as we shall see, in many instances we obstruct our progress with obstacles of our own making.

5.3.1 SOME INTERESTING PROCRASTINATION POINTS

According to Ferrari, Mason and Hammer (2006, p29):

- People in negative moods tend to procrastinate 'in situations where there are interesting (as opposed to boring) stimuli nearby'.
- Generally people procrastinate on tedious tasks (but not all people, indicating other factors in play).
- Procrastinators also tend *not* to focus on future tasks needing attention.
- Procrastinators are often busy with other tasks which are irrelevant to the target task.

Baker and Phillips (2007, p705) raise the very pertinent issue of taking breaks while on the computer by accessing e-mails – what they term e-breaks, as 'they function like a coffee break'. Some individuals (e-breakers) tended to access the e-mail when they should have been doing more important tasks – in other words they were procrastinating. Also, while taking sufficient breaks may be considered beneficial, Baker and Phillips (2007, p707) point out that an e-break is not as relaxing as a normal coffee break and they suggested that e-breakers might also take their usual coffee breaks as well.

5.3.2 PROCRASTINATION AND GOALS

We are often encouraged by senior managers or team leaders to 'buy-in' to what we are doing, whether this is routine or some new project. The implication is that by becoming self-motivated we will do a better job. In motivational terms we talk of intrinsic motivation as opposed to extrinsic motivation: intrinsic motivation is concerned with our personal achievement needs – we want to do something for the psychological boost that doing it gives us; extrinsic motivation concerns

ACTIVITY 5.2

LATE AGAIN?

Take a few minutes to make a (brief!) list of activities that you habitually find yourself putting off or finishing late. Think also of specific examples. How did you feel about the nature of these tasks and of the circumstances of your examples? Have you any explanation for why you delayed or were late in completing your tasks?

factors which influence our behaviour through external rewards and punishments – for instance to gain a pay rise or to please our boss. The suggestion researchers have considered is that perhaps if we are really motivated we will procrastinate less. And perhaps those people who have goals which are intrinsic are less likely to procrastinate than those people who have extrinsic goals. Studies by Saddler and Buley (1999) with college students did, in fact, support the view that extrinsic goals were consistent with procrastination.

Further research by Elliott and McGregor (2001) and Seo (2009) proposes, however, a more complex framework between procrastination and goal achievement, based around (a) our motives for achieving our goals and (b) whether or not we viewed them in a positive or a negative way. In terms of achieving our goals we may strive either for 'mastery' or 'performance': 'mastery' is said to occur when we can achieve the task to some given level – for instance being able to swim 50 metres. This level of competence may be considered as absolute (therefore, it is a set standard) and/or may also be regarded as a measure of our own (internal) standard and subsequent improvements measured against this; by contrast, 'performance' considers our competence compared to that of others (for example, first or second in a race). The researchers suggested that mastery vs performance was one dimension (rather confusingly given the name 'definition') of a 2 x 2 grid which they called the 2 x 2 achievement goal framework. The other dimension (which they named more clearly as 'valence') related to whether we viewed the goal in a positive or a negative way: if we set out to achieve success this was seen as positive and was labelled as 'approaching success', or more simply 'approach'; if our prime motive was to avoid failure, this was regarded as negative and was labelled 'avoidance'. The researchers could now draw their grid of four quadrants, identify each one, and discuss four types of achievement goal. These are listed below:

- **Mastery-approach goal**: Individuals measure the goal in absolute or personal terms. They find that, the tougher the goal is, the more challenging it is for them personally and they will use self-development methods to full effect.

- **Performance-approach goal**: Individuals reference themselves against others, so they are competitive in this sense but still view success as the main aim.

- **Mastery-avoidance goal**: This is sometimes seen in people who measure themselves against previous ability; for instance, people who wish to prove that they are still 'up to the mark', 'have still got what it takes'. They fear not being able to do things they used to do when they were younger/fitter/more expert. They do not want to make basic mistakes. 'They are not ambitious in terms of self-improvement' (Seo 2009, p912).

- **Performance-avoidance goal**: Individuals do not wish to be embarrassed in front of others. Do not wish to be last.

Seo (2009, p916) uses this 2 x 2 grid to explore how people's achievement goal orientations might impact upon their procrastination behaviour and has arrived at the following findings:

- Both mastery-avoidance and performance-avoidance goals are positively related to procrastination. In other words, if you fear failure you are more likely to procrastinate, no matter whether you are comparing yourself against your own standards or against those of others.

- Procrastination is negatively related to the mastery-approach goal. In other words if you adopt a mastery-approach strategy you are unlikely to procrastinate. Good news!

- However, avoidance goals (which are related to procrastination) have a greater impact on the individual than mastery goals. Not so good news.

This leads Seo (2009, p917) to the important statement:

> The results of the present study suggest that the way in which individuals interpret these task features positively or negatively is more important than the task-related features themselves. If students are helped to set positive expectations about a task, interventions designed to decrease students' procrastination might be more successful.

 ACTIVITY 5.3

SWIMMER SAM?

Consider the mini case study overleaf. Show possible mastery and performance goals for Sam relating to him learning to swim as an adult. Also list those outcomes that he wishes to avoid. Suggest how Sam may persuade himself/be persuaded to start a series of adult swimming lessons – something that he has thought about in the past but somehow never got around to doing.

5.3.3 CAN PROCRASTINATION EVER BE A 'GOOD THING'?

Some people say that they work best under pressure. They deliberately do not do something at the earliest opportunity but wait until they feel they need to do it. There is some research in support of this: Chu and Choi (2005) suggest that this behaviour is consistent with 'active procrastination', a different sort of delaying behaviour compared with the more usual concept of procrastination, which they termed 'passive procrastination'.

Active procrastinators enjoy the challenge they get from working to tight

SWIMMER SAM?

CASE STUDY 5.1

Sam sat by the side of the swimming pool feeling dejected. He was on holiday in the Egyptian coastal resort of Sharm al-Sheikh on the Red Sea. The weather was warm and sunny. He was with good friends (all in their early 30s) and physically he was feeling fine. By all accounts he should have been enjoying himself. The problem was that one of the major attractions of the resort was its fantastic snorkelling and diving opportunities – and he could not swim. At first he thought that this would not be a problem as he could sit by the pool and relax with a cool drink and a good book. However, most of his friends could swim and were making the most of the facilities, leaving him on his own. Photographs of his friends, thumbs up,

surrounded by arrays of tropical fish, only made matters worse. He mused that the nearest he had been to such exotic fish species was his own aquarium 'back home'. Not for the first time he wished that he too could swim. He regretted letting a childhood incident in a pool put him off learning (he had fallen upside down in his inflatable ring for what seemed like an eternity before his father had righted him). Now, at 32, he felt rather embarrassed at not knowing how to swim; also, although he was in good health, he was rather flabby and somewhat ashamed of his general physique and was not particularly keen to be seen in a pair of skimpy speedos!

deadlines and the sense of achievement in hitting submission dates (note: they delay yet still hit the target deadlines). By comparison 'passive procrastinators' perform poorly as deadlines approach – to the extent of giving up on occasion, and often do not hit submission dates as they have underestimated the time required for task completion.

Active procrastinators have a high level of self-belief in their ability to achieve their goals (what is known as 'self-efficacy' – see Bandura (1977) for further details). Later work by Choi and Moran (2009, p208) speculated that active procrastinators were very good at re-prioritising and handling the time they had available to them in a highly flexible manner. They suggested that occupations that had tight deadlines and unexpected interruptions (such as management consultants, professors, software engineers) favoured such a flexible approach. It could therefore be argued that this is a very effective time management strategy in certain situations but one that requires a very skilled practitioner!

 ACTIVITY 5.4

ACTIVE PROCRASTINATOR?

Can you think of a time when you acted as an 'active procrastinator', deliberately delaying an activity but ultimately achieving it by the deadline? If so, what are your thoughts now on your strategy? Is it an approach you would use again and if so in what circumstances?

If you have never acted as an 'active procrastinator', suggest possible reasons why you have not done so.

5.3.4 GUARDING AGAINST THE DAMAGING EFFECTS OF PROCRASTINATION

From our previous discussion we can summarise some general rules to help protect us from the worst effects of procrastination. You may also wish to use these as general guidelines for any staff who report to you, or people you are training/developing.

- Free yourself from interesting distractions!

- Restrict your use of e-breaks.

- Think of ways to make tedious tasks more enjoyable.

- Repeatedly ask yourself 'Is what I am doing really important or should I be doing something else?'

- Adopt an 'approaching success' strategy in yourself and others by encouraging and rewarding the undertaking of personal challenges, regarding mistakes as an inevitable part of learning, celebrating subsequent learning and success. Add further 'mastery goals' to whatever it is you are doing.

- Reduce 'avoidance' strategies in yourself and others by not personalising mistakes, feeling humiliated if you make mistakes. If you tend to worry that you cannot cope with a new task, ask for further guidance. If you manage people like this, give them more guidance and encouragement.

5.4 PERSONAL ORGANISATION SKILLS

Personal organisation skills are exactly that – personal. What suits one person may not suit another. Having said this, there is a requirement for some sense of order in our lives. One of the founding figures of management theory, Henri Fayol, had this to say of order, as one of his 14 principles of management (Fayol 1949, revised by Gray 1987, p77): 'The formula for order is ... a place for everything and everything in its place ... a place for everyone and everyone in his place.' Time management, as previously discussed, is one aspect of personal organisation and in its own way gives a sense of order to how we spend our time. Other areas of our working lives that we organise include the way we store and access information and how we arrange our personal working space. We will briefly outline these. However, a more fundamental organisation skill for team leaders and managers is the ability to delegate certain aspects of their job roles. This has direct links with stress management as it allows otherwise overloaded managers to focus on their major contributions to the organisation. Some people try to do this but cannot fully release the reins and end up by meddling in the detail of tasks supposedly delegated to their staff, a situation sometimes referred to as 'micromanagement' (White 2010).

5.4.1 EVERYTHING IN ITS PLACE ...

Look on the Internet under 'declutter your life' and you will find a host of articles with titles such as 'Ten ways to get rid of clutter' – the majority of them written by self-appointed experts, often on the basis on their personal experience or anecdotal tips. The sheer number of articles suggests that clutter is a very real problem. It seems to make sense to keep things where you can easily find them; there comes a point beyond which you can not easily locate information in a disorganised filing system – you can even 'lose' something on a messy desk. Written by specialists Theo Theobald and Cary Cooper (2007), the book *Detox your desk: declutter your life and mind* gives a very practical 10-day 'detox' programme, based on the following steps (Theobald 2007), which you may notice go beyond the simple notion of tidying your desk:

1. Clear the clutter.

2. Wipe as you go.

3. Hydrate – keep a clear mind by avoiding dehydration.

4. Stop! – Stop doing the things that do not matter.

5. Set your own standards.

6. Make a change a day.

7. Stop self-sabotaging.

8. Volunteer for extra. For example, help someone else out – they will repay you.

9. Curb your fear of success.

10. Do the daunting – Do not put off doing things.

ACTIVITY 5.5

DETOX FOCUS

Jot down your feelings about this list. Is there any particular area(s) that need your immediate attention?

5.4.2 SCHEDULES, PLANS AND DIARIES

Where would we be without schedules and plans? It is not easy to keep detailed information in our heads; also, it is much more difficult to convey that information to other people without something written down. However, useful as schedules and plans are, the planning process is arguably of greater importance. Thinking through the logical sequence of activities and allocating resources (for example, staff, materials, equipment, budgets) is an essential management task; monitoring events against the plan as they unfold allows the manager to retain control by applying the necessary corrective actions – which may include an element of re-planning. It is of little use to create a plan and then to consign it to a dusty shelf!

One word of advice on plans in this regard: as they are often subject to change, make sure that each revision is clearly labelled, either by date of issue or by revision number. Then make sure that everyone is given the updated plan to work to. (This advice applies to all quality documentation.) We can create plans for ourselves and for the tasks we are working on. Both types of plan should help us to make the most effective use of our time.

5.4.2.1 Daily 'to do lists'

Daily 'to do lists' may be something that you already write. They are useful as a means of firstly collecting together all of the things that you need to accomplish. You should then prioritise your list. One way to do this is to categorise them as 'must do', 'should do', 'would like to do'. Another way is to list them as 'important' and 'urgent': important things are those which are the few but vital tasks – they may or may not require immediate action; things which require immediate action are the urgent ones which will not wait. Occasionally you will have to deal with tasks which are both important and urgent – clearly these should be tackled as soon as possible.

5.4.2.2 Planners and diaries

On a longer-term basis you may find it useful to use some sort of weekly/ monthly planner, inserting key work-related dates. To be useful this must be readily accessible. You should be able to easily add to your planner and make appropriate changes. This may be done electronically, especially if you need to share diary availability with others in your organisation.

5.4.3 DELEGATION AND MICROMANAGEMENT

At a more fundamental level we are sometimes in the position (and this is usually the case for team leaders and managers) to be able delegate some tasks to others in our organisation. This side of our personal organisation is not always clearly defined so we may have scope to pass some tasks and responsibilities on to others. The advice of Tannenbaum and Schmidt (1986, p129), as given in a classic article in the *Harvard Business Review*, still holds true: although we may delegate responsibility for certain tasks, we are still accountable for them. By delegating certain tasks we can help others develop their skills and at the same time allow ourselves more time to focus on other, more important, central aspects of our job roles. By doing so we may be able to alleviate stress created by task overload. However, implicit in delegation is the question 'Should managers participate with subordinates once they have delegated responsibility to them?' (Tannenbaum and Schmidt 1986, p129). Tannenbaum and Schmidt recommend that managers may participate but should do so in a member role rather than an authority role.

Managers who say that they have delegated but then meddle unnecessarily with the detail of supposedly delegated tasks may be said to be acting as micromanagers. White (2010, p71) states: 'At its most severe level, micromanagement is a compulsive, behavioural disorder similar to other addictive patterns. People who micromanage generally do so because they feel unsure and self-doubting.'

White (2010, p72) goes on to describe 'symptoms' of this 'disease'. The following list outlines the main characteristics of micromanagers:

- oversee their workers too closely
- are control freaks
- go alone to their boss's office as they do not wish subordinates to gain credit
- demand frequent status reports from others but often cause delays themselves as they are so busy
- stretch themselves too thin and take on too many projects
- hate mistakes, seldom praise, consider their employees incompetent.

The advice give in *Management Today*'s 'Brainfood' section (2009, p18) goes some way to counter this approach under the heading of 'Do it right: dynamic delegation', as shown below:

- Delegate for the right reason (not to simply offload tasks).
- Delegate to the right people.
- Brief thoroughly.
- Define results but not method.
- Give them the tools that they need to do the job.
- Keep an eye on how they are doing but resist the temptation to grab the reins back at the first sign of trouble.

 ACTIVITY 5.6

MICROMANAGER

To what extent do you agree with the earlier statement of White's (2010) that micromanagement is a 'disease'? Do you recognise these traits in others at work? If you have a management responsibility for others, take an honest look at yourself – do you recognise any of these micromanagement 'symptoms' in yourself? Finally, how much do you think that the work context/situation influences your/others' ability to delegate?

5.5 STRESS MANAGEMENT SKILLS

5.5.1 STRESS: AN INTRODUCTION

'Stress is likely to become the most dangerous risk to business in the early part of the twenty-first century.'

These are the alarming words of the Health and Safety Executive (HSE), as reported by the CIPD (2009). In the same report the HSE stated that 'one in five workers' and some '5 million in the UK … reported feeling extremely stressed at work.' This does not, of course, mean that 5 million people are off ill with stress – but as many medical conditions are stress-related it is still a shocking statistic. Further, in terms of absence and sickness, the CIPD's absence management survey of 2008 found that the problem was increasing amongst organisations. (CIPD 2009). We shall explore the meaning of stress in this section, but for now a useful way to think of what it means is that repeated exposure to certain pressures may cause some people to feel 'emotionally anxious and exhausted' (Boyd et al 2009, p199).

The general state of awareness regarding linkages between stress and work is part of a larger awareness of the mental health of the nation. A program called 'Foresight' has been established by the Government Office for Science and has published a report entitled *Mental capital and wellbeing: Making the most of ourselves in the 21st century* (Government Office for Science 2008). Again it is worth noting how common mental ill-health is amongst the general population. For instance the above report (p. 21) states:

> Many people experience mental ill-health: for example, about 16% of adults and 10% of children are affected by common mental disorders such as depression and anxiety at any one time. However, whilst all disorders are best detected and treated early, many go undiagnosed or are only treated when advanced, and when the impacts are severe for the individual and families.

One more set of statistics to consider is that:

- In 2000, depression cost more than £9 billion for England, and depression/anxiety was the single most important cause of workplace absenteeism in the UK.

- Over half a million instances of stress resulted in absences from work, costing UK employers £3.7 billion each year (Foresight 2007).

Stressful conditions at work can exacerbate tendencies towards depression and anxiety-related illnesses. From all of the above, understanding and reducing unnecessary stress would therefore appear to be an eminently sensible strategy for managers to adopt within their workplace for both their staff and themselves. As we have both working lives and personal lives we must firstly appreciate that there are strong connections between them

5.5.2 EFFECTS OF MULTIPLE WORK AND FAMILY DEMANDS

Figure 5.3 overleaf is an attempt to show in simplistic terms how work and personal (ie outside work) pressures may compound within the individual. This may seem a fairly intuitive conclusion but verification through research is limited; Melchior et al (2007, p573) state that 'the cumulative effects of multiple work and family demands are not well known, particularly for men' but concluded in their article (2007, p580) that 'Men and women who experience high levels of work and family demands are at increased risk of psychiatric sickness and absence.' Figure 5.3 is therefore for discussion purposes rather than a statement of fact.

Also in Figure 5.3 you will see the inclusion of 'critical incidents' which can give rise to pressure spikes. Some of these are, as you would expect, upsetting events such as a dispute or the death of a friend, but others are what we might want –

Figure 5.3 Potential combination effects of personal life and work life in an individual

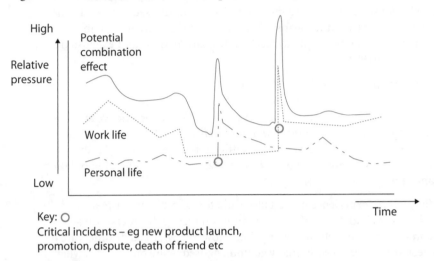

Key: ○
Critical incidents – eg new product launch,
promotion, dispute, death of friend etc

for instance, the launch of a new product, or a personal promotion. This approach reflects studies by Holmes and Rahe (1967), who give a range of life events in a scale, placing the death of a spouse at the top with a value of 100, followed by other events including divorce (73), being fired at work (47), change in residence (20) and so on. You should note that the pressure effect you experience may range from one of excitement to one of stress. However, as we shall see, what stresses one person may be easily accommodated by another.

5.5.2.1 Storing of stress over time

Figure 5.3 also shows the pattern of fluctuation in terms of the overall pressure on the individual. It would appear to show a fairly healthy response in that the effect on this particular individual does reduce when the pressure abates. However, you should be aware that there is evidence to show that the effects of stress can be cumulative over time (Sun et al 2007) – in other words your body does not always return to its unstressed former state after each stressful challenge is encountered; rather it stores up tension somehow and then the next stressful event builds on top of this. This is the basis for the concept of analysing how many stressful events you have encountered in a specific time (for instance a year) and inferring from this a cumulative stress load. In certain conditions we may even become sensitised and struggle to cope with pressures which we previously handled with ease.

ACTIVITY 5.7

PERSONAL PRESSURES

Identify typical personal and work-critical incidents and their associated pressures for yourself over the last year.

5.5.3 STRESS MECHANISMS

5.5.3.1 Fight/flight

The classic model of stress (Selye 1976) describes a natural response of our bodies to a perceived threat. Our ancestors in Stone-Age times might, so we are told, have been faced with the fearsome prospect of a confrontation with a sabre-toothed tiger (why this particular animal features so prominently is open to discussion but those fangs surely must have something to do with it!); faced with the tiger, our ancestor would have had two choices – fight or run (flight). In such circumstances our bodies produce a powerful cocktail of hormones and chemicals that include raising our blood pressure and diverting blood to our muscles ready for action. Some time later, after either killing the tiger or managing to evade it by running away and climbing the nearest tree, our ancestor's bodily state would return to its previous resting state. Fortunately we do not have to fight or run away from tigers today, but the downside is that we still experience the same fight/flight reaction for other perceived threats. Rarely are these life-threatening, but they often have the ability to trigger some or all of the fight/flight reaction. Sometimes this can give us a certain 'edge' which improves our performance – such as the slight feeling of unease/excitement before giving a presentation – but at other times it can be a nuisance and actually detract from our performance. A further consideration is the cumulative effect of what are, in effect, relatively small stressors over the course of the working day but which can lead to a pooling of stress hormones in our bodies when we have no effective way to quickly release them – unlike the case of our ancestor who could expend considerable energy in either fighting or running, effectively dissipating them.

5.5.3.2 Stressors at work

As previously mentioned, what is felt by one person as uncomfortable, demanding or threatening is not necessarily felt in the same way by someone else. All jobs make demands on the individual; by their very nature they must. Also all jobs have a role to be played and specific responsibilities. Typical stress factors are:

- hours worked (it is interesting to note that in the UK we work some of the longest hours in Europe – some 3 million people work more than 48 hours per week (Meade 2009))
- intensity of work
- challenge of tasks/situations
- change situations
- deadlines for task completion
- control over outcomes
- support from others
- responsibility for outcomes
- responsibility for others

- team relationships
- supervisor and subordinate relationships.

In certain cases there may be a tension caused by too many different demands being placed on the individual (role overload) and in others a person may have two or more roles that conflict (for instance a manager may have to discipline someone in one situation but may wish to help them in another) – role conflict.

As mentioned previously, the mere presence of these factors does not automatically mean that an individual feels overwhelmed by them. One explanation is proposed in the effort–reward imbalance (ERI) theory which considers over a period of time the benefits (or otherwise) of an individual taking on a demanding job role, as outlined by the following defining statement:

Effort–reward imbalance describes the perceived mismatch of spent efforts and received rewards in the workplace. ... A situation where an employee is investing overtime hours into completing projects with tight deadlines, but has poor career prospects and fears of being laid off, would be an example of a harmful imbalance. An extended period of harmful imbalance can cause strain reactions that may contribute to various physical and psychological illnesses (Hyvönen et al 2010, p407).

ACTIVITY 5.8

EFFORT–REWARD IMBALANCE

Do you agree with the above statement by Hyvönen et al (2010)? Discuss with a colleague, using examples if possible to support your case.

This is clearly heavily influenced by how we think about our jobs. However, many other factors are relevant. For instance, research on a large sample of Chinese employees (Sun et al 2007, p344) looked at the biological impact (the 'allostatic load') upon the body of chronic (ie long-term) stress and reported that 'at 35 years, the scores began to rise sharply until age 65.' So, the implication is that we need to be better at managing our stress as we age, if we are to avoid illness.

Overcommitment to your job can be a problem, too. If you are ambitious, looking for esteem from others and have a strong need to control, you may be unable to withdraw from work (Hyvönen et al 2010, p407 quoting earlier research) and this can lead to burnout – physical and mental exhaustion and a cynical attitude to work.

5.5.4 WELL-BEING – IT'S NOT ALL NEGATIVE!

If you have the impression so far that all pressure is bad for you, that is hardly surprising, for until relatively recently most studies focused upon people who were suffering from stress-related illnesses, with the emphasis being upon avoiding such consequences. However, as the CIPD points out, 'it is healthy and essential that people experience challenges within their lives that cause pressure and, up to a certain point, an increase in pressure can improve performance and the quality of life' (CIPD 2009, p2). Some researchers are now focusing on improving the well-being of employees who are not already sick. This is a positive approach that seeks to improve working lives. It may not be very fashionable to admit to others that actually you quite like certain aspects of your job, that at times you rather enjoy the stimulation of the challenge and indeed gain a significant amount of satisfaction, even pride from a job well done. This is the opposite side of the coin to burnout: it is called 'engagement'.

A model of work pressure that is consistent with this more balanced approach is the Job Demands–Resources model. This reinforces the view that demands are only negative if they are excessive and introduces the concept of job resources as follows:

> Job resources is defined as those physical, psychological, social or organisational aspects of work context that:
>
> (1) reduce the health-impairing impact of job demand
>
> (2) are functional in achieving work goals
>
> (3) stimulate personal growth, development and learning.
> (Van den Broeck et al 2008, p278)

So, if you have access to these job resources you should be better able to cope with the demands of the job, and hence are more likely to avoid feeling stressed. However, Van den Broeck et al go further to suggest that there is a motivational process at work, that of work engagement. This motivational process appears to meet what they refer to as 'the "ABC": Autonomy, Belongingness, and Competence' (Van den Broeck et al 2008, p279). In other words, being in control of what you have to do at work (Autonomy), feeling part of a community (Belongingness) and feeling that you are doing a skilled job (Competence) are all motivational factors. These lead to individuals feeling more satisfied with their jobs, and when combined with a well-resourced environment enable people not only to handle the pressures of their jobs but to grow psychologically through them.

This approach has obvious links to job design: if we can design jobs (Hackman and Oldham 1976) that are interesting, meaningful, provide us with feedback from others and allow us to achieve our potential, we can provide ABC factors. This is far from being a 'quick fix' method. It may mean a fundamental re-thinking of job roles.

ACTIVITY 5.9

YOUR ABC

Using your present (or a previous) job, assess it using the ABC factors outlined above. What conclusion can you draw from this analysis? If you are feeling dissatisfied with your findings, have you any thoughts on how your job might be improved?

5.5.5 AM I A WORKAHOLIC?

 ACTIVITY 5.10

WORKAHOLIC QUIZ

Take a little time to consider the questions listed below:

Do you:

- Work 50–60 hours per week?
- Work very hard?
- Think about work even when not working?
- Sometime have arguments with your partner that you are working too much?
- Find it difficult to 'switch off'?
- Feel guilty about taking your lunch break/all of your lunch break at work?
- Feel there is always much more to do, even after working hard?
- Have little time for socialising outside of work?
- Frequently not take all of your holiday entitlement?
- No longer have sufficient time for your favourite hobbies/sports?
- Love your job?
- Feel energised and stimulated by your work?

If a lot of your answers to these questions have been 'yes' then alarm bells should ring: you may be a workaholic or on the slippery slopes towards becoming one!

Consider the following definition of workaholism:

> Workaholism (is) an irresistible inner drive to work excessively hard. ... Workaholism includes two elements: a strong inner drive and working hard ... a compulsion (Schaufeli et al 2009, p156).

Workaholism when defined like this is an addiction. It is obsessive. The 'addict' feels compelled to work, feels uncomfortable when not working. Addicts may even realise that this sort of behaviour is likely to isolate them from family and friends and is damaging their physical and mental health through their inability to 'switch' off and relax – yet are still unable to resist the urge to work. In such cases work does provide some respite and satisfaction (though surprisingly little according to some researchers, as outlined by Schaufeli et al 2009, p158, p166) but this does not last long and the 'addict' is soon looking for their next 'fix'.

Schaufeli et al (2009, p166) tell us that many theorists distinguish between 'good' and 'bad' forms of workaholism, and refer to the work of Buelens and Poelmans (2004) who investigated the idea that some workaholics were 'happy hard workers'. (However, their particular study did not support this theory).

Given that some organisational cultures exhort people to work hard, to work long hours, to skip breaks and always be available on text or e-mail, it is easy to see how susceptible individuals may succumb to workaholism. Indeed, their behaviour may be regarded in their companies as 'normal' or even as a role model for others who wish to succeed.

For those who fear that they are taking their work to extreme limits and are in danger of becoming 'workaholics', read on for strategies which go beyond the obvious ones (such as ensuring that you take sensible breaks during the working day and taking all of your holiday entitlement). Many of these can be listed under the heading of 'switching off'.

5.5.6 CALMING AND COPING STRATEGIES

It should be said at this point that if you have been feeling really stressed over a prolonged period of time you should discuss matters with a trained counsellor or your doctor, who will be able to help you. Your goal should be to recover and then learn to recognise symptoms of stress in yourself and be able to apply appropriate coping strategies in the future. Self-awareness, knowledge of what to do and your own self-belief in applying these techniques (what the theorists call 'self-efficacy') are invaluable friends. In fact Boyd et al (2009, p199) state that 'some researchers suggest that the coping style or strategy used may be more important to individual well-being that the presence of the stressor itself.' The following strategies outline some of the work literature (in particular) on dealing with stress in the workplace. Some go further and suggest in a positive sense how to improve well-being in the workplace.

5.5.6.1 Calming fight/flight response

One of the ways to manage stress is to hit the physiological 'relax' button after an unexpected threat has triggered your fight/flight response; alternatively you could activate this in advance of and during a planned experience. The simplest of these is simply to deliberately take a series of slow, deep breaths which counters your natural tendency to tense up under pressure. Control of the breath is one of the fundamental devices used in the much deeper form of relaxation found in meditation and is well documented in guided self-help manuals (eg Williams et al 2007). Another way, if you have sufficient time, is to burn off some of those stress hormones by taking some exercise such as a brisk walk outdoors, away from the immediate work situation. Even getting up from your desk and going to the work cafeteria is helpful.

ACTIVITY 5.11

OFFICE YOGA

There are many short video clips available on YouTube which will show you how to perform simple breathing exercises and yoga stretches. This clip demonstrates some easy but highly effective exercises you can perform in your office and are particularly good at relieving the tension build-up you might be experiencing from sitting too long at your desk or operating a computer. These are the sort of exercises that you could easily adapt to your own working situation (without needing to refer back to the video) so that they become part of your normal work routine. Here is the weblink. Have a relaxing stretch!

http://www.youtube.com/watch?v=4Dxay4McVP8andNR=1 [Accessed 7 May 2010].

5.5.6.2 Relaxing music

Music can help you to relax after a stressful day, but according to recent research (Labbé et al 2007) it is important that it is the right type; typically, music was best selected by the individual and with a relaxing feel to it (classical music was quoted). Heavy metal music appears to have the reverse effect – you can be left feeling more stressed after listening to it.

5.5.6.3 Winding down time: weekends and holidays

This advice will probably sound like the sort of thing your Mum might have told you – but it seems Mum was right in this case! (Rook and Zijlstra 2006). Your body needs time to re-establish its normal unstressed state after each work day – so do not expect to relax if you are still doing work-related tasks at home or (worse?) ruminating over work matters. Good sleep is really important. The traditional weekend break gives you time to recover, Saturday being the most beneficial day, and this effect is carried forward into the working week; however, its effects soon fade. Holidays are also beneficial but research indicates that pre-vacation stress levels tend to return within three days (you probably already knew this too!) (Rook and Zijlstra 2006, p233).

5.5.6.4 Coping strategies

Coping may be defined as 'behavioural and cognitive efforts to deal with stressful situations' (Ben-Zur 2009, p87). These behaviours and thinking may take various forms but can be broadly categorised into either 'problem-focused coping' or 'emotion-focused coping'.

According to Lazarus (1993, p239) 'The function of problem-focused coping is to change the troubled person–environment relationship by acting on the environment or oneself.' Or to put it another way, some people attempt to handle their stress by looking for ways to improve their situation. Here are two examples to illustrate this approach:

- If you are feeling stressed because your office is a mess, then you reorganise it.

- If you are feeling stressed because you feel you do not know enough about a particular aspect of your job, you enrol on a training programme.

Of course you do not have to adopt this strategy. Take the example of your messy office; you could simply decide to avoid facing the mess – or having to tidy it up (quite literally an 'avoidance' strategy) by doing the bulk of your work somewhere else. Alternatively you could adopt a different way of thinking about the so-called 'mess'; people who do this may say that they know exactly where things are – in other words there is an order of sorts which is apparent to them. This really is to deny that the problem exists at all. Both of these strategies are emotion-focused coping strategies, as described by Lazarus (1993, p239), who writes:

> The function of emotion-focused coping is to change either a) the way the stressful relationship with the environment is attended to (as in vigilance or avoidance) or b) the relational meaning of what is happening, which mitigates the stress even though the actual conditions of the relationship have not changed ... for example denial or distancing.

Deciding which approach to take – problem focused or emotion focused – is sometimes your choice, but you cannot always change things. There is a well known prayer (of contested origin) which reflects this dilemma, and whether you are of a religious disposition or not, has a certain ring of truth to it:

God,
Grant me the serenity to accept the things I cannot change;
The courage, to change the things I can;
And the wisdom, to know the difference. (Anon)

Thus, if you have made a mistake you can try to retrieve the situation through some action, and if successful will reduce your stressful feelings. However, some mistakes cannot be corrected. It may be useful then to think about the 'mistake' as an 'experience' from which you will learn and which will guide you in the future.

5.5.6.5 Emotional support – it's good to talk!

It would seem that even project managers (who, unsurprisingly, often use problem-focused strategies to handle stressful situations) most frequently use emotional support as a coping strategy. They talk to others about what is happening on their project, vent their frustrations with the project and other people, and seek advice and a friendly ear. (Richmond and Skitmore 2006, p8, p15; Aitken and Crawford 2007). The research reinforces what to many of us sounds so obvious – if you are stressed or anxious it usually helps to talk to someone.

Depending upon who you talk to you might even gain more than emotional support; the other person may be able to offer you advice on how to solve your problem. They might tell you of a time when they had a similar experience and how they approached it. They may remind you of your strengths and abilities and encourage you to a plan of action. There is evidence that people with a high self-belief (self-efficacy) use more problem-focused strategies (Boyd et al 2009, p200). In many cases it is useful to be able to use problem and emotion-focused strategies in tandem.

5.5.7 GET ACTIVE!

It is official! Exercise is good for both your physical and mental health, according to the Government's Foresight Project, *Mental capital and wellbeing*. To quote from Section 4 of the report:

Moderate activity seems to be most beneficial, with sessions lasting more than 30 minutes, a few times a week. However, benefits were also seen in studies prescribing relatively low intensity and duration of physical activity. ... Low impact physical activity such as stretching, toning and yoga may be effective in reducing depressive symptom and increasing psychological wellbeing (Hendrickx and Van der Ouderaa 2008).

The report goes on to explain that research has shown that these effects may be due to a number of reasons: they provide individuals with a positive 'mastery' method for self-improvement (a problem-focused, self-efficacy approach) whereby they feel in control of managing their stress levels; they lead to increased social interaction with others; there is increased production in the brain of serotonin, whose depletion is linked to depression, and increased levels of endorphins which reduce pain and give a feeling of euphoria.

5.5.7.1 Green exercise – or 'gone fishing'

Getting outside to the natural environment and green space has also been linked to greater well-being. Researchers are now starting to combine this with the effects of exercise and look at activities such as walking, cycling, horse-riding, fishing, canal-boating and conservation activities. Pretty et al (2007, p211) state that in their study 'it was found that green exercise led to a significant improvement in self-esteem and total mood disturbance (with ... tension anxiety improving post-activity).'

ACTIVITY 5.12

BACK TO NATURE

What sorts of natural environment appeal to you? How might you access this natural environment on a more regular basis? Are there any activities you enjoyed in the past and might want to do again? Are there any activities which you have not yet tried but would like to learn more about?

5.6 CONCLUSION

Self-management skills are a 'must have' for anyone at work. As with any set of skills, you may already have a natural aptitude for them – for instance you might already consider yourself to be a good organiser and you may be the sort of person who rarely gets stressed even under pressure. However, the majority of people will benefit greatly from developing these skills through practising the sorts of techniques outlined in this chapter. By managing your work–life balance you will certainly be more effective at both home and work – and perhaps even improve your general well being in the process.

PAUSE FOR THOUGHT

Identify at least three things that you have learned by studying this chapter and engaging with the activities. How will your newly acquired knowledge and skills support your continuing professional development? What value do you expect your learning to have for your daily routines and your further career? In what area have you identified a need for further development and how are you planning to fill that gap? Address these issues in your learning journal and/or CPD log. You may also wish to discuss them with a peer, colleague, mentor or coach to aid your further development.

KEY LEARNING POINTS

This chapter has highlighted some key learning points, which may be summarised as follows:

- Through analysing where you spend your time, you may plan for time management improvement.

- Sometimes you just have to get on and do things, regardless of your mood.

- People put off doing things for a range of reasons – understanding this helps you to plan your action strategy.

- Organisation is probably an underrated skill: even simple use of diaries and schedules or having a clutter-free work environment will make you much more effective at work.

- Delegation is a difficult but important skill, allowing you to focus on your main job role while developing others at the same time.

- Managing stress at both home and work is essential for our general well-being. It should never be underrated as the statistics show it is one of the major factors of absence and sickness.

- We need to be aware that we can use a range of solution and emotional-oriented methods to manage our stress – and be prepared to apply them as necessary.

EXPLORE FURTHER

Here are some more ideas for you to consider:

For some useful tips on day-to-day living look at Times Online: 'Do 5 simple things a day to stay sane, say scientists', available online at http://www.timesonline.co.uk/tol/life_and_style/health/mental_health/article4988978.ece [accessed 11 March 2010].

To look at the Government's Foresight project on mental health and well-being go to the following website: http://www.foresight.gov.uk/OurWork/ActiveProjects/Mental%20Capital/ProjectOutputs.asp [accessed 6 May 2010].

and also

http://www.cabinetoffice.gov.uk/media/cabinetoffice/strategy/assets/mental_capital_wellbeing_071011.pdf [accessed 11 March 2010].

A very interesting area to look at which is receiving a lot of attention at the moment is the concept of 'mindfulness'. This can be a good technique to use if you have difficulty in 'switching off' your mind from work. Mindfulness techniques train your mind to focus on the here and now, rather than dwell on the past or worry about the future. To find out more you could look for YouTube videos featuring Jon Kabat-Zinn (he is also in the reference list, see Williams et al 2007).

The use of meditation is another area which has been shown to have positive effects for reducing stress and you may wish to investigate this further. There are various types of meditation, often linked to relaxation and visualisation exercises. This is an area in its own right and further discussion lies beyond the scope of this book.

As a final activity, go to the following link on You Tube to see a clip with Professor Cary Cooper, one of the UK's leading experts on stress management: http://www.youtube.com/watch?v=-oapmDhrkUU [accessed 11 March 2010]. Make notes of what he says about:

- the role of managers for the health of those in their departments
- how flexible working arrangements can help manage stress
- stress and well-being audits in organisations.

5.7 REFERENCES

AITKEN, A. and CRAWFORD, L. (2007) Coping with stress: dispositional coping strategies of project managers. *International Journal of Project Management*. Vol. 25, No. 7, pp666–673.

BAKER, J.R. and PHILLIPS, J.G. (2007) E-mail, decisional styles, and rest breaks. *CyberPsychology and Behavior*. Vol. 10, No. 5, pp705–708.

BANDURA, A. (1977) Self-efficacy: towards a unifying theory of behavioral change. *Psychological Review*. Vol. 84, No. 2, pp191–215.

BEN-ZUR, H. (2009) Coping styles and effect. *International Journal of Stress Management.* Vol. 16, No. 2, pp87–101.

BOYD, N.G., LEWIN, J.E. and SAGER, J.K. (2009) A model of stress and coping and their influence on individual and organisational outcomes. *Journal of Vocational Behavior.* Vol. 75, No. 2, pp197–211.

BUELENS, M. and POELMANS, S.A.Y. (2004) Enriching the Spence and Robbins typology of workaholism: demographic, motivational and organizational correlates. *Organizational Change Management.* Vol. 17, No. 5, pp440–458.

CHOI, J.N. and MORAN, S.V. (2009) Why not procrastinate? Development and validation of a new active procrastination scale. *Journal of Social Psychology.* Vol. 149, No. 2, pp195–211.

CHU, A.H. and CHOI, J.N. (2005) Rethinking procrastination: positive effects of 'active' procrastination behaviour on attitudes and performance. *Journal of Social Psychology.* Vol. 145, No. 3, pp245–264.

CIPD. (2009) *Stress at work: work-related stress.* Factsheet, revised June. Available online at: http://www.cipd.co.uk/subjects/health/stress/stress.htm?IsSrchRes=1 [accessed 3 March 2010].

ELLIOTT, A.J. and MCGREGOR, H.A. (2001) A 2x2 achievement goal framework. *Journal of Personality and Social Psychology.* Vol. 80, No. 3, pp501–519.

FAYOL, H. (1949) *General and industrial management.* London: Pitman. Revised and updated edn 1987 by Irwin Gray. Belmont, CA: David S. Lake.

FERRARI, J.R., MASON, C.P. and HAMMER, C. (2006) Procrastination as a predictor of task perceptions: examining delayed and non-delayed tasks across varied deadlines. *Individual Differences Research.* Vol. 4, No. 1, pp28–36.

FERRARI, J.R., O'CALLAGHAN, J. and NEWBEGIN, I. (2005) Prevalence of procrastination in the United States, United Kingdom, and Australia: arousal and avoidance delays among adults. *North American Journal of Psychology.* Vol. 7, No. 1, pp1–6.

FORESIGHT. (2007) *Mental capital and wellbeing.* PMSU Lunchtime Seminar, 11 October.

GOVERNMENT OFFICE FOR SCIENCE. (2008) *Foresight mental capital and wellbeing project. Final project report – executive summary.* London: Government Office for Science.

HACKMAN, J. and OLDHAM, G. (1976) Motivation through design of work: test of a theory. *Organisational Behavior and Human Performance.* Vol. 16, No. 2, pp250–279.

HENDRICKX, H. and VAN DER OUDERAA, F. (2008) *State of science review: SR-E24: the effect of physical activity on mental capital and wellbeing.* London: The Government Office for Science.

HOLMES, T.H. and RAHE, R.H. (1967) The social adjustment rating scale. *Journal of Psychosomatic Research.* Vol. 11, No. 2, pp213–218.

HYVÖNEN, K., FELDT, T., TOLVANEN, A. and KINNUNEN, U. (2010) The role of goal pursuit in the interaction between psychosocial work environment and occupational well-being. *Journal of Vocational Behavior.* Vol. 76, No. 2, pp406–418.

KELLY, W.E. (2002) Anxiety and the prediction of task duration: a preliminary analysis. *The Journal of Psychology.* Vol. 136, No. 1, pp53–58.

KELLY, W.E. and JOHNSON, J.L. (ND) Time use efficiency and the five-factor model of personality. *Education.* Vol. 125, No. 3, pp511–515.

LABBÉ, E., SCHMIDT, N., BABIN, J. and PHARR, M. (2007) Coping with stress: the effectiveness of different types of music. *Applied Psychophysiology and Biofeedback.* Vol. 32, No. 3/4, pp163–168.

LAZARUS, R.S. (1993) Coping theory and research: past, present, and future. *Psychosomatic Medicine*. Vol. 55, No. 1, pp234–237.

MANAGEMENT TODAY. (2009) Brainfood: do it right: dynamic delegation. *Management Today*. September, p18.

MEADE, G. (2009) EU fails to curb Britain's work hours opt-out. *Independent*. 28 April. Available online at: http://www.independent.co.uk/news/world/europe/eu-fails-to-curb-britains-work-hours-optout-1675368.html [accessed 3 May 2010].

MELCHIOR, M., BERKMAN, L.F., NIEDHAMMER, I., ZINS, M. and GOLDBERG, M. (2007) The mental health effects of multiple work and family demands. *Social Psychiatry @ Psychiatric Epidiomology*. Vol. 42, No. 7, pp573–582.

MINTZBERG, H. (1990) The manager's job: folklore and fact (HBR Classic). *Harvard Business Review*. Vol. 68, No. 2, pp163–176.

MOORCROFT, R. (2009) Delegation, not relegation. *Manager*. Autumn, pp 4–5.

MURRAY, R. (2005) *Writing for academic journals*. Maidenhead: Open University Press.

OXFORD UNIVERSITY PRESS. (2006) *Compact Oxford English dictionary for students*. Oxford: Oxford University Press.

PEDLER, M., BURGOYNE, J. and BOYDELL, T. (2007) *A manager's guide to self development*. 5th ed. Maidenhead: McGraw-Hill.

PRETTY, J., PEACOCK, J., HINE, R., SELLENS, M., SOUTH, N. and GRIFFIN, M. (2007) Green exercise in the UK countryside: effects on well-being, and implications for policy and planning. *Journal of Environmental Planning and Management*. Vol. 50, No. 2, pp211–231.

RICHMOND, A. and SKITMORE, M. (2006) Stress and coping: a study of project managers in a large ICT organisation. *Project Management Journal*. Vol. 37, No. 5, pp5–16.

ROOK, J.W. and ZIJLSTRA, F.R. (2006) The contribution of various types of activities to recovery. *European Journal of Work and Organisational Psychology*. Vol. 15, No. 2, pp218–240.

SADDLER, C.D. and BULEY, J. (1999) Predictors of academic procrastination in college students. *Psychological Reports*. Vol. 84, No. 2, pp686–688.

SCHAUFELI, W.B., BAKKER, A.B., VAN DER HEIJDEN, F.M. and PRINS, J.T. (2009) Workaholism, burnout and well-being among junior doctors: the mediating role of conflict. *Work and Stress*. Vol. 23, No. 2, pp155–172.

SELYE, H. (1976) *The stress of life*. New York: McGraw-Hill.

SEO, E.H. (2009) The relationship of procrastination with a mastery goal versus an avoidance goal. *Social Behaviour and Personality*. Vol. 37, No. 7, pp911–920.

SUN, J., WANG, S., ZHANG, J.Q. and LI, W. (2007) Assessing the cumulative effects of stress: the association between job stress and allostatic load in a large sample of Chinese employees. *Work and Stress*. Vol. 21, No. 4, pp333–347.

TANNENBAUM, R. and SCHMIDT, W.H. (1986) Excerpts from 'How to choose a leadership pattern'. *Harvard Business Review*. Vol. 64, No. 4, pp129.

THEOBALD, T. (2007) Clear Thinking. *Guardian*, 6 October. Available online at: http://guaridan.co.uk/money/2007/oct/06/work [accessed 24 April 2010].

THEOBALD, T. and COOPER, C.L. (2007) *Detox your desk: declutter your life and mind*. Chichester: Capstone Publishing.

TRACY, B. (2007) *Eat that frog*. San Francisco: ReadHowYouWant.

VAN DEN BROECK, A., VANSTEENKISTE, M., DE WITTE, H. and LENS, W. (2008) Explaining the relationship between job characteristics, burnout, and engagement: the role of basic psychological need satisfaction. *Work and Stress*. Vol. 22, No. 3, pp277–294.

WHITE, R.D. (2010) The micromanagement disease: symptoms, diagnosis, and cure. *Public Personnel Management.* Vol. 39, No. 1, pp71–76.

WILLIAMS, M., TEASDALE, J., SEGAL, Z. and KABAT-ZINN, J. (2007) *The mindful way through depression: Freeing yourself from chronic unhappiness.* New York: Guildford Press.

PART 4

Effective Management of Interpersonal Relationships at Work

CHAPTER 6

Effective team-building and communication

Gillian Watson *and* Ivana Adamson

OVERVIEW

Teamwork is a common feature of contemporary organisations and it is critical for today's and tomorrow's managers to understand how they form and perform and how they can be led effectively. This chapter discusses the key theories of building, managing and working in teams with a particular focus on team roles and the behaviours and skills of individual team members. It also considers the need for communication and giving feedback in a team context. This chapter ends with a discussion of conflict in teams, including the emergence of conflict and different ways of handling it.

LEARNING OUTCOMES

By the end of this chapter, provided you engage with the activities, you should be able to:

- identify various stages in group/team development
- evaluate a range of methods to aid teambuilding and development
- critically evaluate the worth of team role when compiling a team
- explain how a virtual team works and what leadership skills may be employed to manage such a team
- evaluate the need for interactive communication and feedback in teams
- understand the emergence of conflict in teams and how it can be managed.

6.1 INTRODUCTION

Groups and teams are naturally occurring features in organisations, as the notion of organisation itself implies that several individuals work towards a common goal. All members of a group, team or organisation bring in their personalities, life stories and prior experiences, which often results in complex group, team or organisational dynamics. Ideally, these group dynamics lead to improved organisational performance (Jackson and Carter 2000). To achieve its maximum potential, a group or team is more than just a collection of individuals. A group or team is a collection of individuals in which there is social interaction, relatively stable patterns of relationships and the sharing of – and working towards – a common goal. In most instances, however, groups and teams are made up of very diverse individuals – individuals of different age, gender and background (including nationality and culture) that have different knowledge, skills, views and agendas. While this diversity is undoubtedly the strength of groups and teams, it is also often the source of confusion, irritation and conflict.

This chapter introduces you to the theory of working in groups and teams. We begin by distinguishing between groups and teams and examine what it means to work as part of a group or team. We then consider what needs to be done to build a team as well as the different roles that individuals take in teams. We also discuss how team role theory can be applied in practice to build and develop teams, and we introduce the notion of virtual team. We end this chapter with a discussion of communication (including feedback) and with consideration of conflict in team situations.

6.2 WORKING IN GROUPS AND TEAMS

6.2.1 DISTINGUISHING BETWEEN GROUPS AND TEAMS

Groups and teams have long been common types of working in organisations. There are a number of theories about why humans tend to live and work with others, which Clegg et al (2005) summarise as enhancing the safety of individuals in evolutionary terms as well as that need to belong that the 'social animal' called human seems to have. From an organisational perspective, there are significant similarities between groups and teams; for instance, they comprise different members that ideally complement each other, they perform different tasks and roles, and they can contribute significantly to organisational effectiveness and efficiency. This may be the reason why the terms groups and teams are often used interchangeably. There are, however, significant differences between groups and teams, so let consider both terms/concepts in detail.

6.2.2 WORKING IN GROUPS

Groups consist of a number of members who perceive themselves and recognise each other as being part of that group. In mutual interaction, group members define the boundaries of the group and the ground rules (Schein 1988). Group members contribute individually to the group's common goal, and the evaluation of their performance depends on their individual contributions. There are different types of groups. Formal groups – that is, groups that are intentionally created to achieve certain goals – can be permanent (for instance to head a department or unit) or temporary (such as committees and task forces).

The creation of formal groups often leads to the emergence of informal groups which are dynamic and inventive, and can transform organisations into a living, functioning and goal-oriented entity, and could therefore be harnessed by team leaders to support the attainment of organisational goals (Luthans 2005). Formal and informal groups are often regarded as distinctly separate entities, but all formal organisations tend to give rise to informal groupings that eventually resemble formal groups, and some theorists (eg McKenna 1999) refer to them as the emergent organisational structures. Informal groups can enhance the effectiveness of organisational structure, lighten managers' workloads, fill gaps in managers' knowledge and skills, improve communication and provide a safe outlet for sharing thoughts and feelings.

ACTIVITY 6.1

ANALYSING INFORMAL VERTICAL GROUPS

Consider an informal vertical grouping in the workplace, with which you are familiar. Can you identify what characteristics form part of their bond? Also reflect upon an informal group of which you have been a member using the characteristics of power in informal groups. Assess the extent to which they have:

- enhanced the effectiveness of organisational structures
- lightened the managers' workload
- filled gaps in managers' knowledge and skills
- improved communication
- provided a safe outlet for emotions.

Have you been aware of any of these processes taking place? Does your work environment and culture support any of these working practices? Compare and contrast those elements you believe are working and those that are not. Why might this be the case?

Individuals take on specific roles in groups, and Allcorn (1985) identified three types of such roles: group task roles, group maintenance roles and self-oriented roles. In more detail, group task roles focus on productivity and the development and achievement of organisational goals. Group task roles usually involve:

- facilitating – setting goals and procedures for problem-solving activities
- seeking information – initiating discussions, seeking ideas and viewpoints from others
- disseminating information – offering suggestions, information, and own viewpoints
- co-ordinating and monitoring of activities
- energising or motivating the group to achieve higher levels of output.

Group maintenance roles, in contrast, focus on fostering open and positive relationships between group members. In this set of roles, group members act as:

- encouragers to create a friendly interpersonal atmosphere and encourage others

- harmonisers to mediate in conflict situations

- gatekeepers to keep information flowing and facilitate participation

- standard-setters to propose and negotiate standards for group members to adopt

- observers and followers who can provide useful feedback, and willingly follow given direction.

Finally, self-oriented roles refer to each group member's individual needs and personal agendas, which can move the group on or have a negative impact on the group's cohesiveness. In particular:

- Aggressors can be excessively competitive, and thus likely to devalue contributions from others.

- Blockers can be negative and resist agreed-on decisions.

- Recognition seekers crave attention and work primarily to further their own position in and beyond the group.

- Dominators tend to control the group by means of flattery or giving orders.

Allcorn (1985) suggests that the categories are self-contained and mutually exclusive, and that different group members take on different roles. However, while groups need to contain a balanced mix of all the three types of roles, it would be more realistic to conceive that each individual in a group possesses a combination of all three role types. For example, a facilitator may be at the same time an encourager and a recognition seeker. This makes it difficult to objectively evaluate role effectiveness. Moreover, group size is another key contributing factor to group performance. The relationship between group size and group performance is an inverted 'U' shape: as a group grows, so does the level of performance. At some point, the critical mass of group effort exceeds the task needs. At this point, a phenomenon called 'social loafing' or 'self-limiting behaviours' come into play, and individuals begin to withdraw by exerting less effort than they would if they worked alone (Clegg et al 2005).

Hogan et al (1994) observed a number of senior management teams during decision-making and identified a number of reasons for managers' self-limiting behaviours. They found that the presence of someone with more expertise was the major reason for such behaviour (73 per cent), followed by a presentation of a compelling argument (62 per cent), lack of belief in their own ability (61 per cent) and unimportant and meaningless decisions (58 per cent). Almost half of the study participants gave in to team pressure to conform (46 per cent). While these results are somewhat outdated, we can safely assume that similar dynamics are in place today. Self-limiting behaviours or failure to participate in decision-making reduce the group members' ability to offer the kind of dynamic leadership that organisations need to succeed.

6.2.3 WORKING IN TEAMS

A team can be defined as 'a group whose members have complementary skills and are committed to a common purpose or set of performance goals for which they hold themselves mutually accountable' (Greenberg and Baron 1997, p270). Hence, a team depends on both individual and team contributions, and its members take collective responsibility for the results. The notion of collective responsibility thus seems to be the key issue that qualitatively separates teams from groups, and team members enter into a psychological contract with each other that group members do not (Clegg et al 2005).

There have been major changes over recent years in the way in which teams are being perceived, created and evaluated. The following four general types of teams have long been identified (Aranda et al 1998):

- Management teams inspire and integrate the work of the organisations, for example by creating a vision, refining the organisational culture and improving morale, carrying out major change initiatives and improving the organisation's image.

- Task teams tend to be cross-functional teams (ie their members come from different functional units within the organisation) that work on projects for a defined but often extended period of time.

- Work teams are self-contained work units that are responsible for manufacturing a particular product or delivering a particular service.

- Parallel teams work independently but in parallel to the organisational structure and focus on problem-solving or seeking organisational opportunities.

Teams have many advantages, but also many disadvantages, which are summarised in Table 6.1 below.

Early research on team dynamics linked team cohesiveness with stability and higher productivity. Communication in cohesive teams was found to be more

Table 6.1 Advantages and disadvantages of teamwork

Advantages	Disadvantages
Team decisions may deliver a wider choice of solutions.	Team meetings can be costly; this is a hidden cost although important enough to affect the organisation's effectiveness.
Team participation may lead to higher commitment, and ownership of outcomes.	Pressures to conform may lead to premature decisions, and result in poor leadership.
Team discussions increase feedback and can decrease time spent in communication.	Personal agendas may lead to conflict and poor quality of outcomes.
Team membership is known to increase overall effort.	Extremes of cohesiveness may lead to 'groupthink'.

Source: drawing on Haynes (2008), Hall (1991), Janis (1972).

ACTIVITY 6.2

REFLECTING ON YOUR EXPERIENCES OF TEAMWORK

Analyse, using your own experiences, the points made above regarding the advantages and disadvantages of teamworking. Would your evaluation differ if your role in the team was that of a team member or a team leader? Discuss this with others – does their experience differ from yours?

frequent and more satisfying, and team members were found to be more participative when they held similar values. Less cohesive groups experienced more difficulty in enforcing standards of behaviour amongst their members. The key factor influencing their productivity, however, was the teams' performance norms. Highly cohesive teams with high performance norms were found be to highly productive, and their performance levels dropped when they adopted lower performance norms. Highly cohesive teams with low performance norms were by far the poorest performers (Bartol and Martin 1991, Mullen and Cooper 1994). But what makes an effective team?

Traditionally, organisations have used productivity to measure both individual and team effectiveness, but there is increasing scepticism as to whether such measures remain appropriate in an uncertain and rapidly changing business environment. For instance, task teams need to be flexible as they operate within shorter planning and production cycles and often with changing targets. In addition, it has been recognised that different organisational theories perceive and evaluate teams differently, even though competency in problem-solving, technical know-how and the maintenance of relationships within the group have been found to be widespread criteria for performance team performance.

Aranda et al (1998), for instance, identified three types of skills that enhance team productivity. These are team problem-solving skills, team interpersonal skills and task problem-solving skills. Table 6.2 opposite summarises the tasks and outcomes associated with each of these skills.

Ideally, a team comprises individuals with a wide range of skills so that they can tap into each other's strengths and achieve increasingly complex goals in an increasingly uncertain work environment. Hence, team members should be selected on the basis not only of the skills that they already possess but also on their willingness and ability to learn new ones. This poses a challenge to managers and other organisational decision-makers who have traditionally selected team members on the grounds of position and proximity – that is, seniority, association or location. It is also common practice to use the same team over and over again, which results in the team taking the same or similar actions and arriving at the same or a similar outcome. This has far-reaching implications for organisations. Firstly, new organisational problems require fresh thinking that established teams are unlikely to create, and secondly, there is a reluctance to develop potential new team members that might bring in new

Table 6.2 Skills and tasks that enhance team productivity

Skill	Tasks include	Outcomes
Team problem-solving	Identifying alternatives Making and justifying decisions Putting plans into practice	Critical thinking Creativity
Team interpersonal	Encourage communication between team members Consult team members in the decision-making process Analyse and synthesise information	Facilitating Supporting
Task problem-solving	Gathering, analysing and communicating data Prioritising	Analysing Synthesising Discovering

Source: drawing on Aranda et al (1998).

knowledge, skills and ideas. It is therefore imperative that current and aspiring managers know how to build effective groups and teams, which is what we will discuss in the following section.

6.3 BUILDING GROUPS AND TEAMS

In the previous section we saw that organisations require groups and teams that are fluid, that possess a mix of technical, interpersonal and problem-solving skills, and that are able to form and re-form in order to respond to changing organisational needs. It has long been established that groups and teams go through different developmental stages that are relatively predictable. The best known model of group and team development is probably Tuckman's (1965) five-stage model of forming, storming, norming, performing and adjourning.

Tuckman's (1965) model demonstrates that the road to an effective group or team is bumpy. It is satisfying for individuals to know that they contribute to a group or team and achieve outcomes that they would not be able to achieve on their own. It is also desirable for organisations to have effective groups and teams that perform well and contribute to its success. However, it often seems that the ideal of effective groups and teams takes little account of the difficulties and conflicts that groups and teams have on their journey to operating effectively. Current and aspiring managers must therefore have the necessary skill and understanding to facilitate the building of groups and teams to help them to achieve their potential. The team leader's role is paradoxical in that he or she has to demonstrate a strong personal vision while having to balance carrying out the task and maintaining the group/team by allowing group or team members to lead and take responsibility themselves (Quinn et al 2003). Micromanaging and

Figure 6.1 Developmental stages of groups and teams

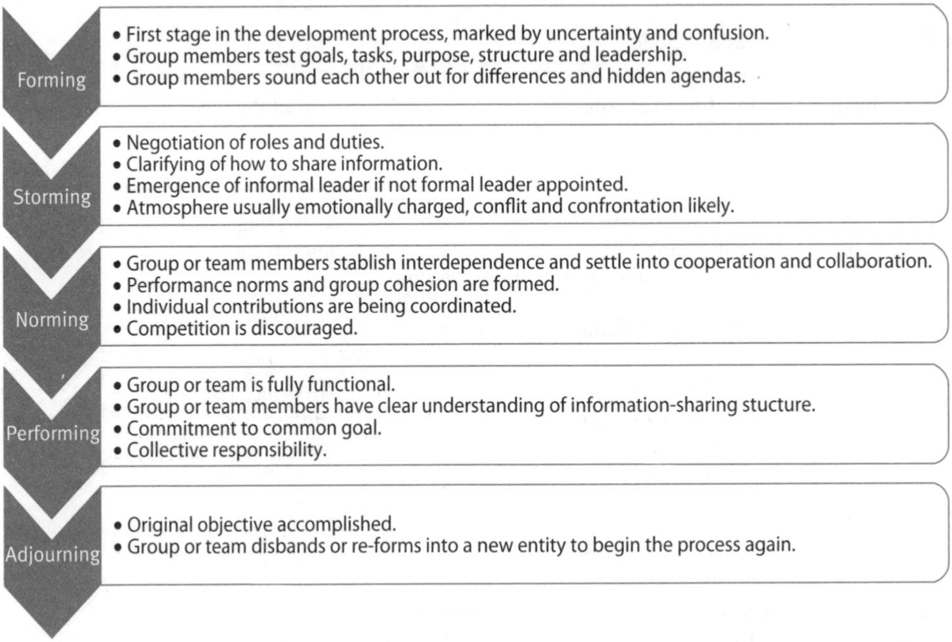

Forming
- First stage in the development process, marked by uncertainty and confusion.
- Group members test goals, tasks, purpose, structure and leadership.
- Group members sound each other out for differences and hidden agendas.

Storming
- Negotiation of roles and duties.
- Clarifying of how to share information.
- Emergence of informal leader if not formal leader appointed.
- Atmosphere usually emotionally charged, conflict and confrontation likely.

Norming
- Group or team members stablish interdependence and settle into cooperation and collaboration.
- Performance norms and group cohesion are formed.
- Individual contributions are being coordinated.
- Competition is discouraged.

Performing
- Group or team is fully functional.
- Group or team members have clear understanding of information-sharing stucture.
- Commitment to common goal.
- Collective responsibility.

Adjourning
- Original objective accomplished.
- Group or team disbands or re-forms into a new entity to begin the process again.

Source: drawing on Tuckman (1965), Quinn et al (2003).

allowing some group or team members to shine at the expense of others can have detrimental effects on team productivity and cohesion.

ACTIVITY 6.3

REFLECTING ON YOUR GROUP OR TEAM

Consider a group or team of which you are a member, either at the workplace, at university or in your leisure activities. Reflect on your experiences as a member and determine whether they tally with Tuckman's (1965) model. Can you identify a particular moment or event when your group or team moved from one stage to another? Were you aware of that happening? Can you think of any evidence to demonstrate this?

6.4 TEAM ROLES

After our discussion of group and team development, let us now focus on the different roles that team members take on (we focus on teams rather than groups because teams have clearer roles and a more strategic approach to their creation than groups; however, this discussion may also be helpful when considering group issues). When leading a team, we need to consider how teams are created and what types of behaviours may be required. The work of Meredith Belbin is important here, as a team-based management approach is constantly advocated in many contemporary organisations. Gunduz (2008) considers this to be the second industrial revolution and indicates that it may also be a milestone on the road to increased organisational productivity. Organisations use all possible means at their disposal to ensure competitive advantage; in order to achieve this they need to be flexible and they need teams that are able to identify activities and associated resources (including people) to react quickly to environmental requirements. Therefore, a well-run, well-managed team should have certain positive aspects that are acceptable to all members and fit in with the organisation's strategic imperatives (Ozbilgin, 2005). The team leader's task is to create the right team atmosphere, make-up of the team, team attitude and behaviour so that the team role concept (Benne and Sheats 1948, Bales and Slater 1955, Belbin 1981, Watson and Gallagher 2005, Belbin 2007) can work successfully. Therefore, a review of what Belbin's work offers to the team leader in order to build a team is relevant to contemporary practice.

Team role theory suggests that people interact with others in different ways and exhibit different behaviours. Belbin (1981, 2007) identifies different roles that team members take, which partly depend on their personality and partly on the team dynamics. These roles can be classified into three different sets: task-related, team-related and individual or thinking-related. Table 6.3 provides details about the different team roles that Belbin's work distinguishes and the characteristics that individuals possess and display.

Belbin's (1981, 2007) process makes many distinctions: for example the need for different team roles being prevalent at various stages of the team's existence, that high-performance teams need a balance of team roles, that individuals show signs of behaviours in many of the roles, and that an overall individual profile can be produced for each team member through team role tests. These tests are designed to assist existing teams, to help form new teams and to be used as a recruitment or promotion tool. Belbin's team role tests assess dominance, intelligence, introversion/extroversion and anxiety/determination, and arguably we all have these attributes in our make-up in various degrees. It is the combination of behaviours and attributes that is the key to determining the individual's place in the team, and possibly how its members are valued or whether they are 'engaged performers' (Stevens 2010): essentially, whether individuals want to feel they belong in the team. The leadership skill in these investigations is to achieve the best fit for the work-related elements and the most attuned social combination; again this joining of people's attitudes and behaviour into a team can prove successful and is highly valued when the team engages and performs well.

Adair's (1986) model enables us to see a more focused context in the differentiation between one role grouping and another (Figure 6.2). The 'task'/'action striving' grouping will use individuals from both the other groupings in the team to start or complete a task; this is the driving force that gives the team energy. The 'team' grouping focuses on the interrelationships within a team and the socialisation that can be present in the team because of those 'team'/'socially' relating individuals within it. The 'individual'/'thinking'

Table 6.3 Team roles

A. Task-related team roles

Team role	Strengths	Weaknesses
Shaper	Challenging, dynamic, goal oriented, has drive and courage	Prone to provocation, often offends people's feelings
Implementer	Disciplined, organised, efficient, turns ideas into actions	Somewhat inflexible, slow to respond to new possibilities
Completer/ finisher	Accurate, conscientious, meticulously prevents error	Inclined to worry unduly, reluctant to delegate

B. The team or social-related team roles

Team role	Strengths	Weaknesses
Resource investigator	Extrovert, enthusiastic, communicative, explores opportunities, develops contacts	Over-optimistic, loses interest once initial enthusiasm has passed
Co-ordinator	Calm, confident, clarifies goals, promotes participative decision-making	Can be seen as manipulative, off-loads personal work
Team worker	Cooperative, caring, diplomatic, sensitive, a good listener, averts friction	Indecisive when faced with tough decisions

C. The individual or thinking-related team roles

Team role	Strengths	Weaknesses
Plant	Creative, imaginative, unorthodox, solves difficult problems	Ignores incidentals, too preoccupied to communicate effectively
Monitor/ evaluator	Logical, analytical discerning, judges accurately	Lacks drive and ability to inspire others
Specialist	Single minded, motivated by the pursuit of knowledge	Contributes on a narrow front, dwells on technicalities

Source: adapted from Belbin (2006, 2007): for further information and access to updated material, please follow the links provided to www.belbin.com and www.belbin.info; printed with kind permission of Belbin Associates.

grouping on the other hand would contribute from what they view as a feeling of self-worth, which in itself emanates from their own particular way of thinking, cognitive style, attitude or specialist ability. These attributes will enable them to accomplish tasks in their own way. Overall the characteristics of all the groupings contribute to the whole; in essence there needs to be a balance of all the roles for the team itself to be successful. The way we interrelate with others in the team does correlate with our tendency to behave in a certain way, principally because certain roles are prevalent in our team role profile. Team role tests offer the opportunity for individuals to assess their overall profile, and to review what are their most preferred as well as their least preferred roles in the team. Critically, identifying an individual's team role (Belbin, 1996, 2007) enables us to:

- improve self-awareness and personal effectiveness
- foster mutual trust and understanding between work colleagues
- engage in team selection and teambuilding
- match people to jobs more effectively.

There is a trend for contemporary organisations to use consultants, assessment centres, in-house trained Belbin assessors and consultants from higher educational institutions to conduct the Belbin analysis with their staff teams. An important point to note is that all Belbin-trained assessors/consultants will

Figure 6.2 Task–team–individual model

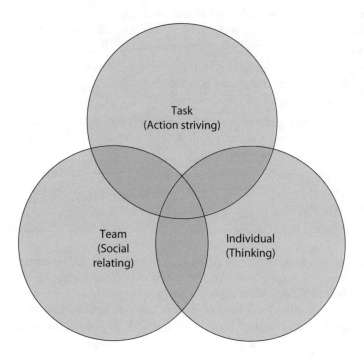

Source: drawing on Adair (1986) and adapted from Belbin (2006, 2007): for further information and access to updated material, please follow the links provided to www.belbin.com and www.belbin.info; printed with kind permission of Belbin Associates.

emphasise the pitfalls of relying on self-reporting alone. Moreover, they will actively seek corroboration of people's self-assessments of their behaviour from fellow team members so as to avoid the team role profile just becoming a self-fulfilling exercise, open to faking and therefore somewhat unreliable. They thus acknowledge that self-perception can be skewed; for example we may be unaware of how we are perceived by others. In amalgamating various sources of data collection, a normalising of the results occurs, enabling the Belbin group to assert that this test has validity and reliability. It is worth emphasising that the Belbin assessment itself aims to enable us to analyse behaviour rather than personality (as in a psychometric assessment). However, our personality is part of our overall make-up and is a constituent part of our behaviours and attitudes, which will be elaborated in Box 6.1 below.

> ### BOX 6.1: UNDERLYING FACTORS TO TEAM ROLE BEHAVIOUR (IN WATSON AND GALLAGHER 2005)
>
> - Psycho-physiological factors, particularly extroversion–introversion and high anxiety–low anxiety, underlie behaviour.
>
> - Nevertheless, high-level thought can override personality to generate exceptional behaviour. This requires the individual to be thinking and reflecting, rather than just reacting to one basic behaviour or instinct, and so to be able to override the underlying inclination someone might have to behave in a pre-determined fashion.
>
> - Cherished values can provide a particular set of behaviours. These are probably developed from our background and the particular traits we might value in ourselves and others, such as loyalty and trust.
>
> - Behaviour can depend on factors in the immediate environment. This may be determined by our reaction to the particular work environment and factors such as deadlines and change.
>
> - Personal experience and cultural factors may serve to conventionalise [individual] behaviour, and behaviour is often adapted to take account of experience and conventions.
>
> - Learning to play a needed role improves personal versatility. This enables individuals to maximise their potential and value to the team and the department.

Developing a team is a quite complicated process, but if conducted accurately it will lead to the norming stage (Tuckman 1965) or a pattern of society within the team. Belbin (1996, 2007) describes this as 'a personality propensity, modified by the thought process, modified still further by personal values, governed by perceived constraints, influenced by experience and added to by sophisticated learning'.

Table 6.4 demonstrates that Belbin's team roles can play a significant part in evaluating personal development and career development choices. The point here

ACTIVITY 6.4

APPLYING YOUR TEAM ROLE PROFILE

If you are fortunate enough to have a personal team role profile, reflect on the result. Try to establish what you and your team intend to do with it. How can it be used effectively? How can relevant personal development strategies become part of the overall outcome? How will you make the most of this knowledge, remembering that roles in your profile could be classified (for personal development purposes) as: least preferred, manageable, preferred (see Table 6.4)?

Table 6.4 Classification of team roles

Least preferred	• Try to avoid using for prolonged periods • Delegate and make use of complementary roles of others • Build a balanced team
Manageable	• Be prepared to adopt these roles if necessary
Preferred	• Develop and perfect role • Plan career to make maximum use of these natural strengths

Source: adapted from Belbin (2006, 2007): for further information and access to updated material, please follow the links provided to www.belbin.com and www.belbin.info; printed with kind permission Belbin Associates.

is that awareness has been raised and therefore there can be a three-tier decision-making process for developmental decisions. The individual will need to make personal decisions, but the team, department and the organisation as whole will need to make strategic decision on how and why teamworking is of value to the organisation and how to utilise their talented individuals. This new awareness also enables team leaders and team members to discuss roles that are manageable, preferred and least preferred; thus individuals have the choice of developing and maximising their strengths and enhancing skills in areas that are least preferred. Indeed it may serve to change a team member's job role in the team.

6.5 TEAM ROLE THEORY IN PRACTICE: MATCHING PEOPLE TO JOBS

Team role profiles can support recruitment and promotion decisions, as the team leader has the option of recruiting the person who fits the demands of the job as well having a relevant 'fit' within the team. While the conventional recruitment process considers eligibility in terms of the relevant entry criteria, Belbin's work

Figure 6.3 Entry and performance criteria

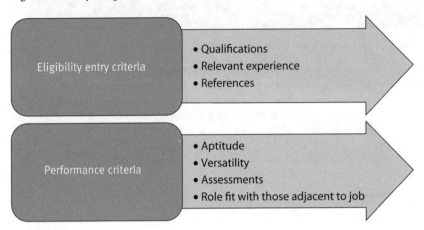

Source: adapted from Belbin (2006, 2007): for further information and access to updated material, please follow the links provided to www.belbin.com and www.belbin.info; printed with kind permission of Belbin Associates.

suggests that performance criteria and the suitability of candidates should also be taken into account when recruiting, selecting or promoting candidates (see Figure 6.3).

There are several crucial elements to consider in selecting an appropriate candidate. At the beginning of the selection process, the manager defines the job or project and compiles a job requirement assessment. In addition, certain team members compile a job observation survey and a job suitability report, which is then used to assess whether a candidate is suitable for the job in question. When selecting a candidate for a particular project or role, managers and those in roles of responsibility must consider not only *entry* criteria like skills, experience and qualifications, but also *suitability* criteria such as aptitude, temperament and behavioural tendencies, which Belbin's test assesses. Entry criteria are critical in actually securing an interview, and assessment of requisite qualifications will always be an essential part of the recruitment process. However, these criteria do not guarantee that the new recruit will be successful in the job and suitability criteria will reduce the 'leap of faith' present in any recruitment decision. Given that the assessment of suitability criteria has been developed through using observation of behaviour, with data reporting variables such as self and others, this process means that the 'suitable' candidate can emerge. Belbin (1996) observes that he would always want to make a case for backing a suitable candidate rather than an eligible one. His argument is that candidates who hitherto may not have been deemed eligible can have their level of eligibility enhanced through undertaking a personal development plan, although as always in today's organisations the cost of this development would have to be worthwhile. Cannall (2009, p1) puts this as follows: 'Team selection is not an exact science. ... A mix of types is necessary, as is a mix of skills.'

To build a diverse and balanced team, other more important considerations are worthy of note: there needs to be a flow of readily available candidates with the right characteristics and the relevant diversity of talent and measure of team roles. Each person on the team would have his or her own role, with a given purpose or terms of reference to achieve results. This would therefore be used to assemble the 'perfect' team.

In his article 'Lights, camera, interaction', Angus Strachan (2004) discusses his view of the importance of team roles. He provides us with an interesting case study in which he highlights the need for a combination of roles with their associated strengths and weaknesses.

ACTIVITY 6.5

REFLECTION ON STRACHAN (2004)

Access Strachan's article on the companion website. Reflect on the case and discuss it with your tutor group or work colleagues. Does it have resonance with your experiences?

In a group consider and discuss several well-known politicians or prominent media celebrities. What attributes do they exhibit and which Belbin team roles do you think apply to them? Analyse each other's opinions and come to a consensus.

Apply the same consideration to a management team with which you are familiar. Can the group pick out certain attributes that are synonymous with the team roles?

6.6 VIRTUAL TEAMS

The concept of the 'virtual team' was created out of the Internet revolution and the subsequent transformation of many business practices, such as e-business, e-learning, and the overall e-economy, which arguably forced businesses to put aside their time-honoured, erstwhile practices and look for a new way of dealing with the globalisation of their business (Townsend et al 1998). The technology that companies used and the way they communicated had to change; therefore, the challenge was to harness the positive aspects of teamworking and translate it into a work team whose members:

- were not necessarily in the same building
- were not – probably – in the same country
- meet face to face very infrequently
- rely on communication through technology to maintain the fundamental nature or spirit of their co-operation.

The virtual team was born, which can be defined as 'geographically dispersed members who communicate with each other using some variant mix of information and communication technologies' (Lee-Kelly and Sankey 2008, p52). Often, a virtual team is created to realise a new project or development, but this does not diminish its worth or negate the challenges that teamwork generally brings. If anything, virtual teams are more complex than other, more traditional types of teams due to geographical and temporal distance (Lipnack and Stamp 2000, Townsend et al 1998), and 'boundary spanning, life cycle and member roles' (Bell and Kozlowski 2002). Cannall (2009, p1) suggests that the virtual team 'may need to communicate by telephone, e-mail and teleconferencing rather than face-to-face. Managing them is particularly difficult, not least because remote working can exacerbate misunderstanding.' Leadership skills can be the critical factor in managing a virtual team; therefore, we must investigate what the key issues are which can support success or condemn the team to failure. Technological processes are critical to the existence of a 'pure virtual team' (Arinson and Miller 2002) and fundamental to influencing how the team works. Therefore, the team leader in this instance relies on the organisation investing in the appropriate technology to support virtual teamworking.

Figure 6.4 Forms of virtual teams

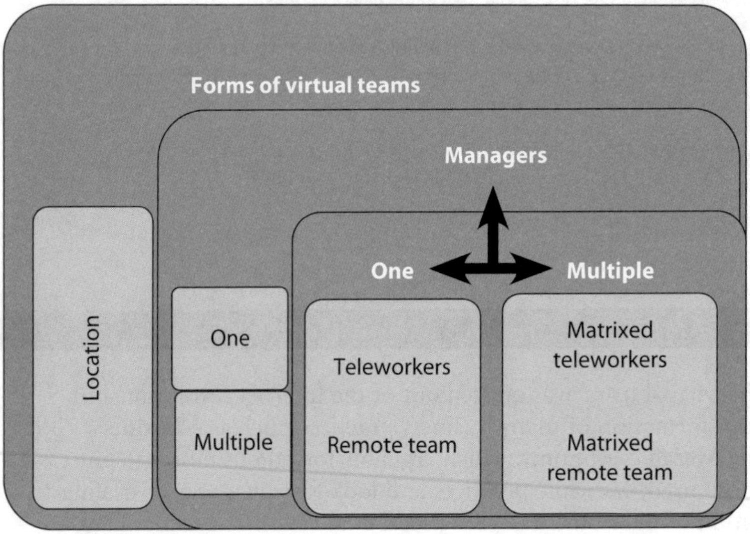

Source: Cascio and Shurygailo (2003).

Cascio and Shurygailo (2003) suggest there are four categories of virtual team: teleworkers, remote teams, matrixed teleworkers and matrixed remote teams as outlined in Figure 6.4.

Cascio and Shurygailo (2003) also note that the other variable is time and shift-working; however, this will only be salient to some specific organisations and therefore is not considered here. Organisations may create hybrid forms of virtual teamworking to suit their requirements. Agreement has not yet been reached about the skills involved in leading a virtual team. One view suggests that managers or leaders of a virtual team need have no particular leadership style (Cascio and Shurygailo 2003); the other view emphasises that any remote leader has little or no control over the virtual team (Kostner 1996 as cited in Lee-Kelly and Sankey 2008).This would suggest that the team's well-being and performance relies on the team exercising voluntary control, and therefore its members need to be self-motivating and to some extent self-managed individuals. In any case, leading a virtual team requires exceptional co-ordination and communication skills, and team leaders and those aspiring to become team leaders in future need to commit themselves to developing their skills.

Let us consider the leadership or co-ordination of virtual teams in more detail. The matrix in Table 6.5 below shows practical approaches that the potential leader of a virtual team may need to adopt in his/her management technique, while having also to take account of creating structure, culture and rules or plans by which the team will adhere.

A particularly neglected area of communication when managing virtually is listening, and Williamson (2009) advocates we should 'listen to silences'. She contends that we need to listen, with care, to every team member when they are

Table 6.5 Co-ordinating virtual teams

	Co-ordinating virtual teams
Shared goals	Clear roles and regular performance feedback are important and need to be explicit.
Standard operating systems	Clear time frames for replying to communication media, and working in a congruent manner, eg defining how team meetings will operate.
Using appropriate technology	Telecommunications, Internet, e-mail, groupware, video conferencing, mobile phones, intranet.
Appropriate communication	Face to face when necessary, for conveying appropriate verbal and non-verbal information (tele-conferencing or webcam could be utilised here); remember: e-mail is relevant for simple tasks.
Building and maintaining interpersonal relationships	Teambuilding activities, possibly together at one venue; this is linked to training the work force to work together, virtually. Also they need to learn how to work and interact in a cohesive and trustworthy manner and, importantly, to respect each other cultural differences.
Selection	Ensure careful consideration is given to team-fit when selecting staff; also be clear about the skill level required in each area of the work, eg technical and interpersonal skills.
Maintaining levels of creativity	Motivate staff – ensure they have attainable goals.

Source: drawing on Axtell et al (2004), Watson and Gallagher (2005).

on the telephone. Remember that it may not be possible to use a webcam or tele-conferencing, and therefore vigilance to the nuances in the speed, quality and pitch in the voice, as well as the silences within the conversation, is especially critical in detecting alleviating any potential problems a member of staff may be experiencing. Figure 6.5, drawing on Williamson (2009), may help illustrate this point.

Figure 6.5 The importance of listening

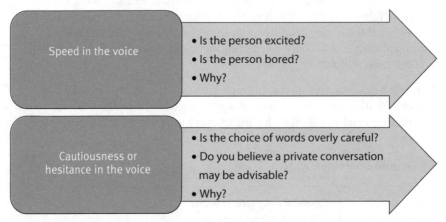

Speed in the voice
- Is the person excited?
- Is the person bored?
- Why?

Cautiousness or hesitance in the voice
- Is the choice of words overly careful?
- Do you believe a private conversation may be advisable?
- Why?

Source: drawing on Williamson (2009).

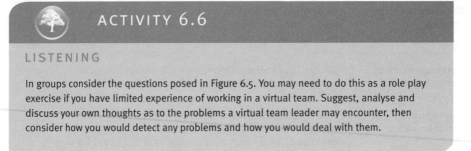

ACTIVITY 6.6

LISTENING

In groups consider the questions posed in Figure 6.5. You may need to do this as a role play exercise if you have limited experience of working in a virtual team. Suggest, analyse and discuss your own thoughts as to the problems a virtual team leader may encounter, then consider how you would detect any problems and how you would deal with them.

The following section will help illuminate many factors relating to group/team communication.

6.7 INTERACTIVE COMMUNICATION IN TEAMS

Communication has long had a key role in an organisation's effectiveness and it is therefore not surprising that managers spend much time communicating with others (Mintzberg 1989). Current and aspiring managers need to develop and hone their communication skills to make use of a wide range of different communication methods and to put information and ideas across more effectively. Both written communication through memos, proposals, reports, and oral communication through presentations, interviews, negotiations, mediation, coaching, and so on are indispensable tools for managerial communication.

Face-to-face (and telephone) communication is fast, personal and offers immediate feedback. However, it can be costly, time-consuming and there is often a need to follow it with a document. Written communication occurs through different media, offers the sender an opportunity to formulate the message prior to sending it, can be widely disseminated, and provides a record. Strategies for group communication need to be driven by three considerations (Praxis Consulting Group 1994):

- the purpose for communicating
- the audience
- the available resources.

The communicator must know his or her purpose but not assume that the audience would automatically share it. The message must be audience-specific, so the vocabulary and the amount of detail must be determined by the audience's needs. For a good fit, the following questions must first be answered:

- How much do the audience know about the subject?
- Are they likely to agree with the presented position or advice?
- What kind of advice have they heard recently on this topic?
- How did they react?

Finally, the scope of communication is defined by available resources such as time, money, energy and available information.

Both oral and written communications are supported by non-verbal elements. Non-verbal communication is not coded into words, but consists of kinesic behaviour, proxemics, paralanguage and object language, and it would be difficult to imagine any type of interaction without it.

- Kinesic behaviour conveys feelings about discussed issues through body movements, posture and facial expressions.
- Proxemics refers to the impact that distance and space has on interaction. This, for example, imposes degrees of formality or intimacy on situations.
- Paralanguage refers to vocal aspects of words, such as timbre, pitch, tone, laughing and yawning.
- Object language refers to the communicative aspects of the personal and physical environment, such as appearance, materials, furniture layout, architecture, and similar.

In communication, 'noise' is always present, threatening to distort the meaning of the message. The reasons for noise are many, including the chosen medium, and the fact that the sender may articulate poorly and the receiver may not be a good listener. Inserting feedback into communication is useful; it acknowledges that the message was sent and received. There are three types of feedback: informational, corrective and reinforcing:

- Informational feedback requires a non-evaluative response; it merely indicates that a message was received. It may include additional information.
- Corrective feedback challenges or corrects the original message.
- Reinforcing feedback requires a response that a message was received.

For communication to be effective, a total listening environment must be created where a message is heard, nonverbal cues are observed, and hidden aspects of a message are not missed. Figure 6.6 shows the three-dimensional aspects of a message: formal to informal, verbal to nonverbal and explicit to hidden meanings are pulled together with a feedback loop.

Figure 6.6   Interpersonal communication in the total environment

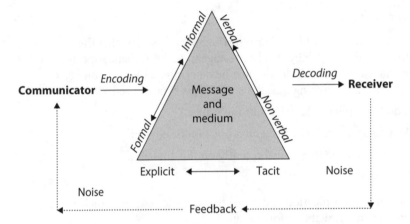

As organisations become larger and or more complex, networking and flattening of structures become necessary. These need to be supported by integrated horizontal communications. Historically, horizontal communication was evident in informal networking activities such as socialising and politicking, although there is need for integration into the formal organisational structure. Giving social support operates well within one level, but fails in upward or downward communications. However, organisations remain comfortable with vertical, 'downward' (management to employees) communication processes. Vertical communication is directive and purposeful, although for teamwork to be effective the communication process must move to more horizontal interaction (Bradford and Kozlowski 2002, Bradley et al 2002, Maznewski and Chudoba 2000, Graetz et al 1998).

There are four reasons for integrated interactive communication (Luthans 2005):

- **Task co-ordination**: For teamwork to be effective and to stay on course, team members must regularly meet and discuss the work in progress.
- **Problem-solving**: The team members use their problem-solving skills to approach a given problem or opportunity, and decide how to minimise potential crisis situations. A number of techniques can be used such as brainstorming, the best and worst scenario.

- **Information sharing**: The team decides on how to access necessary information.
- **Conflict resolution**: The team will meet to share feedback and develop techniques to resolve inherent conflicts arising from their activities.

Praxis Consulting Group (1994) developed a set of effective group communication principles consisting of five stages: Set, Support, Sequence, Access and Polish (SSSAP). The key objective of the principles is to improve the uptake of new ideas in organisations. The assumptions behind the five steps are relatively simple, based on creating an atmosphere for audience acceptance (see Figure 6.7).

The SSSAP principles outline the following techniques:

I.   SET commences with building a rapport between the presenters and the audience, who are usually the decision-makers. Competent presenters are in place, relaxed and friendly when the audience arrives. At the beginning they briefly outline the key issues of the presentation, the timing and/or the 'road map' the presentation will follow.

II. SUPPORT frames the presentation's facts and reasons and aims these at the opinion leaders in the audience. This takes three steps:

The above must be correct, concrete, complete, relevant and logical and supported by two or three examples of supporting evidence. Furthermore, the flow of arguments should mirror the way information is generally processed in the organisation, since unfamiliarity tends to lead to an increase in objections and counter-arguments.

III. SEQUENCE outlines the order of presentation:

Here the presenters must remember that the audience is likely to remember the opening and closing parts.

IV. ACCESS offers a number of steps to make presentations accessible by using appropriate visuals. Visuals must:

V.   POLISH. This last step closes the loop of effectiveness by emphasising that for the maximum impact presentations must be driven by purpose, audience and resources. The presentation must be polished through practice and appropriate attention must be given to details, visuals and the personal appearance of presenters.

Let us now consider another important aspect of communication in teams: the communication of feedback. Feedback is a two-way process that can improve communication among team members. Unfortunately, however, feedback is used in many organisations only to appraise performance or as a control tool. It is therefore not surprising that receiving feedback in particular can be anxious and emotionally charged. Even in the best of circumstances, giving and receiving feedback requires self-confidence and mutual trust. Managers often do not enter feedback situations in the right frame of mind and fail to consider how they feel about the individual about to receive feedback or how they could support him or her. In order to be effective, feedback requires both parties to be in frequent contact and to discuss concrete situations, regardless of whether these are

Figure 6.7 The Set–Support–Sequence–Access–Polish (SSSAP) framework for effective organisational and group communication

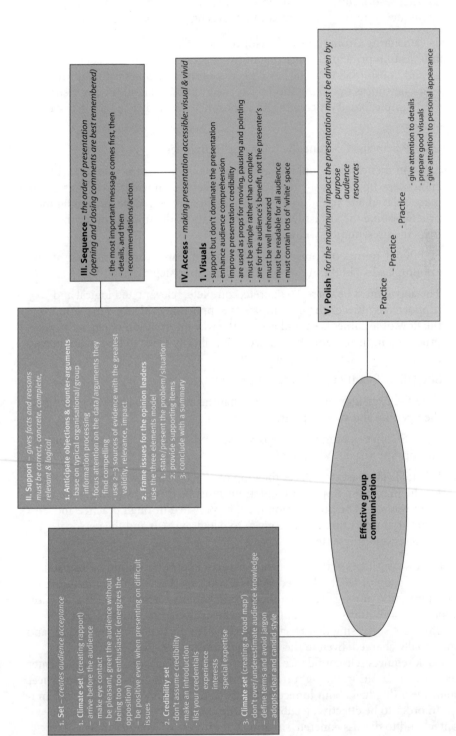

1. Set – *creates audience acceptance*

1. Climate set (creating rapport)
– arrive before the audience
– make eye contact
– be pleasant, greet the audience without being too too enthusiastic (energizes the opposition)
– be positive even when presenting on difficult issues

2. Credibility set
– don't assume credibility
– make an introduction
– list your credentials
      experience
      interests
      special expertise

3. Climate set (creating a 'road map')
– don't over/underestimate audience knowledge
– define terms and avoid jargon
– adopts clear and candid style

II. Support – *gives facts and reasons must be correct, concrete, complete, relevant & logical*

1. Anticipate objections & counter-arguments
– base on 'typical organisational/group information processing
– focus attention on the data/arguments they find compelling
– use 2–3 sources of evidence with the greatest validity, relevance, impact

2. Frame issues for the opinion leaders
use the three elements model
      1. state/present the problem/situation
      2. provide supporting items
      3. conclude with a summary

III. Sequence – *the order of presentation (opening and closing comments are best remembered)*

– the most important message comes first, then
– details, and then
– recommendations/action

IV. Access – *making presentation accessible: visual & vivid*

1. Visuals
– support but don't dominate the presentation
– enhance audience comprehension
– improve presentation credibility
– are used as props for moving, pausing and pointing
– must be simple rather than complex
– are for the audience's benefit, not the presenter's
– must be well rehearsed
– must be readable for all audience
– must contain lots of 'white' space

V. Polish - *for the maximum impact the presentation must be driven by:*
      purpose
      audience
      resources

– Practice

      – Practice

            – Practice

                  – give attention to details
                  – prepare good visuals
                  – give attention to personal appearance

Effective group communication

Source: drawing on Praxis Consulting Group (1994).

positive or negative. Quinn et al (2003 p53) list the following guidelines for giving effective feedback:

- Before giving feedback, check your motivation and make sure the other person is ready and open to hear it.

- Make sure to give the person feedback in a private place that allows for further dialogue.

- Use 'I' rather than 'you'; after all, these are your thoughts, perceptions and feelings.

- Start with the positive, before addressing the negative issues. This sets the tone of the meeting. If only positive or only negative issues are discussed, the feedback loses its credibility.

- Discuss only concrete examples of behaviour; generalised statements say more about your attitude than about the other person.

- The examples discussed must be timely. Old examples may be dated and consequently annoying.

- Ask the other person to clarify, explain, change or correct what you said.

- After giving feedback, give the receiver time to respond.

Like other managerial skills, giving and receiving feedback requires self-awareness, and it is therefore not surprising that many organisations offer training in this, often as part of the appraisal process. In addition to knowledge about how to give and receive feedback, this requires constant practice, and we encourage you to take every opportunity to practise this vital skill.

ACTIVITY 6.7

GIVING AND RECEIVING FEEDBACK

In order to practise giving feedback, write a short evaluation about yourself. Then select someone you consider as 'safe' and friendly, although not someone you are close to. Ask him or her to do the same. Place yourself in the other person's shoes (use empathy and ask yourself how it feels to be that person), and then read his or her self-evaluation. Arrange a joint session with the person at a place and time where you will not be disturbed. Swap your self-evaluations and give the other person feedback on it.

Then ask yourself:

- Did you check that the other person was in the right frame of mind to hear your feedback?

- Were you able to say what you wanted to say? What response did you get?

- Did you have clear idea what you wanted to accomplish before the meeting?

- How were you affected by the feedback you received?

- Would you make any changes in the future?

6.8 BARRIERS TO TEAMBUILDING AND CONFLICT RESOLUTION

As we have seen in previous sections of this chapter, teams do not just happen; they need commitment, investment and training as well as knowledge about effective teambuilding. It must be emphasised that teamwork is destined to fail in many organisations where team activities are not rewarded and in which mistrust, negative feelings and unresolved conflicts are rife. In organisational cultures where team activities are not rewarded and where mistrust, negative feelings and unresolved conflicts exist, teams are unlikely to flourish. The result of ineffective or failed teamwork is often conflict. Indeed, there is evidence that 20 per cent of management time is spent on resolving conflict (Haynes 2008).

One view of conflict, the unitary perspective, considers an organisation to be a happy family, with loyal employees who pull together in harmony to achieve the organisation's goals. Conflict tends to be explained in terms of poor communication, personality clashes or the work of troublemakers. Managers who claim that their work units run smoothly and without any conflict are either exceptionally self-aware and skilful communicators or, more likely, are suppressing conflict. Due to their very nature, suppressed conflicts do not allow resolution and therefore stifle any meaningful interaction between individuals and groups, often with major impact on overall staff morale and productivity. Conflicts may arise from a variety of reasons, such as differences in personal communication styles, levels of inarticulateness, hidden agendas or status. Workplace norms and patterns of communication (values, assumptions, self-image) can lead to insecurity and fear among individuals or groups, which in term may result in a variety of defensive types of behaviour (Argyris and Schön 1996).

Another view of conflict, the pluralistic perspective, accepts conflict as an inherent part of the organisation. Conflict situations can and do arise from the organisational structure, the size of the workforce, standardisation of jobs and increased levels of hierarchy. The word 'conflict' conveys negativity and things being out of control, although conflicts can and often do bring benefits by fostering creative thinking in seeking resolution. Hatch (1997), for instance, argues that a low level of conflict is often associated with poorly focused, unmotivated and ill-integrated teams, while too much conflict leads to a lack of co-operation, distraction from the overall goal and hostility. Hence, the trick for managers and team leaders is to find and encourage a healthy level of conflict that can produce cohesive, productive and co-operative teams. Such an approach requires all parties to jointly identify the sources of any problem, to agree on what the problem is and to seek different solutions.

Situations like this may be familiar to you; there have been minor disagreements that over time have led to conflict through a series of steps or layers (Open University 1985, cited in Senior and Fleming 2006, p221). Many conflicts begin with a simple misunderstanding, followed by the effects of different values, viewpoints and interests of the parties involved, which can lead to interpersonal differences when emotions like irritation, anger and frustration come into play. There are different conflict-handling styles, ranging from the avoidance of

ACTIVITY 6.8

SUE WILLIS AND DAVID BURNS

This activity gives you an opportunity to practise effective communication in a manager–employee situation. This will encourage you to think clearly about the expectations different roles in organisations carry. Access the case study on the companion website and read it carefully. Make notes about the situation presented in this case. The following activity takes two steps:

1. The class is to be divided into dyads to role-play the problem situation simultaneously, in a 'hands-on' way. Each dyad has an impartial observer, who will take notes and give a brief feedback to both role-players. If this proves difficult, then two volunteers may perform for the whole class, while the class attentively observes.

2. At the end of the role-play, carry out a group discussion:

3. At the end of the role-play, carry out a group discussion:

   i.   Identify the main points of the conflict.

   ii. What really happened there? What was (were) the underlying problem(s), if any?

   iii. How easy was it to role-play? Where there some issues, you felt that could not be discussed?

   iv. How difficult was it to communicate a frank feedback?

   v.   Were there situations that were inexcusable?

conflict through competing, compromising and collaboration to accommodating (Thomas 1976). Each manager or team leader will have his or her own style, and different situations and contexts will require different styles of dealing with conflict.

6.9 CONCLUSION

Teambuilding can be enthralling, enjoyable and even exasperating at times. The theoretical and practical situations discussed in this chapter were assembled to assist you in developing the necessary skills to participate and bring together individuals effectively under the banner of 'teams'. We have also discussed the need for good communication and feedback delivered in a relevant and sensitive manner, and explored conflict in team situations.

Groups and teams have long intrigued scholars of management and organisations as well as management practitioners but there is still a long way to go to create effective teams reliably and consistently. One reason for this may be the sheer complexity of human interaction to which team members bring their personalities, life stories and prior experiences, which often results in complex group, team or organisational dynamics. The challenge for managers and team leaders is to turn a group of often diverse individuals into cohesive and functioning teams; team leadership will be discussed in Chapter 16 of this book.

PAUSE FOR THOUGHT

Identify at least three things that you have learned by studying this chapter and engaging with the activities. How will your newly acquired knowledge and skills support your continuing professional development? What value do you expect your learning to have for your daily routines and your further career? In what area have you identified a need for further development and how are you planning to fill that gap? Address these issues in your learning journal and/or CPD log. You may also wish to discuss them with a peer, colleague, mentor or coach to aid your further development.

 KEY LEARNING POINTS

- Recognise and manage the stages in team development.

- Harness the techniques of team development and evaluate which method suits a particular situation.

- Take an enlightened view of team roles and an individual's self-worth within the team.

- Be sensitive to the nuances of co-ordinating a virtual team successfully.

- Having developed a deeper knowledge and understanding of the vital role communication has when building a team show the skills necessary to give quality feedback and reflect on the outcome.

 EXPLORE FURTHER

Belbin Associates: http://www.belbin.com or http://www.belbin.info [accessed 30 May2010].

BELBIN, R.M. (2007) *Management teams: why they succeed or fail*. London: Elsevier Butterworth Heinemann.

CANNALL, M. (2009) *CIPD Fact sheet: team working*. Revised August 2009. London: CIPD.

STRACHAN, A. (2004) Lights, camera, interaction. *People Management*. 16 September, p44. Available online at: http://www.peoplemanagement.co.uk/pm/articles/2004/09/LightsCameraInteraction.htm [accessed 26 May 2010].

STEVENS, M. (2010) Public sector 'intellectually but not emotionally engaged'. *People Management*, 26 January. Available online at: http://www.peoplemanagement.co.uk/pm/articles/2010/01/public-sector-intellectually-but-not-emotionally-engaged.htm [accessed 26 May 2010].

6.10 REFERENCES

ADAIR, J. (1986) *Effective teambuilding*. Aldershot: Gower.

ALLCORN, S. (1985) What makes groups tick. *Personnel*. September, pp52–58.

ARANDA, E.K., ARANDA, L. and CONLON, K. (1998) *Teams: structure, processes, culture and politics*. New York: Prentice-Hall.

ARGYRIS, C. and SCHÖN, D.A. (1996) *Organisational learning II*. Reading, MA: Addison-Wesley.

ARNISON, L. and MILLER, P. (2002) Virtual teams: a virtue for the conventional team. *Journal of Workplace Learning*. Vol. 14, No. 4, pp166–173.

AXTELL, C., WHELLER, J., PATTERSON, M. and LEACH, A. (2004) From a distance. *People Management*. 25 March, p39.

BALES, R.F. and SLATER, P.E. (1955) Role differentiation in small decision-making groups. In T. Parsons and R.F. Bales (eds), *Family socialisation and interaction process issues*. Glencoe: Free Press, pp259–306.

BARTOL, K.M. and MARTIN, D.C. (1991) *Management*. International ed. New York: McGraw-Hill Irwin.

BELBIN, R.M. (1981) *Management teams: why they succeed or fail*. London: Heinemann.

BELBIN, R.M. (1996) *Team roles at work*. London: Butterworth Heinemann.

BELBIN ASSOCIATES (2006) *Cert UK*. Available from: barrie.watson@belbin.info [accessed 20 May 2010].

BELBIN, R.M. (2007) *Management teams: why they succeed or fail*. London: Elsevier Butterworth Heinemann.

BELL, B.S. and KOZLOWSKI, S.W.J. (2002) A typology of virtual teams. *Group and Organisation Management*. Vol. 27, No. 1, pp14–59.

BENNE, K.D. and SHEATS, P. (1948) Functional roles of group members. *Journal of Social Issues*. Vol. 4, No. 2, pp41–49.

BRADFORD, S.B. and KOZLOWSKI, W.J. (2002) A typology of virtual teams. *Group and Organisation Management*. Vol. 27, No. 1, pp14–49.

BRADLEY, L.K., ROSEN, B., GIBSON, C.B., TESLIK, P.E. and MCPHERSON, S.O. (2002) Five challenges to virtual teams success. *Academy of Management Executive*. Vol. 16, No. 3, p67.

CANNALL, M. (2009) *CIPD Fact sheet: team working*. Revised August 2009. London: CIPD.

CASCIO, W.F. and SHURYGAILO, S. (2003) E-leadership and virtual teams. *Organisational Dynamics*. Vol. 31, No. 4, 362–376.

CLEGG, S., KORNBERGER, M. and PITSIS, T. (2005) *Managing and organisations*. London: Sage.

FAYOL, H. (1949) *General and industrial management*. London: Pitman.

GRAETZ, K.A., BOYLE, E.S., KIMBLE, C.E., THOMPSON, P. and GARLOCH, J.L. (1998) Information sharing in face-to-face teleconferencing and electronic chat rooms. *Small Group Research*. Vol. 29, No. 6, pp714–743.

GREENBERG, J. and BARON, R.A. (1997) *Behavior in organisations*. New York: Prentice-Hall.

GUNDUZ, H.B. (2008) An evaluation of Belbin's team roles theory. *World Applied Science Journal*. Vol. 4, No. 3, pp460–469.

HALL, R.H. (1991) *Organisations*. 4th ed. Harlow: Prentice Hall.

HATCH, M.J. (1997) *Organisation theory: modern symbolic and postmodern perspectives*. Oxford: Oxford University Press.

HAYNES, G. (2008) *Managerial communication: strategies and applications*. 4th international ed. New York: McGraw-Hill Irwin.

HOGAN, R., HOGAN, J. and ROBERTS, B.W. (1994) What we know about leadership. *American Psychologist*. Vol. 49, No. 5, pp493–504.

JACKSON, N. and CARTER, P. (2000) *Rethinking organisational behaviour*. Harlow: FT Prentice Hall.

JANIS, I.L. (1972) *Victims of groupthink*. Boston: Houghton Mifflin.

LEE-KELLY, L. and SANKEY, T. (2008) Global virtual teams for value creation and project success. *International Journal of Project Management*. Vol. 26, pp51–62. Elsevier.

LIPNACK, J. and STAMP, J. (2000) *Virtual teams*. 2nd ed. New York: Wiley.

LUTHANS, F. (2005) *Organisational behavior*. 10th international ed. New York: McGraw-Hill.

MAZNEWSKI, M.L. and CHUDOBA, K.M. (2000) Bridging space over time. *Organisation Science*. Vol. 11, No. 5, pp473–492.

MCKENNA, E. (1999) *Business psychology and organisational behaviour*. London: Taylor and Francis.

MINTZBERG, H. (1989) *Mintzberg on management*. New York: Free Press.

MULLEN, B. and COOPER, C. (1994) The relation between group cohesiveness and performance. *Psychology Bulletin*. Vol. 115, No. 2, pp210–232.

MULLINS, L. (1991) Management and organisational behaviour. London: Pitman.

OZBILGIN, M. (2005) *International human resource management: theory and practice*. Basingstoke: Palgrave.

PETZINGER, T. (1999) *The new pioneers: the men and women who are transforming the workplace and marketplace*. New York: Simon and Schuster.

PRAXIS CONSULTING GROUP. (1994) *Presenting with power: a guidebook*. Provo: UT.

QUINN, R.E., FAERMAN, S.R., THOMPSON, M.P. and MCGRATH, M.R. (2003) *Becoming a master manager: a competency framework*. 3rd ed. Chichester: Wiley.

SCHEIN, E.H. (1988) *Organisational psychology*. 3rd international ed. New York: Prentice-Hall.

SENIOR, B. and FLEMING, J. (2006) *Organisational change*. 3rd ed. Harlow: FT Prentice Hall.

STRACHAN, A. (2004) Lights, camera, interaction. *People Management*. 16 September, p44. Available online at: http://www.peoplemanagement.co.uk/pm/articles/2004/09/LightsCameraInteraction.htm [accessed 26 May 2010].

STEVENS, M. (2010) Public sector 'intellectually but not emotionally engaged'. *People Management*. 26 January. Available online at: http://www.peoplemanagement.co.uk/pm/articles/2010/01/public-sector-intellectually-but-not-emotionally-engaged.htm [accessed 26 May 2010].

THOMAS, K.W. (1976) Conflict and conflict management. M.D. Dunette (ed), *Handbook of industrial and organisational psychology*. Chicago, ILL: Rand McNally, 900.

THOMAS, K.W. (2000) *Intrinsic motivation at work*. San Francisco: Berrett-Kohler.

TOWNSEND, A., DEMARIE, S. and HENDERSON, A. (1998) Virtual teams: technology and the workplace of the future. *Academy of Management Executive*. Vol. 12, No. 3, pp17–29.

TUCKMAN, B.W. (1965) Developmental sequence in small groups. *Psychological Bulletin*. Vol. 63, No. 6, pp384–399.

WATSON, G. and GALLAGHER, K. (2005) *Managing for results*. 2nd ed. London: CIPD.

WILLIAMSON, B. (2009) Managing virtually: First, get dressed. *Business Week*. 17 June, p19.

CHAPTER 7

Negotiating and liaising within the political organisation

Ivana Adamson *and* Gillian Watson

OVERVIEW

Organisations are not only social but also political entities and therefore the focus of this chapter is on negotiating and liaising in such a political environment. Power and politics in organisations are the key determinants of negotiated outcomes. Negotiating is a process of combining conflicting positions into a common one – a problem-solving activity in which the outcome is shaped by the process.

LEARNING OUTCOMES

By the end of this chapter, provided you engage with the activities, you should be able to:

- understand the roles of power and politics in organisations
- identify the power bases of individuals and groups
- understand how power and politics can lead to conflict
- apply negotiation skills to resolve conflict situations effectively
- identify the common mistakes that negotiators make.

7.1 INTRODUCTION

Organisations are social entities in which individuals from diverse backgrounds come together to work towards a common goal. Complex systems of rules and procedures seek to govern life in organisations and it is power that helps those in charge to ensure that all members of the organisation comply with these rules and procedures (Clegg et al 2005). Hence, power is a central feature of organisational life that 'forms the core of a tight nexus of ideas that include politics, control, leadership, and conflict' (Gabriel 2008, p231).

It is therefore not surprising that the notion of power has long intrigued organisational leaders and scholars alike and that much work has been done over the last century to understand what power is, how it can be gained and how it is used and abused in an organisational setting. Power in organisations is often regarded as 'the ability to get someone to do something that they do not particularly want to do' (Jackson and Carter 2000, p76) and derives from a variety of sources, which include authority and organisational politics.

The concept of authority is rooted in the work by German sociologist Max Weber's (1978) work on effective organisations and refers to power vested in an individual's position within the organisational hierarchy, which is perceived as legitimate by peers and subordinates. It can derive from the person's charisma, from tradition or from a rational system of rules (as summarised by Gabriel 2008) and is also known as formal position power (French and Raven 1968).

Politics 'is the process through which different groups and individuals seek to promote or defend their interests ... through the use, direct or indirect, of power' (Gabriel 2008, p223). Political behaviour, then, refers to 'what happens when members of organisations behave in ways that are potentially authoritatively illegitimate' (Clegg et al 2005, p161) and often occurs when individuals or groups of organisational members make a claim against those in power (Pettigrew 2002). Hence, power and politics are part of a two-way process flowing simultaneously in a top-down and bottom-up direction, and this will be discussed in more detail later in this chapter.

As power and politics are closely linked with the potential of conflict (Gabriel 2008), they are also closely linked with the need for negotiation and liaising in organisations. The remainder of this chapter will elaborate on this discussion of power and politics before moving on to skills of negotiation required by managers, team leaders and other roles of responsibility and authority.

ACTIVITY 7.1

POWERFUL INFLUENCES IN YOUR LIFE AND CAREER

The purpose of this activity is to reflect on those individuals that have had (or are having) a powerful influence on your life and career. Think as far back in your life/career as you can, then list all influential people in chronological order and describe the context in which they influenced your life. Answer the following questions:

1. Who were these people?
2. What did they do to affect your life or career?
3. Why did that person influence your life or career?

Try to identify an emerging pattern in your list and remember that not all people who are influential in our lives have to have a formal position of power. They could be friends, family members, teachers, neighbours, even total strangers. Keep your answers for the next activity.

7.2 POWER IN ORGANISATIONS

The primary purpose of power in organisations, as outlined above, is to ensure that all members of the organisation comply with its rules, procedures and other systems that govern it (Clegg et al 2005). Power has therefore a central part in the creation of effective organisations. Weber (1978) maintains in particular that the members of an organisation will accept their leaders' or managers' power (or rather authority) and comply with their wishes. This view of organisations is prevalent today, as charts of an organisation's hierarchy will testify.

Individuals and groups in organisations draw their power from a number of sources. Five such power bases in particular have long been identified (French and Raven 1968) and will help you to better understand why some people can exert influence over you and others.

- **Legitimate power** derives from the assumption that an individual or group has the right to make demands, which suggests that they expect compliance and obedience from others in return. This type of power is common between employer and employee or manager and subordinate. Legitimate power is sometimes regarded as part of position power.

- **Reward power** derives from an individual's ability to compensate others for their compliance. This is also a very common power base in organisations, particularly between employer and employee or manager and subordinate, as employers or managers have the ability to pay (or otherwise reward) their employees or subordinates if they do as told. Legitimate power is sometimes regarded as part of position power.

- **Coercive power** derives from the ability to punish others if they do not comply. Again, this is a common type of power between employer and employee or manager and subordinate, as employers or managers have the ability to penalise or punish their employees or subordinates if they do not do as told. Legitimate power is also sometimes regarded as part of position power.

- **Expert power** derives from an individual's knowledge, skills or expertise. This type of power is not generally associated with status or position in an organisation as there will be individuals and groups with expert power at all hierarchical levels. It is this type of power that individuals and groups will use to exert influence through political behaviour, particularly if they perceive themselves as having little power apart from their knowledge, skills or expertise.

- **Reference power** derives from an individual's perceived attractiveness and worthiness. It is the power that makes us strive to become 'just like X' and is a type of personal power.

Individuals and groups in organisations can have more than one source of power (French and Raven 1968) and there is often considerable overlap in the sources of power. Individuals may have position power resulting from their position in the organisation's hierarchy (eg as supervisor, team leader, manager, director), from personal power (eg charisma, expert knowledge and skills) and from networking power that allows them to establish valuable networks of contacts. In many instances, the position that individuals hold is directly related to their legitimate power. In other words, the higher the position, the greater are the opportunity to exercise power by using reward and coercion. Personal power, on the other hand, is exercised through interpersonal relationships, and the individual's success or failure depends on the benefits received from relationships with others, on networking as well as their motivation, efforts and abilities (Baker 2000). These power bases of individuals are graphically represented in Figure 7.1 below.

Figure 7.1 Individual power bases

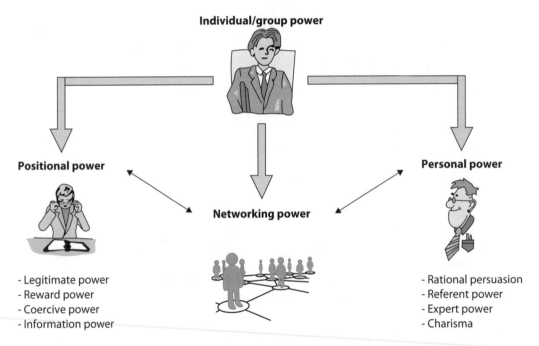

Individual/group power

Positional power

Networking power

Personal power

- Legitimate power
- Reward power
- Coercive power
- Information power

- Rational persuasion
- Referent power
- Expert power
- Charisma

Many an aspiring employee or manager will have wondered how to gain power in organisations, and Luthans (2005) has summarised the following strategies:

- developing knowledge and expertise
- using research to support one's viewpoint
- seeking support
- withdrawing from petty disputes.

This list contains legitimate ways to enhance one's expert, referent and personal power, which many striving to climb the career ladder will employ to enhance their reputation and value as professionals. However, Luthans' (2005) summary does not end here but continues with more dubious activities such as promoting limited communication, controlling access to key information and/or resources, making strategic replacements of key people and keeping other members of the organisation in the dark about one's hidden agenda. These are not only opportunistic, but also unethical and often unlawful. We will discuss these in more detail in Section 7.3 of this chapter.

The trick for managers and leaders is to motivate individuals to seek to enhance their power base through the development of their knowledge, skills and expertise (this is important for developing a pool of talent within an organisation, see Chapter 1) while discouraging them from engaging in damaging political behaviour (Covey et al 1999). Organisational leaders can encourage individuals by:

- listening to their concerns and sharing ideas (this is often done in a collaborative style of leadership)

- clarifying expectations and responsibilities (this includes, for instance, spelling out the steps to promotion)

- giving credit where credit is due (both through saying 'thank you' and through financial and other rewards)

- supporting the individuals' professional development

- acknowledging interdependence.

This implies that organisational leaders and managers must provide a climate in which such behaviours are not only encouraged but can thrive (as summarised by Mullins 2005). This involves recognition of individuals' differences and attributes as well as their needs, their expectations, their hopes and fears. This also involves integration of personal and organisational goals. Finally, it involves just and fair systems and procedures that create and maintain a climate of trust in the organisation in which open discussion and democratic decision-making can take place.

ACTIVITY 7.2

YOUR PERSONAL POWER BASE

In the previous activity, you gained a clearer understanding of the powerful influences in your life and career. Now consider your own power base and those in your own circle of influence. Answer the following questions:

- What makes you influential?

- What have you done recently to influence others?

- How can you increase your circle of influence?

- How political is your behaviour?

Compare your answers with those in Activity 7.1. Is there an emerging pattern?

7.3 POLITICS: THE KEY ORGANISATIONAL MOVER

There is one major problem with Weber's (1978) view of power: the assumption that the members of an organisation behave rationally to achieve the goals set by management, thus making management the facilitators of these goals (Jackson and Carter 2000). In reality, however, few members of an organisation will be rational as each of them bring with them their identities, knowledge, skills, experiences, hopes, fears and aspirations. Individuals and groups in organisations, regardless of their position in the official organisational hierarchy, will have their own ideas of how to go about their work and how to improve the organisation. In many organisations, such a feedback process is encouraged through reports, suggestions, comments and complaints. It is supported through a collaborative style of leadership that includes a wide range of individuals and groups in the decision-making process.

However, in some organisations this formal process of participation breaks down and organisational members may feel powerless and in need of protection for their interests (Pfeffer 1992). They may resort to informal means of getting their views across such as manipulative persuasion, leaking information, whistle-blowing and a host of political games identified by Mintzberg (2002). The latter include insurgency games against the ruling elite, alliance-building games to gain support from peers, budgeting games to secure resources and expertise games to achieve expert power (French and Raven 1968). This informal flow of power (or political behaviour) often leads to conflict due to differences in goals, interests or values of different players in the organisation that cannot be resolved.

We need to bear in mind here that rules, procedures and policies in organisations are subject to interpretation by their members and that this interpretation can differ considerably in line with their identity and prior experiences. Hence, not all disagreement in organisations is political behaviour, and it is often difficult to distinguish between innocent differences in opinion (which can lead to a healthy level of conflict) and potentially damaging political behaviour.

The negotiation of power and influence requires support from other individuals or groups. However, only those individuals and groups that have power – regardless of their source(s) – have the opportunity to get others on their side. Hence, organisations merely mirror the reflections of society at large by being composed of coalitions competing with each other for resources and influence (Nord 1978). Individuals and groups in organisations use a wide range of approaches to influence others and build such coalitions, which Greenberg and Baron (1997, p103–104) summarise as follows:

- Rational persuasion uses logical arguments and facts as a means for achieving desired goals.
- Inspirational appeal uses an emotional approach based on shared personal values and beliefs.
- Consultation is an appeal for participation in the decision-making process.
- Ingratiation is an appeal to an individual's vanity.
- Exchange is seeking something for something else.

- Personal appeal is an appeal for support of loyalty and friendship.

- Coalition-building is seeking support from like-minded others.

- Legitimating is using a position of authority as a legitimate request for assistance or support.

- Pressure is seeking compliance by using personal power.

The main objective of these coalitions is to protect their interests and position of influence and, consequently, the unequal distribution of power in organisations can marginalise some individuals and groups. It can also involve corrupt and therefore unethical and potentially illegal practices such as personally profiting from relationships with one's customers or suppliers, or recruiting or promoting friends or favourites rather than those who are best suited for the job. It is therefore not surprising that organisational politics has been identified as a major stressor in the workplace (Laurance and Radford 2003) that can hinder employees' development and can create division, anxiety and burnout (Ferris et al 2002, Harris and Kacmar 2005).

NORTHERN COLLEGE OF BUSINESS AND INDUSTRY

CASE STUDY 7.1

Northern College of Business and Industry (NCBI) is a small university offering generic business-related degrees to students and tailor-made courses to employers. NCBI is a popular choice for local students as it has a reputation for being easily accessible, friendly, supportive and, most importantly, for offering a good education. NCBI staff hold a review of their programmes of study at the end of each academic year to see whether they still 'fit the bill'. This year, however, there is concern about the personal development module running across all undergraduate programmes. There is general consensus that this module is somewhat outdated and does not meet recent concerns such as enhancing students' employability.

There are three different options of how to take this module further. The first option is to make minor changes to the module content only to include employability and other topics of interest. The second option is to replace it with a specialist skills module developed by a national consortium of skills experts, in which some of NCBI staff are involved. The third option is to replace it with a learning initiative

module.

Charles is in charge of programme development at NCBI and knows exactly which option he favours. He has great regard for Clare, who is behind the learning initiatives option that is largely based on her research. The problem is that this is not his decision alone but a decision in which all heads of programme (HoPs) are involved after consultation with their teaching staff. Charles is a bit annoyed by this – it would be so much easier if he could decide on his own – and has had to spend quite a few weekends drawing up a 'battle plan' of how to get his way.

The six HoPs heads of programme involved in this decision are Bill (human resources), Paul (strategy), Clare (marketing), Les (finance), Sue (management) and Anne (retail). In addition, the head of department thought it necessary to appoint an expert in the field to assist decision-making; this is Mary who is involved with the nationwide skills module.

Charles, who has been with NCBI for many years, knows Bill, Paul and Anne very well; they are colleagues who have become friends. Charles is confident that they will back his plans, as will Clare, who will benefit from the adoption of her module on learning initiatives. Sue is a fairly new member of staff and is likely to go with whatever is decided, while Les, also a colleague for many years, does not belong to Charles's circle of friends. The only 'problem' person in this circle is Mary. She is well liked and respected among colleagues, and she is assertive and stubborn. Charles know that she will be his most dangerous opponent.

Charles decides to 'prepare' his friends for the forthcoming meeting at which the three proposals are due to be discussed. He invites Bill, Paul and Anne for a round of drinks in the local pub and as usual, they 'talk shop' while having a good time. Charles broaches the subject of the personal development module and makes it very clear how he thinks it should be developed further. Much to his surprise, Bill is not very happy about this proposal. He thinks that Clare's learning initiative module lacks substance at present and that they would be better off adopting the specialist skills module. Charles is even more surprised to find that Paul and Anne also have reservations about the learning initiative proposal.

Realising that he is losing ground with his closest allies, Charles decides to take matters one step further. He rings Sue and Anne that evening to get their support. Charles outlines the need to develop the personal development module and praises the learning initiative module to the heavens while ignoring the specialist skills module. At the end of their conversation, Sue and Anne agree to back Charles's proposals. 'That is better,' says Charles to himself, although he is aware that he has yet to solve the problem with Mary. He knows that if Mary is present at the meeting, she will get people behind her proposal – the specialist skills module. Charles cannot afford to lose face!

The next day, Charles goes to the admin office to check when his colleagues will be available for the all-important meeting. Much to his delight, Charles finds out that all colleagues will be free on Wednesday afternoon except Mary, who has a class all afternoon. Things could not go better. Charles is quick to send an e-mail to all colleagues to invite them to the meeting. On the agenda are first a discussion of the learning initiative module, followed by a debate about the personal development module and finally the specialist skills module. Charles expects, of course, that the group will run out of time and not be able to discuss the items further down on the agenda. He, as chair of the meeting, needs to ensure that they spend a long time on the first item.

●●●

'Hello Mary, how are you doing?'

'Not so bad, Sue. How are things with you?'

'Battling on, you know what it is like at this time of the year. By the way, are you going to this meeting on Wednesday afternoon?'

'What meeting?'

'Oh, you know, the meeting Charles is holding about the personal development module. It's on this Wednesday at 2pm.'

'Oh, no, please tell me it isn't. I've got a class all afternoon with executives from our local fire service that I can't miss.'

'That's a shame. Charles seems to be very determined to adopt Clare's learning initiative module and it would be good to have your expert opinion on that.'

'Is he really? Sue, I think we'd better have a cup of tea.'

Mary and Sue go into the cafeteria, and over a cup of tea Sue tells Mary about Charles's phone call and how he praised the learning initiatives module. Mary is fuming as she knows very well that the proposal at present lacks substance and that the specialist skills module would be a much better choice as it addresses a wider range of vital issues.

Mary decides that she will have to rally support against Charles's ideas and has a short conversation with Bill, in which she learns that he is opposed to adopting the learning initiatives module and he knows for sure that Paul is too. However, Bill is unsure about what to do because Charles asked him into his office in the morning to tell him that if he, Bill, did not back his, Charles's, proposals, Charles would give Kevin, a new colleague, responsibility for the human resources programme. Bill is very concerned about his future at NCBI as he has still a number of years left before retirement. Mary is shocked about this as she knows Bill and Charles are close friends. She offers Bill as much support as she can.

Mary also approaches Paul, Les and Anne individually to discuss what they really think about the learning initiative proposal. They are somewhat sceptical because in a meeting just the previous week Clare admitted that preliminary work on the module was not going very well. If Clare knows that it is not working, why take this risk? The specialist skills module, after all, has been developed by a range of specialists and the module is ready to be started.

It is Wednesday afternoon at 2 pm. Charles, Bill, Paul, Anne, Les, Sue and a secretary are assembled in the meeting room and the meeting is about to start.

Questions

- Identify Charles's bases of power and justify your answer.

- Analyse Charles's behaviour. To what extent is it political? Do you have any concerns about it? Justify your answer.

- Identify Mary's bases of power and justify your answer.

- Analyse Mary's behaviour. To what extent is it political? Do you have any concerns about it? Justify your answer.

- Imagine you are Sue, the new girl on the block. What are you making of this situation? How are you going to behave at the meeting? What will determine your behaviour?

- How do you think this scenario is likely to end? Justify your answer...

ACTIVITY 7.3

POLITICAL BEHAVIOUR IN YOUR ORGANISATION

Reflect on your experiences in an organisation or as part of a team. Have you come across political behaviour? Try to describe the situation in detail to identify who did what, how, when and why. How did you feel about that? What did you do?.

7.4 NEGOTIATING IN THE POLITICAL ORGANISATION

Every time we want or need something from others to achieve our aims, we engage in negotiating. We make our case and the other party makes theirs until, in most instances, an agreement is reached. When used well, negotiation becomes a skilful balancing act between maintaining relationships with others and satisfying our own needs. However, when engaging in political strategies or games, the situation can easily get out of hand and waste valuable time, resources and opportunities, as we will see in Case Study 7.3 towards the end of this chapter.

Negotiation is often associated with the resolution of conflict in organisations, which arises 'when people with differing needs or goals are prevented – or perceive that they are being prevented – by others in achieving these needs or goal' (Browaeys and Price 2008, p301). In order to resolve conflict, the parties in question must try to get together and resolve their differences. Power and politics have a key role in this process, as graphically represented in Figure 7.2 below.

We noted in the previous chapter that conflict is not negative per se but that organisations need a certain level of conflict to perform well (Hatch 1997). However, it is equally important to acknowledge that unresolved conflict is likely to increase the amount of political behaviour in organisations as its members may perceive that they have no other alternative to make their views heard, and we discussed the implications this may have on individuals, groups and the organisation as a whole in the previous section of this chapter.

Let us now consider the process of negotiation, which was traditionally regarded in terms of two fundamentally different outcomes: the 'win–lose' and the 'win–win' position (Walton and McKersie 1965). The 'win–lose' position assumes a fixed amount of reward to be had, which implies that one negotiator must win

Figure 7.2 Conflict resolution through negotiating and liaising

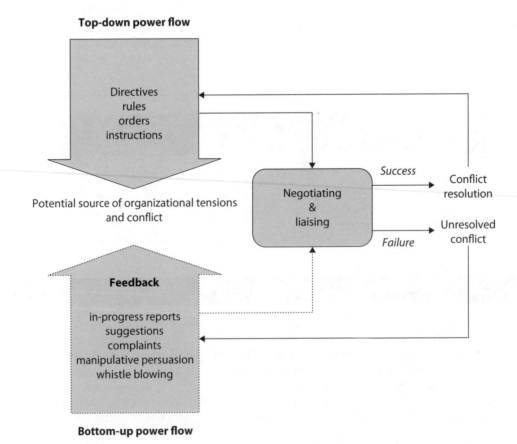

and the other must lose – 'the winner gets it all' is the motto here. The 'win–win' position in contrast focuses on achieving a mutually beneficial outcome for both parties despite there being a fixed reward. The latter is often a form of compromise in which neither party achieves everything they want but is still better off at the end of the negotiations than at the beginning.

There are different approaches to negotiation, which derive from different assumptions. Firstly, position negotiation describes negotiations as a power game, while strategic negotiating regards it as a repetitive game and process negotiating views it as bargaining. Integrative negotiations break the negotiating process into smaller, more self-contained stages, which turns a negotiation into a problem-solving activity. The negotiators' personal characteristics – such as power seeker, persuader, reliable performer or limited performer – have been identified as a major influence in the negotiating process (Gibson et al 2008). The power seeker with his or her prime concern about tasks and results is widely regarded as a good decision-maker, but can also be perceived as confrontational. The persuader uses ambiguity as a negotiating tool and is often seen as a potentially dangerous opponent. The reliable performer, with his or her resistance to sudden change, is regarded as solid and dependable but potentially not easy to convince. Finally, the limited performer, often an introvert, tends to lack self-confidence and is perceived to be indecisive and likely to crack under pressure.

So, what makes a successful negotiator? It has long been known that successful negotiators have three main characteristics: they are ambitious, possess effective negotiation skills and command power (Karrass 1970). Interestingly, highly skilled negotiators were found to be more benevolent, while less skilled negotiators succeeded when both powerful and ambitious. Successful negotiators will also be emotionally intelligent (Goleman 2005), which means that they are able to identify, use, understand and manage their own and other people's emotions (CIPD 2009).

This implies that emotionally intelligent negotiators are able to 'read' the situation in the negotiation process. They will know what kind of influence is acceptable for achieving agreement and commitment. They will strive to achieve the optimal outcomes in the first instance by basing their negotiating approaches on their perceptions of how the opponent is likely to respond. Skilled negotiators hope for and work towards a satisfactory agreement that avoids disaster and improves relationships between the negotiating parties (McKenna 1999). However, while outcomes may be considered successful by all parties, more often than not one party comes out better than the other, for instance in a budget allocation, an extension to a deadline or a better salary. It is therefore imperative for competent professionals to master the skill of negotiation so as to gain the recognition and remuneration they desire and to progress their career. Individuals who are uncomfortable in negotiations may feel demoralised, which in turn might lead to a reduction in organisational productivity (Haynes 2008).

Effective negotiators realise that their skill and technical competence alone will not do the trick. An important aspect of effective negotiation is the negotiator's 'social credit rating' based on the general impression of how competent, supportive and co-operative he or she is (Baker 2000). This rating is not fixed but changes in accordance with levels of trust and respect that an individual commands. We do not learn from those we do not respect, and committing to those we distrust is equally difficult.

Negotiation is a difficult skill to master because of the complex power dynamics prevalent in organisations. It is therefore very easy to make mistakes. Luthans (2005) lists a number of common mistakes by negotiators who hold on to their personal biases, which prevents them from negotiating more rationally and objectively and from achieving an acceptable outcome:

- thinking, acting and being influenced by a prescribed structure of the negotiating situation

- holding onto a previously selected course of action that is no longer appropriate, and thus missing an opportunity to improve the outcome of the negotiation

- holding on to a 'win–lose' approach, and thus missing mutually beneficial 'trade-offs' between the parties that could lead to an acceptable outcome

- accepting as given and working with the initial position

- relying too much on readily available information

- failing to incorporate new information by focusing excessively on the other party's perspective

- being overconfident.

This list of common mistakes by negotiators suggests that a far more fruitful approach to negotiation may be to turn it into a problem-solving activity that draws on the participants' creativity to seek different routes towards a win–win situation. Such an approach implies a concern for the other party (Pruitt and Rubin 1986), which can only support the negotiating process. Let us therefore explore the more productive integrative negotiating approach, also called liaising.

7.5 LIAISING IN ORGANISATIONS

Liaising is about 'cooperation on a matter of mutual concern' (*Oxford dictionary, thesaurus and wordpower guide* 2001), which resonates with notions of reconciling differences and mediating a settlement. Liaising can also be regarded an integrative approach to negotiation that turns bargaining into a problem-solving relationship in which all parties seek to achieve a genuine win–win situation. It is therefore a vital skill for managerial success. Let us illustrate what a successful negotiation may look like using such an integrative approach by the example of the Harvard Negotiation Project (Case Study 7.2).

The Harvard Negotiation Project provides managers, team leaders and others in roles of responsibility who participate in negotiations with a set of important rules that support constructive negotiation. However, negotiations are not always constructive, as numerous industrial strikes around the globe have shown.

THE HARVARD NEGOTIATION PROJECT – AN ILLUSTRATION

CASE STUDY 7.2

The Harvard Negotiation Project focused on the psychology of negotiation and examines why some needs in negotiations are fixed while others are open to negotiation. The approach is called 'principled negotiation' (Fisher et al 2003) and assumes that all negotiators are problem-solvers rather than adversaries. The method arising from this study comprises the following four principles.

- **People:** Separate people from the problem.
- **Interests:** Focus on goals, not positions.
- **Options:** Generate and explore alternative possibilities.
- **Criteria:** Base the outcomes on an objective standard.

Let us consider these four steps in more detail. Firstly, **separating people from problems** is about acknowledging the role of perception and emotion in communication and negotiation. It is not uncommon for negotiations to involve blaming others – their personalities, habits and behaviours – for misunderstandings and bruised egos. This step, therefore, seeks to raise awareness that relational conflicts are destructive and create no value whatsoever in the negotiating process. Once individuals have been blamed, they will feel under threat and spend valuable time defending themselves rather than negotiating or resolving conflict. *Task* conflicts, on the other hand, are positive since they often create new ideas and ways of thinking and working. The trick, then, is to focus on task conflicts by clarifying any situation, by asking questions and by actively listening to all parties involved. It may be necessary, however, to allow participants to let off steam before focusing on the negotiations in a calm and rational manner.

Focusing on interests, not positions, is about respecting the interests of all participants in the negotiation, which more often than not leads to a creative solution. It is imperative, however, that all parties involved communicate their interests to each other; this will avoid that the parties assuming that their interests are the same.

Inventing options for mutual gain is about generating and exploring alternative options in the negotiation process. Good negotiators always try to find ways to reduce their costs and to enhance the other party's benefit, leading to a 'win–win' situation. The trick is not to take the other party's position at face value. Questioning and probing are therefore likely to offer more satisfactory alternatives for all parties. It is important to acknowledge that negotiations can break down, and that in such a situation a process of mediation can help the parties to resume negotiations. Mediation means that 'the people directly in disagreement with each other work out a mutually acceptable solution with the help of a neutral person' (Laurance and Radford 2003). This requires the parties to acknowledge that conflict exists and that they are willing to look for a solution. The mediator has to remain neutral throughout the process and probe the positions and interests of all parties. It is imperative to focus on the problem and its impact on performance rather than on personalities. A skilled mediator will identify areas that all parties agree on and facilitate the reinstatement of the negotiation process.

Finally, **using objective criteria** means that negotiations must be based on principles rather than pressure, because there will be no winner in a negotiation if one party pushes their position in a wasteful 'yes-we-will, no-we-won't' cycle or until the other party backs down. The task for negotiators is to search jointly for objective criteria with which different positions can be evaluated and to be open to new ways of looking at a situation.

In short, 'principled negotiation' builds on the assumption that all parties in the negotiation wish to reach a 'win–win' outcome and that they therefore focus on achieving mutually beneficial outcomes. However, Fisher et al (2003) also acknowledge that negotiators face a range of challenges deriving from an often politically charged context. They refer in particular to one party resorting to dirty tricks and an uneven distribution of power in which the less powerful party has to protect its interests – even if this means walking out on the negotiation.

Industrial conflict is a classic example of a battle of wills over power, often with very little willingness to accept the other party's interests. In some instances, strikes have lasted for years! While it is very difficult to assess what leads to strike action and what could be done to avoid it, it is likely that bruised egos and other emotions have reduced the willingness of all parties to continue with the negotiations in a constructive manner.

ACTIVITY 7.4

CONFLICT AND NEGOTIATION

Research an industrial conflict in the recent past in detail using a variety of news media. Try to identify the parties who have an interest in the situation and the key negotiators. Try to identify also how they reached the point at which strike action was called by analysing the different steps in the negotiation process. What could have been done differently? What can you learn from this example?

There is evidence that the integrative approach to negotiation (or liaising) is more successful than traditional forms of negotiation for the following reasons (Quinn et al 2003):

- *Mutual purpose* is the first step in a dialogue, where a common purpose must be clarified and agreed upon.
- *Mutual meaning* involves establishing that the definitions, words and expressions used are mutually understood and agreed.
- *Mutual respect* is achieved by employing a constructive agreement, focusing on solving the problem at hand and by stopping the 'blaming game'.

The understanding of oneself and of others is an important aspect of liaising, and there are links to emotional intelligence (CIPD 2009). The need for self-awareness among managers and competent professionals has been alluded to throughout the previous chapters of this book, so let us know look at the Johari window (Luft 1984) as a means to enhance self-awareness in individual and group situations.

The Johari window was developed in 1955 as a tool to raise awareness in human behaviour and interpersonal relations. It is a two-by-two matrix that lists factors that are known to oneself and factors that are known to others. The four quadrants, therefore, are open (known to self and known to others), blind (not known to self but known to others), hidden (not known to others but known to self) and unknown (not known to self and not known to others). This is graphically represented in Figure 7.3.

The open area is knowledge about yourself that you is shared with others. This may be, for instance, that you are studying for a postgraduate degree or that you dislike anything to do with maths or figures. The blind area represents things that others may know about you but that you are unaware of yourself. A common example is the use of particular figures of speech, such as 'you know'. Other people tend to be much more aware of such quirks than we are ourselves. The hidden area is knowledge about you that you do not share with others. It may be feelings of inadequacy at work that other people may not be aware of because they see you as a confident person. Finally, the unknown area is about things that neither you nor others will know, and can refer to something deeply hidden inside you. Strictly speaking, the four quadrants do not have the same proportions as illustrated in the figure above; different individuals will have different profiles as their level of self-awareness and the availability of other information will vary. The trick is to increase Field 1 (open) and in that way decrease the blind, hidden and unknown fields. By interacting with each other, individuals will exchange knowledge and information (eg from open to open) and this interaction can also help to make unknown matters known, often leading to more energy and a better availability of personal resources. Mutual trust and skilful communication are the key to this.

Figure 7.3 The Johari window

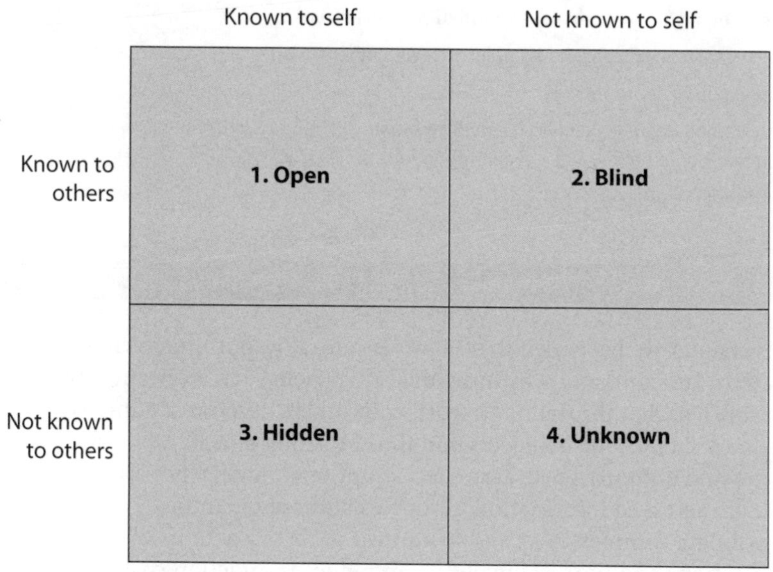

	Known to self	Not known to self
Known to others	1. Open	2. Blind
Not known to others	3. Hidden	4. Unknown

Source: J. Luft (1984), *Group process: an introduction to group dynamics*, 3rd edn., Fig. 7.4, p60. Palo Alto, CA: Mayfield. Reproduced by permission of The McGraw-Hill Companies.

We need to bear in mind that people often find it difficult to learn about themselves. This is partly because we all like to think that we are great and partly because friends and colleagues are often reluctant to be honest with us for fear of embarrassing us or causing conflict. When receiving unwelcome feedback in particular, bear in mind that the other person will only describe their perceptions of you – which, although real, may not be true. We have already discussed feedback in the previous chapter, so it is time now to apply the Johari window.

ACTIVITY 7.5

APPLYING THE JOHARI WINDOW

Before you begin this activity, determine whether you are open to hearing something potentially uncomfortable about yourself. If you are not, then please do not go ahead.

This activity is about increasing your awareness and understanding of yourself through the Johari window, which will help your negotiation and liaising skills and may also help you to become more emotionally intelligent.

Draw a list of what you know about yourself, and distinguish between those issues that you share with others and those that you keep to yourself. Then select two close colleagues with whom you interact frequently and with whom you have a good relationship. Ask them to draw a list of what they know about you (it may be necessary to restrict this information to the main points that are manageable for the purposes of this activity) and ask for a copy of that list, which will include information about you that you already know or that was unknown to you. Draw a Johari window and fill in the individual fields.

Then answer the following questions:

* Were there any surprises when you compared your list with those of your colleagues?
* Were some items from your 'hidden' field known to your colleagues?
* What items on these lists influence how you interact with others in the workplace?
* What have you learned about yourself?
* What have you learned about yourself that would help others to interact with you more effectively and that would help you to interact with others more effectively?

7.6 GAINING AND MAINTAINING POWER IN ORGANISATIONS

Throughout this chapter we have seen that power is central to our understanding of how organisations function and why individuals may behave in a certain way. We have also established that the ability to work with others, to network and to build coalitions is a vital skill for managers and those wishing to achieve positions of power and authority. Self-awareness, emotional intelligence and liaising can facilitate access to information, resources and opportunities. It can also help to co-ordinate complex tasks and to address collective actions like obligations, expectations and norms. Finally, it can reduce transaction costs and create an environment for collaboration, exchange and co-ordination of complementary skills.

An important concept here is networking power: that is, the ability to become part of a coalition that enables the individual to gain access to resources and others with access to even more resources. The number and type of contacts that we develop throughout our (working) lives is believed to contribute to our overall effectiveness and success. Networking is about sharing information and ideas, introducing and referring people we know to others, and giving references and advice.

However, networking in such a potentially constructive sense is not always possible, as different organisational structures and norms impose constraints on personal and interpersonal behaviours. For example, suggesting new ways of working that focus on mutual appreciation in organisations with a strong divide between 'them' (often referring to management) and 'us' (often referring to manual workers) would generally be met with suspicion, disbelief or laughter. Hence, the environment must support any change in an organisation's system of norms, values and beliefs as well as the accompanying systems, structures and procedures.

However, different organisations across the globe have shown that it is possible to make changes to create a more supportive work environment in which individuals and groups can be creative and innovative. Covey et al's (1999) concept of the 'mentality of abundance' suggests a series of steps that organisations can take to encourage good performance by facilitating an attitude of plenty of credit, knowledge and opportunity. These can be summarised as follows:

- Increase trust by listening to individuals' concerns and share ideas.
- Clarify expectations to make sure that everybody knows and accepts what their role entails.
- Give recognition for good performance by pointing out how the performance was helpful.
- Give credit for new ideas and remember that no idea should be shelved without consideration.
- Provide tools and resources to do the job.
- Help to solve problems by checking that there is an adequate 'know-how' to carry out the task. If not, offer help.
- Provide training to encourage personal development (even when resources are scarce) as this is an investment in the organisation's future.
- Never pretend to know something you don't, particularly if you are managing highly skilled professionals or experts – they are likely to know more than you!
- Hold regular performance appraisals that go beyond the formal 'once a year' meetings and are candid discussions that show personal interest.
- Acknowledge interdependence.
- Clarify responsibilities.

Following steps like these will help individuals to motivate others without appealing constantly to the authority of their position. This may be particularly difficult for managers who describe themselves as 'result-oriented' rather than 'people-oriented' (Fisher et al 2003). However, being authentic and conforming to high ethical standards can enhance an individual's expert and personal power, often leading to promotion (ie an enhancement in their position power).

ACTIVITY 7.6

REFLECTING ON POWER IN ORGANISATIONS

Drawing on Activity 7.2, consider how you can enhance your power base in your workplace by following Covey et al's (1999) advice. What are the steps that you need to take to enhance your expert and personal power? What resources do you need? How long will it take to achieve your goals?

7.7 CONCLUSION

Power is inherent in organisations and can have a positive impact on individuals and groups working together. The power structures in an organisation can motivate younger employees to develop themselves so that they can take up these positions in the future, and in that way organisations can grow their own talent from within. Politics is a different matter, however, as it is often used to protect and defend an individual's or a group's self interest, and its implications can have a negative impact on the whole of the organisation.

Negotiation is one way to connect power and politics, to overcome differences and to resolve conflict. More recent approaches to negotiating, which have been found to be successful, require managers and other negotiators to demonstrate genuine concern for the other party and to be willing to search a 'win–win' solution. This requires a high degree of self-awareness and emotional intelligence. However, negotiation is also a difficult task as not all parties always want to play fair. We conclude this chapter with Case Study 7.3, which focuses on power, politics and negotiation.

POWER, POLITICS AND NEGOTIATION AT BRITISH AIRWAYS

Profile and history

British Airways plc is a major international airline which operates international and domestic scheduled passenger flights. The company's principal place of business is London, with a presence at the three major airports of Heathrow, Gatwick and London City; it flies to more than 300 destinations worldwide.

The airline was officially established on 1 September 1974 and took over the operation of two existing airlines which were then dissolved. At that time, British Airways was a nationalised company under the governance of the British Airways Board. In the mid-1980s, as part of the economic strategy of the government of the day, British Airways was privatised and took over a rival carrier, British Caledonian Airlines. The enlarged airline enjoyed a dominant market share in the UK and became a very profitable company. Pay and terms and conditions for British Airways staff are regarded by many as amongst the most generous in the industry.

Problems faced by British Airways

During the 1990s, British Airways continued to be a very profitable company, but as the decade closed its market share was being gradually eroded by an increase in the number and size of newer airlines, including Virgin, with which it has had a long-running rivalry, Ryanair and EasyJet.

In the aftermath of the air attacks on the World Trade Centre in New York on 11 September 2001, the airline industry was rocked to its foundations as, for a time, demand for air travel plummeted and time-consuming and expensive enhanced security checks were introduced. Some airlines went bankrupt but British Airways, although making a financial loss in 2002, remained in business. Unfortunately for the airline, although trade did pick up relatively quickly, the rest of the decade saw a range of problems affecting the industry, including huge rises in the price of fuel; intensifying competition; the negative effects on flying of various natural disasters; and the global economic crisis which began in 2008. In 2009 and 2010 the company announced very substantial losses (www.telegraph.co.uk, 21 May 2010).

Willie Walsh, Chief Executive Officer

In 2005, British Airways appointed a dynamic new chief executive, Willie Walsh, to tackle the problems it faced. Walsh had joined his previous employer, Aer Lingus, as a trainee pilot in 1979. At Aer Lingus, Walsh was not only a pilot, but also gained valuable business and negotiation experience, initially as a representative of the Irish pilots' union and then as the company's chief executive; in that role he earned a reputation for toughness (as 'Slasher Walsh'), having cut 2,500 jobs to make the airline leaner and more competitive (*Guardian*, 21 April 2010, p4).

By the end of 2009, Walsh had achieved a 10 per cent cut in British Airways' cost base through a combination of reduced overtime, part-time working and voluntary redundancy. Nevertheless, the financial situation remained so severe that Walsh believed there was a need to go much further in terms of cost reduction, and BA announced plans to cut 1,700 jobs, to freeze basic pay for cabin crew for two years and to introduce a lower rate of pay for new starters in the company.

Unite the Union

British Airways officially recognises three trade unions for the purposes of collective bargaining about pay, terms and conditions and other matters, one of which, representing many cabin staff, is Unite the Union.

Unite the Union is Britain's biggest trade union and was formed as a result of a merger in 2007 between the unions Amicus and the Transport and General Workers' Union. As a result of this merger, Unite has joint general secretaries, Tony Woodley and Derek Simpson. According to *The Times*, the relationship has been marked by 'rivalry and suspicion.' (www.timesonline.co.uk, 10 October 2008). In addition, Derek Simpson has faced challenges over his continued tenure in his position from other union officials (www.wsws.org, 19 March 2009).

The dispute begins

Unite the Union opposed British Airways' plans and warned that it was prepared to fight the proposals; it particularly disliked the plan to reduce pay for new starters. It held a ballot that endorsed strike action, but this was successfully challenged in court by Willie Walsh as having infringed the statutory framework for industrial action.
Subsequently, there was a lengthy series of talks between British Airways and Unite. The union made some proposals for cost savings which British Airways rejected.

In the meantime, Michael O'Leary, Chief Executive of BA's rival carrier Ryannair, gave an interview where he predicted that British Airways would weaken in the face of strike threats. He is reported to have said, 'The problem for Willie is that the BA board have no balls, no spine and no vision. ... They are not going to take them (unions) on, they will wimp out at the eleventh hour' (www. dailymail.co.uk, 24 February 2010). Shortly after, a group of employee-relations academics sent an open letter to a national newspaper in which they accused Willie Walsh of using the dispute to try 'to break the union' (www.guardian.co.uk, 25 March 2010).

Both Derek Simpson and Tony Woodley were very prominent in the union team which began negotiations with Willie Walsh. The talks broke down and in March 2010 the union called a three-day strike, and this time thwarted British Airways' attempt to obtain a court injunction to prevent it. Willie Walsh announced that any workers who joined the strike would lose their travel perks, including flights at vastly reduced cost, enraging the union.

The dispute escalates

Once flights returned to normal, the dispute entered a further and bitter phase. A series of one-day stoppages began. Derek Simpson and Tony Woodley wrote to British Airways shareholders urging them to put pressure on Walsh:

We want a prosperous company, succeeding in a difficult competitive environment. Without that success, our members won't have jobs. That is why we have worked so hard to get an agreement with BA in relation to the cabin crew dispute. But all these efforts have been thwarted by a management that is, we believe, putting ego and machismo ahead of your interests as investors and shareholders – and playing fast and loose with the airline's future. (www. unitetheunion.com, 20 May 2010)

Walsh for his part announced plans to train up an army of volunteers from across the company to 'keep BA flying' through the dispute. He later claimed he was ready to 'stand firm for as long as it takes' and was willing to stand up to the union: 'We are in an industry that needs to change. We cannot ignore the inefficiency we see' (www. telegraph.co.uk, 8 Jun 2010).

Deadlock

Further talks broke down in May when Derek Simpson was discovered to have been sending messages on Twitter about the negotiations as they were happening (including an accusation that Walsh was being 'vindictive'), which Walsh viewed as acting in bad faith. Walsh also expressed doubts about the ability of Simpson and Tony Woodley to secure the support of their 'dysfunctional' membership should a deal be negotiated (www.telegraph.co.uk, 24 May 2010). The first in a further series of five-day strikes got under way, with BA claiming it could still run a full service at Heathrow by relying on volunteers. Nevertheless, the dispute was taking its toll financially and by early June, the strikes had cost British

Airways an estimated £98 million (www. telegraph.co.uk, 3 June 2010).

Attempts to forge a last-minute deal failed, although the union did offer to suspend its strike if the airline reinstated the travel concessions that had been withdrawn after the earlier strike. BA said it would put these concessions back in place, but not before a final agreement was in place.

By early June, the strikes looked set to continue into the vitally important summer holiday period.

Case study author – Andrew Hambler, University of Sunderland.

Task

- Applying your reading from this chapter, can you analyse why the two sides, British Airways and Unite the Union, have reached such a bitter deadlock? Are any particular details offered in the case study of especial significance?

- Can you suggest how the deadlock might now be resolved?

 PAUSE FOR THOUGHT

Identify at least three things that you have learned by studying this chapter and engaging with the activities. How will your newly acquired knowledge and skills support your continuing professional development? What value do you expect your learning to have for your daily routines and your further career? In what area have you identified a need for further development and how are you planning to fill that gap? Address these issues in your learning journal and/or CPD log. You may also wish to discuss them with a peer, colleague, mentor or coach to aid your further development.

KEY LEARNING POINTS

- Power and politics have complex and dynamic roles in organisations.

- Individuals and groups draw power from different sources, some of which are constructive and some of which may be potentially destructive.

- Power that is perceived as coercive can lead to political behaviour that causes a vicious circle of power and politics interacting that can poison the atmosphere in an organisation.

- Negotiation involves a complex set of characteristics and skills that managers and competent professionals will need to build, hone and practise.

7.8 REFERENCES

BAKER, W.E. (2000) *Networking smart: how to build relationships for personal and organisational success*. Bloomington, IN: iUniverse.

BROWAEYS, M.J. and PRICE, R. (2008) *Understanding cross-cultural management*. Harlow: FT Prentice Hall.

CIPD. (2009) *Emotional intelligence*. Fact sheet revised November. Available online at: http://www.cipd.co.uk/subjects/lrnanddev/selfdev/emotintel?NRMODE=Published&N RNODEGUID={F250EFE3-7D17-434B-9DB6-FBF2E8BC5DE4}&NRORIGINALURL=/ subjects/lrnanddev/selfdev/emotintel.htm? IsSrchRes=1&NRCACHEHINT=LoggedIn&Is SrchRes=1&cssversion=printable [accessed 28 May 2010].

CLEGG, S., KORNBERGER, M. and PITSIS, T. (2005) *Managing and organisations*. London: Sage.

COVEY, S.R., MERRILL, A.R. and MERRILL, R.R. (1999) *First things first: to live, to love, to learn, to leave legacy*. New ed. New York: Simon and Schuster.

FERRIS, G.R., ADAMS, G., KOLODINSKI, R.W., HOCHWARTER, W.A. and AMMETER, A.P. (2002) Perceptions of organisational politics. In F.J. Yammarino and F. Danserau (eds), *The many faces of multi-level issues*. New York: Elsevier.

FISHER, R., URY, W. and PATTON, B. (2003). *Getting to yes: negotiating agreement without giving in*. Revised 2nd ed. London: Random House Business Books.

FRENCH, J.P.R. and RAVEN, B. (1968) The basis of social power. In D. Cartwright and A. Zander (eds), *Group dynamics*. 3rd ed. New York: Harper and Row.

GABRIEL, Y. (2008) *Organising words*. Oxford: Oxford University Press.

GIBSON, J., IVANCEVICH, J.M., DONNELLY, J.H. and KONOPASKE, R. (2008). *Organisations: behavior structure process*. 13th ed. New York: McGraw-Hill Irwin.

GOLEMAN, D. (2005) *Emotional intelligence*. New York: Bantam.

GREENBERG, J. and BARON, R.A. (1997) *Behavior in Organizations*. Upper Saddle River, NJ: Prentice-Hall.

HARRIS, K.J. and KACMAR, K.M. (2005). An investigation of supervisor contracts as buffers on the perceptions of politics-strain relationships. *Journal of Occupational and Organisational Psychology*. Vol. 78, No. 3, pp337–354.

HATCH, M.J. (1997) *Organisation theory: modern symbolic and postmodern perspectives*. Oxford: Oxford University Press.

HAYNES, G. (2008) *Managerial communication*. 4th international ed. New York: McGraw-Hill Irwin.

JACKSON, N. and CARTER, P. (2000) *Rethinking organisational behaviour*. Harlow: FT Prentice Hall.

KARRASS, C.L. (1970) *The negotiating game*. New York: Thomas Y. Cromwell.

LAURANCE, L. and RADFORD, A. (2003) How to ... mediate in a dispute. *People Management*. 25 September. Available online at: http://www.peoplemanagement.co.uk/pm/ articles/2003/09/9435.htm [accessed 29 May 2010].

LUFT, J. (1984) *Group process*. 3rd ed. Palo Alto, CA: Mayfield.

LUTHANS, F. (2005) *Organisational behavior*. 10th international ed. New York: McGraw-Hill.

MCKENNA, E. (1999) *Business psychology and organisational behaviour*. London: Taylor and Francis.

MINTZBERG, H. (2002) The organisation as a political arena. In S.R. Clegg (ed), *Central currents in organisation studies II*. Vol. 5, London: Sage, pp382–392.

MULLINS, J. (2005) *Management and organisational behaviour*. 7th ed. Harlow: FT Prentice Hall.

NORD, W. (1978) Dreams of humanisation and the realities of power. *Academy of Management Review*. Vol. 3, No. 3, pp675–677.

Oxford dictionary thesaurus and wordpower guide. (2001) Oxford: Oxford University Press.

PETTIGREW, A. (2002) Strategy formulation as a political process. In S.R. Clegg (ed), *Central currents in organisation studies II*. Vol. 5. London: Sage, pp337–348.

PFEFFER, J. (1992) Understanding power in organisations. *California Management Review*, Vol. 34, No. 2, pp29–50.

PRUITT, D.J. and RUBIN, J.Z. (1986) *Social conflict: escalation, statement and settlement*. New York: Random House.

QUINN, R.E., FAERMAN, S.R., THOMPSON, M.P. and MCGRATH, M.R. (2003) *Becoming a master manager: a competency framework*. 3rd ed. New Jersey: Wiley.

WALTON, R. and MCKERSIE, R. (1965) *A behavioral theory of labor negotiations*. New York: McGraw-Hill.

WEBER, M. (1978) *Economy and society*. Vol 1. Berkeley, CA: University of California Press.

PART 5

Essential People Management Skills

CHAPTER 8

Interviewing and managing performance

Julie Beardwell

OVERVIEW

Interviews are a common feature of organisational life and are used to gain information and insight into potential and current employees. However, interviews can result in flawed decision-making if they are conducted by people who have not been trained or who lack the skills to identify and obtain the relevant information about individuals. Interviews serve different purposes according to whether the purpose is to select new employees, provide feedback on current performance and agree actions plans for the future or to correct underperformance. This chapter, therefore, identifies the core skills required for effective interviewing and then considers how these skills can be applied to different interviewing situations and to the management of poor performance.

LEARNING OUTCOMES

By the end of the chapter, provided you engage with the activities, you should be able to:

- identify the role and purposes of selection, appraisal and disciplinary interviews
- understand the core skills involved in effective interviewing
- evaluate the effectiveness of different questioning techniques
- explain how to plan and conduct interviews in a range of situations
- understand how interviewing skills can help to manage poor performance.

8.1 INTRODUCTION

Interviews are used in a number of different situations, including selection (which can include appointing new employees or considering existing employees for different roles within the organisation), performance appraisal and employee discipline. This chapter is primarily concerned with the identification and development of skills involved in interviewing. The multiple purposes of interviews are outlined below to highlight the potential damage that can be done if they are not handled correctly, and thus to emphasise the importance of getting them right. The chapter is also concerned with the issue of managing poor performance as many interviewing skills are also applicable here. There are inevitable areas of overlap, as discussions of poor performance are a feature of disciplinary interviews and may also occur during appraisal interviews. However, managing poor performance is treated as a distinct issue because, ideally, it should be addressed informally when it occurs rather than being saved for an appraisal discussion or a disciplinary meeting. Good practice guidelines (for example, ACAS 2009; CIPD 2010) advise that managers should make every attempt to improve poor performance without recourse to disciplinary interviews: 'only when informal options have been exhausted and where there is no alternative should managers enter a more formal disciplinary or capability procedure' (CIPD 2009a).

8.2 THE ROLE AND PURPOSE OF INTERVIEWS

Interviews serve a very useful role as they provide the means of exchanging information and meeting the human and ritual aspects of the employment process (Torrington et al 2005). Human aspects relate to the opportunity to communicate face-to-face whilst ritual elements can reflect custom and practice. For example, you would probably be very wary of accepting a new job without the opportunity to discuss your suitability for the role and to find out more about the organisation and the people you will be working with.

An interview can be defined as a controlled conversation with a purpose. However, that purpose can vary depending on the situation: so a selection interview will have different objectives from an appraisal or a disciplinary interview (Heery and Noon 2000). Before reading further, stop and consider the key purposes of interviews for selection, appraisal and discipline and the key differences between them. The overall purpose of each is as follows:

- **Selection interviews**: to identify and appoint the candidate best suited to the job.

- **Appraisal interviews**: to discuss an employee's performance and establish future goals.

- **Disciplinary interviews**: to improve performance in employees whose conduct or standard of work is unsatisfactory.

In each case, however, interviews serve a number of additional functions. For instance, selection interviews also supply information to the candidate about the job and the organisation. This may be done consciously within the interview, for example through discussing the nature of the job, the work involved, position in the organisational structure, terms and conditions and so on. However, information may also be supplied unconsciously, for example through the friendliness of reception staff and interviewers, the formality of the atmosphere and first impressions of the work environment. A further purpose of selection interviews is to ensure a favourable impression of the organisation so as to encourage the successful applicant to accept the job if offered and not dissuade candidates who may be unsuccessful for one role from applying for future vacancies. The nature of selection means that more people will be interviewed than will be offered a job within the organisation, so creating an unfavourable impression could not only deter preferred candidates but could damage the organisation's reputation as a good employer if those who are unsuccessful complain to friends and family about the way they were treated.

Appraisal interviews can increase levels of employee engagement and commitment if employees feel that their contribution is valued and makes a difference to organisational performance. Conversely, if handled badly, the appraisal interview can demotivate, particularly if employees consider that they have been unfairly assessed or if follow-up action promised in the appraisal, such as training or other development opportunities, does not happen. Although there has been a growth in different forms of appraisal, such as peer appraisal and 360-degree appraisal, downward appraisal (for example, a line manager appraising his or her direct reports) is still the most common method. As a result, an additional purpose of the appraisal interviews is to serve as an employee voice mechanism, providing a formal opportunity for individual employees to put forward their views to management and be heard. More controversially, appraisal interviews can also reinforce managerial control, especially if the appraisal process requires managers to award ratings which are subsequently related to reward.

The overall purpose of disciplinary interviews is to improve unsatisfactory performance, and this is achieved in a number of ways. Firstly, the interview can help to clarify acceptable standards of conduct and performance and the likely consequences of continued failure to meet these standards. Secondly, the interview can identify obstacles that may prevent the individual from achieving these standards and take remedial action. Ultimately, improved performance may be achieved by dismissing employees whose performance continues to be below acceptable standards or whose misconduct is extremely serious. In such circumstances, additional functions of the disciplinary interview include trying to resolve matters without recourse to an employment tribunal or serving as a point of reference for an employment tribunal should someone make a formal complaint about the way they have been dismissed (CIPD 2010).

8.3 CORE INTERVIEWING SKILLS

The effectiveness of interviews and the quality of decisions is heavily dependent on the skills of interviewers. Interviews, particularly for selection and appraisal, have often been criticised for their ineffectiveness. Selection interviews are generally criticised for their low predictive validity, for example their limitations in identifying the person best suited to the job. Appraisal interviews are also criticised for their limited ability to improve employee performance. Indeed, some critics have argued that appraisal interviews are actually detrimental; for example, the US management guru Tom Peters once described the appraisal interview as a ritual humiliation. Despite this, many interviewers rate their interviewing skills as high: three-quarters of respondents to a survey conducted by business leadership consultancy DDI (Woods 2009b) rated their selection interviewing skills as 'A' or 'B', even though the majority worried that they might have missed some important information about the candidate.

Whatever the purpose of the interview, there are a number of core skills that can improve the effectiveness of the process. How each skill is applied and its relative importance may vary depending on the specific overall purpose of the interview, for example to make decisions relating to selection, appraisal or disciplinary matters. The chapter will therefore outline these key skills and then show how they can be applied in a range of different interview situations.

8.4 PREPARATION SKILLS

The starting point for any successful interview is thorough preparation. This will include analysing background information relevant to the purpose of the interview. So, for example, preparation for a selection interview will involve consideration of organisational requirements and details about candidates' abilities and experience; preparation for an appraisal interview should include collecting information about the appraisee's key responsibilities and their performance; and preparation for disciplinary interviews should include investigation into the alleged misconduct or poor performance. Preparation should also include giving careful thought to the issues to be discussed during the interview, the design of questions that will extract the information required and the structure and flow of the interview. At an organisational level, preparation should also include ensuring that everyone with responsibility for interviewing receives appropriate training and that this training is refreshed on a regular basis, particularly for people who only interview infrequently. This can ensure that interviews are handled in a fair and consistent way and that decisions made as a result of these interviews are robust and defensible.

8.5 COMMUNICATION SKILLS

The interview is all about an effective exchange of information, both verbal and non-verbal, so communication skills are crucial. These key skills can be identified as establishing rapport, applying effective questioning techniques and listening.

8.5.1 RAPPORT-BUILDING SKILLS

The interview is a relatively formal event and is likely to engender anxiety and nervousness in the part of the interviewee. It may also provoke anxiety on the part of the interviewer, particularly in situations where a manager has to tackle poor performance and therefore might anticipate resistance and defensiveness. Establishing rapport from the outset can help set a positive tone for the encounter and can encourage interviewees to be open and forthcoming in their answers. Methods of setting the tone can vary depending on the purpose of the interview but some features are common (Torrington et al 2005):

- Speak first.
- Smile, look confident and relaxed (much easier said than done).
- Have brief, harmless exchanges that enable the parties to speak to each other without the answers mattering (weather, travel problems, etc), but always react appropriately to answers.
- Explain your understanding of what is to happen.
- Check that it is understood and accepted.

8.5.2 QUESTIONING SKILLS

Different questioning techniques can be used, depending on the purpose of the interview. However, the broad categories of questions that are recommended for all interviews are open and probing questions.

Open and closed questions: Open (or open-ended) questions are those that cannot be answered with a simple 'yes' or 'no'. Open questions most generally begin with 'what', 'why', 'how' or 'where', though sometimes they might not be questions at all but, for example, 'Tell me about a time when you ...' These questions are designed to encourage interviewees to open up and their use can help the interview to be more like a conversation than an interrogation. Effective interviewers allow the interviewee to do most of the talking, often as much as 70 or 80 per cent in selection or appraisal interviews, and open questions are one of the key means of encouraging this. Closed questions are those that can be answered with 'yes' or 'no'. They should generally be avoided in interviews; if used

ACTIVITY 8.1

OPEN AND CLOSED QUESTIONS

Re-phrase these closed questions into open questions:

- Do you enjoy your job?
- Do you work well in a team?
- Do you often work late?
- Do you work well under pressure?
- Do you like your colleagues?
- Are you proud to tell your friends where you work?

In pairs, ask each other the closed question and then the rephrased open question and compare the quality of the answers. Which do you consider give the best quality of response? Why is this?

too frequently, the result can be 'a stilted dialogue that could prevent any useful exchange of information' (IRS 2003, p154). However, if used selectively, they can have their uses, for example to clarify a factual point or to confirm acceptance of an action that has been agreed during an appraisal or disciplinary interview.

Probing questions: Open questions are useful to invite the interviewee to start talking about a particular topic or event, but these needed to be followed with supplementary questions in order to gain more detail on specific issues. Follow-up questions are likely to feature in all interviews but their use needs to be balanced carefully: too much can be perceived as intrusive whilst too little might mean that the interviewee is able to conceal relevant information. The degree of probing required is likely depend on the purpose of the interview, and the preparation stage should determine the depth of information required. Effective probing can sometimes lead to the interviewee revealing information that he or she would have preferred to keep hidden. A related skill therefore is to successfully close the series of questions and move on to the next topic: in a selection interview this may involve saying something to make the divulged secret seem less awful than the candidate had feared, for example, 'Yes, you must be glad to have put that behind you' (Torrington et al 2005, p74). In an appraisal or disciplinary interview it may be more appropriate to show empathy by asking supplementary questions such as 'That must have been awful. How do you feel about it now?'

8.5.3 LISTENING SKILLS

Asking the right questions will only help interviewers gather relevant data if they actually pay attention to the content and delivery of the answers, so listening is a crucial element of effective interviewing. All too often, however, the quality of information gained during interviews is diminished because interviewers are planning their next question or are distracted by other thoughts. Listening is more than just hearing; it involves paying attention to what is being said and how it is being said, and observing the non-verbal signals that accompany the message. It can also include being aware of what is not said or is only partially addressed by the interviewee. Effective listening requires the listener to concentrate and ask questions to aid understanding. This 'active listening' leads to better comprehension of the interviewee's answers and shows interviewees that their answers matter. The following behaviours demonstrate active listening (Robbins and Hunsaker 2009):

- Maintain eye contact with the person who is speaking.

- Show interest, for example through affirmative head nodding and appropriate facial expressions.

- Avoid distracting actions or gestures that imply boredom, such as fidgeting or doodling.

- Ask appropriate questions; for example: 'So what happened next?'

- Summarise answers using your own words; for example: 'So what you're telling me is that ...'

- Do not interrupt the speaker – let them finish what they are saying before responding or asking the next question.

- Don't talk too much – ideally interviewees should be doing about 70 per cent of the talking.

- Decipher non-verbal messages – including body language, facial expressions and tone of voice.

A key element of active listening is checking understanding, and this can be achieved by using reflective questions and summarising. In reflection, the listener restates the content of what has been said, expressing 'neither approval nor disapproval, neither sympathy nor condemnation' (Torrington et al 2005, p75). Interviewers can also show that they are listening by summarising – that is, selecting the most important aspects out of the answers to a number of questions; for example: 'So what you're telling me is that you've really enjoyed the challenges and responsibilities of your current job but now feel that the time has come to try something new.' Summarising serves a dual purpose: it reinforces the key points that have been made and gives the interviewee the opportunity to correct any false impressions or misunderstandings.

Effective listeners are also willing to allow silence. Many people are uncomfortable with silence, but it is an important aspect of effective interviewing as it provides space for incoming messages and opportunities to observe the other person and think about what is being said (Torrington et al 2005). It also gives the interviewee time to reflect on how to answer the question and this is particularly important if questions are stretching or challenging.

8.5.4 NON-VERBAL SKILLS

Effective communication is not confined to verbal skills. In fact, estimates suggest that over 90 per cent of communication is via non-verbal cues (Quilliam 1995). From the perspective of the interviewer, awareness of the importance of non-verbal communication is important for two reasons. Firstly, interviewers can make efforts to display the non-verbal signs that suggest they are attentive, approachable, confident and in control of the situation; and secondly, they can observe the non-verbal signals shown by the interviewee and use questions and appropriate responses to explore these more fully. Eye contact is seen as a crucial element of interviewing, both to establish rapport and to demonstrate attentiveness. However, competence in eye contact is never easy to establish (Torrington et al 2005) and there is a fine line between focusing on someone and staring intently. The skill lies in maintaining sufficient eye contact to show interest but breaking contact occasionally, to make a brief note or to observe hand gestures for instance.

8.5.5 NOTE-TAKING SKILLS

The purpose of interviews is to collect information on which to subsequently make decisions, so note-taking can act as both an aide-memoire to facilitate the decision-making and as a record should the decision be questioned. For example, candidates who are unsuccessful at interview often request feedback on why they were not offered the post, and a record of the interview can provide useful information. Notes taken during a disciplinary interview can be very important, especially if the ultimate outcome of the disciplinary process is dismissal. However, whilst the taking of accurate notes is important, it can interfere with listening to the answers and with observing the body language and facial gestures of the interviewee.

For example, think about taking notes during a lecture – how well can you remember what the lecturer said? It can also be disconcerting for the interviewee to give answers to someone who appears to be writing everything down word for word, and this can lead to a very stilted encounter. Ideally, note-taking should be kept to a few key words or points during the interview and then supplemented with fuller notes immediately after the interview. This does require effective preparation so that the interviewer can identify the information that is most important and pay less attention to irrelevancies.

8.5.6 DECISION-MAKING SKILLS

Decision-making is the act of choosing between two or more courses of action (see also Chapter 14). The overall purpose of the interview will determine the types of decisions that need to be made, for example, to select or reject candidates, identify performance targets or decide appropriate disciplinary action. The skills involved in effective decision-making include analytical skills, enabling the interviewer to dissect and evaluate the information that has been collected; and assessment skills, in order to compare this information consistently and accurately with the relevant selection criteria or performance standards. If handled well, interviews can contribute to the effectiveness of decision-making by ensuring that interviewers have an appropriate amount of information on which to make reasoned, justifiable decisions. In practice, however, decisions are often based on inappropriate judgements of incomplete, inaccurate data (Walley and Smith 1998).

8.6 SELECTION INTERVIEWING

A range of selection tools can be used but interviews remain the most common, and the interview process is expected by both candidates and managers (CIPD 2009a). Most interview practitioners and researchers agree that formal interview training is essential to successful recruiting and selection practices (Chapman and Zweig 2005) but, all too often, selection interviews are conducted by people who have had no training and lack the relevant skills. Online research conducted by the interview skills website Recruitsure.com found that eight out of 10 managers had not received any training in how to interview prior to recruiting (Woods 2009a).

Selection interviewing is undertaken by almost all organisations but the format can vary considerably from a loosely structured, traditional interview, which may be little more than a conversation, to a highly structured, regimented format where all questions are pre-determined and answers are systematically recorded

Table 8.1 Comparison of traditional and structured interviews

Traditional interviews	Structured interviews
Loosely structured	Highly structured
Emphasises candidate characteristics	Emphasises job-related behaviour
Dynamic interchange – amendment of overall agenda	Consistency predominates
Sequence of questions often haphazard – ad hoc format	All candidates asked identical questions or the same number of questions from a predetermined base
Closed questions	Open questions
Limited information	Encouragement of in-depth probing
Answers jotted down	Answers scored on checklists and rating scales
Content frequently unrecorded	Systematic recording
Evaluations often subjective and impressionistic	Structured evaluations
Social encounter with potential for stereotyping and bias	Formal encounter with limited capacity to establish rapport

Source: adapted from Walley and Smith (1998: 82).

in line with predefined rating scales. Table 8.1 compares the components of traditional and unstructured interviews.

Structured interviews have a higher predictive validity (for example, ability to predict future job performance) than traditional interviews (see, for example, Anderson and Shackleton 1993) but they can be perceived to restrict interviewers' discretion. Two other interview formats are also popular: the 'focused' interview, where topics for discussion are set but not the specific questions, and the 'semi-structured' interview, where topics and questions are determined in advance but interviewers can use their discretion and ask additional or follow-up questions if necessary.

8.6.1 PREPARATION AND PLANNING SKILLS

Preparation for selection interviewing is primarily focused on two key areas: content and process. Content preparation is concerned with identifying the information that is required during the interview and preparing the questions that are most likely to elicit it. Questions are generally based on a combination of organisational requirements and information on each candidate's application form or CV. Information about organisational requirements can be gained from a variety of sources including job descriptions, person specifications and competency frameworks. Job descriptions provide information about the key purpose of the job, where it fits within the organisational structure and the tasks that the successful candidate will be expected to undertake. Person specifications outline the skills, experience and qualifications that are required for the job and usually clarify which of these elements are essential to do the job and which are merely desirable. Competency frameworks provide information on the behavioural and technical abilities that are expected in the organisation and also articulate the level of skills and abilities required for different jobs.

This information is analysed to determine the key areas of questioning and the level of competence that needs to be demonstrated by the candidate before the interviewer or interviewers have enough evidence to move on to the next aspect. For example, person specifications and competency frameworks frequently include reference to team skills (see, for example, CIPD 2007). However, the amount of probing about experience of and attitudes to teamwork are likely to vary, depending on whether the job-holder is required to work closely with other members of a self-directed team or behave collaboratively with colleagues in a loosely-defined team. Effective decision-making can be aided by the explicit identification, at the preparation stage, of what constitutes 'good', 'satisfactory' or 'poor' performance for each of the selection criteria.

The second component of content preparation includes studying the data provided by candidates on the application form or CV to determine suitable question topics. One would expect that in short-listing candidates for interview, the applicants who do not meet the essential criteria have already been rejected, so interview preparation is primarily concerned with identifying aspects of the candidate's experience or knowledge that might benefit from fuller explanation or any gaps in information that need to be followed up.

The relative importance attached to organisational requirements or candidate information is largely determined by the type of interview that will be conducted. Traditional interviews are most likely to follow a biographical format and base the questions around the information supplied on the application form or CV, whereas structured interviews will ask candidates the same (or similar) questions based around the demands of the job and the competencies required. In focused or semi-structured interviews the balance is more likely to be even; in other words, organisational requirements are likely to determine the broad topic areas but the specific questions are likely to be tailored to the candidate's own circumstances. The CIPD's annual survey of recruitment and selection practice (CIPD 2009b, p10) shows that the rank order of popularity of different interview formats is: competency-based (69 per cent), biographical (68 per cent) and structured (59 per cent).

Whatever format is applied, effective interview preparation should include planning the questions to be asked or, at the very least, the topic areas that need to be covered. This can help ensure that all necessary information is covered and that all candidates are treated fairly and consistently. The ordering of questions should also be planned to ensure that there is a logical flow to the interview, especially in the case of panel interviews where several people will be involved. Ideally, the interview should be planned to start with simple questions and move on to more complex areas as the interview progresses and the interviewee (and possibly the interviewer) becomes more relaxed.

Planning and preparation skills also include consideration of the interview process, such as the number of candidates to be interviewed, the format, duration, time and location of interviews and how they fit into the overall selection process. For example, will the selection decision be based on a single interview or on two or more interview stages? Will information gathered during the interview be supplemented by other data, for example from selection tests? Last but not least, preparation needs to include inviting candidates to attend and providing them with information so that they know what to expect and have the opportunity to make their own preparations.

ACTIVITY 8.2

INTERVIEWING

Review the last selection interview you conducted or participated in and consider the amount of preparation that you undertook.

To what extent might the interview have benefited from more preparation?

What could you do differently in future?

8.6.2 QUESTIONING SKILLS

Different types of interview questions can contribute to an effective selection interview. As discussed in the section on core skills, open-ended questions are an effective means of ensuring that interviewees do more talking than interviewers. The main purpose of the selection interview is to find out the extent to which candidates have the necessary skills and experience to do the job, so the key skill is to ask open-ended questions focused on the specific job requirements or candidate's knowledge and experience rather than just open-ended questions per se; for example, 'What are your key responsibilities in your current job?' rather than 'Tell me about yourself.'

Two types of questions that have been widely studied in relation to selection interviewing are *behavioural* and *situational* questions. *Behavioural* questions are frequently used in competency-based interviews. They are based on the assumption that past performance predicts future performance and so interviewees are asked to give examples of behaviour in past situations. An example of a behavioural question is 'Tell me about a time when you had to make a difficult decision; what did you do?' Asking for in-depth evidence about actual behaviour makes 'faking' by candidates less likely and the quality of evidence more robust (Barclay 2001). However, the expectation that interviewees can describe occasions when they have enacted the competency required has been criticised as not necessarily appropriate for everyone. Candidates with limited work experience or who have been in jobs where the competency has not been necessary can be disadvantaged by behavioural questions: 'these might be candidates with significant potential, incisive intelligence, fecund ideas and admirable values which match those of your organisation but such things are beyond the scope of the typical competency-based interview' (Martin and Pope 2008, p82).

Situational questions

Situational or hypothetical questions are often used in structured interviews. Here, the interviewer poses a hypothetical problem and asks the candidate how he or she would behave. The situation will usually reflect an issue likely to be faced in the job for which the candidate is applying but there may be situations when examples from outside work are used in an attempt to obtain evidence about a candidate's typical reactions to pressured or unusual circumstances (Taylor 2008). The hypothetical nature of the question can help to overcome the problem of lack of experience as candidates are able to discuss what they would do rather than what they have done. However, there are also inherent problems in this style of questioning as candidates may exaggerate or falsify their answers and say what they think they should do, rather than what they actually would do. They can provide some insights; for example, situational questions about people management issues can establish how much candidates know about best practice or legal requirements.

 ACTIVITY 8.3

DESIGNING BEHAVIOURAL AND SITUATIONAL QUESTIONS

The Apprentice is an award-winning British reality TV show in which a group of aspiring young businessmen and women compete for the chance to win a £100,000 a year job as apprentice to the British business magnate, Alan Sugar (now Baron Sugar).

Interviews are held across the country before the series begins, attracting thousands of applicants. The business skills required are sales ability, negotiation, leadership, teamwork, organisation and screen presence. You have been asked to propose the questions that will be asked during these interviews.

- Design a behavioural and situational question to test each competence.

- In each case, identify which you prefer and why.

Probing questions

Asking well-designed behavioural and situational questions will only aid the decision-making process if they elicit sufficient information to make reasoned judgements about candidates' abilities. One of the frequent criticisms of interviews is the tendency of interviewers to accept the first answer to a question. Candidates can obtain advice about good interviewing techniques from a variety of sources, including recruitment websites, careers' offices, and consultants. These recommend that candidates anticipate typical interview questions and give guidance on the types of answers that will help candidates to show their experiences in the best light. Preparing for an interview is a positive sign of commitment to the job and should be welcomed. Macan (2009) reviews findings from a number of studies which show that the use of behavioural and situational questions does not limit the tendency for candidates to apply impression management techniques as previously thought. The interviewer, therefore, has to minimise the risk of being overly influenced by candidates who are good at interviews and be able to identify the extent to which the candidate has the ability to do the job. This is often easier said than done: even experienced interviewers report difficulties in breaking through the candidate's prepared answers and dealing with evasive and polished candidates (Goodale 1989).

The best way to minimise risk is to supplement behavioural and situational questions with probing questions, designed to elicit more detail and, at the same time, establish whether the candidate is exaggerating their achievements or being 'economical with the truth'. In selection interviews, this combination can be referred to as a funnel (see Figure 8.1 below). Experienced interviewers will not necessarily ask all of the supplementary questions or might reword them

Figure 8.1 Example of a question funnel

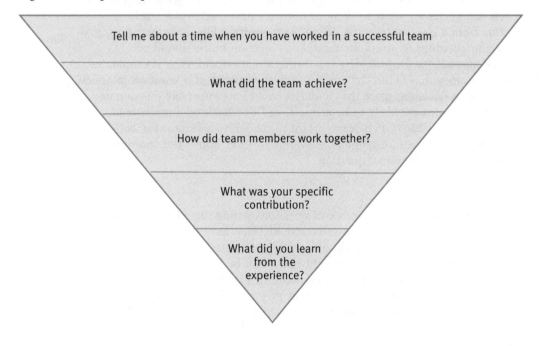

Tell me about a time when you have worked in a successful team

What did the team achieve?

How did team members work together?

What was your specific contribution?

What did you learn from the experience?

depending on the candidates' responses (Whiddett and Hollyforde 1999). An interview is likely to consist of a series of funnels on different topics that can be broken up by the interviewer, who summarises the answers to each 'funnel' before moving on to the next.

Questions to avoid

Interviewers have considerable freedom of choice when it comes to determining the most appropriate interview questions. Good questions elicit answers that enable interviewers to accurately determine the extent to which candidates match the selection criteria. By the same token, questions to avoid are those that add little to the process because they provide irrelevant information or encourage candidates to be 'economical with the truth'. For example, the question 'What are your strengths and weaknesses?' is a common feature of many interviews and so is likely to be anticipated by many interviewees. Candidates may be unaware of their weaknesses or may be unwilling to disclose accurate information during a competitive selection process. For example, few are likely to say something like 'My main weakness is a tendency to push difficult work to one side in the hope that someone else will deal with it,' but are more than likely to project a 'weakness' that shows them in the best possible light, such as being a perfectionist. Indeed, many recruitment websites provide guidance on the type of answers to give to questions like this. Furthermore, the purpose of the interview is to identify strengths and weaknesses in relation to the specific selection criteria, so it is better to explore this via more focused questions.

Leading questions

Leading questions are those that give a strong indication of the desired answer; for example, 'Teamwork is very important to us; are you a good team player?' Few candidates are likely to disagree but the interviewer will learn little of value from a positive response. Some interviewers deliberately ask provocative leading questions to assess the candidate's reaction but it should be remembered that the interview is a formal situation and, even if candidates disagree, they may be unlikely to say so in the context of a selection interview. Such stress questions place the candidate in an uncomfortable position and the reactions shown are likely to be artificial and unreliable as a measure of behaviour (IRS 2003). If it is important to the job to ascertain someone's willingness to take an unpopular view, this is better done via a more neutral behavioural or situational question.

Multiple questions

Multiple questions are a number of questions strung together, for example: 'Why did you choose that course of action? What have you learnt from the experience? What might you do differently next time?' These questions may each be legitimate in their own right but, when bundled together, can be confusing to interviewers and interviewees. In likelihood, candidates will answer the last question or the one that they consider easiest, so the other questions in the sequence may go unanswered. This is not necessarily

ACTIVITY 8.4

IMPROVING THE QUALITY OF QUESTIONS

The recruitment website www.monster.com lists a number of questions that they consider should be avoided as they could take the interview off course or create an unprofessional image of the organisation:

- Tell me about yourself.

- Where do you want to be in five years?

- What can you do for us that others can't?

- If you were an animal which one would you be?

- What salary are you hoping for?

To what extent do you agree that these questions should be avoided? Justify your answer.

How might you rephrase the questions to get more focused answers?

For CPD purposes, review your own questioning techniques and make a note of changes that could improve overall effectiveness.

problematic, as the interviewer can always repeat the omitted question but, more often than not, the discussion moves on, leaving a gap in the information obtained. Some interviewers often have favourite or pet questions which they believe are the key to identifying the best candidates. These questions are often ones that they themselves have been asked in the past, are often not relevant to the job and are 'unlikely to have been validated for their actual effectiveness' (IRS 2003, p156).

Leading and multiple questions may not add anything to the interview but are not necessarily detrimental. In contrast, personal questions, such as those asking about domestic circumstances, intentions to have a family or sexual orientation, are potentially unlawful as well as unethical and so should be avoided at all costs.

8.6.3 ACTIVE LISTENING

Demonstrable active listening can be an important contributor to selection interviewing in a number of ways. Firstly, eye contact and affirmative nods can help to put candidates at ease and encourage them to be open and honest in their responses. Secondly, it shows candidates that their responses are being given serious consideration so that, even if they are unsuccessful, they can feel that they were given a reasonable opportunity to demonstrate their abilities in relation to the job. Thirdly, it provides the opportunity to clarify any potential misunderstandings or ambiguities in the candidate's answers. As we discussed in the core interviewing skills section of this chapter, active listening involves questioning and summarising as well as listening; summarising the answers to each 'funnel' gives the candidate the opportunity to correct any inaccuracies at an early stage.

If candidates can anticipate the questions they are likely to be asked then they may prepare answers in advance, possibly with some coaching, which may not give an accurate reflection of a candidate's skills and abilities. Active listening enables interviewers to pick up cues from the answers given and then pose more probing questions using the funnel technique described in Figure 8.1. For example, if a candidate frequently refers to 'we' rather than 'I' when talking about achievements, this could indicate a strong team focus or could imply that the candidate is claiming achievements in which he or she has only made a marginal contribution. A series of more probing questions, such as 'Who was involved in achieving this goal?' and 'What were your specific responsibilities?' can help to paint a fuller picture. Listening can also help interviewers ensure that they get as balanced a picture of candidates as possible. For example, if the candidate is giving answers that indicate they are a high-achiever, then a question about a time when, despite their best efforts, they have not been able to achieve their goal can help to create a more rounded image.

It is also important to allow silence in selection interviewing, especially if asking behavioural questions which are likely to require the candidate to take some time to recollect a suitable example from their past. Silence can also encourage candidates to respond to questions relating to issues that they may find a little awkward and would prefer to avoid, such as reasons for leaving a previous job or a gap in their work history. However, silences should not be allowed to go on too long so it is important to observe non-verbal signals to determine whether the candidate is struggling. In this case, rewording the question might help to restore the flow.

Active listening also involves being aware of non-verbal behaviours. These are assumed to be an important element of the selection interview and there have been a number of studies into various non-verbal cues, including eye contact, smiling, posture and handshakes (for example, Stewart et al 2008). Studies suggest that these non-verbal cues influence interviewers' assessments of communication ability, intelligence and self-confidence (for example, McGovern and Tinsley 1978) so interviewers need to be aware of how they personally interpret these behaviours. They also need to be aware of how they may be unduly influenced by a candidate's appearance. Two common errors that can distort interviewers' assessment of candidates are the 'halo' and 'horns' effect (Searle 2003). The halo effect occurs when one highly rated aspect of the candidate's qualities boosts the entire assessment and the horns effect occurs when over-attention to one negative aspect of the candidate reduces the overall assessment. Physical characteristics are key contributors to the halo and horns

ACTIVITY 8.5

REFLECTING ON YOUR LISTENING SKILLS

How 'active' a listener are you? Reflect on how your listening behaviour alters in different situations. Which approach is most effective at getting the other person to open up? Note down your reflections in your CPD and/or learning log.

effect: candidates who are considered attractive are more likely to receive high ratings whilst 'ugly' but capable candidates tend to be marked down (Searle 2003). Searle (2003) also cites studies (for example Pingitore et al 1994) which found that interview assessments were more likely to be biased against overweight applicants.

8.6.4 NOTE-TAKING

It is important to take notes on candidates as 'after a few interviews have taken place, they can blur into each other in the mind of interviewers' (Pearce 2007, p21). However, it is important that the note-taking is not so extensive during the interview that it prevents an interviewer from maintaining eye contact. The best way to achieve a reasonable balance is to note down key words or triggers during the interview and supplement these with fuller notes immediately after the interview. Note-taking can be made easier by the use of checklists that enable the interviewer to make notes against the selection criteria.

8.6.5 DECISION-MAKING

The key decision involved in selection interviewing concerns which candidates, if any, to select and which to reject. Ideally, this should be based on a reasoned assessment of the evidence presented during the interview and other parts of the selection process, but more often than not 'gut feeling' or intuition plays a significant part. A recent survey of 1,900 interviewers (Woods 2009b) found that nearly half (47 per cent) consider candidates' results for less than half an hour before making a decision. Anderson and Shackleton (1993) suggest a number of factors that might affect the objectivity of interviewers and thus reduce the rationality of the decision-making process:

- **Similar-to-me effect**: Some interviewers may favour candidates who they consider to have a similar background, personality or characteristics to themselves.

- **Personal-liking effect**: Some interviewers are influenced by whether or not they personally like the candidate.

- **Prototyping effect**: Some interviewers may give preference to a particular personality type, regardless of job-related factors.

ACTIVITY 8.6

REFLECTING ON DECISIONS

Reflect on successful and less successful interview decisions you have made. What factors have contributed to these decisions and what could you do to replicate the successful decisions and minimise the risks of making the wrong decisions in future? Note down your reflections in your CPD and/or learning log.

- **Contrast effect**: Some interviewers may compare candidates with other candidates rather than with the selection criteria for the job.

About two-thirds of recruitment errors can be attributed to two interviewing mistakes: hiring people who are competent but not motivated, and recruiting people who are only partially competent (Adler 2005). The first mistake happens because interviewers judge on the basis of the candidate's CV and their interview performance and thus run the risk of appointing people who are motivated to get the job, but not necessarily do the work. The second is caused by giving too much weight to interviewer intuition and assuming that candidates who are confident and articulate are more competent than candidates who are nervous. This second error is also known as the 'temporal extension effect' (Anderson and Shackleton 1993), whereby interviewers assume that a candidate's behaviour at interview is typical of general performance.

In order to overcome these problems, decision-making skills need to involve objectively analysing the information that has been presented and comparing it against the selection criteria. Explicit identification, at the preparation stage, of what constitutes 'good', 'satisfactory' or 'poor' performance for each of the selection criteria can help in the decision-making process. It is also helpful if interviewers are aware of the potential sources of bias discussed above, so that they can consider the extent to which they might have been influenced by any of these areas. Where there is significant doubt or ambiguity, it is better to invite the candidate back for a further interview than to offer the job to the wrong person.

 COMPETENCY-BASED INTERVIEWING

CASE STUDY 8.1

A major bank used competency-based interviewing as part of its selection process for customer service staff. More than a hundred staff were recruited using the interview as part of the process. Only accredited interviewers, trained in a very disciplined approach to interviewing, were used to conduct the interviews.

Assessment records indicated that the interviews had actually collected very little evidence relating to the competencies required. Further analysis showed that decisions to select or reject a candidate were not specifically based on any of the core competencies.

Interviewers had been misguided in how to structure their questions – the process itself did not allow an interviewer the necessary freedom to keep the interview focused on the competencies. In fact, most of them were simply reading out each question and noting the reply; no probing or supplementary questions were being asked.

(*Source:* S. Whiddett and S. Hollyforde (1999), *The competencies handbook*, CIPD, London, p70)

Questions

- Why, in this instance, have competency-based questions failed to collect accurate information on the competencies of candidates?

- What might be done to improve the quality of interviews?

- To what extent might these criticisms be true of interviewing in your own organisation?

8.7 APPRAISAL INTERVIEWING

Performance appraisal comes in a variety of shapes and forms, but its most typical incarnation involves the formal appraisal of an employee's work performance over a set period by his or her immediate line manager (Taylor 2008). The interview is a key aspect of performance appraisal as it provides the opportunity for the appraiser to engage the appraisee in a discussion about his or her performance and agree on development plans to support performance improvements. However, appraisals rarely seem to achieve the improvements they're supposed to (Goodge and Coomber 2009). A recent survey (CIPD 2009c) found that the majority of respondents do not consider that performance management improves performance. Less than a third (30 per cent) think that performance management enables individuals to better understand what they should be doing and how to do it, and only a fifth (20 per cent) think that performance management has a positive impact on individual performance. Poor interviewing skills are one of the main reasons why appraisal systems fail (McMahon 1999). A survey conducted by YouGov for Investors in People (IiP) found that 44 per cent of employees do not think their manager is honest during appraisal and a quarter believe that their manager sees the annual review purely as a tick box exercise (Soriano 2007).

Some of these perceptions may stem from a general reluctance among managers to carry out appraisals. A number of reasons have been put forward to try to explain this (Taylor 2008), including a dislike of passing judgement on others, an inability to handle emotional responses that can arise when appraisal ratings are less impressive than the employee expected, and the perceived lack of fit between the appraisal interview and individual managers' preferences for managing people. Performance appraisal remains a common feature of organisational life, so developing the necessary skills can help to improve effectiveness and reduce management reluctance to participate in the process.

Armstrong and Baron (2005, pp329–330) suggest that there are five key elements to appraisal meetings:

1. **Measurement**: assessing results against agreed targets and standards.

2. **Feedback**: providing information on how a person has been doing.

3. **Positive reinforcement**: emphasising what has been done well so that it will be done even better in the future, and making only constructive criticisms (for example, those that point the way to improvement).

4. **Exchange of views**: ensuring that the discussion involves a full, free and frank exchange of views about what has been achieved, what needs to be done to achieve more and what appraisees think about their work, the way they are managed, and their aspirations.

5. **Agreement**: jointly reaching an understanding about what has to be done by both parties to improve performance, knowledge and skills and overcome any work problems raised during the discussion.

So let us now look at how the core interviewing skills identified earlier in the chapter can be applied to ensure that appraisal interviews incorporate these elements.

8.7.1 PREPARATION AND PLANNING SKILLS

Discussions need to be evidence-based if the process is to be considered as a valid, fair, rigorous and reliable approach to managing the performance of staff. Piggot-Irvine (2003) cautions that, in the absence of objective, factual information, appraisals may be perceived as a poorly constructed process, leading to inadequate, inaccurate and subjective decision-making. However, in practice, preparation is often less than adequate: a fifth of respondents to the IiP survey believe that their manager does not even think about the appraisal before the meeting (Soriano 2007).

Latham et al (2008) draw on a number of studies to show that people have difficulty in providing an appraisal that accurately reflects a person's performance over the relevant time frame. Common sources of error are difficulties in recalling information on performance and a lack of opportunity to observe all dimensions of an individual's performance. As a result, appraisals may be based on only partial evidence of performance and give undue weight to recent events.

ACTIVITY 8.7

MEETING APPRAISAL

Before reading further, consider the sources of information that may be used in preparing for an appraisal meeting in your organisation:

- What can be done to ensure that this information covers the whole period under review and not just the weeks leading up to the appraisal meeting?

- How might managers be persuaded to collect information on an ongoing basis?

Reflect on your interviewing practice: to what extent do you follow your own recommendations? Please include your reflections in your CPD and/or learning log.

Armstrong and Baron (2005, pp330–331) suggest that the appraiser should prepare for the meeting by considering:

- how well the appraisee has done in achieving work objectives and meeting performance standards since the last appraisal meeting

- to what extent, and with what effect, the personal development plans agreed at the last meeting have been implemented

- the feedback to be provided at the meeting and the evidence that that will be used to support it

- the factors that have affected performance, both those within and outside the appraisee's control

- the points for discussion on the possible actions that might be taken by the appraiser and appraisee to further development or improve performance

- possible directions that the appraisee's career could take

- possible objectives for the next review period.

The appraisee should also be encouraged to give some thought to these issues in advance of the meeting.

8.7.2 RAPPORT-BUILDING

The appraisal interview is part of an ongoing employment relationship and so managers may sometimes see this stage of the meeting as unnecessary. However, it should be recognised that the appraisal is a relatively formal encounter, and taking a little time to break the ice and relax the atmosphere can help to set the right tone and get the meeting off to a good start. 'The bottom line here is that if you can't discuss EastEnders, the football results or the weather, it's hard to see an open discussion of someone's shortcoming developing' (McMahon 1999, p60).

8.7.3 QUESTIONING SKILLS

Questions in the appraisal should be open-ended to encourage the appraisee to talk and to create an atmosphere of calm and friendly enquiry (Armstrong and Baron 2005). Whilst the selection interview is primarily focused on extracting information about individual's behaviour and skills, the appraisal is also likely to be concerned with an individual's opinions and feelings. So open questions can be focused towards emotional aspects of performance, for example, 'How did you feel at the end of the project? How do you think things have been going?' As with selection interviewing these can then be followed with a series of probing questions to extract more detail as required. Where possible, it is best to avoid starting probing questions with 'Why' as this can seem confrontational. If necessary, 'why' questions can be rephrased into 'what' questions which makes them seem less accusatory, for example, 'What are the reasons for …?' or 'What causes you to think that?' (Gilbert and Chakravorty 2005, p56).

Open-ended appraisal questions can be used to help the appraisee self-review: for example, 'What have you been particularly proud of this year?', 'What could have gone better?' They can also be used to encourage appraisees to identify their own solutions to issues and to determine future actions: for example, 'What could you have done to avoid missing that deadline?' 'How could you build on the success of that particular project?'

8.7.4 ACTIVE LISTENING

A good appraiser can spend up to 80 per cent of the time listening. Active listening is a crucial element of the appraisal interview, particularly focusing on the facial gestures, body language and tone of voice used in answering questions. Voice characteristics can reflect different feelings, as identified in Table 8.2.

Allowing silence after asking a question or providing feedback may be necessary to allow appraisees time and space to reflect on what they have heard and consider how they are going to respond. As with selection interviewing, being attentive to body language can help to determine whether they are thinking, if which case the interviewer should keep quiet for a little longer, or if they are

Table 8.2 Probable meanings of voice characteristics

Characteristics	Probable meaning
Monotone voice	Boredom
Slow speech, low pitch	Depression
High voice, emphasis	Enthusiasm
Ascending tone	Astonishment
Abrupt speech	Defensiveness
Terse speed, loud tone	Anger
High pitch, drawn-out speech	Disbelief

Source: Torrington et al (2005, p72).

stuck, in which case it might be helpful to ask a further question such as 'What are some of your thoughts?' (Gilbert and Chakravorty, 2005, p66).

Reflecting back to the appraisee can help to show that the interviewer is paying attention to what is being said and, as with selection interviewing, can provide the opportunity for any misunderstandings to be addressed. Summarising is also important, but its use in appraisal interviewing is different from the way it is used in selection interviewing. At the close of the appraisal interview it can be a good idea to let appraisees summarise first and then help them to focus on any important points they may have missed (McMahon 1999, p61). This is an effective technique for identifying how far the appraiser and appraisee share a joint understanding of what has been agreed.

8.7.5 GIVING FEEDBACK

A key element of the appraisal interview involves giving two types of feedback: observations about what areas met or exceeded expectations, and information about what fell short of expectations (Gillen 2007). Appraisers are generally more willing to give positive feedback because it is usually well received and readily accepted. Negative feedback can be perceived as more problematic due to a fear that it may cause offence or meet with resistance (Robbins and Hunsaker 2009). There are a number of techniques that can improve the quality of feedback and thus the likelihood that it will be accepted, even if it is negative:

- **Be specific**: Even when referring to good performance there can be a tendency for generality – for example, 'You've worked really well.' More specific examples of tasks that have been performed particularly well can help the appraisee feel that their contribution has been recognised. Equally, specific examples of poor performance are better than vague criticisms as they help to pinpoint the aspects of performance that need to improve.

- **Select key issues**: Restrict the feedback to the issues that really matter. 'There is a limit to how much criticism anyone can take. If it is overdone, the shutters will come down and the discussion will get nowhere' (Armstrong and Baron 2005, p336).

- **Focus on what can be changed**: Constructive feedback needs to focus on aspects of performance that can be improved, so concentrate on job-related behaviours that are in the individual's control rather than personality traits or characteristics.

- **No surprises**: Feedback is most meaningful when it is given soon after the behaviour on which it is based has occurred: 'If you have to spend time recreating a situation and refreshing someone's memory of it, the feedback you're providing is likely to be ineffective' (Robbins and Hunsaker 2009, p109). Appraisal interviews may involve discussions of incidents that happened some time ago but this should not be the first time the situation or performance has been discussed. Rather the appraisal discussion should build on ongoing feedback to create a balanced picture of an individual's performance over the appraisal period.

8.7.6 RECEIVING FEEDBACK

It is good practice for the appraiser to ask for feedback at the end of an interview; after all, 'appraisal is a two-way process and if you're big enough to give feedback you should be big enough to take it' (McMahon 1999, p61). This may relate to your skills as an appraiser or more generally as a manager or work colleague. In practice, many appraisees may find this difficult or awkward, especially if they feel the appraisal interview has not been a pleasant experience. As a consequence, appraisers rarely get feedback on the appraisals they conduct and so bad appraisers believe they are fine and continue to be bad (Goodge and Coomber 2009).

 APPRAISALS

CASE STUDY 8.2

You receive the following email from your Chief Executive Officer:

'I have just attended a seminar on Performance Management. One of the speakers reported that her company had improved the quality of appraisals by asking all appraisees to complete questionnaires on the appraisal experience. A summary of views was then fed back to each manager. This enabled managers to learn more about their appraisal skills and identify areas to improve.'

Questions

- How effective might this approach be in your organisation?

- What would you need to do to encourage appraisees to give open and honest feedback?

- What else could you do to improve the quality of appraisals?

8.7.7 PROBLEM-SOLVING SKILLS

Open and honest feedback should mean that problem areas of performance are confronted rather than avoided. Once problems have been confronted, creative problem-solving skills may be required to help identify solutions to the areas of performance that need to be improved. Problem-solving involves defining and analysing the problem before determining a solution. Assumptions about the causes of problems can lead to confusion between symptoms of the problem and its causes (Robbins and Hunsaker 2009) so it is good practice to ask open questions to encourage the appraisee to identify the root causes of the problem. Many of the active listening skills already discussed, for example listening, observing non-verbal clues, asking probing questions, reflecting and summarising, are likely to be applied where someone is experiencing problems: 'a considerable amount of questioning and listening may be required before the point becomes clear, because clarity of expression and strong emotions seldom go together' (Armstrong and Baron 2005, p340).

After the problem has been analysed, the next step is to develop a course of action that will help improve the situation. This involves two steps: generating a range of possible solutions and then evaluating the relative merits of these possibilities to select the most effective course. The appraiser should not attempt to impose a solution but ask questions that can help the appraisee identify a number of options and then choose the best. There are two types of open questions that can help in this respect: those that engage the imagination and those that focus the mind (Gilbert and Chakravorty 2005). Questions that engage the imagination – for example, 'What might you possibly do to overcome this situation?', 'What would happen if you ...?' – can help to change the way the appraisee looks at the problem. Questions that focus the mind – for example, 'which is most important to you?' – can help them to determine priorities and make choices.

In summary, effective questions in appraisal interviews are those that encourage appraisees to reflect on their own performance and identify their own solutions to problems. These questions also need to be supplemented by probing questions and reflective statements that demonstrate active listening.

Average reviewers are likely to be doing more talking than listening: they spend almost twice as much time proposing or giving information as expert reviewers. At the same time, expert reviewers spend much more time 'actively listening'

ACTIVITY 8.8

REFLECTING ON APPRAISALS

Reflect on a recent appraisal interview that you have conducted or participated in. What could you do to improve your appraisal interviewing skills? Note down your thoughts and observations in your CPD and/or learning log.

(testing understanding and summarising) and encourage appraisees to identify their own future actions (seeking proposals). They also appear more constructive as they spend more time building on the answers and suggestions of appraisees. However, this does not make them a soft touch as expert reviewers are no less likely than average reviewers to disagree with the appraisee.

8.7.8 OBJECTIVE-SETTING SKILLS

Objective-setting is one of the most common features of performance reviews but also one of the more problematic: 'too often, the annual performance appraisal is the meeting when managers and staff "discover" that the performance achieved bears little or no relation to many of the goals set at the beginning of the year' (Evans 2007). This is because objective-setting may be viewed as nothing more than a 'box-ticking' exercise to be completed and then ignored. Even if acted upon, objectives tend to be short term and can often give too much weight to relatively minor aspects of performance whilst downgrading the factors that are actually important (IRS 2003). This 'surface' approach to objective-setting can be described as 'one that is concerned with getting the objective out of the way as quickly as possible rather than focusing substantially on something that results in considerable improvement' (Piggot-Irvine, 2003, p175). In contrast, 'deep' approaches to objective-setting require more detailed action plans that identify the aspect of performance that needs to change, the interventions required to realise this change and how the degree of change can be measured.

Effective practice in objective-setting concentrates on the objectives being SMART. This acronym is commonly used on organisations although the initials can be applied in a number of ways:

S = Specific or Stretching

M = Measurable

A = Achievable or Agreed

R = Realistic

T = Time-bound.

Objectives need to be agreed between the appraiser and the appraisee. The appraiser's agreement can help ensure that objectives are consistent with organisational objectives and values, whilst the appraisee needs to accept personal responsibility for future actions. Effective objective-setting requires the appraiser to understand and be able to explain the standards of performance required, to focus on objectives related to important aspects of performance, and to ask appropriate questions that will encourage the appraisee to identify his or her own objectives. Armstrong and Baron (2005, p291) suggest that information on objectives can be obtained by asking the following questions:

- What do you think are the most important things you do?

- What do you believe you are expected to achieve in each of these areas?

- How will you – or anyone else – know whether or not you have achieved them?

ACTIVITY 8.9

CHARACTERISTICS OF GOOD OBJECTIVES

Armstrong and Baron (2005, p290) outline the characteristics of good objectives:

- **Consistent**: in line with the values of the organisation and with departmental and corporate objectives.
- **Precise**: clear and well defined, using positive words.
- **Challenging**: to stimulate high standards of performance and to encourage progress.
- **Measurable**: related to quantified or qualitative performance measures.
- **Achievable**: within the capabilities of the individual, taking account of any constraints that may affect the individual's capacity to achieve the desired result.
- **Agreed**: by the appraiser and the appraisee.
- **Time-related**: achievable within a defined timescale.
- **Team-oriented**: emphasise teamwork as well as individual achievement.

Consider these characteristics and answer the following questions, justifying your answers:

1. To what extent do you agree that these characteristics reflect good objectives?

2. What additional characteristics would you include?

3. To what extent could application of these characteristics improve the effectiveness of objective-setting within your own organisation?

8.7.9 NOTE-TAKING

It can be useful to take discrete notes during the appraisal interview, particularly if an appraisal form has to be completed. The fact that you are going to do so should be mentioned at the start of the meeting. It can also be a good idea to encourage the appraisee to take notes, especially about agreed actions, as this can show their willingness to take personal responsibility (Gilbert and Chakravorty 2005).

8.7.10 DECISION-MAKING

The decisions made as a result of the appraisal interviews are likely to be dependent on the overall purpose of the appraisal system, for example whether it is primarily developmental or evaluative. In the latter case, decisions are likely to involve recording specific aspects of performance and providing an overall rating, which may or may not be linked to reward. Both developmental and evaluative systems are likely to include an action plan that consolidates the objectives agreed during the appraisal discussion. In order for appraisees to have confidence in the system, it is critical that the appraiser follows up any agreed actions: 'there is no better way of undermining the system than by agreeing actions that you then fail to take' (McMahon 1999). However, it appears in practice that lack of follow-up is a fairly common feature of appraisals: a fifth of respondents to the IiP survey say their manager 'rarely' or 'never' follows up on their concerns (Soriano 2007).

8.8 MANAGING POOR PERFORMANCE

Sooner or later, most managers encounter a staff member whose performance or behaviour is below par (Gillen 2007). Reducing the incidence of underperformance is a key priority for organisations so it is important for managers to deal with poor performance as and when it occurs rather than delaying discussion until the appraisal interview or avoiding tackling the issue until it becomes serious enough to warrant disciplinary action. Armstrong and Baron (2005, p344) suggest that 'managing underperformers is a positive process which is based on feedback throughout the year that looks forward to what can be done by individuals to overcome performance problems and, importantly, how managers can help.' Thus, the feedback and problem-solving skills involved in appraisal interviewing are also relevant to managing poor performance, albeit on a more informal basis.

8.8.1 FEEDBACK SKILLS

Providing ongoing feedback is key to ensuring that employees understand what is expected of them and appreciate how their performance measures up to expectations. However, this is an area in which managers often fail to deliver. Swinburne (2001) argues that managers tend to give little feedback to their staff and rarely take action over their behaviour until it becomes necessary to challenge them or even start disciplinary proceedings. She goes on to say that 'regular constructive feedback reduces the need to challenge and discipline people in this way,' and instead focuses on helping them to learn what they are good at as well as where they are going wrong. Some guidelines to providing effective feedback in an appraisal context were outlined earlier in the chapter. In addition, Swinburne suggests some points that can help improve the quality of feedback, to ensure that even negative feedback is constructive:

- **Be respectful**: The acceptability of any feedback depends on how it is given, so tone of voice and body language are as important as the words used.

- **Get the balance right**: Although many people have been taught that negative comments should be 'sandwiched' between two pieces of positive feedback, this can be counterproductive if recipients see the positive comments as nothing more than a sop to make the negative comments more palatable. When feedback is given regularly, it should be focus on whatever is relevant at a particular moment, whether it is positive, negative or mixed. What counts is the balance of positive to negative feedback over time.

- **Invite a response**: Asking questions such as 'What was happening here?' can help the recipient to think through and learn more from the feedback.

Used regularly in this way, feedback can be seen as a key component of coaching to help individuals to become aware of how they are doing and where they need to improve. Once individuals have recognised and accepted the need for improvement, the next stage involves helping them identify how they might achieve this.

CASE STUDY 8.3

AGAINST COMPANY POLICIES

You need to have a discussion with Matt, one of the people in your team. For the most part, Matt's performance is good but he gets easily distracted and, more than once, you have walked into his office to find him booking cinema tickets online or taking a personal phone call. Strictly speaking, this is against company policy but you've not taken issue with it before now as he always delivers results and works extra hours if the job demands it. He is also a rather prickly person who takes offence easily. However, you've now received complaints from other members of the team who had agreed to take on some of Matt's more routine work in order to help him finish an important project. Whilst doing this extra work, they overheard Matt chatting on a number of personal phone calls and feel that if he had time for those calls then he had time to do the work that they have been doing on his behalf.

Questions

- How would you tackle this issue?
- What problems might you anticipate?
- What questions might you ask to help Matt appreciate how his actions might be perceived by others?
- How would you secure his commitment to work differently in future?

For CPD purposes, reflect on a recent performance problem you have encountered and include your reflections in your CPD and/or learning log.

- How well did you handle it?
- What might you do differently next time?
- What impact might this have on the outcome?

8.8.2 PROBLEM-SOLVING SKILLS

In order to manage poor performance, managers need to confront the problem and then work with the individual to identify the causes and seek possible solutions. Thus the creative problem-solving techniques discussed in the section on appraisal interviewing can also be effective here. However, it is important for managers to recognise that their behaviour may actually exacerbate the issue. Manzoni and Barsoux (2004) suggest that management perceptions that someone is a poor performer can become something of a vicious circle. Their research indicates that managers tend to monitor the poor performer more closely and that this more controlling style of management can undermine the confidence of the person being 'micro-managed', which in turn leads to underperformance and increased tension. The way to avoid this is to engage in genuine dialogue about mutual behaviours and intentions: 'there can be no real discussion until the boss acknowledges his or her role in shaping the subordinate's attitude and action; nor can there be a real discussion until the subordinate recognises that his or her misery is, in part self-inflicted' (Manzoni and Barsoux 2004, p27). This joint problem-solving requires both parties to reflect on their own attitudes and behaviours, to try to understand the other person's point of view and to engage in open and honest discussions in order to agree a way forward.

8.9 DISCIPLINARY INTERVIEWING

In cases where individuals are unresponsive to coaching-based methods of performance improvement, managers may need to resort to disciplinary measures. The choice of disciplinary route should not be taken lightly. Taylor (2008, p490) highlights the inherent tensions in using a formal disciplinary process to improve problems of poor performance: 'The very act of setting up a formal hearing ... signals a breakdown in trust. However positive and helpful the managers present at the hearing try to be, invariably the fact that the procedure has started at all will have the opposite effect.'

The purpose of the disciplinary interview is to deal with misconduct or improve underperformance that has not been satisfactorily addressed by more informal means. In order to fulfil this purpose, the interview must enable the manager to establish the facts under investigation and give the employee an opportunity to explain the conduct or performance. Decisions that will be taken as a result of the interviews are whether disciplinary action is required and what the employee needs to do to achieve the required standard of conduct or performance. A disciplinary interview can be stressful for the person conducting it as well as the employee who is subject to the investigation, and the impact of getting it right or wrong can be significant. When handled well, a disciplinary interview can have a positive impact on the individual and the organisation. At an individual level, an effective disciplinary interview can resolve issues of underperformance or misconduct and thus prevent more serious action having to be taken against the employee. At an organisational level, effective disciplinary action can raise employee morale as standards are seen to be maintained in a fair and just way. However, if handled badly, there can be negative implications for individuals and the organisation. Disciplinary action that is seen as arbitrary and unfair may ultimately result in tribunal claims for unfair or constructive dismissal. It is also argued that applying disciplinary measures lowers trust and demotivates employees, leading to less commitment and higher staff turnover (Taylor 2008). This section will consider how the application of core interviewing skills can help to improve the quality of disciplinary interviews.

8.9.1 PREPARATION SKILLS

At an organisational level, appropriate training should be provided to ensure that everyone involved in disciplinary action knows the disciplinary procedure and understands the importance of adhering to it. At an individual level, thorough preparation before a disciplinary interview is extremely important. ACAS guidelines (ACAS 2009, p19) recommend that preparation should include:

- collecting all relevant facts, such as disciplinary records, other relevant documents and written statements
- checking whether any special circumstances need to be considered
- considering explanations that may be offered by the employee and, if possible, checking them out in advance
- planning the structure of the interview and key points to be covered.

Employees should also be given advance notice of when the interview is to take place so that they have sufficient time to prepare their case and arrange to be accompanied if required.

8.9.2 RAPPORT-BUILDING

The purpose of the meeting is to establish facts and then seek resolution through an open and frank discussion. The context of the situation may mean that it is inappropriate to engage in the same level of initial small-talk as in appraisal or selection interviews but, nevertheless, it is important to set a non-confrontational tone from the start of the interview. ACAS (2009, p20) again provide useful advice here, recommending that the interviewer:

- introduces those present and explains why they are here
- explains that the purpose of the meeting is to consider whether disciplinary action should be taken in accordance with the organisation's disciplinary procedure
- explains how the meeting will be conducted.

ACTIVITY 8.10

REFLECTING ON YOUR OWN EXPERIENCES

For CPD purposes, reflect on your own experience. How well is this stage of the process handled? What could be done to ensure that all involved appreciate its importance?

8.9.3 QUESTIONING SKILLS

Open questions should be used to try and encourage the employee to speak freely so that facts can be established. Given that the outcome of the interview might be disciplinary action, employees might be reluctant to be forthcoming or may try to withhold information, so probing questions are also likely to be necessary to extract sufficient information to make a reasoned and justifiable decision. As with appraisal interviewing, softening 'Why?' questions may help reduce the risk of the interview becoming confrontational. Supplementary questions can also be used to clarify issues and minimise the risk of misunderstanding or misinterpretation. In some instances it might be appropriate to use a closed question to establish a specific fact – for example, 'Did you have authorisation to do that?' A closed question may also be appropriate to establish that the employee accepts he or she may have done something wrong or is not performing to the required standard, before trying to agree a suitable solution. At the end of the discussion the interviewer should summarise the main points to remind all parties of the nature of the offence, the arguments and evidence put forward, and to ensure that nothing is missed

(ACAS 2009). The employee should then be asked if he or she has anything further to add.

8.9.4 LISTENING SKILLS

The disciplinary interview helps to establish facts and uncover the causes of poor performance or misconduct, so it is important not to pre-judge the outcome. The interview discussion may reveal that employee has a reasonable explanation for the event in question. Active listening can help ensure that appropriate and sufficient probing questions are asked. Allowing silence can also be effective in a disciplinary context: 'listen carefully and be prepared to wait in silence for an answer as this can be a constructive way of encouraging the employee to be more forthcoming' (ACAS 2009, p21).

8.9.5 DEALING WITH EMOTIONS

It is important that the interviewer remains professional and polite even if the employee gets upset or angry. Focusing the questions on behaviour rather than personality and concentrating on facts rather than being judgemental can potentially take some heat out of the situation but, nevertheless, there are likely to be times when employees get distressed. Allowing time for the employee to regain composure can be helpful but, if the level of distress prevents the employee from continuing, then the meeting may have to be adjourned to a later date. During the meeting there may be some 'letting off steam' and this can be helpful in finding out what has actually happened (ACAS 2009). If the employee is angry or aggressive then the first instinct of the interviewer may to respond in kind but this is unlikely to lead to a constructive discussion. Better for the interviewer to acknowledge the employee's feelings – for example by saying 'You're obviously upset/angry about this' – and then ask questions to explore the cause of these feelings in more depth.

8.9.6 NOTE-TAKING SKILLS

Notes taken during a disciplinary interview form an important record of what has occurred and good practice guidelines suggest that these notes should be taken by a manager who is not directly involved in the meeting. This enables the person conducting the interview to concentrate on listening to what is being said and observing body language and facial expressions without the added distracted of needing to capture the key issues in note form. The note-taker can also act as a witness to what is being said. These notes will provide a record of the meeting (the employee or person accompanying them may also have taken notes) and should be kept for a reasonable length of time after the meeting.

8.9.7 DECISION-MAKING SKILLS

Employees should be notified of the outcome of the meeting as soon as is reasonably possible but an adjournment after the meeting is recommended to allow time for reflection and proper consideration (ACAS 2009). The decision should be based on the information gathered during the preparation stage and any explanations provided during the meeting. In the case of poor performance, the decision is likely to include the steps that can be taken to improve performance as well as any punitive action, such as an oral or written warning.

To sum up, questioning and listening skills are as important in disciplinary interviews as in selection and appraisal interviews. In addition, interviewers may be faced with emotional or angry employees and will need to maintain calm control of the process. The formality of the process means that the disciplinary process should be seen as a last resort rather than a common feature of tackling poor performance. As a result, managers will hopefully have less experience of disciplinary meetings than of selection or appraisal interviews, so it is essential that preparation is thorough and involves consideration of the steps necessary to ensure a fair and effective interview.

8.10 CONCLUSION

Interviews play a key role in organisational decision-making relating to who to employee, how to get the best out of current employees and how to deal with those who are underperforming. It stands to reason, then, that if interviews are not conducted well, these decisions are likely to be flawed. Nevertheless, it seems that, in practice, interviews are often undertaken by people who lack the necessary skills. The skills that make someone a good interviewer can all be learned but regular practice is necessary to embed and build on the basic level of skills. Interview training is an important contributor to skills development at a number of levels: firstly, it can raise awareness of the key skills and common pitfalls; secondly, it can provide a safe context in which to practise these skills; and thirdly, it can enable interviewers to gain feedback on their own performance and areas that would benefit from fuller development. Interviewing is a prime example of where reflective thinking, self-analysis and requests for feedback from others can help to deliver continuous professional development.

 PAUSE FOR THOUGHT

Identify at least three things that you have learned by studying this chapter and engaging with the activities. How will your newly acquired knowledge and skills support your continuing professional development? What value do you expect your learning to have for your daily routines and your further career? In what area have you identified a need for further development and how are you planning to fill that gap? Address these issues in your learning journal and/or CPD log. You may also wish to discuss them with a peer, colleague, mentor or coach to aid your further development.

KEY LEARNING POINTS

Five learning objectives were identified at the start of the chapter. The key learning points for each objective can be summarised as:

- Interviews can be defined as a controlled conversation with a purpose, but that purpose can vary depending on the situation. Selection interviews aim to identify and appoint the candidate best suited to the job, appraisal interviews aim to discuss an employee's performance and establish future goals, and disciplinary interviews aim to improve performance in employees whose conduct or standard of work is unsatisfactory. In each case, interviews serve a number of additional functions and their quality can impact on employee morale and organisational reputation.

- The core skills involved in effective interviewing are preparation, rapport-building, questioning, active listening, note-taking and decision-making. Additional skills in some situations include problem-solving, giving and receiving feedback, objective-setting and dealing with emotions.

- The effectiveness of different questioning techniques depends on their purpose. Open questions are applicable to all interview situations and are designed to encourage the interviewee to talk freely. Probing questions are also universally applicable although the depth of probing may vary depending on the situation. Closed questions may be used to clarify a point.

- Thorough preparation is crucial to ensure the effective planning and conduct of interviews in a range of situations. This preparation should include collecting appropriate data on the person to be interviewed, planning the questions to be asked and giving some thought to the logical order of questions to ensure that the interview flows well. Preparation should also include giving interviewees adequate notice so they can prepare to facilitate a two-way flow of information in the interview.

- Many of the skills required for effective interviewing skills can also be applied to the management of poor performance. Ongoing feedback means that employees know what is required of them, what they are doing well and what needs to improve. Questioning and listening skills can help to identify the root causes of problems and agree possible solutions.

8.11 REFERENCES

ACAS. (2009) *Discipline and grievances at work: the ACAS guide*, London: ACAS.

ADLER, L. (2005) Outside chance. *People Management*. 10 March. pp38–39.

ANDERSON, N. and SHACKLETON, V. (1993) *Successful selection interviewing*. Oxford: Blackwell.

ARMSTRONG, M. and BARON, A. (2005) *Performance management: the new realities*. 2nd ed. London: CIPD.

BARCLAY, J. (2001) Improving selection interviews with structure: organisations' use of 'behavioural' interviews. *Personnel Review*. Vol. 3, No. 1. pp81–101.

CHAPMAN, D. and ZWEIG, D. (2005) Developing a nomo logical network for interview structure: antecedents and consequences of the structured selection interview. *Personnel Psychology*. Vol. 58, No. 3. pp673–702.

CIPD. (2007) *Learning and development*. Annual Survey, April. London: CIPD.

CIPD. (2009a) *Selection interviewing*. CIPD Factsheet. February. London: CIPD.

CIPD. (2009b) *Recruitment, retention and turnover*. Annual Survey. London: CIPD.

CIPD. (2009c) *Performance management in action: current trends and practice*. Hot Topics. November. London: CIPD.

CIPD. (2010) *Discipline and grievances at work*. CIPD Factsheet. April. London: CIPD.

EVANS, J. (2007) *Goal-setting in a one-to-one coaching environment*. CIPD Member Resource. London: CIPD.

GILBERT, A. and CHAKRAVORTY, I. (2005) *Go MAD about coaching*. Woodhouse Eaves: Go MAD Books.

GILLEN, T. (2007) The people skills behind the appraisal process. *Strategic HR Review*. Vol. 6, No. 4, p4.

GOODALE, J. (1989) Effective employment interviewing. In R. Eder and G. Ferris (eds), *The employment interview: theory, research and practice*. London: Sage. pp 307–323.

GOODGE, P. and COOMBER, J. (2009) How to ... improve appraisals. *People Management*. Vol. 29, January. pp57–58.

HEERY, E. and NOON, M (2000) *A dictionary of human resource management*. Oxford: Oxford University Press.

IRS. (2003) *IRS best practice in HR handbook*. Croydon: Lexis Nexis.

LATHAM, G., BUDWORTH, M-H., YANAR, B. and WHYTE, G. (2008) The influence of a manager's own performance appraisal on the evaluation of others. *International Journal of Selection and Assessment*. Vol. 16, No. 3. pp220–228.

MACAN, T. (2009) The employment interview: a review of current studies and directions for future research. *Human Resource Management Review*. Vol. 19. pp203-218.

MANZONI, J.F. and BARSOUX, J.L. (2004) Rescue remedy. *People Management*. Vol. 14, October. pp26–28.

MCGOVERN, T. and TINSLEY, H. (1978) Interviewer evaluations of interviewee non-verbal behaviour. *Journal of Vocational Behaviour*. Vol. 13, No. 2. pp163–171.

MCMAHON, G. (1999) A lovely audience. *People Management*. 25 March. pp60–61.

MARTIN, P and POPE, J. (2008) Competency-based interviewing – has it gone too far? *Industrial & Commercial Training*. Vol. 40, No. 2. pp81–86.

PEARCE, C. (2007) Ten steps to conducting a selection interview. *Nursing Management*. Vol. 14, No. 5. pp21.

PHILPOTT, L. and SHEPPARD, L. (1992) Managing for improved performance. In M. Armstrong (ed), *Strategies for human resource management*. London: Kogan Page.

PIGGOT-IRVINE, E. (2003) Key features of appraisal effectiveness. *International Journal of Educational Management*. Vol. 17, No. 4. pp170–178.

PINGITORE, R., DUGONI, B., TINDALE, R. and SPRING, B. (1994) Bias against overweight job applicants in a simulated employment interview. *Journal of Applied Psychology*. Vol. 79, No. 6. pp909–917.

QUILLIAM, G. (1995) *Body language*. Godalming: Carlton Books.

ROBBINS, S. and HUNSAKER, P. (2009) *Training in interpersonal skills*. 5th ed. London: Pearson.

SEARLE, R. (2003) *Selection and recruitment: a critical text*. Milton Keynes: Palgrave Macmillan.

SORIANO, K. (2007) Appraisals seen as a 'box-ticking' exercise. *People Management*. 3 December. Available online at: http://www.peoplemanagement.co.uk/pm/articles/2007/12/appraisalsseenaboxtickingexercise.htm [accessed 29 May 2010].

STEWART, G., DUSTIN, S., BARRICK, M. and DARNOLD, T. (2008) Exploring the handshake in employment interviews. *Journal of Applied Psychology*. Vol. 93, No. 5. pp1139–1146.

SWINBURNE, P. (2001) How to use feedback to improve performance. *People Management*. 31 May. Available online at: http://www.peoplemanagement.co.uk/pm/articles/2001/05/730.htm [accessed 29 May 2010].

TAYLOR, S. (2008) *People resourcing*, 4th ed. London: CIPD.

TORRINGTON, D., HALL, L. and TAYLOR, S. (2005) *Human resource management*. 6th ed. Harlow: FT/Prentice Hall.

WALLEY, L. and SMITH, M. (1998) *Deception in selection*. Chichester: Wiley.

WHIDDETT, S. and HOLLYFORDE, S. (1999) *The competencies handbook*. London: IPD.

WOODS, D. (2009a) Managers' lack of interviewing skills puts employers at risk of discrimination claims. *Human Resources*. 14 July. Available online at: http://www.hrmagazine.co.uk/news/919916/Managers-lack-interviewing-skills-puts-employers-risk-discrimination-claims/ [accessed 29 May 2010].

WOODS, D. (2009b) Interviewers don't spend enough time weighing up candidates' pros and cons. *Human Resources*. 16 February. Available online at: http://www.hrmagazine.co.uk/news/881149/Interviewers-dont-spend-enough-time-weighing-candidates-pros-cons/ [accessed 29 May 2010].

CHAPTER 9

Learning professional and training skills for the contemporary business environment

Gillian Watson *and* Ivana Adamson

OVERVIEW

This chapter seeks to give you a relevant and contemporary view of learning and training-related issues as they affect individuals and the organisations in which they work. There are the fundamental training strategies to consider such as analysing need, delivery methods and evaluation. There are also wider implications for organisations to contend with, for example decisions as to whether to train or not. Relevant skills are required to enable you and your team to benefit from learning, training and development initiatives. To achieve this, however, the skill of advocacy is an important consideration, as by harnessing delivery methods and presentation skills you should be able to advocate a business case for training and learning. We also discuss the various trainer roles and highlight in what scenarios they may be used as well as reviewing the role of the learning professional. The purpose of this chapter is to enable you to develop the relevant skills so as to enhance your ability to develop others or/ and to get your point across when presenting all necessary skills for people in, or aspiring to be in, a leadership role.

LEARNING OUTCOMES

By the end of this chapter, provided you engage with the activities, you should be able to:

- understand current training, learning and development issues
- conduct an analysis of training provision
- analyse individual and departmental learning/training needs
- evaluate learning/training provision
- improve your presentation skills
- understand the business imperatives linked to development issues
- support organisational effectiveness through development initiatives.

9.1 INTRODUCTION

Learning, training and development is a vast subject, and therefore not all aspects can be covered here. However, what we can achieve is an overview of recent research and CIPD-led surveys that have discussed learning and training, in particular what contemporary organisations are expecting from their learning professionals/trainers and the subsequent impact on their staff. We will consider what these individuals do and the skills and techniques they could employ. In today's business environment the aptly named 'global re-think' (CIPD 2007a) must be evaluated in relation to the strategic development of staff. In fact, skills in producing the business-case arguments are significant in maintaining and realising relevant staff development in any organisation.

This chapter therefore seeks to show the relationship between learning and training and to enable you to develop skills of the learning professional. Reynolds (2004, p1) offers his definition of training and learning thus: 'training was defined as "an instructor-led, content-based intervention, leading to desired changes in behaviour", and learning as "a self-directed, work-based process, leading to increased adaptive capacity"'. Therefore this chapter is part of a continuum of learning highlighted by Reynolds which has aspirations to enable changed behaviours, encourage self-directed learning and increase capacity and performance.

9.2 LEARNING PROFESSIONAL/TRAINER ROLES

The title 'trainer' can be used or understood to explain a variation of roles and a myriad of actual job-related skills. Certainly the complexity of the tasks related

Figure 9.1 Role and skills elements of the learning professional/trainer

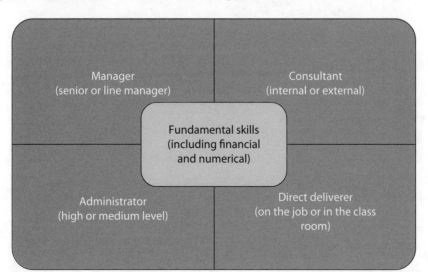

Source: drawing on Bureau of Training (1970) as cited in Johnson and Geal (2009, p49).

to training can be both expansive and eclectic. Therefore the title 'trainer' itself can have a different meaning in a number of organisations. These roles can range from a direct trainer, a HR generalist who has some accountability for staff training or performance, an internal or external consultant, a line manager, a training administrator (high or medium-level job role) or a director of learning and development (Johnson and Geal 2009).

Figure 9.2 Developing the learning professional

Developing the learning professional	

Administrator	• The role may include the production of a range of paper work:
	   o Training notes
	   o Joining instructions
	   o Course lists
	   o Letters to: venue – clients – suppliers
	• Could act as clerical assistant to the trainer, consultant or manager
	• Manages the library – loan of learning materials
	• Manages the learning interface – officiates over the rules of attendance and certification
	• Problem-solver and handler – everyone needs information or help – now!

Direct deliverer or trainer	• Skills of: Insightfulness, reliability, dealing with people
	• Needs a systematic approach to the task therefore, initially they develop skills in:
	   o Conducting learning needs analysis
	   o Defining entry level behaviour
	   o Producing learning objective
	Designing the learning event using the appropriate delivery methods
	• Delivering the event and assessing the results
	• Initially trainers train from their own experience – pass on their skill to others
	• Teach what is new – trainees do as they are instructed

Figure 9.2 continued

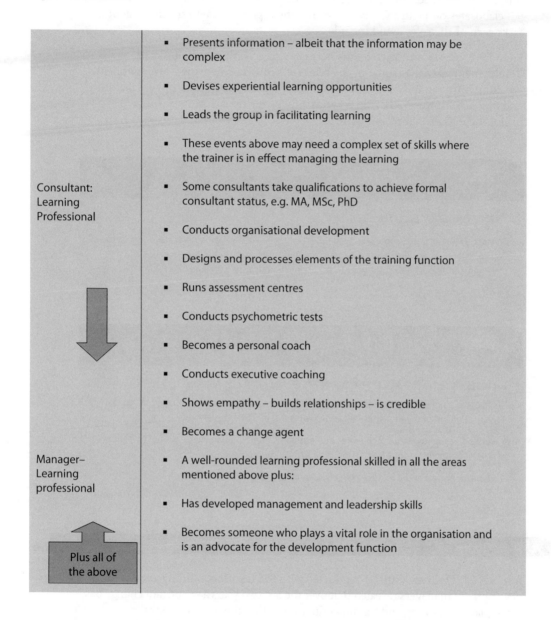

	■ Presents information – albeit that the information may be complex
	■ Devises experiential learning opportunities
	■ Leads the group in facilitating learning
	■ These events above may need a complex set of skills where the trainer is in effect managing the learning
Consultant: Learning Professional	■ Some consultants take qualifications to achieve formal consultant status, e.g. MA, MSc, PhD
	■ Conducts organisational development
	■ Designs and processes elements of the training function
	■ Runs assessment centres
	■ Conducts psychometric tests
	■ Becomes a personal coach
	■ Conducts executive coaching
	■ Shows empathy – builds relationships – is credible
	■ Becomes a change agent
Manager– Learning professional	■ A well-rounded learning professional skilled in all the areas mentioned above plus:
	■ Has developed management and leadership skills
	■ Becomes someone who plays a vital role in the organisation and is an advocate for the development function
Plus all of the above	

There are some fundamental skills learning professionals/trainers should possess, which include a good level of intellect as well as relevant knowledge and a synthesis of the materials – in short, attributes that enable them and others to perform. They would also be expected to possess good numerical and communication skills and require personal qualities that allow them to relate to others in order to facilitate learning, always remembering that the reason we encourage staff to engage in training is to ensure that they learn and consequently, develop. Professionals/trainers therefore need to learn and develop into a well-rounded professional in order to progress their own careers. Figure 9.2 elaborates on Figure 9.1 by expressing the type of behaviours and practical tasks each of the roles could include.

Figure 9.2 focuses on the elements necessary to accomplish the tasks of development as well as some of the relevant skills. The items we have highlighted are numerous and to become proficient and experienced in them will take time and practice. However, they do serve as a focus for the aspiring learning professional as described in Figure 9.2.

ACTIVITY 9.1

SKILLS DEVELOPMENT

Consider Figure 9.2 as an opportunity to reflect on the skills that you already have and those that you intend to acquire. Use it as a checklist for part of your continuing professional development process. Incorporate your results into your learning log and/or CPD log.

ACTIVITY 9.2

TRAINING OR/AND LEARNING IN ORGANISATIONS

To give you an overall perspective as to how training or/and learning is managed in your organisation (or an organisation with which you are familiar):

- Evaluate whether some of the roles and attributes mentioned in Figure 9.1 are present in the department/wider organisation in which you work or study.

- Consider whether the roles are largely accomplished by line managers.

9.3 CURRENT LEARNING AND DEVELOPMENT ISSUES

A recent CIPD survey (2010a) conducted with 859 learning, training and development managers revealed that over the last two years a significant change has taken place in learning and training initiatives within the organisations they surveyed. More respondents are opting to introduce programmes to develop the role of the line manager (61 per cent) as well as taking forward innovations that enable the development of a learning and development culture (50 per cent) across the organisation. In addition, 47 per cent of respondents maintain that coaching by the line manager is an improvement on learning and development approaches that already exist in their organisation. This aligns with a view expressed by 65 per cent of respondents who believe that learning and development activities will continue to integrate with business strategy, while 60 per cent suggest that in future more emphasis must be put on evaluating the effectiveness of the development function.

This is probably no surprise given the current economic climate, in which organisations are finding it necessary to become more efficient and effective with fewer resources. Even more critical for a manager of the learning, training and development function is to make the business case, which would argue that any learning and development initiative such as training, mentoring and coaching is in line with the organisational strategies.

The same CIPD survey suggests an inclination towards optimism for the future in relation to organisations earmarking resources for development of their staff. However, development budgets are always constricted when the economic outlook is uncertain; consequently organisations will be scrutinising the 'value-addedness' of their development departments. The survey endorses this level of caution by alerting us to the fact that on a positive note 70 per cent of organisations who took part in the research had kept a training budget for 2009; however, this budget had decreased from the 2008 level. This, in quantitative terms, is quoted as the median spend for 2009 being £220 per employee – a decrease of £80 from the 2008 expenditure of £300. Concurrently these organisations registered an increase in take-up of government assistance for enhancing employee skills; for instance, 47 per cent of respondents indicated that they had engaged in (or had thought about engaging in) the 'Train to Gain' initiative (a UK government initiative to train a high volume of the country's workforce), an indicator that organisations are exploring every opportunity at their disposal to protect developmental imperatives. Other European Union and overseas countries will be forging their own responses to supporting training; however, this may be tempered by their respective economic circumstances.

 ACTIVITY 9.3

CHANGES IN TRAINING PROVISION

Review whether your organisation (or an organisation that you are familiar with) has:

- increased or decreased its training provision in the last year
- applied for or used government-led initiatives to help fund the development provision
- invested in developing its line managers.

Why, or why not?

Discuss your findings with others; compare and contrast to establish whether the organisation you have investigated is following the current trends.

Economic considerations are essential when addressing the skills that professionals will need for their current and future career enhancement, as in conjunction with numerical and financial skills they need 'commercial awareness and business acumen' (CIPD 2010a). They must combine this with excellent communication and interpersonal skills, the ability to persuade and the art of facilitating learning. Johnson and Geal (2009, p49) express their views as to what behaviours a trainer or development professional should exhibit thus: 'Trainers need the foundations of behaviour as expounded through behaviourism, psychodynamics, the humanist approach, social behaviour, personality and learning theory.' Therefore, they suggest that skills development in this area of work has its own complexities.

9.4 GROWING TALENT

All organisations aspire to attract the 'best' people. Talent can be bought in by recruiting new people or it can be grown from within the organisation. It is critical, therefore, for an organisation to be fully aware of its skills gaps and learning and training needs, and how they might be filled. The problem is that these issues have been a somewhat short-term interpretation of actual requirements rather than part of continuing sustainable strategic developments. The CIPD contemporary survey, in discussing the 'war on talent', suggests: 'Our professional engagement should be with issues of sustainability and substance. This will be a much better defence against future meltdown than any war' (Butler 2010, p1). In this quote Butler was expressing some concern regarding the paths organisations have hitherto taken in regard to developing talent, and contends that a more co-operative attitude is required to grow the talent of the future. This also heralds the change in focus from training to learning as a development tool that has greater focus on individuals and how they can be engaged, motivated and prepared for a range of learning experiences at the workplace. The *Helping People Learn* survey (Reynolds 2004) characterised the changing focus of the training professional in terms of: 'The progressive movement from the delivery of content to the development of learning capabilities as a people development strategy' (Reynolds (2004) as cited in Butler 2010, p1), thereby highlighting the focus on learning and skills development.

Therefore, this chapter refers to 'learning' in a wider context than 'training', as the former relies on the transfer of development on a more permanent basis that encompasses the build-up of capabilities and attributes which have the potential to support and enhance the career of the individual learner. This is not to denigrate 'training' as it has a vital role in meeting the immediate needs of the individual, department or organisation, focusing on a specific area that assists the overall development strategy. It is not enough for organisations to provide learning and training opportunities. Employees must be willing to learn, to transfer and use any newly acquired knowledge and skills for the greater good of themselves and others in the organisation.

All too often the debate regarding sustainability, employability and skills concentrates on the views of employers and the government (see Leitch 2006) and neglects to involve the workforce. The CIPD (2008) survey *Who learns at work* sought to include workers in the debate, and therefore the findings are worthy of examination. Of those respondents who do not receive training on a regular basis, 24 per cent worked in the private sector, and 11 per cent and 12 per cent in the public and voluntary sectors respectively (CIPD 2008). Those respondents employed by large organisations were more likely to receive training than those employed by small firms (ie those with 20 or fewer employees). Out of those questioned (751 individuals), 18 per cent had not received training in the previous year. Of that 18 per cent, the largest group (27 per cent) who had not received training were over 55 years old. Those in the lowest economic groups accounted for the same percentage (27 per cent) who (as in the case of the over-55-year-olds), did not have the opportunity to train. These factors are worrying from a diversity management perspective (see Chapter 1). The survey informs us that the most frequent forms of delivery are off-the-job training (64 per cent) which takes place in classrooms or meeting areas. Training delivered on the job was enjoyed by 51 per cent of respondents; here the researchers did not discriminate between employer-led or externally led deliverers. A constructive characteristic of this survey was that the data showed an increase in employees receiving training from their line managers, from 21 per cent in 2005 to 36 per cent in 2008. Training or coaching from someone else rose from 20 per cent to 23 per cent and training by electronic methods ('e-learning') rose from 18 per cent to 26 per cent (see also Chapter 13). This suggests:

- Increasingly line managers need to exhibit a breadth of training skills.

- More line managers than ever before need to be aware of coaching or mentoring initiatives and be prepared to engage in this activity.

- The somewhat obvious connotation, however, is that less direct trainer-led activity is taking place.

- E-learning continues to grow but perhaps not at a fast pace: the increase is less than was previously predicted (Harrison 2002, Reynolds 2002).

- Organisations use a range of blended learning (see Section 9.8, Learning and training).

- There are some definite questions regarding opportunities for employees aged over 55 years; it might have been desirable to ask whether the training policy aligned with any diversity policy in the organisations surveyed.

- The line manager as well as the learning-professional needs to be knowledgeable and gain experience in a wide range of learning techniques.

- And, possibly to have the ability to persuade others that training and development is necessary and meaningful is a valuable communication skill to acquire.

9.5 DEVELOPMENT PROCESS

The learning, training and development process must be delivered as part of an overarching strategic development process. Several writers (eg Harrison 2002,

Figure 9.3 Organisational development strategy

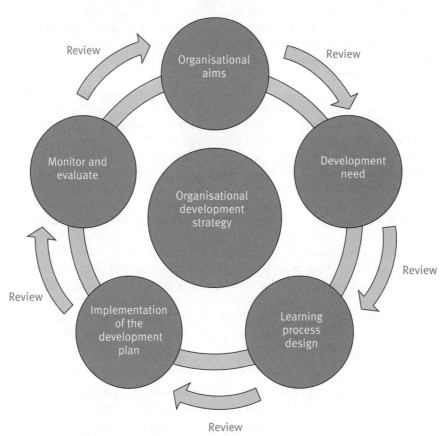

Reid et al 2004) offer a model for such development; the adaptations below (see Figures 9.2 and 9.3) draw from those sources.

From an organisational perspective it is vital that a clear development strategy is devised and that there are adequate opportunities to monitor review and evaluate. This strategy should be established upon a definitive identification of need linked to the organisations aims and strategic objectives. However, for the purposes of this text we will concentrate on the operational aspects of such a plan.

A central focus of contemporary organisations is sustainable performance. To achieve this organisations must create effective processes to organise the development of their staff (see Figure 9.3). These processes and plans should be monitored and reviewed continuously so that the organisations' learning and training needs can be met. Core elements of this process are the identification of learning and training needs, crediting prior learning and creating action plans, designing and planning the learning, delivering and implementing the plan, and critically evaluating the whole process. We assume therefore that organisations are undergoing perpetual change and their learning and development practices will transform and adapt accordingly.

Figure 9.4 Operationalising the learning and training process

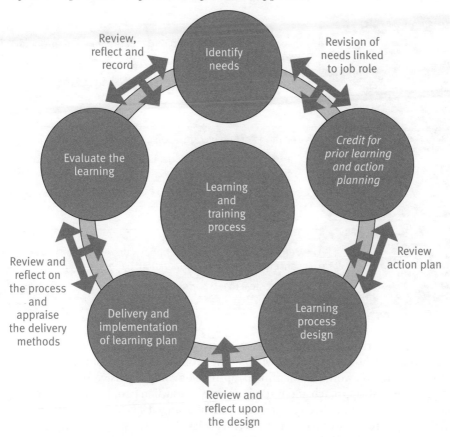

9.6 LEARNING AND TRAINING NEEDS ANALYSIS

The identification of learning and training needs is aligned to the analysis of the gaps in skills and knowledge. This analysis should identify individuals who will need to learn and/or train to have the required competencies for present and future performance. The issue of identifying needs is really a process that enables the organisation to fill the development gaps. This can involve both formal and informal provision encompassed in a course of action that delivers opportunities for learning and allows individuals to gain relevant experience. The CIPD (2009a, p1) suggests training and learning needs analyses are a 'health check on skills, talent and capabilities in the organisation'. They go on to say it is a 'systematic gathering of data to find out where the there are gaps in the existing skills, knowledge and attitudes of employees'. The overall aim of this data gathering is to enable learning professionals to produce a plan so that ongoing business capacity can be maintained and potentially exceeded.

Methods of data collection include problem-centred analysis as well a process that compares the individual's competency and performance with that for the role profile or key tasks. A performance-centred approach therefore reviews problems

Figure 9.5 Components of the learning gap

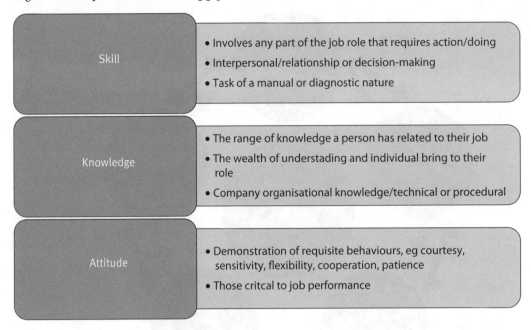

Skill	• Involves any part of the job role that requires action/doing • Interpersonal/relationship or decision-making • Task of a manual or diagnostic nature
Knowledge	• The range of knowledge a person has related to their job • The wealth of understading and individual bring to their role • Company organisational knowledge/technical or procedural
Attitude	• Demonstration of requisite behaviours, eg courtesy, sensitivity, flexibility, cooperation, patience • Those critcal to job performance

or difficulties experienced by individuals or those within a department or organisation as a whole. It considers whether the problem is due to a skills gap, in which case the reason would be identified. A profile or comprehensive analysis takes a broad-brush approach and is used in some cases when people are new to a job or when new jobs have been created, because of changed strategic imperatives. Key task analysis relates to a particular or critical task that relates to the overall job or role held by an individual. Harrison (2002, p269) suggests: 'Job training analysis is a process of identifying the purpose of a job and its component parts, and specifying what must be learned in order for there to be effective work performance.' The learning gap may be in one of three areas in Figure 9.5.

All of the above have relevance to the development of skills required by the organisation and to the methods used in the delivery of learning and training. Table 9.1 opposite sets out an overview of the types of data collection methods that may be employed, the knowledge, skills and attitude (KSA) required of the learning/training professional and where it is most typically used (adapted from Harrison 2002, p273–278).

Learning, training and personal development undertaken by individuals in organisations should result in an improvement in their performance. However, it should also be cost-effective and measurable.

9.7 CREDITING ACHIEVEMENT

In order for learning and training to be cost effective, the needs analysis must be integral to the individual, role and organisational status. However, most

Table 9.1 Analysis of data collection methods

Comprehensive or profile analysis	Examination of all tasks in the job role usually compartmentalised into knowledge, skills and attitudes (KSA). Measuring objectives, standards and frequency of performance. KSA in this context is time consuming and requires skill. Typically used for: manual repetitive tasks, unchanging tasks; could have many job-holders in the organisation.
Problem-centred analysis	Definition of the problem that requires learning or training interventions. Finding what caused the dilemma and the characteristics of the problem and the KSA relevant to the issue. Can be combined with key task analysis. KSA requires good interpersonal and communication skills as the job holder should be involved in the analytical process. Typically used when: intervention is urgent, job holder needs help in a limited area of development.
Key task analysis	Proficiency in certain performance levels is critical to the job overall. Requires focus on an area of the learner's job specification; the intervention will only focus on those tasks. KSA requires good interpersonal and communication skills as the job holder should be involved in the analytical process. Analysis carried out on a regular basis. Typically used where: tasks vary and have non-critical components, job has a wide variety of tasks, intervention needed in key tasks, Also when the job changes in content, priorities, emphasis and skill level
Competency-based analysis	Analysis is both job and person related. Clearly defined standards of performance can relate to one or more groups in an organisation, Need to relate interventions to a national standard, eg NVQ. When the main problem is to identify the core behavioural attributes needed to perform across a job sector. Use of a competency framework. KSA needs meticulous analytical skills, patience and resilience, along with good interpersonal and communication skills. Typically used when; a statement of the general role or category of the job is needed, eg managerial at first-line level. A breakdown of the role in discrete components is needed. Statement of competence needed. A criteria for the measurement of competency is required.

interventions tend to be directed at individuals and their immediate workplace, so the benefits tend to be more localised. We need to keep in mind that training is not carried out in a 'tabula rasa' or neutral environment. 'Tabula rasa' is Latin for 'scraped table' and often refers to one's having a 'clean slate' or the mind of a newborn. Organisations are therefore far removed from the concept of 'tabula rasa', as they are environments with their own distinctive histories and cultures, formal structures, technology, reward systems and work practices. All these have an impact on the relationships within an organisation, on how employees are selected for further development, on how information is disseminated and on how learning/training is perceived and supported. Individuals also come with a raft of previous learning achievements, which may include NVQs, degrees or/and a professional accreditation. Therefore, whatever development we may embark upon, we do not start with a clean slate; we have views and opinions as to the value of such undertakings.

It should be emphasised that, on the one hand, models of training are rooted in educational practices where knowledge and skills are closely linked. The formal educational system aims to equip individuals with the ability to learn, for example, to change a situation and act autonomously. On the other hand, in organisations individuals are often expected to modify their behaviour to support the organisational aims and objectives, for example to become part of the system. Therefore, individuals need to feel part of the system. One aspect of this is the recording of their achievements, recognising their prior learning and creating personal learning action plans for ongoing development, thus ensuring that individuals feel valued and see the organisation as supporting their development on to other programmes.

Some of these other programmes may involve attendance or distance learning through a university or professional body; these will align with the Quality Assurance Agency's (see website: http://www.qaa.ac.uk) mapping across programmes. However, no formal agreement actually exists between various awarding bodies, and it can therefore be problematic if a potential student wishes to use recognised credits when applying for a higher education programme. That said, most higher education establishments in the United Kingdom will try to accredit prior achievement/learning, allowing wider participation in Bachelor's or Master's degrees. Furthermore, universities will have a mapping process for recognising qualification from overseas students following internationally recognised guidelines on to other programmes (for instance, the European Qualifications Framework is recognised by OECD).

9.8 DESIGNING LEARNING AND TRAINING

We need to establish the link between other elements of the learning/training cycle. Firstly, we analysed need linked to the job/role an individual possesses and how setting learning objectives helps to clarify precisely the purpose and expected outcome of a learning process. Secondly, we must, when designing learning or training events, consider the current accomplishments of the learners. However, as we have indicated previously there are many methods of engaging the workforce in a range of learning initiatives. Table 9.2 categorises some of the methods that enable the design of the learning process to take place.

Table 9.2 shows a range of activities and methods that could be used to augment the design process. A further example of a step-by-step design structure may help here, as illustrated in Figure 9.6 (p265).

Table 9.2 Design methods

Learning and training strategy	Design methods used
Instruction – work based	At the work place: • The learner may have needed preparation time; this will have taken place before the trainer-led development. • Assemble the necessary learning materials and aids. In terms of resources machinery may need to be available for on-job development. • For simple tasks the key point will need to be emphasised and learner progress catalogued.
Managerial – work based	May take the form of coaching from a senior individual or an external consultant. Preparation will take place with the learner reflecting on an aspect of the job role. Other examples may include work-shadowing good practice. Key learning points will be agreed and a learning plan developed.
Focused in-company experience	Designed using existing company initiatives: may be in or out of the department. In short, a planned experience that supports the individual's ongoing development: eg special project or assignment, new product development, problem-solving group and the like. These activities, backed by the organisation, are most likely to allow a convincing transfer of learning. Coaching and mentoring may also factor in the overall learning design.
Regular in-house courses	Most large organisations have in-house learning and training programmes. Here the design may factor-in refreshing the learner's awareness of new techniques or general up-dating. These may also include in-house discussion forums, conferences. and/ or tele-conferencing calls to another part of the organisation. Other in-house programmes may be designed to fit a particular qualification or standard, eg NVQs. Computer-based design may also feature; this would take a process of progressing from one unit to another until all elements have been successfully completed. Key learning points are firmly organisationally based, although most individuals will capable of transferring this knowledge to other work settings.

Table 9.2 continued

Blended learning	Many definitions of this method exist. However, the main consideration is that the learning is designed using more than one method of delivery. For example, a distance-learning programme may use the following: • computer-based – Internet/intranet-focused package • lecture – seminar – discussion with tutor • DVD. These programmes are usually cost effective and utilise in-house experience with externally developed packages. Key reason for using this design is that it can harmonise an individual's learning preferences with appropriate delivery methods; it also expands and enhances development opportunities for all employees.
A planned external organisational experience	This involves planned visits to external partners, eg suppliers, customers, other parts of the organisation (overseas). May be resource intensive so the design must conform closely with the development need as well as the organisational imperatives. Here the transfer of knowledge may largely depend on the value the learner places on the experience.
External courses	All organisations are bombarded with external literature advertising courses. They can be categorised as a) the short 'quick hit' variety run at an external venue – usually staffed by consultants, and b) the longer term – possibly part-time – programme which will end in a qualification. The design therefore is external: the organisation's input is to decide whether it fits in to an agreed learning plan, and if so to allocate resources.
Self-oriented learning	Here learners are reliant on their own management and design skills to facilitate their own development, although these may be linked to the individual's work role. In some organisations staff may be actively encouraged to self-manage their learning, although in this circumstance it must be supported by an organisational culture which values development and learning. A CPD-recording system is of value here (see Chapters 1 and 18).

 ACTIVITY 9.5

REVIEW DESIGN STEPS

Either:

• Review the design steps of a course or programme of which you are familiar.

or:

• Consider an aspect of behaviour (managerial, administrative, shopfloor) taking place in an organisation of your choice and think how it can be improved. Design a learning or training process to enable improvement to take place.

Figure 9.6 Step-by-step design structure

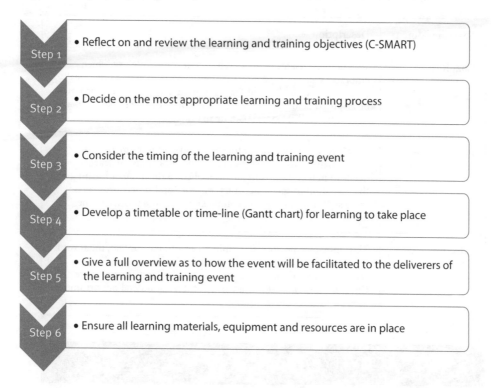

Step 1
- Reflect on and review the learning and training objectives (C-SMART)

Step 2
- Decide on the most appropriate learning and training process

Step 3
- Consider the timing of the learning and training event

Step 4
- Develop a timetable or time-line (Gantt chart) for learning to take place

Step 5
- Give a full overview as to how the event will be facilitated to the deliverers of the learning and training event

Step 6
- Ensure all learning materials, equipment and resources are in place

It is always preferable to ensure such step-by-step design features are present in any learning design structure you may undertake. Used as a checklist they help to organise the whole process and make sure certain elements are not omitted. The process itself is used to enable us to move to the next stage and it also ensures the previous stages in the learning cycle have been utilised correctly.

9.9 LEARNING AND BEHAVIOURAL OBJECTIVES

Writing behavioural objectives is an important part of the training process. However, it is worth reflecting purposefully on the learning domain in which they occur. We refer here to knowledge, skills and attitudes which are manifest in the cognitive, psychomotor and affective domains respectively. Table 9.3 overleaf gives an overview of the type of behavioural objective that may be established in a particular learning domain.

Learning development objectives are an essential part of the training process; they allow both the learner and the trainer to assess whether the learner behaviour has changed in the light of the development process. In writing a learning objective the trainer is required to describe what the learner will have achieved at the end of the training or study period. This helps to set targets for achievement; therefore, producing guidelines on how to write objectives for use in organisations and

Table 9.3 Learning domain descriptors

Learning domain	Description
Cognitive (knowledge)	This domain relates to the development of the intellect which embraces conceptual skills, which in its basic form includes recall of data and recognition of facts and patterns. The basic forms must be acquired before the later-stage categories can be undertaken and more advanced categories can be mastered.
Psychomotor (skills)	This involves the use of motor skills: physical movement and co-ordination. To achieve good psychomotor skills the learner needs to practise; measurements applied to this type of learning are the execution of speed, accuracy, distance and procedures. Again these skills may increase in complexity the more proficient the learner becomes.
Affective (attitude)	This domain is positioned within an emotional context, the way in which we handle or cope with events. It involves our feelings, values, appreciation, enthusiasm, motivation and attitudes (see also Chapter 4). All are vital as an array of developmental opportunities used to acquire leadership skills.

ACTIVITY 9.6

WRITING LEARNING OBJECTIVES FOR A TRAINING EVENT

From the insight you have gained thus far, practise writing a set of learning objectives for a training session on one of these topics:

- A briefing for your team who are meeting a new overseas client.
- A departmental change, eg merging with another department.
- A situation in your own practice.

You may choose to do this task in groups or on an individual basis. Compare and contrast your attempts with others in the study group..

formal study is an important skill a manager should acquire. 'SMART' objectives are often used, and some managers or trainer might add 'C' to form 'C-SMART', thus: Challenging, Specific, Measurable, Achievable, Relevant and Time-bound/defined. Arguably, adding the C – challenging – helps to focus the intellect on the more stimulating and exacting form of a SMART objective.

9.10 LEARNING AND TRAINING DELIVERY OPTIONS

Essentially the learning professional must be aware of the level at which the learning and training is pitched/aimed. If a first-year nursing student, for

Table 9.4 C-SMART objectives

C-SMART	Written in terms of what the individual should be able to do
Challenging	Allowing the learner a good level of challenge and enabling him/her to engage in activities that are both stimulating and motivating.
Specific	The objective should be as specific as possible. It should describe what the individual should be able to do or demonstrate after the training or learning event.
Measurable	Written so that an explicit (yes or no) answer can be given as to whether the objective has been attained or not.
Achievable and	By definition objectives should be achievable yet challenging and describe what the individual is currently unable to accomplish. They should not demoralise; to be precise, should not be too far removed from what a trainee will be capable of undertaking.
Agreed with the individual learner	Learning objectives can be a negotiated/agreed process between the learner and the trainer or line manager. Some appraisal systems operate a process where the appraisal concludes with a set of agreed development objectives, although in many cases the appraisee is responsible for the first draft.
Relevant	Relevant to the needs of both the individual and the department/ organisation, whereby the achievement of the learning objectives will enhance performance and be a factor in the attainment of organisational targets.
Time-bound	Learning objectives are often rendered useless if they are open ended, which removes the learner's sense of urgency and thus his/her motivation to achieve. Therefore a target time or date should be set whereupon the learner should be able to carry out the task, test, assessment, demonstration, etc.

example, was due to attend a lecture and went to the midwifery module by mistake, she/he would be very aware that the relevant learning and underpinning had not yet taken place for the full value of the learning to be apparent. Yet another equally important factor is whether the training is on a one-to-one basis or delivered in heterogeneous groups. The overview in Table 9.5 (overleaf) endeavours to raise awareness of a number of learning and training options that may be available, although this is not an exclusive compilation.

The CIPD highlights the use of e-learning and blended learning by describing them thus:

- **E-learning**: 'developed online development topics, with exercises and diagnostic tools which are accessible to all'.

- **Blended learning**: 'main focus on blended learning increasing the use of e-learning and e-packages for mandatory training, for example induction, risk management'. (CIPD 2010b, p16)

In Chapter 18 there are many examples of the project assignment type of development as well as several case studies that help to illuminate the points raised above.

Table 9.5 covers relevant learning and training options for working in groups, and shows a range of method and types of activities that can be employed.

Table 9.5 Overview of learning and training options

Learning and training options		
Description of the learning or training	Delivery method	Advantages and disadvantages
One-to-one: tell–show–do	Sitting with 'Nellie': involves the trainee sitting alongside an experienced worker and observing the relevant behaviour before trying it out for themselves. Often also describes as the 'tell–show–do' method.	Usually more sophisticated approaches are adopted; however, this does introduce a trial-and-error process that enables the trainee to learn from experience, have one-to-one guidance and acquire basic skills. Caution is needed here as the new operative takes on the skills of the existing worker, including all his/her mistakes or short-cuts. In other words, the learning professional needs to be credible and truly skilled at the work.
One-to-one: coaching (see also Chapter 17).	Coaching: an individual with this could be his/her senior manager or more likely an external consultant. Work-related events and developments can form a basis for reflection and monitoring of personal improvement. Because of the direct work relationship the impact can be immediate and enhancing for both the individual and the department. Executive coaching is also delivered on a one-to-one basis, although this is usually through a planned personal and professional development process for senior managers and is delivered, in most cases, through engaging an external consultant.	Advantages include: • Remedial training can be offered if the required performance is not being achieved. • Taking on a new challenge, the individual may need assistance to meet the range of new work or extended skill set. • Job enhancement to stretch the individual abilities and attributes. • Consolidation of a range of developments or courses already experienced or achieved, the individual is encouraged to put the new skills into practice. Disadvantages: • The main disadvantage here is cost ie the line manager's or a consultant's time must be budgeted as part of the overall training cost. • If there is no follow up process the initiative/skill set can be diminished.

Table 9.5 continued

Description of the learning or training	Delivery method	Advantages and disadvantages

Combination 'blended learning': project assignment (see chapter 18)	Project assignment has increasing worth as a training method; however it is not readily recognised as a direct development process. The projects therefore should be chosen so that the individual's capabilities can be stretched but not over-stretched. The task may involve addressing a particular problem or a relevant enhancement and enrichment. Fundamentally to enable this type of initiative to become successful organisations must conscientiously adhere to the values and concepts involved in this type of development, notably as part of the prevailing culture of continuing enrichment.
	
	This level of development can be internally costly and some organisations take the view that to hire a consultant to do the task or to send the trainee on a course on 'project management' would be the less expensive option.
		Advantages:
		• Involves the individual with his/her coach or development manager in addressing a work related issue.
		• Can be used as part of a Master's degree programme where active research methods are being used to construct the dissertation.
		• Allows the learner to acquire a considerable breadth of skills (see Chapter 1).
		• Can try new methods; be creative, review change-related initiative, be a change-agent, eg pilot project.
		• Has the potential to be career enhancing.
		Disadvantages:
		• Problematic unless you have the full backing of the management hierarchy as the project may extend over many departments.
		• Problems also occur unless you have:
		  – relevant level of understanding from staff in the various departments
		  – good preparation and planning and regular reviews
		  – good access to the senior/strategic manager who is your guide or mentor for the life of the project (it may be your line manager)
		  – a guide that possesses the right skill set
		  – the relevant awareness of the personal demands project work can create; and willingness to acquire new skills.

Table 9.6 Overview of group learning and training

Learning and training options: learning in groups		
Description of the learning/ training	**Method**	**Advantages and disadvantages**

Learning in groups	There are many methods associated with learning in groups. The method chosen will depend on the desired learning outcomes.	Generic advantages:
		• Large numbers of people can be trained in one place.
		• The specialist, lecturer or trainer can impart new ideas or techniques to a large group.
		• Cost-effective.
		• Issues can be discussed.
		• People can support and learn from each other.
		• The merits of new ideas can be analysed and evaluated.
		Generic disadvantages:
		• Problematic if the learners are not progressing at the same speed; a compromise rate is often found.
		• Restrictive issues which are often present in a heterogeneous group:
		  – Motivational differences (some individuals may not want to take part).
		  – Some people have different learning preferences and may not want to learn in a group environment. This seriously minimises the effectiveness of the group's ability to learn.
		  – Some may have personal reasons why active participation alongside others is felt to be uncomfortable.

Problem-solving groups	Case-study-based.	• Ensures the group members have an opportunity to practice/simulate experience of a certain technique or incident and to discuss the outcome with the facilitator. • The plenary is important as it allows the group to discuss the different solutions, challenge other groups' results, or evaluate the different methods of approaching a particular problem. • Some participants may refute the reliability or credibility of the facilitator or the findings of another group.

Table 9.6 continued

Description of the learning/ training	Method	Advantages and disadvantages
Discussion group	Usually easy to find a forum for discussions to occur. If the groups are quite small in number it allows the more reticent members of the group to feel comfortable to discuss their ideas.	• Enables a more focused discussion to take place, possibly as a follow-up to a previous session, a lecture or in preparation for a tutorial. • Useful for work groups to consider applying their learning to the work environment in a reflective style.

Planned activities	The process by which each activity is undertaken can be reviewed, eg self-analysis and observation or group analysis and observation.
	
	The role of the observer is significant, though choosing the observer can pose problems. However, if the observer role can be interchanged between the individuals in the group taking part in the activity, it can be a powerful learning tool.
		There are various forms of this type of activity; for example:
		• A simple task, non-job related.
		• A complex task which is job-related, possible in two or more phases:
		  – plan and construct relevant objectives
		  – operationalise the plan and evaluate the outcome.
		
		An advantage in playing the observer role is that it gives the individual a chance to observe the activities more closely, which will enable them to analyse and evaluate the various events much more successfully. Remember the observer has more of an overview than those taking part in the activity.
		The observer must give relevant feedback to the participants.

ACTIVITY 9.7

GROUP INTERACTION

Plan a group interaction to brainstorm the redesign of a local coffee-bar:

• What new feature can you agree upon?

• What features are unacceptable to all the participants?

• Who emerged as leader of the group, and why?

9.11 DELIVERING LEARNING AND TRAINING

It would be futile to suggest that 'there is one right way' to deliver training. However, some trainers will deliver by using one method repeatedly, and often these approaches are destined to disappoint. Learners are diverse: they will have differing learning styles, various motivations and attitudes to learning, and they will come from a range of educational backgrounds. They may have varied cultural and national identities, which may mean their educational experiences will again be varied; some overseas students/employees may be used to didactic methods rather than the more participative approach common in the Anglo-Saxon education system (see also Chapter 1). In reality, then, 'one size fits all' does not apply to the design and delivery of learning and training; hence a more blended approach may be sensible, particularly in the modern globalisation-driven business community (Simmonds 2003). It is necessary to consider the needs of the learner. Simply put: to enable learning to take place it should be learner-centred.

Whetton and Cameron (2007) cite research by the NTL Institute for their view of learning retention; Figure 9.7 is an adaptation of their configuration. It gives the average retention rate a trainer can expect from the learning methods cited in the text. The emphasis, however, is on the 'teaching others' figure: it suggests that by teaching/training others one can gain a greater level of insight into the subject

Figure 9.7 Retention rates against particular forms of delivery

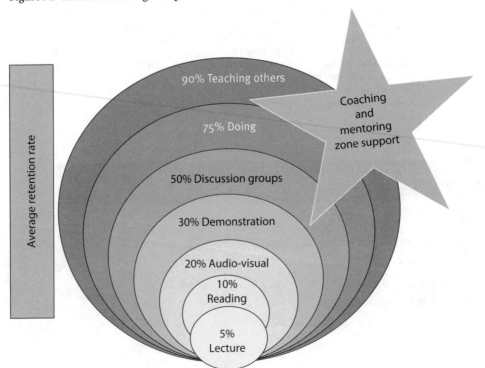

matter. Prominence is also given to the coaching and mentoring zone; these are the interactive relationship-building approaches favoured by advocates of learner-centred training.

One of the keys to delivering a successful learning and training programmes is planning. Hours spent in preparation will be deemed worthwhile if evaluation of the event shows that the audience found it valuable.

9.12 EVALUATING LEARNING AND TRAINING PROVISION

In the current business environment training providers/line managers and others will find that there is a renewed imperative for evaluating training, as the money spent on it will need to be justified. It is always easy for organisations to cut their training budgets. However if value to the organisation can be proven the decision-makers are more likely to continue developing their staff. There are many and varied other reasons why evaluation should be carried out on any development programme, some of which are indicated below.

9.12.1 EVALUATING LEARNING AND TRAINING INITIATIVES

Consider the following questions and relate them to a recent training or development programme that you have delivered or attended:

- Why should we evaluate training programmes?
- Who should carry out the activity?
- What elements should be evaluated and when should this task be completed?
- What kind of measurement tools will be used?

Your answers should mirror the following suggestions (drawing on Reid et al 2004).

9.12.1.1 Why should we evaluate the training/learning programme?

- It will give an indication as to whether the training objectives have been met and whether any additional training or remedial action is warranted.
- It will give feedback to the trainers regarding their performance (although this can controversial), methods and the learners' opinion about the whole experience.
- It may sanction the trainer to make change to the programme to initiate (ongoing) improvements.
- From the individual learners' point of view, it will allow them to evaluate in-progress achievements as part of their continuing development.
- From the organisation's standpoint, it enables a review of its expenditure on training and an opportunity to judge the outcomes. This may ameliorate the tendency of organisation to see training as intangible.

9.12.1.2 Who should carry out the activity?

- A crucial decision. Any hint of favouritism or bias could invalidate some very good work (results) or render the training worthless. Therefore, no single person evaluation is advisable.

- Tolerance, care and sensitivity should also be considerations when giving feedback.

- Involve the learners (eg happy sheets ☺, longer forms that are designed to collect data to enable the whole programme evaluated).

- From the organisation's perspective, the line manager and the employee should make it part of an appraisal and co-operate together in evaluating the benefits.

- Others may be involved, eg external consultant, evaluator, examiner, training manager.

9.12.1.3 What elements should be evaluated and when should this task be completed?

Several writers (Hamblin 1974, Bramley 19991, Reid et al (2004) suggest levels at which learning and training can be evaluated:

- Levels 1 and 2 focus on the opinions of trainees about the content and methods used in the training and learning programme realised by the trainees. They are fairly straightforward to evaluate.

- Level 3 relates to the perceived or actual change in the trainee's behaviour after the learning and training period has ended.

- Level 4 is concerned with whether the training has had a beneficial effect on the work of the department, eg measurable improvement.

- Level 5 relates to the question whether the learning and training programme has had a positive effect on the organisation as a whole. This is the most difficult level to evaluate but may link directly to issues of enhanced profitability or survival (Reid et al 2004).

9.12.1.4 What kind of measurement tools will be used?

- Varying method of measurement will be needed depending upon the level and type of learning and training undertaken.

- Timing the measurement tool to coincide with the staged completion of the training is advisable; for example the 'happy sheet' is often used at the end of a course. Further evaluation is necessary when the trainee is back in the workplace and using the new techniques, although trainees may not know for several weeks whether there new learning has been helpful.

- At Level 1 of evaluation it is reasonable to use questionnaires, interviews, group discussions, individual interviews or written reports by the trainer.

- At Level 2 evaluation tools may be part of the assessment process. These include phase tests, final tests, concluding examinations, projects, case studies, exercises, structured activities and taking part in discussions. All these techniques can be used to assess how the learner is progressing during or at the end of the course. The trainer would make an assessment of the learner's development.

- Level 3 concentrates upon improved job performance. Before-and-after measurements can be taken if the training is in an operational area of work.

- The higher up the organisational structure the trainee is, the more complex the evaluation can be. The point of the training may have been about reflecting on a new behavioural technique. The measurement of success may simply by questioning superiors or colleagues about changes in behaviour, although the function of the learned behaviour may not materialise for some time.

- Generally the more care that has been taken over the assessment of need, the greater the possibility of effective evaluation.

- Level 4 and 5 are notoriously difficult to evaluate as the evaluation is dependent on several individuals who will all have an opinion regarding levels of improvement. Evaluation is therefore carried out more on a general scale, for example through an organisational survey. Another recognisable method is seeking evidence from other internal sources, for example fewer customer complaints, employers holding a favourable attitude to training, greater profitability, higher organisational profile of the development, performance, appraisal and internal promotion (you may think of others).

ACTIVITY 9.8

CRITICAL EVALUATION

- Using Section 9.12 above, critically evaluate a course, training programme or conference you have attended during the past year.

- Consider an area of behavioural development you would like to enhance, for example, presentation skills:

  – Compile a suitable training programme for 'using presentations as a tool of persuasion'.

  – Create the learning outcomes and justify your plan. Outline the methods to be used.

  – How would this be evaluated?

9.13 PRESENTATION SKILLS

9.13.1 EFFECTIVE PRESENTATIONS

In organisations, individuals' success depends to a large extent on their ability to organise and present ideas confidently, to stay focused and to show enthusiasm and clarity. Oral presentations, whether formal or informal, can be a powerful communication tool that helps to inform or persuade others. At the same time, they can produce immediate feedback. However, just like everything else in life, variables such as resources, time, audience and place may determine the outcome, so skilful presentation may contribute to our success.

9.13.2 PREPARING FOR A PRESENTATION

The first step in preparing an effective presentation at the right pitch begins with getting to know the audience. This may make a difference between being successful or failing. The presenter thus needs to find answers to the following questions:

- Who is the audience? Technical experts, generalists, mixed audience?
- What are their knowledge and skills? How much background to introduce?
- What are their preferences? Formal or informal presentations?
- What is the size of the audience? What facilities are available? What time?
- What are their attitudes? Interested, hostile, indifferent?
- What are their demographics? Men, women, mixed audience? Young and inexperienced? Position in the organisation?

The second step is to help the presenter to establish his or her credentials, by asking the following questions:

- What is the purpose of the presentation?
  – General purpose: to inform, to persuade, to entertain.
  – Specific purpose: whom to influence, how, when and where.
- What message is to be delivered, and what response is desired?
- What is the speaker's knowledge or expertise? How authoritative is his or her knowledge? Does she or he have all the important and up-to-date information/figures?
- How does he or she feel about the presentation? Enthusiastic, indifferent, reluctant? We need to remember that it is difficult to sell an idea or a product we do not believe in.

The third step is to develop a credible and realistic key idea. This should be in a form of a statement, which is then periodically repeated and supported by the main body of presentation. Unfocused presentations confuse listeners, who are then likely to lose interest or not realise the true intent of the presentation. To highlight this, sometimes sales people hide the purpose of their presentation by stating that while they do not want to sell anything, they are concerned about the consequences of the audience not having what the presenter has to offer or is selling. This is clearly unethical behaviour and indicates that presentations are not always to the listener's benefit.

Presentations may take a number of different formats, although a generic presentation consists of the following three parts:

1. Introduction.

2. Main body.

3. Conclusion.

Key words such as 'the next important ...', 'another reason ...', 'to conclude, ...' act as bridges and are important in progressing ideas, promoting clarity, emphasising key points and keeping audience interested (see also Chapter 3). These should refer to both the most recent and the next idea, showing the relationship between the two.

ACTIVITY 9.9

BUILDING PRESENTATION SKILLS (1)

You have been asked to give a five-minute presentation on one of the following:

- interviewing for a job in another department
- asking for a pay rise
- briefing two new employees on the key operating procedures in your department.

9.13.2.1 The introduction

The purpose of an introduction is to get attention from the audience, who may not be attending because they are interested in the topic. Often, on-the-job presentations have an audience whose attendance is mandatory. It is therefore vital to build a rapport with the audience by convincing them that the presentation is worthwhile and that they will find it interesting. An introduction should last about one-fifth of the whole presentation and consists of the following steps:

1. The opening remarks should put the audience in a good mood and get their attention.

2. If the speaker has not been introduced and is not known to all present, they need to establish their credibility and demonstrate their competence.

3. The introduction is concluded by briefly outlining the major purpose for the presentation using a short summary format.

ACTIVITY 9.10

BUILDING PRESENTATION SKILLS (2)

Prepare an introduction for the following topics. Each presentation should last no more than eight minutes:

1. Getting funding for an interesting and from your point of view important conference.

2. Your department is planning to upgrade the software you are currently using and you have been asked to introduce different products for the employees to choose from.

3. Introduce new safety procedures after a recent accident.

4. Lead a discussion on reducing employee absenteeism.

9.13.2.2 The main body

Presenters often find the opening statements of the main body difficult. Thus, if the audience and the topic are familiar, only a brief background may be needed instead of a formal introduction. By now, the presenter should have the audience's attention, although the interest has to be retained. This requires pitching the tone at the right level, the remarks must be related to the topic at hand, and the topic has to build seamlessly on the introduction. Adler and Elmhorst (2002) suggest a number of steps for opening statements of the main body:

- Involve the audience by asking them a question and establish its importance.
- Lead the audience into the topic by telling them a story.
- If appropriate, present a quotation, making sure that it is relevant.
- Make a startling statement (but be sure not to offend your audience).
- Refer to the audience by mentioning their needs, concerns or interests.
- Use humour. A timely joke or an amusing remark may be effective in retaining attention, making a point and/or making the audience like the speaker more. Once again, humour must be appropriate to the topic and to the occasion. Risky jokes of all kinds are not worth the laugh they generate; remember humour does not always travel across cultural boundaries.

When the opening part is over, then the speaker may concentrate fully on the key topic of the presentation. The main points in the body of presentation should be stated in complete sentences, and should support the key topic. The body of the presentation should not exceed five points, and each point should contain only one idea. The main body may be presented with the following approach:

- The ideas must be presented in chronological order.
- The ideas must be topical, spatial and focused.
- If appropriate, the 'cause–effect' approach can be used.
- If appropriate, the 'problem–solution' approach can be used.

ACTIVITY 9.11

BUILDING PRESENTATION SKILLS (3)

Plan an opening sentence for the following presentations:

1. A discussion on the topic of 'what your organisation expects from graduates'.
2. An appeal for involving your organisation with the local community.
3. The second in a series of five talks on uptake of new technology in your organisation.
4. The management announced a round of redundancies.

9.13.2.3 The conclusion

The conclusion should include the following two parts:

1. A restatement of the purpose of the presentation and a summary of the main points.

2. The conclusion, or a closing statement. People usually remember the beginning and the end of presentation, thus strong closing remarks help the audience to remember the presentation favourably. The closing statement may, if appropriate, challenge the audience to take action. The opening statements to the main body of presentation listed above may work well too.

All presentations follow more or less this basic structure. In establishing a purpose and a statement of the purpose, the first step in the preparation is to compile a list of all points that need to be covered by the presentation. These then have to be organised into parts as suggested in this chapter. After the main body has been developed, the introduction and conclusion should be added, using transitions for clarity and progression. Presentations must be focused and logical if they are to be understood, be persuasive, and establish the speaker's credibility.

ACTIVITY 9.12

BUILDING PRESENTATION SKILLS (4)

Use the topics from the previous activity and prepare concluding remarks for all of them.

9.14 CREATING VALUE

We as individuals place worth and value on every enterprise or activity in which we engage; therefore it is no surprise that organisations do the same. The difference is that organisations must justify their actions to chief executives and stakeholders, whereas individuals have only themselves to answer to. One of the worst aspects of any economic 'belt-tightening' is a lack of understanding regarding the worth and value of the role learning and development performs in an organisation. Consequently managers of the development function or those at line manager level may need to justify, advocate and persuade decision-makers of the worthwhile contribution development makes to the existence and well-being of the organisation. Therefore, the art of promoting and even marketing the development function is worthy of discussion, as conveying the relevant business case for any development is an overriding factor of contemporary organisational life (CIPD 2007a). A CIPD study (2007a) suggests that because of the global rethink about the direction and purpose of organisations, learning and talent development has never been more important. However, again there will need to be justification, as organisations do not always make the relevant connection that learning and development has had an impact on organisational success. The following activity brings this issue to the fore as it asks you to relate the questions to your own organisation.

ACTIVITY 9.13

CREATING AN IMPACT

Consider the following questions, originally posed by the CIPD study (2007a). Relate them to your organisation, answer them honestly (or if you do not know the answers, try to find out and share them with others as to whether or how you could justify development).

- Would you know how to demonstrate the impact of a customer service programme, for example, to your marketing department?
- Could you defend a coaching programme that may be considered by your managing director as 'nice to have' in terms of its bottom-line impact?
- Do you really know how the costs and benefits of e-learning compare with other methods when your finance director says, 'Why don't we just give everybody a DVD; it's a tenth of the cost?'
- Do you know what methods and approaches are considered most effective? Is it classroom training, blended learning, e-learning? (CIPD 2007a)

The CIPD report emphasises the need to show 'relevance, alignment and measurement' and cites the example of the finance department of a local authority, which illustrates a process of measurement and rationalisation that can be defended (see Table 9.7 opposite).

ACTIVITY 9.14

ORGANISATIONAL DEVELOPMENT STRATEGY

1. Adapt Table 9.7 opposite to align with a department in your organisation, or one of which you are familiar with; ensure you link your table to the current organisational development strategy.
2. Can you now justify any expenditure on development?
3. Prepare a presentation to senior management for a new/essential training initiative.

'Employers who invest in their own staff are best placed to save money, improve staff motivation and increase employee retention' (Parry as cited in CIPD 2009b, p2). Parry emphasises the opinion that knowledge-led learning companies are best placed to not only preserve their business but also extend their capacity. They do this by developing talent, which enables the organisation to exploit its human capital, which in turn furnishes the organisation with the wherewithal to compete in current and future markets. In a recent CIPD study (2009b, p1) the following suggestions are made in order to help managers argue a case for development:

- putting the relevance and impact of learning and development (L&D) at the centre of the business, therefore building the business case for effective L&D
- helping to connect the importance of L&D with key people in the business by ensuring that you can align your approach to the organisation's goals and objectives
- helping you to provide the most effective measures and metrics to help prove the impact of L&D on the business.

Table 9.7 Promoting the value of learning in adversity

Measuring the value of learning: council finance and resources department	
What matters to the organisation?	Measurement option(s) (for different staff groups)
How is learning contributing directly to the achievement of our organisational targets?	• time taken to gain competence, data for finance centre staff • proportion of employees with required competence level • customer feedback data on handling of council tax bills • employee engagement data measured by staff survey • number of individuals able to move into key positions • council member satisfaction with finance function • the number achieving professional qualifications (ACCA, and so on)
To what extent are employees achieving their performance targets?	Achievement against performance appraisal targets for council budget
How cost-effective are the learning and training opportunities we provide?	Employee reaction and learning data (levels 1 and 2 evaluation) Management feedback data
What economic benefits does our investment in training provide?	Cost–benefit data for specific learning interventions measured against costs and productivity: • SAGE training • Advanced Excel • Accounting technician stage modules
Is learning contributing directly to the achievement of HR targets?	Performance data on relevant HR targets; for example: • absence • retention • number of internal promotions

Source: adapted from CIPD (2009b, p12).

9.15 CONCLUSION

This chapter has given what we hope you will consider to be a well-founded view of the challenges facing the training and development arm of any business. It has also alluded to the skills learning professionals need to be effective. Principally, we have painted a picture of the current business environment and how accurate research, information, valuing people and good presentation skills are essential when advocating the importance of learning and training to decision-makers in the business.

PAUSE FOR THOUGHT

Identify at least three things that you have learned by studying this chapter and engaging with the activities. How will your newly acquired knowledge and skills support your continuing professional development? What value do you expect your learning to have for your daily routines and your further career? In what area have you identified a need for further development and how are you planning to fill that gap? Address these issues in your learning journal and/or CPD log. You may also wish to discuss them with a peer, colleague, mentor or coach to aid your further development.

KEY LEARNING POINTS

- In any development situation we should take account of the process of development the managers and leaders of the learning and training function have undergone to become learning professionals.

- Government in any country will have development strategies; it is important to be aware of their impact.

- The strategic development process has a bearing on the operational learning and teaching strategy.

- The learning and training cycle is an invaluable tool to review, reflect on and analyse:
  – the learning and training need
  – the prior achievement of the learners
  – the methods of design and delivery
  – and, importantly, the evaluation process.

- Skills in presenting are vital.

- Making the link from learning and training to business success is of prime consideration.

EXPLORE FURTHER

CIPD. (2009) *A barometer of HR trends and prospects 2010*. London: CIPD Publishing

CIPD. (2009) *Promoting the value of learning in adversity*. April 2009. London CIPD

QCF Readiness programme. (ND) Available online at: http://www.qcda.gov.uk/qualifications/qcf/58/.aspx

Review your government's website on their development initiatives.

Visit the Quality Assurance Agency website: http://www.qaa.ac.uk.

9.16 REFERENCES

ADLER, R.B. and ELMHORST, J.M. (2002) *Communicating at work: principles and practices for business and the professions*. 7th ed. New York: McGraw-Hill.

BRAMLEY, P. (1991) *Evaluating training effectiveness*. London: McGraw-Hill.

BUTLER, M. (2010) The talent of the future. *People Management Online*. Available online at: http://www.peoplemanagement.co.uk/pm/articles2010 [accessed 30 March 2010].

CIPD. (2007a) *The value of learning*. Research report in collaboration with the University of Portsmouth. London: CIPD.

CIPD. (2007b) *Learning and the line: the role of line managers in training, learning and development*. Available online at: http://www.cipd.co.uk/researchinsights [accessed 30 April 2010].

CIPD. (2008) *Who learns at work? Employees' experiences of training and development*. Survey report, March 2008. Available online at: http://www.cipd.co.uk/surveys, [accessed 30 April 2010].

CIPD. (2009a) *Identification of learning need*. Fact sheet. London CIPD

CIPD. (2009b) *Promoting the value of learning in adversity*. London: CIPD

CIPD. (2010a) *Overview of CIPD surveys: a barometer of HR trends and prospects*. Available online at: http://www.cipd.co.uk/surveys, [accessed 30 April 2010].

CIPD. (2010b) *Innovative learning and talent development*. London: CIPD.

HAMBLIN, A.C. (1974) *Evaluation and control of training*. Maidenhead: McGraw-Hill

HARRISON, R. (2002) *Learning and development*. London: CIPD.

JOHNSON, B. and GEAL, M. (2009) The complete trainer. *Training Journal*. November, pp48–52.

LEITCH. (2006) *Prosperity for all in the global economy: world class skills*. Final report; HM Treasury Leitch review of skills. Available online at: http://www.dcsf.gov.uk/furthereducation/index.cfm?fuseaction=content.view&CategoryID=21&ContentID=37 [accessed 30 April 2010].

MEZIROW, J. (1990) *Fostering critical reflection in adulthood*. San Francisco, CA: Jossey-Bass.

REID, M.A., BARRINGTON, H. and BROWN, M. (2004) *Human resource development: beyond training interventions*. 7th ed. London: CIPD.

REYNOLDS, J. (2002) *How do people learn*. London: CIPD

REYNOLDS, J. (2004) *Helping people learn: strategies for moving from training to learning*. London: CIPD.

SIMMONDS, D. (2003) *Designing and delivering training*. London: CIPD.

WHETTON, D.A. and CAMERON, K.S. (2007) *Developing management skill*. New Jersey: Pearson.

PART 6
Finance Skills

CHAPTER 10

Interpreting financial information

Donglin Pei

OVERVIEW

This chapter is designed to give you basic but essential knowledge of three major kinds of financial statement, as well as other related issues such as corporate governance, creative accounting and interpretations of financial statements by computing key performance ratios. You will find that the chapter is helpful to answer your questions such as why, when and how to prepare and interpret financial statements. This chapter will also help you to define a close relationship between three financial statements and understand the key elements in each of them. You will appreciate the fact that accounting is a practical discipline which is regulated by accounting standards and that the accounts are read and interpreted by shareholders and other stakeholders with a view to making decisions.

LEARNING OUTCOMES

By the end of this chapter, provided you engage with the activities, you should be able to:

- discuss agency theory and explain the different objectives of directors and share-holders

- discuss underlying reasons for creative accounting

- outline a historical development of the International Accounting Standards Board (IASB) and major contents of the conceptual framework

- describe the relationship between three main financial statements and understand relevant accounting concepts

- outline essential elements in three financial statements and acquire key skills to prepare financial statements by using given data

- calculate and interpret financial ratios.

10.1 INTRODUCTION

Accountants are communicators. Financial statements are final products from accountants which are used as a tool by a business entity to communicate with its users of financial information. In this chapter we will consider the format and key elements of main three financial statements: major financial ratios which are used to interpret financial statements, and corporate governance and creative accounting which are related with financial reporting, under the following headings:

- corporate governance
- creative accounting
- definitions and purposes of financial statements
- structure and contents of a statement of financial position
- structure and contents of a statement of income
- structure and contents of a statement of cash flows
- interpretation of financial statements.

10.2 CORPORATE GOVERNANCE AND CREATIVE ACCOUNTING

10.2.1 CORPORATE GOVERNANCE

In order to understand the background to the need for a robust system of financial reporting we need to take a quick look back through history. There have been a series of financial scandals that have, over the centuries, presented a less than perfect picture of the world of finance. The following list includes some famous ones but not all:

- the Victorian railway boom of the 1840s
- the Wall Street crash of 1929
- the Barings Bank scandal in the 1990s
- the collapse of Enron in 2001 and of WorldCom in 2002.

There is no doubt that you can add more to it from your own reading of world events, particularly very recent ones from the current global banking crisis.

ACTIVITY 10.1

FINANCIAL SCANDALS

Use an Internet search engine such as Google to find:

- details of the events mentioned above
- more examples of financial scandals past and present.

Financial scandals like those listed above highlight the need for careful review of both the role that directors and managers play in corporate affairs and the nature of the financial reports that corporate entities produce for their shareholders. Such a review was carried out in the UK in 1991, and in 1992 the Committee on the Financial Aspects of Corporate Governance produced its report of this review. This report, known as the *Cadbury report* (1992), defines corporate governance as: 'the system by which companies are directed and controlled in the interest of shareholders and other stakeholders' (p14).

Financial reporting is the process by which directors meet the accountability requirements of the system of corporate governance: directors report to shareholders regularly on their stewardship, with a system of independent auditing providing a check on the 'truth and fairness' of those reports.

Shareholders own a company; directors control it. The Figure 10.1 shows how the delegation of control by shareholders to directors leads to those groups having distinct sets of objectives.

Figure 10.1 Agency theory

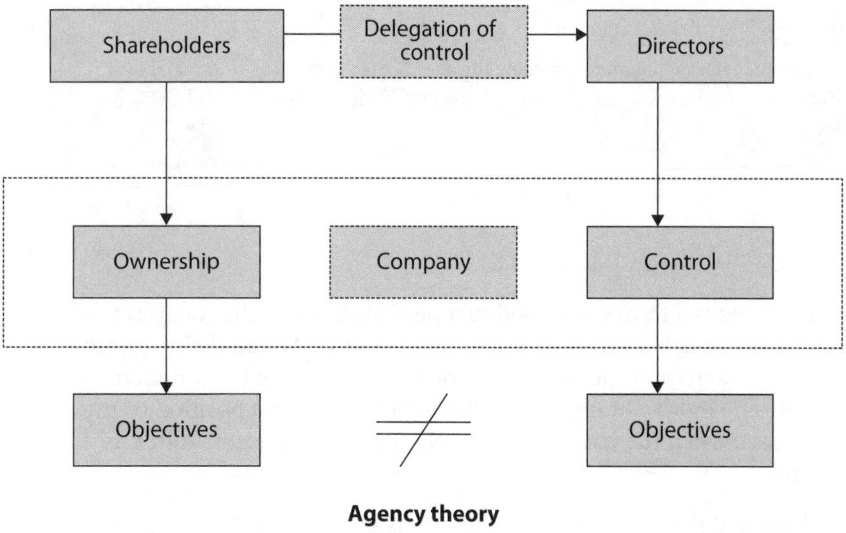

Agency theory

Note the label 'agency theory' below these two sets of objectives: we now need to explore what the term 'agency theory' means.

10.2.2 AGENCY THEORY

The relationship between shareholders and management is an example of the principal–agent relationship, and has given rise to agency theory. An agent may be defined as 'a person used to affect a contract between his/her principal and a third party'. So the owners or shareholders are the principals, the directors and senior managers are their agents and the third parties are those with whom the company deals: customers, suppliers, lenders and so on.

The objective of a shareholder's investment is to maximise profit by receiving dividends and capital gains from increased share prices. This can be achieved by an enterprise's long-term business growth, merger and acquisition activities, or preferring high-risk projects with high returns. However, differing from the shareholder's objective, a director may focus on his/her own benefits and job security by enhancing short-term business performance, avoiding merger and acquisition activities, or avoiding high-risk projects.

Therefore, agency theory leads to an important problem: what happens when the agent-directors have a different view or different agenda from that of the principal-owners? If the goals of the two parties are different or they have a different view of the risks involved in a course of action, then the maximisation of shareholder wealth may not be achieved. It is beyond the scope of this chapter to explore the solutions to this problem but you should be aware that agency theory is a contributory factor in our next topic: creative accounting.

ACTIVITY 10.2

AGENCY THEORY

By drawing on the relevant literature regarding the agency theory, how could you deal with the conflicts between the management and shareholders if you were a director of a business?

10.2.3 CREATIVE ACCOUNTING

Creative accounting is a term often used in a pejorative sense; dictionaries tend to define it using words like 'exploitation' or 'misleading'. We can define creative accounting as the exercise of (legitimate) choice in accounting for transactions and events with the motive of improving the performance and position of the business. It is used when the interests of shareholders and directors differ, as described above.

Let us now look at different types of presentations of financial statements:

- **True and fair view/fair presentation**: Financial statements use the flexibility within accounting to give a true and fair picture of the accounts so that they serve the interest of users.

- **Creative accounting**: Financial statements use the flexibility within accounting to manage the measurement and presentation of the accounts so that they serve the interests of preparers.

- **Fraud**: Financial statements deliberately step outside the regulatory framework to give a false picture of the accounts.

This is graphically represented in Figure 10.2.

Figure 10.2 Regulatory framework

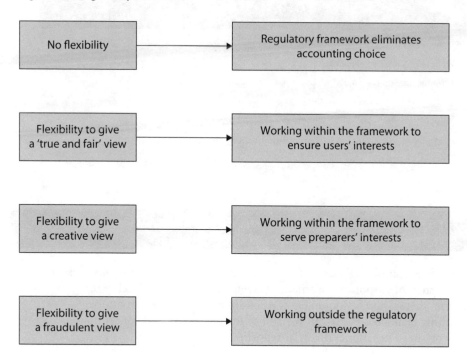

For example, management may want to improve ratios such as the earnings per share (EPS) and/or the gearing ratios, or they may want to suggest an inefficient stock market.

Creative accounting can arise because of the agency relationship in business that we referred to earlier or there may be problems with the regulatory framework, gaps in accounting or an underlying assumption of 'economic consequences'. More in-depth knowledge regarding creative accounting is available from relevant accounting literatures.

10.2.4 PRESSURES ON THE SYSTEM OF CORPORATE GOVERNANCE

There are pressures on the system of corporate governance from the increasing divorce of ownership and control and from a change in the assumed information needs of users towards a decision-useful perspective. There are two issues relevant to financial reporting:

- **Content issues:** relating to creative accounting that appeared not to be effectively addressed by the audit function or the efficiency of the stock market.

- **Context issues:** relating to the nature and effectiveness of the regulation of accounting in curtailing creative accounting; this presupposes that regulation of the system is the most appropriate approach.

ACTIVITY 10.3

SELF-ASSESSMENT QUESTIONS (1)

- What is corporate governance?
- How and why do the objectives of shareholders and directors differ?
- How do we define creative accounting?
- What are the main pressures on the system of corporate governance?

Suggested answers to these self-assessment questions are available on the companion website.

10.3 THE REGULATORY AND CONCEPTUAL FRAMEWORK OF INTERNATIONAL FINANCIAL REPORTING

The previous section suggests that a natural consequence of the various pressures on the system of corporate governance is regulation. We shall develop this further in this section by looking at the development of the International Accounting Standards Board (IASB) and of the regulatory and conceptual framework of international financial reporting.

10.3.1 HOW MIGHT WE REGULATE FINANCIAL REPORTING?

Financial reporting is, as we have seen, an important part of the international system of corporate governance. However, there are arguments both for and against the regulation of financial reporting, and recent decades have witnessed concerns relating to the context and content of financial reporting. So the first step in this sector is to ask how we might regulate financial reporting. History tells us there might be a combination of ways that financial reporting can be regulated:

- **The market**: Each company might choose its own rules, pressured by the capital markets.
- **Associationism**: Rules are developed by organisations formed to represent the interests of their members.
- **Corporatism**: Rules are developed by organisations that are licensed by the state and incorporated into a state-sponsored system of regulation.
- **The state**: Statutory rules are developed, with an enforcement mechanism.

Within each of these possible regulation mechanisms there is also the need to consider how the rules are first created and approved, and then enforced. Bearing all this in mind, we can say that the most important types of regulation are the law and accounting standards. It is useful, first of all, to look briefly at the history of the IASB.

10.3.2 IASB: A HISTORY

In 1973 accountancy bodies from nine countries (Australia, Canada, France, Germany, Japan, Mexico, the Netherlands, the UK and the United States) formed the Board of the International Accounting Standards Committee (IASC), and until the late 1980s the Board's activity involved codifying best practice in a set of International Accounting Standards.

In 1989 the Board published a conceptual framework of International Accounting Standards (IASs), the *Framework for the preparation and presentation of financial statements*, and began initial discussion with the International Organization of Securities Commissions (IOSCO) regarding the acceptance of IASs as applicable to the financial statements of cross-border multinationals. This period also saw the development of a 'comparability project' to eliminate certain options in IASs and/or to incorporate the expression of a preference (a benchmark treatment).

From 1993 IASs began to be adopted by a number of continental companies for their consolidated statements, and in 1995 IOSCO and the IASC agreed to develop a 'core set' of IASs. In 1998 certain countries legally allowed the use of IASs for consolidated statements, and in 2000 IOSCO endorsed the use of IASs. In 2001 the IASC reformed as the International Accounting Standards Board (IASB). The reformed IASB consists of the IASC Foundation (which has two main bodies – the IASB and the advisory trustees), the IASB (which initially adopted extant IASs but issues its own IFRSs), the International Financial Reporting Interpretations Committee (IFRIC) and the Standards Advisory Council (SAC).

We referred above to the conceptual framework approved by the IASB in April 1989. We now need to explore this in more detail.

10.3.3 WHAT IS A CONCEPTUAL FRAMEWORK?

The Financial Accounting Standards Board (FASB) defined a conceptual framework as 'a coherent system of interrelated objectives and fundamentals that can lead to consistent standards and that prescribes the nature, function and limits of financial accounting and financial statements' (FASB 1976, p1).

Financial reporting needs such a framework in order to:

- ensure consistency and coherence in standard setting
- identify and rank issues, and allow for a proactive approach to standard setting
- encourage 'rational' debate
- aid interpretation of standards by those who prepare and audit accounts
- enhance the credibility of financial reporting
- legitimate the standard setting process.

The framework covers four main areas of:

- the objective of financial statements

- the qualitative characteristics that determine the usefulness of information in financial statements
- the definition, recognition and measurement of the elements from which financial statements are constructed
- concepts of capital and capital maintenance (Technical Summary 2009).

According to the framework, the main objective of financial statements is to provide financial information about the reporting entity that is useful to present and potential investors and creditors in making decisions in their capacity as capital providers. Thus the objective is to provide information about financial position, performance and changes in financial position to a range of users, but the priority user is the investor group and the main purpose is for economic decision-making.

ACTIVITY 10.4

BUSINESS PERFORMANCE

Are there any other means except financial statements a company can use to provide stakeholders information about its business performance? Make yourself a list.

From the framework we have also noticed that the framework states that financial statements are prepared with the underlying assumptions:

- of the accruals (or matching) basis of accounting
- that the entity is a going concern.

The qualitative characteristics referred to in the framework are:

- understandability
- relevance (including materiality)
- reliability (including faithful representation, substance over form, neutrality, prudence, completeness)
- comparability.

The framework also covers other important issues of definitions, recognitions and measurements of the elements from which financial statements are constructed for example:

- An asset is defined by the summary as a resource controlled by an enterprise as a result of past events and from which future economic benefits are expected to flow to the entity.
- A liability is a present obligation arising from past events, the settlement of which is expected to result in an outflow of resources embodying economic benefits.
- Equity is the residual interest in the assets of the enterprise after deducting all its liabilities.

- Income is defined as increases in equity (other than transactions with the owners).

- Expenses are decreases in equity (other than transactions with the owners).

An element should be recognised if it is probable that any future economic benefit associated with the item will flow to or from the entity, and the item has a cost or value that can be measured with reliability. The elements of a set of financial statements must be measured, and here the choice is between historical cost, current cost, realisable value or present value.

10.3.4 WHY A REGULATORY FRAMEWORK?

There is a need for regulation of financial statements because they need to:

- provide direction

- provide guidance

- ensure quality

- meet users' requirements.

The issue of quality is crucial, and can be represented by the concept of the 'true and fair view' or 'fair presentation'.

Finally, we should note that there are various global standards:

- EU regulation imposes endorsed IFRSs on the consolidated statements of all companies listed in the UK on 1st January 2005.

- Currently, the US Financial Accounting Standards Board (FASB) and the IASB are working together on 'convergence'.

- The aim for 2009 is to eliminate the Stock Exchange Committee (SEC) requirement for foreign private issuers to reconcile International Financial Reporting Standards (IFRS)-based financial statements to US GAAP.

The goal is harmonisation of national financial reporting frameworks: a response to the globalisation of business, but whether harmonisation will be based on a particular view (the conceptual framework) that is appropriate for other countries remains to be seen.

In summary, in this section we developed the idea from Section 10.1 that a natural consequence of the various pressures on the system of corporate governance is regulation. We looked at the development of the IASB and of the regulatory and conceptual framework of international financial reporting. We also explored the notion of the 'true and fair view'. On the companion website there is a list of IFRS and IAS summaries.

ACTIVITY 10.5

SELF-ASSESSMENT QUESTIONS (2)

In this unit we want you to check your progress by exploring the 'true and fair view' concept.

- What definitions are there of this term?
- Where is the term used most frequently?
- What is the historical development of the concept?
- Why is a 'true and fair' view required?
- How is the 'true and fair' view achieved?
- What is the relationship between 'true and fair' and harmonisation?

Suggested answers to these self-assessment questions are available on the companion website.

10.4 THE PRESENTATION OF FINANCIAL STATEMENTS (IAS 1) 1

This is where we begin to look closely at the International Accounting Standards. In this and the next sector we shall focus on IAS 1, the standard that deals with the presentation of financial statements. In this section we shall concentrate on the balance sheet.

10.4.1 INTRODUCTION

From the technical summary of IAS 1 we can see that IAS 1 covers (Technical Summary 2009b):

- the objective, scope and purpose of financial statements
- the components of financial statements: balance sheet, income statement etc
- aspects such as fair presentation and compliance with IFRS, the 'going concern' and 'accrual' basis of accounting, consistency of presentation, materiality and aggregation, offsetting, comparative information
- the structure and content of financial statements
- the basis for conclusions
- guidance on implementation.

We can see from IAS 1 that the three basic financial statements are:

- **The balance sheet:** showing the accumulated wealth of the entity at the end of the accounting period. It is a statement at one point in time and can be regarded as a snapshot of the entity's position.
- **The income statement:** showing the profit (or loss) generated over the period. It is a record over time rather a snapshot of one moment.
- **A cash flow statement:** showing cash movements over the period.

Figure 10.3 Accounting period

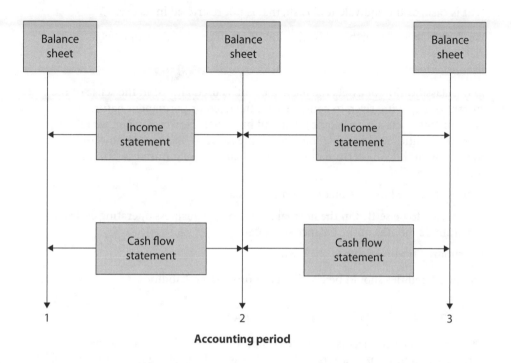

Accounting period

All three statements provide an overall picture of the financial health of the entity. The relationship between the statements can be summarised in Figure 10.3.

10.4.2 THE BALANCE SHEET

As mentioned previously, the purpose of the balance sheet is to set out the financial position of a business at a particular moment in time. It is therefore a position statement showing a picture of financial strength (or weakness) with, on one hand, the assets of the business and, on the other, claims (liabilities) against the business.

There is an important distinction to be made when discussing either assets or liabilities and that is between those that are current and those that are non-current.

10.4.2.1 Assets

A current asset is one that is bought or acquired for non-permanent use in the business. Alexander et al (2007) describe a current asset as having the following features:

- It is expected to be realised in, or is held for sale or consumption in, the normal course of the operating cycle of the business.

- It is held primarily for trading purposes.

- It is expected to be realised within 12 months of the balance sheet date.
- It is cash, or the equivalent of cash, that is not restricted in its use.

We shall look at the further classification of non-current assets in later sections.

10.4.2.2 Liabilities

In the classification of assets the term 'current' is used almost in the sense of the current of a flowing river, to contrast with the fixed or permanent nature of non-current assets such as equipment and buildings. However, when we refer to current liabilities we are using the term in the sense of 'happening now' to contrast with the long-term nature of some liabilities of a business. So, current liabilities are:

- those that the business incurs from day to day
- expected to be settled in the normal course of the business operating cycle and within 12 months of the balance sheet date
- primarily trading debts of the business.

All other liabilities should be classified as non-current liabilities.

10.4.3 MAJOR ITEMS IN THE BALANCE SHEET

Of course a balance sheet is far more complex than our distinction between current and non-current assets and liabilities would so far suggest. From an overview of a range of balance sheets from different business entities you should have drawn up a list similar to this:

- property, plant and equipment
- investment property
- intangible assets
- financial assets
- inventories (stock or work-in-progress)
- trade debtors and other receivables
- cash and cash equivalents
- trade creditors and other payables
- tax liabilities and assets
- provisions
- financial liabilities
- minority interests
- issued capital and reserves
- other elements.

There is also a wealth of additional information in most balance sheets. Key items will be subject to further classification and analysis, for example:

- tangible/intangible assets: see IAS 16 Property, Plant and Equipment
- the sub-classifications of inventories: see IAS 2 Inventories
- operating leases or finance leases: see IAS 17
- borrowing costs shown as an expense or capitalised: see IAS 23.

You will also have noticed the often substantial notes to the financial statements.

10.4.4 THE BALANCE SHEET EQUATION

One way of looking at a balance sheet is to conceptualise it as an equation. A mathematical equation states that everything on the left is equal to everything on the right; a modern balance sheet says that the total of everything in the top section is equal to the total of everything in the bottom section. Let us explore this using a series of simple examples in which no goods are sold but the asset and liability situation of the business changes.

EXAMPLE

A trading entity starts as a small business with £4,000 of the owner's own money. At this point, it is easy to see that £4,000 in a bank represents what the business is worth, since the business owes nothing. The balance sheet 'equation' is therefore:

Bank = Capital

£4,000 = £4,000

If we assume the following transactions:

1. The owner spends £1,000 of the money on a van.
2. The owner then obtains stock on credit of £2,000.
3. The owner introduces some more capital in the form of a computer at a cost of £3,000.

The equation will change at each step as follows:

1. After the owner spends £1,000 of the money on a van (another asset), the equation becomes:

Bank + Van = Capital

£3,000 + £1,000 = £4,000

2. After obtaining the stock on credit the equation is a little different, since there is now a liability in the form of the supplier of the stock, but the balance on the capital account remains the same:

(Bank + Van + Stock) − Creditor = Capital

(£3,000 + £1,000 + £2,000) − £2,000 = £4,000

3. After the further injection of capital, the equation becomes:

$$(Bank + Van + Stock + Computer) - Creditor = Capital$$

$$(£3,000 + £1,000 + £2,000 + £3,000) - £2,000 = £7,000$$

In this last step the net worth of the business increased because of the introduction of new capital; whatever happens to one side of the net worth equation also affects the other side.

In addition, following mathematical principles, the equations can be manipulated. The last one would be exactly the same if it had been expressed as:

$$Bank + Van + Stock + Computer = Capital + Creditor$$

$$£9,000 = £7,000 + £2,000$$

We can summarise this in the following diagram:

Assets	=	Capital	+	Liabilities
OR				
Assets	-	Liabilities	=	Capital

Non-current assets	+	Current assets	=	Capital	+	Non-current liabilities	+	Current liabilities
OR								
Non-current assets	+	Current assets	-	Capital	-	Non-current liabilities	=	Current liabilities

The balance sheet is not without its limitations. It provides us with a snapshot of the strength (or weakness) of the business at one point in time but this means that inevitably:

- It can provide no details of what happened during the period.
- It can give little information about performance and cash flows during the period.
- Being composed of historical data, it may be seen as being of little use for the future.

The balance sheet focuses on the resources that go into and out of the business, and we need to be aware that the valuation of some of those resources may be subjective. This will become apparent when we look at topics such as depreciation and the valuation of inventory. We will now be looking at the accounting concepts that underpin financial statements.

ACTIVITY 10.6

BALANCE SHEET

If you are a departmental manager of a business (any department other than an accounting/ finance department), do you think that the information in a balance sheet is useful for you? Can you summarise any usefulness and limitations of a balance sheet?

10.4.5 ACCOUNTING CONCEPTS

The recording of accounting information and the preparation of accounts has always been governed by a number of accounting concepts that may relate to the ethics of the profession, the rules of measurement of financial transactions or the rules that govern the content of financial statements. These concepts are briefly summarised below.

Entity

The business is, for the purpose of accounting, a separate legal entity from its owners. In English law a limited company is a separate legal person but the accounting concept also applies to the financial statements of a sole trader, in that personal financial matters are kept separate. In the event of bankruptcy this is no longer the case, but this topic is not within the scope of this chapter.

Time interval

Financial statements are prepared at regular intervals. This is usually, though not always, done annually.

Duality

Every transaction has a two-fold effect: one is credited, the other debited. For example, when the entity sells goods on credit, the sales account is credited and the customer's account is debited.

Money measurement

Financial accounting, as the term suggest, can only deal with items capable of being expressed in money terms.

Accruals

Transactions and events are recognised when they occur, not when cash is received or paid for them. If the entity has consumed electricity but not paid for it at the date of the balance sheet, this consumption is included in the expenses of the profit and loss account and shown as an accrual on the balance sheet.

Going concern

Financial statements are prepared on the assumption that the business will continue trading.

Consistency

Consistency of presentation of the accounts should be retained from one period to the next.

Materiality and aggregation

Material items should be shown separately, but immaterial items may be aggregated with amounts of a similar nature.

 PHOENIX PLC

CASE STUDY 10.1

Phoenix plc's trial balance at 30 June 2008 was as follows:

	£000	£000
Freehold land	2,400	
Other property, plant and equipment	1,800	(depreciation) 540
Furniture and fittings	620	(depreciation) 360
Inventories (30 June 2007)	1,468	
Sales revenue		6,465
Administrative expenses	1,126	
Ordinary shares of €1 each		4,500
Investments (non-current)	365	
Revaluation reserve		600
Development cost	415	
Share premium		500
Receivables	947	
Payables		592
Cost of goods sold	4,165	
Distribution Costs	669	
Dividend received		80
Profit and loss account		488
Bank	150	
	14,125	14,125

Corporation tax for the year is estimated at £122,000.

Insofar as the information permits, prepare the balance sheet as at 30 June 2008 in accordance with international financial reporting standards (IFRS). The answer is available on the companion website.

Offsetting

Assets should be shown separately from liabilities, and income from expenses. There should be no offsetting.

Comparative information

Comparative information for the previous period should be shown alongside that for the current period.

10.5 THE PRESENTATION OF FINANCIAL STATEMENTS (IAS 1) II

In this section we continue our work on IAS 1 and look at the other major financial statements: the income statement and the cash flow statement. After completing this section you should be able to:

- describe the nature and purpose of an income statement and cash flow statement

- discuss their format and presentation

- explain the key issues for preparing the statements

- comply with the main accounting conventions

- prepare an income statement and cash flow statement.

10.5.1 INTRODUCTION

In the previous section we saw that the income statement and the cash flow statement form a link in that they show, respectively, the profit (or loss) generated and the cash movements over the period between any two successive balance sheets (refer to Figure 10.3, p297).

Let us look at each of them in turn.

10.5.2 INCOME STATEMENT

The purpose of the income statement, according to IAS 1, is to measure and report how much profit (wealth) the business has generated over a period. It is therefore an instrument for measuring performance. It will show:

- the total revenue generated during the period

- the total expenses incurred in generating that revenue

- the difference between them, which is the profit or loss for the period.

You will recall that in the previous sector we explored the balance sheet equation, which is, at its most basic:

$$\text{Assets} = \text{Capital} + \text{Liabilities}.$$

Since the profit or loss made over an accounting period adds to or reduces the capital account, we can rewrite this as:

Assets = (Capital + Profit) + Liabilities; or

Assets = (Capital + (Revenue – Expenses)) + Liabilities.

In the previous unit you carried out an activity changing the balance sheet equation. It finished like this:

Assets = Capital + Liabilities

£9,000 = £7,000 + £2,000.

During the next accounting period this business makes a profit of £5,000, which will be added to the capital account. How might it be reflected in the other components of the equation to make it balance?

The profit has been generated throughout the period through the use of both assets and liabilities of the business. For example, stock has been used and replaced, creditors have been paid and new liabilities incurred, and fixed assets will have depreciated. These changes are reflected in the accounts, so that the assets and the liabilities figures will also change.

Let us now look at the key elements of an income statement.

10.5.3 KEY ELEMENTS OF THE INCOME STATEMENT

It is convenient to think of an income statement as consisting of three parts:

- the revenue, that is, the sales of the entity, also referred to as the turnover
- the cost of sales during the period
- other key elements.

Revenue (sales or turnover)

IAS 18 defines revenue as 'the gross inflow of economic benefits during the period arising in the course of the ordinary activities of the enterprise'. In order to report income as revenue, it must be earned during the period: the work must be completed, or be realised and verifiably measured. If it has been completed, this increases the likelihood of conversion into cash.

Cost of sales

The cost of goods sold during the period is determined by adding together the opening stock and purchases during the period, then deducting closing stock.

Other key elements

These might include:

- gross profit, being the sales less the cost of sales
- any other operating income
- distribution costs: transport, postage etc
- administration expenses: light, heat etc

- other operating expenses
- profit from operating activities, obtained by deducting all the expenses from the gross profit
- notes to the income statement.

The format of an income statement can be seen later in the text (see Case study 10.2). Before we look at cash flow statements, we shall say a little more about the term 'profit'. This term has been mentioned several times and it is important that you realise two factors:

- it is not the same as cash
- its calculation is rarely simple.

These points are illustrated in the next two case examples.

EXAMPLE: SOCIAL VENTURE

Imagine that you are involved in running a social venture where you have to raise some money, such as a sports club or charity. A series of fund-raising events raises £1,000 worth of income during a month. Why might not all of this income be donated to the club/charity?

Not all of the income is donated to the club/charity because there may be expenses to pay out of the money during the month, such as the hire of the room where the events took place, refreshments for any helpers, printing costs for sponsorship forms and advertising posters. There might have been other things you can think of, but the point is that the cash received is not the same as the profit made on a venture. The profit made is the income less the expenses.

EXAMPLE: RETAILER PROFIT

A retailer wants to know how much profit she has made during a single month. However, she has electricity and telephone bills that cover three-month periods and rates that cover six-month periods. On the last day of the month she takes delivery of some stock, but does not have to pay for it for another month. She makes sales on credit and does not receive the cash until two months have passed. How does she know how much profit has been made during the month?

In order to calculate profit it is necessary to deduct expenses related to the venture from the income, as you saw in the first scenario. However, the income for a given period must have set against it only the expenses for that same period. This is the basic accounting convention of accruals (also known as matching) and it requires a variety of adjustments to be made to the figures in a trial balance before an income statement can be produced that will provide the profit for a particular period. The retailer in our scenario will need to adjust her expenses.

The other financial statement that we have to deal with is the cash flow statement.

10.5.4 CASH FLOW STATEMENT

The cash flow statement is a primary financial statement showing the movement of cash, and cash equivalents, over a period. It is regulated by IAS 7. The objectives of the cash flow statement are to provide information about the historical changes in cash and cash equivalents, to classify cash flows from various business activities, and to provide information for users to enable them to assess the ability of the entity to generate cash and cash equivalents and assess the timing and certainty of this generation.

Cash is defined as 'cash on hand and demand deposits'. Cash equivalents are defined as 'short-term, highly liquid investments that are readily convertible to known amounts of cash and which are subject to an insignificant risk of changes in value'(Technical Summary 2009). Examples of cash equivalents are treasury bills and money market funds.

IAS 7 requires the cash flows from three areas of activity to be shown:

- operating activities
- investing activities
- financing activities.

These are added together to show the net changes in cash and cash equivalents. Let us look at these three areas.

Cash flows from operating activities

These include cash flowing:

- in from the sale of goods and rendering of services
- in from revenues of royalties, commissions etc
- out via payments to suppliers and employees
- in and out via receipts or payments of income taxes or contracts held for dealing or trading purposes.

Cash flows from investing activities

These include cash flowing in/out from:

- receipts or payments from disposal or acquisition of fixed assets
- receipts from interests in joint ventures or payments to joint ventures or the acquisition of equity or debt instruments in other enterprises
- receipts or payments from/to loans to other parties
- payments to other financial instruments: futures, forward options or swaps.

Cash flows from financing activities

These include cash flowing in/out from:

- the issue of shares and other equity instruments
- payments to the owners to acquire or redeem the enterprise's shares
- the proceeds of issuing loans, notes, bonds and other short and long-term borrowings
- repayments of amounts borrowed.

IAS 7 describes two methods of showing the cash flows:

- The direct method: this shows gross cash receipts and payments.
- The indirect method: this starts with the pre-tax profit and adjusts it for the effects of non-cash charges and credits, deferrals/accruals of past/future operating cash flows and income or expenses associated with investing or financing cash flows.

IAS 7 encourages the direct method, but the indirect method is an alternative option. We shall use an example showing operating activities of an entity as an illustration of both methods. The same statement is shown in the two different ways in Tables 10.1 and 10.2, and might also be given as shown in Table 10.3.

Table 10.1 Direct method

	£
Cash received from customers	X
Cash payments to suppliers	(X)
Cash paid to and on behalf of employees	(X)
Other cash payments	(X)
Net cash inflow from operating activities	X

Table 10.2 Indirect method

	£
Profit before tax	X
Adjustments for:	
Depreciation	X
Investment income	(X)
Interest expense	X
Operating profit before working capital changes	X
Increase in inventory	(X)
Increase in trade receivables	(X)
Increase in trade payables	X
Cash generated from operations	X
Interest paid	(X)
Income taxes paid	(X)
Net cash inflow from operating activities	X

Table 10.3 Both direct and indirect methods

Direct method		Indirect method	
	£		£
Cash received from customers	15,424	Profit before tax	6,022
Cash payments to suppliers	(5,824)	Depreciation charges	899
Cash paid to and on behalf of employees	(2,200)	Increase in inventory	(194)
		Increase in receivables	(72)
Other cash payments	(511)		
		Increase in payables	234
Net cash inflow from operating activities	6,889	Net cash inflow from operating activities	6,889

The direct method has some advantages in that it provides extra information for users and shows the true cash flows involved in the trading operations. However, the extra information is obtained at a cost. The indirect method shows the 'quality' of earnings and incurs a low cost in obtaining the information, but it lacks information on the trading cash flows.

The IASC encourages the use of the direct method but the indirect method is acceptable. However, in Australia and New Zealand the direct method has been mandatory since 1992; the indirect method is not allowed. In the UK and United States both are optional.

ACTIVITY 10.7

DIRECT AND INDIRECT METHODS

You may want to think about options of the direct and indirect methods in your country.

There are some differences between IAS 7 and the UK accounting standard FRS 1. IAS 7 is similar to FRS 1 before its revision in 1996. The current FRS 1 has eight headings whereas IAS 7 requires only three. Also, IAS 7 includes cash and cash equivalents whereas FRS 1 requires cash only (short-term investments are reported separately).

The use of different headings makes it more difficult to compare cash flow statements of UK GAAP-adopted companies with those of IASs/IFRSs-based companies. The different definition of cash and cash equivalent includes/ excludes some items to be recognised in the cash flow statement. Therefore, we

ACTIVITY 10.8

DIFFERENCES BETWEEN IAS 7 AND FRS 1

What do you think are the consequences of these differences?.

will have different cash flow statements for the same company if it adopts different accounting standards. You may, therefore, want to consider the question of which accounting standard shows a 'true and fair view' of the cash flow statement: UK GAAP or IASs/IFRSs.

10.5.5 USEFULNESS AND LIMITATIONS OF THE CASH FLOW STATEMENT

The cash flow statement is useful in that it:

- enables users to make decisions based on a forecast of future cash flows
- shows the relationship between profitability and cash-generating ability
- has uses in the research and analysis of assessment models
- shows liquidity, viability and adaptability, in conjunction with the balance sheet
- is less difficult to 'manipulate' than the balance sheet.

However, there are limitations. A cash flow statement shows historical information, which is not a necessity in forecasting future cash flows, and there are still possibilities for the manipulation of cash flows. Cash flow is critical for short-term survival; profit is for long-term survival, so a negative cash flow does not always mean that there is a problem. After all, a substantial cash balance may indicate bad management.

ACTIVITY 10.9

DIFFERENCES BETWEEN PROFIT AND CASH

By analysing various firms bankrupted in the financial crisis, could you tell what differences between profit and cash are? And why is cash so important for a company's survival?

INCOME STATEMENTS

CASE STUDY 10.2

1. Using the information in Phoenix plc's trial balance at 30 June 2008 given in the self-assessment question in Case study 10.1, insofar as it permits, prepare the income statement for the year ended 30 June 2008.

2. The draft financial statements of Max Plc for the year ended 31 December 2008 are as follows:

Income statement for the year ended 31 December 2008

	£
Sales revenue	30,650
Cost of sales	(26,000)
Gross profit	4,650
Depreciation	(450)
Administration & selling expenses	(950)
Interest expenses	(400)
Investment income (dividends received)	500
Profit before tax	3,350
Income tax expense	(120)
Profit for the year	3,230

Balance sheet as at 31 December 2008

	2008		2007	
	£	£	£	£
Assets				
Cash and cash equivalents		490		160
Accounts receivable		1,800		1,200
Inventory		1,000		1,950
Long-term investments		2,500		2,500
Property, plant & equipment at cost	3,810		1,910	
Accumulated depreciation	(1,510)		(1,060)	
Property, plant & equipment net		5,790		5,810
Total assets		8,090		6,660
Trade payables	250		1,890	
Interest payable	230		100	
Income taxes payable	400		1,000	
Long-term debt (including finance leases)	2,300		1,040	
		3,180		4,030
Total net assets		4,910		2,630
Shareholders' equity				
Share capital		1,200		1,100
Share premium		300		150
Retained earnings		3,410		1,380
Total shareholders' equity		4,910		2,630

Dividends paid were £1,200.

Prepare a cash flow statement for the year ended 31 December 2008 using the indirect method illustrated in IAS 7 (ie starting the cash flow statement with the profit before tax). The answer to this case study is available on the companion website.

10.6 INTERPRETATION OF FINANCIAL STATEMENTS

We will now interpret financial statements by using key ratios which are calculated from the balance sheet, income statement and cash flow statement which we introduced in the previous sections of this chapter. After completing this section you should be able to undertake:

- classification of various financial ratios
- calculation and interpretation of important ratios
- utilisation of ratios in helping to assess financial performance
- limitations of ratios as a tool of financial analysis
- production of reports analysing results over time or between entities by ratios.

10.6.1 PERFORMANCE MEASUREMENT

A financial statement is the final product of an accountant. However, it tells little about business performance of an enterprise if we simply read these absolute numbers without a further analysis. This requires us to do a financial analysis, which is a process involving reclassification and summarisation of information through the establishment of ratios and trends.

A financial analysis can be an analysis of financial statements for the purpose of acquiring additional information regarding the activities of the business. The objectives of a financial statement analysis are to examine a firm's financial position and returns in relation to risks, by forecasting the firm's future prospects.

A popular technique which is used to analyse financial statements is horizontal analysis (or comparative analysis). The horizontal analysis examines changes in individual categories on a year-to-year or multiyear basis: a comparison of ratios between accounting periods over several years reveals the direction, speed and extent of a trend(s). By using financial ratios, we can:

- express the relationship of one figure to some other figures
- examine various aspects of financial position and performance
- conduct management planning, control, and other management decisions, and
- inform investors for investment decision-making.

ACTIVITY 10.10

NON-FINANCIAL FACTORS

Other than financial ratios, do you think there are non-financial factors which can be used to analyse a business's performance?

10.6.2 CLASSIFICATION OF FINANCIAL RATIOS

Table 10.4 summarises major ratios which are commonly used.

Table 10.4 Summary of commonly used major ratios

Type	Reflect	Examples
Profitability	Performance of company and managers	ROCE, ROE, gross and net profit margin
Liquidity	Ability to meet short-term financial obligations	Current ratio, quick ratio, and cash ratio
Efficiency	Efficiency of asset usage	Stock turnover period, average settlement period, etc
Gearing	Long-term solvency	Gearing ratio, interest cover ratio
Investment	Returns on shareholders' investment	EPS, PE ratio, dividend yield, dividend cover, etc

Source: ACCA, *The official text for the professional qualification: Financial Reporting (International) Study Text,* Decemnber 20904/June 2004, FTC Foulks Lynch, p291.

10.6.2.1 Profitability ratios

Return on capital employed (ROCE)

ROCE exams the relationship between the size of the profit figure relevant to the size of the business. The ratio is designed to assess how efficiently a business is using its resources.

ROCE = profit/capital employed x 100%

Here, the profit is the net profit before interest and taxation. Capital employed comprises share capital plus reserves plus long-term loans.

ROCE can be used to compare with the firm's previous years' figures, its cost of borrowings, its own target ROCE as well as other companies' ROCE for a performance measurement.

Return on equity (ROE)

ROE is another ratio to measure business performance. Differing from ROCE, ROE focuses more on ordinary shareholders' return. Therefore, the ratio is more relevant for existing or prospective shareholders than management.

ROE = Profit after tax and interest and preference dividends/
(ordinary share capital + reserves) x 100%

Here, the profit is the amount of profit which is available to the ordinary shareholders.

Gross profit margin (GPM)

GPM relates the gross profit of the business to the sales generated for the same period.

GPM = gross profit/sales x 100%

GPM is a measure of profitability in buying and selling goods before any other expenses are taken into account. When compared with average GRM in the same sector, a low GPM may indicate a poor business performance and need for improvement. A high GPM may evidence a good management but may attract more market entries into the industry sector.

Net profit margin (NPM)

NPM relates the net profit for a period to the sales during that period.

NPM = Net profit before interest and tax/sales x 100%

NPM is a measure of net profit from trading operations before any costs of servicing long-term finance are taken into account. Different industry sectors have different types of NPM. For example, a supermarket usually has a low rate while a jewellery shop has a high one. There are a number of factors, such as competition, customer, economic climate and industry characteristics, which can influence the NPM ratio.

10.6.2.2 Efficiency ratios

Efficiency ratios are used to examine the ways in which various resources of the business are managed.

Stock (inventory) turnover

Stock turnover measures how well a company converts stocks into revenues. The ratio can be calculated in times or in days.

Stock turnover (times) = cost of sales/inventory OR

Stock turnover (days) = Inventory/cost of sales x 365 days

Days increased (or times decreased) may indicate a lack of demand (outdated or obsolescence) for the goods or a poor inventory control. However, days increased (or times decreased) maybe resulted from a large stock quantity which is ordered with trade discounts. Similar to the net profit margin, stock turnover ratios could be significantly different between the different industry sectors. For instance, stock turnover ratios for milk in a supermarket are much lower than for a building construction in a house developer company.

Accounts receivable collection period (ARCP)

ARCP measures the average number of days that accounts receivable are outstanding.

ARCP = trade receivables/credit sales revenue x100%, OR

ARCP = trade receivables/credit sales revenue x 365 days

A number of factors may increase the ARCP ratio, such as a lack of a proper credit control, a firm's strategy of attracting more trade by extending credit period or conducting different terms for major customers. A decreased ARCP ratio is usually a good sign if the business is not in a cash shortage. However, an ARCP ratio could be decreased by using factoring of accounts receivable. In that case, the ARCP ratio is of little use in measuring efficiency of credit control.

Accounts payable payment period (APPP)

APPP measures the average number of days that accounts payable are outstanding.

APPP = accounts payable/credit purchases x 365 days

A long payment period provides a business with a source of free finance. However, a long payment period may also indicate that the business has a liquidity problem. In addition, if the business is a slower payer of its payables, its reputation may be damaged and consequently supplies may be discontinued.

10.6.2.3 Liquidity ratios

Liquidity ratios are used to determine a company's ability to pay off its short-terms debt obligations.

Current ratio

Current ratio measures the adequacy of current assets to meet short-term liabilities.

Current ratio = current assets/current liabilities

The higher the ratio, the more liquid the business. For most businesses, an ideal current ratio is at or higher than 1.5, although an appropriate level actually depends on the nature of business. However, a high current ratio may result from a high level of inventory and/or receivables rather than cash and/or low liabilities. In this case, the quick ratio (see opposite) can be used to make a further analysis.

Some other factors need to be considered in terms of managing a current ratio. For example, the availability of further finance such as overdraft can compensate for a lower current ratio. The seasonal nature of a business can also distort the interpretation of current ratio. For example, there is usually a high inventory level in a Christmas season for retailing firms. One more factor is the nature of long-term liabilities.

Quick ratio (acid test ratio)

If the total value of inventory is significant against the total value of current assets and the nature of inventory is slow moving (ie difficult to convert into cash), quick ratio is a more appropriate way to measure the liquidity.

Quick ratio = (current assets – inventory)/current liabilities

Quick ratio measures the adequacy of current assets (receivables and cash) to meet immediate liabilities. For most businesses, an acceptable figure is in a range of 0.7 to 1.0.

10.6.2.4 Gearing ratios

Gearing ratios are used to determine a company's ability to pay off its long-term debt obligations.

Gearing

Gearing, or leverage, describes the mix of long-term funding provided internally (by shareholders) and that contributed externally (by lenders).

Gearing ratio = loan capital/total capital employed x 100%

Here, loan capital is long-term (non-current) loans. Capital employed is share capital plus reserves plus long-term loans.

A high gearing ratio indicates a high proportion of money borrowed and therefore a big financial risk (eg capital repayment when due and interest burden) of whether the business can meet its obligations. A high gearing ratio may also indicate a more tightened loan covenant, such as further restrictions on the firm's further loans and operating actions. As a consequence, shareholders may require a higher return from the increased financial risks.

However, there are also advantages from a high gearing ratio. For example, loans are cheap finance compared with other financing sources such as equity due to the tax relief benefit (loan interest is an allowable expense for taxation). Therefore, a high gearing ratio may increase returns for shareholders.

Interest cover

Interest cover measures the amount of profit available to cover interest payable.

Interest cover ratio = operating profit/interest payable

Here, operating profit is the profit before interest and taxation.

A low interest cover may indicate a high risk that interest payments will not be met as well as a high risk to the shareholders that the lenders will take action against the business to recover the interest due.

10.6.2.5 Investment ratios

Earnings per share (EPS)

EPS is a measure of profitability: the portion of a company's profit allocated to each outstanding share of common stock.

EPS = earnings available to ordinary shareholders/number of ordinary shares in issue

As a major component of the price/earnings (P/E) ratio, EPS is a fundamental measure of share performance. The trend of EPS may indicate the investment potential of a firm. However, there are limitations to an EPS ratio. EPS could be decreased by a new share issue in the short term although the funded project is profitable in the long term. In this case, EPS may not be an appropriate indicator to assess the investment potential of a firm. In addition, users of EPS need to be aware that the earnings figure is subjective, which may result in a subjective EPS.

Price/earnings (P/E) ratio

The P/E ratio is a market confidence ratio, and relates the market value of a share to the EPS.

P/E ratio = market value per share/earnings per share

The higher the P/E ratio, the faster the growth the market is expecting in the firm's future EPS. P/E ratio is particularly useful in comparing different businesses.

Dividend yield ratio

Dividend yield ratio measures the cash return from a share in relation to its current market value.

Dividend yield = dividend per share/market value per share x 100%

Dividend yield ratio provides investors with information about how much dividends are paid by the company to shareholders.

10.6.2.6 Trend analysis

By using financial ratios, a trend analysis can be conducted by comparing current data with prior periods, to indicate the overall financial position or strength of a company. There are a number of methods which can be used in trend analysis, such as 'scattergraphs' and other graphical techniques, time-series analysis, and statistical regression (eg calculating the 'line of best fit') by using a computer program.

However, there are a number of limitations in a ratio analysis. For example ratios could be misleading if they are calculated in a less uniform manner. Ratios calculated may not be representative if seasonal trading activities are significant for a firm. Other factors may limit the usefulness of ratio analysis; these include subjective accounting figures used in ratio calculations, inconsistent accounting policies adopted and applied in preparing financial statements, and other non-monetary items excluded from ratio analysis. Finally, complex business patterns may not be solved solely by ratios.

LORRY PLC

CASE STUDY 10.3

Using the figures given below and overleaf, you are required:

1. To calculate relevant ratios for Lorry plc between 2007 and 2009:

    Gross profit margin, ROCE, net profit margin; receivables collection days, payables payment days, stock turnover days; current ratio, quick ratio; gearing ratio, interest cover.

2. To analyse the performance of Lorry plc from 2007 to 2009.

The answers to this case study, and the IFRS and IAS summaries 2009, are available on the companion website.

Summarised income statement of Lorry Plc for the year ended 31 December

	2007 £m	2008 £m	2009 £m
Revenue	840	981	913
Cost of sales	(554)	(645)	(590)
Gross profit	286	336	323
Expenses	(186)	(214)	(219)
Profit before interest	100	122	104
Interest	(6)	(15)	(19)
Profit before taxation	94	107	85
Taxation	(45)	(52)	(45)
Profit after taxation	49	55	40
Dividends	24	24	24

Summarised balance sheet as at 31 December

	2007 £m	2008 £m	2009 £m
Assets			
Non-current assets			
Intangible assets	36	40	48
Tangible assets	176	206	216
	212	246	264
Current assets			
Inventories	237	303	294
Receivables	105	141	160
Bank	52	58	52
	394	502	506
Current liabilities			
Trade payables	53	75	75
Other payables	80	105	111
	133	180	186
Net current assets	261	322	320
Non-current liabilities			
Long-term loans	74	138	138
Total net assets	399	430	446
Equity			
Ordinary share capital	100	100	100
Retained earnings	299	330	346
	399	430	446

10.7 CONCLUSION

Financial data can be complex. Those reading this text who are unfamiliar with some of the concepts highlighted above should seek help from a tutor.

PAUSE FOR THOUGHT

Identify at least three things that you have learned by studying this chapter and engaging with the activities. How will your newly acquired knowledge and skills support your continuing professional development? What value do you expect your learning to have for your daily routines and your further career? In what area have you identified a need for further development and how are you planning to fill that gap? Address these issues in your learning journal and/or CPD log. You may also wish to discuss them with a peer, colleague, mentor or coach to aid your further development.

- Agency theory identifies the different objectives of shareholders and directors that can lead to creative accounting.

- Creative accounting exerts pressure on accounting standard-setters who, typically in companies or governments or professional bodies, work hard to eliminate creative accounting activities by using corporate governance or government interventions or improved accounting standards, for example IFRSs/IASs.

- Key elements in financial statements, which create a close relationship between main financial statements, are regulated by accounting standards and accounting concepts.

- The objective of financial statements is to provide useful information to users of financial statements. Different financial statements provide different financial information to users for their decision-making.

- A series of financial ratios can be calculated by using given data in financial statements, and can be interpreted by users to support their decision-making.

EXPLORE FURTHER

ALEXANDER, D., BRITTON, A. and JORISSEN, A. (2007) *International financial reporting and analysis*. 3rd ed. London: Thomson.

ELLIOTT, B. and ELLIOTT, J. (2008) *Financial accounting and reporting*. 12th ed. Harlow: Prentice Hall.

10.8 REFERENCES

ACCA. (2004/2005) *The official text for the professional qualification: financial reporting (international)*. Wokingham: FTC Foulks Lynch.

ALEXANDER, D., BRITTON, A. and JORISSEN, A. (2007) *International financial reporting and analysis*. 3rd ed. London: Thompson.

COMMITTEE ON THE FINANCIAL ASPECTS OF CORPORATE GOVERNANCE. (1992) *Report with Code of Best Practice [Cadbury Report]*. London: Gee Publishing.

CADBURY REPORT. (1992) *Report of the Committee on the Financial Aspects of Corporate Governance.* Online version available at: http://www.ecgi.org/codes/documents/cadbury.pdf [accessed 17 May 2010].

Conceptual framework for financial accounting and reporting: elements of financial statements and their measurement (1976) **FASB discussion memorandum** the "scope and implications of the conceptual framework project" section (Stamford, CNN: FASB, p1).

EVANS, L. (2003) The 'true and fair view' and the 'fair presentation override' of IAS 1. *Accounting and Business Research.* Vol. 33, No. 4, pp311–327.

FRS AND IAS SUMMARIES. (2009) Online version available at: http://www.iasb.org/IFRSs/IFRS+technical+summaries/IFRS+and+IAS+Summaries+-+English+-+%282009%29.htm [accessed 17 May 2010].

IASB. (2009) *Technical summary: framework for the preparation and presentation of financial statements* as issued at 1 January 2009. Online version available at: http://www.iasb.org/NR/rdonlyres/4CF78A7B-B237–402A-A031–709A687508A6/0/Framework.pdf [accessed 17May 2010].

IFRSs and IASs summaries. (ND) Available online at: http://www.iasb.org/IFRSs/IFRS+technical+summaries/IFRS+and+IAS+Summaries+-+English+-+%282009%29.htm [accessed 17 May 2010].

TECHNICAL SUMMARY. (2009a) *IAS 7 Cash flow statement.* Available online at: http://www.iasb.org/NR/rdonlyres/8C532526–9CE7–49B6–84BB-446BEDA65541/0/IAS7.pdf [accessed 17 May 2010].

TECHNICAL SUMMARY. (2009b) *IAS 1 Presentation of financial statements.* Available online at: http://www.iasb.org/NR/rdonlyres/80B373BF-BB16–45AB-B3F7–8385CD4979EA/0/IAS1.pdf [accessed 17 May 2010].

WALTON, P. (1993) The true and fair view in British accounting. *European Accounting Review*, Vol. 2, No. 1, Introduction, pp 49–58.

CHAPTER 11

Managing financial resources

Mike Ashwell

OVERVIEW

Chapter 11 builds on Chapter 10, intending to further the understanding of financial information and in particular its use as a key element of business decision-making. This is covered within the overall activity of management accounting. Management accounting is conducted primarily within an organisation, and much of the information gathered is not disclosed to outside parties due to commercial sensitivity. An important exception is key information, like the business plan for example, which will be shared with funders in support of an application for a loan or other financing. Management accounting has a wide scope, ranging from business plans and budgets, through performance reporting and measurement, to calculation of detailed costs. Unlike external financial reporting, there is no statutory requirement for organisations to maintain management accounts, but this chapter will demonstrate clearly the value of such information, and the risk to the business if this area is neglected or poorly applied.

LEARNING OUTCOMES

By the end of this chapter, provided you engage with the activities, you should be able to:

- identify the objectives and key elements of a business plan
- explain the purpose of a budget, and identify the key steps in the budget process
- understand how different types of costs behave, and the importance of this for business decisions
- understand the importance of cash management within an organisation
- evaluate a capital expenditure proposal using a variety of techniques
- understand the significance of performance monitoring within an organisation, and the application of a range of measurement and control techniques
- have a clear appreciation of the value and application of management accounting information to the organisation.

11.1 INTRODUCTION

Management accounting is essentially a forward-looking activity that aims to predict the future of an organisation by firmly establishing its current position and gaining a clear understanding of past events. The management information determined by this process has a key purpose: that of monitoring and controlling the progress of the organisation and enabling appropriate decisions to be made. Reference will be made throughout this chapter to the 'control loop': the business process by which plans are established, decisions made, results gathered, and plans and decisions reviewed and evaluated. This process is illustrated in Figure 11.1.

Figure 11.1 Control loop

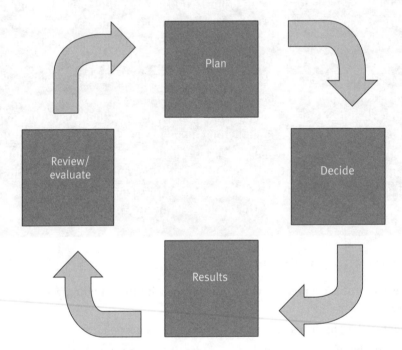

These decisions are usually taken at a variety of levels, from overall strategic issues to detailed pricing and costing choices for individual products or services. In the increasingly complex and fast-moving world of modern organisations, it is essential to establish and communicate a clear view of the overall strategy and direction of the organisation. This is the role of the business plan, with which we will commence our study of the management of financial resources.

11.2 BUSINESS PLANNING

One of the most difficult and time-consuming activities within an organisation is the establishment of a business plan. However, it is also an essential feature of business life – the old military saying 'If you fail to plan, you plan to fail' is still of the greatest relevance in today's organisations. The business plan addresses a number of key points:

- It enables the business to be reviewed thoroughly in a logical and considered format. The key objectives and direction of the business can consequently be established.

- It provides targets and a framework against which the performance of the organisation may be monitored and controlled.

- It establishes the resources required to fulfil the agreed objectives, and the times when they will be needed.

- It provides a framework for communication with all employees about the business objectives and provides a 'common currency' for discussions on such issues.

- It enables current or potential investors in the business to gain a clear understanding of both the overall objectives and the detailed mechanisms by which these are to be achieved.

- It provides the framework on which annual budgets are based – and enables those budgets to be checked for consistency with the long-term aims.

The business plan should have a number of key components. These may be presented or combined in different ways according to the exact nature of the business, but the overall contents will always follow a similar pattern. The following structure is based on recommendations on the UK Government website www.businesslink.gov.uk

11.2.1 THE EXECUTIVE SUMMARY

1. This should include a clear mission statement and the objectives of the business. A wide variety of mission statements are currently produced, ranging from a few words to several paragraphs. The best mission statements are lively and attractive and include key aspects of the product or service, the customers, the employees and the financial objectives of the organisation. A mission statement for Fusion 99, a fictitious restaurant, might look like:

> We aim to make Fusion 99 a great place to eat, combining a fun atmosphere with Eastern and Western-influenced food. By serving delicious meals and retaining happy and motivated staff, we will delight our customers and develop an efficient and profitable organisation.

2. The highlights and key points of the plan should also be presented. The objective should be to present information accurately, but in an attractive style and format which encourages the reader to examine the details of the plan. The summary should not include unsupported 'hype' as this may encourage unjustified expectations in the casual reader or simply cause an experienced evaluator to move on to a more realistic proposal.

11.2.2 THE BUSINESS OVERVIEW

1. Key points in the business history and structure.

2. Details of the business products or services.

3. Key features of the industry or sector in which the business operates.

11.2.3 MARKETS AND COMPETITORS

1. Overall size of the market, how it has been developed, and is anticipated to change in the future.

2. Target customers – current and proposed.

3. Competitors – evaluation of their number and size, with estimates of market shares.

4. Overall market environment and potential risks and opportunities.

11.2.4 MARKETING AND SALES

1. Given the factors established in Section 3 of this plan structure – Markets and competitors – a clear description of the marketing strategy, including identification of customer needs, pricing policies an differentiation, promotion and selling techniques.

11.2.5 BUSINESS OPERATIONS

1. Detailed analysis of the business operations and location(s).

2. Facilities and requirements for production/operations/logistics.

3. Management information systems – both to meet operational and statutory accounting requirements, and to provide management accounting information.

4. IT infrastructure – to support financial information systems requirements and other applications such as production control, design etc.

5. An evaluation of the environmental implications of the business, including pollution controls, waste management and any necessary licences or consents.

11.2.6 HR REQUIREMENTS

1. Management structure, organisation and skills.

2. Employee numbers and structure and ongoing training and development requirements.

11.2.7 FINANCIAL FORECASTS

1. These should be the direct and logical result of all the other elements of the plan and will include forecast profit and loss accounts, balance sheets and cash flow statements, together with the key additional assumptions used.

2. Detailed analysis should be provided for the first financial year, with clear summaries, with working papers available, for future years. Business plans typically cover three to five years, but in the case of industries with very long lead times for establishment of activities, such as a nuclear power station, a plan would extend over a much longer period.

ACTIVITY 11.1

MISSION STATEMENT OF YOUR OWN ORGANISATION

Find the mission statement and objectives for your organisation (if you do not currently work or have no work experience, please move on to Activity 11.2) and consider the following questions:

- How easy was this to find?
- Is it publicly visible – websites, notice boards, prompt cards, communications etc?
- Does it address key aspects of the product or service, the customers, the employees and the financial objectives of the organisation?
- Is it employed to assist with agreeing or reviewing personal objectives, for example during personal development reviews?

ACTIVITY 11.2

MISSION STATEMENTS FOR MAJOR ORGANISATIONS

- Find the mission statement – it may be listed as 'purpose', 'objectives', or 'vision' – for major organisations in the UK and overseas, for example:
  - http://www.shell.co.uk/home/content/gbr/aboutshell/who_we_are/our_purpose/
  - http://www.alcoa.com/global/en/about_alcoa/vision_and_values.asp
  - http://www.coca-cola.co.uk/Mission_Vision_and_Values/
- Consider:
  - Is it clearly written and understandable by all stakeholders?
  - Does it address key aspects of the product or service, the customers, the employees and the financial objectives of the organisation?

11.3 BUDGETS

11.3.1 BUDGET FUNDAMENTALS

Once an organisation has established a clear business plan, then to operate effectively it should create an annual budget. The budget for an organisation is a key part of the 'control loop' described in Section 11.1 above as well as a further building block in the management of an organisation. The budget should always be aligned with the overall strategy and objectives and therefore fully consistent with the business plan, otherwise achieving the budget may not move the organisation in the right direction and could lead to sub-optimal behaviour.

There are a number of key purposes for the creation of a budget:

- **Targets**: The most obvious purpose is setting targets and agreeing action plans by which they can be addressed. The targets may be in the form of costs, for example a finance department budget of £20,000 per month, or may include other measures, for example a sales department budget of 600 units per month.

- **Control**: By matching actual results, both financial and other measures, with the agreed budget, management can identify divergences from budget at the earliest possible stage, take corrective action, and monitor the effectiveness of this action.

- **Resources**: It helps allocate resources and improving investments. In all organisations there are limits on resources, and the budget process enables the available resources to be aligned towards the key objectives. Resources issues can be identified in advance and crucial decisions made in a considered manner.

- **Co-ordination**: It allows the departments or teams who interact within the business to ensure that their plans match. For example, the sales director may be planning to sell 5,000 units of a product during the budget year, but the process identifies that the production department can currently only manufacture 4,000 units in the period. This must be resolved by changing sales targets, revising production plans and resources, sourcing purchased products, or a combination of these actions.

- **Communication**: The budget document provides a sound basis on which to explain to employees the details of the organisation's objectives for the coming year and the role of themselves or their department/team in the achievement of these objectives.

- **Delegation and rewards**: By identifying key responsibilities of teams and individuals as part of the budget process, delegation may be effectively achieved, and where appropriate, this may be link to an evaluation and reward process.

Given that the budget clearly has far-reaching impacts on an organisation, it is vital that the budget process is effectively planned and managed. Successful organisations agree and communicate a budget timetable well in advance of the actual requirement and allocate clear responsibilities for each stage. As with all key activities, it is vital that the budget is shown by management at all levels to be of crucial importance to the organisation rather than simply a necessary evil which must be despatched as quickly as possible. Each organisation will develop an appropriate process, but as Dyson (2007) suggests, a general process may be described as follows:

1. Identify the current mission and objectives of the organisation and ensure that these fully reflect the latest position – they will form the keystone of the budget.

2. Identify limiting factors, for example a production constraint, space limitation, or pollution limit, which cannot be changed during the budget year.

3. Prepare an initial forecast of the key factors – for example sales values/ quantities and production/service quantities. Perform an initial match and resolve any fundamental discrepancies.

4. On the basis of the agreed key data, prepare departmental cost and performance information.

5. Prepare an initial budget – identify mismatches, or shortfalls in required profit or cash.

6. Review the initial budget and agree management actions to resolve the issues identified. Where necessary, corrective actions must be communicated and resolved between departments/groups to ensure efforts are co-ordinated and not contradictory.

7. Consolidate the updates to the budget and gain final approval – several iterations may be required before this point is reached!

8. Communicate appropriate budget summary and details to all those affected. Senior management will require the full overview and details, but individuals may require a simple overview, together with the specific targets and impacts for their roles. This information can be effectively discussed during personal development reviews as an aid to objective-setting, monitoring and feedback.

11.3.2 BUDGET TECHNIQUES

The details of the budgets which are prepared in the process described above may be addressed by a number of different approaches. The two extreme approaches and a practical compromise are described below.

- **The incremental approach**, as described by Gowthorpe (2005, p384). This approach was historically employed in public organisations and is still prevalent today. The approach is based on using the previous year's data and adding an agreed percentage for inflation. This approach may be made slightly more sophisticated by using a variety of percentages dependent on the data type, for example differing percentages for salaries, administration costs and IT costs. The advantages of this approach are that is generally quick and simple, but it does not address changes to the internal and external environment of the organisation or its key objectives. It may also lead to pressure for managers to spend up to their budget level to ensure that the full value is subject to the inflation uplift for the following year.

- **The zero-based or bottom-up approach**, as described by CIPFA (ND) starts with a 'blank sheet' and the budget is produced solely on the basis of the long-term objectives of the organisation and the means by which these can be addressed in the budget year. All items of sales and revenue are built up on the basis of these objectives and the current environment with very limited initial assumptions. Clearly this should result in a very detailed and accurate budget, but it is extremely time-consuming and there is a risk that key items may be omitted if there is not sufficient reference and validation with historic information.

Best practice is to adopt a practical approach which is a combination of these two extremes. This involves the combination of overall organisational objectives and the current environment with detailed knowledge of previous budgets and actual results. Where necessary, structural changes can be made to incorporate new departments or methods of working. The overall budget is checked for completeness and consistency against both long-term plans and previous history.

Recent criticisms of the limitations of a fixed budget process have led to the development of 'beyond budgeting' techniques as described by Hope and Fraser (1999) where an organisation adopts a less structured approach that includes flexible targets in response to the ever-changing external environment. This has been adopted successfully by a number of major international organisations such as Handelsbanken based in Sweden, but it has proved unsuccessful in others. The key issue has proved to be the increased requirement for very strong management to provide strong leadership and decision-making input to direct a fluid internal organisation with an absence of the traditional budget structure based on functional departments or 'silos'.

11.3.3 PRACTICAL BUDGET ISSUES

Without the effective engagement and co-operation of management and staff, budgetary control can be at best ineffective and at worst can cause demotivation and the opposite effects to those that were intended. The following case study illustrates a number of these issues

 SNACKS LTD

CASE STUDY 11.1

Snacks Ltd manufactures a variety of pre-packed food products. Responsibility for the manufacturing costs of each product is given to individual product managers. They have responsibility for the purchasing and production functions for their products but have no say in machine replacements or labour rates. The selling and distribution aspects are the responsibility of the sales manager.

The company has recently seen a large increase in both the demand for its products and the breadth of its own product range, and in order to achieve better control has instigated a 'responsibility accounting' system.

This involves senior management in association with the accounts department setting pre-determined budgets based on anticipated activity levels and costs. The budget is divided into 12 accounting periods, and at the end of each of these the budget managers' individual performances are highlighted through the comparison of actual costs incurred in the period with the predetermined budgets. Any adverse variance in excess of 5 per cent has to be explained to senior management at the monthly management board meeting.

An example of such a performance report (for the De-luxe sandwich department for month 5) is shown opposite.

The budget was prepared two months prior to the start of the year.

The manager concerned, Eddie Bowyer, is a little upset. He has just been heavily criticised for the adverse performance of this department. He has been with the company for 20 years, working his way up to manager from junior assistant, and has always felt he has given the company his best. He is now feeling rather disgruntled and is considering his future with the company.

Questions

- What are the key issues that have upset Eddie Bowyer?
- How could the report be improved to reflect the quantities of products that he has been required to make and the areas of cost that he can actually control?
- Revise the report to illustrate your views.

- Comment on problems that you have identified with the budget process and suggest improvements.

A suggested answer to this case study is available on the companion website.

Performance report

Production centre: De-luxe sandwich manager – E Bowyer

Productive activity	Budget 6,000 units	Actual 8,000 units	Variance		
Costs	£	£	£		%
Sandwich fillings	3,000	3,900	900	Adverse	30
Bread	1,000	1,250	250	Adverse	25
Direct labour	800	950	150	Adverse	19
Indirect labour	500	500	–	–	–
Depreciation	200	200	–	–	–
Other attributable costs	300	310	10	Adverse	3
Selling and distribution	250	280	30	Adverse	12
Apportioned overhead	1,000	1,100	100	Adverse	10
Total	7,050	8,490	1,440	Adverse	20

11.4 COST TYPES AND COST BEHAVIOUR

In order to make effective decisions, it is crucial that the behaviour of different types of costs is clearly understood. There are a number of different cost types and their nature is easily explained with reference to practical examples:

- **A fixed cost:** This does not change when there are changes in the level of activity. This level of activity may be defined in terms of production, sales or usage – but always in some form of units. A domestic telephone bill provides a helpful example. Most domestic telephone bills comprise two main elements, a line rental charge and a call charge. A line rental charge is a fixed cost. It does not vary with the number of call minutes. The line rental charge may be illustrated on a chart as in Figure 11.2.

Figure 11.2 A fixed cost

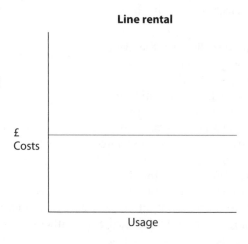

Line rental

£ Costs

Usage

Many business costs are fixed, for example rent, rates, insurance, administration salaries. These do not vary with changes in the level of activity or output of the organisation.

- **A variable cost**: This varies in proportion to the level of activity. Using our domestic telephone bill as an example, the call charges will usually be variable costs. Another indicator of a variable cost is that the cost is usually zero when the level of activity is zero – when we make no calls we would expect no call charges. A variable cost is shown in Figure 11.3. Note that the cost line starts at the origin, and steadily rises as usage increases.

Figure 11.3 A variable cost

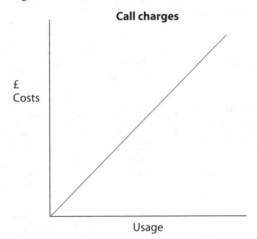

In a business, such items as raw materials and sometimes direct labour costs are variable costs.

- **A semi-variable cost**: Some charges, such as the overall package for our domestic telephone, are combined so as to create an overall semi-variable cost – one that has both fixed and variable elements. This may be illustrated in Figure 11.4, where the two elements of the charge are combined.

Figure 11.4 A semi-variable cost

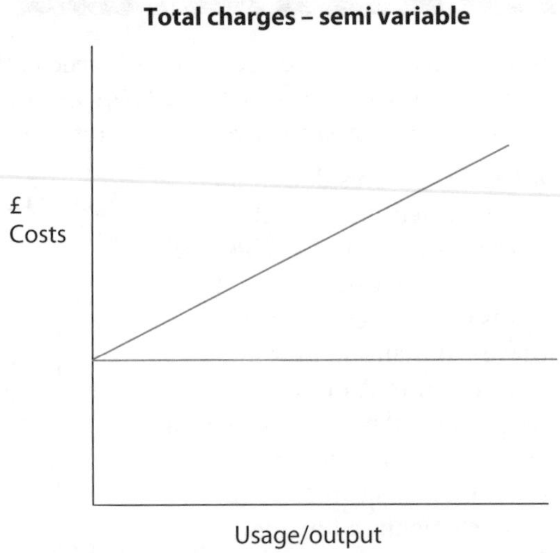

This diagram may also be used to illustrate the overall cost position of an organisation. Where, as is usual, the organisation has a combination of both fixed and variable costs, the overall fixed costs may be illustrated by the horizontal line, and the variable costs by the slope. Note that even when there is zero usage or output, fixed costs are still incurred, therefore the variable cost slope is added to the fixed costs, rather than starting at zero.

- **A stepped fixed cost**: In some circumstances, an organisation may have costs that are fixed until a certain output or usage level is reached, when there is a step rise in costs. This may arise, for example, where a manufacturer has three distinct production bays in the factory, each of which can be used to produce 100 units per week. At demand levels between 0 and 100 units, heating and lighting is only required for one bay; between 101 and 200 units, two bays are used; and over 200 units, three bays are used. The heating and lighting costs will therefore step up to the next cost level as each level of production is reached. Note that this is a distinct shift in costs, rather than a smooth progression as with variable costs. This is shown in Figure 11.5.

Figure 11.5 A stepped cost

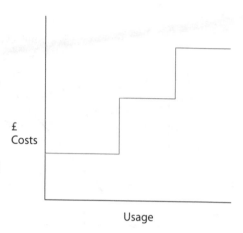

11.4.1 BREAK-EVEN POINT

The calculation of a break-even point for an organisation is very useful for management decision-making. 'The break-even point is the point at which no profit and no loss is made' (Gowthorpe 2005, p449). Any increase in output from that point should yield a measurable profit, whereas a decrease will produce a loss. The break-even point may be illustrated on a graph simply by adding a revenue line to our overall cost chart (Figure 11.6 overleaf).

The point at which the revenue line intersects the total cost line is the break-even point, and the break-even level of output is simply shown by projecting that point downwards to the output axis. This shows the level of output required to break even. Practical business information requires a quicker and more accurate process than drawing graphs, and the break-even point may be readily found by calculation.

The break-even point can be calculated by first determining the contribution per unit sold. Contribution per unit is calculated as the sales (revenue) per unit, minus the variable costs per unit. The break-even point is then given by dividing the contribution per unit by the fixed costs.

For example, if a business made light fittings at a variable cost of £6 per unit and sold them for £10 per unit, the contribution would be £4 per unit. If the overall business fixed costs were £8,000 per annum, then the number of fittings required to break even would be:

8,000/(10–6) = 2,000 units

Figure 11.6 Total costs, total revenue, break-even

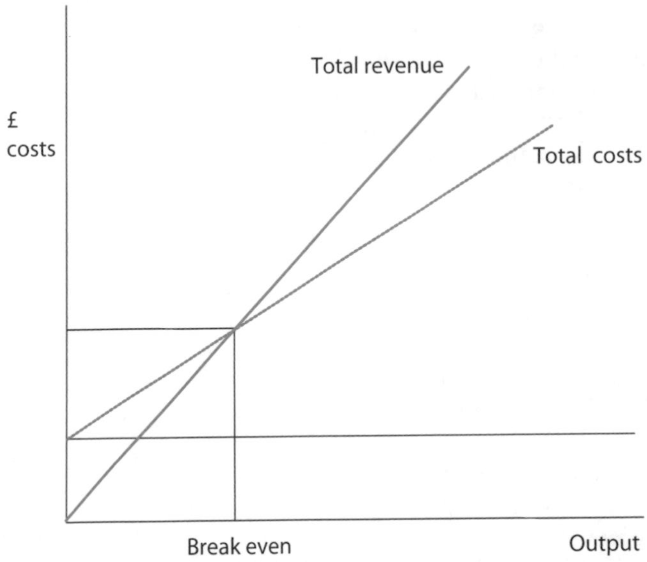

Chart: vertical axis labelled "£ costs", horizontal axis labelled "Output". Lines for "Total revenue" and "Total costs" intersect at the "Break even" point.

ACTIVITY 11.3

FIXED COSTS, VARIABLE COSTS AND BREAK-EVEN

As the owner of Woodlands Taxis, you are faced with intense competition in your local area and you are worried because you do not know how many passenger miles need to be achieved in order to break even. You first need to confirm your understanding of fixed and variable costs, and break-even points.

Sketch a simple chart for the taxi firm, including labels on axes, showing:

- total costs – including both fixed and variable costs
- revenue
- break-even point.

Your fares are £2 per mile and you have the following annual costs:

- Fuel: 20p per mile.
- Insurance: £10,000.
- Drivers' wages: (fixed contract) £50,000.
- Administration Costs: £20,000.
- Depreciation of vehicles: £10,000.

Part 1

Determine which of these items are fixed, and which are variable.

Calculate how many passenger miles need to be driven to reach the break-even point.

Remember that the break-even point is calculated using the formula:

Break-even point = $\dfrac{\text{Fixed costs}}{\text{Contribution per unit}}$

Contribution per unit = Selling price per unit – Variable costs per unit

Part 2

Using the information in Part 1, how many passenger miles will be needed for you to make an annual profit of £10,000?

Part 3

You have been offered some more efficient vehicles, for which the fuel cost will only be 10p per mile but whose total annual depreciation will be £30,000. How will this affect your break-even miles, and the miles required to make £10,000 annual profit?

A suggested solution to this activity is provided on the companion website.

11.4.2 SHORT-TERM DECISION-MAKING

It is important to note that the definition of fixed and variable costs described above is principally related to short-term decision-making. In the longer term, all costs may be considered variable; for example local authority rates are fixed in the short term, but in the longer term the organisation may choose to move or expand premises and hence the rates bill will change.

A clear understanding of cost behaviour is very valuable for managers making short-term tactical decisions about pricing or operations. A company may usually sell its products for £100 per ton, with variable costs of £60 per ton. If it has spare capacity and receives a short-term offer to purchase product at £80 per ton, the first instinct would be to refuse the offer as it is significantly below the usual price. The offer is, however, above the level of variable costs and hence every additional ton sold yields a contribution of £80 –£60 = £20 towards the existing fixed costs. If the offer was at £50 per ton, then it should not be accepted as, in this case, each additional ton loses the company an additional £50 –£60 = £10 per ton.

11.5 CASH MANAGEMENT

The discussion of the cash flow statement in Chapter 10 demonstrated that this is a relatively simple financial statement, not unlike a bank statement that an individual receives for a bank current account. It may be tempting to think that if a monthly balance sheet and profit and loss account are available for an organisation, then the cash flow statement is probably superfluous. This is very far from the truth, as many organisations have found to their cost.

It is also important to note that the meaning of the term 'cash' in this context extends far beyond notes and coins, which have only a limited place in most modern businesses, but also to bank deposits, both in local and foreign currencies, and short-term investments which may be readily converted into current bank balances.

In everyday conversation, the terms 'profit' and 'cash' are often used interchangeably, but in business they are very different, and this may be illustrated by two simple and contrasting examples.

- Bob the Builder has a one-man business as a jobbing builder, carrying out small construction work and repairs for householders, for which he insists on cash payment. The materials that he uses are bought on credit from a builders' merchant, nominally on 30-day payment terms, although he usually manages to stretch that to 45 days or more. He always has plenty of cash and seems to be running his business successfully. At the end of the year, he takes his box of receipts and cheque book stubs to his accountant and is amazed to learn that he has actually made a small loss for the year. He has been underpricing jobs, but has not realised it because of favourable timing of his cash flows – generally receiving payment 45 days before paying his bills. He therefore has cash, but no profit.

- Stadium Enterprises is a major building company specialising in the construction of sports stadia. Its managers pride themselves on their construction skill and efficiency and are delighted to be offered a two-year contract to build a football stadium. The contract price, at £20 million, looks fine, and all their projections indicate a healthy profit. They neglect to focus on the payment terms, however, which indicate that 40 per cent of the contract value will be paid only on final completion. Work progresses very well on the contract, but with a high proportion of the overall expenditure being required in the first year of the project, the company runs up a large cash deficit, which had not been forecast, and is forced to go into liquidation. It has a good forecast profit, but no cash.

These examples clearly demonstrate that profit and cash are not the same and that an organisation must carefully monitor and manage its cash resources. There are many reasons for the divergence between profit and cash, and we will examine those that are of particular importance from a practical financial management viewpoint.

Organisations very frequently sell goods and services on credit terms. The sale will be recorded in the profit and loss account in the period in which the sale takes place, but in the cash flow statement in the period when the payment is received. It is vitally important that this time lag is recognised and closely monitored. It is also crucial that every reasonable effort is made to check the customers' ability to make payment when due – and the typical steps in this process, as described by the government's Business Link website www.businesslink.gov.uk are as follows:

1. The organisation should have clear terms of sale which define precisely when payment should be received for invoices. These terms must not be ambiguous, eg 'payment in 30 days' is not sufficiently precise; 'payment into the designated bank account within 30 days of the date of product delivery'

is much better as it is more precise. If an individual sales contract is made, then these terms must be specifically referred to.

2. The organisation should have a detailed and consistently enforced credit management policy. This will include obtaining references and credit checks for new customers, and regularly monitoring the position of existing customers.

3. The credit management process for existing customers should include both periodic credit checks to ensure their ongoing credit worthiness, and could also include subscriptions to organisations providing business information, such as Dun and Bradstreet Limited which provides both ad hoc information and ongoing customer monitoring and alerts.

4. Internally, the organisation's credit management policy and processes should include detailed monitoring of payments, at an individual customer level and for the organisation as a whole. One measure that is very frequently used is the accounts receivable collection period (ARCP) described in Chapter 10, usually defined in numbers of days. This provides a very rapid measure of debt collection efficiency; for example, if the standard company payment terms are 30 days after delivery and the ARCP shows a current value of 45 days, then there is clearly a payment problem which must be followed up urgently in detail. It may be just a few customers who are severely overdue or a general late payment problem.

5. If payments are severely delayed then the credit management policy should define a range and sequence of actions to be taken, for example stopping supply to the customer until payment is received, referring the company to a debt collection agency, or direct legal action.

A second major variation between profit and cash is the purchase of goods and services on credit terms. Many of the principles that apply to this process are similar to those described above.

1. The organisation should establish a clear contract with the supplier, including a detailed description of the terms of payment.

2. The organisation should have a supplier payments policy and process which ensures that supplier payments are made on the due date, unless there is a documented dispute in process.

3. This may be effectively monitored using the accounts payable payment period (APPP) calculation described in Chapter 10. By reviewing the number of days yielded by this calculation, the organisation can identify overall supplier payment issues and focus on the specific accounts where problems are arising. In practical terms, this often occurs, not as a deliberate company policy, but because individual managers are simply failing to approve and pass on invoices for payment. Clearly a simple training process, followed by effective monitoring, could address this issue.

4. In the short term, it might be argued that it is of benefit to the company's cash flow to delay payments to suppliers beyond the contractual due dates. This not only gives rise to problems of business ethics, but also can result

in practical difficulties. Delay in payments may result in the company being placed on the supplier's 'stop-list', with no supplies being made until payment is received. This may result in a number of problems, including disruption to business activities due to the shortage of key materials or services, and an impaired credit rating, which may reduce the ability of the company to gain credit accounts with other suppliers.

The other key area where company managers can influence the variation between profit and cash is in the level of stocks held. By reducing stocks, the company may be able to improve cash flow, even though profit may be unaffected. As described in Chapter 10, the stock turnover, calculated as a number of days, can vary widely between different types of organisations. The key area of management decision-making and control in this area is to monitor and critically review the levels of stocks held, and make crucial decisions on stock-holding levels and possible alternative strategies. This requires accurate data, in terms of numbers of days stock held for each item, clear information about the exact purpose and criticality of each stock item, and a good understanding of the supply chain and lead time for each item. Careful analysis of all these features may result in quite different decisions being made for the wide range of stock items. For example, a major manufacturer may identify three key stock areas:

- An item in stock, costing £50,000, which is a unique spare part for a custom-built production line machine. To order and receive a replacement would take several months. Clearly, although the stock turnover of this item may be measured in years, rather than days, the value of cash tied up appears to be fully justified, to provide 'insurance' against major business disruption in the unlikely event of the failure of the installed part.

- Production components, with a typical value of £500,000, which are delivered weekly by the supplier, with an average lead time of two weeks. The overall stock holding could be reviewed in detail, ensuring that the number of different components is rationalised where possible, and agreement made to share the company production schedule with suppliers so that components could be delivered on a daily 'just-in-time' basis where this is beneficial.

- Several hundred items of maintenance spares, with a total value of £100,000, and a stock turnover up to 60 days, all of which are readily available on a daily basis from a local supplier. This appears to be an example where, by making a specific agreement with the local supplier to hold stocks of a designated list of spares, the stockholding effort and cash holding could be significantly reduced.

There are other reasons for differences between profit and cash, covered in Chapter 10, such as depreciation, provision for bad debts and company financing transactions which are significant for the organisation as a whole, but not within the remit of the day-to-day operational management of the organisation. By closely monitoring and managing the position with debtors, creditors and stocks, the management of an organisation can significantly influence the cash flow statement of the organisation and be in a much stronger position to contribute to an accurate cash flow forecast. Further details on this topic are covered by Gowthorpe (2005).

Why is it so important that an organisation maintains and effective cash flow forecast?

1. To avoid surprises, which can be costly both in direct terms and in lost opportunities. By having a clear forward view of its cash position, the company can identify, for example, that there will be a cash shortage of £50,000 for a week at the end of July, and appropriate steps can be taken to bridge that gap with a short-term loan or bank overdraft, which can usually be agreed more easily, and at better rates, than if it were a last-minute crisis request.

2. Similarly, the identification of a forecast cash surplus in a future period enables plans to be made to invest the cash at the best possible rates – again, these are likely to be more favourable when planned and agreed in advance.

3. Many transactions are now made in currencies which are not that of the usual company transactions, and by predicting such inflows and outflows, decisions can be made on currency sales and purchases, and where appropriate these can be made in advance so as to hedge the exposure to exchange rate movements and remove uncertainty and risk.

11.6 CAPITAL EXPENDITURE EVALUATION

Capital investments are major long-term investments fundamental to the organisation. Dyson (2007, p421) notes that all entities would find it difficult to survive if they did not invest in some form of capital expenditure. Whereas many decisions have relatively short-term impacts, capital expenditure involves the appraisal of profits and cash flows generated, often over several years. The key objective of capital expenditure is to directly or indirectly generate extra profits for the business. Funds for capital expenditure are never unlimited, so in considering the potential return on the investment, the opportunity cost should be taken in to account. The opportunity cost is a measure of the return that could be earned if the funds were invested elsewhere.

In making decisions on capital expenditure, managers must make two linked decisions – whether the proposed project meets the basic criteria for financial return, and what is the ranking of the project among the other projects under consideration. Clearly if availability of capital was unlimited, all projects meeting the return criteria would be approved, but this is never the case, and a defined means of project ranking is crucial.

A number of evaluation techniques may be used to assess capital expenditure proposals. The techniques and process chosen by a company should be clearly documented, as illustrated later in this section, in some form of capital expenditure policy manual, to ensure that the approved processes are consistently followed and that decisions between expenditure requests are made logically and fairly. This section will examine the four most common techniques, all of which are widely used:

- accounting rate of return (ARR)
- payback
- net present value (NPV)
- internal rate of return (IRR).

11.6.1 ACCOUNTING RATE OF RETURN (ARR)

This method compares projected accounting profit for the project with the capital invested in the project or asset. The calculation is as follows:

$$\frac{\text{Average expected return (accounting profit)} \times 100}{\text{Average capital employed}} = \text{ARR per cent}$$

It should be noted that accounting profit for the project takes into account the depreciation of the assets, unlike the cash flow principle on which the other three evaluation techniques are based. The average capital employed is calculated by taking the initial expenditure at the start of the project, calculating the depreciated value at the end of each year, totalling each of the annual values for the life of the project, and dividing by the number of years, as follows:

	Accounting profit £'000	Capital employed £'000
Year 0		100
Year 1	20	80
Year 2	15	60
Year 3	10	40
Year 4	10	20
Year 5	5	0

Average accounting profit = 60/5 =   £12,000

Average capital employed = 300/6 =   £50,000

$$\text{ARR} = \frac{12,000 \times 100}{50,000} = 24\%$$

This return may be compared with the minimum return required in the company's capital investment procedures, or with its return on capital employed, as calculated in Chapter 10. If the project return meets or exceeds the criteria, then it is placed in a 'pool' to be compared with other projects whose return is calculated in exactly the same way. Projects with the highest returns are selected in descending order or returns, to the point where the organisations capital budget is fully committed.

11.6.2 PAYBACK

Payback is a technique which is simple to understand and apply. It involves estimating the length of time it will take for the cash inflows from the project to exceed the initial outflow.

	Cash flow £'000	Cumulative £'000
Year 0	−100	−100
Year 1	20	−80
Year 2	30	−50
Year 3	30	−20
Year 4	20	0
Year 5	10	10

In this example, the project repays its capital costs by the end of Year 4.

The payback technique has the advantage that it can be readily understood by non-financial staff and focuses on the payback in the early years of the project, thus reducing the effect of uncertainty. It does, however, ignore the time value of money, which will be explained in Section 11.6.3 below, and ignores potentially large cash inflows and outflows of cash after the payback period. This may be potentially misleading, particularly if there will be major cash outflows at the end of the project to restore the land to its original condition before the project commenced.

11.6.3 NET PRESENT VALUE (NPV)

This technique uses the concept of the time value of money. The principle involved is that £1 now is more valuable than £1 in a month's time or £1 in a year's time. The net present value method therefore discounts all cash flows to the same terms, adjusting for the time value of money. This calculation is dependent on the choice of a discount rate. The company might choose to apply a discount rate that reflects the cost of borrowing, for example a bank rate of 4 per cent, but few capital investment projects are risk free, so the company is likely to apply a risk premium to give a total discount rate of, say, 10 per cent.

Using the cash flows from the example in the previous section, the discount factor at a 10 per cent rate is applied to each year's cash flow. Note that the discount factor increases each year, as £1 in 5 years time is worth much less than £1 next year.

	Cash flow £'000	Discount factor (10%)	Discounted cash flow £'000
Year 0	−100	1.000	−100
Year 1	20	0.909	18
Year 2	30	0.826	25
Year 3	30	0.751	23
Year 4	20	0.683	14
Year 5	10	0.621	6
			−15

This calculation indicates that at the selected discount rate this five-year project has a negative discounted cash flow, and therefore should not proceed.

If the value had been positive, then the return would be compared with other potential projects, evaluated on the same basis, to provide a ranking list for access to the available capital. The NPV technique takes into account all cost and revenues over the full life of the project and hence should avoid issues around remediation costs, which are a significant problem with the payback method.

11.6.4 INTERNAL RATE OF RETURN (IRR)

Some organisations use the internal rate of return technique. This is best described as the inverse of the NPV method, in that using the cash flow information prepared on the same basis, a discount rate is calculated which brings the net value of the project to zero. For example, using a discount rate of 13 per cent a project may have a negative net value of £10,000, while at a rate of 12 per cent the net value may be zero, and at a rate of 11 per cent it may have a positive net value of £5,000. It can therefore be said that the IRR of the project is 12 per cent. If the company discount rate was 10 per cent, then the project would qualify to be ranked for approval.

ACTIVITY 11.4

EVALUATING CAPITAL EXPENDITURE

Examine the following cash flow information from a project proposal. The project is to extract gravel from a greenfield site, which must be returned to its original condition after five years. Note that there is a cash outflow in Year 5 which includes the expense of this remediation. Evaluate the project using both the payback and NPV methods described in this section. The company payback criterion is that a project must repay its capital cost within four years. It uses a 10 per cent discount rate for NPV calculations. The discount factors to be used can be taken from the example in Section 11.6.3 above.

	Cash flow £'000
Year 0	−200
Year 1	120
Year 2	80
Year 3	60
Year 4	50
Year 5	−120

Do both evaluation techniques yield the same decision? Consider why differences might arise. A suggested answer to this activity is available on the companion website.

11.6.5 CURRENT PRACTICE: TECHNIQUES ACTUALLY USED

Research shows that organisations often use a combination of approaches to decision-making on capital investment. Larger companies often use a payback criterion to 'weed out' projects that do not pay back sufficiently rapidly, and then apply IRR, NPV or ARR techniques to rank the short-listed projects. Smaller companies often use the payback method to make their initial selections and then use a less formal process of management judgement to make the final choices. This judgement incorporates a view of the project risk, which is usually more formally incorporated in the discount rates by larger organisations. The key principle should be that a consistent approach is adopted to every proposed and approved project, and this is the purpose of the creation and implementation of a capital expenditure policy manual, which is described in the next section.

11.6.6 CAPITAL EXPENDITURE POLICY MANUAL

Such a manual is essential to ensure that capital investment proposals are correctly and consistently reviewed, and that once a decision has been made the ongoing investment process is fully managed and reviewed. The policy manual should include specifications for:

- an annually updated forecast of capital expenditures – to be included in the overall cash flow forecast for the organisation
- the appropriation steps – processes to and forms to be used
- the appraisal method(s) to be used to evaluate proposals, with a clear definition of the sequence and documentary evidence required
- the minimum acceptable rate(s) of return or payback periods on projects of various risk
- the limits of authority for approval of each defined project size
- the mechanism for reporting and control of capital expenditures
- the procedure to be followed when accepted projects will be subject to a post-completion audit and performance review after implementation.

11.6.7 POST-COMPLETION AUDITS

It is vital that capital expenditure projects are monitored through from the approval stage to final completion, to provide evaluation and feedback on decisions. The post-approval audit plan should be established at the project authorisation stage. It should not be seen as threatening to managers, as this would have an undesirable impact of deterring managers from putting forward all but the safest of investment schemes. It should have a very positive effect in that thorough and realistic project appraisal is undertaken before a project is finally proposed, as the sponsoring manager will be clearly aware that both the decision process and the ongoing project costs and benefits will be thoroughly audited. By making a much more comprehensive database of reviews available to managers, this will improve the quality of decision-making by making past experience available to decision-makers – this is a significant contribution to knowledge management within the organisation.

A positive but sometimes unwelcome result of post-approval audits is that decisions can be made at an early stage to modify or even terminate a project which is not meeting its planned outcomes. Rather than this being the result of an ad hoc decision, it can be made with full explanation and justification.

There some further practical difficulties with the post-approval audit process. One is simply the problem of isolating the specific costs, revenues and cash flows resulting directly from the project. This can be particularly difficult in a rapidly changing external environment, and some practical estimates may need to be made to enable a reasonable statement of the project performance, compared with the plan, to be produced. Post-approval audit may prove to be time consuming and unwelcome to some managers, particularly when it is first introduced, but nevertheless, it is an important tool to facilitate improvements in capital expenditure management and decision-making.

11.7 PERFORMANCE MONITORING

We have seen how budgets and budget monitoring and control are one aspect of the way that companies monitor their performance. As previously indicated, management accounting covers more than just financial data, and recent developments in performance monitoring have seen it adopt an expanded remit to cover much wider aspects of the organisation. Why should this be?

Current thinking is that traditional performance monitoring was unduly focused on budgetary financial control, which although it produced widely understood measures and information, concentrated on only a few aspects of the overall organisation. It was argued by Kaplan and Norton, among others, that a much wider view of the organisation and its strategy was required. They devised the balanced scorecard approach which enables managers to obtain a fast but comprehensive view of the business's performance and the progress towards its strategic aims. The scorecard addresses the key areas of the organisation and shows how important the linkages are between those areas. The key areas initially chosen by Kaplan and Norton (1996) are as follows:

- **Financial**: 'To succeed financially, how should we appear to our shareholders?'

- **Customer**: 'To achieve our vision, how should we appear to our customers?'

- **Internal business processes**: 'To satisfy our shareholders, what business processes must we excel at?'

- **Learning and growth**: 'To achieve our vision, how will we sustain our ability to change and improve?'

These key areas are all clearly linked and are all targeted at the vision and strategy of the organisation. Kaplan and Norton intended the four initial areas to be indicative suggestions, and indeed other writers have added further dimensions, for example supply chain and technology. Once the key aspects of the scorecard have been devised, based on the mission and values that we discussed earlier in the chapter, then a number of key objectives and measures for those objectives should be devised. Overall, this means that groups and individuals have specific targets that are directly aligned with the overall strategy of the organisation and are not, as often happens, working hard but actually 'pulling in the wrong direction' through no fault of their own.

By identifying objectives and specific measures, and monitoring performance against targets, management can have a clear picture of the overall success of the organisation and can readily identify areas where improvement is required. For each of these problem areas, an improvement project can be identified, and the total of these improvement projects should encompass all the initiatives in progress in the organisation. Any company initiatives not directly linked to the scorecard objectives are simply contributing to 'initiative overload' and should be removed.

An example of the application of the balanced scorecard approach to performance monitoring follows. If we analyse the mission statement from our imaginary restaurant Fusion 99, as introduced in the Section 11.2, then we might identify the key dimensions of the business as:

- customers
- operations
- human resources
- finance.

Within those dimensions, the objectives might be:
- delighted customers
- effective operations
- happy staff
- sustainable profits.

A range of measures and targets could be selected to monitor performance, for example:

- a weekly customer survey, with a target of 95 per cent of customers rating the restaurant as 'good' or 'excellent'.
- an employee turnover measure, with a maximum target of 20 per cent per annum turnover.

Several measures may be chosen to address each of the dimensions, but it is important that these should not proliferate so that the effect of each is devalued. A practical maximum of four measures per dimension is usually recommended. By monitoring performance against specific and closely defined measures, the management of the organisation have a concise and accurate overall view of the progress of the organisation, and team leaders can provide clear briefings on their section's progress, with the knowledge that their objectives are fully integrated with the overall business strategy.

An example of an improvement project that might be identified is if the customer survey indicates a lower level of satisfaction than targeted. A multifunctional improvement team should be identified to analyse the areas of shortfall, recommend improvements and oversee their implementation. For example, a problem with the customer satisfaction results might be identified as relating to small portion sizes. Representatives of the finance, marketing and operations teams would meet to identify how this can be resolved in the most effective way, in line with the overall organisation objectives. It might just require the purchase of smaller plates!

The argument is sometimes raised that not all objectives can be effectively measured, but the counter-argument is that those that really cannot be measured are perhaps not appropriate objectives, or are at least very difficult to communicate to managers, and individual staff.

The balanced scorecard (Kaplan and Norton 1996) is an example of a popular technique used for performance monitoring. It is widely used by commercial organisations and also in the public and not-for-profit sectors. It also serves to illustrate the means by which finance closely integrates with other aspects of the organisation. Many performance measures are not finance based, but all of the items measured contribute directly or indirectly to the financial performance of the organisation. A good example of this will be illustrated in the following section on 'Environmental management accounting', in which many non-financial measures are reported and monitored alongside conventional financial measures as part of the overall management process of the organisation.

ACTIVITY 11.5

DEVELOPING FUSION 99'S BALANCED SCORECARD

Examine the mission statement for Fusion 99, and the suggested objectives noted above, and create some additional measures and targets which could help to monitor the progress of the organisation towards its key objectives:

We aim to make Fusion 99 a great place to eat, combining a fun atmosphere with Eastern and Western-influenced food. By serving delicious meals and retaining happy and motivated staff we will delight our customers and develop an efficient and profitable organisation.

ACTIVITY 11.6

APPLYING THE BALANCED SCORECARD

Take the mission statement for your own organisation, identified in Activity 11.1, or for an alternative organisation, as identified in Activity 11.2, and consider the key dimensions of the organisation – you should identify between four and six dimensions. Define the objectives, and hence measures and targets that you consider to be appropriate.

11.8 ENVIRONMENTAL MANAGEMENT ACCOUNTING

Before the 1990s, environmental accounting was generally considered to be the preserve of a few specialist researchers, and environmental issues as a whole were examined by individuals or very small groups within major companies. The costs of pollution and waste were often not recorded against particular activities or departments, and were 'lost' in overheads. For example, costs of disposal of waste created throughout a manufacturing site were often collected and reported within a single transport or waste-disposal department, rather than being identified as relating to specific production activities or products. Since these costs were not identified as being the responsibility of a specific manager, there was little incentive to reduce the cost or environmental impact of the waste created. These specific issues are now often handled by environmental management accounting and are seen to be a key current concern for organisations for a number of reasons, as noted by Gray and Bebbington (2001).

- **Regulations**: International, national and local environmental regulations are now in place with which organisations must comply or risk major fines or restrictions on their ability to operate. The cost of fines or effect of restrictions could be prohibitive.

- **Customers and suppliers**: The overall supply chain is now much more environmentally conscious, and companies may refuse to work with potential partners who, for example, are unable to offer the facility to return packaging for recycling.

- **Trade organisations**: Having appropriate and auditable environmental procedures in place may be a condition of membership of a trade organisation which is vital to the company.

- **Cost benefits**: Awareness and investigation of potential benefits, including cost savings, of waste reduction can yield a competitive advantage to the organisation.

- **Financing**: Providers of finance, including banks and other financial institutions, are increasingly conscious of the importance of reviewing the environmental impact of their investments. Many shareholders and potential shareholders factor environmental impacts into their investment decisions.

The role of management accounting in these processes is to enable the effects to be measured, using both financial and non-financial data. This is proving to be a significant challenge. Often environmental departments are not fully integrated with the cost structure of the organisation. Many environmental costs are hidden within overheads and are not attributed to the department actually generating the waste or pollution. Despite increasing focus on control and stewardship, many organisations do not fully track the flow of materials through their processes, and are simply unaware of all the losses and waste that are occurring. Many capital investment decisions do not follow the guidelines indicated earlier in this chapter, and hence do not include the overall lifetime costs of a project, including all pollution and remediation impacts.

Given these potential pitfalls, how should a modern organisation identify and handle environmental costs through its management accounting processes? Some key steps are as follows:

1. Analyse the flow of products and services through the organisation, so as to fully identify all costs of delivering products or services through from the initial supplier to the customer. Where these costs include elements of waste, then these must be separately recorded against the operation and product or service to which they relate.

2. For companies using physical materials, use a mass balance process to accurately track flows of materials through the process, so as to identify where waste and pollution are occurring. This could also result in significant cost benefits.

3. Implement some form of reporting tool, such as the Rhone-Poulenc Environmental Index, through which all waste costs are reported back to the manager or department with which they originate, on the principle of 'polluter pays'. For example, rather than having overhead costs for waste disposal collected within a transport department, all such costs should be analysed and charged directly to the departments where these items originated, thus enabling the true cost of their product or service to be identified, and corrective action taken if required.

4. Analyse all capital expenditure proposals with full recognition of the overall life cycle costs of the project.

Creating a budget for an organisation which recognises the key impacts of accounting for environmental costs and waste is thus a more complex activity, but the benefits in terms of management awareness and control should significantly outweigh the costs. When environmental data are captured within the routine management reporting of the organisation, decisions can be fully integrated into day-to-day operations, and annual company reporting, including environmental impacts, should prove to be easier and with more positive initiatives to be presented.

11.8.1 MANAGEMENT ACCOUNTING: KEY EMPLOYEE ATTRIBUTES

This chapter has illustrated a number of ways in which management accounting information is vital to the management and control of any organisation. In the current ever-changing environment, reliance on periodic financial accounting reports is not sufficient – an organisation needs to have effective measures, based on strategy, measures, budgets, and forecasts that incorporate accurate, timely information. This vital information must be fully communicated to empowered and well-trained staff. An enlightening study by Dearman and Shields (2005) investigated how individuals in an organisation reacted to a fundamental change in the accounting principles used to determine product pricing. They found that:

- Seventy-eight per cent of managers did not change their decision model.

- Twenty per cent of managers changed their decision model in the right direction.

- Two per cent of managers changed their decision model in the wrong direction.

Their conclusions on investigating these managers in detail was that those who reacted in the correct way to the change were those properly equipped to take on the change; that is:

- Unless people have the correct attributes, then they are not likely to change their behaviour appropriately in response to changes in management accounting.

- Because employees often lack enough of at least one of these attributes, many firms are not likely to realise benefits from changes in management accounting.

This research indicates clearly that the implementation of one or more of the important management accounting techniques described in this chapter does not provide a guarantee of improvement in performance. Staff must have sufficient ability to understand both the details of the new techniques and their wider importance. They must be appropriately trained in the new techniques and their application. Most importantly, they should be sufficiently motivated to drive through the changes successfully.

11.9 CONCLUSION

Management accounting information is fundamental to the internal decision-making process of an organisation. The value of the information extends far beyond the traditional accounts department and is of essential importance both to the management teams within all departments, and to multifunctional teams working on projects or key initiatives. The all-encompassing nature of the financial and non-financial information provides the lifeblood of the control loop circulatory process described at the start of this chapter. The ever increasing rate of change in both organisations and the external environment in which they operate means that it is even more important that accurate and consistent information is available on a timely basis, to enable the decision-making processes to be swiftly but rigorously applied.

PAUSE FOR THOUGHT

Identify at least three things that you have learned by studying this chapter and engaging with the exercises and activities. How will your newly acquired knowledge and skills support your continuing professional development? What value do you expect your learning to have for your daily routines and your further career? In what area have you identified a need for further development and how are you planning to fill that gap? Address these issues in your learning journal and/or CPD log. You may also wish to discuss them with a peer, colleague, mentor or coach to aid your further development.

KEY LEARNING POINTS

- The importance of a long-term plan and annual budgets for a business, and the relationship between these items.

- The presentation of budgetary data and its importance to the overall control of the organisation.

- The reliance of an organisation on cash flow, and the means by which this can be monitored and improved.

- The key approaches to the evaluation of capital expenditure proposals, and the additional data which is relevant to these decisions in the current environment.

- The design of performance monitoring processes in an organisation, and the crucial role of non-financial data.

- The increasing importance of environmental management accounting in influencing the financial decision-making process.

- The importance of management accounting information and processes in the management and control of an organisation, and the key role of selecting, fully training and empowering staff to correctly respond to the information provided.

If you wish to explore further the management of financial resources, then there are a range of activities and materials that can be recommended. There are a number of very helpful texts which expand on the key topics covered by this chapter and are particularly targeted at managers and students who are not finance specialists, but who aim to develop further their theoretical and practical knowledge of this key area. The works listed in the references section by Broadbent and Cullen (2003), Dyson (2007) and Gowthorpe (2005) should prove very useful in expanding on topics that are inevitably covered rather briefly in this general chapter. You may also want to explore Duncan Williamson's website that introduces the key numerical techniques required for capital budgeting (see http://www.duncanwil.co.uk/invapp.html).

It is also strongly recommended that you take every opportunity to be involved in budgetary meetings and financial communication sessions within your organisation and that you volunteer for multifunctional project teams, where you will gain enormously from exposure to staff from across all specialisms, including finance. You should also consider taking part in business simulation activities, which will not only enhance your financial understanding but will also develop your awareness of the linkages between finance and the other key business areas. There are many such 'games' which, although usually great fun, also have a very serious business and educational purpose. An example may be found at http://www.venturesimulations.co.uk.

11.10 REFERENCES

BROADBENT, M. and CULLEN, J. (2003) *Managing financial resources*. Oxford: Butterworth-Heinemann.

CIMA Global. (2005) *A practitioner's guide to the balanced scorecard*. Available online at: http://www.cimaglobal.com/Documents/ImportedDocuments/tech_resrep_a_practitioners_guide_to_the_balanced_scorecard_2005.pdf [Accessed 25 May 2010].

CIPFA. (ND) *Zero based budgeting*. Available online at: http://www.cipfa.org.uk/pt/download/zero_based_budgeting_briefing.pdf [Accessed 25 May 2010].

DEARMAN, D. and SHIELDS, M. (2005) Avoiding accounting fixation: determinants of cognitive adaptation to differences in accounting method. C*ontemporary Accounting Research*. Vol. 22, No. 2, pp351–384.

DYSON, J. (2007) *Accounting for non-accounting students*. 7th ed. Harlow: FT Prentice Hall.

GOWTHORPE, C. (2005) *Business accounting and finance for non-specialists*. 2nd ed. London: Thomson.

GRAY, R. and BEBBINGTON, J. (2001) *Accounting for the environment*. 2nd ed. London: Sage.

HOPE, J. and FRASER, R. (1999) Beyond budgeting: building a new management model for the information age. *Management Accounting*. Vol. 77, No. 1, pp16–21.

KAPLAN, R. and NORTON, D. (1996) Using the balanced scorecard as a strategic management system. *Harvard Business Review*. Vol. 74, No. 1, pp75–85.

MILLS, R. and KENNEDY, J. (1993) Experiences in operating a post-audit system. *Management Accounting*. Vol. 71, No. 10, p26.

Proficiency in Information Technology

CHAPTER 12

Handling statistical data using IT

Jeff Evans

OVERVIEW

This chapter considers a concise account of the fundamental statistics required by human resources professionals. The chapter is designed for study by people who have a limited or no background in statistical analysis. There are a number of statistical concepts contained in this chapter which are explained and examples provided to test the studied knowledge. The chapter commences with a section of a fundamental computer-based human resource database as used by a typical company and suggests that the information contained within it does not appear to be easy to quantify. The chapter continues by considering the type of data to use for ease of manipulation and demonstrates how the data can be pictorially represented. A discussion on how to determine measures of central tendency and the dispersion of the data from the mean value follows. The five basic statistical descriptors are introduced and discussed as are the 'Normal' and 'Students' "t"' distributions and how we can use these distributions to help us to resolve hypothesis tests. Basic probability theory is introduced and the chapter concludes with a discussion of basic forecasting using the two variable linear regression models.

LEARNING OUTCOMES

By the end of this chapter, provided you engage with the activities, you should be able to:

- identify the difference between qualitative and quantitative data
- organise data into a suitable format to use as information to assist with the decision-making process
- create pictorial representations of a distribution of ungrouped data either by freehand or by the use of a spreadsheet
- find the values of central tendency and spread of the data set in any given distribution of ungrouped data
- understand and apply the concepts of the normal distribution, basic probability theory, and hypothesis testing with data relating to a population or to a sample of data from the population
- understand and apply the concepts of linear correlation and regression analysis

and feel confident enough to undertake a forecast of one variable when given another variable

- feel comfortable with the use of IT as a medium to help with the statistics.

12.1 INTRODUCTION

In the current business environment, technology is becoming more sophisticated and a major part of commercial activity. Various available computer software packages are designed to produce supplementary statistics of data, so a fundamental knowledge of statistical skills and interpretation of statistical data is becoming very useful to provide the competent manager with an ability to develop alternative strategies and/or reinforce current strategies and objectives. Rather than leave the responsibility of interpretation to a subordinate, managers who are able to directly interpret the statistics will provide themselves with a competitive advantage in terms of time.

This chapter is primarily designed to provide the fundamental concepts of statistical analysis of data and is set up for readers who have few or no statistical skills. Readers seeking a more robust grounding in statistical analysis are directed to and encouraged to read selected texts from the vast range of the (business-related) statistical literature (see 'Explore further' at the end of the chapter for details).

12.2 FUNDAMENTAL CONCEPTS OF STATISTICAL ANALYSIS

Let us begin with a straightforward example from a human resource perspective to introduce the benefits of statistical analysis. Please be aware that the principles applied to this example can be applied to data from other domains.

Consider the data as captured in Table 12.1 opposite. These data are likely to represent part of a company database relating to (sensitive) employee information, and nowadays is usually stored in a secure electronic format such as Microsoft Access or bespoke database software.

The first (collective) observation of the data is that there are various fields (columns) attributed to each of the records (rows) and that a record (row) can be identified by a unique number (in this case the employee number). Typical electronic databases come complete with an automatic (unique) record identifier. Databases are traditionally more secure than spreadsheets for storing electronic records because their built-in safety checks reduce the risk of deleting data by mistake.

Table 12.1 An extract of employee data from a company database

First name	Last name	DOB (dd/mm/yr)	Gender	1st line of address	2nd line of address	Employee number	Start date (dd/mm/yr)	Salary grade
Kirstie	Adams	12/11/1977	F	27 Maughan St	Newtown	60374	01/01/1999	E
David	Fletcher	17/01/1971	M	313 Sycamore Dr	Newtown	60466	01/01/2006	G
John	Smith	03/07/1950	M	14 Curlew Way	Newtown	60355	01/04/2007	G
John	Ahmed	09/05/1958	M	'The Mill'	Oldtown	60152	01/01/1995	C
Alan	Wright	22/05/1985	M	37 Peel St	Newtown	60102	01/07/2004	F
Sonia	Jones	04/06/1971	F	141 The Avenue	Newtown	60786	01/10/1991	B
Robert	Wood	19/01/1973	M	89 Hallside	Newtown	60983	01/01/2002	F
Angela	Thompson	30/08/1973	F	3 Disraeli St	Newtown	60588	01/07/1990	B
Thomas	Ross	16/12/1966	M	46 Walsham Rd	Oldtown	60986	01/04/1997	D
John	Smith	19/09/1959	M	31 Park View	Oldtown	60481	01/01/1994	C
Simon	George	29/11/1973	M	9 The Avenue	Newtown	60235	01/01/1990	B
Lin Li	Wong	14/08/1972	F	32 Oldtown Rd	Newtown	60713	01/04/1994	C
Derek	Edwards	13/04/1976	M	15 Princes St	Oldtown	60430	01/10/2002	C
Craig	Smith	26/07/1985	M	14 Curlew Way	Newtown	60178	01/01/1996	F

Another (collective) observation of the data is that the information does not look too easy to qualify or quantify. For example, the data would need to be sorted into alphabetical or numerical order to help to determine the minimum, maximum or average values, and this can only be undertaken on specific fields such as date of birth. Finding average values for the employee number, for example, would not be of any use. And, similarly, what would be the average salary based upon a letter identification?

So, rather than discuss the negative aspects of observations of the data, we will discuss what we can do to organise it so as to help us process it more effectively. This chapter considers the fundamentals of statistical analysis, including aspects from descriptive statistics and inferential statistics. We commence with the understanding of the types of data, how to display data pictorially, measurements of central tendency and dispersion (including an introduction to the normal distribution of data), the five basic statistical descriptors of a data set, elementary probability theory, hypothesis testing and simple correlation, and regression of the linear line. Throughout this chapter there are activities to help you to understand the necessary concepts.

ACTIVITY 12.1

STORING PERSONNEL DATA

Think about the set-up of a database to store personnel data. Identify the necessary information you believe would be useful to store and consider the aspects for the ease of handling (or manipulation) and analysis of the data. Could numerical data be better for data analysis than non-numerical data? Could non-numerical field descriptor values become numerical? How could you achieve this?

Data is traditionally split into two specific types: qualitative (or categorical) and numerical (or quantitative). We will discuss these in turn in the next sections.

12.2.1 QUALITATIVE (CATEGORICAL) DATA

This type of data is typically countable and can be summarised and presented in a table. For primary data sources (for example, data collected from a primary source such as a questionnaire), it is up to the data collector to use what s/he believes would prepare the data for better understanding and interpretation. Secondary data sources – that is, data already available (for example, data published elsewhere) – are usually already summarised and presented in some tabular or pictorial format.

Data can be presented either through univariate methods (for example, when one variable is analysed) or through multivariate methods (where two or more variables are analysed). Typical descriptive statistical formats include those shown in Table 12.2.

Table 12.2 Total employment categories of a company

Employment category	Count	Percentage
Managerial	47	12 (= 47/407 * 100%)
Clerical	350	86
Technical	10	2
Total	407	100

The data set presented above is univariate since it represents the total employment categories of a company. Employment in this example is split into three broad areas – managerial, clerical and technical – for analysis; other organisations may require different categories. These data can be represented in graphical form through pie charts, bar charts and histograms, as shown in Figures 12.1–12.3.

Figure 12.1 Pie chart for total employment categories

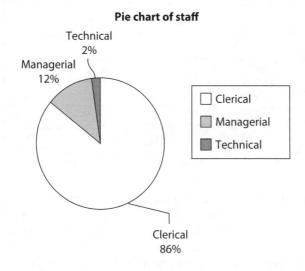

Figure 12.2 Bar chart for total employment categories

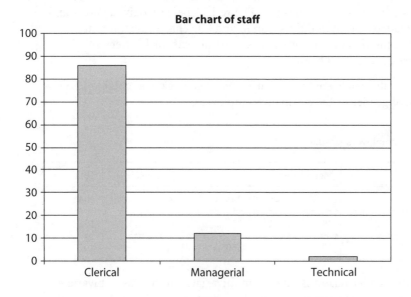

Figure 12.3 Histogram for total employment categories

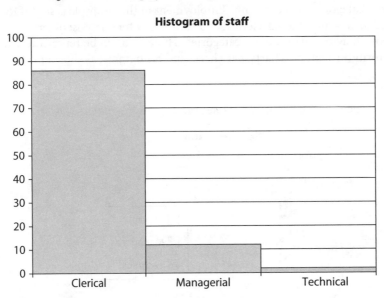

Notice how a histogram is very similar to a bar chart, but is more pleasing to the eye since it provides an element of perspective relating to the total area contained by each of the data series. With a histogram, the area is proportional to the frequency of the data and, with equal class intervals (or widths) (for example, the width of the bars), the vertical axis will represent the frequency. With unequal class widths, the vertical axis will represent the frequency density. Histograms typically, are of more use with quantitative data.

There are other pictorial data presentations available in addition to the above, and these include frequency polygons (see Figure 12.6 below), ogives, Pareto and line charts. For a description of ogives, Pareto and line charts, the interested reader is directed towards one of the many statistical texts for further information (see Section 12.8 below).

Presentation of multivariate data is similarly undertaken. Consider Table 12.3's summary table of gender of the company's employees.

Table 12.3 Data of employees' gender

Gender	Management	Clerical	Technical	Total
Female	9	293	2	304
Male	38	57	8	103
Total	47	350	10	407

We can depict the gender relationship on a multivariate (in this case a bivariate – female and male) pictorial presentation in a bar chart (Figure 12.4). Analysis of the bar chart indicates a clear visual comparison for the gender of the three

Figure 12.4 Bar chart of employees' gender

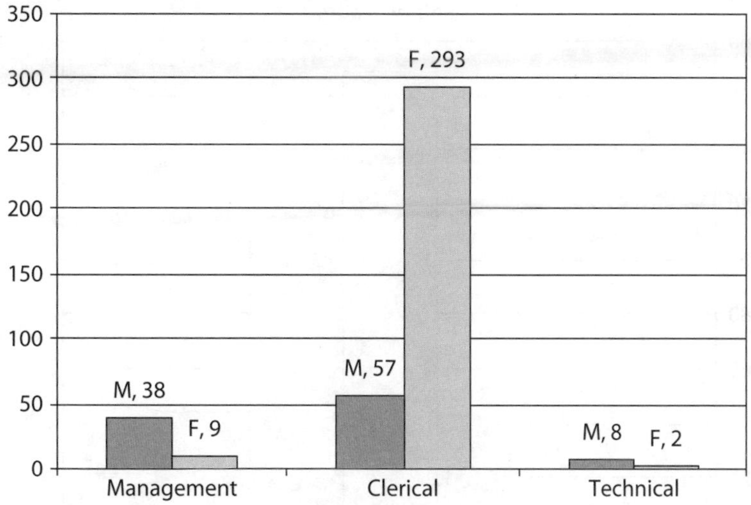

employee categories: The management employment category is dominated by males and the clerical by females.

ACTIVITY 12.2

PICTORIAL PRESENTATION OF CATEGORICAL DATA

Are there any other diagrams you could think of or perhaps conceive, to use to analyse the data? Which ones would you use for which purposes?

12.2.2 QUANTITATIVE (NUMERICAL) DATA

Quantitative data is measurable and after collection it is usually summarised and presented in an appropriate frequency table or frequency distribution chart. The fundamental forms of frequency tables include frequency, relative frequency (for example, percentages) and cumulative frequency tables. Consider Table 12.4, a frequency table of salary grades and the number of employees per grade.

Such information is appropriately displayed as a histogram (see Figure 12.5).

Table 12.4 Frequency table of salary grades

Salary grade	A	B	C	D	E	F	G
No. employees	0	9	43	169	121	44	21
£000 pa	>55	45–55	40–50	35–45	30–40	25–35	<25
Average	N/A	50	45	40	35	30	20

Figure 12.5 Histogram for salary grades

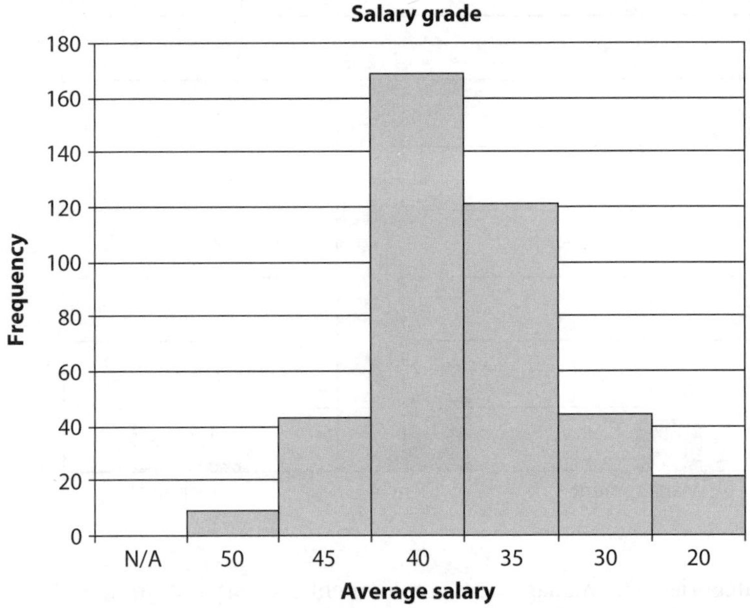

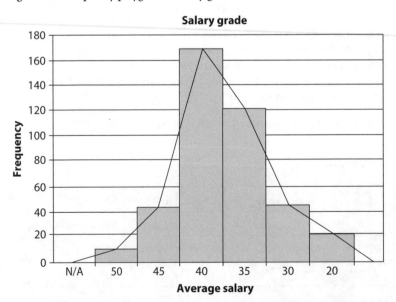

Salary grade

Just by examining the histogram, it is clear that the highest proportion of employees are receiving an average salary somewhere in the region of £40k. Similarly it is clear that the right-hand side of the histogram depicts more employees than the left-hand side of the histogram indicating that there are more lower-than-average earners than there are higher-than-average earners.

It is also possible to apply a frequency polygon to the data in the histogram (see Figure 12.6).

Figure 12.6 Frequency polygon for salary grades

Notice how the frequency polygon captures the mid-points of the bars of the histogram. Similarly, and to close off the frequency polygon, it is terminated at either side of the histogram at a point that is equal to half of the width of each of the class intervals.

A cumulative frequency distribution (Figure 12.7) is useful for determining a number of observations that are greater (or less) than a set amount. Typically expressed in percentages on the vertical axis (to identify proportions), the cumulative distribution simply sums up the observations per class. In this case, the distribution is set up on actual numbers. All 407 (100 per cent) of employees earn a salary of at least Grade G. We can identify that there are 50 employees who earn a salary of at least Grade C (for example, grades A, B and C).

Figure 12.7 Cumulative frequency distribution for salary grades

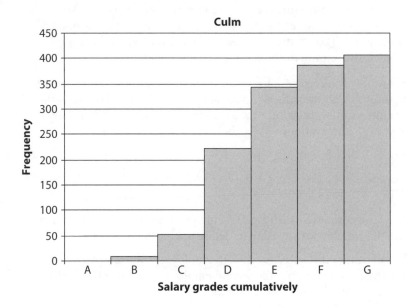

Before proceeding to other useful statistical measures, it is worth understanding the principles of producing graphs similar to those produced above. Microsoft Excel (v2007) was used to produce the graphs above, and interested readers are directed to Section 12.6, where a step-by-step guide to creating a graph in Excel is provided.

Microsoft Excel also provides fundamental statistical tools for use in analysis (possibly sufficient for a non-statistician). Readers interested in statistical tools are directed towards statistical software packages such as SPSS, Minitab and SAS. For readers interested in programming their own statistical analysis commands, I would recommend the software package 'R', (currently available free from the CRAN-R project website (http://CRAN.R-project.org)). Programming is relatively easy to do in 'R' and an example is provided later in this chapter. For this chapter, we will make use of the various statistical functions available in Microsoft Excel.

When given a full quantitative data set it is possible to analyse the data into measures of central tendency and dispersion and, by arranging them in numerical order, to summarise the data by the five basic statistical descriptors.

12.3 MEASURES OF CENTRAL TENDENCY AND DISPERSION

Central tendency and dispersion works for both grouped data (data that are presented in grouped form and not as individual data points) and ungrouped data (data that are presented as individual data points). This section will consider ungrouped data only.

12.3.1 CENTRAL TENDENCY

The six basic central measurements relating to ungrouped data are the mean, the median, the mode, the trimmed mean, the weighted mean and the geometric mean. This section will concentrate on the mean, the median and the mode, which are the most common of the central measurements.

The **mean** is simply the average value of our data observations, and we calculate its value by summing all the values of our data observations and dividing that sum by the number of observations. As an example, suppose our data consisted of the following 15 observations of salaries (in £10,000s):

2, 5, 1, 5, 7, 5, 2, 8, 3, 5, 4, 2, 5, 4 and 5

then the mean would be $(2 + 5 + 1 + 5 + 7 + 5 + 2 + 8 + 3 + 5 + 4 + 2 + 5 + 4 + 5)/15 = 63/15 = 4.2$ (ie £42,000)

For shorthand purposes, we usually express the mean value by a horizontal bar, placed above the variable we are using to define the mean, for example: $\overline{X}$

Suppose X_i determines the salary for the i'th employee (for example, X_1 implies the first employee, X_2 determines the second employee etc), then the statistical formulae to determine the mean is as follows:

$$\overline{X} = \frac{(X_1 + X_2 + X_3 + ... + X_n)}{n}$$

The **median** is the middle value of a set of data observations when arranged in ascending or descending order. As an example, we can look at the previous set of 15 data observations for example:

2, 5, 1, 5, 7, 5, 2, 8, 3, 5, 4, 2, 5, 4 and 5

The first step when dealing with the median is to arrange the data into numerical order, for example:

1, 2, 2, 2, 3, 4, 4, 5, 5, 5, 5, 5, 5, 7 and 8

(The Excel 'Data/Sort' command will do this for you!).

When there is an odd number of data observations, we use the following formula to determine the position of the median:

$$\text{MEDIAN} = \frac{X_{n+1}}{2}$$

(where X_n represents the total number of data observations and, in the above case, $X_n = 15$ so $X_n+1 = 16$ and, the median must lie at the $16/2 = 8$th position).

We use the value of 8 to count from either side of the distribution, to the eighth data observation. So counting from left to right in the data set, the eighth observation is a value of 5 (for example, the first occurrence of the 5 in the ordered data set). Hence, the median of this data set is 5.

If there is an even number of data observations, we use the following formula to determine the position of the median:

$$\text{MEDIAN} = \frac{X_{n/2}+X_{(n/2)+1}}{2}$$

Using the same data observations as before (but including one additional observation of (another) 3), for example:

1, 2, 2, 2, 3, 3, 4, 4, 5, 5, 5, 5, 5, 5, 7 and 8

There are now 16 data observations, hence n = 16. Applying the formula for an even number of data observations to the median for example:

n/2 = 16/2 = 8; and (n/2) + 1 = 9.

Hence the median = (eighth + ninth data values) divided by 2:

For example, (4 + 5)/2 = 9/2 = 4.5.

As the median of the data simply divides the ordered data set into two sections with an equal number of data observations in each section, we can in effect find the median of each of the two sections. The values we find are called quartile one and quartile three respectively (also known as Q1 and Q3) and they simply identify the values in the data set represented at the 25 per cent and 75 per cent positions of the ordered data set.

Since the median is found by ordering the data, we can use the median value with the two quartile values, and by identifying the minimum and maximum observational values, we can explain the data set by five basic numerical values: for example, minimum, Q1, median, Q3 and maximum. Many of the statistical software packages provide these summary statistics as normal practice and these values form the basis of other pictorial representations of data such as box and whisker diagrams (see Figure 12.12).

The **mode** is simply the value of a data set that occurs most often. More than one mode can exist. For example (using the previous 15 data observations):

2, 5, 1, 5, 7, 5, 2, 8, 3, 5, 4, 2, 5, 4 and 5

The mode in this case is 5 (occurs six times).

Another example: 7, 3, 4, 4, 3, 8, 5, 4, 7, 1 and 7

This time, both 4 and 7 occur on three occasions each. Hence 4 and 7 are the modes. Just to recap, any data set contains only one value for the mean and only one value for the median, but there may be more than one value for the mode.

For further examples on the mean, median and/or mode (some using Excel), please see the following references (by author):

Albright et al (2002) – p88.

Anderson et al (2003) – p64.

Levine et al (2005) p132.

Mason and Lind (1993) – p74 onwards.

Sandy (1990) – p74 (quite technical).

Swift and Piff (2010) – p280 onwards.

Webster (1992) – p92 onwards.

Whigham (1998) – p301 (quite technical).

12.3.2 DISPERSION

Given that the central measurement of the data set is determined, we may also want to know about how the dispersion of the data set relates to the central measure. The dispersion of the data provides the relationship of where the observations occur relative to the central value. Dispersion is also known as the spread of the data and it is normally referred to as the standard deviation or as the variance of the data set. Consider the spread shown in Figure 12.8.

The diagram represents a plot of the data set and highlights the average or mean value and the spread of a data set. This diagram appears to be symmetrical around the central axis (the mean), but it should be noted that not all plots of data will appear to be symmetrically displayed. For a symmetrical distribution such as the

Figure 12.8 Data spread

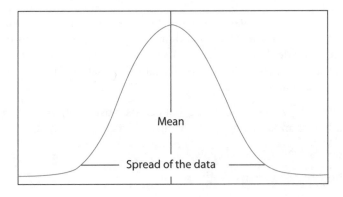

ACTIVITY 12.3

EXERCISES ON THE MEAN, MEDIAN AND MODE

In order to help you to understand the concepts of the mean, median and mode of a data set, determine these three measurements for the examples below.

17, 43, 14, 7, 20, 32, 30, 23, 9, 23, 27, 31

Solution: the mean, median and mode = 23

(Mean: (17 + 43 + 14 + 7 + 20 + 32 + 30 + 23 + 9 + 23 + 27 + 31)/12 = 23)

(Median: arrange the data into numerical order):

(7, 9, 14, 17, 20, 23, 23, 27, 30, 31, 32, 43) and n = 12 hence the median is the average of the 6th and 7th data observation values for example, (23 + 23)/2 = 23

(Mode: select the value (or values) that occur more frequently than any other value(s) and in this case, there are two observations of 23 while each other observational value occurs only once. Therefore the mode is 23.)

EXCEL

(The following relates to Excel version 2007.)

Input the unsorted data from the beginning of this activity into column A, row 1 to row 12. Highlight your data in column A from row 1 to row 12 inclusive (ie click and hold the mouse button in the cell identified by column A and row 1 (for example, cell A1) and drag to row 12 then release the mouse button).

On the 'HOME' tab, click the mouse button ('click') on the 'copy' icon (ie the icon below the 'scissors' icon in the 'Clipboard' section) (or simply depress the 'CTRL' and 'C' keys together). Click in cell C1, then (on the 'HOME' tab) click on the 'Clipboard' icon ('Paste') (or simply depress the 'CTRL' and 'V' keys together). This will copy the data from column A rows 1 to 12 to column C rows 1 to 12.

In cell B13, type 'average'. In cell B14, type 'median' and in cell B15, type 'mode'.

Highlight your data in column C from row 1 to row 12 inclusive.

Click on the 'DATA' tab, then in the 'Sort & Filter' section, click on the 'smallest to largest' icon (the icon with 'A' above 'Z' complete with a downward pointing arrow). If a 'Sort Warning' dialogue box appears, check the box for 'Continue with the current selection' and click on 'Sort'. (Your data should now be sorted).

In cell C14, input the following command: =average(c1:c12) , and press 'ENTER'

In cell C14, input the following command: =median(c1:c12) , and press 'ENTER'

In cell C14, input the following command: =mode(c1:c12) , and press 'ENTER'

(the '=' sign is part of the command)

The results should display the mean (average), median and mode values as given above. (Be wary of finding the modal value with Excel as it usually only finds the first mode if there is more than one!)

Save your data; we can make use of it when we come to find the standard deviation.

Figure 12.9 Mean, mode, median

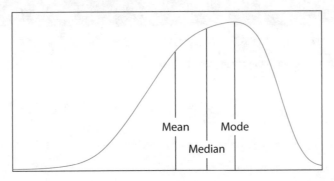

Mean   Mode

Median

above, the mean, median and the mode are expected to be equal in value to each other. However, other data sets may appear as shown in Figure 12.9.

The mean is dragged to the left by a few extreme values in the left-hand tail. The mode will exist under the curve peak, while the median will simply divide the data into two equal parts. This type of distribution is referred to as being skewed, and in this case it is left skewed.

We measure the dispersion of the data by what is known as the standard deviation from the mean (or as how the data set varies (hence variance) from the mean). Before we consider this in any more detail, it is worth understanding the reason why we need to consider the dispersion of the data from the mean value. Consider the following two small distributions of raw data relating to ages of patients at a clinic:

(a) 26, 27, 28, 29, 30
(b) 9, 15, 28, 38, 50

The mean (average) value for data set (a) is given as (26 + 27 + 28 + 29 + 30)/5

or 28.

The mean (average) value for data set (b) is given as (9 + 15 + 28 + 38 + 50)/5

or 28.

So the mean value for data set (a) is the same as the mean value for data set (b), yet the data range (ie minimum value to maximum value) for data set (a) is closer to the mean value than that of the data range for data set (b). Therefore, knowledge of the mean value is not sufficient to help us to interpret how the data actually relate to the mean value.

The Excel functions to provide the mean and the standard deviation of the data are given as:

'=average(*data range*)' and '=stdev(*data range*)'

(where '*data range*' relates to the row or column block of Excel cells where the data are housed).

The standard deviation is usually denoted as 'σ' and represents the horizontal distance the data are dispersed from the mean value. Values of the standard deviation greater than the mean value are attributed to be positive values, while standard deviations less than the mean value are attributed to be negative values.

Figures 12.10 and 12.11 are designed to support the understanding of the standard deviation. Figure 12.10 represents what the statisticians call the *normal distribution* of data, and is a bell-shaped curve that is symmetrical around its central axis.

Figure 12.10 Characteristics of normal distribution

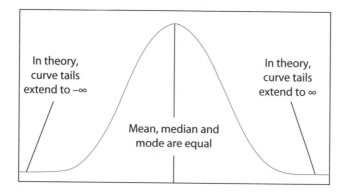

The normal distribution has the following characteristics:

- The distribution is bell shaped and symmetrical about the vertical axis at the mean or average value.
- The left-hand and right-hand tails extend to infinity.
- The area under the curve = unity (as for all continuous probability distributions).
- The curve is defined by its mean and standard deviation (σ) values.
- Approximately 68 per cent of the values of the random variable lie within ±1σ from the mean.
- Approximately 95 per cent of the values of the random variable lie within ±2σ from the mean.
- Approximately 99 per cent of the values of the random variable lie within ±3σ from the mean.

 ACTIVITY 12.4

NORMAL DISTRIBUTION

Suppose the normal distribution above represented the intelligence of a workforce. What could you infer from the distribution? As a hint, consider the mean (average) value; this value has the highest frequency of observations.

Figure 12.11 Normal probability distribution

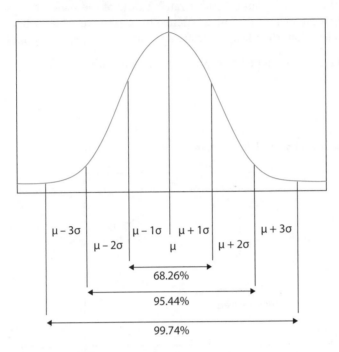

The normal probability distribution is a continuous distribution that measures the general population of the variable under discussion. For example, we can illustrate the curve shown in Figure 12.11 by discussing UK female fashion sizes. Assume that the average size of ladies fashions is size 14. One standard deviation above the average size will be a ladies' fashion size of 16 while, similarly, one standard deviation below the average size will be a ladies' fashion size of 12. Fashion sizes from size 12 to size 16 will be sufficient for about 68.26 per cent of all ladies in the UK. If we consider female fashions for ±2 standard deviations from the mean value, we have size 10 (-2σ) to size 18 (+2σ). This would accommodate and be sufficient for about 95.44 per cent of all ladies in the UK. Hence, a ladies' fashion buyer for one of the larger chain stores would purchase the same fashion in sizes from size 10 to size 18 inclusive, knowing that this range would be sufficient to accommodate over 95 per cent of UK ladies. The normal distribution curve can be applied to other examples of a general population.

Earlier, it was mentioned that the variance was a measure of the dispersion of the data. The variance is simply the square of the standard deviation value, thus ridding the data of any negative values. The variance for a sample can be calculated via the following sequence of steps:

1. Find the mean value of the data set.

2. Subtract each value from the mean value of the data set.

3. Square each of the values as calculated in (2) above.

4. Sum up all of the squared values as calculated in (3) above.

5. Divide the value calculated in (4) above by the number of observations less 1.

For example, given the data set from Activity 12.3 above:

17, 43, 14, 7, 20, 32, 30, 23, 9, 23, 27, 31

We can set the data and the necessary information as required above in a table (see Table 12.5).

Table 12.5 Determining the variance and standard deviation of ungrouped data

	Data	Data – Mean	(Data – Mean)^2
	17	-6	36
	43	20	400
	14	-9	81
	7	-16	256
	20	-3	9
	32	9	81
	30	7	49
	23	0	0
	9	-14	196
	23	0	0
	27	4	16
	31	8	64
SUM =	276		1188
n =	12	n–1 =	11
MEAN =	23	Variance =	108

Hence, the variance of the data set is 108. By taking the square root of the variance, the standard deviation (σ) (for a sample = 's') can be calculated for example, $\sigma = \sqrt{108} = 10.39$.

ACTIVITY 12.5

WORKED EXAMPLE: VARIANCE AND STANDARD DEVIATION

This activity is designed to help you to understand and recap the concepts of the variance and the standard deviation of a data set. Given the following data sample, determine the variance and the standard deviation of each set:

(a) 26, 27, 28, 29, 30

(b) 9, 15, 28, 38, 50

Solution: as the mean value of both data sets is 28 (see the two small distributions of data above), then the variance of the sample (s^2) of each set is found as follows:

(a), $s^2 = [(26 - 28)^2 + (27 - 28)^2 + (28 - 28)^2 + (29 - 28)^2 + (30 - 28)^2]/4$

$s^2 = [4 + 1 + 0 + 1 + 4]/4 = 10/4 = 2.5$ and $s = \sqrt{2.5} = 1.58$

(b), $s^2 = [(9 - 28)^2 + (15 - 28)^2 + (28 - 28)^2 + (38 - 28)^2 + (50 - 28)^2]/4$

$s2 = [361 + 169 + 0 + 100 + 484]/4 = 1114/4 = 278.5$ and $s = \sqrt{278.5} = 16.69$

EXCEL

(The following relates to Excel version V2007.)

For data set (a) – on a new worksheet, input your data into column B, row 1 to row 5.

In cell A6, type 'Variance'. In cell A7, type 'stdev' (standard deviation).

In cell B6 input the following formula: =VAR(B1:B5).

In cell B7, we take the square root of the variance by inputting the following formula: =SQRT(B6).

For data set (b) – input your data into column C, row 1 to row 5.

In cell C6 input the following formula: =VAR(C1:C5).

In cell C7, input the following formula: =SQRT(C6).

Notice the values for the variance and the standard deviations of both data sets are different, despite both data sets having the same mean value. The spread of data set (a) is much closer to the mean value than the spread of data set (b).

In mathematical terms, the standard deviation for a sample(s) is given by the following formula:

$$s = \sqrt{\frac{\sum_{i=1}^{N}(x_i - \bar{x})^2}{N - 1}}$$

(where $\sum$ represents the 'summation' sign)

Earlier, the five basic statistical descriptors relating to data were mentioned (see Section 12.2 above). We will consider them in a little more detail here. To identify the five basic descriptors by hand, the data would need to be sorted into numerical order. However, by using a statistical software package, the five basic descriptors can be automatically found without the requirement for the data to be sorted.

The five basic statistical descriptors of a data set are defined by the:

Minimum value, Q1 value, median value, Q3 value and the maximum value.

By definition, the minimum and maximum values of a data set are the smallest and largest values contained within the data set. We have already looked at the median value – it is the middle value of a set of data observations when arranged in ascending or descending order (see Section 12.3.1 above).

Hence, the Q1 and Q3 values need to be defined. 'Q' represents 'quartile' and the Q1 (Q3) quartile represents the data observation(s) at the point where the first 25 per cent (75 per cent) of the data (in numerical order) is isolated or identified (for example, the first quarter and the last quarter of the data). We calculate the position of the lower quartile by the following formula: Q1 = 0.25(n + 1)th value and the position of the upper quartile by: Q3 = 0.75(n + 1)th value. So, for the ordered data set from Activity 12.3:

> 7, 9, 14, 17, 20, 23, 23, 27, 30, 31, 32, 43

the lower quartile is identified as follows:

n = 12 hence n + 1 = 13 and 0.25(13) = 3.25 and the 3.25th value is found by identifying the 3rd lowest value (= 14) and calculating 0.25 of the distance from 14 to the next successive value (17) (= 0.75). Hence, Q1 = 14.75 and similarly, Q3 = 0.75(13) = 9.75 and is found by identifying the 9th value (30) and calculating 0.75 of the distance from 30 to the next successive value (31) (= 0.75). Hence Q3 = 30.75.

I have checked these answers in Excel, and the results are given as Q1 = 16.25 and Q3 = 30.25. I suspect the formula used in Excel is incorrect. Clearly, the Excel value for Q1 as given is 75 per cent of the distance from 14 to 17, and the Excel value for Q3 as given is 25 per cent of the distance from 30 to 31.

Knowledge of the quartile information is relatively useful since it is possible to explain a data set by the five basic statistical descriptors. For example, consider the data set from Activity 12.3 above:

> 17, 43, 14, 7, 20, 32, 30, 23, 9, 23, 27, 31

And rearranging the data into numerical order:

> 7, 9, 14, 17, 20, 23, 23, 27, 30, 31, 32, 43

We can identify the five basic statistical descriptors, for example:

Minimum value = 7,

Q1 value = 14.75

Median = 23

Q3 value = 30.75

Maximum value = 43

So what use is this? By drawing a pictorial representation of the data, it is possible to gain knowledge of how the data are distributed by observation and by value. Figure 12.12 represents a 'box and whisker' diagram (also known as a 'boxplot').

The 'box' contains the median value and represents the mid-range of the data (the mid 50 per cent of the data numerically ordered). The 'whiskers' are represented by the lower and upper ranges of data and these represent the lower and upper 25 per cent ranges of the data. In the case of the 12 observations of the data set from Activity 12.3, the boxplot would look more like the one shown in Figure 12.13.

Figure 12.12 Box and whisker diagram

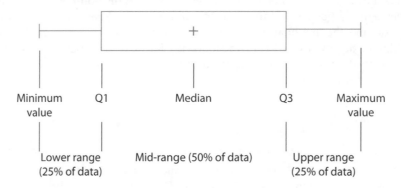

Figure 12.13 Box and whisker diagram of the data from Activity 12.3

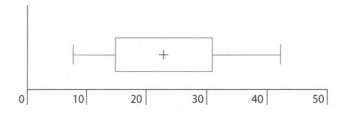

Notice how the lower range of the data (the left hand-side 'whisker') is shorter in length than that of the upper range of the data (the right hand-side 'whisker'). This indicates the data in the lower range is less spread out than that in the upper range of the data. Typically on a time series plot of the data observations (say for salaries), recent changes (increases) in salaries tend to be greater in value than corresponding increases during earlier times.

Plotting the quartile values in Excel (for example, the command is =quartile(data range,1) for quartile No. 1 and =quartile(data range,3) for quartile No. 3) provides slightly differing values than those given above (for the reasons given above).

 ACTIVITY 12.6

FIVE STATISTICAL DESCRIPTORS

For a quick and brief analysis of any data set, would the five basic statistical descriptors be useful? Are there any other descriptor values that we could use to enhance the data set for a quick and brief analysis?

For further examples on the dispersion of data (some using Excel), please see the following references:

Albright et al (2002) – p88 (includes central measurements of data).

Anderson et al (2003) – p71.

Levine et al (2005) – p159 (includes boxplots).

Mason and Lind (1993) – p144 onwards.

Sandy (1990) – p68 (includes boxplots, but quite technical).

Swift and Piff (2010) – p286 onwards.

Webster (1992) – p92 onwards (includes central measurements of data).

Whigham (1998) – p301 (includes central measurements of data, but quite technical).

12.4 PROBABILITY THEORY

What would be the probability of selecting one person from the workforce and finding that person to be 50 years of age or more? What would be the probability of employee unrest occurring? What would be the probability of selecting one person from the workforce of 50 years or more and finding that person to be responsible for the causation of the employee unrest? These are some simple questions to introduce the theory of probability. Probability provides policy and decision-makers with the tools for taking rational decisions based upon limited knowledge of uncertainty.

There are only two rules to probability theory:

- Probability values lie between (and including) 0 and 1 and the mathematical expression is given as $0 \leq P \leq 1$. If an event is impossible, we usually assign it a value of 0. If an event is certain to occur we usually assign it a value of 1.

- The sum of all probability values is equal to unity and the mathematical expression is $\sum P = 1$.

Fundamentally, probability is all about identifying the number of particular sample points in a sample space. The sum of these points, divided by the total sum of the points in the sample space, is the probability value. A **sample space** contains every possible outcome associated with an experiment. An **experiment** can be viewed as a process of attempting to prove or disprove a theory. Each outcome from attempting to prove or disprove a theory is referred to as a **sample point**, and the sample space simply consists of every possible sample point that could occur with an experiment. The selection or occurrence of a sample point is referred to as an **outcome**.

An example to assist the understanding of a sample space and sample points is given by the sample space for throwing two unbiased, six-sided dice and recording the sum of the scores on the uppermost faces. For this experiment, the dice are thrown and scores recorded until every conceivable set of differing scores have occurred. In this sample space, there are 36 possible outcomes and once all 36 possible outcomes have been achieved, then further experiments will simply supply outcomes that have already occurred and thus are available in the sample space.

For example, assume that on the throw of the first die, it will always land with the upper face depicting 'one'. (In reality this is very unlikely to occur but by imposing the restriction, it should help us to understand the concepts of sample points and sample spaces). The second die is free to fall on any number. Continual throwing of the two dice will then produce the following scores:

> 1:1. 1:2, 1:3, 1:4, 1:5 and 1:6

(on the assumption that the first die always lands with the upper face depicting 'one').

These six outcomes then become part of the sample space for the throw of two dice. Let us now assume that on the throw of the first die, it will always land with the upper face depicting 'two'. The second die is free to fall on any number. Continual throwing of the two dice will then produce the following scores:

> 2:1, 2:2, 2:3, 2:4, 2:5 and 2:6.

These six outcomes then also become part of the sample space for the throw of two dice. So up to now, by forcing one die to land on a 'one' or a 'two', we have identified 12 sample points within the sample space. We repeat the above scenario, but assuming the first die will land on a 'three' then 'four' then 'five' then 'six'. By doing so, we create another 24 sample points to join the previous 12 in the sample space.

Having identified a sample space of 36 points in a sample space for the throw of two dice, then the result of further experiments with two dice will supply a score that has already occurred previously. The sample space and sample points for the throw of two dice are given below (see Table 12.6).

Table 12.6 The sample space and sample points for the throw of two dice

Die	1	2	3	4	5	6
1	1,1	1,2	1,3	1,4	1,5	1,6
2	2,1	2,2	2,3	2,4	2,5	2,6
3	3,1	3,2	3,3	3,4	3,5	3,6
4	4,1	4,2	4,3	4,4	4,5	4,6
5	5,1	5,2	5,3	5,4	5,5	5,6
6	6,1	6,2	6,3	6,4	6,5	6,6

Table 12.7 The sample space and sample points for the combined scores of the throw of two dice

Die	1	2	3	4	5	6
1	2	3	4	5	6	7
2	3	4	5	6	7	8
3	4	5	6	7	8	9
4	5	6	7	8	9	10
5	6	7	8	9	10	11
6	7	8	9	10	11	12

The sample space and sample points for the combined scores of the throw of two dice are given in Table 12.7.

So if we are asked to determine the probability of throwing a combined score of nine from one throw of two dice, we simply look into the sample space and count the number of time that '9' occurs, and then divide that number of times by the total number of sample points in the sample space. Hence, '9' occurs four times (for example, 3:6, 4:5, 5:4 and 6:3 where the first number refers to the score occurring on the first die). Dividing the number of times a '9' occurs (four times) by the total number of sample points in the sample space (36) we find that the probability of throwing a combined score of nine from one throw of two dice = 4/36 or one ninth.

Consider the casino game of craps, where a win occurs on the combined score of seven or 11 from one throw of two dice. From the sample space, '7' occurs on six occasions and '11' occurs twice and hence the probability of the combined score is 8/36 = 2/9.

The above concepts relate to what is known as the classical school of probability theory. There are two other schools of probability theory, which are the relative frequency method and the subjective method. The relative frequency method is discussed later in this section. The example of the game of craps introduces the concept of the addition rule of probability theory, and the reader seeking a more robust grounding in probability theory (and/or the subjective method) is advised to undertake further reading of numerous available statistical texts (see 'Explore further' at the end of this chapter).

Sample space sizes in classical probability are fairly easy to determine. Consider the throw of a single die – there are six possible sample points (outcomes) in the sample space. Hence, for one die, we can write the number of outcomes to the power of (the one die) as 6^1 (or 'just' 6). When we have two dice to throw together, the size of the sample space is set to the number of possible outcomes from one die, raised to the power of two dice or 6^2 (or 6 squared, giving a sample space containing 36 sample points). So, the number of sample points in the sample space for the combined throw of three dice is 6^3 (or 216 sample points in the sample space), and so on.

The same principle applies to coins. The throw of one coin will result in either a head or a tail so there are two possible outcomes. If we raise the two outcomes to the number of coins (in this case a single coin), we arrive at 2^1 (or just 2, for example a head or a tail). For two coins, the sample space contains 2^2 or four possible sample points for example, H:H, H:T, T,H and T,T. For three coins, we have 2^3 or eight sample points in the sample space for example, H:H:H, H:H:T, H:T:H, H:T:T, T:H:H, T:H:T, T:T:H and T:T:T.

ACTIVITY 12.7

PROBABILITY EXAMPLES

This activity has been designed to help you to understand and recap the concepts of classical probability. The following questions relate to an unbiased die (dice) or a normal deck of 52 playing cards:

Determine the probability of the following events:

1. Throwing a score of '2' with a die.

2. Selecting a red card from a deck of cards.

3. Throwing a score of '3' with two dice.

4. Selecting a 'ten' from a deck of cards.

5. Selecting a red king from a deck of cards.

Solutions

1. (One die) hence the probability is 1/6

2. Twenty-six red cards out of 52 cards, hence the probability is 26/52 or 1/2

3. (Two dice) hence a '3' is found by 1:2 and 2:1 or probability = 2/36 or 1/18

4. Four '10s' in a deck of cards, hence the probability = 4/52 or 1/13

5. Two red 'kings' in a deck of cards, hence the probability is 2/52 or 1/26.

Relative frequency probability occurs when the rules of classical probability (or subjective probability) cannot be used. Consider the situation of an office containing a number of employees. What is the probability that one or more of the employees will leave the office, for whatever reason? Similarly, what is the probability that there will be two employees of the same gender leaving the office in succession? Classical probability theory is unable to answer questions such as these so we introduce the concepts of relative frequency, where observations across time are recorded and used to help the policy/decision-maker to reach an informed decision.

As an example, an experiment concerns the interviews of married couples without children living at home. The question is asked whether either individual

Table 12.8 Interview experiment

Husband	Wife
Employed	Employed
Employed	Unemployed
Unemployed	Employed
Unemployed	Unemployed

or the couple are employed or not. The sample space for this experiment is shown in Table 12.8.

We can re-write this sample space in shorthand as:

$$S = \{(W, W) (W, U) (U, W) (U, U)\}$$

where 'S' is the sample space, 'W' ('U') indicates a person is employed (unemployed). Note that the husband's response is (in this case) placed first.

The first question we could ask is, what would be the probability of interviewing a couple at random and finding that they are both employed? That is, what is the probability that (W, W) has occurred? (The mathematical expression is P(W, W))

For the purpose of demonstration, let us assume the following:

P(W, W) = 0.313 ; P(W, U) = 0.213 ; P(U, W) = 0.188 (the probability that both are employed, the probability that the husband (wife) is employed (unemployed) and the probability that the husband (wife) is unemployed (employed)). Let us further assume that the probability of finding at least one of the couple to be working (that is, either one or both) is given by P(A).

Hence P(A) = 0.313 + 0.213 + 0.188 or P(A) = 0.714. Similarly, P(U, U) = 1 − 0.714 = 0.286

We could let B imply the event that the woman is unemployed,

for example, B = {(W, U) (U, U)} and P(B) = P(W, U) + P(U, U). Therefore, P(B) = 0.213 + 0.286 or P(B) = 0.499

Given this information, the policy or decision-maker could use this to assist her/him to make an inference about future married couples.

Another example: assume that a supermarket manager has checked the previous two days till receipt rolls from the wine department. He finds that out of 600 customers, 120 spent £40 or more. Suppose now, that the supermarket plans to give away a set of wine glasses to anyone who spends £40 or more in its wine department. The manager would be interested to know the number of sets of wine glasses he should hold. Therefore, he would be interested to learn the probability of a customer spending £40 or more. Associated with this experiment is the outcome of each customer decision. For example, a customer (or consumer) may or may not spend £40 or more, and each customer is assumed to be independent and to not be influenced by other customers.

Hence 120/600 customers spent £40 or more, which implies 20 per cent of all customers spent £40 or more. Thus the probability of a consumer spending £40 or more = 0.2.

0.2 is known as the relative frequency of the £40.00 or more class.

The general formula for relative frequency is as follows:

$$P(E_i) = \frac{\Sigma f_i}{f_i}$$

where f_i is the total frequency associated with event E_i and Σf_i is the sum of the observed frequencies.

Using the data from the supermarket example, if $f_i = 120$ and $\Sigma f_i = 600$, then $P(E_i) = 120/600 = 0.2$

The manager would then have to estimate his future customers to wine department (say 400), and multiply that figure by the probability of a customer spending £40 or more (0.2). The answer of 80 (400 * 0.2) becomes the number of sets of wine glasses the manager should hold.

This method is particularly suitable when past frequency data from similar experiments are readily available.

ACTIVITY 12.8

A SIMPLE FORECAST USING THE RELATIVE FREQUENCY PROBABILITY METHOD

The next time you are in a room containing a finite number of people, try counting the number of people in the room (gender wise – including yourself). Divide the number of females/males by the total number of people and determine the relative frequency probability of each gender. Use those probabilities as a guess to forecast the gender of the next person to leave the room. How confident would you be with this forecast and why?

For further examples on probability theory (some using Excel), please see the following references:

Aczel (2002) – the probability chapter contains a series of problems throughout, but be aware that some of them may be quite technical.

Albright et al (2002) – p135 onwards.

Anderson et al (2003) – p109 onwards.

Levine et al (2005) – p175 onwards.

Mason and Lind (1993) – p163 onwards (exercises throughout the chapter).

Sandy (1990) – p83 onwards (exercises throughout the chapter, quite technical).

Swift and Piff (2010) – p311 onwards (exercises throughout the chapter).

Webster (1992) – p177 onwards (quite technical).

12.5 HYPOTHESIS TESTING

Suppose a policy or decision-maker were to make a statement about a theory. The statement could be considered to be true or false by using the rules of hypothesis testing, coupled with the strength of statistical analysis to help us to prove or disprove the theory. To help us to study hypothesis testing, we need to learn how to read the statistical tables to support our interpretations when we come to make a decision on whether or not a statement is fundamentally true or false.

We will use two types of statistical tables: the normal distribution tables and the student's 't' distribution tables. Both sets of distributions are very similar except for the slight differences in the tails. We have already considered the normal distribution above, where we learned about the mean value and the standard deviation (see Section 12.3.2).

What we aim to study now is how to read probability values from the tables and perhaps given probability values, and how to read off the associated standard deviation values. The two sets of tables are supplied on the companion website (and it should be noted that for simplicity, the normal distribution tables are standardised to mean of 0 and a standard deviation of unity).

Before we study how to read the tables, it is worth emphasising when we would use the normal distribution tables and when we would use the student's 't' distribution tables. When we know the values of the resident population mean and standard deviation values, we would use the normal distribution tables. If however, we do not know the value of the resident population's standard deviation value (but know the mean value), we would use the student's 't' distribution tables. The student's 't' distribution is typically used when we deal with a sample.

There is a slight difference with the reading of either of the tables supplied on the companion website, while otherwise there is an element of similarity. We commence with a probability value of committing a type-one error (for example, the chances of accepting a hypothetical statement to be false when it is, in fact, true) and we determine a critical value from the tables. The critical value is what we use to compare with a test statistic to help us to accept or reject a hypothetical statement. Before we discuss the test statistic let us consider how to identify the critical value from the tables. The 'tail(s)' of the distribution are typically where the critical value will lie.

12.5.1 THE STUDENT'S 'T' DISTRIBUTION

Let us consider the student's 't' distribution first. The 't' distribution tables are supplied on the companion website, and the values indicated in the Table refer to the percentages (probabilities) or the area under the distribution (the curve) from the fixed value to the tail of the distribution. The Table is a little easier to read since both one-tailed and two-tailed test probabilities of making a type-one error (significance value) are given. If the hypothesis test is one tailed, we read the top row of the tables to determine our significance value. Suppose our significance value is given as 5 per cent or 0.05. We identify the column headed by $\alpha = 0.05$ and we read down that column. The value of 'υ' degrees of freedom relates to the number of observations of the variable under scrutiny, minus 1. Hence, if we had for example 25 observations, then our degrees of freedom would be equal to $25-1 = 24$. We search down the column for $\alpha = 0.05$ and stop at the row where 'υ' degrees of freedom = 24. At this point, our critical value is equal to 1.711. With a little caution, this value can be looked upon as 1.711 standard deviations from the mean value.

If, however, the test is two tailed, we read the second top row to determine our significance value. Suppose our significance value is given again as 5 per cent or 0.05. This time we are dealing with a two-tailed test where half of our significance value (ie 2.5 per cent) will lie in each tail. We identify the column headed by $2\alpha = 0.05$ and we read down that column. Again, the value of 'υ' degrees of freedom relates to the number of observations of the variable under scrutiny, minus 1. Hence, if we had the same 25 observations as before, then our degrees of freedom would be equal to $25-1 = 24$. We search down the column for $2\alpha = 0.05$ and stop at the row where 'υ' degrees of freedom = 24. At this point, our critical value is equal to 2.064. Since this is a two-tailed test, we really should indicate our critical value as ± 2.064.

Having determined how to find the critical values from the tables, we now need to set up the hypothesis, calculate the test statistic, compare the result to the critical value(s) and conclude with either a non-rejection or a rejection of the null hypothesis.

We set up a hypothesis test as follows:

1. Set up the null and alternative hypotheses (H_0 and H_1 respectively).

   (The null hypothesis needs to include the equality (=) sign but it could read as 'less than or equal' ($\leq$) or 'more than or equal' ($\geq$)).

2. Select a value for 'α' (the significance level) for example, 0.01 etc.

   (Remember to correctly identify whether or not you are using a one-tailed test or a two-tailed test.)

3. Find the critical value from the 't' tables.

4. Calculate the test statistic value by use of the following formula:

$$\frac{(\overline{X} - \mu_0)}{\sqrt{(s^2/n)}}$$

where $\overline{X}$ = sample mean, s^2 = sample variance,

n = sample size, μ_0 = hypothesised value.

5. Compare the critical value determined from the 't' tables with the solution found in (4) above.

6. Given the hypotheses, then the solution to (5) above, is found as follows:

If H_O = a theoretical value (and hence, $H_1 \neq$ a theoretical value) then the test is two tailed. If the test statistic value is greater than the right-hand-side critical value (or if the test statistic value is less than the left hand-side critical value), we REJECT the null hypothesis and conclude that the statement linked to the null hypothesis is incorrect. Otherwise we may assume the statement linked to the null hypothesis is correct.

If H_O = a theoretical value (and hence $H_1 >$ a theoretical value) then the test is one tailed (at the right-hand side of the distribution). If the test statistic value is greater than the right hand-side critical value, we REJECT the null hypothesis and conclude that the statement linked to the null hypothesis is incorrect. Otherwise we may assume the statement linked to the null hypothesis is correct.

If H_O = a theoretical value (and hence $H_1 <$ a theoretical value) then the test is one tailed (at the left-hand side of the distribution). If the test statistic value is less than the (left-hand-side) critical value, we REJECT the null hypothesis and conclude that the statement linked to the null hypothesis is incorrect. Otherwise we may assume the statement linked to the null hypothesis is correct.

On one-tailed tests, the direction of the greater or less sign in the alternative hypothesis indicates the direction of the test. For example, $H_1 <$ a theoretical value – the '<' sign is pointing to the left, indicating a left-hand-side test.

For further examples on hypothesis testing using the student's 't' test, (some using Excel), please see the references.

ACTIVITY 12.9

WORKED EXAMPLE: HYPOTHESIS TESTING

The government health department releases the following statement: 'The average wait for an operation does not exceed 20 weeks.' The National Patients' Care Society, are sceptical and decide to test this statement. Their findings are as follows:

- Sample average waiting time = 21.6 weeks.

- Sample variance = 22.5.

- Number of patients in the sample = 25.

Given this data, is the government correct ? (Use α = 0.1 and α = 0.05)

SOLUTION

The null hypothesis becomes associated with the '20 weeks' and the government indicates: 'The average wait for an operation does not exceed 20 weeks.' Hence, the average wait is at the most 20 weeks. So, the null hypothesis indicates the wait could be less than or equal to 20 weeks.

1. $H_0 \leq 20$, and $H_1 > 20$ (the sign on the alternative hypothesis points to the right, hence we have a one-tailed test at the right-hand-side of the distribution).

2. We are given two significance values to work with, ie $\alpha = 0.1$ and $\alpha = 0.05$

   When $\alpha = 0.1$ and $N = 25$, the critical value (from the 't' tables) is 1.318 (did you remember to look at the top row of the 't' tables for $\alpha = 0.1$ and subtract 1 from the sample size?). For $\alpha = 0.05$ and $N = 25$, the critical value is 1.711.

3. $\overline{X} = 21.6$, $\sigma^2 = 22.5$, $\mu_0 = 20$ and $N = 25$

   Hence, $(21.6 - 20)/\sqrt{(22.5/25)} = 1.6/0.949 = 1.687$

4. For $\alpha = 0.1$ and $N = 25$, the critical value is 1.318 and we can simulate this information in the following diagram:

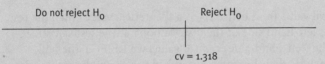

We can now add the test statistic value (tsv) to the same diagram (reproduced below):

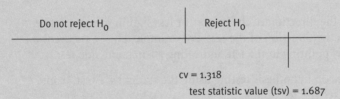

and clearly, the test statistic value falls in the 'reject H_0' side of the diagram, indicating that we reject the null hypothesis, suggesting the government are incorrect with their statement.

5. For $\alpha = 0.05$ and $N = 25$, the critical value is 1.711 and we can simulate this information in the following diagram:

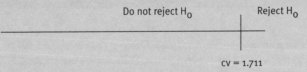

We can now add the test statistic value (tsv) to the same diagram (reproduced below):

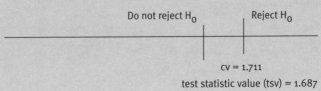

and clearly, the test statistic value now lies in the 'do not reject H_0' side of the diagram indicating we DO NOT reject the null hypothesis suggesting the government may well be correct with their statement.

Notice that in the first case when we rejected the null hypothesis, the significance value of 0.1 implies that we have a 10 per cent chance of committing a type-one error. By reducing the significance value to 0.05, we have reduced the probability of committing a type-one error.

ACTIVITY 12.10

SETTING UP HYPOTHESES

Think about how you would set up the null hypothesis (and the alternative hypothesis is then easily identified). In each of the following situations say whether a one or two-tailed test is appropriate and state the null and alternative hypothesis:

1. A study to test whether the durability of a product has changed

2. A study to check the assumption that the average hours of overtime worked per employee are more than 5 hours a week

3. A bank manager wishes to test whether the average number of cheques written by current account holders per quarter has decreased

4. A test to check whether a machine is running out of control and producing too large a number of items which fail to meet specification

5. A study to test the view that the average number of miles driven by 'senior citizens' is less than the average for the population as a whole

SOLUTIONS

1. Two-tailed; H_0: $\mu = \mu_0$, H_1: $\mu \neq \mu_0$

2. One-tailed; H_0: $\mu \leq 5$, H_1: $\mu > 5$

3. One-tailed; H_0: $\mu \geq \mu_0$, H_1: $\mu < \mu_0$

4. Two-tailed; H_0: $\mu = \mu_0$, H_1: $\mu \neq \mu_0$

5. One-tailed; H_0: $\mu \geq \mu_0$, H_1: $\mu < \mu_0$

12.5.2 THE NORMAL DISTRIBUTION

We have discussed the normal distribution in Section 12.3.2, so let us now consider the tables associated with the normal distribution. As the normal distribution is symmetrical, only one half of the probabilities is supplied. We use these probabilities to determine the corresponding probabilities in the other half of the distribution. The total sum of the probabilities under the distribution is unity (as in all probability distributions) but we are working with half of the distribution, hence the tables indicate a maximum probability of 0.5. The values

ACTIVITY 12.11

HYPOTHESIS TESTING USING A 'T' TEST (WORKED EXAMPLE)

Current average annual salaries for employees at a company are set at £30,000 pa.

A sample of 28 employees were surveyed and the following information was determined:

(sample mean) $\overline{X}$ = £29,600; s^2 = 1,500,000 (sample variance)

Use the student's 't' tables to determine whether or not the average annual salaries = £30, 000 pa.

SOLUTION

The average annual salary is set a £30,000 (not at least or at the most, but equal to). Hence, this is a two-tailed test.

$H_0 : \mu$ = £30,000; H1 : $\mu \neq$ £30,000 (two-tailed test)

using α = 0.1 and on a two-tailed test, we read the second top line in the 't' tables to determine for 2α = 0.1 (since we apply half of the significance value to each tail).

From the 't' tables we read the critical value as ±1.703 (2α = 0.1, n−1 = 27)

Using

$$\frac{(\overline{X} - \mu_0)}{\sqrt{(s^2/n)}}$$

where $\overline{X}$ = sample mean, s^2 = sample variance,

n = sample size, μ_0 = hypothesised value.

$$\frac{29\ 600 - 30\ 000}{\sqrt{(1\ 500\ 000/28)}} = -1.728$$

and -1.728 is outside the limits of ±1.7033 => reject Ho @ α = 0.1, concluding that we have evidence to suggest that the salaries may well be not equal to £30,000 pa.

When α = 0.05 and on a two-tailed test, we read the second top line in the 't' tables to determine for 2α = 0.05 (since we apply half of the significance value to each tail).

From the 't' tables we read the critical value as ±2.052 (2α = 0.05, n-1 = 27)

and -1.728 is inside the limits of ±2.052 => DO NOT reject Ho @ α = 0.05, concluding that we have evidence to suggest that the salaries may well be equal to £30,000 pa.

Reduction of the significance value from 0.1 to 0.05 reduces the probability of the occurrence of a type-one error.

indicated in the normal distribution tables refer to the percentages (probabilities) or the area under the distribution (the curve) from the mean value towards a value that can be fixed.

The normal distribution was introduced earlier (see Figure 12.11) and if it is studied in more detail, we can identify the percentage under the curve between plus and minus one standard deviation as 68.26 per cent (or as a probability 0.6826). Since the probability tables reflect only half of the distribution, we can identify the percentage under half of the curve and in this case for plus one standard deviation from the mean value, the percentage will be 34.13 per cent (or as a probability 0.3413). We locate this value in the normal distribution tables by moving down through the first column until we find '1.0'. The value immediately to the right of '1.0' (and under the column headed by '00') is 0.3413. If 0.3413 represents the area under the curve from the mean value to one standard deviation, then the remaining area under the curve to the right of one standard deviation is 0.5 (half of the distribution) minus 0.3413 = 0.1587. This analysis holds true for the remainder of the work considered here.

Now consider the percentage under the curve between plus and minus two standard deviations as 95.44 per cent (or as a probability 0.9544). Using the half of the distribution, we can identify the percentage under half of the curve for plus two standard deviations from the mean value as 47.72 per cent (or as a probability, 0.4772). We locate this value in the normal distribution tables by moving down through the first column until we find '2.0'. The value immediately to the right of '2.0' (and under the column headed by '00') is 0.4772.

This analysis holds true for the third standard deviation. If we need similar percentages/probabilities to the left-hand side of the mean value (for example, -1 standard deviation etc.), we simply use the above rules and use the same percentages/probabilities we would find in the tables for the positive standard deviation values, but infer them to the left-hand side of the distribution.

Suppose we needed to identify the percentage under the curve at say 1.24 standard deviations from the mean value. We do exactly the same as we have undertaken before but this time scrolling down the first column until we find '1.2'. Then we read along the row at '1.2' until we find the value in the column headed by '0.04' (total is 1.24). The result is 0.3925.

We may be likely to require the standard deviation value if we are given a percentage. This is also relatively easy to do. Suppose we are working with a significance value of 5 per cent (or 0.05). The first thing to do is to identify whether or not we are working with a one-tailed test or a two-tailed test, since working with a two-tailed test means that we will have to split our significance value into two to compensate for each tail. Let us assume we are working with a one-tailed test.

Since we need 5 per cent in the tail of the distribution, we need to subtract 5 per cent from 50 per cent (half of the distribution) and search in tables for the remainder (45 per cent), or as a probability value, 0.45. So we search through the general body of the tables until we locate 0.45 (or as close as we can, for example, between 0.4495 and 0.4505) and then we can read off the standard deviation value as being between 1.64 and 1.65 (say 1.645) – read the value in the first column corresponding to 1.6 and read off the corresponding value from the figures provided in the first row.

If we are working with a two-tailed test, then after splitting our significance value into two, we subtract the new value from 50 per cent (47.5 per cent or 0.475) and then we search for 0.475 in the tables. In this case we locate 0.475 as 1.96 and since it is a two-tailed test, we represent it as ±1.96

We have already considered hypothesis tests with the student's 't' distribution so let us now consider the use of the normal distribution to solve similar related issues.

ACTIVITY 12.12

WORKED EXAMPLE: HYPOTHESIS TESTING USING NORMAL DISTRIBUTION

Let the mean of a factory payroll be £1,000 (μ) and the standard deviation (σ) = £100. Assume the payroll follows a normal distribution. Find the area under the normal curve between £1,000 and £1,150 and interpret your result.

SOLUTION

In this case we standardise the value between £1000 and £1150 by applying the following formula:

$$z = \frac{X - \mu}{\sigma} \quad \text{and } z = \frac{£1,150 - £1,000}{100} = £1.50$$

By standardising the values, we can use the standard normal distribution table, to determine the area under the normal curve, for z = 1.50

We do this by looking in the table for z = 1.50σ; When z = 1.50σ the area under the normal distribution is 0.4332.

We know the area under the standardised normal distribution is unity (or 100 per cent) (as for all probability distributions), hence 0.4332 then becomes 43.32 per cent.

This means that 43.32 per cent of the payroll have an income between £1,000 and £1,150. Also, the probability of selecting an employee at random and finding an employee who falls into this income bracket is 0.4332.

For further examples on hypothesis testing (some using Excel), please see the following references:

Aczel, A. D. (2002) – the chapters on confidence intervals and on hypothesis testing contain a series of problems throughout, but be aware that some of them are quite technical.

Albright et al (2002) – p378 onwards (exercises throughout the chapter).

ACTIVITY 12.13

HYPOTHESIS TESTING USING NORMAL DISTRIBUTION

1. The average number of calls per hour undertaken by staff operating in a call centre is assumed to follow a normal distribution with a mean (μ) of 10.2 and a variance (σ^2) of 0.09 (standard deviation (σ) of 0.3). What percentage of staff are expected not to exceed 10.7 calls per hour?

2. Determine the maximum number of calls the lowest 20 per cent of staff will receive.

SOLUTION

1. We should really standardise the values and we know that the mean (μ) is 10.2 and a standard deviation (σ) is 0.3 hence, we can calculate the required (standard deviation) value for 10.7 fairly easily. For example, $(10.7 - 10.2)/0.3 = 0.5/0.3 = 1.67\sigma$.

   The question asks what percentage of staff are expected not to exceed 10.7 calls per hour. This means we need to find all of the area under the curve up to 1.67σ.

   From the normal distribution tables, from the mean value to 1.67σ is 0.4525 (or 45.25 per cent of the observations) and we take into account the left-hand side of the distribution (0.5 or 50 per cent). So the answer is that 95.25 per cent of staff are expected not to exceed 10.7 calls per hour.

2. Question 2 gives a percentage towards the (left-hand) tail of the distribution and we need to identify a relevant standard deviation value. The 20 per cent in the tail indicates we have 30 per cent between the mean value and the standard deviation value we are attempting to find. Hence we search for 0.3 in the normal distribution tables and read off the standard deviation value (= 0.84 approximately (or -0.84 since it is in the left-hand side of the distribution)).

   The corresponding number of calls per hour we require is therefore the mean value less $0.84 * \sigma = 10.2 - (0.84 * 0.3) = 10.2 - 0.252 = 9.948$ calls per hour. So 20 per cent of the call centre staff will take fewer than 9.948 calls per hour.

Anderson et al (2003) – p288 onwards (exercises throughout the chapter).

Levine et al (2005) – p345 onwards (exercises throughout the chapter).

Mason and Lind (1993) – p370 onwards (exercises throughout the chapter).

Sandy (1990) – p318 onwards.

Swift and Piff (2010) – p489 onwards (exercises throughout the chapter).

Webster (1992) – p445 onwards (quite technical).

Whigham (1998) – p428 (includes probability, but quite technical).

12.6 LINEAR CORRELATION AND REGRESSION

Suppose we had two sets of data that we thought could be related to each other. Could we do anything with them to help us to make an informed decision? The easy answer is yes, but we need to be careful when we interpret our findings. Linear correlation and regression analysis simply looks at two sets of variables and how they correlate to each other when they are plotted on a two-dimensional graph. The vertical axis of the graph traditionally displays the 'dependent' variable while the horizontal axis traditionally displays the 'independent' variable. It is assumed that changes in the dependent variable 'depend' upon changes in the independent variable.

Once we plot the data, we sketch a linear line through the data plots to provide an idea of how the data relate to each other. A linear line comes with its own mathematical model for which we can use to make a forecast. The mathematical model for a linear line is y = mx + c and we will explore this model later in this section. Let us consider the followed worked example.

ACTIVITY 12.14

WORKED EXAMPLE: TUITION FEES

The raw data in Table 12.9 opposite relate to tuition fees (in £000) at a sample of 15 preparatory schools in District A and of 15 preparatory schools in District B during a recent academic year.

Determine a regression equation that would enable a policy-maker to estimate the tuition fees at schools in District B based upon the tuition fees of schools in District A.

Calculate the linear coefficient of correlation. Does the result obtained indicate that tuition fees at schools in the District A are good predictors of the tuition fees of schools in District B?

Estimate the tuition fees for schools in District B based upon a tuition fee of £1,1000 offered by the schools in District A.

SOLUTION

The first step is to plot the data and 'see how it looks' – in other words, are we able to determine any trends in the data? We are asked to estimate the school fees in District B based upon the school fees in District A. Hence, we may assume that the school fees in District B are the dependent variable. Figure 12.14 displays a graph of the co-ordinate relationship between each pair of fees for the schools in District A and District B.

There appears to be a downward trend in the data according to the linear line of best fit drawn by the Excel software. The data appear to be scattered around the linear line and there appears to be little evidence of linearity of the data (see Figure 12.14).

Excel has also provided the values of the parameters for the mathematical model of Y = mx + c, and these are given as Y = -0.1689X + 10.816. This is called the regression equation of the variable 'Y' as a function of the variable 'X'.

The parameter values are best explained as follows:

Table 12.9 Tuition fees

District A	N	District B
10.5	1	7.9
10.1	2	8.2
10.0	3	9.1
11.0	4	9.3
9.8	5	8.8
8.9	6	10.6
9.3	7	10.1
9.7	8	8.5
10.4	9	7.5
10.0	10	9.3
9.6	11	8.4
9.1	12	9.2
11.2	13	10.7
10.5	14	9.5
9.9	15	9.8

- 10.816 is the point on the vertical axis where the linear line would commence from when the value for X = 0 – this value is known as the **intercept term**.

- 0.1689 indicates that for every one unit change that occurs in the independent variable, the dependent variable will change by 0.1689 units. The minus sign indicates that the direction of the change will be inverse to the respective change in the independent variable. (Also, the negative sign indicates that in this case that the line of best fit will slope downwards.) This value is known as the **slope term**.

The Excel commands to determine the parameter values of the regression equation are given as:

- (Intercept) '=intercept(*known y's, known x's*)'

- (slope) '=slope(*known y's, known x's*)'.

The second step is to decide whether or not the model is capable of being used to forecast (ie can an efficient forecast of the dependent variable be made by using an additional observation of the independent variable?).

My personal experience suggests that this model does not appear to be efficient and is likely not to provide too good a forecast. If the data observations had been closer than they are to the linear line, then a different interpretation – that of a reasonable model – could have been undertaken.

Figure 12.14 Graph of x and y

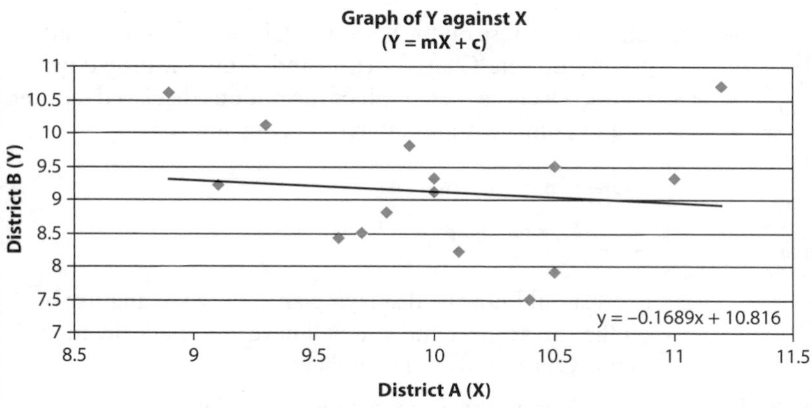

Graph of Y against X
(Y = mX + c)

$y = -0.1689x + 10.816$

District B (Y)

District A (X)

So, does a test exist to help with the interpretation of how good or how bad the model is? (For example, to test the linear strength of the association between the variables.) Yes, there is one, but the result needs to be interpreted with caution since it would be very easy to assume that a causal relationship exists if the result of the test indicated a strong linear association occurred between the two sets of variables. In reality we assume a non-causal relationship exists between the two sets of variables.

Step 3: The linear correlation coefficient as a test to determine the strength of the linear relationship between the variables. There is a simple command in Excel to determine the correlation coefficient between two sets of variables and it is '=correl(*data array1, data array2*)'.

For the two sets of variables, the linear correlation coefficient is -0.1172. The correlation coefficient value lies between ±1. When the correlation coefficient value is -1, all of the data will lie on a linear line sloping down-over from left to right. When the correlation coefficient value is +1, all of the data will lie on a linear line sloping up-over from left to right. When the correlation coefficient value is 0, the data will lie randomly scattered on the graph and it will be difficult to interpret whether or how a linear line could be inserted on to the graph.

The linear correlation coefficient value of -0.1172 is very low, and hence the interpretation is that this model would not be an efficient model to use for the purposes of prediction.

Consider why we need to find these values. What questions could be asked of us and how could these values help us to answer those questions?

The following is a step-by-step guide on how to use Excel (V2007) to plot a graph and to test the linear correlation coefficient.

Given the information in Table 12.9:

X	Y
0	32
10	50
20	68
30	86
40	104
50	122
60	140
70	158
80	176
90	194

1. Input these data into Excel. Use column A for the 'X' values and column B for the 'Y' values. Commence both sets of data at row 1.

2. Highlight cells A1 to B10 inclusive ('click' and hold the mouse button in cell A1 and 'drag' to cell B20 then release the mouse button).

3. Click the mouse on the 'INSERT' tab and select the 'Scatter' graph from the 'Charts' section and. From the drop down menu, select the first graph of the options displayed (scatter plot of points without interconnecting lines).

4. Excel should now be displaying an 'empty rectangular box' on the spreadsheet and you will have automatically moved to the 'Chart Tools' – 'Design' tab.

5. Click on the 'Select Data' icon in the 'Data' section and a 'Select Data Window' dialogue box will 'pop up'. Ensure that the information in the 'Chart

data range' window is flashing (if not, double click in this window to highlight it).

6. Click on and highlight the range from A1 to B10). Ensure that this range is displayed in the window of the dialogue box and click on 'ok'.

7. The graph of your data should now be displayed and it is possible to add titles etc. by clicking on the 'Layout' tab under the 'Chart Tools' tab.

8. Consider how the data appear on the graph and ask yourself if this would be a good model to use for forecasting.

9. In cell D1, input/type 'Correlation'.

10. In cell D2, input the following command: '=correl(A1:A10,B1:B10)' and press 'enter'. Did your correlation coefficient formula return a value of unity? (It should have done!) With a value of unity, how good do you think this model would be for forecasting? (It should be an excellent model for forecasting!).

11. On the 'Chart Tools' and 'Layout' tabs, search for the 'Trendline' icon and click on it and then select 'Linear Trendline' and a linear line of 'best fit' should appear on your graph. Notice how it passes through every data point!

12. On the 'Chart Tools' and 'Layout' tabs, again select the 'Trendline' icon and click on it and then select 'More Trendline Options'.

13. 'Check' the box for 'Display Equation On Chart' and click on 'Close'.

14. In addition to the linear line passing through all of the data observations, the graph of your data should now include and display the equation of the line of best fit. Your equation should read as Y = 1.8X + 32.

15. To forecast, let X = 100 and use this value to multiply to 1.8 (= 180) and add 32 (= 212). Hence, the forecast for Y when X = 100 is 212. The correlation coefficient should be unity, so this forecast is assumed to be very strong.

16. Interestingly, this example is based upon the relationship between Celsius and Fahrenheit temperature scales where the boiling point of water for Celsius (Fahrenheit) is 100° (212°) and it highlights the point that correlation and regression is not a causal relationship since (in this case) both Celsius and Fahrenheit both depend upon heat (or the lack of it) rather than on each other.

For further examples on correlation and regression (some using Excel), please see the following references:

Aczel (2002) – the chapter on simple linear regression and correlation contains a series of problems throughout but be aware that some of them are quite technical.

Albright et al (2002) – p560 onwards (exercises throughout the chapter).

Anderson et al (2003) – p478 onwards (exercises throughout the chapter).

Levine et al (2005) – p536 onwards (exercises throughout the chapter).

Mason and Lind (1993) – p467 (correlation) and p501 onwards (exercises throughout the chapters).

Sandy (1990) – p536 onwards (quite technical).

Swift and Piff (2010) – p515 onwards (exercises throughout the chapter).

Webster (1992) – p632 onwards (quite technical).

Whigham (1998) – p376 (quite technical).

12.7 CONCLUSION

In this chapter we have addressed pictorial representations of data, the central measurements of data and the dispersion of the data from the mean value, which together with the standard deviation are usually addressed as descriptive statistics. Such statistics are useful to help us make informed decision. For example, a company could calculate the average age and standard deviation of its workforce to help it plan for future recruitment if the average age appears to be too high and the standard deviation is very small; an example might be an average age of say 55 years with a standard deviation of say 0.5 could imply an age range of staff between (approximately) 53 and 57 years. We also considered the normal distribution as an example of how the data can be dispersed from the mean value. It is possible to further examine the attributes of the normal distribution since we can use its properties to help us to undertake inferential statistics, such as hypothesis testing, correlation and regression. Hypothesis testing allows us to use a statistical formula to support a 'test' of validity about a spurious statement. Correlation and regression analysis permits us to forecast a value of one variable, based upon another variable (regression analysis) and to 'test' the strength of that forecast by use of correlation analysis.

ACTIVITY 12.15

USING STATISTICS IN YOUR CAREER

Reflect upon the concepts you have studied above and ask yourself if you could use any of these to help you become more effective and efficient in the management of your role in the company structure.

PAUSE FOR THOUGHT

Identify at least three things that you have learned by studying this chapter and engaging with the activities. How will your newly acquired knowledge and skills support your continuing professional development? What value do you expect your learning to have for your daily routines and your further career? In what area have you identified a need for further development and how are you planning to fill that gap? Address these issues in your learning journal and/or CPD log. You may also wish to discuss them with a peer, colleague, mentor or coach to aid your further development.

- The most common central measurements of ungrouped data are the mean, the median and the mode.

- The five basic statistical descriptors of a data set are minimum value, Q1 value, median value, Q3 value and maximum value.

- Probability is about identifying the number of particular sample points in a sample space.

- Hypothesis testing, linear correlation and regression are key measures to assist decision-making in organisations.

- Hence, non-specialist managers and professionals are able to interpret statistical data confidently.

EXPLORE FURTHER

You should at this stage have a fundamental grounding in statistical analysis to support any work that you will be involved with at a non-statistician level in a commercial enterprise. The texts contained in the reference section are specific texts that are useful for business activity for non-statisticians. Most (if not all) of the texts will complement the work provided for in this chapter and will also provide additional exercises – with solutions in most cases and, will provide the interested reader with further theory in statistical analysis.

12.8 REFERENCES

ACZEL, A.D. (2002) *Complete business statistics*. 5th ed. New York: McGraw-Hill/Irwin.

ALBRIGHT, C.S., WINSTON, W.L. and ZAPPE, C. (2002) *Data analysis and decision making with Microsoft Excel*. London: Duxbury.

ANDERSON, D.R., SWEENEY, D.J. and WILLIAMS, T.A. (2003) *Statistics for business and economics*. 3rd ed. Mason, OH: Thomson/South-Western.

LEVINE, D.M., BERENSON, M.L. and STEPHAN, D. (2005) *Statistics for managers using Microsoft Excel*. 4th ed. Upper Saddle River, NJ: Prentice Hall.

MASON, R.D. and LIND, D.A. (1993) *Statistical techniques in business and economics*. 8th ed. Homewood, ILL: Irwin.

R DEVELOPMENT CORE TEAM. (2006) *R: a language and environment for statistical computing*. Vienna: R Foundation for Statistical Computing.

SANDY, R. (1990) *Statistics for business and economics*. New York: McGraw Hill.

SWIFT, L. and PIFF, S. (2010) *Quantitative methods for business, management and finance*. 3rd ed. Basingstoke: Palgrave Macmillan.

WHITE, J, YEATS, A. and SKIPWORTH, G. (1985) *Tables for statisticians*. Cheltenham: Stanley Thorne.

WEBSTER, A. (1992) *Applied statistics for business and economics*. Homewood, ILL: Irwin.

WHIGHAM, D. (1998) *Quantitative business methods using Excel*. Oxford: Oxford University Press.

12.9 APPENDIX: 'R' COMMANDS

Simple formulation of the commands to produce a graph in 'R' statistical software language (Note, the command prompt in 'R' is given as '>'):

(Assuming there are two files of data (file1.txt and file2.txt) stored within the 'my documents' folder on the computer).

> data1<-scan("c:/my documents/file1.txt")

> data2<-scan("c:/my documents/file2.txt")

> plot(density(data2))

> lines(density(data1),lty=2)

The relationship is displayed as follows (where the dotted lines relate to data1):

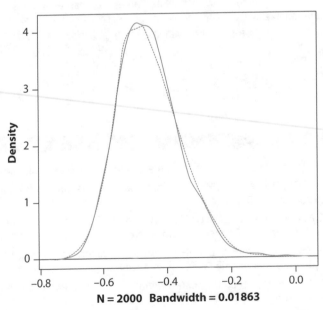

Density.default(x = theta2)

N = 2000   Bandwidth = 0.01863

Line 1 of the commands reads the data file (file1.txt) into the 'R' software.

Line 2 of the commands reads the data file (file2.txt) into the 'R' software.

Line 3 of the commands plots the data2 file (renamed from file2.txt) in the graph ('density' is an 'R' command to produce the type of plot of the data).

Line 4 of the commands overlays the data1 file (renamed from file1.txt) in the graph ('lty = 2' refers to the type of line to plot and in this case it is a dotted line).

The software is free and the commands are relatively simple to perform once you have experienced the software.

A more advanced diagram can be displayed via the following commands:

> x <- seq(-10, 10,
length= 30)

> y <- x

> f <- function(x,y)
{ r <- sqrt(x^2+y^2);
10 • sin(r)/r }

> z <- outer(x, y, f)

> op <- par(bg = "white")

> persp(x, y, z, theta = 30,
phi = 30, expand = 0.5,

col = "lightblue")

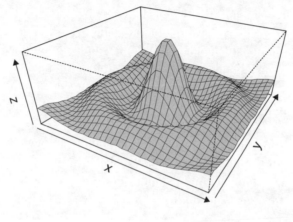

CHAPTER 13

Integrated IT skills

Sue Stirk *and* Stefanie C. Reissner

OVERVIEW

Information technology (IT) has become an integral part of the way in which organisations across the globe operate. Employees and managers alike need to be able to use information technology confidently and competently as part of their daily routines. Through its focus on the integrated nature of information technology, this chapter seeks to provide you with a new perspective on the use of IT skills in postgraduate study, continuing professional development and your everyday career. You will be given the opportunity to reflect on your current use of information technology and the skills to use information technology to stay up to date with recent developments and to work smarter. You will also be encouraged to look at how information technology can be employed in your organisation to support operations and to use resources efficiently.

LEARNING OUTCOMES

By the end of this chapter, provided you engage with the activities, you should be able to:

- use everyday software packages to support your studies and career development
- access online materials confidently
- raise your self-awareness using online questionnaires
- analyse organisational requirements through the use of online tools
- understand the impact information technology can have on the wider organisation.

13.1 INTRODUCTION

Information technology (IT) is prevalent and all-pervasive in the social and leisure world as well as professional life. This is seen through the everyday use of common software such as the Internet, e-mail, word processing, spreadsheets and databases as well as through the more recent growth of social networking sites (such as Facebook), chat rooms, discussion forums, blogs, wikis and the like. At work, you will spend considerable amounts of time in front of a computer screen and the same will apply to your studies. Indeed, some parts of the modules that you are studying will be delivered through IT: that is, online through virtual learning environments (see also Chapter 2). These newer means of communication are becoming part of everyday life and can be seen as an advantage in a professional context, too. Some organisations have realised that they can use the social dimension of IT for their benefit, for example in collaborative working, sharing of good practice and in brand building (IBM 2007). The accountancy firm Ernst & Young, for instance, became one of the first employers to have a recruitment profile on Facebook, resulting in a greater connection with potential graduate recruits (for details, please go to http://www. facebook.com/ernstandyoungcareers).

On the other hand, there are potential problems with the use of such sites. Firstly, there is the potential for posting inappropriate material; a CIPD survey, for instance, revealed that 62 per cent of their respondents were concerned about damaging comments being posted on social network sites and blogs (CIPD 2008a) or about inadvertent leaks of data. Secondly, there is the potential for loss of productivity through e-breaks, in which e-mail and social networking sites are accessed for private reasons during work hours in lieu of the traditional coffee break (see also Chapter 5). Thirdly, people can, and do, bring into the professional environment practices and habits from the social technology world, which are not always appropriate. For example, the use of e-mail is often social and chatty, probably because it is thought to be private and somewhat anonymous. This is inappropriate in many professional situations, as you will be well aware. However, organisations have responsibility for their employees' use of e-mail and the Internet and increasingly develop an Internet and e-mail usage policy to protect their employees.

The Internet is not the only medium that can be used inappropriately. Common applications with which most of us are familiar in our professional lives can equally have negative as well as positive effects. For example a recent *New York Times* article reported on the use of PowerPoint in the US military and their operations in Iraq and Afghanistan. It is, of course, not surprising that the US military should be using PowerPoint. After all, modern armies are complex organisations which are highly reliant on the rapid processing and dissemination of vast amounts of information. Yet the *New York Times* (Bumiller 2010) reported that when General Stanley A. McChrystal was shown a PowerPoint slide summarising strategy in Afghanistan he was recorded as saying: 'When we understand that slide, we'll have won the war.' Even more striking was the comment of General Brigadier H.R. McMaster, who handled an important military campaign in Iraq in 2005. According to McMaster 'PowerPoint is dangerous because it can create the illusion of understanding and the illusion of control,' and 'Some problems in the world are not bullet-izable.'

Despite these potential drawbacks, IT has become an integral part of everyday working life for many of us (CIPD 2008b). In fact, a CIPD survey suggests that 75 per cent of the British workforce use computerised or automated equipment, that software applications are getting increasingly sophisticated and that IT systems are being adapted to an organisation's unique requirements (CIPD ND). It is important to note that IT is neither inherently good nor inherently bad. IT depends upon the use to which we put it and how well we understand both its benefits and potential risks in complex organisations and the social world that we inhabit.

Proficiency in IT is not simply about being able to use software packages and information systems, but also about understanding the context in which IT is used and its impact on the organisation. It is therefore not the intention of this chapter to teach you how to use common software packages. Instead, this chapter is about giving you a new perspective on the use of common IT applications in managing your talent through continuing professional development (see also Chapter 1) and in developing your professional identity (see also Chapter 4), as well as about understanding the impact of the use of IT for your organisation.

13.2 IT FOR PROFESSIONAL DEVELOPMENT

13.2.1 HOW IT SYSTEMS CAN SUPPORT CPD

In recent years, the focus has shifted from information technology per se to IT systems: 'integrated complex[es], consisting not only of the computer system at heart, but also of the social and operational systems of which [they are] part' (Gourlay and Baily as cited in CIPD 2008b, p5). Hence, the computer systems and associated IT skills are only part of IT competence. More importantly, we need to understand how IT can support our continuing professional development and how it relates to other systems and activities in the organisation if we are to make most of what IT has to offer. The challenge, however, is to recognise the role that IT has in our professional and private lives because it is so pervasive.

ACTIVITY 13.1

ANALYSING THE USE OF INFORMATION TECHNOLOGY

Think about your own use of information technology both at the workplace and at home. How competent are you in handling commonly used applications (such as e-mail and Internet, word processing, spreadsheets, databases and graphic programmes)? How confident are you in using them? Do you spend a great deal of your time answering e-mails, or do you just read them once or twice a day? Do you have e-mail alerts sent to your phone? Do you prioritise how you reply to e-mails? Does your organisation have an e-mail or Internet usage policy? (See CIPD 2009 on why such a policy might be necessary.) Consider whether there are ways in which you could use social networking sites (such as Facebook or LinkedIn) or blogs to aid your professional development. Is there any area that you think ought to be developed further?

Answering these questions will help you to reflect on the IT skills that you already possess as well as on your strengths and weaknesses with regard to your use of information technology. This, in turn, will allow you to take stock of your skills and how they are integrated in your daily work in order to argue your case for a promotion or new employment as well as to identify further development opportunities. Your answer to these questions will partly depend on how long you have been working with IT and how aware you are of the opportunities and risks associated with it.

However much you have used IT, you will already have realised that it serves a number of different purposes. For example, you might have used it to monitor budgets or operational processes, to communicate with people in your organisation and externally, or to produce management reports which have utilised charts created in a spreadsheet, imported them into a word processing document and then e-mailed them to relevant colleagues. In short, much of the time you will be integrating IT into your daily routines without even realising it. You may already be utilising newer communication methods such as social networking not only in your private but also in your professional life. Whatever your role in an organisation, you will have to continuously learn to use new software, computer systems and other technology to keep up to date with the latest advances. The use of IT is now a core activity for most people in work or study. Both as a postgraduate student and as a professional you will be using traditional skills of organising and handling information, analysing situations and data, critical thinking and writing, but now you may be combining these with knowledge of how to use IT for researching sources, accessing a variety of information, connecting to experts for advice, and communicating and disseminating ideas and results throughout your organisation or network of contacts.

Information technology has a crucial role in supporting learning and development in a professional context, in formal study and in informal learning. Gourlay and Baily (ND) have identified four learning situations that you may encounter in any learning context. These are graphically represented in Table 13.1.

Table 13.1 Learning situations

	Formal training and learning	Informal training and learning
Individual, cognitive learning	Formal training	Informal learning
Group, communicative learning	Learning in the classroom or other groups	Situated and reflective learning

Source: adapted from Gourlay and Baily (ND).

Each of these four learning situations can be supported by different types of IT that are widely available. Firstly, formal training such as training courses or professional study is increasingly being complemented by online activities, virtual learning environments (VLEs) and online portals, as operated by many university libraries (see also Chapter 2). There have been major developments in VLE technology to turn VLEs into interactive tools to support formal learning. For example, some products provide a live VLE that includes audio and video content, video conferencing facilities, quizzes, whiteboards and live chat as well as content from PowerPoint, Word, Excel and other software, all of which, when combined, enable a lecturer and a learner to engage interactively just as they could in a classroom.

Secondly, informal learning can be supported by the use of online resources such as electronic newspapers, news magazines or specialist journals as well as online tools (see Activity 13.5). Thirdly, learning in the classroom or other groups can be supported by e-mail and social networking, and by online discussion forums

ACTIVITY 13.2

UPDATING YOUR CPD RECORD

Do you have an up-to-date CPD record?

Yes? Congratulations! Keeping an up-to-date CPD record may be a requirement of your professional body or your employer, so we tend to use it as a 'tick-box exercise'. You may now want to see how effective it is, as it has benefits beyond 'ticking the box'. Do you think it will impress your current or future employer to offer you promotion or a new job? Please do not say 'yes, of course' straight away but be critical with yourself and answer the questions below.

No? Well, here is your chance to bring it up to date. List all CPD measures of (depending on how far you are behind) anything up to five years. Include formal study, work-based training courses, short courses, and any mentoring and coaching that you have given or received, as well as professional memberships and conferences or networking events that you may have attended. Give details about what it was, who facilitated it and where it took place. You may also want to add who financed it, particularly if you received third-party funding. You can either do this for each year or in blocks of activities (for example, in our work as university lecturers we can distinguish between research-related CPD, teaching-related CPD and other, more general CPD measures, and we expect something similar will apply to you whatever your role is). Each way has its advantages and disadvantages, so it is down to you to decide what works best for you. Alternatively, you may want to draw on Table 13.1, looking at different learning situations and how well you use IT to complement them.

You may also want to ask yourself the following questions: Has there been an underlying theme to your continuing professional development or does it seem something of a patchwork? Does it draw on a variety of CPD measures or are there any gaps? For instance, some of us are very good at receiving training but less so at more unstructured CPD measures. Others may prefer mentoring and coaching over training courses. An effective CPD record will contain a wide range of measures, regardless of the role involved, even though at the early stages of one's career or job role, training may be more important. You may also want to ask yourself if you have left out something that ought to be part of your CPD record, such as membership in professional bodies (like the CIPD) or other associations, any networking events that you have been doing, any speeches that you were invited to make, any awards that your work has won and so on.

and blogs, which most of you will be already familiar with through your personal use of IT. Finally, situated and reflective learning can take the form of blogs (in lieu of more traditional forms of reflective writing, see Chapter 1) as well as online CPD records.

Much of what we put into our CPD record tends to be individual and formal learning: that is, training, often off-the-job. Undoubtedly, this is an important part of learning and continuing professional development. However, we may learn more through other means, such as informal learning and learning in groups. The difficulty with this type of learning is that we often do not have evidence as there are no attendance certificates or anything like that. However, such learning is an integral part of our continuing professional development and there may be evidence that serves as a substitute. For instance, networking events, professional conferences and development measures such as coaching will help us to learn in a more informal and communicative way and should therefore be included in a comprehensive CPD record.

While the traditional, paper-based CPD record will continue to be important, there is a move towards online management of continuing professional development. For instance, CIPD members have the opportunity to keep an online CPD record (https://www.cipd.co.uk/cpdonline/_RecordList.htm), and other professional bodies may have similar offers. You may wish to check what options are available to you and, after consideration of the benefits and potential risks, to transfer your manual record onto an online one. The advantages and potential disadvantages of online CPD records are summarised in Table 13.2 below.

Table 13.2 Advantages and disadvantages of online CPD records

	Advantages	Disadvantages
Individual learner	• All CPD evidence in one place. • Ready availability • Easy accessibility • Format of CPD record provided	• CPD record may be no longer private
Professional body (eg CIPD)	• Ready record of different CPD measures for research purposes • Voice of the members	• Development and maintenance of system • Support function (help desk) required • Data security and protection – monitoring potential abuse, legal responsibility (Data Protection Act)

Keeping an online rather than a traditional paper-based CPD record can offer many advantages to individual learners and we encourage you, after careful scrutiny of the terms and conditions (with particular focus on security and data protection), to consider transferring your CPD record online. Examples like this demonstrate how increasingly virtual our private and professional lives are becoming. This section has therefore emphasised the importance of seeing IT as part of a wider social and professional environment.

13.2.2 COMMONLY USED SOFTWARE: A CPD PERSPECTIVE

Word processing, spreadsheets, databases, presentation software, graphics programmes and the like may be an old hat for you and you may wonder what else there is to learn. Probably little from a technological skills perspective and more from a systems perspective (CIPD 2008b). Gourlay and Baily (ND) suggest that the challenge is not to learn new software applications but to integrate new IT skills in one's daily routines. In this section you are encouraged to explore applications like simple spreadsheets and small databases to record sources of reading, either for your university work or job-related projects. These activities may be easy for many of you from a technical viewpoint but more beneficial from a learning and career development perspective.

We suggested in Chapter 2 of this book that you could use simple spreadsheets or small databases to record any readings for your studies or other information required for a larger project at work. We have noted that keeping track of sources can be challenging in the current climate of information overload, yet it is vital for the success of tasks. Being organised is becoming an increasingly important skill for managers and professionals (see also Chapter 5), and generic software packages can help you with this.

ACTIVITY 13.3

MAKING USE OF SIMPLE SPREADSHEETS OR DATABASES

Most of you will have one common characteristic: you are studying for a postgraduate degree in business and management, so let us take your studies as an example. (If you find that a particular project at work lends itself to this exercise, please feel free to use it as the underlying principles remain the same.) Collect as many sources as possible that you have been using as part of your studies – books, journal articles, magazines, websites, reports – either for your whole programme of studies or a particular module or task.

First of all, consider what type of information you will need to include in your spreadsheet or database (see also Chapter 3 for details on referencing). You will need the author's name, the date of publication, the title of the item, possibly the title of the publication, the place of publication and name of the publisher. You may want to add the type of publication so that you can sort them into different categories; you may want to add means of accessing the item (different library sites, different libraries, academic databases, items you borrowed from relatives or friends and so on); you may also want to add ISBN and ISSN numbers or you may want to add where you are keeping this item (at work, at home, on your memory stick). You may find that not all of this applies and that other information is important, such as key words, subject terms or the name of the module or course for which the item was most relevant.

Secondly, with these details at hand, start your spreadsheet or database and type in the information. This should be an easy task with the experience and expertise that you will already have. Once you have finished, start sorting the entries according to different characteristics. If your database is small, you may find it useful to sort all entries alphabetically according to the author's name or title but if your database has a lot of entries, sorting according to key words, module or course name may be more useful.

If you are doing a lot of formal study (or are planning to continue formal study beyond your current studies, for instance for a doctorate degree), you may benefit from using specialist bibliographic software. One such package, which is available free of charge and in different languages, is Zotero (www.zotero.org). It allows you to store bibliographic information, websites and files in one easy-to-access database and to cite any reference in a written piece of work. You may need to devote some time to learning how to use this programme but it may be worth your while.

Did you choose to use a spreadsheet or a database for this activity? The choices you make can have a big impact when processing large amounts of data. A spreadsheet is fine if you just want one list of information and if you are not going to have to repeat data. For example, if an author is only going to have one book or article then it is fine to use a spreadsheet. But if you think about it, what happens when an author has several articles in the same year – then you are going to have to write in the author's name and the year several times. So you can save yourself work by choosing to use a database. If you use a database then it is easy to link related data, such as suppliers and their products, customers and their orders, authors and their works.

If you chose to use a database, then how did you design it? Did you store your data in a single table or did you use more than one table and link them together? Storing data in a single table or in a spreadsheet can often become cumbersome and encourage mistakes. When using a database, therefore, it is important to think about how you will design it because this will have an impact on how well you can use the information and on how efficiently you work. There are numerous textbooks on how to design databases, but mainly you need a way of working out which tables you will need and what data will be in each table. As students, you will be aware that your university or place of study will keep records in which they store your name, address, date of birth and other details along with the modules you study, and the marks you obtain for each module. If they just used a spreadsheet or one table then they would have to repeat your details against every module you studied. If your personal details changed, such as your address, then they would have to change the address on every record – this is inefficient and prone to error. It would be much more sensible to have two tables, one for your personal details and one for the modules you study, and then link them together with some piece of common information. If they gave you a unique code, like a student number, then they could store that in both tables. In this way, if they wanted to know your marks on a module they could find your student code and then retrieve all your module details. Although they would have two tables, all of your information is stored only once. This is a very simple example, but it serves to illustrate the necessity for thoughtful database design.

We would hope that you have made a good start with this activity on your journey to become a smart student and professional, drawing on the skills that you have learned in Parts 2 and 3 of this book. We can only encourage you to keep up to date with your spreadsheet or database and to reflect on the value of it as your studies or other projects progress. We tend to take such things for granted but it may be one way to demonstrate that you possess good organisation skills when applying for promotion or a new job or role. This is continuing professional development and talent management in practice.

13.2.3 ONLINE RESOURCES

As you will be aware, the Internet gives you access to a wealth of information resources. An increasing number of journals, magazines and other traditionally printed materials are available online, many free of charge. The advantages of online provision are clear: items can be accessed at any time from any location (subject to Internet access, of course), there is no heavy paper to be carried around, it is cheaper and more environmentally friendly to produce, there are no packaging and shipping costs, there is less waste. In short, online provision makes better use of resources.

Being able to locate information efficiently online is crucial. There are numerous search engines that help you with this. Google is probably the one that you have heard of the most and no doubt you will use Google Scholar to search for academic sources to aid your study. Search engines classify information on the Internet and search webpages automatically. They look for information based on key words before displaying matches. They do not display every webpage they find but they create indexes of the pages they visit. The search engine then finds the pages to match your keywords by searching that index. When you search for information you can make your searches more efficient by choosing key words carefully.

For example, try searching for the words 'integrated IT skills' on the Internet. You will probably find tens of pages of sites listed. Now search for the same thing but place the words in double quotes – '"integrated IT skills"'. This time you will not see as many sites listed. The first search will find all sites that contain any of the words. The second search will only find sites that have all three words listed exactly as specified. Therefore you do not have to read through as much information to find what you want. It can be quick and easy to use Internet resources but there are two main challenges to our ability to use online resources with confidence.

The first is the possible unreliability or poor quality of resources, because the Internet is not controlled and so you should always be aware that some information may not be as accurate as you might hope (see also Chapter 2). It is usually possible to trust public body websites (such as governments and non-governmental organisations), websites of professional bodies (such as the CIPD), reputable publishers of journals, and established educational websites – though even then you should take care.

The second challenge is that of security. Security measures for an organisation will usually be the responsibility of an IT department, but nevertheless it is important to be aware of the risks and to ensure that in your own use of the Internet you keep your antivirus software up to date and that you use an appropriately configured firewall. You should also consider how you store material – personal, study and work related. As Baldin (2010) points out 'On average, 10,000 mobile phones and 1,000 other tech gizmos including iPods, laptops and memory sticks are left in the back of London taxis every month.' Losing a data stick may not be the end of the world if it contains journal articles, but it could be much more serious if it contained corporate data. Therefore security is just as much about people and awareness of security issues as it is about policies and procedures.

ACTIVITY 13.4

REFLECTING ON YOUR USE OF ONLINE RESOURCES

Think for a moment about how much use you make of online provision of print materials on a daily or weekly basis, and for which purposes. We would also like you to think about whether you tend to access materials free of charge or materials that carry a subscription (though that may be part of your membership of bodies like the CIPD). Are you surprised by the findings? Is there anything that you would like to do differently in the future or see being done differently by your employer or other stakeholders? Take some time, too, to think about the security issues that could be associated with your use of online materials. Take a few minutes to read an item found on the British Computer Society website – Bleaken (2009) – which describes how an online attack can take place. What can you do to stay safe online?

We have included this activity as an opportunity to practise access to online resources safely – particularly if you have not used them as part of your previous study – and to raise your awareness of your use of online materials and your reading habits and how they may impact on your organisation and on your career. Smart managers and professionals know what they are doing and how that affects other aspects of their lives. For instance, you may be commuting on public transport and find that reading a print newspaper en route to work keeps you up to date with the latest news. However, you may realise that you less frequently access additional materials from specialist trade journals, trade associations or professional bodies that are easily available online, and that this may have negative impacts on your career. Do you know what you are missing?

13.2.4 ONLINE QUESTIONNAIRES AND INTERACTIVE TOOLS

The key to personal and professional development is raising your level of self-awareness (see Chapters 1 and 4). Many development measures, particularly at managerial level, will encourage you to raise the level of your own self-awareness in order to build awareness of others. There is a wide variety of personality tests on the market which aim not only to raise self-awareness but also to give managers the cognitive abilities and the language to understand their own and their subordinates' behaviour and take appropriate action. Particularly in advanced development measures like coaching, such tests have a vital role (see also Chapter 17). These tests are usually administered by accredited professionals and carry a charge, and we appreciate that not all of you will have the opportunity to access such tools through your employer or have the financial means to pay for them yourself. However, simplified versions of the most common personality tests are available free of charge on the Internet. They tend to make use of a simple questionnaire in which you click on the answer that applies to you.

ACTIVITY 13.5

LEARNING MORE ABOUT YOURSELF ONLINE

If you want to learn more about your personality, you may find it useful to type 'free personality tests' into your search engine. You will then be given a wide range of websites that offer commonly used personality tests free of charge. However, you are advised to check the following issues before embarking on a 'free' test:

1. Do you get the results of your test free of charge?

2. How much detail about yourself are you required to provide?

3. Can you identify the people or organisation behind the website?

4. Is there a privacy and security policy?

As with any other online activity, you need to take care to protect your identity, your anonymity and confidentiality. We cannot accept liability for any damage or loss incurred in this activity. The BBC offer a free personality test on http://www.bbc.co.uk/science/humanbody/mind/index_surveys.shtml. Alternatively, www.learnmyself.com is a website which operates as a not-for-profit organisation, which does not require you to sign in and which explains your results using psychological theory. These tests are based on the 'Big Five' theory (see also Chapter 4), and you may find the tests both useful and fun. In addition, you may find it interesting to test your emotional intelligence (EI) (see Chapter 4), and there is a free online test available through the Institute of Health and Human Potential on http://www.ihhp.com/quiz.php.

You need to be aware that your personality will be far more complex than any personality test can reveal and you should not take any test results at face value; they are only an indication of your preferred behaviours. The results of any test will depend on how truthfully you answered the questions, whether you were thinking about all aspects of your life or only a few (eg your working life), whether you had something particular in mind when answering the questions and how reliable the interpretation is. You may not like the results and you may not agree with them. If you don't, you may want to let the test rest and go back to it at a later stage, perhaps with the support of a close colleague or friend who may give you his or her interpretation. We often do not recognise certain behaviours in ourselves but may be encouraged to watch for them as a result of such tests. It may not be comfortable to find out that we are not as nice as we thought we are or would like to be, but this self-awareness is the first step to doing something about it.

The implications of personality tests for our professional life are not always obvious at first glance but they are often significant. For instance, the test that Stefanie, one of the authors of this chapter, took on the BBC website showed a low level of agreeableness and the results of the Learn Myself website confirmed this with a particularly low score for co-operation in comparison with other females of her age group in the United Kingdom. You will all be aware of the need for co-operation in today's business environment (see also Chapters 6 and 16). So the fact that Stefanie does not appear to be agreeable and does not like (or is not very good at) co-operating with others may hinder her ability to work effectively in teams and with others, which may in turn have significant negative effects on her further career. However, she is already aware that co-operation is a weakness of hers which means that she can and does make extra efforts to engage in more collaborative work, of which this book is an example. Your weak spot will probably be elsewhere, but knowing about it can help you take the important steps of remedying it. You may want to seek help from work colleagues, your mentor or a coach to explore ways to improve any areas that you have identified for further development. The converse is equally true, of course: knowing your strengths can help you to position yourself better at the workplace by actively seeking roles and activities that suit your personality and play to your strengths. After all, if you wanted to compete in the forthcoming Olympic games, would you try to enter in your strongest or weakest discipline?

Online provisions are becoming increasingly interactive and allow users to develop and reflect on their professional practice. Users can rate elements and aspects of a particular situation as well as typing in their comments, reflections and action points to consider at a later stage. Due to their flexibility, interactive online tools can be used for a variety of purposes, such as the development of individuals or discussions in groups. The CIPD have developed a range of online tools that serve both analytical and developmental purposes, a selection of which are available on the companion website of this book (see also Activity 13.6 on p402).

13.3 IT FOR ORGANISATIONS

13.3.1 ANALYSING ORGANISATIONAL IT REQUIREMENTS

The previous section of this chapter has given you examples of how IT can support your professional development, which may benefit not only you personally but also your work colleagues in other parts of the organisation (see also Chapter 1). Let us now focus on how IT can support the business needs of an organisation.

The use of IT in any organisation depends upon understanding business needs, along with the organisation's strategy and objectives. When there is a requirement for an IT system in the organisation, it will be necessary to analyse it carefully. This analysis would normally be carried out by an IT department, but it is nevertheless useful to understand how you might be involved in this. For example, you may be the person who identifies the need for a system and therefore commissions it, or you may be involved in helping IT staff to elicit information that would be required. In either case, you would not be passive, but would be a participant in the analysis. If you are someone who might commission an IT system, the CIPD provide a tool *Technology in HR* (CIPD 2007) that can help you to understand better how IT can help your organisation. The focus of the tool is HR, but the general principles are applicable to other areas of business. As the authors of the tool point out, the successful use and implementation of technology requires that you understand your own organisation's strategy and business objectives. IT professionals are dependent on managers and users in order to collect information and to understand the requirements of the system and its possible impact on other parts of the organisation. Any professional can have major input in developing or commissioning IT systems.

ACTIVITY 13.6

USING ONLINE TOOLS

Access the CIPD online tools *Technology in HR* (CIPD 2007) and *Helping people learn IT systems* (CIPD 2008b), which are available on the companion website, and see how information technology can support human resources and other functions in your organisation. In which areas is there evidence of good practice? What other areas would benefit from development?

While IT systems may be more prevalent in some parts of an organisation (for example, design departments have long used CAD to support their work), others have only recently begun to implement sophisticated IT systems. Research conducted for the CIPD suggests that functions like human resources can benefit from technological advances to facilitate their operations and strengthen the support that they offer to their clients (Martin 2005, Parry et al 2007). An example of these benefits can be seen in the BOC Gases case study reproduced here from the CIPD tool *Technology in HR* (CIPD 2007).

This example demonstrates perfectly the integrated nature of IT. BOC Gases are using an SAP HR system, a payroll system, a recruitment database, a corporate website, an intranet, and Excel files and reports which all work together to support the needs of their HR function.

13.3.2 HOW IT CAN MAKE A DIFFERENCE TO ORGANISATIONS

Information systems – ie information technology and the people using it – can make or break an organisation's success in the twenty-first century, and alignment of IT with all aspects of an organisation is crucial (Martin 2005). According to a study on people management and technology conducted by the CIPD (2005), technology is used across a range of HR functions, such as absence management, training and development, rewards, and recruitment and selection.

BOC GASES – AN ILLUSTRATION

CASE STUDY 13.1

BOC Gases have used as SAP HR system since 1999. This system holds HR data and allows managers to access them. The employee information contained in the system includes cost centre, role, pay and benefits, absence and leave. SAP also stores the organisational tree and personnel actions, such as salary changes and departmental moves, as a piece of history. Managers access this system via the line manager desktop. They are responsible for recording absence, and for entering bonus ratings on a quarterly basis and salary review details annually. One part of the business also uses the system to record hours under the annualised hours system. The system drives the payroll process (though an SAP payroll system is not used) through a monthly report that interfaces with the payroll system. The reward team use the SAP system to produce reports.

BOC Gases introduced an e-recruitment system in 2003 to increase the visibility of its spend on recruitment and to improve the efficiency of the recruitment process. There is a recruitment database that sits centrally and is connected to a number of different career centres, each with a different URL. Each career centre also has its own behind-the-scenes processing and application form. The system has different levels of access for vendors, managers,

administrators and HR recruiters. Managers or resourcing staff can create vacancies in the system and a corresponding advertisement. This goes through an approval process and is then posted on the corporate website, intranet and on a number of external jobs boards. Applicants complete a form online, which is then saved to the database. It is also possible to add multiple-choice questions on which the applicant will be screened automatically. Managers can then log in to look at the applications. The system sends out automated acknowledgements and will generate rejection letters once the manager or recruiter has entered that a candidate has been rejected. This can be done in batches rather than individually. A summary of candidates can be viewed on screen and reports can be produced as Excel files or as a printout.

The HR intranet has recently been relaunched; the previous system was out of date and difficult to navigate. The site is accessed via the intranet homepage and contains HR information, forms, news and tools such as 360-degree feedback. All of the HR policy and procedure information is now on this site and is current. The system can be navigated using menus or search functionality; it is aimed primarily at the HR team but is also used by managers and employees with different levels of access.

The same survey found that IT is usually used to improve the quality of information (91 per cent), improve the speed at which information is available (81 per cent), to improve service to employees (56 per cent) and for cost reduction (35 per cent). The implementation of technology may also have implications for how organisations work and for the role(s) of professionals. For example, the Internet has become the foundation for new business models and new ways of distributing knowledge and of doing business (Laudon and Laudon 2002). More and more work is now carried out electronically and there has been a significant increase in the number of mobile workers. Communications technology has removed distance as a barrier for many types of work. For example, a salesperson can have up-to-date information on a hand-held computer and so spend more time with customers and less on paperwork. IT has had an impact on organisational culture, the nature of work, job roles and indeed on the workplace itself. An example of this can be found in the CIPD (2007) report *HR and technology: impact and advantages,* which noted the implications for HR practitioners of the implementation of HR information systems. The report outlined the necessity for new capabilities within the HR function and suggested that the use of technology could facilitate a change in role away from administration to a more strategic contribution to the organisation.

The human resources function in particular, then, can contribute to an organisation's success through the effective use of information technology (Parry et al 2007). Martin (2005), for instance, highlights the following five areas in which the human resources function in particular can contribute to an organisation's success through the use of IT:

- improving information provision
- fostering intellectual integration and knowledge-sharing
- encouraging organisational learning and knowledge management
- creating new forms of communities at work and of organisations
- supporting innovative business models and participative organisational cultures.

But what does this look like? Let us consider the following case study.

CASE STUDY 13.2

EMBEDDED E-LEARNING IN THE CROWN PROSECUTION SERVICE

Background: the role of the CPS

The Crown Prosecution Service (CPS) is the government department responsible for prosecuting people in England and Wales who have been charged with a criminal offence. The CPS has 7,700 staff across 42 geographical areas, which are aligned with the boundaries of the police authorities and headquarters. Some 3,000 of the staff are lawyers and the CPS could be described as the biggest law firm in the country – it is certainly the biggest recruiter in the field, recruiting up to 400 lawyers with a range of experience in any given year.

Technical legal knowledge is of critical importance. New legislation is appearing continually and CPS staff need to keep abreast of complex legislation and

understand its consequences as quickly as possible. Given this need for instantaneous and accurate updating, e-learning has attractions as a means of delivery. In 2002 the CPS commissioned and deployed a bespoke e-learning module 'Speaking up for justice'. This considered the consequences of a Home Office report on the treatment of vulnerable and intimidated witnesses. This was intended to be part of a blended solution involving e-learning and classroom elements; it was also intended to be made available to partners across the criminal justice system.

The experience of 'Speaking up for justice' has convinced the CPS that it is only customised e-learning material that will be valued within the organisation. However, it is now recognised that this first module was insufficiently rigorous in its technical content (rigour is essential in a legal environment), it was also insufficiently interactive, and there was not enough support given to the module. Sharron Hughes, E-Learning Manager at the CPS, regards this last point as critical. In her words: 'Don't put anything online if you don't want to support it.'

The lawyer induction modules

In 2005 the CPS established an online Prosecution College. This is organised into a number of faculties, each of which offers a series of online modules.

The first range of programmes that were developed and tested were components for lawyer induction. Here the modules concentrate on technical subjects like the Bail Act, identification, custody and evidence. Completion of these modules, which will take approximately four hours, is compulsory for all newly recruited lawyers before they attend classroom sessions.

Support and monitoring is provided by line managers and internal lawyer-induction tutors. However, there are clear standards on what is to be expected and these are issued to all learners, with the name of their immediate manager identified. Most importantly, induction appears in the performance targets that are set for CPS areas. Such learning and development targets were introduced for the first time in April 2005 and are reviewed on a quarterly basis.

One other interesting approach to embedding their use within the organisation is a feature of the design of the modules themselves. At some stages learners are presented with a scenario: an example would be an outline of an exchange that has taken place between a suspected shoplifter, a store detective and a police officer. The learner is invited to submit a short free-form text commentary on the exchange, highlighting its conformance to the CPS guidelines. This commentary is sent immediately to the learning and development team, who forward the

individual's assembled commentaries to one of 80 internal tutors or mentors who are employed by the CPS. These tutors have committed to respond to the learner within a certain time period (five days).

The CPS approach

There are three principles that underpin the CPS approach to developing e-learning:

- Effective e-learning products should be customised or bespoke rather than generic.
- Any e-learning material must be adequately supported.
- E-learning should be an integral part of the wider organisational objectives

The CPS Learning and Development Team is firmly of the view that unsupported, generic material made available on a user-choice basis is unlikely to make a significant contribution to the wider training effort.

The CPS has aimed for what it describes as medium technology. Although the modules incorporate audio commentary at some stages, and quizzes and scenarios, they do not adopt high-level graphics or interactive facilities. This choice reflects a view on both what the CPS technology infrastructure will support and what is acceptable for the learner in that framework. The material included within the modules is specified by an internal CPS expert and the CPS Learning and Development Team, and production is undertaken by Futuremedia, a Brighton-based e-learning consultancy.

Costs of production at this level work out at about £16,000 an hour of module time – low-level interaction would cost about £11,000 and high-level about twice as much as low-level. Current feedback on the modules is positive and efforts are now focused on their use in the organisation rather than on improving their design.

Sharing with a wider audience

A number of other modules are under production and some of these will be of particular value to partner organisations in the criminal justice system. One example is a module on the proceeds of crime that will be of value to those involved in asset recovery. Another concerns the care of witnesses who are of particular value to the police.

The CPS intends to give all appropriate parties access to the Prosecution College via the Internet. However, the monitoring and support – considered essential to effective learning – must be conducted by the user organisations.

Sharron Hughes feels that senior management are convinced of the value of e-learning and the Prosecution College is now seen as an essential element in learning provision. She envisages no great changes in the pattern of e-learning, but a gradual growth until it provides between half and three-quarters of learning time. The CPS is currently assembling data on the extent of take-up, but with 5,000 users she estimates that they are perhaps half-way to their target usage. In her words: 'We must carry on the way we are and show the business the value

of e-learning. We will however never replace the need for face-to-face interpersonal skills for topics like advocacy.'

Other initiatives under development at the Prosecution College include:

- A features and articles session on the Prosecution College home page. Podcasts may be piloted in 2007.

- The gradual extension of external access. This will be mainly for organisations that fall into the category of Law Officer Departments under the Attorney General. Discussions are ongoing with the Bar Council and there is growing international interest.

- More emphasis on pre-course assessment and post-course assessment.

- Renewed efforts to determine the most appropriate techniques for evaluation.

Source: CIPD (ND), *Embedded e-learning in the Crown Prosecution Serice*, case study.

Please note: A further case study is available on the companion website.

The focus of these case studies is clearly on training and staff development, but you will recognise that the initiatives have wider implications for the way in which the respective organisation operates. At the BBC, the system comprises electronic training, virtual learning resources and information about further development measures, all of which emphasise the importance of training and development within the organisation. At CPS, the e-learning initiative is supported by a team of tutors or mentors that help staff to stay up to date. It is a strong signal that continuing professional development is an integral part of working within the organisation and the sector as a whole. There are potentially wider implications for the organisations in question as such e-learning activities become an integral part of training and staff development. For instance, staff may be more willing to share knowledge and to engage in other learning activities. New forms of work and organisation may evolve, such as virtual study groups, which may complement more traditional ways of working.

13.4 CONCLUSION

You will have seen in this chapter that IT skills need to be seen in their wider context (CIPD ND), particularly with regard to training, learning and development in organisations. There is a personal dimension to this learning and development as information technology can help you increase your self-awareness and support the development of your professional identity. However, there is also an organisational dimension to training, learning and development, as effective strategies will try to align different organisational members' learning in a complementary fashion. The use of IT has potentially significant impacts on the way in which an organisation operates and how it is structured and governed as its members' expectations may change through exposure to a range of IT systems and applications (Martin 2005). For instance, fostering knowledge-sharing and virtual-learning teams through IT can change the culture of an organisation, and consequently styles of leadership, control and reward (among others) may have to be adapted. However, as we become extremely reliant on IT, there are dangers of losing productive time when there are power cuts or system failures, and also of cyber-fraud. IT systems must therefore be used in a strategic and thoughtful way and they must be tailored to the organisation's unique needs, and you may be able to get involved.

ACTIVITY 13.7

REFLECTING ON THE EFFECTIVENESS OF IT SYSTEMS

Consider what IT systems are prevalent in your organisation and how effective they are in supporting both operational and developmental aspects. What can your organisation learn from the two examples above?

PAUSE FOR THOUGHT

Identify at least three things that you have learned by studying this chapter and engaging with the exercises and activities. How will your newly acquired knowledge and skills support your continuing professional development? What value do you expect your learning to have for your daily routines and your further career? In what area have you identified a need for further development and how are you planning to fill that gap? Address these issues in your learning journal and/or CPD log. You may also wish to discuss them with a peer, colleague, mentor or coach to aid your further development.

- Information technology has a personal dimension and can support the development of professional identity.

- Information technology, particularly Internet technology, can provide open access to a wide range of tools and techniques which support continuing professional development.

- Information technology can help organisations to train and develop their staff effectively at comparatively low cost, and potentially to make the organisation more participative and innovative.

EXPLORE FURTHER

BBC Surveys and Personality Tests: http://www.bbc.co.uk/science/humanbody/mind/index_surveys.shtml.

CPD Online: https://www.cipd.co.uk/cpdonline/_RecordList.htm.

Zotero Citation Management: http://www.zotero.org.

13.5 REFERENCES

BALDIN, A. (2010) *Managing people, policies and privacy.* British Computer Society. Available online at: http://www.bcs.org/server.php?show=conWebDoc.34663 [accessed 20 April 2010].

BLEAKEN, D. (2009) *Anatomy of an attack.* Swindon: British Computer Society. Available online at: http://www.bcs.org/server.php?show=conWebDoc.33653 [accessed 20 April 2010].

BUMILLER, E. (2010) We have met the enemy and he is PowerPoint. *New York Times.* 26 April. Available online at: http://www.nytimes.com/2010/04/27/world/27powerpoint.html?scp=1&sq=powerpoint&st=cse [accessed 23 May 2010].

CIPD. (2005) *People management and technology: progress and potential.* London: CIPD. Available online at: http://www.cipd.co.uk/NR/rdonlyres/6A49F28D-9EC5-4A85-

B739–F4F4A759BF44/0/peoplmantechsr05.pdf [accessed 23 May 2010].

CIPD. (2007) *Technology in HR.* Available online at: http://www.cipd.co.uk/NR/rdonly. London: CIPD res/B3018E59–CD65–4099–9EFB-D789702B9443/0/techinhrpractool. pdf [accessed 24 February 2010].

CIPD. (2008a) *Recruitment, retention and turnover survey.* London: CIPD. Available online at: http://www.cipd.co.uk/NR/rdonlyres/BE3C57BF-91FF-4AD0–9656–FAC27 E5398AA/0/recruitmentretentionturnover2008.pdf [accessed 20 April 2010].

CIPD. (2008b) *Helping people learn IT systems.* London: CIPD. Available online at: http://www.cipd.co.uk/NR/rdonlyres/074AAD3D-EEBC-4593–BD3F-D29763C5C26A/0/helpingpeoplelearnIT.pdf [accessed 24 February 2010].

CIPD. (2009) *Internet and e-mail policies.* CIPD Factsheet. London: CIPD. Available online at: http://www.cipd.co.uk/subjects/hrpract/general/webepolicy.htm [accessed 19 April 2010].

CIPD. (ND) *How do people learn IT systems?* Discussion paper. London: CIPD. Available online at: http://www.cipd.co.uk/helpingpeoplelearn/_hdpl.htm [accessed 26 February 2010].

GOURLAY, S. and BAILY, C. (ND) *How people learn systems.* Report for CIPD. London: CIPD. Available online at: http://www.cipd.co.uk/helpingpeoplelearn/_hwpplrn.htm?Is SrchRes=1 [accessed 26 February 2010].

IBM (2007) *Achieving tangible business benefits with social computing.* Available online at: http://www-935.ibm.com/services/de/cio/pdf/wp-cio-empower-benefits-of-social-comp.pdf [accessed 23 May 2010].

LAUDON, K.C. and LAUDON, J.P. (2002) *Management information systems.* Upper Saddle River, NJ: Prentice-Hall.

MARTIN, G. (2005) *Technology and people management.* Research Report. London: CIPD.

PARRY, E., TYSON, S., SELBIE, D. and LEIGHTON, R. (2007) *HR and technology. Research into Practice Report.* London: CIPD.

PART 8

Effective Decision-Making and Problem-Solving at Work

CHAPTER 14

Effective decision-making and creative problem-solving

Fred Yamoah

OVERVIEW

Decision-making is a core managerial and leadership responsibility. Making a decision is to choose a course of action from a range of alternative decision options. A decision once made commits resources required for its implementation. The decision-making process is constrained by financial and human resources, relationships and other factors over which managers do not always have full control. Decision-making becomes more complex when it is at a group level or borders on ethical considerations. Decisions can have positive or negative consequences. Inaction or procrastination is not a prudent alternative as it mostly results in missed opportunities. To the manager or leader, decision-making is not a matter of choice but a requirement and personal responsibility, which goes to determine both the viability and future profitability of the business. Continuous development of decision-making skills is a matter of priority for managers and other decision-makers.

An equally essential managerial responsibility is problem-solving. It involves finding the root cause of problem(s) through analysis, exploring possible solutions through evaluation, and selecting the most suitable solution. Creative problem-solving skills enhance one's ability to resolve problems by stimulating imaginative thoughts to produce innovative remedies that ensure business survival. Creativity has been traditionally associated with the creative arts, but has become a key quality that differentiates leading organisations from their less innovative counterparts in today's highly competitive business environment. It is the core element driving processes that facilitates innovation, flexibility and competitiveness. Creative problem-solving skills improve the quality of solutions to problems, motivate staff and enhance satisfaction of management. Acquiring decision-making and creative problem-solving skills will enhance the capacity of managers to make effective decisions based on innovative ideas that will gain acceptance and the resources needed to carry them through. In this chapter students will learn about decision-making and problem-solving in the context of: underpinning knowledge, creative methods, group approaches, techniques to deal with ethical dilemmas, and guidelines for communicating decisions.

LEARNING OUTCOMES

By the end of this chapter, provided you engage with the activities, you should be able to:

- understand decision-making and creative problem-solving
- apply creative methods of decision-making and problem-solving
- understand the importance of developing mental skills to be creative and proactive
- apply ethical decision-making and problem-solving techniques and ways of resolving ethical dilemmas
- explain approaches to communicate and justify decisions and problem-solving options.

14.1 INTRODUCTION

Central to decision-making is the element of choice among alternative course of actions. A decision is therefore a chosen course of action from alternatives (Harrison 1996). The choice is informed by the decision-maker's knowledge, his or her understanding of the issues at stake, and conviction about the solutions available. This means the decision-maker determines the relative attractiveness of each option, and selects the 'best' to meet the decision-making criteria. Every decision option will lead to either a positive or a negative outcome. It is possible to have a collection of decision options that provides positive outcomes to a different degree. The decision-making process is also constrained by financial and human resources, requisite technology, the quality of data and information available, and relationships, legal and ethical considerations. Hence, the key issue is the ability of the decision-maker to choose the option that offers the best outcome out of all the options available. This is why it is important to shift the emphasis from decision-making to effective decision-making and the supporting techniques available. Effective decision-making aims at ensuring that the most efficient and effective decision is made by utilising the best information possible within a given timescale. It is also essential that the decision can be communicated and justified to respective stakeholders.

Creative problem-solving involves the application of imaginative thoughts to produce innovative remedies that create competitive advantage and ensure business survival (Titus 2000). At the operational level, it serves to motivate employees and increases the credibility of managers and decision-makers. The total effect of creative problem-solving techniques is improved satisfaction through the implementation of innovation ideas. It is therefore very important for decision-makers to acquire creative problem-solving skills to find solutions to problems, and increase motivation and the performance of the organisation. Many management science writers have used creativity and innovation interchangeably but others (Heap 1989, Titus 2000) have argued that they are fundamentally different but part of a continuous process. For example, Titus (2000) suggests that creativity results in the generation of new ideas. According to Heap (1989) creativity leads to the creation of new ideas but innovation relates to putting into practice the ideas produced from creativity. This means that creativity involves coming up with new ideas. It is then followed by the innovation process, which involves sorting out and applying the refined ideas within an organisational setting. This distinction is very important for a better understanding of the two key terminologies and how managers and decision-makers can take the correct steps to enhance their creative and innovative skills.

14.2 CREATIVE METHODS OF DECISION-MAKING AND PROBLEM-SOLVING

Managers and leaders of organisations operating within any sector of the economy will find it valuable to have a guide to decision-making and problem-solving. These skills and techniques prepare managers to be able to reduce risks and enhance the rewards accrued from the decisions they make. For decision-makers to succeed and achieve organisational objectives, it is important for them to resolve problems creatively. There are simple as well as complex decision-making and problem-solving tools and techniques. This discussion will cover Six Thinking Hats (De Bono 2000) and lateral thinking, storyboard exercises, benchmarking creative leadership skills, mental imagery, mind mapping (Buzan 2010), Pareto analysis and the Plus-Minus-Interesting (PMI) technique as key methods to enhance the decision-making and creative problem-solving capabilities of managers. It will explain the nature and scope of these techniques, illustrate how they work and provide opportunity for practice and reflection.

14.2.1 DE BONO'S SIX THINKING HATS

The 'Six Thinking Hats' technique, also known as 'De Bono's Coloured Hats', (Table 14.1) is noted as a key decision-making tool because it helps the decision-maker to look at making a decision from various perspectives. Approaching decision-making from different perspectives does not come naturally when one has to make a decision. Rather, decision-makers are more inclined to stick to the status quo by adhering to what they know and believe works for them. This tool therefore is very handy for decision-makers as a good background skill that encourage them to explore all possibilities for a more comprehensive solution. By so doing, decision-makers are enabled to explore, in addition to rational decision capabilities, their creativity and intuitive abilities to deal with the problem at issue. It enables decision-makers to explore opportunities outside their comfort zone for solutions without overplaying the rational approach, and to be less defensive of the status quo. The Six Thinking Hats technique is applicable to both group and individual decision-making.

Table 14.1 Description of De Bono's Six Coloured Hats technique

Hat	De Bono's prescription
White	Always focus on data, information or facts available, explore knowledge gaps, draw lessons and attempt to bridge knowledge gap or find remedy.
Yellow	Stands for optimism and brightness and focuses on positive thinking, points to benefits and value of the decision, encourages forward thinking and not giving up even when encountering challenges.
Black	Wear the hat of pessimism, play the devil's advocate, spot the weaknesses and dangers, minimise the tendency for complacency, enhance one's preparedness to resolve potential difficulties.
Red	Espouses expression of intuition, emotion, and conviction, positive or negative feelings, reading into possible emotional and intuitive feedbacks from other people likely to judge the decision.
Green	Advocates creativity, creation of new ideas and perceptions, offers every idea an opportunity for consider without initial criticism and possible elimination (see also discussion on lateral thinking).
Blue	Worn to manage the thinking process towards a consensus, usually associated with facilitators of the decision-making process at team meeting sessions, directs compliance with the directives on the thinking hats. For example, this hat will emphasize Green Hat to serve as a catalyst for creativeness.

Source: adapted from De Bono (2000).

Using De Bono's Six Hats technique will prop up decisions and plans with a combination of ambition, skill in execution, sensitivity, creativity and good contingency planning. In a nutshell, exploring the six different points of view to make decisions helps groups and individual decision-makers to identify potential pitfalls, reduce risk of a backlash and enhance the possibility of arriving at a viable solution to a problem. It minimises the tendency to becoming a victim of unforeseen possibilities by helping the decision-maker to test the waters.

ACTIVITY 14.1

APPLYING THE SIX THINKING HATS TECHNIQUE

Apply the Six Thinking Hats technique to diagnose a case where you have been selected as the chairperson of a committee set up by your organisation to plan a redundancy programme in the wake of a global recession.

AN ILLUSTRATION OF THE SIX THINKING HATS TECHNIQUE

CASE STUDY 14.1

The scenario

The management of an insurance company is considering whether to acquire a new office building. The economic indicators are all positive and the company is growing. They are recruiting many new staff and this is putting a lot of pressure on office space for staff. At a committee meeting to decide the way forward, the management team decided to use the Six Thinking Hats technique as a planning tool.

Suggested application of the De Bono's Six Thinking Hats to the scenario

Assessing the issue with the *White Hat*, the team analyses data at their disposal. They reviews staff office allocation reports that confirm the need for more office space. They recognise that the time required to complete the new office acquisition will be adequate to solve the problem since the majority of the new recruits are starting in the next three months. The financial bodies are predicting increasing growth for at least the next three years in the light of the economic recovery and the reducing cost of credit.

Looking at the issue with the *Yellow Hat*, the team sees exciting moments ahead. The benefits likely to accrue to the business will outweigh the cost of acquisition as the economy and the business are all expected to grow. If there is any prospect of economic downturn, the company is not likely to suffer from acquiring the new office space because they would have made significant profit in the three years of growth. They also have the option of freezing recruitment of new staff after three years.

When evaluating the problem from the point of view of the *Black Hat*, they have anxieties about how reliable the economic projections of the financial institutions are. Competitors could undercut prices and they might lose clients. Economic decline and intense competition may mean downsizing and hence the new office building would not be put to good use.

Thinking with the *Red Hat*, some members of the management team think acquiring the new office will mean many of the current middle managers located at their present office will have to be moved into the new office to manage the new staff, who are primarily client advisers. This change may not be well received by the affected middle managers although analyses show that the acquisition is cost effective.

With *Green Hat* thinking the management team focuses discussion around office arrangement and design to ensure efficient use and to offer a pleasant and safe working environment for staff. They further consider changes required to make their clients as comfortable as possible, and the need to ensure that if the new office is to be rented out at some point it will be attractive to other office users. They may also consider whether the possibility of redesigning their current building to increase its capacity is a viable option. They could also explore office sharing through flexible working arrangements.

The *Blue Hat* has been used by the meeting's chairperson to co-ordinate the step-by-step application of the different thinking styles. He or she may have needed to ensure that team members have equal opportunities to contribute and share ideas, and have had to build consensus when all points have been expressed.

14.2.2 LATERAL THINKING

Lateral thinking a way of thinking that explores non-conventional remedies and ideas in order to solve problems (De Bono 1970). It is a cognitive approach that sidelines the generally acceptable logical means of thinking in order to generate creative ideas. It is characterised by bringing together unfamiliar elements, looking at the other side of the coin, recombination and drilling out for new connections from existing ideas. Conceptually, it is similar to the 'Green Hat' thinking approach in the Six Thinking Hats technique discussed earlier. In the context of problem-solving, lateral thinking espouses indirect rather than direct methods to provide solutions. Flexibility is one key element in lateral thinking. It is important to emphasise that lateral thinking principles do not seek to replace logical or traditional thinking methods, but rather play a complementary role to enhance decision-making and problem-solving. Some of the operative phrases that convey the differentiation between lateral and traditional logical thinking are:

- to think of as many solution options as possible and thus go beyond the obvious or the status quo

- to avoid sequence by approaching issues from several directions (order reversal) and then linking them up

- to break down problems into as many parts as possible to give equal attention to all parts

- to encourage cross-fertilisation of ideas, where another person's idea is viewed as a different solution option from existing ones and not an opposing idea.

Thinking laterally leads to the creation of new mental representations as the problem-solver accepts all other suggested solution options, which are treated as alternatives. Lateral thinking problems are encountered in everyday life. The popular case of describing a glass half full of water as being half empty is a typical lateral thinking example. Clearly, both views are correct and applicable. Hence, from the point of view of lateral thinking the two options are not opposing views but a collection of views that offer many decision options from a variety of creative ideas. Another interesting example is where in a child custody case in the United States, the judge, in deciding how much time the children involved will spend with each parent, ruled that the children will stay at their current address but the parents will come in alternately to spend time with them.

Lateral thinking is also very useful in solving problems in management practice. This is because management problems by nature can be approached from so many perspectives. Creative solutions to management problems mostly emanate from lateral rather than vertical thinking. Think about the threat of a hung parliament prior to the 2010 election in the UK, and the solutions offered by contesting political party leaderships. A common argument was that the electorate should ensure that they voted in such way that one party would gain an absolute majority of 326 seats. Do you think the only solution was to avoid a hung parliament, or there were other means of resolving this issue?

14.2.3 STORYBOARD EXERCISE

Organisations with the history of creativity and innovation are noted for encouraging the creation of ideas, and believe in attaining competitive advantage through innovation to meet the needs of their customers (Twiss 1974). The organisation needs to be receptive to creativity and innovation if it is to unearth the potential of management and staff towards creative problem-solving. McAdam and McClelland (2002) have stressed the need to build an organisational culture which cherishes continuous generation of ideas, and always seeks to reward creativity and innovative ideas. This contextual creative environment is consistent with the social constructionist approach, which does not see a researcher and a subject differently and questions all assumptions to create knowledge.

The storyboard exercise is a planning tool that helps users to explore their creative capabilities so as to generate ideas which are expressed in both words and pictures to bridge the gap between an existing state and an expected future state. It covers the series of events that need to happen to ensure that the expected end state is achieved. It is commonly used in website design and video production. It is also used as a planning tool for learners to help them organise their thoughts to achieve a learning outcome. Project managers also use this tool to understand the various parts of the project and aid in rearranging sections of the project to achieve the total deliverables of their projects. Apart from helping the user to creatively capture an expected future state, storyboard uses pictures to connect images to words. Organisations that accept and encourage creativity would potentially benefit most from storyboard exercise.

The global pharmaceutical giant Glaxo's executive development programme epitomises the creative working environment in action. A key component of this development programme is to support Glaxo's leaders in exploring new ways of unearthing their creative potential so as to build cutting-edge competitive advantages (Godfrey 1998). For the purpose of illustration Glaxo's storyboard exercise is used to show how skills can be built from a creative activity. The expected end state in this example is a successful management career at Glaxo. (See Case Study 14.2 overleaf.)

ACTIVITY 14.2

APPLYING THE STORYBOARD EXERCISE

Using an organisation you have worked for or are familiar with, outline the benefits of the storyboard exercise for building creative skills.

STORYBOARD EXERCISE (COURTESY OF GLAXO WELLCOME)

The objectives of the storyboard activity are:

- to help participants express their future ambition
- to allow them to see the gap between current and future state
- to enable participants to generate some transitional steps
- to encourage participants to tap into their subconscious wisdom.

Storyboard activity process

Step 1: Participants are supported by a facilitator to draw a picture of the future in the designated box on the storyboard (Table 14.2).

Step 2: Participants then capture how things are at present in the box designated as the present on the storyboard.

Step 3: Transition steps are then drawn on the storyboard. It is important to note that the number of transition phases varies from one exercise to another. It is determined by both the issue that the technique is being applied to and the discretion of the individual or the team using it. In the particular case of Glaxo they created four transitional stages.

Step 4: When the storyboard is fully completed participants are then invited to share their hopes, dreams and aspirations.

Lessons

During the sharing process participants within the group are offered the opportunity to assess commonalities and differences across their views and perceptions for the present and the future of the organisation. At the individual level, participants are led on a journey to explore 'transitional steps' towards the future.

Table 14.2 The storyboard

The present	Transition 1	Transition 2
Transition 3	Transition 4	The future

14.2.4 BENCHMARKING CREATIVE LEADERSHIP SKILLS

Many organisations undertake skills audits to assess skills gaps for continuous professional development. Leadership skills are important for managers and decision-makers because they influence the acceptance and smooth implementation of decisions. One would come across various leadership attributes in management literature. Of special interest to this discussion are the common attributes for creative leadership developed by Peter Cook (1998).

Benchmarking leadership skills in terms of creativity is a novel idea proposed by the writer of this chapter to provide the reader with the opportunity to assess his or her creative leadership ability and subsequently design a plan for improvement. Benchmarking creative leadership characteristics was developed using the common attributes of creative leadership described by Cook (1998) as the criteria for leadership skills. It is envisaged that it will be beneficial to users. This exercise offers baseline criteria (Cook's (1998) six common creative leadership attributes) for personal assessment and reflection on one's creative leadership skills. The six creative leadership attributes are presented in the box below as a general measure of creativity for business leaders and decision-makers.

BOX 14.1: CREATIVE LEADERSHIP ATTRIBUTES

- Ability to set a direction that excites others, rather than bland 'mission' statements.

- Being an idea advocate, sensing and moving ideas around the organisation to attract resources and gain acceptance.

- Ability to give a tangible example for the concept that failure is a learning opportunity and encouraging risk taking.

- Ability to build teams with level of trust and conflict resolution.

- The capacity to enable others to make meaning and sense out of their environment.

- The competence to move rapidly from one role to another without losing credibility.

Source: Peter Cook (1998), *Sex, leadership and rock'n'roll*, reproduced by permission of Crown House Publishing Ltd.

Benchmarking process

A decision-maker can make a self-assessment on the scale of 1 (Low) to 5 (Very high) across the six characteristics outlined in the box above. For each attribute scored, the participant will have to cite at least two examples as evidence. A total score greater than or equal to 18 is deemed a satisfactory creative ability. A score below 18 shows a need for improvement. It is however important to undertake a thorough analysis of the relative scores for each attribute so as to be able to identify specific competences that require improvement. It is also highly recommended for individuals engaging in this activity to involve colleagues, peers, mentors, coaches or a line manager.

ACTIVITY 14.3

APPLYING CREATIVE LEADERSHIP ATTRIBUTES

Carry out an assessment of your leadership skills using Peter Cook's six creative leadership attributes, and design a personal creative leadership development plan for the next six months. It is always helpful for the effectiveness of this activity to seek the co-operation of your line manager, mentor or a colleague.

14.2.5 MENTAL IMAGERY TECHNIQUES

The essence of adopting a proactive approach to decision-making and problem-solving is reflected in how successful proactive decision-makers and organisations are relative to their less proactive counterparts. Being proactive means creating one's own circumstances by undertaking entirely new events or changing existing ones, rather than waiting to react to situations as they occur (Bateman and Crant 1999). Self-awareness, conscience, independent will and creative imagination are important personal qualities that determine how proactive a person is (Pavlina 2004). It is a common saying that being creative means being proactive. As described earlier, creativity is seen as the vehicle that generates innovative ideas to enable individuals and decision-makers to act proactively. Mental imagery techniques are used to illustrate the importance of proactive problem-solving and how it enables decision-makers to become more creative and subsequently act proactively.

Mental imagery techniques are built on the principle that people in general, and decision-makers in particular, have a natural tendency to stick to the status quo. This habit has found expressions in popular phrases such as 'stick to the knitting', 'why reinvent the wheel', 'if it's not broken why fix it', and 'a bird in the hand is worth two in the bush'. It is striking also that such tendencies cut around different cultures and jurisdictions. The limiting factor is the lack of capacity to think outside the box. This human condition is described as the inability to go outside subjectively created boundaries and is the reason why the better part of management knowledge is not used (Bennett et al 1999).

Behind this background, the proponents of mental imagery techniques advocate that creative and innovative solutions only emerge after an internal representation of the problem or issue is constructed. Therefore, the key to opening the door to stimulating imaginative thoughts is the ability to visualise and transcend personal boundaries. It is viewed as the process of integrating the right and left-brain thinking abilities. This will then release thoughts across more divergent and creative ideas.

Mental scenario rehearsal is regarded as a key activity, and it has been found to improve mental imagery. Typical examples include:

1. Many athletes mentally practise their events either the night before the competition or minutes before they participate in it (McWhirter and McWhirter 1985).

2. Taking a mental walk through a presentation as part of preparation has proven to enhance the presenter's knowledge and the quality of responses to questions during the actual presentation session (Bennett et al 1999).

3. It is common for an individual to mentally picture walking around the house to answer a question as to the number of windows there is in it (Bennett et al 1999).

4. Many a prospective bride and groom have drawn on their mental imagery to visualise themselves at the altar (Moulton and Kosslyn 2009), and how their great day will look to ensure that everything is in place for the occasion.

These examples show that mental imagery is a common activity. However, it seems that the benefits have been overlooked or not appreciated. This is because of the lack of understanding of its usefulness to creative decision-making and problem-solving. Mental imagery brings together a variety of cognitive processes such as opinions, perceptions, memory, and voluntary and involuntary actions and thoughts (Hunt 1985) to indirectly observe a behaviour scenario. The direct effects of these processes are observed in the quality of ideas generated to solve problems.

Individuals, and especially management decision-makers, stand to gain a lot from practising mental imagery. In fact, management skills taught in the various business schools follow the theoretical concepts of management functions, namely planning, controlling, organising, communicating, staffing, problem-solving and leading. In reality, management practice takes place mostly outside the school setting, where managers undertake a specific task. Therefore, the development of mental imagery techniques would enhance management performance because they address real management challenges. It is also important to note that it is safe, convenient, not time bound and a less expensive means to enhance management performance.

ACTIVITY 14.4

APPLYING MENTAL IMAGERY TECHNIQUES

On the basis of your understanding of mental imagery write a brief outline of how imagery can help in your personal development. Indicate how imagery can help you overcome your personal assumptions and biases to become more creative in decision-making and problem-solving.

14.2.6 BUZAN'S MIND MAPPING TECHNIQUE

The Mind Map is one of the most effective thinking tools to enhance creativity and communication for decision-making as well problem-solving. It helps both individuals and organisations to improve learning, efficiency and productivity. The Mind Map is a graphical expression of connected thought processes that begins from a central point. It 'creates an exterior mirror of what is happening inside the mind during ideas generation, and repeats and mimics thought processes and amplifies the functions of the brain' (Buzan 2010, p31).

The developing Mind Map shown in Figure 14.1 expresses the author's thoughts whilst generating ideas on what makes employees happy.

The developing Mind Map starts from a central image (a), which in this illustration is an image representing a happy staff. The next stage (b) shows initial four basic ideas on what makes employees happy. It then expands the four initial ideas to another level of branches shown in (c), and further sub-branches in (d) and (e). Examples of fully completed Mind Maps can be found at www.iMindMap.com and www.novamind.com.

Figure 14.1 Graphical illustration of a developing Mind Map

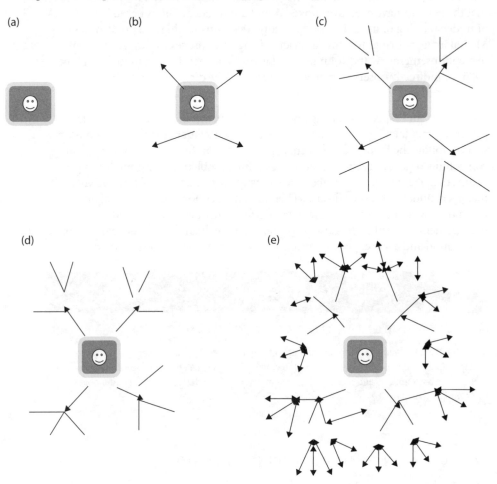

14.2.6.1 Key principles behind Mind Mapping

The Mind Mapping technique relies on research into understanding the nature and operations of the human brain and its potential to boost memory by enhancing receiving, holding, analysing and controlling information (Buzan 2010). Of special interest to this section are two of such principles stemming from how the human brain thinks:

- Mind Mapping is underpinned by the principle that the human brain thinks multilaterally and not linearly or sequentially like a computer (Buzan 2010). Therefore, the Mind Map follows the same pattern as the brain by creating branches outwards to form sub-branches and in so doing creating more ideas. The connection of thoughts in a multilateral thinking pattern of the brain is followed in Mind Mapping. This is achieved through linking all ideas on the Mind Map, which provides good understanding and insight through associations. Many people who have adopted Mind Mapping techniques have found that word association is a key to generate more ideas. It is likened to online searches where finding and reading a piece of information leads to others. Mind Mapping applies this same principle to trigger avenues for linkages to ensure a free flow of ideas.

- Mind Mapping also relies heavily on the fact that human beings think with images and their associations and not in words as presumed for so many years. It must however be emphasised that the period prior to print technology depended heavily on images, signs and symbols for communication. According to Buzan (2010) the words we use are just the vehicles that covey our images out from our own minds to other peoples' minds. This has been confirmed by many research findings that found the human brain is able to efficiently recognise images in three-dimensional space. Buzan (2010) further asserts that pictures are more important than words when it comes to the effective functioning of the mind because they make use colour, form, line, dimension, texture, visual rhythm and imagination. This is another reason why Mind Mapping places emphasis on the use of images instead of words.

ACTIVITY 14.5

APPLYING MIND MAPPING

Use plain paper and coloured pens for this exercise. In the middle of one piece of paper write the name of your organisation or an organisation that you are familiar with. Around the name write out words that you associate with your organisation. At the centre of another piece of plain sheet use the coloured pens to draw an image of what the organisation looks like. Out of this image draw, with different coloured pens, thick branches to represent each of the words you associate with your organisation. On each branch draw an image that you think best represents the word you associate with that branch.

It is envisaged that this exercise will give you a basic introduction to Mind Mapping and also provide you with an opportunity to compare how your mind perceives what you have represented in words and images. Using two sheets of paper ensures that you start both the word and image representations from the centre of the page.

Mind Mapping can be applied to personal life, learning and work. This section is interested in how the application of Mind Map techniques can improve work through management decision-making and problem-solving. It is particularly helpful to decision-making and problem-solving because it sets out the needs, expectations, preferences and challenges of the decision-maker. It ensures decisions are made on the basis of a clear understanding of matters at stake. The following discussion will focus on how mind mapping helps in making simple as well as complex decisions.

The Mind Mapping technique follows a set of guidelines in making a simple dyadic decision involving clear cut choices like: Yes or No, Viable or Not viable, Good or Bad, Beneficial or Not beneficial, and Appropriate or Inappropriate.

The process begins with a central image, followed by drawing main branches and then sub-branches as shown in the graphical illustration of a developing Mind Map above (Figure 14.1). Having reported and expressed all ideas, emotions and thoughts across the main and all sub-branches of the Mind Map, five methods are used to arrive at a decision (see Buzan 2010, pp101–102). Note that these methods can be used in a sequential manner; that is to say the second, third, fourth or fifth method is used only when the preceding one does not yield a decision. These decision-making methods from Mind Mapping are: the process-generated method, number-weighting, intuition, incubation and option if the weightings are equal (Buzan 2010).

- In the *process-generated* method a decision emerges as the Mind Map developer (decision-maker) gets a clearer picture from the ideas gathered and presented in the Mind Map. The decision becomes obvious from the detailed overview. Take note that this is dyadic decision-making using the Mind Map created.

- The *number-weighting* method is applied if a decision has not emerged at the end of the Mind Map development. With this method every specific word on all sides of the Mind Map is assigned a number from 1 to 100. Scores are then added for both 'yes' and 'no' sides. The side with the highest score wins. That is, the decision option corresponding to the highest score is adopted. When this second method does not also work the third one is used.

- With the *intuition method*, the decision-maker's gut feeling determines the decision. Traditionally, intuition has played a key role in decision-making in crisis management, in situations of uncertainty and when there is a lot of data to be processed (Patton 2003, Novicevic et al 2002). What is unique about intuition application for decision-making through Mind Mapping is that Mind Maps provides a large pool of information that serves as a background for intuitive decision.

- The decision-maker activates the *incubation method* when the first three have failed to yield a decision. It is a simple approach whereby the decision-maker takes a break to allow the brain to 'incubate' the idea. It is a fact that the human brain generates ideas and decisions when at rest. It is expected that through such a resting phase a decision will emerge.

- Beyond incubation, is a basic coin tossing or balloting approach (*option* if weightings are equal method), which is used to make a choice as any of the alternatives is deemed satisfactory. The clue here is for the decision-maker to assess his/her reaction to the outcome of the coin tossing or balloting: that is, seeing whether your initial reaction is a feeling of disappointment or of relief will help you confirm whether the outcome reflects your true feeling.

The Mind Mapping technique does not rule out indecision after all the five methods have been exhausted. However, the occurrence of indecision is rare. If it happens, then a third decision option –'Continue thinking about the choice' – ensues, in addition to Yes and No options, and therefore the nature of the decision is no longer dyadic but triadic (three-option).

The key to using Mind Maps to tackle complex decisions is an improved ability to choose relevant 'basic ordering ideas' in good time. The basic ordering ideas are the main branches that are drawn from the central image. Buzan (2010, p105) recommends choosing a maximum of seven basic ordering ideas because the average human brain 'cannot hold more than seven major items of information in its short-term memory'. He further recommends 11 basic ordering ideas that are helpful in developing good Mind Maps. The cautionary rule is that a maximum of seven can be chosen for each Mind Map and this means that you choose the ones that best reflect the subject.

The 11 basic ordering ideas suggested by Buzan (2010, p105) are as follows:

- **Basic questions**: how/when/where/why/what/who/which.
- **Divisions**: chapters/lessons/themes.
- **Properties**: Characteristics of things.
- **History**: chronological sequence of events.
- **Structure**: forms of things.
- **Function**: what things do?
- **Process**: how things work.
- **Evaluation**: how good/worthwhile/beneficial things are.
- **Classification**: how things are related to each other.
- **Definitions**: what things mean.
- **Personalities**: what roles/characters people have.

When you have mastered generating basic ordering ideas, you can then take the steps outlined earlier to create a Mind Map that will aid in decision-making to tackle complex decisions. Mind Mapping techniques can be applied to enhance many other management activities such as presentation and meetings. The coverage in this chapter serves as an introduction to draw the reader's attention to the enormous possibilities of developing Mind Mapping skills.

ACTIVITY 14.6

MIND MAP ABOUT STAFF WELFARE

Imagine you have been asked for advice by management on the key issues to be considered in the design of new staff welfare package for your department. Outline the relevant basic ordering ideas (main branches) to be drawn from the central image (staff welfare), which you find suitable for the design of a mind map.

14.2.7 PARETO ANALYSIS

This analytical technique thrives on the principle that the majority of the problems that organisations face, especially in the area of quality management, are generated by a minority of problems which are the key causes of the entire set of problems (Craft and Leake 2002). This is expressed as the '80/20 rule', whose central idea is that when a decision-maker is able to identify the few major problems (20 per cent) and provides the appropriate solutions, that will enhance the chance of successfully dealing with the entire problem set (Kock 2007). This tool is also referred to as the 'law of vital few' (Daniel 1983). It was developed by the renowned quality management consultant J.M. Juran and named after Vilfredo Pareto, an eminent Italian economist (Craft and Leake 2002). Pareto analysis has been applied to other disciplines over time. In business, Pareto principles tie in nicely with the business idea that 80 per cent of an organisation's sales is generated from 20 per cent of its customers (Guerreiro et al 2008). Pareto analysis can be useful to both a decision-making team and a manager to ensure that they concentrate their efforts on the major key problems (Craft and Leake 2002). The technique becomes the important next step after a cause-and-effect analysis to determine how often the varieties of problems occur.

We will use the example below to demonstrate how decision-makers can apply the principle to decision-making processes. This guides the reader through applying the tool to a typical decision-making scenario.

 LABOUR TURNOVER: AN ILLUSTRATION

CASE STUDY 14.3

Background

A newly appointed human resource manager has found that the organisation has experienced increased labour turnover for the past five years. In view of this she has commissioned a piece of research to help identify the causes of the problem in order to address it.

Feedback from a survey conducted on current and some former employees indicated that seven causes (a, b, c, d, e, f, g) listed below account for the high turnover rate. The accompanying scores on the scale of 1 to 20 also indicates the importance the respondents attached to the factor as contributing to staff not completing their contracts with the organisation.

(a) Low morale due to lack of teamwork (2).

(b) Excessive bureaucracy (2).

(c) Poor communication between management and operational staff (3).

(d) Lack of performance incentives (3).

(e) Absence of a flexible working arrangement (1).

(f) Limited opportunities to acquire new skills (17).

(g) Absence of a clear staff development policy (13).

The causes identified in the survey were grouped under main three headings namely:

- **Lack of staff training and development:** Limited opportunities to acquire new skills (f) and Absence of a clear staff development policy (g).

- **Poor reward systems:** Lack of performance incentives (d).

- **Inappropriate work practices:** Low morale due to lack of teamwork (a), Excessive bureaucracy (b), Poor communication between management and operational staff (c) and Absence of a flexible working arrangement (e).

The groups and the respective scores expressed in percentages are presented in Table 14.3.

A careful observation of the nature of these causes show that issues relating to staff training and development contribute largely to the high turnover rate. When the management team concentrates attention on continuous professional development, close to 73 per cent of the problems will be resolved. It is also expected that when staff training and development help improve staff skills and confidence, their performance will also improve. With improved performance management could

Table 14.3 Causes of high turnover

Group	Complementary causes	Total score (%)
Lack of staff training and development	f and g	30 (73%)
Poor reward system	d	1 (2%)
Inappropriate work practices	a, b, c & e	10 (24%)

afford an attractive reward package to help retain staff. This initial action could be followed up with a review of current work practices to embrace flexibility, improve communication and encourage better teamwork. Thus, by applying Pareto analysis the decision-maker can concentrate on training and development as an immediate priority instead of focusing attention on all the causes identified by current and former employees.

ACTIVITY 14.7

APPLYING PARETO ANALYSIS

Using the interview results presented in Table 14.4 below on a sample of 50 users and 20 staff members of an Accident and Emergency section of a health centre, apply Pareto analysis to determine the key causes/problems (20 per cent) to solve. Recommend the important change(s) to be made given reasons for your suggestions.

Table 14.4 Interview results

Possible causes of long waiting times	Percentage of total	Possible causes of long waiting times	Percentage of total
Policies require excess information on users	01	A&E personnel have insufficient training	02
Policies require complicated procedures	01	A&E personnel aren't motivated	01
Too much paperwork	02	A&E personnel are careless	01
Not enough funding	02	A&E personnel don't follow the schedule	16
Inadequate planning of activities	13	Users forget ID cards	01
Inadequate policies	02	Users don't follow instructions	02
A&E personnel have no tea breaks	02	Users are uncooperative	01
A&E personnel have other jobs	02	Delay in handing over data within the department	14
A&E personnel lack punctuality	06	Outdated methods	12
		Lack of automation	08
		Procedures take too long	11

14.2.8 PLUS—MINUS—INTERESTING (PMI) TECHNIQUE

The Plus–Minus–Interesting (PMI) technique is a straightforward but very useful tool which enables a decision-maker to judge the value of a decision option after assessing the positive and negative effects and the implications of the decision. Although it utilises subjective scores on pros and cons to evaluate decision implications, it is another useful tool developed by Edward de Bono to highlight the possible risks and benefits of a decision prior to its implementation (Mind Tools 2009).

Steps to use PMI (Mind Tools 2009)

1. Draw a table with the headings Plus, Minus and Interesting.

2. State all positive effects under the Plus column, negative effects under the Minus column, and the implications of the decision under the Interesting column.

3. A trend may emerge at this stage, suggesting whether to go ahead with the decision or consider an alternative. The decision rule at this stage is to observe and compare the number of pluses and minuses.

4. If no clear trend emerges, then consider assigning scores between 1 and 10; positive for points under the Plus column and negatives under the Minus column. State the total marks for positive and negative under plus and minus tables and state the total score under interesting as well.

5. Sum up scores which will reflect either a 'strong positive' or 'strong negative' score to inform decision direction.

Consider the example below to illustrate the use of PMI technique.

ACTIVITY 14.8

APPLYING THE PMI TECHNIQUE

Imagine the appraisal report on the middle managers of your organisation has revealed an urgent need for postgraduate study in management to enable them take up senior management positions in the future. Management need to choose between granting postgraduate study leave (full time) and a part-time option (day release plus weekend) option. Design a PMI table to reflect the possible Plus, Minus and Interesting factors and suggest an option to management.

14.3 CREATIVE TEAM-BASED DECISION-MAKING AND PROBLEM-SOLVING TECHNIQUES

It is worth noting that all the techniques already discussed can be used in both individual and team or group contexts. The following discussion on creative team-based decision-making and problem-solving will be restricted to techniques that are only applicable in a team or group setting.

CASE STUDY 14.4

HOSPITALITY SERVICES — AN ILLUSTRATION

A growing hospitality services provider in the Midlands is deciding where to locate a branch in south east England. The choice is between a big city and a rural setting, and managers are inclined towards a big-city branch. A PMI table is designed to consider this option under the headings Plus, Minus and Interesting.

The PMI table score reads 17 (Plus) – 10 (Minus) + 1 (Interesting) = (+ 8)

By referring to the steps suggested by Mind Tools (2009) above, the PMI table is interpreted as follows. Firstly, without recourse to the scores we assess whether a clear decision emerges after completing the plus, minus and interesting columns. Comparing the three points raised under plus and the four under minus, it does not appear there is a clear decision. This is because minuses like noise pollution and less parking space could be controls to a large extent. We will now move to the second stage where we will factor the score into making a decision. The PMI table score shows a positive balance of eight. We conclude that, for this hospitality services provider in the Midlands, the benefits of locating the south east England branch in a big city are greater than those of locating it in a rural setting.

Table 14.5   PMI Table to aid location decision-making for a hospitality services provider

Plus	Minus	Interesting
Vibrant business environment in the city (+7)	High property rental and council tax (−4)	Attract more customers? (+4)
Easier to partner and network with related businesses (+4)	More noise pollution (−2)	Increased profit level? (−1)
Good transport and communication facilities (+6)	No countryside attractions (−2)	Staff relocation? (−2)
	Less space, eg parking restrictions (−2)	
+17	-10	+1

Creative knowledge is essential for development of new products and services, and for solving complex business problems. One way to approach such tasks is through the use of problem-solving teams. However, creative and team-based decision-making presents a different challenge to decision-makers because of the need to have a cutting-edge decision and also build consensus among the entire team.

Two key features of creative and team-based decision-making and problem-solving techniques are:

- The elements of creativity and innovation are embedded in them (Cook 1998).

- They provide a broad acceptability among all stakeholders (team) to facilitate a decision's implementation (McAdam and McClelland 2002).

This is another reason why creative team-based decision-making tools and guidelines are essential in enhancing decision-makers' skills. Group decision-making is constrained by struggle for recognition, a feeling of intimidation on the part of less vocal team members leading to non-contribution, destructive attitudes and excessive criticism. To illustrate this point we will explore the following examples of group decision-making approaches and guidelines:

- the stepladder technique
- brainstorming skills
- group decision facilitation skills.

14.3.1 THE STEPLADDER TECHNIQUE

This is a group decision-making technique which helps to minimise the tendency for team members not to contribute to the decision-making process (Orpen 1995, Mind Tools 2009). Through this technique team members are given the opportunity to make inputs to the decision-making process in their individual capacities before any group interaction begins. The stepladder technique thus ensures the decision-making process is more enriched with a diversity of ideas (Orpen 1995).

14.3.1.1 How to apply the stepladder technique

This is a straightforward tool that follows four simple steps (see Orpen 1995, Mind Tools 2009):

1. **Task administration prior to group meeting.** At this first stage, the issue for discussion is given out in good time for each member to think through it and develop a possible solution.

2. **Group formation stage**. Forming the groups begins with the pairing of two members who discuss the problem and come up with their provisional decision.

3. **Additional member introduction.** A third member is introduced to the existing two-member group. The new member shares his/her ideas and the three collectively discuss their ideas and select a provisional decision. A fourth member is then introduced and the process is repeated, and this continues until all team members have joined.

4. **Final collective decision-making stage**. At this stage the whole group engages in a final discussion and the final decision is taken.

ACTIVITY 14.9

APPLYING THE STEPLADDER TECHNIQUE

As part of a four-member group, apply the stepladder technique above to explore the challenges that global economic recession pose to human resource management. Provide specific examples to support your point of view. Make recommendations as to how human resource practitioners can face these challenges through continuous professional development.

14.3.2 BRAINSTORMING SKILLS

Brainstorming is a common but important technique used to generate verbal ideas among groups or teams involved in decision-making and problem-solving (see also Chapter 16). The rules outlined below illustrate the key features, merits and demerits of brainstorming. The rationale for its use is to ensure total involvement of all group members in the decision-making process. Its usage is traced back to Alex Osborn's *Applied Imagination*, published in 1962.

Osborn's rules for brainstorming technique, cited by Stech and Ratliffe (1985) are:

- Criticism is ruled out. Both positive and negative evaluation of ideas must be withheld during the brainstorming process.

- 'Free-wheeling' is encouraged. The wilder the idea, the better. It is much easier to tame down than to think up an idea.

- Quantity is encouraged. The greater the number of ideas, the greater the likelihood that several of them will be workable.

- Combinations of ideas are encouraged. The participants may combine two or more stated ideas in still another idea.

- 'Hitchhiking' is encouraged. This involves suggesting an idea similar to or triggered by someone else's idea.

The brainstorming technique is noted for generating loads of ideas. It is less expensive and requires a moderate amount of time relative to other idea-generating techniques. However, creating many ideas without first screening is seen as a big demerit of the brainstorming technique. Nonetheless, it is very useful in small teams which are homogenous in status. You may also come across 'brainwriting' as another technique for group decision-making; this differs from brainstorming because it encourages silent generation of ideas in writing whilst brainstorming requires a verbal discussion of ideas with others (Wilson and Hanna 1990).

14.3.3 GROUP DECISION-MAKING AND PROBLEM-SOLVING FACILITATION SKILLS

The above guidelines for group decision-making and problem-solving have highlighted the importance of decision-making teams (see also Chapters 6 and 16). But effective group decision-making thrives on excellent group-facilitation skills. Some of the characteristics associated with disorganised decision-making groups are lack of direction and focus, boredom, apathy, and absence of motivation and commitment. The major source of these problems is poor facilitation skills on the part of managers. There is also evidence that the role of facilitation among UK businesses is changing (Berry 1993). In addition to acquiring skills through creative and team-based decision-making techniques, it is important for decision-makers involved in group decision-making and problem-solving to be conversant with tested facilitation guidelines.

A useful example of such guidelines for facilitating a group problem-solving session is that of Nelson and McFadzean (1998), which covers the tasks and responsibilities of the facilitator during the pre-planning session, group session, post-session report and post-session review. They suggested among other things that during pre-planning sessions the facilitator should be conversant with problem-solving techniques, consult on the agenda and structure it accordingly, design standards and meeting procedures, and understand group dynamics. At group sessions, they recommend that the facilitator promotes teamwork, is flexible and neutral, and gives feedback from previous sessions. At this stage communication and presentation skills are important for the success of the session. Post-session reports should describe the outcome of the session and issues to be followed up, and provide an implementation timetable. A post-session review is also suggested for the facilitator to reflect on the meeting and find out areas that may need to change for future sessions.

ACTIVITY 14.10

TEAM FACILITATION

Investigate the team-facilitation activities undertaken in your organisation or an organisation with which you are familiar.

- Tabulate team facilitation activities undertaken by your decision-making team or management team under the headings: Pre-planning session, Group session, Post-session report and Post-session review.

- Report on any difference in activities between your team and those suggested by McFadzean and Nelson (1998), and explain why there are differences in activities.

14.3.4 FACILITATOR COMPETENCES

In addition to knowing and understanding the variety of activities involved in group-facilitation processes, it is important for managers and meeting facilitators to appreciate the salient attributes of a team facilitator. Knowing these attributes helps in two ways. Firstly, the team leader or facilitator can carry out a self-assessment on the specific attributes, discover gaps and then work on those areas so as to be a better facilitator. Secondly, it is usually assumed that once a person is appointed into a managerial position, he/she will be able to effectively facilitate meetings and group discussions. This is particularly true for organisations that appoint senior managers on the basis of their qualification and experience in the organisation and not necessarily their management experience, or for that matter team facilitation skill. Development of group or team-facilitation skills does not appear to be a common training programme offered to new managers across the world. Mosaic Management Consulting Group's key team-facilitation competences (Nelson and McFadzean 1998) outlined in the box below is a good example to study.

BOX 14.2: FACILITATOR COMPETENCES

- **Understanding context**: understanding of problem-solving theories, methodologies and techniques, business environments, particular problem situations and why they arise, learning processes, and group dynamics.

- **Technical competences**: time management, planning and preparation; management and use of visual aids; managing physical environment; management and use of computer-based group decision support tools; the use of integrated software packages to feedback/present information and produce post-group-session reports.

- **Rational competences**: objectivity, judgement, making rapid and quality decisions, and being specific.

- **Interpersonal competences**: communication (verbal and non-verbal); active listening and hearing; clarifying, questioning, summarising; persuasiveness; emphatic, respectful elicitation of information; observation; presentation and feedback.

- **Task process competences**: development of a structured group problem-solving agenda; guidance and support throughout the whole problem-solving process; flexibility, going with the flow; process intervention management; and action and results orientation; establishing expectations, maintaining focus; pacing and congratulating people.

- **Human process competences**: establishing trust; conflict resolution and management; management of internal group relations, treating people as equals, recognising and respecting differences, addressing people's fears; and positively confronting difficult issues.

- **Personal characteristics**: ability to learn, friendliness, tact, sensitivity, sincerity, intellectual agility, genuineness, sense of humour, self-awareness, modesty, emotional stability, humanity and integrity.

ACTIVITY 14.11

DEVELOPING TEAM FACILITATION SKILLS

Justify the inclusion of understanding context and personal characteristics as essential elements to consider in developing team facilitation skills.

14.4 ETHICAL CONSIDERATIONS IN DECISION-MAKING

The point has been made about the challenges confronting decision-makers in today's competitive business environment. The challenge is exacerbated when the decisions to be made and problems being resolved border on ethical considerations. In the light of this, decision-makers require the same level of understanding and skills to help solve ethical dilemmas which are encountered regularly in management and other decision-making contexts. In fact, however, ethical decision-making techniques have not received a lot of attention in management training programmes. Most of the discussions have centred around general ethical guidelines and research findings on the views of decision-makers on the subject. For an illustration, we will consider conclusions of an ethical decision-making strategies model (Holian 2002, p866) which is based on practising managers' experiences of and views on ethical decision-making. This model is very useful because the study on which it is based combined intensive case studies involving over 200 managers and in-depth interviews of 39 managers from 32 organisations in Australia. This model categorises skills related to ethical decision-making and problem-solving into four classes.

These skills categories are:

- judgement
- integrity
- courage
- humanity.

A combination of these skills lead to four distinctive ethical decision-making approaches: namely, the legalistic, entrepreneurial, navigation, and worried modes (Holian 2002), as outlined in Figure 14.2.

Figure 14.2 Holian's model of ethical decision-making strategies

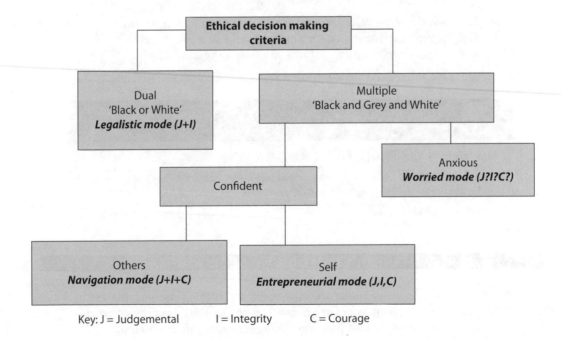

14.4.1 Model interpretation

According to the model when a decision-maker is faced with making an ethical decision where the issues involved are clear (dual: black or white), the best option to consider is the legalistic mode. Under this condition, managerial elements at play are judgement and integrity. When the issues are not that clear cut, then the decision-maker may assume the entrepreneurial mode and make a decision by combining the three elements of judgemental, integrity and courage. The other option under this scenario is to take the navigation mode by involving others in the decision. The 'worried' mode ensues when the decision-maker is anxious because the issues are not clear.

Examples of high-profile management decisions that made the headlines in the first quarter of the year 2010 in the UK include:

- Four hundred Cadbury workers were sacked one week after Kraft had taken over Cadbury with the promise to keep the factory open in the UK. Clearly, the new management would have taken a look at the ethical implications of their decision, which fell within the multiple (black and grey and white) domain. They however, decided to apply the judgemental, integrity and courage entrepreneurial mode, knowing very well the consequence of their actions. Kraft management could have reclined into a worried mode by delaying making a decision.

- Another example is the resignation of Lord Triesman – former England Football Association (FA) boss – after publication of his accusation that Spain and Russia had engaged in bribery, though in a private conversation. Once the issue was out, it was clearly in a black and white domain. Thus, the FA's trustees rightly compelled him to leave. If he had persisted they would have exercised a legalistic mode to get him out to save the FA and England's bid to host 2018 World Cup.

- The court ruling on British Airways (BA) cabin crew strike as illegal on technical grounds is another interesting case. Consider how the elements (judgment, integrity, courage and humanity) informed this (see also Case study 7.3):
  - BA management's decision to seek a court order to restrain cabin crew from embarking on strike
  - The decision by the cabin crew's union to embark on a strike at the time of peak holiday travels of BA passengers.

Decision-makers in the 'worried mode' are challenged by generating decision options because they focus more on the ethical problems than on finding solutions. Whereas judgement and integrity are classified as prime requirements for ethical decision-making, courage is seen as a necessary precursor. Excessive use of the legalistic mode for ethical decision-making could be problematic because it cannot be said in all cases that a course of action that is legal is also ethical. The rule of thumb here is for managers and decision-makers to make decisions that are sensitive to ethical ramifications, and to temper judgement and integrity modes with courage and humanity, in order to minimise worry, delays and resentment about ethical decisions.

In addition to making ethical decisions by looking at the clarity or otherwise of the issues at stake, managers will find that ethical decisions are influenced by the prevailing conditions. These include the perceived opportunity to commit an unethical act, the perceived incentive for the individual to commit an unethical act (the magnitude of the personal gain envisaged if the unethical act is committed), and the perceived risk of being caught (Perri et al 2009). Perri et al used ethics-based scenarios that mimic real-life ethical choices to help explain the personal factors that precipitate an ethical dilemma and influence ethical decision-making. The lesson here is that managers or decision-makers need to recognise that their personal views and ideas about business ethics play a key role in helping them resolve ethical dilemmas in decision-making and problem-solving. One way of ensuring that personal ethical opinions do not unduly influence decisions is for managers to review their ethical positions in line with corporate and industry ethical standards.

ACTIVITY 14.12

SAMPLE SCENARIO FOR PRACTICE

You are the executive director of a human resource management consultancy. Numerous recruitment agents regularly contact your organisation to encourage the placement of their professionals with leading financial institutions whose recruitment and selection is handled by your company. Your organisation has just placed three professionals from a new recruitment agent with two leading financial institutions. The new agent passed by your office, and as a way of showing his appreciation for placing his professionals, and knowing you are a big fan of the hometown professional football team Sunderland, offers you a ticket to Sunderland's next home game. Your company's code of practice prohibits any employee from accepting gifts beyond a value of £20, but there is almost no chance that anyone would find out about you accepting the ticket (which has a face value of £40). Given the circumstances, would you accept the offer? Please indicate your choice from among the following alternatives and give reasons for your answer.

definitely yes		probably yes	
probably no		definitely no	

14.5 APPROACHES AND GUIDELINES TO COMMUNICATING DECISIONS

A creative and innovative decision which can be described as 'good' may not succeed if it is poorly communicated and justified to stakeholders. Management is in essence an act of communication, for management processes are linked to the receipt of information and its valid interpretation which results in effective decision-making (David 1995). Satisfaction with management communication has been reported to be strongly related to staff responses (positive or negative) to organisational change (Nelissen and van Selm 2008). Effective communication is vital for all aspects/stages of decision-making and problem-solving. Keeping in line with basic principles of communication – such as ensuring relevance and accessibility, and being as precise as possible – is always a sensible thing to do when communicating decisions. But it must be emphasised that different decisions may require different approaches to communicate and justify them. Sample guidelines and warnings about communicating decisions are explored in this section.

There are traditional means of communicating decisions across businesses and work groups such letters, minutes, memos and reports. With the turn of the millennium however, electronic systems of communication have become the most common means of communication. It is against this background that a conscious effort is required on the part of decision-makers to ensure a good balance between modern means of communication and the more traditional ones. This has become important because there is an evolving communication culture of overdependence on electronic systems, for example e-mail, to the exclusion of achieving greater impact through simple but extremely effective means such as speaking and listening to stakeholders. Christopher Connolly of Sporting Bodymind Ltd, a leading teambuilding and organisational development consultancy, strongly recommends that decision-makers must be at the forefront of efforts to develop the personal communication skills of stakeholders to enable them participate effectively in information exchange (Connolly 1996). Core interpersonal skills essential in the decision-communication mix include listening, questioning and giving feedback to ensure that all stakeholders accept joint ownership of the decision (Connolly 1996).

Another discipline that can potentially enable modern decision-makers to communicate their decisions effectively is communication ethics. This is a vehicle that provides a language to build trust in shared knowledge and in relations between organisations and people (Beckett 2003). Being conversant with and skilful in communication ethics will help decision-makers to evaluate their decisions for their ethical content. The result of such an evaluation will inform the choice of language and other communication processes to ensure the clarity and acceptability of decisions.

Effectively communicating decisions among business teams is absolutely essential. In terms of cost, speed and time, modern communication methods have huge advantages over the traditional ones. Yet it still appears that simple personal and team communication skills – such as taking ample time to listen and offer the appropriate feedback – are very effective in achieving corporate ownership of decisions for successful implementation. This highlights the need for decision-makers and managers to be conversant with the use of both modern and traditional communication methods. A good blend is recommended.

ACTIVITY 14.13

REVIEWING COMMUNICATION

In the light of the above discussion, undertake a review of the communication methods used by your organisation in communicating decisions and make recommendations for improvement.

ACTIVITY 14.14

REFLECTIVE ACTIVITY

How do the techniques and skills covered in this chapter relate to your job role and responsibilities?

Can you identify specific area(s) of your work that could benefit from the application of any of the skills and techniques outlined in this chapter?

Which of these techniques, tools and guidelines would you recommend to your colleagues, working group or organisation to be incorporated or adopted for their continuous professional development?

Reflect on the potential benefits that your knowledge and acquisition of specific decision-making and problem-solving techniques could bring to your professional career and organisational development.

Using the skills pool identified across the various techniques and tools covered in this chapter, carry out a decision-making and problem-solving skills audit. Identify the skills that you posses at present and others that you think are lacking, and classify them as 'decision-making and problem-solving skills gaps.

Set out a decision-making and problem-solving skills and techniques development plan for yourself by outlining which skills you require, when you need them, and how you can acquire them and master their use. Indicate how you intend to monitor your skills acquisition and implementation plan to ensure progress.

14.6 CONCLUSION

The chapter has shown that the amount and variety of decision-making skills and techniques that a manager or a decision-maker possesses will determine the level of achievement of organisational and career goals. The chapter has covered the Six Thinking Hats and lateral thinking, storyboard exercises, benchmarking creative leadership skills, mental imagery techniques, mind mapping technique, Pareto analysis, and the Plus–Minus–Interesting (PMI) technique as key creative techniques of decision-making and problem-solving. It has also explored exclusively team-based techniques, comprising the stepladder technique, brainstorming skills and group-facilitation skills. Guidelines and techniques beneficial to resolving ethical dilemmas and communicating decisions have also been addressed. Clearly, placing the acquisition and practice of decision-making and problem-solving skills at the centre of continuous professional development is the best way forward for management professionals and organisations to achieve corporate success, career aspirations and sustainability.

PAUSE FOR THOUGHT

Identify at least three things that you have learned by studying this chapter and engaging with the activities. How will your newly acquired knowledge and skills support your continuing professional development? What value do you expect your learning to have for your daily routines and your further career? In what area have you identified a need for further development and how are you planning to fill that gap? Address these issues in your learning journal and/or CPD log. You may also wish to discuss them with a peer, colleague, mentor or coach to aid your further development.

KEY LEARNING POINTS

- The capacity of managers to use effective and efficient decision-making and problem-solving skills and techniques is important to their professional career success and the performance of the organisations they represent.

- The acquisition and practice of decision-making and problem-solving skills are central elements for effective human resource development, and for that matter continuous professional development programmes.

- Despite the peculiarities surrounding their operations, De Bono's Thinking Hats and lateral thinking, storyboard exercises, mental imagery techniques and Buzan's mind mapping techniques enhance one's capacity to make innovative and effective decisions and resolve problems creatively. They are applicable in both personal and group decision-making and problem-solving contexts.

- Pareto analysis and Plus-Minus-Interesting (PMI) techniques and skills prepare managers to be able to reduce risks and enhance the rewards accrued from the decisions they make.

- Benchmarking creative leadership skills, the stepladder technique, brainstorming skills, and group-decision-facilitation skills are core skills and techniques for effective team decision-making and problem resolution.

- Being familiar with guidelines and acquiring skills in dealing with ethical dilemmas is the best way to minimise anxiety and worry, delays and resentment towards decisions. Communicating techniques and skills are the means to build trust in shared knowledge and in strengthening relations between organisations and their staff.

EXPLORE FURTHER

Books and other works of E. Paul Torrance provide a good source of materials for further reading on lateral and creative thinking.

The 80/20 principle: the secret to achieving more with less by Richard Kock, 2nd edition (2007, London: Nicholas Brealey) is recommended for further reading of the 80/20 principle.

Wilson and Hanna's work on *Groups in context* (1990, New York: McGraw-Hill) is a good source for further reading on brainwriting.

Papers in the *Journal of Communication Management* are recommended for further reading, particularly Beckett (2003).

14.7 REFERENCES

BATEMAN, T. and CRANT, J.M. (1999) Proactive behaviour: meaning, impact, recommendations. *Business Horizons*. Vol. 42, No. 3, pp63–70.

BECKETT, R. (2003) Communication ethics: Principle and practice, *Journal of Communication Management*. Vol. 8, No. 1; pp41–52.

BENNETT, R.H., WHEATLEY, W.J., and MADDOX, E.N. (1999) The mind's eye and the practice of management, *Management Decision*. Vol. 32, No. 2, pp21–29.

BERRY, M. (1993) Changing perspectives on facilitation skills development. *Journal of European Industrial Training*, Vol. 17, No. 3, pp23–32.

BUZAN, T. (2010) *The Mind Map book*. Harlow: Educational Publishers LLP.

CONNOLLY, C. (1996) Communication: getting to the heart of the matter. *Management Development Review*. Vol. 9, No. 7, pp37–40.

COOK, P. (1998) The creativity advantage. *Industrial and Commercial Training*. Vol. 13, No. 5, pp179–184.

CRAFT, R.C and LEAKE, C. (2002) The Pareto principle in organisational decision-making. *Management Decision*. Vol. 40, No.8. pp729–733.

DANIEL, E.A. (1983) Quality control of documents. *Library Trends*. Vol. 41, No. 4, pp644–708.

DAVID, W. (1995) *Managing company wide communication*. New York: Chapman & Hall.

DE BONO, E. (1970) *Lateral thinking: creativity step by step*. New York: Harper & Row.

DE BONO, E. (2000) *Six thinking hats*. Revised and updated ed. London: Penguin.

GODFREY, S. (1998) Are you creative? *Journal of Knowledge Management*. Vol. 2, No. 1, pp14–16.

GUERREIRO, R., BIO, S.R. and MERSCHMANN, E.V.V. (2008) Cost-to-serve measurement and customer profitability analysis. *The International Journal of Logistics Management*. Vol. 19, No.3, pp389–407.

HARRISON, W.G. (1996) A process perspective on strategic decision-making. *Management Decision*. Vol. 34, No. 1, pp46–53.

HEAP, J. (1989) *The management of innovation and design*. London: Cassell.

HOLIAN, R. (2002) Management decision-making and ethics. *Management Decision*. Vol. 40, No.9, pp862–870.

HUNT, M. (1985) *The universe within*. New York: Simon & Schuster.

KOCK, R. (2007) *The 80/20 principle*. London: Nicholas Brealey.

MCADAM, R. and MCCLELLAND, J. (2002) Individual and team-based idea generation within innovation management. *European Journal of Innovation Management*. Vol. 5, No. 2, pp86–97.

MCFADZEAN, E. (2002) Developing and supporting creative problem-solving teams: part 1 – a conceptual model. *Management Decision*, Vol. 40, No. 5, pp463–476.

MCWHIRTER, J. and MCWHIRTER, M. (1985) Increasing human potential. *Personnel and Guidance Journal*. Vol. 62, pp135–143.

MIND TOOLS. (2009) *Essential skills for an excellent career*. Available online at: www.mindTools.com [accessed 4 December 2009].

MOULTON, S.T. and KOSSLYN, S.M. (2009) Imaging predictions: mental imagery as mental emulation. *Philosophical Transactions of the Royal Society Biological Sciences*. Vol, 364, pp1273–1280.

NELISSEN, P. and VAN SELM, M. (2008) Surviving organisational change. *Corporate Communications: An International Journal*. Vol. 13, No. 3, pp306–318.

NELSON, T. and MCFADZEAN, E. (1998) Facilitating problem-solving: facilitator competences, *Leadership & Organisation Development Journal*, Vol. 19, No. 2, pp72–82.

NOVAMIND CONNECT (2010). Available online at: www.novamind.com [accessed 5 February 2010].

NOVICEVIC, M.N., HRENCH, T.J. and WREN, D.A. (2002) Playing by the ear … in an incessant din of reasons. *Management Decision*. Vol. 40, No. 10, pp992–1002.

ORPEN, C. (1995) Using the stepladder technique to improve team performance. *Team Performance Management*. Vol.1, No. 3, pp24–27.

OSBORN, A.F. (1972) *Applied Imagination*. Waco, TX: Success Motivation Institute, Inc.

PATTON, J.R. (2003) Intuition in decisions. *Management Decision*. Vol.41, No. 10, pp989–996.

PAVLINA, S. (2004), *Be proactive*. Available online at: www.stevepavlina.com [accessed 17 March 2010].

PERRI, D.F., CALLANAN, A., ROTENBERRY, P.F. and OEHLERS, P.F. (2009) Education and training in ethical decision-making. *Education and Training*. Vol. 51, No. 1, pp70–83.

STECH, E. and RATLIFFE, S. (1985) *Effective group communication*. Lincolnwood, IL: National Textbook Company.

TITUS, P.A. (2000) Marketing and the creative problem-solving process. *Journal of Marketing Education*. Vol. 22, No. 3, pp225–235.

TWISS, B. (1974) *Managing technological innovations*. London: Pitman.

WILSON, G. and HANNA, M. (1990) *Groups in context*. New York: McGraw-Hill.

CHAPTER 15

Decision-making and problem-solving in practice

Gillian Watson *and* Stefanie C. Reissner

OVERVIEW

Studying theory is one thing and applying it in practice is often another. This chapter has been specifically designed to give you the opportunity to practise a range of skills developed in this book on a series of case studies. These vary in length, type, content and context to appeal to a majority. Each of these case studies relates to more than one chapter to mimic real business situations.

LEARNING OUTCOMES

By the end of this chapter, provided you engage with the activities, you should be able to:

- analyse complex business situations
- apply business and people skills to complex business situations
- decide what course of action to take and justify your answer.

15.1 INTRODUCTION

Making decisions and solving problems are among the key tasks and key skills of managers. While there are numerous techniques to facilitate decision-making and problem-solving, which were discussed in the previous chapter, decision-making and problem-solving are difficult tasks. This chapter seeks to provide you with real-life case studies (although some names are disguised for reasons of confidentiality) to hone your decision-making and problem-solving skills in practice.

This chapter includes several case studies and you will find more on the companion website of this book.

15.2 COLLABORATION AND LEADERSHIP: THE UNIVERSITY OF SUNDERLAND AND ONE WATER

COLLABORATION AND LEADERSHIP: THE UNIVERSITY OF SUNDERLAND AND ONE WATER

This case study relates to Chapters 7, 16, 17 and 18 and explores what can be achieved by collaboration between two organisations. It also examines the impact of partnership working between change agents in one organisation and innovative leadership in the other.

The University of Sunderland

The University of Sunderland's vision of being recognised as one of a new generation of great civic universities is expressed thus: to be innovative, accessible, inspirational and outward looking; with international reach; and with great local impact. This university has long been aware of its social responsibilities and in many areas goes beyond what is expected of an organisation. It has been on a journey towards corporate social responsibility for a number of years, but prior to 2006 had not taken conscious leaps forward. However, a new outlook began to immerge as its corporate social responsibility principles became more apparent. Under these principles, an organisation's internal and external practices can influence its employees, customers, partners, community and environment in a positive manner. It is this positive change and its influence on staff members and the further implications for partners that this case study addresses.

Between 2006 and 2009 a number of work strands began to link together from the point of view of the individuals and the disparate examples of good practice already taking place throughout the institution. Further work ensued which bound many of these elements of good practice together with new initiatives, which helped to foster a corporate culture underpinned by ethical principles and one which gave a good grounding for the corporate social responsibility (CRS) ethos.

One initiative that exemplifies this change in corporate consciousness is the ongoing collaboration between the university and One Water.

One Water

In 2003 the compassion and imagination of Duncan Goose was stirred when he read about the one billion people around the world who do not have access to clean drinking water. He drew up his own business vision and left his job in 2004 to work full time on getting his new project off the ground.

Tichy and Ulrich (2008) refer to a new breed of transformational leaders who develop a vision, gather support and buy-in from stakeholders, and guide their organisation into institutionalising a clear value base. In 2005 the vision of Duncan Goose became a reality when the first bottles of One Water began to roll off the production line. One Water is a not-for-profit organisation which aims to deliver clean drinking water for some of the people hardest hit by a shortage of drinkable water.

The revenue generated via the sale of bottles of One Water funds mechanical spinning wheels known as 'PlayPumps' in different regions of Africa. The effect of children using these PlayPumps is that in the villages they can draw clean water from below ground, as opposed to the children having to several miles to collect unclean water from rivers. This ready access to clean water brings significant health benefits to villages and to the children's ongoing education.

Working in partnership

The University of Sunderland achieved Fairtrade status in 2006. The policy not only covered every cup of tea and coffee in the university's outlets, but also a range of innovative sport and leisure goods. The

Fairtrade branding extended to catering concessions, with the university's Greggs Bakery outlet becoming the first Fairtrade Greggs in the UK. The success of this arrangement led to Greggs embracing Fairtrade across all its outlets within a two-year period. Fairtrade status proved extremely popular with students and staff alike and became part of the university's branding. The university was a key contributor to the City of Sunderland achieving Fairtrade status in 2007.

The two main drivers behind the university's Fairtrade profile, Catering Manager Sharon Olver and Equality and Diversity Manager Paul Andrew, wished to go a step further in ethical sourcing and also saw the potential benefits to the university and its wider communities. In early 2007 they asked Duncan Goose to deliver a guest lecture on the story of his new company and invited an audience drawn from the university and region. In this lecture Duncan outlined the philosophy and impact of his organisation. It was very well received and paved the way for the university to strike an initial catering contract with One Water. Within six months, One Water became the sole water supplier for all the university's hospitality and retail outlets.

Zadek (2001) asserts that 'partnerships are a means of getting things done that individuals would be unable to achieve alone.' The collaboration between the two organisations proved fruitful for both parties.

In 2009 the university achieved the installation in Africa of its first water wheel, or PlayPump, funded solely by the sale of One Water at its outlets. In collaboration with One Water the PlayPump was installed in the village school in Lerato, Lesotho, Southern Africa. Lerato is a village in which 20 per cent of children are orphans due to the high prevalence of HIV/ Aids. The clean water is greatly assisting with the treatment of the disease. It is also enabling the children, who used to spend three hours per day collecting water from elsewhere, to spend more time at school.

The Principal of the school, Ms Malikhoele Letsie, commented in 2009:

The PlayPump has made a dramatic impact not only on the pupils of Lerato Primary School, but the wider community too. Thanks to the support of Sunderland University, they now have a reliable source of fresh, clean drinking water, which means that rather than spending hours every day collecting water, children can go to school, learn and also have fun!

The PlayPump captured the imagination of staff and students alike. To highlight this, a group of self-funded drama students visited Lerato school to see the PlayPump for themselves and carried out drama workshops with the schoolchildren. Simply by buying the water, the students had appreciated their own contribution to the water wheel. Moreover, they recognised the role of their university in making this happen.

To both internal and external stakeholders, the university is now seen as a socially responsible and fair organisation. In the 2009 staff survey, 81 per cent of staff rated the university as a responsible organisation, compared with 56 per cent in 2007. This brings benefits to the organisation in terms of employee commitment and also places it strategically in terms of being seen as a good business partner. Cannon (1994) asserts that 'when competing for resources, firms with a good corporate reputation in the wider society will find themselves in an advantageous position.'

Leadership styles

In an organisation's structural context, Middleton (2007) argues that many organisations operate in silos. They need leaders who can see across the whole organisation and make the sum of the parts greater than the whole. These leaders understand the value of networks which extend beyond the traditional confines, and they know how to lead them. Middleton's concept of 'leading beyond authority' is not about pre-existing perceived levels of authority. It is about earning legitimacy with ideas that resonate, and using an approach that means that people and organisations willingly grant authority to turn the ideas into deliverable objectives.

At the university, Paul Andrew and Sharon

Olver had acted as change agents in their institution, leading beyond authority by turning one-off initiatives into general practice and helping to formally embed ethical principles into corporate culture. Significantly influenced by their input, the University of Sunderland in 2009 launched its first Corporate Responsibility Statement, which set out ethical organisational values and outlined how it is making a difference to its stakeholders.

This was the second corporate social responsibility (CSR) statement issued by a UK university, and the first to be international in scope, and placed the institution at the forefront of CSR developments in higher education. Within 12 months the CSR principles were embedded into the university's Corporate Plan 2009/10 to 2013/14.

The leadership style at One Water is reflected in the work of Collins (2001), who explored the role of leadership in turning an organisation's performance from mediocre to excellent. This 'good to great' leadership is epitomised at the highest level by the executive 'who builds enduring greatness through a paradoxical blend of personal humility and professional will'. The impact of the personal leadership of Duncan Goose meant that by 2009 One Water had become a global organisation, with sales in four continents across the world. Distribution of One Water has progressed from small sympathetic organisations to national supermarket chains, and its partnership initiatives now involve a number of global organisations. In 2010 the One Water product range has expanded to include vitamin water, condoms, toilet tissues and hand-wash, with over 500 clean water projects extending across the African continent.

An ongoing relationship

The relationship between the university and One Water has benefited from taking what Goyder (1998) describes as an inclusive approach to both internal and external stakeholders. 'The inclusive approach differentiates Tomorrow's Company from Yesterday's Companies. Tomorrow's Company values reciprocal relationships, understanding that it can improve outcomes. It works to build relationships with customers, suppliers and other key stakeholders, through a partnership approach.' The university and One Water fit Goyder's description as companies of tomorrow, ones that have clear values that encourage commitment and deliver successful business partnerships.

Their relationship was further strengthened with the awarding of an honorary doctorate from the university to Duncan Goose in 2009. The recognition was returned with Duncan making a public endorsement of the university's approach to corporate social responsibility in One Water's *Annual Review 2009*, which is circulated to business partners and to a range of UK and worldwide organisations.

With a second PlayPump being installed in 2010, the collaboration between the University of Sunderland and One Water is now an integral part of both organisations' operations.

Questions

- Have you been involved in a change programme? If so:
  - Did it influence others in the organisation?
  - Did it change the culture?
  - Did it have an impact on how the organisation is perceived externally?
- What leadership qualities were evident here?
  - Analyse Duncan and his vision.
  - Analyse Paul and his vision and motivation.
- Research theories of CSR and consider how they fit with issues in this case.
- Evaluate the impact this initiative had had on both organisations.

Case study by Paul Andrews (Diversity Manager, University of Sunderland) with Gillian Watson.

15.3 HEALTH AND SAFETY DAY: A TEAM-BUILDING EXERCISE

 HEALTH AND SAFETY DAY: A TEAM-BUILDING EXERCISE

CASE STUDY 15.2

This case study relates mainly to Chapters 1, 6, 7, 16 and 17.

It is a glorious spring day, warm and sunny. Scores of people have gathered in small groups on a giant lawn, many sitting in camping chairs in front of small tents in which traditional South African stews are bubbling away in the midst of a wave of delicious smells. It is a friendly and relaxed atmosphere, with people chatting, visiting those in the neighbouring tents and also playing football or rugby. In the background is Steel Corp., one of South Africa's biggest steel companies. It is Health and Safety Day, when production is staffed at minimum levels (and only to keep the machinery going) to allow the majority of employees to have a fun day with a serious message. This message is that Steel Corp. employees have to work together as a team to improve relationships between different groups of employees, to improve their mediocre health and safety record and, most importantly, to improve productivity.

Steel Corp. is experiencing a difficult transition – the transition from an exclusive, racially divided organisation to a more inclusive and team-based one that is profitable, effective and efficient. The firm was founded shortly after the Second World War and thrived under the Apartheid regime, providing work for many white men from the local community. Black manager Adam recalls that:

Steel Corp. was a purely Afrikaans-dominated company, influenced by ideas of racial segregation and discrimination. All managers were white and Afrikaans was the official company language even though many blacks didn't understand the language. The perception was that a black guy is inferior and useless and not going to survive. At certain colour lines, your job prospects would end, that was that. You would spend the rest of your life slaving away at the furnaces.

After the end of the Apartheid regime, South Africa began a transition to a more inclusive, democratic society and Steel Corp. had to follow suit. There are several official company languages now, including English and the most widely spoken native South African languages. Social facilities like canteens are open to all employees, regardless of their position and their ethnic origin. An increasing number of black employees are being promoted to supervisory and managerial positions as a result of the government's Employment Equity programme, which prescribes that organisational hierarchies have to mimic the country's ethnic composition (ie 80 per cent black, 15 per cent white and 5 per cent Asian). Employees like Adam have much improved job prospects and do not face any major obstacles in getting to the top of an organisation's hierarchy.

However, this transition has been painful for Steel Corp. employees and the local community. In the course of only a few years, 65 per cent of employees from all ethnic groups were made redundant in an attempt to make the company more profitable in a very competitive environment. The efforts have paid off, and Steel Corp. has become a respected player in the global steel industry. It is a leaner organisation that operates like a business and not a charity as in the past, as many employees acknowledge today. However, unemployment in the local community is high and few former Steel Corp. employees have found alternative employment. Many white employees are facing a glass ceiling when striving up the career ladder but lack better prospects elsewhere. Adam's experiences of job prospects ending at a certain colour line, it seems, has become a reality for those who previously dominated supervisory and managerial positions. It is therefore not surprising that relationships between different ethnic groups in the plant remain difficult with many falling back on old prejudices.

After a successful turnaround in financial terms, Steel Corp. management is devoting much energy to softer aspects of the business. Teamwork, particularly in multi-disciplinary teams across hierarchical boundaries, has become more prevalent and decision-making has become more participative. However, the greatest challenge to these efforts is to rid employees of the baggage of the past; in other words, to overcome old prejudices with regard to racial segregation and discrimination. This baggage was visible on Health and Safety Day: white employees would visit former colleagues in other tents, while black employees would do the same – strictly along the old colour lines. The football teams would be almost exclusively black, while the rugby teams would be almost exclusively white. The friendly and relaxed atmosphere that characterised Health and Safety Day, however, might have been the first step to a more inclusive and team-oriented way of working at Steel Corp. where every employee is given a fair chance, regardless of background and ethnic origin.

Questions

- How would you describe group dynamics on Health and Safety Day? Which kind of group – formal or informal – is the most cohesive and therefore most difficult to change in an organisation required to turn around its fortunes?

- How have the levels of power and authority of white employees and black/Asian employees respectively changed over time? What can managers do to promote a different balance of power in organisations?

- Evaluate the benefit of measures such as Health and Safety Day to promote teamwork and cross-cultural understanding. What other measures might complement or replace Health and Safety Day?

- What role do leaders have in a transition like the one that Steel Corp. is going through? What knowledge and skills do they require?

Case study by Stefanie C. Reissner.

15.4 INTERCONTINENTAL HOTEL GROUP: KEYSTONE DEVELOPMENT PROJECT

INTERCONTINENTAL HOTEL GROUP: KEYSTONE DEVELOPMENT PROJECT

CASE STUDY 15.3

This case study relates to Chapters 1, 9 and 18.

IHG business employee development offering

The InterContinental Hotels Group (IHG) is a global hotel organisation comprising 4,438 hotels globally (as of February 2010). It is an umbrella organisation for seven brands, namely Holiday Inn, Holiday Inn Express, Crowne Plaza, InterContinental Hotels, Staybridge Suites, Hotel Indigo and Candlewood Suites. The hotel portfolio comprises a mixture of business models, including franchised, managed and company-owned hotels. The 66 properties discussed in this case are the 'managed' UK and Ireland estate.

To help deliver IHG's core purpose – 'Great Hotels Guests Love' – the company is committed to developing employees to help them excel today in their current role as well as to prepare them for future roles. The training offer across all hotels includes:

- facilitator-led training with specialist IHG trainers and IHG subject matter experts

- online learning through its partners: Harvard Business online, eCornell, E-Advisor, Rosetta Stone® (language learning), Element K (technology and management training) and Risk (online modules)

- leadership development at Ashridge executive education business school.

This commitment to employee development formed part of the element which won the business a 2010 *Sunday Times* '25 Best Big Companies to Work For' award, which is based on surveys of employees in large companies in the UK and officially recognises companies that

'Provide their people with an outstanding place to work'. (Times Online 2010)

Introduction and historical background to the case

This very successful organisation has an excellent track record in developing its staff, yet along with many other major hotels groups trading in the UK it was experiencing some labour turnover issues, including among the general manager population. This, coupled with IHG's commitment to create opportunities for their employees to have 'room to grow' (which forms part of the IHG employee brand commitment), required some attention.

The business was incurring costs in refilling positions when staff left, and recognised that immediate action was needed to reduce recruitment costs and also to develop the pipeline of internal talent, both of which were motivators for change. Management were keen to highlight how heavily recruitment agencies were being used to fill positions, and were also aware of how much exceptional talent the business might be losing. Even more concerning was that in the majority of cases, these senior managers were moving to IHG's competitors. It was decided that action needed to be taken in order to retain those employees who were performing well and were of key value to the business. The following strategy was adopted:

- a ban on the use of agencies (only with authorisation from the Area General Manager were positions permitted to be advertised using agencies)

- investment in succession planning software

- a relaunch of the existing (outdated) talent management matrix, which was to be collated and aligned to individual personal development plans (PDPs), mobility, and performance reviews.

Introduction of a development programme to support 'growing our own' general manager talent

The company identified a need to train and develop the existing operations manager population with the aim of creating a 'bank of home-grown talent' that could move up to general manager (GM) level. This would present the company with the opportunity to promote internally through a structured succession plan.

The task

A project leader was appointed and was tasked to design and implement an internal development programme, named Keystone. It was envisaged that the project's success would result in an increase in GM positions being filled internally.

Expected programme return on investment (ROI)

By the end of the project the following results were anticipated:

- At the end of the 18 months, a 'high impact' development programme would be embedded into the business.

- This would result in 15 per cent of general manager positions being filled by internal candidates in the two years following completion of the programme (depending on vacancies within the business).

- The programme would support the development of the operations manager population, and would furnish them with the core skills and knowledge needed in the role of general manager.

The problem

Despite this investment, philosophy and training opportunities, several resignations from the general manager population were received. Interestingly most leavers had secured new positions within the hospitality sector. Subsequent analyses of exit interviews from these employees revealed that there were four key factors for their decisions to leave (Figure 15.1). The main reason for leaving was a 'belief' that IHG offered limited career progression for this target group. More in-depth probing and questioning with existing managers revealed that they were disillusioned by vacancies being filled externally. These findings fully supported Charan et al (2001) and Hirsh's report (2000) which discussed the need for developing internal talent as opposed to

Figure 15.1 Staff perceptions of personal development planning

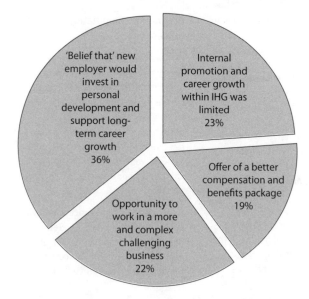

'Belief that' new employer would invest in personal development and support long-term career growth
36%

Internal promotion and career growth within IHG was limited
23%

Offer of a better compensation and benefits package
19%

Opportunity to work in a more and complex challenging business
22%

'buying it in' and that this is key to career planning. Priding itself in strong employee engagement survey scores and low labour turnover (LTO), the business was concerned at these findings.

Primary research conclusions

Competitor analysis findings and primary research in the business resulted in the following conclusions:

- IHG needed to address comments made by the exiting GMs relating to succession planning opportunity and personal development.

- Investment and provision of a structured development route for GMs could have significant ROI benefits to all stakeholders.

- Such a programme would be most effective if delivered as 'off-job' training.

- Existing GMs believed that all of the subjects identified were critical to success, and therefore the syllabus should contain all of them.

- As competitors were not offering development programmes specifically aimed at talent management (TM) IHG could benefit from working on talent management and talent development as a recruitment tool.

- Action needed to be taken to reduce the risk of business being lost though the 'brain-drain' of GM tacit and intellectual knowledge.

Recommendations and actions

The preliminary research conclusions helped to inform the business case for moving forward, which was presented to the executive team for approval and backing. With this approved, an inaugural meeting was held with the objective of creating working parties, using a knowledge management (KM) approach to communicate the subject content. This delivery model was primarily selected because it would give ownership of the writing and delivery of the modules to the specialists in the business; this it was hoped would achieve the best results.

Another aspect of the approach was that the delegates would tutored by experts in each subject; colleagues therefore were enlisted on the basis of their individual skills, competencies and subject knowledge, which were matched to the needs of each module.

The inaugural planning meeting established the identity of the programme was given, which was given the name *Keystone*. The thought process behind this was that the 'keystone' of a building is the stone that supports the rest of the structure, just as this programme would underpin the business. A was designed logo to market the programme (Figure 15.2).

Figure 15.2 Logo 'Building for the Future'

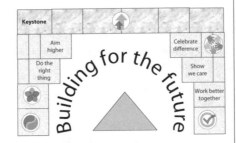

Over the following months the working parties designed their specialised assigned programmes.

Programme nomination and selection process

As Keystone's main objective was to provide the business with a 'pipeline' of next-generation GM talent, the target audience for the programme were operations managers (Ops). As this population are best assessed, and their performance is best reviewed by their direct reports, their GMs, the GMs were asked to nominate potential candidates on the basis of specified success criteria.

It was clear that this process was vital to the success of his programme. Selecting the right delegates would be a major factor in achieving a successful outcome to the project. It was imperative that the selection process was fair, had clearly defined eligibility and success criteria and was challenging enough to attract *high-potential* candidates. Delegates were required to have reached an overall score in their last performance review of Level 4, (defined as '*Strong* – Employee demonstrates effective performance in this competency and exceeds it on some occasions'). This was set as the minimum entry criterion, effectively eliminating weaker candidates from applying and increasing the chances of those accepted being successful in securing a GMs position within the 18-month duration of Keystone. Nominations then needed to be supported by the candidate's general manager, the HR manager, area general manager and vice president of operations. This ensured that everyone had 'bought in' and committed to the candidates nomination.

A short interview and presentation by each candidate based around the title 'What will I do to give a return on investment to the company, if I am selected for Keystone?' This process proved to be very challenging in several ways. Firstly, due to the company's financial results being released late, the review process was subsequently held up (the financial results are needed to score performance objectives, which form part of the review process). As the criteria required the nominees to achieve a score of 4 in their annual performance review there was a time lapse before the review process could be completed. This was done to prevent any tampering with the scores.

For those candidates not successful in getting onto the programme, one-to-one feedback was given to identify areas of development, and direction to help them to be successful in the future.

Keystone: the programme

Over the subsequent 18 months, the Keystone delegates attended nine off-job modules. After each module delegates were set an assignment in order to consolidate the module learning and to put learning into practice. Consequently there was a strong emphasis on continuous professional

development (CPD)and reflective learning (CIPD ND). The purpose of this was to make the learners take responsibility for their own development, and to link their learning experience to business needs (ibid).

To support CPD and to enable all learners to have a 'help line', each delegate was assigned a trained mentor from the business. The aim of offering this long-term tailored relationship (CIPD 2010) was to allow the learner or 'mentee' access to ongoing support outside the Keystone modules and the opportunity of to reap all of the benefits of access to a personal mentor. Mentors and mentees attended awareness sessions to make sure the relationship was steered to success. These sessions followed Alred et al's three-step model:

- exploration – to explore issues which are identified by the mentee
- new understanding
- action planning.

The results: ROI and programme achievements – evaluation of programme objectives

- The project aimed to have 15 per cent of general manager positions filled by internal candidates in the two years following completion of the programme (depending on vacancies within the business).

- At the end of the 18 months, a 'high-impact' development programme would be embedded into the business.

On completion of the programme all the delegates and all those involved in Keystone were invited to attend a Graduation Ball to celebrate the successes of the programme, and the 'feeling' was that the programme has been a huge success.

Twenty-two delegates completed the programme, and the original objective/target of 15 per cent of delegates becoming GMs was exceeded. In fact 25 per cent of the delegates were promoted to GM positions.

Some of the other successes were: two

delegates were offered GM positions externally (arguably not business successes, but success for the individuals). One of delegates was successful in securing a general manager position covering maternity leave for 12 months, four delegates were either promoted to larger, more challenging and complex hotels in the same role, or moved into corporate roles (two individuals) aligned to their PDPs.

One delegate confidentially informed the project leader that she had been offered a position with a competitor's hotel group but had declined because of the prospects that Keystone would offer her, and that she is working on her personal development plan. The remaining 12 delegates remained in their current roles. However, all were given programme exit interviews and attended an additional day's 'debrief' which was devoted to formulating their career plans so that they would fully understand those plans and would leave the programme feeling motivated and with a clear vision for the future. It was of vital importance that these delegates felt they had been successful and had benefited from the programme.

Keystone: set-up for success and the results

It is important to acknowledge that Keystone was, by its design, created to be a success. The programme manager was selected because of her tenacity and creativity, coupled with skills in networking and influencing people, as well as a proven track record in project management and a background in leadership development. From the business prospective, delegates were selected using a set of criteria of behavioural competencies and attitudes, as well as demonstrating high potential abilities and desire to become general managers. From the outset, all of the resources needed to meet the challenges were provided to ensure that there were no barriers to success, and this also included allowing the rare and valuable commodity of time to plan, deliver and evaluate.

As previously discussed, the high-level sponsorship of the programme was undoubtedly a critical contribution factor to Keystone. Throughout the project senior management were visible; they opened the programme and told the delegates of their vision for Keystone and the commitment from the company.

Questions

- From a talent management perspective, evaluate the Keystone programme's aims.

- Comment on how participants were recruited for the development. Did this have an impact on the success of the programme?

- Do you agree that the objectives were met? Why/why not?

- Evaluate the value of the programme from the participants' point of view (there are distinct pluses and minuses here). In particular consider the career development process.

- Evaluate the level of support given by executive/senior managers to the Keystone project.

- Evaluate the success of the initiative.

- Where should the company go from here? What decisions need to be taken? What criteria for decision-making will you use?

Case study by Debbee Forster and Gillian Watson.

15.5 EXPERT BANK

EXPERT BANK

CASE STUDY 15.4

This case study relates mainly to Chapters 1, 6, 7, 14, 16, 17 and 18.

Expert Bank is an international commercial bank with its headquarters in Germany. It has specialised in supporting the international operations of its corporate clients – typically small and medium-sized manufacturing firms seeking to sell German technology abroad. Expert Bank will accompany this core client group on all steps on their way into operation internationally through providing financial advice as well as offering the necessary financial products for this process, either as own products or together with partners.

For this purpose, Expert Bank has established small units of local finance experts in the developing markets of this field, among others in India. The Indian unit, which is the focus of this case study, accounts for about 50 per cent of the bank's market share and therefore contributes significantly to Expert Bank's performance. The Indian unit is headed by Gurjeet Singh, a very experienced and well-networked finance expert in his early 50s. He is a self-motivated and very sales-oriented professional, making him the ideal candidate for this role. Gurjeet Singh is supported by a secretary looking after administrative matters and, as typical in India, by an office boy who does the errands.

Traditionally, Expert Bank's core client group only sought to sell their products in India, which involved export financing and the accompanying bank-to-bank services required for such deals. Gurjeet Singh is an expert in this field and has developed considerable know-how and expertise over his many years in banking. His unit is doing extremely well and has reached the upper limits of its capacity. However, there is a trend among German manufacturers to expand their international operations. Many choose to set up their own distribution networks in their target markets while others venture into setting up production facilities for purchasing in the Indian markets. This requires new and different financial products and services (eg new current accounts, investment financing), which would stretch Gurjeet Singh's unit beyond capacity.

Gertrude Muller is Gurjeet Singh's manager at German headquarters and very happy with his performance. She is an economist by training and has managed Expert Bank's international operations for the last 15 years. It is her task to take the Indian unit forward as Expert Bank cannot afford to lose the new opportunities presented by their clients' expansion plans and the associated potential for Expert Bank's expansion in India. This involves expanding Gurjeet Singh's unit to create new capacity for the new products and services to be offered.

Her many years in international management have taught Gertrude Muller that she will have to tread carefully to achieve her goal. Although she has only been responsible for the Indian unit for the last two years (and therefore did not have a close relationship with Gurjeet Singh), she is aware that she cannot just hire an additional member of staff for Gurjeet Singh's unit to look after the new products and services because he would be offended by having to work with a probably younger and less experienced employee and concerned about losing his knowledge and expertise to him or her, thus reducing his own market value as export finance expert. This is a crucial concern for Gurjeet Singh because the value of employees in India is measured by their knowledge of the market, their knowledge of the customers, their know-how and expertise in their field of specialism as well as their network of contacts. Gertrude Muller is therefore well aware that Gurjeet Singh is a much sought after export finance expert whom competing organisations would be more than willing to hire. If Gurjeet Singh chose to leave Expert Bank, it would lose a major part of the export finance business in India – a risk that it can ill afford in the present economic climate. She needs to find a way to expand the Indian unit without losing Gurjeet Singh in the process.

Questions

- Imagine you are Gertrude Muller. How would you go about resolving this dilemma? How would you approach it – on your own, with the help of your colleagues (all international managers themselves) or in consultation with Gurjeet Singh?

- Using the creative decision-making and problem-solving techniques discussed in Chapter 14 and drawing on your knowledge of international issues introduced in Chapter 1, identify the different options that Gertrude Muller has. Discuss these options and their viability with a peer or in small groups and devise an action plan. Justify your decisions at all stages.

- Consider how you will approach this dilemma from a management and leadership perspective – will you discuss your options with Gurjeet Singh or will you make that decision on your own and communicate it to him? Devise a strategy of how to communicate with Gurjeet Singh. If this case study is being used in a classroom setting, the discussion between Gertrude Muller and Gurjeet Singh might be brought to life through role play.

Case study by Stefanie C. Reissner.

15.6 DEVELOPMENT INTERVENTION AT GULPS HOTELS

 DEVELOPMENT INTERVENTION AT GULPS HOTELS

CASE STUDY 15.5

This case study relates mainly to Chapters 1, 9, 11 and 18 and consists of three parts. Please answer the questions on each part before moving on to the next.

Part 1

Gulps Hotels is a small hotel chain that has 12 establishments, predominantly in the north of England, although there are two hotels in the south of England and a further two in Scotland. They all have four or five stars and consequently quality is central to the company ethos. Madeline is the newly appointed development and quality advisor. She is a university graduate who completed her studies at master's level, and has worked for other hotel chains in the past.

The hotel group has two regional managers who cover the areas of 'North and Scotland', and 'Midlands and the South', managing seven and five hotels respectively. The northern regional manager has designated Madeline's first task – or indeed problem – which he wants her to resolve: a hotel in Newcastle that is experiencing problems. He tells her that in his opinion the hotel manager is nearing retirement (in eight months' time), so there needs to be a planned change regarding the management of the facility. Furthermore, there may need to be a progression process enabling career development for some of the staff; the hotel chain has had a practice of appointing the assistant manager to the post.

The information given to Madeline is certainly somewhat vague; however she is undaunted and always ready for a challenge. The information is as follows:

- Bookings have remained unchanged over the last year although the rest of the group has enjoyed a small rise.

- Unlike other hotels in the region of a similar star rating, this one has few bookings for special events such as conferences, occasional parties or weddings.

- Complaints have grown over the last three months; some of these include:
  - rooms being unclean when guests arrive
  - misplaced luggage
  - unanswered telephone calls to the hotel or potential customers having wait long periods before calls are being answered
  - bills being incorrect.

Having stayed at the hotel for two days Madeline conclude that:

- The manager is extremely complacent about the service offered.

- The assistant manager has been given no real responsibility for a particular area of work or a particular function, and has been used very much as an office junior.

- The assistant manager has been employed at the hotel for 2½ years, has a business degree and is very eager and interested in all aspects of the business.

Questions 1

Given the information that can only be described as very limited:

- What do you identify as major areas of training and development need?

- What additional information would you seek?

- What intervention/s would you consider implementing and what strategies would you adopt?

- Plan how you would evaluate whether your interventions will be effective.

Discuss and evaluate the case in groups and arrive at a consensus for moving forward.

Part 2

Madeline has examined the situation in the hotel at Newcastle. It is tellingly obvious to her that she must discuss her findings with the hotel manager. At first the hotel manager is reluctant to acknowledge any of the issues Madeline has brought up, but during the session the assistant manager walks into the office highlighting another problem; fortunately it is a minor consideration. The assistant manager joins the discussion and Madeline wishes she had thought to ask her to attend in the first place. From that point on the discussion goes well, with the hotel manager agreeing with Madeline that there are quality and customer care issues that need to be resolved. Because of the volume of customer complaints, Madeline is also concerned that any development in that area will just be the tip of the iceberg. Nonetheless, customer care remains the primary concern. With that in mind Madeline, having consulted with her manager, agrees to a regime of staff training. This will effectively develop the whole workforce in customer care issues. Gulps Hotel allocates £3,500 for this task. Madeline considers running the training programme herself as she has had experience of running such courses.

The staff complement of the hotel is as follows:

- Receptionists: two full-time and three part-time.

- Cleaners: ten part-time and one full-time cleaner/supervisor.

- Porters/caretakers: four full-time.

- Bar staff: two full-time, four part-time and one full-time drinks manager.

- Kitchen staff: three chefs, six assistants six ancillary staff – all are full-time under a head chef.
- Restaurant staff: six waiters full-time and eight part-time – all under a head waiter.
- Administrative staff: four full-time reporting directly to the hotel manager.
- Maintenance staff: one full-time, two part-time.

The hotel has a three-shift system. Any part-time work may be a whole shift or a part of a shift. The shifts are:

a. 9.00 am to 5.00 pm (A shift)

b. 5.00pm to 1.00 am (B shift)

c. 1.00 am to 9.00 am (C shift)

Madeline has to make a decision. If she decides to take on the training herself she will have the task of designing, implementing and evaluating how effective the customer care programme has been.

Questions 2

- What would you do?
- Devise an implementation plan for training the hotel's workforce.
- Design the customer care training sessions
- Plan an evaluation strategy
- Consider the cost of your training plan. Can it stay within the budget?
- Calculate the full learning cost
- Consider the cost benefit analysis of carrying out this extensive training programme.

Appendix 15.1: Calculating learning and training cost

From Reid et al (2004, p106).

Tables 15.1 and 15.2 depict the type of items that could be used to calculate each element of the training process.

Table 15.1 Examples of learning costs

Payment to employees

The cost of materials wasted, sales lost or incorrect decision making

Supervision/management costs in dealing with problems of incompetence

Cost of reduced output/service/sales

Cost attributed to accidents caused by lack of knowledge and 'know-how'

Costs resulting from employees learning:
- work too difficult
- no planned learning
- no prospects

You may think of others as appropriate to a particular circumstance/environment.

Table 15.2 Examples of training costs

People costs:
- Wages or salaries of the trainees
- Managers' salaries while training/coaching
- Fees to external providers
- Fees to external assessors
- Travel and subsistence

Equipment costs:
- Training equipment and aids
- Depreciation of training buildings and equipment

Administration costs:
- Wages and salaries of administration – back up staff
- Postage and telephone calls
- Office consumables
- Systems and procedures
- Room hire

Materials costs:
- DVDs, downloads
- Distance-learning packages
- Materials used in practical sessions
- Protective clothing
- Books and journals

You may think of others as appropriate to a particular circumstance/environment.

Part 3

Madeline has come to a decision: the problems at the Newcastle Gulps Hotel are too deep to be solved by a customer care training programme that only gives each member of staff one training session. The problems are widespread and the skill levels of some staff must be in question. As Madeline has herself delivered several training sessions for the staff, she knows the complexity of the overriding problems. She also has to consider the general staff attitude to any development plan.

Madeline has unearthed some disturbing characteristics of the hotel's practice:

- The staff usually receive no feedback on their tasks and no reference is made to their abilities; thus there is no individual or group performance record. For this reason the hotel management cannot possibly know how things are going.

- Staff are not encouraged to develop new skills nor are they expected to pass on their skills to other, less experienced staff.

- Staff at times make suggestions for improvements: for example, reporting a problem or improving a service. They are not listened to and consequently nothing gets done.

Because of her close involvement with the customer care training course, all the staff at the hotel believe it is Madeline's job to solve all their problems and that all issues have a training solution. As the hotel

Case study by Gillian Watson.

manager remarked: 'Madeline, you did such a good job dealing with customer care!'

Madeline feels extremely pressured and also believes she has been 'trapped' at Newcastle long enough. After all she has another 15 hotels to oversee, and her family bemoan the fact that she is never at home. The journey across the Pennines seems to get longer and longer. However, she still needs to complete her work here. There is a growing imperative to use the skills, knowledge and experience of the hotel staff to ensure all have an opportunity to develop and learn: after all they cannot rely on Madeline for everything.

Questions 3

- Madeline is feeling a great deal of pressure. What steps can she take overcome this?

- What practical suggestions do you have to help Madeline enable the hotel to make the best use of the staff's skill base?

- Develop a training plan for either:
  - the administrative and reception staff
  - the deputy manager
  - the cleaners.

- Develop a strategy to ensure the other hotels in the business have a career/succession plan.

15.7 CONCLUSION

This chapter has provided you with a series of case studies on the basis of which you can practise vital managerial and leadership skills. All scenarios are presented are complex in that they relate to a business situation with multiple stakeholders, unique team and organisational dynamics, and no right answers.

PAUSE FOR THOUGHT

Identify at least three things that you have learned by studying this chapter and engaging with the activities. How will your newly acquired knowledge and skills support your continuing professional development? What value do you expect your learning to have for your daily routines and your further career? In what area have you identified a need for further development and how are you planning to fill that gap? Address these issues in your learning journal and/or CPD log. You may also wish to discuss them with a peer, colleague, mentor or coach to aid your further development.

KEY LEARNING POINTS

- Complex business situations require thorough analysis, and a creative team approach can help decision-makers to consider a range of views.

- Complex business situations can only be tackled through an appropriate mix of business and people skills.

- Complex business situations require sound decision-making as well as justification and communication.

EXPLORE FURTHER

For details about Steel Corp, please consult:

REISSNER, S.C. (2008) *Narratives of organisational change and learning: making sense of testing times*. Cheltenham: Edward Elgar.

REISSNER, S.C. (2010) Change, meaning and identity. *Journal of Organisational Change Management*, Vol. 23, No. 3, pp287–299.

15.8 REFERENCES

ALRED, G., GARVEY, B. and SMITH, R. (1998) *Mentoring pocketbook*. Alresford: Management Pocketbooks.

CANNON, T. (1994) *Corporate responsibility*. London: Prentice Hall.

CHARAN, R., DROTTER, S. and NOEL, J. (2001) *The leadership pipeline: how to build the leadership-powered company*. San Francisco, CA: Jossey-Bass.

CIPD. (2010) *Mentoring*. Available online at: http://www.cipd.co.uk/subjects/lrnanddev/ coachmntor/mentor.htm?IsSrchRes=1 [Accessed 20 May 2010].

COLAN, L.J. (2008) *Engaging the hearts and minds of all your employees*. McGraw-Hill.

COLLINS, J. (2001) *Good to great*. New York: Harper Collins.

GOYDER, M. (1998) *Living tomorrow's company*. London: Gower.

HIRSH, W. (2000) *Succession planning demystified*. Report 372. Brighton: Institute for Employment Studies.

MIDDLETON, J. (2007) *Beyond authority: leadership in a changing world*. Basingstoke: Palgrave Macmillan.

ONE WATER. (2009) Press release. 9 June 2009.

ONE WATER. (ND) [website], available online at: http://www.Onedifference.org/water.

REID, M.A., BARRINGTON, H. and BROWN, M. (2004) *Human resource development: beyond training interventions*. 7th ed. London: CIPD.

TICHY, N.M. and ULRICH, D.O. (2008) The leadership challenge. In J.S. Ott, S.J. Parkes and R.B. Simpson (eds), *Classical readings of organisational behaviour*. Belmont, CA: Thomson-Wadsworth.

TIMES ONLINE. (2010) *Top 25 big companies to work for*. Available online at: http:// business.timesonline.co.uk/tol/business/career_and_jobs/best_100_companies/ article7029136.ece [accessed 20 May 2010].

UNIVERSITY OF SUNDERLAND. (ND) *Corporate social responsibility* [website]. available at http://www.sunderland.ac.uk/university/social/.

UNIVERSITY OF SUNDERLAND. (2009) *Annual Review 2008/09*. Available online at: http:// www.sunderland.ac.uk/dvc/dvc-sureview.pdf [accessed 30 May 2010].

UNIVERSITY OF SUNDERLAND. (2009) *Corporate Plan 2009/10 – 2013/14*. Available online at: http://www.sunderland.ac.uk/dvc/dvc-uoscorporateplan.pdf [accessed 30 May 2010].

ZADEK, S (2001) *The civil corporation*. London: Earthscan Publications.

PART 9
Effective Leadership

CHAPTER 16

Leadership and team dynamics

Gillian Watson *and* Ivana Adamson

OVERVIEW

Leading a team can be a considerable challenge as there are complex team dynamics at play that need to be handled skilfully. This chapter seeks to help you to understand and apply the skills required to lead successfully in a team environment in order to enhance the team's performance. Building on our discussion of teamwork in Chapter 6 and the political organisation in Chapter 7, we will focus on team leadership here, and in particular leadership, delegation, chairing meetings and co-ordinating discussions, and resolving conflict between team members as well as on decision-making.

LEARNING OUTCOMES

By the end of this chapter, provided you engage with the activities, you should be able to:

- understand the key aspects of leadership in a team environment
- apply people's skills to the management of staff in work teams
- understand how team leadership can enhance performance
- understand the characteristics of effective meetings
- apply appropriate modes of handling conflict.

16.1 INTRODUCTION

Teams have a central role in any organisation as they can improve its creative and innovative potential as well as its overall performance. But teams do not just happen; they need to be purposefully created and constantly maintained through social relationships. Although all its members are collectively responsible for the working and outcome of a team, the team leader has a particular role to play. He or she has to lead by example, manage the collective processes and resolve conflict whenever necessary within the constraints of the organisation's rules, procedures and control structures. In many instances, the team leader faces a balancing act between ensuring that tasks get done and maintaining the team's morale and productivity. There are different styles of leadership that team leaders can employ to do so and it is their responsibility to choose the right approach for a particular situation.

'People skills' such as fostering collective effort, building cohesion and morale in teams, and effectively resolving interpersonal conflicts are an intrinsic part of the team leader's role. An experienced team leader is able to relate well to others, to build trust, manage conflict, promote participation and design and chair meetings. Very importantly, team leaders are responsible for developing leadership skills within their team, thus contributing to the development of staff within their organisation. Effective team leaders engage with and empower their employees and in that way reduce dissonance between individuals and groups within the organisation. More importantly, quality team leadership through engagement with others is a significant predictor of performance in organisations (Alimo-Metcalfe et al 2007). However, such a style of team leadership needs to be supported by the organisation's culture and systems (Alimo-Metcalfe and Bradley 2008).

It has become accepted wisdom to distinguish between management and leadership. Management is generally associated with efficiency, planning, procedures, regulations and control. Leadership, in contrast, is associated with providing direction, guidance and vision (Gabriel 2008). The latter is sometimes connected to self-knowledge (Boyatsis et al 2008), as the Greek oracle temple in Delphi had inscribed upon it 'know thy self'. Boyatsis et al (2008) argue that understanding oneself is a precursor to understanding one's dreams and aspirations, without which one cannot create a vision for a team nor lead convincingly.

Throughout history, the study of leadership has employed different methodologies that reflect the prevalent thinking in different periods of time. However, the focus was invariably on a leader's personal characteristics, such as charisma. Greek themes helps us again when remembering the term 'charisma' as it comes from classical Greek, meaning 'gift', and traditionally charismatic leaders were seen to derive their authority from their personal qualities like self-confidence and their ability to communicate with others. In organisations, charismatic leaders help to develop a vision, energise action by setting high expectations and enable others to become effective. The concept of charismatic leadership remains a popular subject in management writing and even among managers.

However, there are other approaches to leadership that have long been identified, and this chapter will provide you with an overview of the most important ones. We will also look at team decision-making, effective conduct of team meetings, team problem-solving and handling conflict in a team environment.

16.2 STRATEGIC FIT AT TEAM LEVEL

In this chapter we take a more strategic view of team leadership simply because, regardless of who we are or what our role in an organisation, we probably work in a team. Examples include the Cabinet (a high-level government team), an executive board or board of directors (a team charged with overseeing the direction of the organisation), a senior management team (a team consisting of department heads who must fit, rather like a large jigsaw puzzle, with each element dependent on the others to create a whole.) The team and its leadership, therefore, need to effectively manage its own work yet also must look beyond itself, linking with others, in order to be truly successful.

Ulrich et al (2009) in developing the Ulrich model of HR give a similar message, suggesting it is not enough just to get HR practices right. Instead, the HR function should look to its customers' needs in order to help their organisation succeed. They prescribe that so-called 'transformational' initiatives are unlikely to succeed unless they are linked to relevant business objectives (Ulrich et al 2009), and consequently success is not about doing the work more effectively, it is about building business success. To initiate such a transformation Ulrich et al (2009) have created a four-phase model of HR transformation:

1. Building the business case.

2. Defining the outcome.

3. Redesigning and engaging line managers and others in defining.

4. Delivering the transformation.

Although this model of redesigning a department focuses on the HR function, it can also be used to analyse other organisational functions such as finance and marketing. The model, in effect, shows how a functional area can be embedded into the corporate plan, and therefore offers a method of evaluating strategic fit even on a team level. Using Ulrich et al's (2009) model can therefore initiate team discussion on the flow of people, performance and any work in which the team engage.

ACTIVITY 16.1

GROW YOUR OWN

Read the article 'Grow your own' from *People Management* magazine (23 December 2009) provided overleaf and answer the following questions:

- Consider how this model could be applied to your organisation:
  - What would be the positive aspects involved in this process?
  - What would be the negative aspects or 'sticking points' of using this method?
- How would staff in the department react to organising and working in a different context?
- If you were the team leader how would you prepare staff for such changes?
  - What type of learning and development might need to take place?
  - How would the training needs be implemented?
- Analyse the merits of this model in the context of involving staff in more strategic and company-wide initiatives.

BOX 16.1: GROW YOUR OWN (ULRICH AND ALLEN 2009)

The Ulrich model of HR has attracted numerous followers, but Dave Ulrich himself and his co-author Justin Allen warn that transformation efforts will fail if they focus only on the function and not on wider organisational aims.

At workshops with HR professionals, we often begin by asking: 'What is the biggest challenge you face in your job today?' As we go around the room, the challenges mentioned usually range from getting HR practices right and relating to business leaders to managing the increased personal demands of the job. Heads generally nod in agreement until we say that all these answers are wrong – or, at least, incomplete. Silence then ensues.

Our point is that HR professionals often focus internally on their own function and roles, rather than externally on what their customers need. We believe that the biggest challenge they face today is helping their organisations succeed. That's not to say that activities such as hiring people, developing leaders or building incentive programmes do not matter. They obviously do. However, our argument is that HR professionals should be at least as concerned with the outcomes of these activities – the value they create – as with the activities themselves.

The same goes for efforts to transform the HR function. Initiatives such as implementing e-HR, restructuring the function or designing new HR practices are often described as transformational. However, our experience of working with many thoughtful and innovative HR executives, combined with over 20 years of research, suggests that these actions will not be transformational and are unlikely to be sustained unless they are tied to clear business objectives. HR transformation, in other words, is not about doing HR more effectively, but about building business success.

To help practitioners achieve this goal and avoid the mistakes that are often made along the way, we have developed a four-phase model for HR transformation. Phase one consists of building the business case for transformation, phase two of defining the outcomes, phase three of redesigning HR, and phase four of engaging line managers and others in defining and delivering the transformation.

Phase one addresses the question: why carry out transformation? We believe that HR transformation should begin by making sure that all those involved in the process have a clear understanding of the context of the business. When HR professionals start thinking about the outcomes of their work as defined by the business context, they change their conversations with line managers and are able to justify and build a business case for the transformation. They are also more likely to avoid the common mistake of seeking to implement internally focused ideas that come across as solutions looking for problems.

The approach we propose has a number of practical implications. For example, many HR leaders launching transformation programmes call an all-hands meeting to share the vision and goals of the new HR organisation. We strongly recommend beginning this event with a detailed discussion of the business and the challenges it faces, as this will set the agenda for the entire HR transformation.

The second phase of a transformation programme involves defining its expected outcomes. We recommend that you start by picking the stakeholders you are most worried about, be they customers, employees, investors or the wider community, and then discuss and define the outcomes that will be most important to them. These stakeholder outcomes should be tracked over time to measure the progress of your HR transformation.

HR transformation should also change the fundamental identity, culture, or image of the organisation. We refer to this outcome as defining and building capabilities. These capabilities become the identity of the firm, the deliverables of HR practices, and the keys to implementing business strategy. For a retail firm, for example, service might be the critical capability, while for a firm moving into Asia, it might be the ability to collaborate with business partners. Senior leaders must be clear about the two or three most critical capabilities the firm must have in order to execute its strategy.

Our experience suggests that while there is no magic list of desired or ideal capabilities, certain capabilities seem to be inherent in most well-managed firms. For example, they are good at building leaders who generate confidence in the future, at creating a shared agenda around business strategy, at fostering enduring relationships of trust with customers and at working together across organisational boundaries. They also tend to have a strong reputation for corporate social responsibility, innovation, efficiency and accountability.

The third phase of our transformation model focuses on redesigning the HR function to make sure that it is aligned with business strategy. We have found that the most successful designs are those where the structure of the HR function reflects that of the business organisation. So if the business has a centralised structure, HR should also be centralised, or if the business is decentralised, the HR function should be similarly decentralised. The HR organisation should also mirror the structure of any professional service organisation. This means that there will often be centres of expertise where specialists with distinct knowledge – of learning and development or reward, for example – are charged with turning that knowledge into productivity. Lastly, the redesigned HR function needs to differentiate between transactional and transformational HR work.

These design principles can result in an HR organisation with five distinct – and at times overlapping – elements or channels. These are corporate HR, which oversees the whole function; operational executors, responsible for implementing initiatives; embedded HR, including both strategic business partners and generalists; centres of expertise, and service centres carrying out transactional work (see Figure 16.1 overleaf).

Using a new HR information system. This can increase the efficiency of HR administration, but it will not be a complete HR transformation unless the other roles are also redesigned.

When the HR function is redesigned, HR practices may need to be revamped as well. First, however, they need to be described. So we have divided the vast array of HR work into four domains representing the flows or processes central to organisational success:

- **Flow of people:** how people move in, through, up, and out of the organisation.

- **Flow of performance management:** what links people to work, including standards, measures, feedback and financial and non-financial rewards.

- **Flow of information:** the information people need to do their work can flow up, down, or laterally, and from the outside in or from the inside out.

- **Flow of work:** who does the work, how and where work is done, and how business and operating processes turn individual efforts into organisational outputs.

To transform HR, work in each of these four flows of HR practices needs to be innovative and aligned to customers. The flows should also be integrated with each other.

Ultimately, HR transformation depends on the quality of HR professionals, who may need to upgrade their competencies in order to perform their roles in the new organisation. HR transformation has therefore raised the bar for the profession. Using data from just over 10,000 people around the world, we have identified the competencies required of today's HR

Figure 16.1 Redesigning the HR department

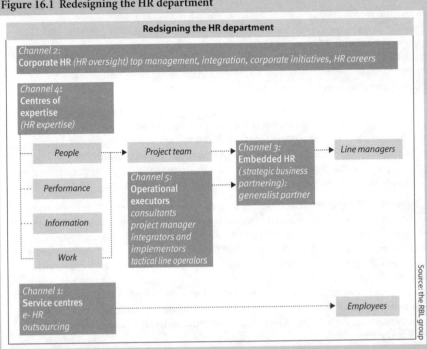

professionals. They include the ability to form relationships of trust with others, to contribute to the formulation of strategy and to make change happen. These competencies are not standards for entry into the profession but the differentiators of those who succeed in delivering value from HR.

The fourth and final phase in our HR transformation model is concerned with accountability. Four groups of stakeholders should be involved in any HR transformation: HR, line managers, customers and investors, and external consultants. HR's role is to design the process and facilitate the implementation of the transformation. However, it is line managers who are ultimately accountable for ensuring that the organisation has the right talent and right structures in place to deliver on the expectations of customers, shareholders and communities. So line managers need to work with HR on implementing the transformation and on making sure it is aligned to business goals. Another group of stakeholders, external customers and investors, can play a role in guiding HR decisions throughout the transformation. Lastly, consultants and advisers can work as partners to advance the transformation. Clear role definition and rigorous accountability will help an HR transformation succeed.

Although we have listed the four phases of a transformation sequentially, in reality they are likely to occur concurrently. For example, while knowledge of business conditions has to frame the HR transformation (phase one), having the right transformation team (phase four) is critical to initiating the process. The challenge for HR professionals throughout is to remember that HR transformation is not an end in itself but a means to helping their organisations succeed.

Further information

This article draws on the book *HR Transformation* by Dave Ulrich, Justin Allen, Wayne Brockbank, Jon Younger and Mark Nyman, published by McGraw Hill, 2009.

16.3 APPROACHES TO LEADERSHIP

There have been many attempts over the last decades to understand what leadership is and how leaders can be distinguished from followers. The trait approach to leadership was one of the earliest attempts to shed light on the mysterious and somewhat nebulous concept of leadership. It suggests that leaders have particular personality traits that distinguish them from the rest of the population, which has given it the nickname 'great person theory' (Barker 2001). The traits that have been identified (as summarised by Clegg et al 2005) include self-confidence, a drive for achievement, honesty, integrity and the ability to motivate people towards a common goal as well as intelligence, creativity and the ability to adapt. While certain traits have been identified as being present in good leaders (House et al 2004), however, there is no evidence to suggest that leaders are born. In fact, it is far more likely that leaders gain their skill and knowledge over time. Moreover, trait theory holds little predictive value, since leaders can be only understood in the context in which they operate. A leader may be excellent in one organisation and fail in another.

The trait approach to leadership was followed by the situational approach, in which leadership is regarded as emerging from the situation. In a formal group, an appointed leader achieves his or her legitimacy from the position he or she holds, while emergent leaders achieve their authority from the group members (Brown 1965, Turner 1991, Gross 1993).

The behavioural approaches attempt to identify behaviours associated with leadership. Fiedler (1967) studied patterns of behaviours that result in effective group performance and identified two basic orientations that leaders engage in to influence their subordinates: relationship-oriented and task-oriented behaviours. Relationship-oriented leaders build trust, show respect and generally care about their employees. These leaders are concerned with developing good relations with their subordinates and in return tend to be liked and respected. Task-oriented leaders, on the other hand, are primarily concerned with employees performing at their best so that the job gets done. Both leadership behaviours are independent variables, thus supervisors can be high or low on both orientations.

Fiedler's (1967) theory of leadership, also known as the contingency theory, incorporates the situation and the group as key variables in effective leadership. The leader's effectiveness is seen as contingent upon the situation, and it is the situation that determines whether a leader is successful. In Fiedler's contingency model, the following variables are considered as the key determinants of leadership effectiveness:

- The relations structure determines how much workers like and trust their leader.

- The task structure determines the extent to which employee tasks are made clear, and how positive the situation is for effective leadership.

- The position power structure (legitimate, reward, and coercive power) determines the leader's ability to influence. When the leader's position power is strong, his or her leadership effectiveness becomes more influential.

Fiedler's model purports to identify situations in which different managers have the opportunity to perform at their best. The preferred leadership style is relatively stable (Adamson 1997), and managers are likely to be effective when:

- They are placed in situations that suit their leadership style, or
- The situation is adapted to fit the manager's leadership style.

Fiedler's contingency model further proposes the following steps of an effective influencing approach:

1. There must be clearly defined job outcomes.
2. Rewards for high-performance and goal attainment must correlate with employees' values.
3. Obstacles to effective performance must be removed.
4. Confidence in employees' ability must be shown.

Transformational leadership focuses on the basic difference between leading for stability and leading for change. In particular, effective leaders are able to recognise and guide organisational changes (Burns 1978). Transactional leaders, on the other hand, are known for their use of reward and coercive powers to encourage a high performance from employees.

The collective or substitute leadership approach assumes situations where the need for leadership is superfluous (Sims 1987). Collective leadership arises from accepting the following:

- the characteristics of the employees with their skills, experience, motivation
- the characteristics of the context in which work is interesting, challenging and satisfying
- employee empowerment or self-managed work teams
- that there is not always the need to directly exert influence over others.

Empowerment can be of benefit to managers, since empowered employees feel they are an integral part of the organisation. This then increases employees' motivation levels, which reflects back on the manager by releasing him or her from controlling to concentrate on other activities. This notion of empowering and engaging staff conforms to Alimo-Metcalfe et al's (2007) research of how staff perceive the quality of leadership displayed by their team leaders. These are categorised as having three dimensions: engaging with others, visionary leadership and leadership capabilities (Alimo-Metcalfe et al 2007, Alimo-Metcalfe and Bradley 2008). Table 16.1 sets out to show the 'how' or by 'what' method these dimensions could be addressed as well as offering a view of the effect, the researchers suggest, these approaches would have on your staff team.

Interestingly, the importance of engagement and the need for a supportive organisational culture highlighted above are supported by Boyatsis et al (2008). Their research also, though, leads them to advocate the importance of optimism,

Table 16.1 How staff perceive the quality of leadership

Dimension	'What'	'How'	Effect on the team
Leadership capabilities	Understanding and using overall strategy to achieve goals and objectives. Ensuring clarity of roles. The goals and/or targets and criteria of success. Establishing, maintaining and being committed to high standards of service delivery and quality outcomes. Having well-thought-out systems and procedures that support the effective use of resources.		Motivation, job satisfaction, strong sense of team effectiveness.
Visionary leadership		Having a clear vision of what the team was aiming for. Being sensitive to the agenda of a wide range of stakeholders. Inspiring them with the team's passion and determination.	Significantly positive effect on motivation, and on aspects of well-being, a sense of fulfilment. Also the researchers reported this approach reduced stress and exhaustion.
Engaging with others		Concern for the needs of staff. Empowering them by trusting them to take decisions. Listening to others' ideas and being willing to accommodate them. Finding time to discuss problems and issues despite being very busy. Supporting others by coaching and mentoring. Inspiring all staff to contribute fully to the work of the team. Actively promoting the achievements of the team to the outside world.	Significantly affected all aspects of positive attitudes to work, and all aspects of well-being, a strong sense of team spirit backed by the organisational culture.

Source: adapted from Alimo-Metcalfe and Bradley (2008).

honesty and emotional intelligence (Goleman et al 2002) as leadership attributes, which they add, can be learnt. However, the current thinking from this team of researchers is endorsing and even encouraging for managers wishing to become 'resonant leaders' (Boyatsis et al 2008); the opposite of this style is dissonance. Obviously, dissonant environments would be classed as negative places to work, and Boyatsis et al suggest emotions such as fear, anxiety, anger, pessimism and individualism would abound. The management style applied to this would be command and control, possibly micromanagement and a lack of trust. In contrast, in environments where resonant leadership is practised we could expect 'powerful collective energy that reverberates among people and supports higher productivity, creativity, a sense of purpose and better results' (Boyatsis et al). Boyatsis et al (2008) suggest:

> Resonant leaders need to know what inhibits effective individual and team performance and how to address these issues. In other words leadership requires emotional and social intelligence and a deep understanding of social systems – and the people in them must work together to achieve complex and challenging goals.

Leading teams therefore, is complex, challenging and engaging; to be successful, it requires positive participation from team members and their managers alike.

16.4 PARTICIPATIVE DECISION-MAKING

The participative management approach used in organisations today reflects the values embraced by the world's developed democratic societies. The concept of democracy became a basis for the human relations management model after Elton Mayo's research at the Western Electric Company between 1924 and 1934 (also known as 'the Hawthorne studies') became generally known and accepted. The human relations model that was developed on the basis of this research focuses on the following three areas of group functioning: commitment, cohesion and morale, where the key values are participation, consensus building and conflict resolution. Participative decision-making should be evident in the following areas:

- the decision-making processes
- decisions about who should participate, to what extent and when
- effectively managed meetings.

Supervisors constantly face decisions regarding their own and their subordinates' work, and in deciding when it is appropriate and to what degree to involve employees in the day-to-day operations. The boundaries of the decision-making process are determined by the overall organisational structure and the degree of authority a manager holds. In terms of competitive advantage, participative decision-making offers two broad benefits to organisations. Firstly, the front-line employees possess detailed knowledge concerning their work, and thus have the competency to take decisions. Secondly, the more information is shared amongst employees, the better the decision-making outcomes.

In Figure 16.2, the decision-making process is expressed as a bipolar continuum with the individual decision-maker (control orientation) positioned at one extreme and the participative decision-making at the other. At the control-oriented end decisions are made by the top management without involving the employees. At the opposite end decisions are made by employees. In reality, the participative decision-making always takes place within the boundaries determined by management (Lawler 1992).

There is no general agreement on whether managers functioning as individual decision-makers are more or less effective than those who function as members of decision-making teams. The collective knowledge of a team is diverse and exceeds that of any individual. Team decision-making offers more approaches to the decision-making process, but team consensus takes longer to reach and high team cohesiveness has been found to be inherently problematic. Further, pooled judgments of non-experts were found less competent than those of a best-qualified team member, and team members were found to accept risk and uncertainty more readily than individual decision-makers. There is a general belief that greater participation in the decision-making increases the acceptance of the final choice (Janis 1982, Campbell 1968, Stoner 1968, Tattersall 1984).

A recent example of individual decision-making is Roger Carr, chairman of Cadbury, the British confectionery company founded in Birmingham in 1831. Carr negotiated a hostile takeover bid by the American Kraft Foods and secured a 'good' price for the company and recommended that the shareholders accept the settlement. In an interview, he stated that as a chairman, he was employed and paid by shareholders to get the best deal for them, and in the prevailing financial markets £11bn is considered a good deal. The winners of this deal are

Figure 16.2 The decision-making process in organisations

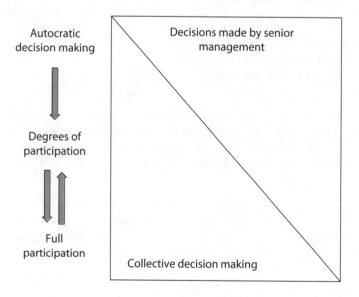

the senior managers, who will get pay-offs or bonuses; the fund managers, whose performance (and therefore remuneration) will be boosted by a short-term blip as a result of selling out to a hostile bidder; and the bankers and lawyers, who have made bumper fees (over £200m) out of the whole business, 'as per usual' (Corrigan 2010). The likely losers are Cadbury employees losing their jobs; the UK taxpayers, who will finance the redundancy benefits; and Kraft Foods, which took on considerable debt to finance the takeover. Cadbury's chairman confirmed to the BBC that job losses are inevitable. Workers past and present voiced their concerns, with some describing the move as 'a disgrace', while others believe the brand's profile could grow in the United States' (BBC News, Corrigan 2010).

ACTIVITY 16.2

MANAGING THE KRAFT FOODS TAKEOVER OF CADBURY

You are a newly appointed a line manager at Kraft Foods. You have been briefed to use the concept of participative decision-making during the process of streamlining Cadbury operations in line with those of Kraft Foods.

- Where will you begin?
- What do you need to know?
- Who do you need to talk to?

You already have a fair understanding of how your unit feels about the changes and also of the overall morale among your staff.

- What do you need to achieve?
- How will you go about it?

Write a short in-progress report to your superiors stating your objectives, actions and times of implementation.

Then answer the following questions:

- How difficult did you find the activity?
- How easy was it to use the participative approach in this particular situation?
- What interpersonal skills did you find most useful?
- What in particular did you find difficult?
- How useful were your past experiences?

Using Figure 16.2, decide where you position yourself in managing the above situation. Remember, there are both advantages and disadvantages in involving employees in the decision-making process. The approach cannot be arbitrary, but depends on the context of socio-cultural values, the nature of the workforce and the external environment.

Research suggests that team decision-making benefits unpredictable, non-routine and one-off situations, while individual decision-making is more appropriate in routine and recurring situations. Harrison (1995) proposed the following six guidelines for the full utilisation of both individual and team decision-making strengths:

GROUP DECISION-MAKING AT A GLASS-
MANUFACTURING COMPANY

Douglas McDougal, a manufacturing line manager, was sent by his medium-sized glass-manufacturing company to attend a week-long workshop on participative leadership organised by a well-known and respected training consultancy.

Douglas was impressed by the 'hands-on' style of delivery and was active during group discussions and decision-making activities. The workshop's main message was that employees, given the opportunity, would responsibly discuss problems, and then arrive at quality decisions.

On return, Douglas decided to follow the principles he had learned at the workshop, and called a meeting with his employees. He frankly discussed the recent low production levels, which he attributed both to the recently introduced working practices and the need to upgrade the present manufacturing equipment. Without increased production output, the company was unlikely to have a future in today's fierce global competition. After having presented all the possible scenarios on the future of the company, he left his employees to discuss and to decide among themselves what steps are to be taken to remedy the situation. Douglas was confident that the group would find a rational solution that would lead to increased production, and thus ensure the company's future.

After a discussion lasting several hours, Douglas was presented with the group's unanimous decision. They declared that the working conditions were already far too demanding, and since they had been given the authority to decide their own standards, they were making a reduction in output by 5 per cent. Douglas found the decision deeply disappointing, since even the present level of production output would fail to deliver a fair profit on the owner's investment. Without implementing radical changes the company's future was uncertain. He felt let down and placed in a 'no-win' position since he could not present the decision to the company owners.

Before taking a course of action, Douglas called the workshop organisers to discuss the situation.

Questions

- What do you think happened at the group meeting?

- Should Douglas have anticipated the group decision-making outcome? Justify your answer.

- Given the current situation, was Douglas right to use participative decision-making in this way?

- What would be your advice to Douglas? Be specific in your suggestions and justify your decision.

- The combined knowledge of team members is superior in setting organisational objectives.

- In searching for alternatives, pooled individual efforts offer a wide variety of options.

- The collective judgment is best utilised in evaluating options proposed by individuals.

- In situations of high risk, the team decision is likely to be accepted as a result of participation of those who will be affected by its consequences.

- Decisions made by both individuals and teams must be implemented by individual managers, who are then responsible for the outcomes.

- Follow-up and control procedures also must be carried by individual managers at the point of implementation.

16.5 LEADING MANAGEMENT MEETINGS

Team decision-making more often than not takes place during meetings, even though meetings are not always very popular among staff. Meetings are conducted to inform, to instruct and to persuade. Barrett (2006, p213) states that 'meetings matter because that's where an organisation's culture perpetuates itself.' Meetings can take many forms and are the settings for communicating strategy, management planning, organising and resolving problems. As meetings take up a significant amount of working time, they need to be effective and productive.

ACTIVITY 16.3

MY RECENT MEETING ...

Remind yourself of a recent meeting that you attended and answer the following questions about it:

- What was the topic of the meeting?
- Who chaired the meeting?
- Did you receive an agenda prior to, or at the beginning of, the meeting?
  - What were the ground rules?
  - How were the ground rules presented?
  - Were you satisfied with the procedure?
- What preparations did you make for the meeting?
- Did you contribute to the discussion? Was contribution encouraged?
- Was the meeting well structured?
- What decisions were taken? Did you agree with them?
- Were the participants satisfied with the meeting?
- How was the meeting concluded?
- Were any follow-up measures proposed?
- If you had chaired the meeting, what differences would you have made?

In order to conduct meetings effectively, you need to be able to determine whether a meeting is an appropriate forum for your activity in the first place and whether it will deliver the desired outcome. Barrett (2006) suggests a four-step approach for small-group meetings in organisations:

1. **Deciding whether a meeting is the appropriate forum**: This is the first step in conducting a productive meeting. One of the first considerations is the purpose, the audience and the desired and likely outcomes. The following questions have to be answered before the next step can take place:
   – Is a meeting necessary and what is to be accomplished?
   – Are there other more suitable alternatives?
   – What is the expected outcome from the meeting?

2. **Planning the meeting**: Once the above questions have been satisfactorily answered, the meeting can be planned. The following questions need to be answered:
   – Selecting the appropriate participants. The selected attendees must have an important stake in the outcome of the decision, and contribute towards the meeting objectives outcomes in terms of diversity and expertise.
   – Information and materials needed for the meeting. Circulating in advance prepared and distributed agendas with supporting information increases the likelihood of achieving the meeting's planned outcomes.
   – The items on the agenda to be included need to follow from the objectives. The time for each must be realistic and not allowed to overrun.
   – The place, settings and timing for the meeting must be appropriate for the purpose. Seating arrangements can be critical in determining the flow of interaction. Holding a meeting in an office carries a different message from using a dedicated room. For example, the organisation's culture may play a part and in some organisations the most senior member of staff in the meeting may always be seated at the head of the table, while others are seated according to rank. If disagreements or hostilities are expected, then key individuals can be interspersed around the room to prevent forming power groups and similar groupings. Timing too is important, and attendees' schedules and commitments should be taken into account.

3. **Conducting the meeting**: for a meeting to be productive, the following activities must take place:
   – The meeting must start on time, participants must be introduced to each other if they do not know each other already, the agenda must be presented and any actions agreed on the previous meeting must be discussed. The roles and responsibilities of the leader, the facilitator, the minute-taker and the time keeper must be determined ahead of or at the beginning of the meeting. The agenda of the meeting must be followed. However, an organisation's culture will often determine the format of a meeting, the decision-making process and the discussion.
   – The standing ground rules for each meeting need to be established. The number of interruptions must be minimised and valid contributions to be encouraged. Again, different organisational cultures may determine whether active participation and contributions are encouraged. Figure 16.3 provides a checklist for conducting an effective meeting. Box 16.2 (on p487) summarises a number of problem-solving activities commonly used by teams. These provide a creative way of dealing with unusually complex or politically sensitive problems.

4. **At the end of the meeting:**
   – Action and responsibilities agreed on at the meeting are to be assigned to appropriate individuals.
   – Summarise the meeting, including the assigned deliverables.
   – Jointly agree on the date of the next meeting.
   – Close the meeting.

5. **After the meeting:**
   – Distribute the meeting minutes in a timely manner.
   – Follow up on actions in-progress.

A prescriptive approach to holding a meeting, as suggested above, may look like an attempt at micromanaging. This may well be the case, but we all will have attended badly managed meetings which left us feeling dissatisfied and which wasted valuable organisational resources. Well-structured meetings, on the other hand, tend to finish on time, encourage fuller participation and have more productive outcomes.

Running an effective meeting does not come naturally but is a learned skill. A meeting is effective when well structured and mindful of the participants' time. Effective meetings result in higher-quality solutions, and thus can improve participants' morale. Let us return now to Barrett's (2006) four-step model.

Figure 16.3 Checklist for conducting an effective meeting

- Start on time
- Introduce:
  - the leader
  - the facilitator
  - the minutes taker
  - the timekeeper.
- Review the agenda
  - Check for adjustments if necessary.
- Introduce all attendees if necessary.
- Follow the agenda.
- Eliminate or minimise interruptions
  - In a virtual meeting minimise background noise
  - Avoid:
    - side-conversations.
    - tapping of pens
    - shuffling of papers.
- Encourage participation
  - The level depends on the organisation's culture and the meeting's purpose.
- Conclude the meeting
  - Review decisions reached.
  - Assign activities to be carried out.

BOX 16.2: PROBLEM-SOLVING ACTIVITIES FOR TEAMS

There are many useful activities available to teams for generating new ideas. The activities range from relatively simple ones such as brainstorming – a fast generation of an exhaustive list of ideas – to relative complex ones such as the scenario, an evaluation of a preferred alternative at the end of the strategic decision-making process (see also Chapter 14).

Some of the activities have their basis in the means–end analysis (MEA), using a general heuristic strategy of gradual reduction in distance between the current situation and the current goal. The major aim of this heuristic is to divide a problem into manageable parts that are then dealt with by trying different methods, and incorporating progress checks that indicate whether the problem-solvers are on the right track (Simon 1979). Another approach is a state-space theory developed for use when one situation needs to be changed into another. Here the solution takes a sequence of action akin to travelling along tree branches towards the desired goal (Garnham 1988).

The advantages of team problem-solving activities are twofold: efficiency and creativity. Efficiency is gained through encouraging teams to work together using a common approach and arriving at a joint solution, which is likely to save time and money (Barrett 2006). Creativity utilises knowledge, intellectual abilities and personality characteristics, such as self-confidence and an ability to handle criticism (Godfrey 1986).

Brainstorming

This is a technique intended to produce new ideas and solutions to problems that are new to the organisation by simulating creativity and encouraging group members to build on the contributions from others (see also Chapter 14).

Session 1

1. Team members are presented with a problem.
2. The team members then generate ideas with brief explanations.
3. Each idea, however risky or impractical, is recorded for all to see.
4. No evaluating comments are allowed.
5. Each member is asked to generate as many ideas as possible.

Session 2

6. The alternatives ideas are evaluated for their usefulness.
7. The team members then end up with a few realistic alternatives.

Brainstorming is unlikely to provide resolutions to problems; it provides a few realistic alternatives for further consideration.

The nominal group technique (NGT)

This is used in a later stage of brainstorming by offering a means with which to identify a problem and select appropriate criteria for evaluating alternatives.

1. The team convenes to address an issue.
2. Each individual writes a list of ideas. The activity is timed.
3. Team members present their ideas to the rest. This could be done anonymously if appropriate.

4. All the ideas are recorded for all to see.

5. More ideas are generated from the shared list.

6. A discussion of the ideas on the list takes place.

7. Team members then anonymously rank the presented ideas.

8. The generation–discussion–vote process may continue until a decision is reached.

The nominal group technique offers an advantage in using anonymity for generating ideas (and/or voting), thus minimising the negative effects of power and status differences between members.

The Delphi technique

This is similar to the nominal group technique and is used to gather judgments from experts in the forecasting process (see also Chapter 3). This technique uses questionnaires to generate and evaluate alternatives and is often deployed when experts are geographically dispersed.

Other techniques

Techniques such as the **SWOT** (strengths, weaknesses, opportunities and threats), **'from–to'** (current to desired future situation), and **force-field** (current to desired future situation, and driving/restraining forces) analyse attempt to deal with organisational changes (see also Chapter 17). They evaluate the current position against the desired new state, taking account of the organisation's background of strengths (or drivers), weaknesses (or restraining forces) and the impact of the external environment. The objective of the exercise is twofold: to seek new opportunities and to effectively manage the change.

Opposition and analyses

Opposition and the scenario analyses force the team members to evaluate both the risks and benefits inherent in the preferred. The outcome of the evaluation then determines the future action to be taken.

 ## ACTIVITY 16.4

MANAGING A MEETING ABOUT ORGANISATIONAL PRACTICES

For this activity form a group of up to six members. Enact a meeting for the following scenario and employ any participative decision-making skills that you think can be used safely in this situation.

You have been selected to chair a quality task team meeting. The task team was formed to discuss and make suggestions about policies and procedures to deal with employees doing personal business during office hours. Over the past few months, senior management became aware that some employees spend a substantial amount of time doing personal business from work. They came to a conclusion that this accounts for substantially decreased output. When the unit managers were approached about the problem, some responded that their employees would reasonably argue that some personal business can be done only during office hours; thus it would not be fair to expect them to take personal leave to sort out things that usually take only a few minutes. Other managers dismissed the concern, saying that the amount of time lost wasn't worth worrying about. What is more, they argue, taking any punitive action would likely result in negative feelings toward the organisation.

In your meeting, discuss the following issues:

- How can you monitor and change staff behaviour?
- How can you improve working practices to ensure employee productivity generally?

Once you have conducted the meeting, reflect on the following issues:

- How did you prepare for the meeting?
- How did you run the meeting?
- What happened during the meeting?
- Did all task force members participate in the meeting?
- Did your team propose any follow-up measures?
- Would you run future meetings differently? If so, what would you change?

4. **Managing problems and conflicts**: Conflicts occur when the values, norms, beliefs and attitudes of individuals and groups clash. In a situation of interdependence when departments and individuals have incompatible goals and interests but cannot accomplish tasks independently, individuals can experience both internal and intrapersonal conflict. Other conflict situations may arise when having to choose between two equally desirable options, when outcomes carries both positive and consequences, or when having to choose between two or more negative outcomes (Lewin et al 1939).

Sometimes problems discussed at meetings turn into conflict. When this happens, the meeting must be interrupted and the conflict has to be negotiated there and then if it is not to spill into the working environment. Conflicts are an inherent part of both organisational and private lives; they are not always dysfunctional but can be positive by acting as agents of change (see also Chapter 6 and Chapter 7). In organisations, conflict arises mainly from organisational structures and communication errors. Managers spend up to half of their working time on dealing with conflict.

Conflict progresses through a number of stages (Quinn et al 2003):

Stage 1: Conflict is latent; the situation is set up for conflict, for example due to the organisational structure, although neither party senses the conflict.

Stage 2: There is a perception of a potential conflict by one or both parties. This could be cognitive or/and emotional, where the concerned individuals or groups become aware of their differences. The other party gets the blame, and emotional reactions such as hostility, frustration, anxiety and pain take place.

Stage 3: Cognitive or/and emotional feelings lead to action, where conflict becomes overt, and steps are taken to resolve the conflict either explicitly or implicitly. This may be demonstrated as aggressive behaviour, both verbal and physical. At this stage the conflict can be resolved only if both parties are positive (see also Chapter 7).

Stage 4: Functional resolution of the conflict fosters a better understanding, improved quality of decision, increased attention to creativity and innovation, and most importantly, positive self-evaluation. Dysfunctional outcomes include continued anger and hostility, reduced communication, destruction of team spirit, and can snowball into new conflicts.

16.6 TEAM EFFECTIVENESS AND CONFLICT

Conflict situations in a team can be rooted in a wide range of human emotions felt by one or more of the members. These emotional states can include resentfulness, anger, hurt feelings and defensiveness, to name but a few that in turn can lead to friction, mistrust, ego-clashes, tension and open personal disagreement (Jehn, 1997). A team experiencing relationship conflict (Guetzkow and Gyr 1954) may become dysfunctional. The imperative for the team leader is to have the necessary people skills to turn relationship conflict into task conflict or to design the team so that the likelihood of relationship conflict does not emerge. As outlined in Chapter 6, Belbin's (1993, 2008) team role theory may be utilised to compile a potentially effective team.

However, not all team leaders have the luxury of designing their team. This is why the more constructive task conflict is crucial to developing team cohesiveness. For many in leadership roles, managing task conflict (or managing an open debate) is thought of as difficult and potentially risky. The essence of managing task conflict over a period of time (Jehn and Mannix 2001) is to have the team focus on a particular project, plan or task. They can then debate the merits of one method for achieving the team's goals over another, thus offering an outlet for tension and for the most part avoiding personalising an argument (see also Chapter 7). A major element of team cohesion is to agree on the common goals and to share the vision; it is only by sharing the vision that a team can become homogeneous. Agreeing common goals helps to define the ground rules or decisions about how the team will operate, whereas creating or sharing a vision can enlist 'buy-in' to where the team want to be and what they all want to achieve. This is where a skilled leader would employ factors that promote collective interest, for instance an attempt to instil and communicate a common identity leading to a team culture, be aware of shared threats, harmonise jobs/work, and encourage relationships and friendships both within the team and with other, similar teams. The latter can help to ensure that the team is not isolated and thus can avoid the harmful effects of 'group think' (Janis 1982).

16.7 CONFLICT-HANDLING STRATEGIES

Thomas (1976) developed a conflict negotiating approach involving different levels of assertiveness (ie the degree to which a party is concerned with their own interests) and co-operation (ie the degree to which a party is concerned with the other parties' interests). Each of the resulting five conflict-handling modes, which are discussed in more detail in Table 16.2, will have its use in handling different conflict situations.

Table 16.2 Conflict-handling modes

Mode	Criteria	Explanation	Appropriate use
Avoidance	Low assertiveness Low co-operativeness	Recognises but does not address the conflict, thus satisfies neither party. Both parties withdraw and put up a barrier. Avoidance is useful during the 'cooling-off' period, although the conflict remains unresolved. Later all the problems tend to surface again, and important management issues will not be addressed.	• When an issue is trivial. • When there is no chance of satisfying own concerns. • When potential disruption outweighs the benefits. • When gathering information supersedes immediate decision. • When others can resolve the conflict more effectively. • When issues seem tangential and symptomatic of other issues. • When cooling down.
Accommodation	Low assertiveness High co-operativeness	Act only to satisfy the other party's concerns by preserving harmony, and avoiding disruptions. Accommodation exploits the individual's willingness to sacrifice personal needs. Although it is useful in the short term, in the long term, it stifles creativity and innovation.	• When wrong-footed. • When issues are more important to others. • When building social credits for later use. • When minimising losses after being outmatched and losing. • When harmony and stability are very important. • When learning from mistakes.
Competing	High assertiveness Low co-operativeness	Satisfies one party's own goals only, relies on authority structures and formal rules, and is used in 'win–lose' situations. Competing can be appropriate for quick and decisive action, but limits creativity and new ideas.	• When quick, decisive action is needed. • When unpopular actions need implementing. • When issues are vital to the organisation's interests. • Against those who take advantage of non-competitive behaviour.

continued overleaf

Table 16.2 continued

Mode	Criteria	Explanation	Appropriate use
Collaborating	High assertiveness High co-operativeness	Concerns both own and others' interests. There are no underlying assumptions of fixed resources and giving something up in order to gain. It offers a 'win–win' situation, is good for cohesion and morale, but may not always work.	• When seeking an integrative solution. • When the objective is to learn. • When sharing insights. • When gaining commitment. • When working with negative feelings.
Compromising	Medium assertiveness Medium co-operativeness	Is first in the solution approaches, depends on giving up something in order to get something else, and neither party wins or lose.	• When goals are not worth the effort to disrupt. • When dealing with an equal opponent. • When seeking temporary settlements to complex issues. • When seeking an expedient solution under time pressure. • As a back-up when collaboration fails.

Source: drawing on Thomas (1976, 1977).

We have seen that these five conflict-handling modes can be used to approach a wide range of conflicts in organisations. One problem we may face, however, is that we tend to be blind to our problems and often resist resolving personal conflicts. Although painful, we may sometimes find ourselves prolonging the conflict by refusing to see the other person's point of view. However, the above approaches can be learned and require practice, which will enhance our ability to deal with conflict in both our professional and private lives more constructively. It becomes clear from Table 16.2 that the collaborative approach is the only one of the five styles that can create a genuine 'win–win' situation beneficial to all parties involved (see also Chapter 6).

16.8 CONCLUSION

Leading and managing people in a team context can be motivating, interesting and at times exasperating. It requires a diverse set of people skills to deal with the individual team members' expectations, behaviours and emotions, to encourage participation and creativity and to deal with conflict. This skill set operates at different levels – the strategic, the operational and the personal – and team leaders have to work very hard to build the very diverse skills required to lead effectively. We also have to remember that team leadership and team dynamics do not happen in a vacuum, but that they are influenced by the organisation's culture, dynamics, rules, systems and procedures. Hence, a leader can be extremely effective and successful in one organisation, but then fail miserably in another. Nevertheless, an effective leader in a wide range of contexts will be confident, honest, intelligent, creative, will have a drive for achievement and the ability to motivate others and to adapt. Generally effective leaders will also be emotionally intelligent, being able to read different team situations in order to identify and manage emotions.

PAUSE FOR THOUGHT

Identify at least three things that you have learned by studying this chapter and engaging with the activities. How will your newly acquired knowledge and skills support your continuing professional development? What value do you expect your learning to have for your daily routines and your further career? In what area have you identified a need for further development and how are you planning to fill that gap? Address these issues in your learning journal and/or CPD log. You may also wish to discuss them with a peer, colleague, mentor or coach to aid your further development.

KEY LEARNING POINTS

- Leadership theories have looked at leaders' personality traits and the different situations in which leaders tend to operate.
- Team leaders require a wide range of people skills to be effective.
- Good team leadership can enhance a team's and an organisation's performance.
- Effective meetings make good use of resources and are a valuable tool for managing and making decisions in team situations.
- Conflict can be handled using five distinctive modes that will be effective in different situations and for different purposes.

EXPLORE FURTHER

BELBIN ASSOCIATES. (ND) [website], http://www.belbin.com, http://www.belbin.info

16.9 REFERENCES

ADAMSON, I. (1997) Management consultants' intervention styles and the small organisation. *Journal of Small Business and Enterprise Development*. Vol. 4, No.2, pp55–65.

ALIMO-METCALFE, B., ALBAN-METCALFE, J., SAMELE, C., BRADLEY, M. and MARIATHASAN, J. (2007) *The impact of leadership factors in implementing change in complex health and social care environments*. Department of Health NHS NIHR SDO project 22/2002.

ALIMO-METCALFE, B. and BRADLEY, M. (2008) Cast in a new light. *People Management*. 24 January. Available online at: http://www.peoplemanagement.co.uk/pm/articles/2008/01/castinanewlight.htm [accessed 30 May 2010].

BARKER, R.A. (2001) The nature of leadership. *Human Relations*. Vol. 54, No. 4, pp469–494.

BARRETT, D.J. (2006) *Leadership communication*. Singapore: McGraw-Hill.

BBC NEWS. Available online at: http://bbc.co.uk/news.

BELBIN, R.M. (1993) *Team roles at work*. London: Butterworth-Heinemann.

BELBIN, R.M. (2008) *Management teams: why they succeed or fail*. 2nd ed. Oxford: Butterworth-Heinemann.

BOYATSIS, R., MCKEE, A. and JOHNSTON, F. (2008) *Becoming a resonant leader*. Boston, MA: Harvard Business School Press.

BROWN, R. (1965) *Social psychology*. New York: Free Press.

BURNS, J.M. (1978) *Leadership*. New York: Harper and Row.

CAMPBELL, J.P. (1968) Individual versus group problem solving in an industrial sample. *Journal of Applied Psychology*. Vol. 52, No. 3, pp205–210.

CLEGG, S., KORNBERGER, M. and PITSIS, T. (2005) *Managing and organisations*. London: Sage.

CORRIGAN, T. (2010) Available online at: http://www.telegraph.co.uk/finance/comment/tracycorrigan [accessed 19 January 2010].

FIEDLER, F.E. (1967) *A theory of leadership effectiveness*, New York: McGraw-Hill.

FIEDLER, F.E. (1971) Validation and extension of the contingency model of leadership effectiveness. *Psychological Bulletin*. Vol. 76, No. 2, pp128–148.

GABRIEL, Y. (2008) *Organising words*. Oxford: Oxford University Press.

GARNHAM, A. (1988) *Artificial intelligence: an introduction*. London: RKP.

GODFREY, R.R. (1986) Tapping employees' creativity. *Supervisory Management*. Vol. 31, No. 2, pp17–18.

GOLEMAN, D., BOYATSIS, R. and MCKEE, A. (2002) *Primal leadership*. Boston, MA: Harvard Business School Press.

GROSS, R.D. (1993) *Psychology: the science of mind and behaviour*. 2nd ed. London: Hodder and Stoughton.

GUETZKOW, H. and GYR, J. (1954) An analysis of human conflict in decision-making groups. *Human Relations*. Vol. 7, No. 3, pp367–382.

HARRISON, E.F. (1995). *The managerial decision making process*. 4th ed. Boston: Houghton Mifflin.

HOUSE, R.J., HANGES, P.J., JAVIDAN, M., DORFMAN, P.W. AND GUPTA, V. (2004) (eds.) *Leadership, culture and organisations: the GLOBE study of 62 societies*. Thousand Oaks, CA: Sage.

JANIS, I.L. (1982) *Groupthink*. 2nd ed. Boston: Houghton Mifflin.

JEHN, K.A. (1997) A qualitative analysis of conflict types and dimensions in organisational groups. *Administrative Science Quarterly*. Vol. 42, No. 3, pp530–557.

JEHN, K.A. and MANNIX, E.A. (2001) The dynamic nature of conflict: a longitudinal study of intragroup conflict and group performance. *Academy of Management Journal*. Vol. 4, No. 2, pp238–251.

LAWLER, E.E. (1992) *The ultimate advantage: creating the high involvement organisation*. San Francisco, MA: Jossey-Bass.

LEWIN, K., LIPPITT, R. and WHITE, R. (1939) Patterns of aggressive behaviour in experimentally created social climates. *Journal of Social Psychology*. Vol. 10, pp271–299.

LIKERT, F.E. (1967) *A theory of leadership effectiveness*. New York: McGraw-Hill.

QUINN, R.E., FAERMAN, S.R., THOMPSON, M.P. and MCGRATH, M.R. (2003) *Becoming a master manager: a competency framework*. 3rd ed. New Jersey: Wiley.

SIMON, H.A. (1979) Information processing theory of human problem solving. In W. Estes (ed), *Handbook of learning and cognitive processes*. Vol. 5. Hillsdale, NJ: Laurence Erlbaum.

SIMS, H.P. (1987) Leading workers to lead themselves. *Administrative Science Quarterly*. Vol. 32, No. 1, pp106–128.

STONER, J.A.F. (1968) Risky and cautious shifts in group decisions. *Journal of Experimental Social Psychology*. Vol. 4, pp442–459.

TATTERSALL, R. (1984) In defense of consensus decision. *Financial Analysts Journal*. Vol. 40, No. 1, pp55–67.

THOMAS, K.W. (1976) Conflict and conflict management. In M.D. Dunnette (ed), *Handbook of industrial and organisational psychology*. New York: Wiley.

THOMAS, K.W. (1977) Toward multi-dimensional values in teaching. *Academy of Management Review*. Vol. 2, No. 3, pp487.

TURNER, J.C. (1991) *Social influence*. Milton Keynes: Open University.

ULRICH, D. and ALLEN, J. (2009) Grow your own. *People Management*. 3 December. Available online at: http://www.peoplemanagement.co.uk/pm/articles/2009/12/grow-your-own.htm [accessed 29 May 2010].

ULRICH, D., ALLEN, J., BROCKBANK, W., YOUNGER, J. and NYMAN, M. (2009) *HR Transformation*. McGraw Hill.

CHAPTER 17

Leading change and development in organisations

Stefanie C. Reissner

OVERVIEW

Organisational change is a constant reality and its management is a key challenge for managers and employees alike. The stakes are high, it seems: if an organisation does not change, its future prosperity and even survival may be under threat. Yet, managing organisational change is a complex task that involves two main aspects: the business processes that govern an organisation, including strategic and operational considerations, and cultural aspects such as the roles and relationships of the organisational actors (ie all those working for an organisation). In contrast to other accounts of organisational change, this chapter focuses on the interplay of business and people aspects as well as the skills and key tools that managers and employees will need to manage organisational change successfully. It will also explore the use of consulting and coaching to facilitate change and associated skills that each manager will benefit from when tasked with leading a change programme.

LEARNING OUTCOMES

By the end of this chapter, provided you engage with the activities, you should be able to:

- understand the key aspects of organisational change
- appreciate the importance of the context of change
- apply business skills to the management of change
- apply people skills to the management of change
- understand how consulting and coaching can support the management of change.

17.1 INTRODUCTION

ACTIVITY 17.1

ORGANISATIONAL CHANGE

What comes to mind when you hear the term 'organisational change'? Are you dreading the mere mention of it or are you excited about what is to come? Why do you think you react the way you do? What are your experiences with organisational change? Take a few minutes to jot down some thoughts; you will need them later for the activities of this chapter.

Organisational change is a complex interplay between business processes that can be designed and implemented and the meanings that organisational actors (ie those working for an organisation) attribute to it. Hence, it can only be understood and managed through the experiences of those involved (Dawson 2003b). The challenge is that organisational change means different things to different organisational actors. For some, it is an exciting opportunity to turn around an organisation or parts of it, to make their name or just to do something new. For others, change means unsettling times, a break with routines and old truths, and the fear of pay cuts and redundancy. Due to the major differences in the ways that organisational actors understand and experience organisational change, managing it is a difficult and complex task. Organisational change is often a rigid and controlling process of renewal and it is therefore not surprising that many change initiatives fail (Beer and Nohria 2000). In order to succeed at managing organisational change, managers and change agents need to focus their attention on reading situations of change and respecting the organisation's context, history and culture; this requires a complex set of skills including analysis of business processes, self-awareness and people skills.

This chapter explores the key aspects of organisational change and essential strategies for its management by focusing on both business and people aspects. Business aspects of organisational change will be discussed in Section 17.2 below. I propose a five-stage model of organisational change and consider contextual issues that affect the organisation and the way it changes. Section 17.3 of this chapter will examine people issues, including an understanding of the perceptions, experiences and skills of different organisational actors. I will introduce tools to raise awareness in individuals and teams to support change and development within the organisation. In Section 17.4, I will bring business and people aspects of change together and discuss issues of leadership, agency and sustainability of organisational change. Section 17.5 will explore consulting and coaching as means to facilitate change and to develop both managers and staff. Each section will be complemented by reflective activities to help you to understand yourself and your role in organisational change better.

17.2 BUSINESS SKILLS FOR CHANGE

17.2.1 CONCEPTS OF ORGANISATIONAL CHANGE

Organisational change has been understood in a multitude of ways and is regarded here as 'a process by which an organisational entity alters its form, state, or function over time' (Stevenson and Greenberg 1988, p742). This definition comprises anything from systematic continuous improvement (Drucker 1999) through fine-tuning activities to major programmes of transformation (Dunphy and Stace 1993). It comprises change that has been planned as well as change that has emerged naturally (Wilson 1992). It also comprises change programmes that are reactive as well as those that anticipate external changes (Dawson 2003a). The processual nature of organisational change makes it a dynamic and fluid phenomenon that is challenging to manage. Each change programme involves a unique mix of factors and there is no recipe for the management of change, even though the management literature often seeks to create that impression. The good news is that studies of organisational change have identified factors that increase the likelihood of successful change management (or, put differently, the absence of which increases the risk of failure). Drawing on Plant (1987), Kotter (1995) and Murray and Richardson (2003), I propose the following process of organisational change (Figure 17.1).

The first step in this process is the detailed analysis of (1) the organisation's context (ie its external and internal environment) to establish any opportunities and threats that the organisation may face and (2) the change challenge to create a detailed understanding of what the change programme seeks to establish; this is vital to provide direction. The second step is to devise vision and mission (Plant 1987), a shared understanding of the change challenge (Murray and Richardson 2003) and a sense of urgency (Kotter 1995) as well as strategies and tactics which will increase its chances for success (Ulrich 1997). This is usually done by a change team (Kotter 1995) which will prepare the organisation for the changes to come (Armenakis et al 1993) and manage the change process. The third step focuses on communicating the vision, mission and urgency of the change programme to the organisational actors and to develop a shared understanding of what lies ahead (Murray and Richardson 2003). It is vital that communication at this stage goes beyond a single meeting or vast amounts of

Figure 17.1 A five-step model of organisational change

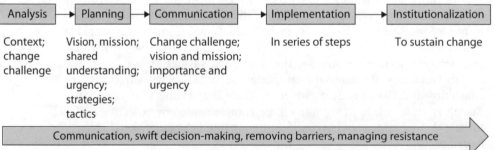

Analysis	Planning	Communication	Implementation	Institutionalization
Context; change challenge	Vision, mission; shared understanding; urgency; strategies; tactics	Change challenge; vision and mission; importance and urgency	In series of steps	To sustain change

Communication, swift decision-making, removing barriers, managing resistance

Time

written materials. Kotter (1995) emphasises that change programmes need to be communicated in a way that reflects their importance and urgency within the organisation over a sustained period of time to capture the hearts and minds of those affected and to get their involvement in making change happen. The fourth step is about implementing the change programme, ideally in stages with clearly defined milestones so that each stage can build on the momentum of the previous one. It is important to build in flexibility, both in design and implementation (Ulrich 1997), so as to be able to respond to any unforeseen circumstances. The fifth step is about institutionalising the change programme to make it an established part of the organisation and the way it operates; this is the key to sustaining change. It is also crucial to the potential success of a change initiative to remove any obstacles and barriers (such as structural and cultural issues) and to speed up decision-making in the communication, implementation and institutionalisation phases so as to prevent the organisation from falling back into old habits before new routines have taken root (Murray and Richardson 2003). This will require a detailed action plan and sustained commitment from all organisational actors, particularly HR professionals (Ulrich 1997), as well as changes in personnel policies and practices (Senior and Fleming 2006, drawing on Mabey and Pugh 1995).

Effective communication of any change programme, both as a step in its own right and an ongoing activity, is a vital ingredient for the management of change, and Scott and Jaffe (1989) recommend the following strategies. Firstly, organisational actors should initially be addressed in person and be given an opportunity to raise their opinion and have their questions answered. Written communication (such as newsletters or blogs) can be a useful means of further communication to support the change process. Armenakis et al (1993) suggest that external information such as press cuttings or reports may also support the message the change team wishes to communicate. Secondly, organisational actors should be informed about all aspects of the change programme, particularly those changes that may have a negative impact on their working lives. The change team may want to encourage questions in order to minimise the amount of uncertainty among organisational actors; this may help to reduce resistance. Thirdly, the change team should express their feelings as this will often reflect what other organisational actors think and feel; this can be a powerful tool to build rapport and provide a bond between different groups in the organisation

ACTIVITY 17.2

IDENTIFYING A CHANGE ISSUE

Identify a change issue in your organisation which you are involved in or contribute to. This can be anything from the introduction of a new computer system to a major restructuring exercise. Describe the change programme in detail, including what it is expected to achieve, who initiated it, how it is being implemented, how long it will take to accomplish, how the key stakeholders have reacted to it and so on. You may also want to consider your role, perceptions and experiences of this change programme. Please write down your answers as this exercise is the first step of a reflective process which will continue throughout this chapter.

(Scott and Jaffe 1989). The most powerful message of all, however, will be the change team's actions (Armenakis, Harris and Mossholder 1993). The key to successful organisational change, it seems, is to make it happen in a joint effort.

17.2.2 CONTEXT OF CHANGE

A prerequisite for the successful management of change is the analysis and understanding of the organisation's context (Reissner 2008). It consists of the organisation's external and internal environment, with the external environment comprising social, political, economic, technical and legal factors as well as industry, supply chain, market and other considerations (such as geographical location or the country's education system). The internal environment comprises the organisation's history and culture, the organisational actors' qualifications, skills, roles and relationships, their expectations, hopes and fears, values and beliefs. It is important to bear in mind that these contextual factors are dynamic and often in flux, which can make their interpretation, analysis and management difficult. One key task of managers and employees involved in shaping organisational change is the analysis of the organisation's present context (Plant 1987) as well as any anticipated changes in its external and internal environment, and there is a wide range of tools and techniques available.

A popular tool for the analysis of an organisation's external environment is PESTEL (Johnson et al 2005), which is an acronym for political, economic, social, technological, environmental and legal factors. The central premise of this model is that small changes in an organisation's environment can have a major impact on the organisation (Carruthers 2009). For each category, the key factors influencing the organisation are listed, identified as being an opportunity or threat, and rated according to how strong an impact that factor may have on the organisation. It may also be a good idea to compare the current state of the PESTEL environment with an anticipated future one so that the key factors can be identified and their impact on the organisation evaluated in more detail. PESTEL provides an overview of the wider environment in which an organisation operates and is likely to useful in most change situations. More importantly, such analysis can help an organisation to anticipate changes in its wider environment and to be proactive (Carruthers 2009). Depending on where the stimulus for a change initiative originates, more specific analysis of the competitive forces in an industry, the marketplace, distribution channels and sources of finance may have to be conducted. A detailed discussion of these is beyond the scope of this chapter. Suffice to say that techniques originating in strategy such as five forces analysis (Porter 1980), life cycle analysis and growth-share matrix, in finance (breakeven analysis, cost-benefit analysis, profit analysis and ratio analysis) and in marketing (like three Cs or four Ps) are widely used by organisations and consultants alike (Biswas and Twitchell 2002).

The analysis techniques mentioned above tend to use statistical and other quantitative data for analysis (see also Parts 6 and 7 of this book). The advantage of using established analysis techniques is that they break a phenomenon into its constituent parts for detailed examination through a structured approach. However, such techniques will rely to a large extent on the interpretation of information and forecasts, and any results will therefore be subjective. Hence, these analyses are best conducted in a team setting or in conjunction with a consultant to get a more balanced view of the situation and to get expert knowledge where appropriate. Additionally, the relatively rigid factors of established analysis tools can be a hindrance in understanding how different factors are connected to other factors within a model or how different models may complement each other. It is also important to bear in mind that analysis tools are unlikely to provide an answer as to which course of action to take. Nevertheless, such techniques will allow managers to think in a more structured manner and focus the analysis on the key factors expected to impact on the change programme and the organisation's future prospects.

An organisation's internal environment is essentially about its culture, which can be defined as its personality (Hofstede 1980) or 'patterned ways of thinking, feeling and reacting' (Kluckhohn 1951, p86). These patterned ways of thought, emotion and behaviour (which can collectively be called paradigms) derive from an organisation's history and heritage and are usually taken for granted by the organisational actors. As they are reflected in various domains of an organisation's fabric, these are made explicit in models like the cultural web, which consists of six interrelated elements that define the paradigm in which the organisation operates (Johnson and Scholes, 1992). These are:

- **Stories** or the events and characters of the past which are still talked about today, and other rhetorical means of bringing other, impersonal organisational aspects to life.

- **Rituals and routines** or daily actions and behaviours that are regarded as acceptable within the organisation. They are often described as 'the way things are done here'.

- **Symbols** or visual representations of what the organisation stands for (such as the company logo, dress code, any displays and organisation-specific jargon).

- **Organisational structure**, both as defined on organisational charts and as lived out in daily interaction.

- **Control systems** to manage finance, quality, rewards and acceptable behaviours.

- **Power structure**, or who matters in the organisation regardless of their formal position.

For analysis purposes, each element is considered in its own right and in the present time. The cultural web can be employed at different levels of an organisation, such as functions, divisions, departments or other subunits as well as the organisation as a whole. It is often a good idea to determine which aspect is crucial for each element: that is, which aspect would create the biggest difference if it was changed or taken away. (For instance, the performance of a department would suffer if George retired because he knows everything about the department and other parts of the organisation. Without George, nobody would know where to look for information or whom to ask. George is therefore in a position of great power within that department and there may be ways of sharing that power with other organisational actors.) Then the analysis can move on to what the organisational culture should be after successful completion of the change programme to determine an appropriate course of action. (For instance, the language used to address each member of a department might be changed to incorporate less swearing and to show more respect to each individual instead. Such a step would address rituals and symbols that are central to the department's way of working.) The cultural web is usually graphically represented in overlapping bubbles, which can be modified in size, position and level of overlap according to the relative importance of each element.

Tools like the cultural web can help to break down the complex phenomenon of organisational culture into smaller parts to aid detailed analysis; however, the outcome will differ depending on who conducted the analysis. It is therefore imperative to establish the views of a multitude of organisational actors so as to create the shared understanding of the change initiative that Murray and Richardson (2003) regard as vital for the success of a change programme. It is usually beneficial to seek the views of organisational actors from different parts, backgrounds and positions to get a picture that reflects reality more accurately, even though it may unearth some uncomfortable truths for management. You will also need to be aware that many of the deeper issues involved here, such as organisational actors' values and beliefs, may be difficult to uncover. There are techniques that can help to make these otherwise invisible aspects of organisational culture explicit, which are frequently used in coaching (please refer to Section 17.5 below for details).

The external and internal environments of an organisation are interdependent entities and there is usually a strong link between an organisation's environment, particularly the industry in which it operates, and the type of culture it has established. Plant (1987), for instance, suggests that organisations that receive slow feedback from their environment (such as government departments, education institutions, public utilities, pharmaceuticals and heavy industry) tend to be procedural and bureaucratic, whereas organisations that receive feedback from their environment fast (such as IT, retail, sales, construction and entertainment) tend to be more dynamic and agile. Each type of culture has to be appropriate for the environment in which an organisation operates.

The analysis of an organisation's context will determine the 'substance of change' (Dawson 2003b, p47). This term comprises a range of factors, such as the content of change, the time frame in which change needs to be completed and the criticality of change to the prosperity and survival of the organisation. It also comprises the depth of change: that is, whether the change programme works at operational, strategic, cultural or paradigmatic level. Murray and Richardson (2003) argue that each of these levels of change has a different purpose and is best achieved with a particular set of measures (see Table 17.1 opposite). Two issues need to be highlighted here: firstly, the deeper the change programme, the more difficult it will be and the longer it will take to achieve it (Hersey and Blanchard 1972 as cited in Kubr 2002, p89) and secondly, measures which are frequently advocated in the management literature in a 'one size fits all' approach may not be appropriate for the type of change required.

In summary, the analysis of an organisation's context will provide vital

Table 17.1 Depth of change and appropriate action

Level of change	Focus on	Frequently employed measures
Operational	Efficiency	Restructuring Downsizing
Strategic	Effectiveness	Improvement of business planning Restructure of product portfolio
Cultural	Attitudes, beliefs, behaviours	New leadership New vision and values
Paradigmatic	Survival	New purpose Redefinition of success

Source: adapted from Murray and Richardson (2003, p23).

information for the further change process and will determine what kind of change programme will be required and what measures are likely to yield the best results. Each change initiative will be unique in the type of opportunities and threats coming from the external environment, in the type of organisational response that will be appropriate given the organisation's history and culture, and in the ways in which a change programme will be implemented. Managers frequently look for straightforward answers when facing complex situations, but there are no recipes for managing organisational change successfully. The key skills that change agents require to manage business aspects of organisational change are numerical skills (such as finance and statistics), analysis, synthesis, evaluation, interpersonal and communication skills.

ACTIVITY 17.3

CONTEXTUAL ANALYSIS

Drawing on the change issue that you identified for Activity 17.1, determine which factors in the organisation's external or internal environment were central to the initiation, implementation and outcome of the change programme. You may want to draw on the models introduced above to aid your analysis and work with a peer or in small groups.

17.3 PEOPLE SKILLS FOR CHANGE

17.3.1 SENSEMAKING: AN ALTERNATIVE VIEW OF CHANGE

The definition of organisational change provided in the previous section lacks one crucial element: the personal dimension of organisational change: that is, the organisational actors' perceptions and experiences. Organisational change is best understood as socially constructed (Reissner 2008), which means that organisational actors ascribe meaning to events such as change, which derives from their knowledge, experiences, values and beliefs. The creation of meaning (or sensemaking, Weick 1995) is intensely personal and will differ between groups and individuals. However, the creation of meaning is central to the way in which organisational actors think and behave (Reissner 2008), and therefore needs to be taken into account when planning, designing and implementing organisational change. This is often easier said than done because many of the factors that determine the meaning of change are tacit and unacknowledged. Internal analysis using tools like the cultural web (Johnson and Scholes 1992) may provide some insights into how an organisation ticks and how any intervention may be interpreted by the organisational actors.

ACTIVITY 17.4

REACTIONS TO CHANGE

Consider the following questions: How do you react to change in your personal and professional life? Do you embrace whatever comes your way with open arms or are you more sceptical and reluctant to make any changes? You may want to draw on your experiences with change with the change issue identified above. Write down your answers; you will need them later on.

Organisational actors are often hesitant at first to commit to a programme of change and you may understand why this is the case. However, in many instances their perceptions, attitudes and behaviours change over time and many organisational actors will take an active role in making change happen. This can be after initial communication by the change team or once a change programme has begun. In my research (Reissner 2008), one manager described this process as beginning with disbelief and ridicule about the change programme, assuming that something like that just could not work. However, as the first results became evident, an increasing number of organisational actors started to acknowledge that there might indeed be something worthwhile in the initiative and began to show more commitment towards the change programme. As further results became evident, organisational actors began to take the new way of working for granted and even started to question those who remained unconvinced. This three-step process is graphically illustrated in Figure 17.2.

Figure 17.2 **Making sense of change**

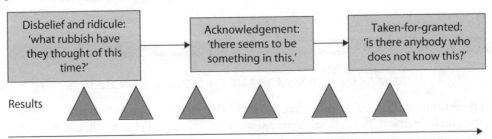

The two imperative factors in this process seem to be time and results. Few organisational actors will be convinced about the need for change merely by hearing about it from their managers, and initial scepticism is often important as a safeguard against rash decisions. While good communication may convince organisational actors to give the change programme a chance (Plant 1987, Kotter 1995, Murray and Richardson 2003), they need to see results as they go along if they are to commit more fully and over a sustained period of time to the initiative (Reissner 2008). In order to see results that shape this process, organisational actors need the time to reflect on what is happening and to make sense of it. The achievement of targets and results will enhance the credibility of the change programme and it is therefore imperative that any initiative be implemented in steps or phases.

17.3.2 UNDERSTANDING ONESELF

One major complaint among organisational actors is that change is being done to them and that they have little input into what is happening within the organisation. In an ideal world, every organisational actor has an input into a change programme and will be fully committed to its successful implementation and sustainability; change would really be a joint effort. However, most organisations do not operate in an ideal world. Many organisational change programmes will be conceived with only marginal consultation and involvement by those at the coalface, particularly in the early stages of the process. While organisational change may be an unpleasant reality for those involved, and one that is beyond their control, they can change their reaction to the initiative with some self-awareness. Throughout this book we have attempted to help you to increase your level of self-awareness, that is, the awareness of your personality traits, your skills and your expertise as well as other contributions you may make to your team and wider organisational environment. The reflective activities in this chapter will further support you on your learning journey.

Cameron and Green (2004) recommend analysis of one's personality type through the Myers–Briggs Type Indicator method (MBTI to the insider) to learn more about oneself and one's behaviour in times of change. MBTI is an application of Carl Jung's psychological type theory (Jung 1971), which is based on the assumption that each individual has natural behavioural preferences. This theory was developed further into 16 specific personality types or MBTI and is one of the most established and best-researched tools of its kind (Myers-Briggs Foundation 2007). MBTI is about preferences and not associated behaviours. This is best illustrated through the example of left and right-handedness. While left-handed people prefer to use their left hand and right-handed people prefer to use their right hand for certain tasks, they can learn to use the other hand if required. Behaviour preferences based on our personality type are no different as we can learn to behave differently if required, for instance by our role at work.

MBTI has four dimensions which, if combined in different ways, make up the 16 personality types it distinguishes. The first dimension is about where we draw our energy from. Is it a crowded shopping centre or a quiet beach? Extrovert individuals (E) tend to get a buzz out of crowds, while introvert individuals (I) tend to recharge their batteries on their own. The second dimension is about what we pay attention to and how we come to know. Is it our five senses or a detailed analysis of information? Sensing individuals (S) rely on their experiences, while intuitive (N) individuals focus on possibilities and patterns. The third dimension is about a preference of how to make decisions. Is it following an objective, logical, rational and structured process or is it based on one's gut feeling? Thinking individuals (T) prefer the structured way, while feeling individuals (F) rely more on personal values and empathy in their decision-making. The fourth dimension is about one's lifestyle. Is it structured and organised or is it flexible and spontaneous? Judging individuals (J) are drawn to the former, while perceiving individuals (P) are drawn to the latter. Each personality type is represented as four letters, which are made up by the characteristics an individual exhibits. (For instance, a test taken two years ago suggests that my personality type is ENFJ.) The MBTI framework is non-judgemental: each personality type is as valuable as any of the others (or, put differently, none is better than any of the others), and it is inappropriate to use MBTI or similar models to put individuals in rigid boxes and expect particular behaviours from them.

MBTI works with a detailed questionnaire that is used to determine one's preferences, which is only available through accredited practitioners and at a charge. However, a detailed description of the 16 personality types is available on the Myers-Briggs Foundation website and can help us to determine fairly accurately what our preferences may be – if we do not know already. Many management development programmes and coaching initiatives use MBTI as a framework to help managers to explain some of their behaviours and those of their peers and subordinates. Our personality type will influence many factors of our life which we are often unaware of, and MBTI can help to reveal such tacit factors. In the context of organisational change, MBTI can help us to explain why we react to an initiative in a particular way. Cameron and Green (2004), for

Figure 17.3 Personality and change

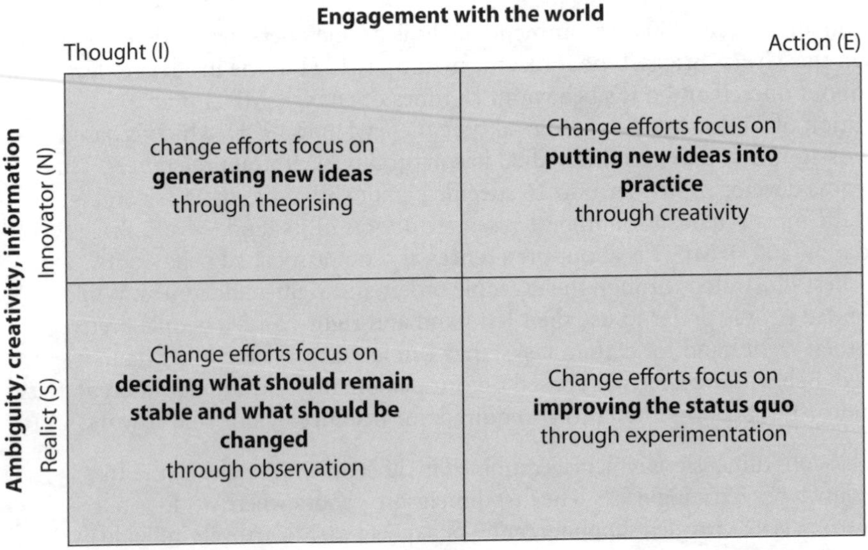

Source: adapted from Cameron and Green (2004, p45).

instance, distinguish between four types and their preferred ways of dealing with organisational change (see Figure 17.3). The introvert or thoughtful types will focus on observation, analysis and theorising, while the extrovert or action-oriented types will want to be creative, experiment and implement. The intuitive or innovative types will focus on what is new while the sensing or realist types will be drawn towards stability and the status quo.

In particular, thoughtful innovators (IN) will excel in generating new ideas for the future of the organisation, drawing on their ability to analyse and synthesise information. Action-oriented innovators (EN), in contrast, will excel at implementing change with a team of others, drawing on their creative potential. Thoughtful realists (IS) will carefully consider which aspects of the organisation need to remain untouched and which areas need to change. They are the people who will quietly observe what is going on and caution against any rash action. Action-oriented realists (ES) will focus on improving the status quo in a practical manner. Each approach to change will have its place in a multitude of change situations, and I will come back to team aspects of MBTI under the next heading.

ACTIVITY 17.5

IDENTIFYING PERSONALITY TYPES

Check the detailed descriptions of personality types on the Myers-Briggs Foundation website (http://www.myersbriggs.org/my-mbti-personality-type/mbti-basics/the-16-mbti-types.asp) and try to establish your own preferences. Please be aware that you are likely to have characteristics that feature in different categories (which are represented on the MBTI questionnaire as a continuum), so choose that side of the continuum that you think is dominant. Drawing on the 'guestablishment' of your personality type, can you explain your opinions and experiences of organisational change that you identified in Activities 17.1 and 17.3?

Armed with knowledge about their skills, expertise and personality type, each organisational actor should ask what he or she can bring to a change programme. Organisational change, after all, is a joint effort. The contributions of each organisational actor to the change effort will of course depend on their position, their role, their qualifications and skills as well as their self-awareness. Those in managerial positions and other positions of responsibility may get involved in planning, designing and implementing organisational change, conducting analyses and gathering information, or champion a particular part of the change programme. In contrast, those not in managerial positions may support their colleagues by continuing to give their best in their daily routines. I suggest that every organisational actor will have personal characteristics or skills that are valuable for change in their immediate team or wider organisation. These characteristics or skills may look insignificant but can have a big impact on morale and ways of working. The challenge for the change team will be to know who the individuals with the biggest contribution may be and actively involve them in the change programme.

17.3.3 UNDERSTANDING THE TEAM

Like individuals, teams can contribute to organisational change, and the key question should be: 'What can we bring to the change programme?' A team is a group of people who work together towards a particular goal, who determine the structure of the team and who negotiate rituals and traditions, and each team member has a role to fulfil (Luft 1984). Knowledge about the role which each team member fulfils is crucial to achieve maximum performance and satisfaction, particularly about those roles that do not appear on any official list or chart (see also Chapter 6). The trick is to identify the characteristics and skills that each team member has and their contribution to the team to raise awareness among team members. There is a simple yet powerful exercise to reveal these otherwise often hidden characteristics and skills, which is as follows. Team members ideally sit in a circle or square, this is purely for practical reasons. Each team member takes a sheet of paper, writes their name at the bottom and passes it to the person sitting on their right. The person receiving their neighbour's sheet of paper writes something he or she values about the person whose name is on the sheet, starting at the top, folds the sheet over the comment so that all contributions remain anonymous and passes it on again to the person sitting on their right. This process continues until the sheet of paper reaches the person whose name it bears. It is imperative to focus on the positive contributions of each team member rather than spending time complaining about each others' faults and weaknesses. If team dynamics allow, team members may be willing to share what has been written about them, which helps to make the different contributions explicit and makes it possible to take appropriate action. In the context of organisational change, this exercise may be used to distribute any tasks required for the initiative or to put forward any names for a role to be filled. It is vital that this process takes place in a safe and trusting environment and remains positive and non-judgemental throughout.

Knowledge of models like MBTI can also support the analysis of team situations, particularly if a team has been newly created, if roles within the team are to be redistributed or if there is conflict in the team. An understanding of different people's preferences in behaviour can help other team members to appreciate, for instance, why Paula is such a spoilsport, always asking questions about how our great ideas for change can be put into practice. It is vital in such circumstances to remain non-judgemental, as it is Paula who provides a reality check for potentially unworkable ideas, and such a contribution can be crucial for the success of a change programme. The trick is twofold: firstly, to be aware of one's own and each other's characteristics and skills, and secondly to appreciate rather than condemn differences. Knowledge of personality types can also explain why reactions to organisational change can differ considerably from team member to team member. Murray and Richardson (2003) suggest that 20 per cent of employees will actively support any change programme, while 70 per cent remain uncommitted (it is they that are often perceived to resist change), with the remaining 10 cent opposing any changes. You may be able to see the connection to Cameron and Green's (2004) application of MBTI to organisational change discussed in the previous section. The action-oriented types are more likely to support any change programme, while the thoughtful types are more likely to remain uncommitted or maybe even oppose change. You can also see that the realists may be more suitable for analysis roles while the innovators may be more suitable for design roles within the change process. The understanding of why other team members react in such ways can help you to make these issues explicit, discuss them and decide on a course of action. The challenge, however, is finding the time and space to do so.

In summary, the key skills involved in the people aspects of organisational change are self-awareness, appreciation of different traits, skills and roles, and understanding of how individuals and teams can contribute to the change effort. Other important skills include communication, analysis, synthesis and evaluation. Analysis and synthesis are likely to be based on qualitative factors deriving from reflection, observations and experiments that will be more difficult to capture than quantitative factors. Tools like MBTI are frameworks to understand and express some of the often tacit issues involved here. However, any initiative to raise self-awareness among individuals and teams requires authentic commitment and a culture that enables and supports such a process. Some organisations are better at nurturing the continuous development of their employees through training, coaching and other measures, while in other organisations such moves would be destined to fail. Again, the key to success, it seems, is to judge the appropriateness of any measure to be employed.

17.4 MANAGING CHANGE

17.4.1 CHANGE AGENCY: DRIVING CHANGE

Let us now combine business and people aspects of organisational change and consider further issues in the management of organisational change. Business and people aspects are best regarded as interdependent entities that need to complement each other if a change programme is to be successful. Business aspects tend to be relatively easy to analyse, manage and control, but people aspects can develop a life of their own that are difficult to predict and manage. If business and people aspects develop in different ways, the success of a change programme will be severely compromised. Figure 17.4 is a graphic representation of the process of organisational change and highlights potential interactions of the business and people aspects as change unfolds. For instance, the announcement that a change programme is to be launched is likely to be met with disbelief and ridicule, while communication about the need for change may

Figure 17.4 Business and people aspects of change

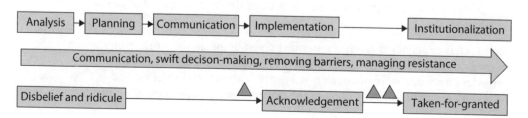

move some organisational actors to acknowledge its importance. Results in the implementation stage are likely to convince more organisational actors of the benefits of the change programme.

This figure also illustrates that it often takes a long time to get organisational actors on board and that the change team has to adapt their approach to the communication and implementation of the change programme to people's reactions, perceptions and behaviours. Change agents, the drivers of organisational change who provide direction and are involved in all stages of the change process, require a wide range of business and people skills. These include clarity, flexibility, tolerance of ambiguity, interpersonal skills, motivation, enthusiasm, sensitivity and political awareness (Buchanan and Boddy 1992) as well as credibility, trustworthiness, sincerity and expertise (Armenakis et al 1993). In addition, good change agents will have excellent communication skills and high levels of self-awareness (Plant 1987), which means that they will know when to trust themselves and when to trust others, when to talk and when to listen. Good change agents also find the right balance between the consensus required to implement change and the creative potential of difference that shapes the change process (Olson and Eoyang 2001) and fosters innovation and experimentation in the organisation (Kubr 2002) – everything needed to provide direction to an organisation in critical times.

There are a number of different approaches to change agency. Caldwell (2003), for instance, distinguishes between change agents who are senior managers, change agents who are middle managers, teams of change agents and external change agents (eg consultants). Each approach has its advantages and disadvantages, and the organisation's context and the substance of change will determine which one will be most appropriate. Regardless of the approach, the human resources function in an organisation will ideally have a central role in supporting organisational change due to its detailed knowledge of the organisation and its context, as well as the range of skills available among HR professionals. According to Ulrich (1997), four roles appear to be particularly important to support and facilitate organisational change:

- **Strategic partner**: aligns human resource strategies and practices with the overall business strategy and the way it is being executed.

- **Administrative expert**: designs, implements, maintains and evaluates human resource systems.

- **Employee champion**: builds skills and capabilities to manage organisational change and that communicates employees' concerns and needs to management.

- **Change agent and consultant**: drives change in the organisation and identifies other groups within and outside of the organisation that can drive change.

Hence, change agency is rarely about one person doing all the work, even though in many instances a change programme will have a visible figurehead that provides direction. More often, change agency is about collaboration and teamwork between different parts of the organisation and perhaps also outside parties like coaches and consultants. Poole (2004) even suggests that actions taken by someone behind the scenes may prove fundamental to the success of a change programme and that factors originating in an organisation's external environment – such as a change in government policy or an economic downturn – may limit change agents' ability to provide direction and drive organisational change. Nevertheless, sound analysis of the organisation's context and the substance of change as well as multiple initiatives and a focus on the work that promises the best results may support the change agents' work (Shepard 2005).

17.4.2 MAKING CHANGE STICK

One key challenge for managers is to institutionalise change and sustain any improvements that an initiative may have achieved, as all too often organisations slip back into established routines. The problem is, however, that there has been little research into the sustainability of change (Buchanan et al 2005) which could inform managerial practice. Nevertheless, there are several factors that are likely to determine the success or failure of an organisational change programme and whether it can be sustained in the medium or longer term. Many change programmes are destined to fail from the outset due to a lack of realistic analysis, planning, design and implementation. For instance, a change programme needs to be appropriate for an organisation and the context in which it operates, there need to be clear and stable goals as well as support for the initiative by change agents, managers, key organisational actors and trade unions as well as systems and procedures (Jacobs 2002). Moreover, it is often easier to sustain organisational change if the difficult issues are tackled first (so that organisational actors do not perceive change to get harder over time), if management commitment remains the same or increases over time, and if a change programme is perceived to be tackling problems rather than symptoms only (Senge et al 1999). In short, any change initiative needs to be properly thought through, have a strong rationale that is being communicated to all organisational actors effectively and have the buy-in from organisational actors to be sustainable.

Sustainability also requires commitment by the majority of organisational actors to do things differently on a permanent basis (Lewin 1951) and needs to be supported by managers and change agents (Kotter 1995). Cameron and Green (2004), for instance, highlight the paradoxical nature of reward systems in this context. While teamwork and collaboration are highly desirable features in many organisations, reward systems often focus on the best-performing team member. The same applies to innovation and creativity (where rewards are reaped for making no mistakes) as well as employee involvement (which is often coupled with tight operational and financial controls). Such a mismatch is counterproductive and needs to be eradicated. Hence, a change in behaviour – the behaviour of all organisational actors as well as the structures, systems, policies and procedures that govern life in an organisation – is essential for making change stick (Plant 1987). Early involvement of key organisational actors in the change programme through clear and focused communication can also facilitate the sustaining of organisational change (Kotter 1995). It is imperative that the change team pay attention to the steps of the change process outlined above as well as any others that may be specific to their organisation. As there is no recipe for successful organisational change, it is also imperative that the change programme be evaluated against expectations from time to time to detect and tackle any mismatch at an early stage. Implementing and sustaining organisational change successfully is a joint effort by all organisational actors and therefore requires an approach that reflects the collectiveness of the process.

ACTIVITY 17.6

DRIVERS OF CHANGE

Relating to the change issue you worked with above, consider agency and sustainability. Who are the drivers of change? Is there a change team that has been specifically appointed for the task? What skills, characteristics, experiences and background do they have? What part does the HR function play in designing, planning and implementing the change programme? How likely is it that the organisation will slip back into its old ways? Again, you may want to draw on the models discussed above and share your ideas with a peer or in a small group.

17.4.3 UNDERSTANDING RESISTANCE TO CHANGE

ACTIVITY 17.7

RESISTANCE TO CHANGE

One common complaint among managers and change agents is that employees resist change. Why do you think this is the case? Referring to the change situation above, identify the forms of resistance that organisational actors employ as well as any reasons for resistance. What kinds of issues feature on your list? Are they understandable or are they unreasonable?

There is a big difference between non-commitment and resistance (Murray and Richardson 2003), although the associated behaviour is often difficult to distinguish. Non-committed employees will initially remain neutral and get on with their work, while those who oppose change may do so through non-compliance. To an outsider, their behaviours may look identical and both employees may be perceived to resist change. However, the non-committed employee may yet have to be convinced of the value of the initiative to gain his or her full commitment, while it will be more difficult to convince anybody opposing change. Resistance to organisational change, whether real or perceived, is often due to a lack of knowledge and information (Plant 1987), particularly about the substance of change (Dawson 2003b), and this, in turn, is often due to a lack of appropriate communication by the change team (Kotter 1995). In such circumstances, it is understandable that organisational actors remain cautious initially. The trick, it seems, is to get sufficient backing to create the momentum to start off change, and to win an increasing number of organisational actors through results.

Other common reasons for resistance are the perceptions and assumptions of organisational actors that have been shaped by bad experiences with organisational change (Plant 1987). Key examples are the level of trust in the organisation and the strength of relationships and group norms. It is very difficult to overcome a culture of distrust in an organisation (Reissner 2008), which, however, is a key factor in making change happen. Rather than engaging in open conflict, organisational actors often disengage from the change process and demonstrate high levels of energy and creativity to counteract change in their organisation. According to Keen (1985), common initiatives include reducing the change agent's credibility and influence, bringing in representatives from different functions to reduce the impact of plans, and keeping a low profile. However, resistance to change is not limited to employees as often management pays lip-service to a change programme rather than making it happen through active leadership (Cockman et al 1999). The challenge for the change team is to identify such behaviours and address them appropriately, which is often done more successfully with outside help (see also Section 17.5).

One tool to investigate the balance of power, to identify the key organisational actors as well as the opponents and allies in a change situation, is force field analysis (Lewin 1947). It starts off with a description of the current and desired state and tries to identify how a situation will develop if no action is taken. Then, all driving and resisting forces will be listed and rated according to strength. It is important to scrutinise this list to see whether these forces are forces in their own right, if they are critical to the success of the change programme and if they can indeed be changed. A tool that can complement force field analysis is what Plant (1987) calls 'key relationship mapping'. This involves asking four questions about a proposed change programme:

- Who are the winners?
- Who are the losers?
- Who has information?
- Who has power?

It is important to bear in mind that both force field analysis and relationship mapping deal with the perceptions of those involved. Those employees who perceive themselves as winners of a change programme may need little convincing, but it may be more difficult to convince those employees who perceive themselves as losers. It may be useful for the change team to view the change process and its implications for organisational actors through their employees' eyes, as managers and employees tend to have different views of change. Management tend to focus on the opportunities and benefits of a change programme, while employees are more likely to focus on the threats and disruptiveness associated with change (Strebel 1996). The result is often a breakdown in communication, difficulties in implementing a change programme and a lack of tangible results, which will further reduce the credibility of the change programme and increase any resistance that may have developed. To increase the chances of success, managers need to examine the reciprocal obligations and commitments between the organisation and its employees and to balance the needs of different organisational actors (Duck 1993). Any intervention may be fruitfully targeted at those with information and power; persuading an organisational actor who is well respected by his or her peers to participate more actively in the initiative can make a big difference. However, dealing with people, particularly in the context of organisational change, needs to be done with utmost sensitivity and respect.

Several barriers to organisational change have been established that go beyond resistance. Carnall (2003, drawing on Adams 1987) suggests that there are five areas which can potentially block any change initiative. Firstly, perceptual blocks are about the way in which organisational actors perceive the change effort; these include the inability to view a situation from more than one viewpoint or the inability to identify a problem in a complex scenario. Secondly, emotional blocks are about the way in which organisational actors feel about change; they include fear of failure, inability to cope with ambiguity and an overcritical attitude towards any suggestions for change. Thirdly, cultural blocks are about the norms, values and beliefs that are accepted in an organisation and its wider context. These include, for instance, a tension between reason and intuition, and between tradition and change. Fourthly, cognitive blocks are about the way in which language impacts on perception; they include a lack of flexibility and creativity in the implementation of change as well as a lack of information. Finally, environmental blocks are about the support for a change initiative within an organisation, and include a lack of acceptance of alternative or deviant points of view.

In conclusion, organisational change is a minefield. A multitude of issues, both external and internal, need to be taken into account when planning, designing and implementing a change initiative. An almost infinite number of factors can make or break any change programme, some of which can be anticipated and some of which are beyond the control of those involved. Managing organisational change is less about methods, tools and techniques and more about trust, respect, honesty and transparency. It is the organisational actors that will (and will have to) make change happen together, but often it is worth seeking outside help.

 ACTIVITY 17.8

BARRIERS TO CHANGE

Drawing on your change issue, what are the barriers to change in that instance? How can they be overcome? You may want to work with a peer or in a small group again and draw on the issues discussed in this section.

17.5 FACILITATING CHANGE AND DEVELOPMENT THROUGH CONSULTING AND COACHING

17.5.1 CONCEPTS OF CONSULTING AND COACHING

The management of organisational change often benefits from support through consultants and coaches, both external and internal. A consultant is a 'person providing professional advice' (*Oxford dictionary for the business world* 1993, p175) and requires expert knowledge in a particular field (Neilson 2002). Consultants tend to work on business aspects of organisational change, aiding an organisation with the analysis of contextual data and providing expertise in the management process. A coach, in contrast, is a person who facilitates performance, learning and development (drawing on Downey 2003) and will tend to work on people aspects of organisational change. This is a crude picture, however, as roles, approaches, methods, tools and techniques that consultants and coaches employ may have considerable overlap. It may therefore be best to view consulting and coaching services as a continuum of the provision of advice and the facilitation of learning (see Figure 17.5).

Figure 17.5 The consulting–coaching continuum

Hence, in reality there are consultants who facilitate learning and development through the use of creative and open-ended methods (see the case study available on the companion website) and there are coaches who provide advice through the use of more rigid processes. For instance, what Cockman et al(1999) call the accepting and catalytic style of consulting is more about facilitating learning and development. In a similar fashion, Caplan (2003) identifies instances when coaches may be offering expert advice as part of a coaching assignment or when consultants may employ coaching techniques. For reasons of simplicity, however, I will maintain the distinction between consulting as providing advice related to business aspects of change and coaching as facilitating learning and development related to people aspects of change. Both concepts will be discussed in more detail in the remainder of this section, and the overlap between them is illustrated by the case study 'Leading Bold Change™' on the companion website.

17.5.2 CONSULTING FOR CHANGE

Consultants help managers to solve problems, improve performance, implement change and take new opportunities (Kubr 2002). While traditionally consulting has focused on analysis and research, project management, relationship management, new business development and governance issues (Biswas and Twitchell 2002), more recently the focus has shifted towards innovation, knowledge-sharing and issues related to organisational change (Czerniawska 1999). There is a vast array of consultancy firms a client organisation can choose from, including large multinational consultancy firms that provide a wide range of services, strategy and general management consultants, specialist consultancy firms, sole practitioners and small partnerships, networks and academics offering consulting services (Kubr 2002). Many consultancy firms and practitioners, regardless of their type and size, have specialised in a particular area or method, and specialisation is expected to continue (Czerniawska 1999). An increasing number of large organisations provide consulting services in-house through designated specialists and experts, which is called internal consulting. The advantages of internal consultants is that they can provide services at shorter notice and lower cost than their external counterparts and that they can instantly draw on detailed knowledge about the organisation. Internal consultants will share the same value system as the client organisation and be able to identify the key stakeholders in the consulting assignment (Cockman et al 1999). However, the disadvantage of internal consultants is that they may lack the ability to provide an outside view as only a true third party can. They may also find it difficult to be truly independent in their judgement and to get the credibility and authority that their work deserves (Kubr 2002). Internal consultants often also face ethical dilemmas about confidentiality, role conflict and information about the client that they may have gained from other assignments (Cockman, Evans and Reynolds 1999). It may therefore be beneficial to employ both external and internal consultants to support change in organisations. A range of innovative and creative approaches to consulting for change have been developed to help managers and change agents make change a reality (see, for example, the case study available on the companion website).

Consulting assignments tend to follow a series of clearly defined steps, which typically include: (1) entry to identify clients' needs, (2) diagnosis of the problem or issue in question, (3) action planning to resolve the problem in question, (4) implementation of the action plan, and (5) closure of the consulting assignment (Kubr 2002). A multitude of other processes have been developed, which follow a similar pattern of steps. Consultants can take a variety of roles, ranging from planning, organising, directing and controlling to being a leader, figurehead, spokesperson, negotiator and troubleshooter (Wickham 2004), each of which requires a distinct set of skills. Despite this vast diversity, there are at least six basic skills that every consultant needs to master (Kubr 2002). These are:

1. **Interviewing skills** to identify the client's needs and to obtain information from the organisational actors and other parties

2. **Analysis skills** to diagnose problems and issues in the client organisation and to assist in contextual analysis

3. **Organisation skills** (sometimes called project management skills) to plan the work to be done and to complete it within the allocated time frame (Wickham 2004)

4. **Interpersonal skills** to build rapport and trust with the client, to share knowledge and information and to manage the relationship with the client effectively

5. **Communication skills** to communicate problem, analysis and solution to the client organisation

6. **Presentation skills** to present proposals, action plans and conclusions.

The relationship between consultant and client is central to the success of a consulting assignment. Ideally, it is a collaborative relationship that is based on high levels of trust in which the consultant takes the role of a trusted advisor who focuses on the client and on ways of adding value to its service (Maister et al 2000). Moreover, consultants need to be independent to help their client effectively, They must be financially independent – which means they will not benefit financially from the course of action the client organisation is advised to take – and also emotionally independent, remaining detached and objective throughout the consulting assignment (Kubr 2002). Consultants have economic, legal and moral responsibilities towards the client organisation so that the organisation can improve and develop (Wickham 2004). Consultants also need to be professional, which means that they need to be competent, avoid any conflict of interest, be impartial and objective, respect confidentiality and provide value for money (Kubr 2002). Cockman et al (1999) suggest that consultants share their knowledge and expertise with the client so that they are a resource for the client, whether the latter is an individual, group or part of an organisation.

There is no doubt that consultants provide valuable services to organisations, particularly in times of change when consultants can reinforce the change message that management wishes to communicate (Wickham 2004). However, there are a few pitfalls that client organisations need to be aware of. Firstly, consultants are not always responsible for the outcome of the task or project for which they provided advice (Kubr 2002). Secondly, despite efforts to devise a system of certification (International Council of Management Consulting Institutes 2004–2008), consulting is an unregulated profession, which means that anybody can call themselves a consultant and provide advice. Thirdly, consultants can usually only be held liable for gross negligence or fraud, not for an error of professional judgement (Kubr 2002). Hence, organisations seeking the help of a consultant need to select him or her carefully as they will not only

ACTIVITY 17.9

CONSULTING FOR CHANGE

Referring to the change issue identified above, consider the involvement of consultants, both actual and hypothetical. If consultants are involved, what role do they have? What style do they use? How successful is their intervention? If consultants are not involved in this instance, consider how the scenario would differ if they were. What type of consulting would be most appropriate? What would help the organisation most with the change issue?

buy a professional service but also enter into a relationship with the consultant. Maister (1993) suggests that in their first encounter, a good consultant will be well prepared, listen to what the client has to say, be helpful and empathetic, tell the client something new and demonstrate his or her creative potential. The consultant should also prepare a proposal of how he or she seeks to address the issue in question before a contract is entered into (Kubr 2002).

17.5.3 COACHING FOR CHANGE

Coaching seeks to help organisational actors to maximise their potential, achieve their goals, improve their confidence and remove barriers to performance and achievement (Kubr 2002); it is about empowerment (Whitherspoon and White 1996) and change (Hudson 1999) rather than correcting behaviour (McManus 2006). Coaching builds on the premise that it is people that change organisations (Malone 2001) and is often used to create a culture that fosters learning and development (Burdett 1994). Such a coaching culture is open to new ways of leading and managing people, particularly in the context of knowledge management (Caplan 2003) and the sustainable success of an organisation (Clutterbuck and Megginson 2005). Hence, coaching can make lasting changes to organisations at a cultural level and overcome performance problems, increase productivity, improve staff retention, develop skills and create a positive working culture (Luecke 2004). It can be employed at executive level, particularly to support change agents in their often challenging work, at middle and lower management levels for career progression, and at specialist level to help employees to achieve their potential through specialist skills (Caplan 2003).

Coaching has its roots in athletics, and many characteristics stemming from sports coaching continue to define business coaching (Peltier 2001). For instance, trust, integrity and communication are at the heart of coaching both in sports and organisations. Coach and coachee will have a closer relationship than consultant and client, and communication is a true two-way process. Individuality, flexibility, intuition and exploration are key issues in finding what helps the coachee most to improve and develop. Visualisation, daydreaming and other creative techniques are commonly used to set goals and examine past, present and future scenarios. Coaching is often described as 'holding up the mirror' for coachees to increase their self-awareness (Wilson 2007). It is the coachee who determines which issue to explore, and the coach's task is to challenge, stretch and support. The relationship between coach and coachee is crucial in this process and needs to be based on values like respect, discovery, exploration, empathy, sharing and trust (Burdett 1994).

Interpersonal and communication skills like listening, questioning and building relationships are vital for coaches, as are analysis and synthesis skills. In the context of coaching, listening goes beyond taking in words and questioning goes beyond eliciting information. Coaches need to listen in a way that asks for more (Wilson 2007), picking up hopes, fears, expectations and other emotions that might be unacknowledged (Luecke 2004). Coaches will typically use open-ended questions that are free of judgement (Wilson 2007), challenge destructive and establish constructive thought patterns and behaviours (Malone 2001). Clarke and Dembkowski (2006) suggest that best practice in coaching is about using questions that presuppose knowledge and resourcefulness in coachees rather than putting them down. Good coaches will also know when to listen and when to talk and which question to ask in which situation (McManus 2006). Information deriving from conversations with the coachee will also need to be analysed, interpreted, synthesised and fed back to the coachee. It is often beneficial to highlight any observations, offer tentative explanations and make explicit any hidden assumptions in feedback to the coachee, in a process that needs to be sincere, timely and positive, and focus on future performance and behaviours (Luecke 2004). In order to do this effectively, coaches need to be emotionally intelligent (Hudson 1999).

A coaching assignment will follow a four-stage process (Reissner and Du Toit forthcoming): the contracting stage, selection stage, coaching stage and dissemination stage. At the coaching stage, the coaching contract will be established, which usually includes the parties to the contract and their roles, the objectives of the assignment, an initial meeting to discuss the practicalities of the assignment, a development plan containing the goals of the assignment, practicalities (eg timing, frequency, duration and location of coaching sessions), confidentiality, feedback and evaluation of the coaching assignment, payment and any external resources required (Caplan 2003).

The contracting stage is essential for the potential success of a coaching assignment and the coach needs to find out exactly what the client wants. This may sound like common sense, but it is not for three reasons. Firstly, coaches may have preconceived ideas of what an assignment is about and need to approach it with an open mind (McManus 2006). Secondly, the purpose of a coaching assignment is often not clearly defined or expressed by the client, and coaches need to find out if coaching is indeed the right measure for the person(s) and issue(s) in question (Caplan 2003). Thirdly, coaching often involves multiple stakeholders, including the person receiving coaching (coachee), a line manager, HR and potentially other sponsors, each of whom may have their own agenda. Clutterbuck and Megginson (2005) refer to this web of stakeholders and relationship as an energy field that also includes previous experiences of coaching, the capability of coaches, the beliefs and values of the stakeholders, integration of coaching into the HR system and a culture of open dialogue. In preparation for a coaching assignment, coaches need ensure that they understand the reasons for their services and what the desired outcomes will be (McManus 2006). Coaches need to be aware of the power dynamics often played out in this process and any hidden roles that the client may want the coach to take (Reissner and du Toit forthcoming).

In the selection stage, the coachee will be selected and matched with the coach in terms of style, approach and personality as well as knowledge and expertise in a particular area (Caplan 2003). Although coaching seeks to enhance and maximise the coachee's potential, there is often resistance by organisational actors to engaging in coaching. Clutterbuck and Megginson (2005, drawing on Wynne), for example, suggest that reluctance to admit weakness or a learning need, lack of clarity and lack of self-belief are common individual barriers, while excessive workloads, unwillingness to face up to uncomfortable truths and cultural issues are common organisational barriers. Potential coachees need to be receptive to coaching and motivated to change their behaviour (Jarvis et al 2006). It is customary for coach and coachee to meet at this stage to discuss the coaching assignment if this has not happened in the contracting stage. Ideally, the coachee will have asked for coaching as part of his or her development. However, in some instances the coach will have to explain to the coachee what coaching is, what the coaching assignment entails and what the potential benefits may be. The coachee needs to understand that coaching is a focused yet flexible form of development that is tailored to and owned by him or her (Jarvis et al 2006). It is at this stage that the coach needs to decide if the assignment is viable and can go ahead.

The coaching stage involves hands-on work with the coachee, usually in a series of up to six regular sessions, and focuses on questioning and challenging (Jarvis et al 2006). Coach and coachee will set targets for the overall coaching assignment and each coaching session, and break them down into smaller, achievable steps (Clutterbuck and Megginson 2005). The coaching stage may involve formal diagnostic measures (Jarvis 2004) as well as time for reflection both during and between coaching sessions to raise the coachee's self-awareness (Jarvis, Lane and Fillery-Travis 2006) and to open up pathways for learning and development. It is customary to use different techniques to facilitate coaching (for a summary of the most popular ones, see Megginson and Clutterbuck 2005). Good coaches will take every opportunity to learn and develop themselves (McManus 2006), both by reflecting on the coaching sessions and by regularly engaging in continuing professional development to improve their ability to design effective coaching, adapt their methods and approaches to the individual coaching assignment, motivate the coachee, encourage new perspectives, assist in sensemaking, identify patterns of thinking and behaviour, promote action and build resilience in the coachee (Jarvis et al 2006).

The dissemination stage refers to the period after the coaching assignment in which the coachee will disseminate new ideas and behaviours within the organisation (Reissner and Du Toit, forthcoming). A coaching assignment typically ends after the agreed number of coaching sessions (usually four to six) to give the coachee an opportunity to put his or her learning into practice and to reduce the risk of dependence on the coach (Berglas 2002). The dissemination stage is crucial for organisations to gain the full benefit of coaching, particularly when coaching is employed to support change in an organisation or to build a coaching culture (Clutterbuck and Megginson 2005). However, the dissemination of new ideas and behaviours gained through coaching depends on a culture of trust, respect and sharing, which is not available in all organisations.

A considerable challenge in coaching is the evaluation of a coaching assignment, as results are difficult to quantify. Kirkpatrick's framework for evaluating training (as cited in Caplan 2003) is often used for coaching. It distinguishes between the learner's reaction, learning, behaviours and the results of the coaching assignment and relies on subjective data. In addition, a lack of shared understanding of what is being evaluated and why, who the audience for the evaluation is and how the results may be used do hamper evaluation efforts. The benefits of coaching may therefore have to be evaluated using a range of measures that are susceptible to the often subtle yet powerful changes coaching can achieve (Gray 2004). Studies on the effectiveness of coaching have provided tentative evidence that coaching indeed improves performance and effectiveness in organisations (Sherwood 2004) and it is therefore not surprising that coaching is increasing in popularity.

The key drivers for coaching are the need for continuous development and lifelong learning, the need to attract and retain good staff, the need for targeted and timely staff development, the increasing demand for people skills among managers, a shift in cultural values and employees' demand for different types of development (Jarvis 2004; Jarvis et al 2006). Organisations wishing to employ the services of a coach should look out for the following criteria (Caplan 2003):

- qualifications, CPD, accreditation/certification
- experience and specialisation
- chemistry and style
- ways of measuring success.

Coaching is a profession in the making, with a number of formal coaching qualifications and accreditation of experience becoming more widely available, and these need to be checked prior to hiring the services of a coach. The HR function of an organisation is instrumental in supporting coaching and often fulfils coaching roles itself (Caplan 2003). In particular, HR are involved in championing and managing coaching assignments, often sponsoring or leading them (Clutterbuck and Megginson 2005). Moreover, HR are a key stakeholder in selecting coaches and coachees and bring in their expertise in selection interviewing. HR are often also responsible for evaluating any coaching assignments and for integrating coaching with other HR activities and business goals (Jarvis et al 2006). As with many other development initiatives, coaching is not effective as a one-off, tick-box exercise. It must have the full support of management and HR function as well as of potential coachees from different parts of an organisation. Most importantly, it must be the right initiative for the situation in question and have the right coach with the right approach to make coaching a success (Berglas 2002).

To bring this discussion of consulting and coaching to a conclusion, I will introduce an innovative and creative approach to supporting the management of change that combines consulting and coaching as defined above (see the case study available on the companion website). It is the *Leading Bold Change*™ workshop (ISB Worldwide

ACTIVITY 17.10

COACHING FOR CHANGE

What role does coaching have in your organisation? Do you think it would be accepted or perhaps even embraced by managers and employees? What areas of development would coaching be most appropriate for? What might be the barriers to using coaching to support change in your organisation?

2007–2009), a client-centred training programme that is being delivered to organisations across the globe. It is based on Kotter and Rathgeber's (2006) fable 'Our iceberg is melting,' a development of Kotter's (1995) eight-step model that works with story, image and metaphor. The fable is about a colony of penguins which discovers that its habitat is under threat and accordingly adapts its way of life. It includes both business and people aspects of organisational change and allows participants to explore the opportunities and challenges of change in their own organisation in a creative and playful way. For details, please refer to the case study 'Leading bold change™' on the companion website.

17.6 CONCLUSION

Organisational change is often seen as the biggest challenge that managers are currently facing, and with good reason. On the one hand, it is an impersonal phenomenon consisting of business processes that need to be re-engineered, while on the other hand, it is a very personal affair that provokes intense emotional reactions among organisational actors. It is the people aspects of organisational change that can make or break a change initiative, and although they are difficult to control they must be aligned to business aspects. The management of the business aspects of change requires different skills from the management of people aspects, and therefore organisational change is often best managed by a change team that encompasses individuals with different skills and strengths. Organisational change should focus on the improvement of the organisation, in particular on creating a culture that encourages and supports learning and development for the future survival and prosperity of the organisation. There are many pitfalls in designing, planning and implementing organisational change, some of which can be avoided by taking into account the experiences, perceptions and wisdom of organisational actors. Others may be more difficult to predict and manage, and often organisations would benefit from the support of consultants and coaches to facilitate change.

Through the activities in this chapter, I have attempted to help you to reflect on your own experiences and reactions to change and to bring them together with other, more impersonal aspects of organisational change. To be successful, organisational change is a joint effort and each organisational actor has to contribute his or her unique skills and capabilities. This, however, requires a high level of self-awareness both as individuals and in teams. The theories presented and discussed above will provide a framework for analysis and interpretation and will provide a language to express otherwise tacit issues. The challenge is to increase organisational actors' self-awareness despite time pressures and excessive workloads. This is where HR professionals have a fundamental role: they can champion organisational change and facilitate it through formal and informal development measures. By providing new experiences for organisational actors, which lead to new perceptions and behaviours, HR can be instrumental in making change happen and in developing the organisation for sustained prosperity and success.

ACTIVITY 17.11

CHANGE AND CONTINUING PROFESSIONAL DEVELOPMENT

Revisit the change issue that you identified at the beginning of this chapter and identify how your understanding of change has developed. How can you contribute to the success of change in your organisation? You may want to add your reflections to your CPD log.

PAUSE FOR THOUGHT

Identify at least three things that you have learned by studying this chapter and engaging with the activities. How will your newly acquired knowledge and skills support your continuing professional development? What value do you expect your learning to have for your daily routines and your further career? In what area have you identified a need for further development and how are you planning to fill that gap? Address these issues in your learning journal and/or CPD log. You may also wish to discuss them with a peer, colleague, mentor or coach to aid your further development.

KEY LEARNING POINTS

- Organisational change is a complex interplay between business and people aspects and requires a complex set of skills.

- Organisational change can only be understood or managed through the organisational actors' experiences.

- Consulting and coaching can support change and development in organisations if used appropriately.

EXPLORE FURTHER

ASSOCIATION FOR COACHING. (ND) [website]: http://www.associationforcoaching. com

EUROPEAN MENTORING AND COACHING COUNCIL. (ND) [website]: http://www. emccouncil.org/

MYERS-BRIGGS FOUNDATION. (ND) [website]: http://www.myersbriggs.org/.

NICKOLS, F. (2004) *Change management 101: a primer.* Available online at: http://home.att.net/~nickols/change.htm [accessed on 30 May 2010].

KOTTER, J.P. and RATHGEBER, H. (2006) *Our iceberg is melting: changing and succeeding under any conditions.* London: PanMacmillan.

REISSNER, S.C. (2008) *Narratives of organisational change and learning.* Cheltenham: Edward Elgar.

17.7 REFERENCES

ARMENAKIS, A.A., HARRIS, S.G. and MOSSHOLDER, K.W. (1993) Creating readiness for organisational change. *Human Relations.* Vol. 46, No. 6, pp681–703.

BEER, M. and NOHRIA, N. (2000) Cracking the code of change. *Harvard Business Review.* Vol. 78, No. 3, pp133–141.

BERGLAS, S. (2002) The very real dangers of executive coaching. *Harvard Business Review.* Vol. 80, No. 6, pp86–92.

BISWAS, S. and TWITCHELL, D. (2002) *Management consulting.* 2nd ed. New York: Wiley.

BUCHANAN, D. and BODDY, D. (1992) *The expertise of the change agent.* Hemel Hempstead: Prentice Hall.

BUCHANAN, D., FITZGERALD, L., KETLEY, D., GOLLOP, R., JONES, J.L., SAINT LAMONT, S., NEATH, A. and WHITBY, E. (2005) No going back: a review of the literature on sustaining organisational change. *Journal of International Management Reviews.* Vol. 7, No. 3, pp189–205.

BURDETT, J.O. (1994) To coach, or not to coach – that is the question. In C. Mabey and P. Iles (eds), *Managing learning.* London: Thomson, pp133–145.

CALDWELL, R. (2003) Models of change agency. *British Journal of Management.* Vol. 14, No. 2, pp131–142.

CAMERON, E. and GREEN, M. (2004) *Making sense of change management.* London: Kogan Page.

CAPLAN, J. (2003) *Coaching for the future.* London: CIPD.

CARNALL, C.A. (2003) *Managing change in organisations.* 4th ed. Harlow: Pearson.

CARRUTHERS, H. (2009) Using PEST analysis to improve business performance. *In Practice.* Vol. 31, No. 1, pp37–39.

CLARKE, J. and DEMBKOWSKI, S. (2006) The art of asking great questions. *The International Journal of Mentoring and Coaching.* Vol. 4, No. 2. Available online at: http://www. emccouncil.org [accessed 11 December 2007].

CLUTTERBUCK, D. and MEGGINSON, D. (2005) *Making coaching work.* London: CIPD.

COCKMAN, P., EVANS, B. and REYNOLDS, P. (1999) *Consulting for real people.* 2nd ed. London: McGraw-Hill.

CZERNIAWSKA, F. (1999) *Management consultancy in the 21st century*. Houndmills: Macmillan Business.

DAWSON, P. (2003a) *Reshaping change*. London: Routledge.

DAWSON, P. (2003b) *Understanding organisational change*. London: Sage.

DOWNEY, M. (2003) *Effective coaching*. London: Texere.

DRUCKER, P. (1999) *Management challenges for the 21st century*. New York: Harper Business.

DUCK, J.D. (1993) Managing change: the art of balancing. *Harvard Business Review*. Vol. 71, No. 6, pp109–118.

DUNPHY, D. and STACE, D. (1993) The strategic management of corporate change. *Human Relations*. Vol. 46, No. 8, pp905–920.

GRAY, D.E. (2004) Principles and processes in coaching evaluation. *International Journal of Mentoring and Coaching*. Vol. 2, No. 2. Available online at: http://www.emccouncil.org/ [accessed 13 December 2007].

HOFSTEDE, G. (1980) *Culture's consequences*. London: Sage.

HUDSON, F.M. (1999) *The handbook of coaching*. New York: Wiley.

ISB WORLDWIDE (2007–2009) Available online at: http://www.isbworldwide.com/training.html [accessed 29 March 2010].

INTERNATIONAL COUNCIL OF MANAGEMENT CONSULTING INSTITUTES. (2004–2008) Available online at: www.icmci.com [accessed 21 January 2010].

JACOBS, R.L. (2002) Institutionalising organisational change through cascade training. *Journal of European Industrial Training*. Vol. 26, No. 2/3/4, pp177–182.

JARVIS, J. (2004) *Coaching and buying coaching services: a guide*. London: CIPD.

JARVIS, J., LANE, D.A. and FILLERY-TRAVIS, A. (2006) *The case for coaching*. London: CIPD.

JOHNSON, G. and SCHOLES, K. (1992) Managing strategic change. *Long Range Planning*. Vol. 25, No. 1, pp28–36.

JOHNSON, G., SCHOLES, K. and WHITTINGTON, R. (2005) *Exploring corporate strategy*. 7th ed. Harlow: Pearson.

JUNG, C. (1971) *Psychological types*. Princeton: Princeton University Press.

KEEN, P. (1985) Information systems and organisation change. In E. Rhodes and D. Wield (eds), *Implementing new technologies*. Oxford: Blackwell, pp361–373.

KLUCKHOHN, C. (1951) The study of culture. In D. Lehner and H.D. Lasswell (eds), *The policy sciences*. Stanford, CA: Stanford University Press, pp85–101.

KOTTER, J.P. (1995) Leading change: why transformation efforts fail. *Harvard Business Review*. Vol. 73, No. 2, pp59–67.

KOTTER, J.P. and RATHGEBER, H. (2006) *Our iceberg is melting: Changing and succeeding under any conditions*. London: PanMacmillan.

KUBR, M. (ed). (2002) *Management consulting*. 4th ed. Geneva: International Labour Office.

LEWIN, K. (1947) Frontiers in group dynamics. *Human Relations*. Vol. 1, No. 1, pp5–41.

LEWIN, K. (1951) *Field theory in social science*. London: Tavistock.

LUECKE, R. (2004) *Coaching and mentoring*. Harvard Business Essentials. Boston, MA: Harvard Business School Press.

LUFT, J. (1984) *Group processes*. 3rd ed. Palo Alto, CA: Mayfield.

MAISTER, D. (1993) *Managing the professional service firm*. New York: Free Press.

MAISTER, D., GREEN, C. and GALFORD, R. (2000) *The trusted advisor*. New York: Free Press.

MALONE, J.W. (2001). Shining new light on organisational change. *Organisation Development Journal*. Vol. 19, No. 2, pp27–36.

MCMANUS, P. (2006) *Coaching people*. Boston, MA: Harvard University Press.

MEGGINSON, D. and CLUTTERBUCK, D. (2005) *Techniques for coaching and mentoring*. Amsterdam: Elsevier.

MURRAY, E.J. and RICHARDSON, P.R. (2003) *Organisational change in 100 days*. Oxford: Oxford University Press.

MYERS-BRIGGS FOUNDATION. (2007) *MBTI Basics*. Available online at: http://www.myersbriggs.org/my%2Dmbti%2Dpersonality%2Dtype/mbti%2Dbasics/ [accessed 13 December 2007].

NEILSON, G. (2002) The work of consulting. In S. Biswas and T. Twitchell (eds), *Management consulting*, 2nd ed. New York: Wiley, pp60–64.

OLSON, E.E. and EOYANG, G.H. (2001). *Facilitating organisational change*. San Francisco, CA: Jossey-Bass/Pfeiffer.

OXFORD DICTIONARY FOR THE BUSINESS WORLD. (1993) Oxford: Oxford University Press.

PELTIER, B. (2001) *The psychology of executive coaching*. New York: Routledge.

PLANT, R. (1987) *Managing change and making it stick*. London: Fontana Paperbacks.

POOLE, M.S. (2004). Central issues in the study of change an innovation. In M.S. Poole and A.H. Van de Ven, (eds), *Handbook of organisational change and innovation*. Oxford: Oxford University Press, pp3–31.

PORTER, M.E. (1980) *Competitive strategy*. New York: Free Press.

REISSNER, S.C. (2008) *Narratives of organisational change and learning*. Cheltenham: Edward Elgar.

REISSNER, S.C. and DU TOIT, A. (forthcoming) Power and the tale: coaching as story-selling. *Journal of Management Development*, Special Issue on The Use and Abuse of Stories in Organisations.

SCOTT, C.D. and JAFFE, D.T. (1989) *Managing organisational change: a guide for managers*. London: Kogan Page.

SENGE, P., KLEINER, A., ROBERTS, C., ROSS, R., ROTH, G. and SMITH, B. (1999) *The dance of change*. London: Nicholas Brealey.

SENIOR, B. and FLEMING, J. (2006) *Organisational change*. 3rd ed. Harlow: Pearson.

SHEPARD, H.A. (2005) Rules of thumb for change agents. In W.L. French, C.H. Bell Jr. and R.A. Zawacki (eds), *Organisation development and transformation*, 6th ed. Boston, MA: McGraw-Hill Irwin, pp336–341.

SHERWOOD, I. (2004) Does coaching actually work? The Bristol & West coaching experience. *International Journal of Mentoring and Coaching*. Vol. 2, No. 2. Available online at http://www.emccouncil.org/[accessed 13 December 2007].

STEVENSON, W.B. and GREENBERG, D.N. (1988) The formal analysis of narratives of organisational change. *Journal of Management*. Vol. 24, No. 6, pp741–762.

STREBEL, P. (1996) Why do employees resist change?. *Harvard Business Review*. Vol. 74, No. 3, pp86–92.

ULRICH, D. (1997) *Human resource champions*. Boston, MA: Harvard Business School Press.

WEICK, K.E. (1995) *Sensemaking in organisations*. Thousand Oaks, CA: Sage.

WICKHAM, P.A. (2004) *Management consulting*. 2nd ed. Harlow: Prentice Hall.

WILSON, C. (2007) *Best practice in performance coaching*. London: Kogan Page.

WILSON, D.C. (1992) *A strategy of change*. London: Thomson.

WHITHERSPOON, R. and WHITE, R.P. (1996) Executive coaching: a continuum of roles. *Consulting Psychology Journal*. Vol. 48, No. 2, pp124–133.

PART 10

The Use of Skills Acquisition

Developing your leadership skills through project management and managing your career

Gillian Watson, Kevin Gallagher *and* Stefanie C. Reissner

OVERVIEW

Perhaps you have never considered yourself to be a 'project manager' but in many working situations today project management is likely to be an area that you are involved in, either as a project team member or in the role of a project manager. Project management is no longer the sole preserve of large construction projects – any complex, one-off organisational undertaking may use project management techniques. Increasingly, projects are also focusing upon internal change within organisations, and so are clearly of importance to HR strategic change initiatives. Developing your skills as a project manager will therefore be beneficial to your career development and may be particularly so if you are considering managing your career, as such skills will broaden your personal portfolio.

LEARNING OUTCOMES

By the end of this chapter, provided you engage with the activities, you should be able to:

- define the scope of project management
- understand the concept of hard and soft changes
- recognise organisational change management projects
- analyse the four phases of projects
- apply stakeholder analysis to projects
- draw typical project organisational structures
- construct Gantt charts
- argue the importance of employee engagement in successful projects
- explain the nature of culture and virtual teams within multinational project teams
- analyse typical communication barriers within such project teams

- apply various aspects of career enhancement, with particular reference to links with personal and professional development, personal performance, and progression.

18.1 INTRODUCTION

The approach taken in this final chapter of the book differs somewhat from the previous chapters. It starts by covering a specific subject area (in this case project management) but then goes on to explore how a typical project may be tackled. It draws upon the earlier sections in the book, in particular upon change management, team dynamics, leadership, problem-solving and decision-making. The title of this chapter, 'Developing your leadership skills through project management and managing your career', has been carefully chosen. It implies that, no matter what your job title is, when you are involved in projects (ie complex, one-off undertakings) you will need to use project management skills. Typical 'projects' would include: setting up a new company operation, amalgamating sites, organisational restructuring, a new staff development programme and introduction of a quality assurance system. You should note that your involvement may be in either a leading or supporting role. You should also note that, although specific 'project' skills such as 'project control' have been identified in the chapter, in reality you will be using many of the skills from the other chapters in this book. That is one reason for locating this chapter as the final one, as you will now be able to integrate your previous knowledge and skills and apply them as one.

This chapter consists of two sections. The first section focuses on project management and discusses the different phases of a project, stakeholder analysis, organisational structure, project control and project teams as well as learning, training and change. It illustrates project management with the Mountech Gear case study, in which a 'green' project will be implemented across three countries. Projects are synonymous with change and there are clear links to corresponding requirements in professional development. The case study highlights the need for particular aspects of professional development for various staff members, thus giving typical examples of CPD. You are encouraged to then consider the importance of CPD within your own professional context and your own CPD in particular. You may wish to include your course of study and the skills outlined in this book as part of this process.

Section 2 of this chapter focuses on talent management, career enhancement and continuing professional development with a special emphasis on what you can do now that your studies with this book have come to a close.

18.2 WHAT IS PROJECT MANAGEMENT?

Project management as a separate discipline has its roots in large civil engineering and construction projects, complex military projects (eg missile development) and oil exploration. With advances in information technology, the advent of large IT projects has also featured prominently in the project management literature. The emphasis within these areas has been upon ensuring that the project runs to budget and on schedule, and delivers optimal performance. Within these industries the role of a dedicated project manager has emerged, in some cases even within a particular department – for instance project planning. These project managers have access to computer software to assist them in co-ordinating a multitude of data in the most efficient manner; they may also use sophisticated project management systems (such as PRINCE – projects in controlled environments – (Maylor 2005, p399). A growing research culture is supplying academic papers for consideration by both academics and practitioners; the *Project Management Body of Knowledge* (often referred to as *PMBOK*, Project Management Institute 2009) heralded a milestone in this quest for information with which to expand the project manager's command of the discipline. The Project Management Institute (www.mpi.org) offers a comprehensive website for professional managers. Key journals are the *International Journal of Project Management* and the *Project Management Journal*. If you are already one of these professional project managers, then skip the first section of this chapter. However, many of you will not be in such jobs; it is for you that this chapter is written, for – as outlined in the introduction – if you are involved in a complex, one-off undertaking at work, you are probably doing the role of the project manager. Consider the following statement from one of project management's gurus, Jeffrey Pinto:

> At one time, project management was almost exclusively the property of civil and construction engineering programs where it was taught in a highly quantitative, technical manner. ... Project management today is a holistic 'management' challenge requiring not only technical skills but a broad based set of people skills as well. Project management has become the management of technology, people, culture, stakeholders, and other diverse elements necessary to successfully complete a project. (Pinto 2007, pxvii)

Then consider what Harvey Maylor, another well-respected project management author, says:

> Many managers have not recognised that they are project managers, despite the statistics from those who study such things that the average manager now spends upwards of 50 percent of their time on projects or project-related issues. Their line responsibilities (finance, marketing, design) involve them in a variety of day-to-day activities plus longer term projects. ... The more enlightened organisations will provide a basis skills grounding in the best way to run projects, and help, coach and mentor individuals in recognising and developing their project roles. (Maylor 2005, p10)

18.2.1 PROJECT DEFINITION: A MORE DETAILED CONSIDERATION

Something that you do everyday as part of your normal activities, such as producing goods or services, is not a project; it is a process. So if you are an accountant producing the usual end-of-month accounts, a sales manager selling your usual range of products, or a university lecturer marking students' scripts, you are engaged in your normal, everyday work activities. We would not describe these as projects.

Now that is not to say that accountants, sales managers or university lecturers do not become involved in projects, nor that they cannot be project managers. Pinto (2007, pp3–5) describes a project in the following terms:

> A project is a unique venture with a beginning and end, conducted by people to meet established goals within parameters of cost, schedule, and quality [that are:]
>
> 1. Complex, one time
>
> 2. Developed to resolve a clear goal(s)
>
> 3. Customer focused
>
> [and]
>
> 4. Are ad hoc endeavours with a clear life cycle
>
> 5. Are responsible for the newest and most improved products, services and organisational processes
>
> 6. Provide a philosophy and strategy for the management of change ...crossing functional and organisational boundaries.

Here are a few real examples that illustrate the scale and scope of project work:

- a major construction project such as the Lesotho Highlands Water Project – a major hydro-electric construction project in the mid-1980s (Gallagher 2006)

- introduction of Quality Assurance System ISO 9001 to an organisation

- amalgamation of two NHS hospitals within the same trust

- GP's surgery IT project to locate all patients records and create a communications hub

- the TEMPUS project – university staff developing managers in Egypt.

Consider these examples in the light of Pinto's points 1–6 listed earlier (Pinto 2007). The Lesotho Highlands Water Project (LWHP) is typical of the large, complex projects that you would automatically tend to think of when the word 'project' is mentioned. The LWHP was unique in terms of the terrain, requirements of construction – eg the number of dams and their location – and the political situation (this was a project between the adjoining countries of Lesotho and South Africa); and the costs were applicable only at that time. Its goal was to provide South Africa with water and Lesotho with electricity and revenue. The customers were the governments and ultimately the peoples of these countries. It had a definite start and end date; many amendments/ alterations were made along the way as the project developed to overcome unforeseen circumstances. The series of waterways and tunnels built to pipe the water remains one of the most technologically advanced examples of tunnelling in the world. Although not a 'change project' as such, in a political sense it crossed boundaries with its mutual benefits.

The introduction of ISO 9001 in contrast is something that many organisations have done. However, each organisation is unique and must analyse its own operations. It is true that it must ensure that its systems then meet the requirements of the ISO 9001 system and use accepted standards – but how it does this is not prescribed. For instance, it is a requirement for the organisation to ensure that it has a customer feedback system in place but the exact set-up is not dictated; rather the emphasis is upon satisfying criteria such as the system's ability to identify problem areas. So, although this sort of project is not likely to have the same scale of unknowns as the previous example (the LWHP), it will still have many lesser unknowns. Experienced ISO 9001 consultants may advise or assist organisations and thus cut down some of the 'guesswork' but there is still a great deal of work to be done, not least in ensuring that staff 'buy in' to the new system.

The amalgamation of two hospitals into one, again, is something that various trusts have done over recent years, usually for reasons of service efficiency. However, no two situations are the same. There is a start and end date, ad hoc arrangements must be made and arrangements for the amalgamation are often intricate. In such cases there may be resistance from various quarters – staff objecting to the move, the possibility of staff grade restructuring and redundancies, and patients objecting to the loss of their 'local' hospital.

The GP's surgery IT support system is typical of the gradual linking of patient/ customer information for monitoring and control purposes. Establishing and implementing the system is a one-off activity. Such systems have various 'users' as 'stakeholders' (more on these later): the GP, practice nurses, local hospitals, and the patients. Such systems replace the traditional paper record cards and communication methods for arranging appointments and requesting repeat prescriptions, and even queries to the GP or practice nurses; however, this requires the patient to 'buy in' to the system and to be trained to use it, and this is also part of the project.

The last example relates to a 'Tempus' project. Tempus is the European Union's programme which supports the modernisation of higher education in the Partner Countries of Eastern Europe, Central Asia, the Western Balkans and the Mediterranean region, mainly through university co-operation projects' (Executive Agency Education, Audiovisual and Culture 2009). This particular example concerned a UK and an Egyptian university devising a project for the management development of staff working for the Suez Canal Authority in Egypt. This was not that complex a project but it was very customer oriented and, more significantly, it was aimed at Pinto's point 6 (Pinto 2007) as organisational change was a major requirement.

18.2.2 HARD AND SOFT CHANGES

Occasionally projects are purely technical in nature; for instance, a construction company carrying out yet another project is just doing what it always does. The challenges it faces will be different but will relate to technical matters. Such changes are sometimes called 'hard' changes. However, many changes in other sorts of organisations affect the end-user (the customer) and those working for the organisation. Take, for instance, the hospital amalgamation project outlined above; the operation of the amalgamated hospital will be changed but there are also many other changes of leadership, communication and working behaviours. Such changes are sometimes called 'soft' changes. In reality many projects embody both hard and soft changes. IT projects sometimes receive bad press for introducing technical improvements without sufficient consideration for staff development in the new processes, but they are far from being alone in this regard. This view is backed by research with one study stating that 'human factors [of] change management (the most important factor identified), internal staff adequacy, training, project team, consultants, prioritisation/resource allocation, ownership, senior management support' are the source of a staggering 57 per cent of difficulties and obstacles in the implementation of the certain types of IT project implementation (Legris and Collerette 2006, p65).

18.2.3 ORGANISATIONAL CHANGE MANAGEMENT PROJECTS

It is not possible to discuss project management without also considering 'change'. From a traditional project point of view (Briner et al 1996, p126) projects are dynamic and thus change within the project is to be expected. They suggest that the project team carries out successive cycles of plan–do–review with project team, and discusses and agrees revisions to plans with relevant stakeholders. Construction projects are characterised by updated plans (it is very important to give all plans clear issue status so that everyone is working to the same documents).

Going a stage further, some projects only have provisional plans in place as the final outcomes are unknown. In particular, IT projects which involve the creation of software are examples of what Cockburn (2002) describes as incremental

 ACTIVITY 18.1

MY PROJECTS

- Make a list of various projects that you have been involved in over the last two years. Now, select a maximum of three projects.
- Describe each project in a single sentence outlining its main aim(s).
- Next, list hard and soft aspects of these projects.
- Would you describe any of them as having significant organisational change aspects? Explain.
- Finally, what do you think your role(s) (eg team member, specialist, project leader, other) was in each of these projects?

learning, as the team progresses towards its final goal through a succession of developmental stages during design and implementation.

Some projects, however, are deliberately established to bring change to the ways in which organisations behave or the behaviours of people within them: internal change projects. Others have this as a 'knock-on' effect of some primary technical change. When people talk of 'managing change' they are often referring to these sorts of changes. Thus quality systems projects such as ISO 9001 incorporate the technical changes relating to documenting systems and adhering to quality standards, but to work they need to bring about an attitude change to quality – an awareness that quality is not the sole responsibility of the quality manager but of everyone in the organisation from the managing director downwards. This is an example of organisational change.

18.2.4 PHASES OF PROJECTS

The project management writers appear to agree that there are four main stages to any project. Pinto (2007, p11) uses the terms 'Conceptualisation, Planning, Execution, and Termination' while Lockyer and Gordon (2007, p4) refer to 'Conception, Development, Realisation, and Termination'. These stages overlap each other as they progress from one stage to the next. This basic framework can be used to great effect to analyse various aspects of projects – for instance the people involved at each stage – and is a feature of research into project management.

Let us take the writing of this book as a project to illustrate each of the four stages.

18.2.4.1 Conception

The beginning – an idea is born. This book is a natural accompaniment to the new CIPD standards, providing a core text for the Developing Skills for Business Leadership module, so the idea of producing a book is hardly a surprise. However, the exact format of such a book is very much open to further ideas. Like many projects a business case has to be put forward and agreed before further development can take place. In publishing terms this means the acceptance of a book proposal. Typical questions reflect those of any business project:

- What is the scope of the project? In other words what areas will it cover, in what depth, what size (eg aim of the book, level and type of book, intended readers, outline of content)?

- Who is likely to be involved? (In this case two editors and a team of writers.)

- How does the project case compare to the competition (eg other existing books, books about to be published)?

- What is the financial case for the project (eg projected sales versus costs)?

- How does the project 'fit' the organisation's business strategy (eg is this the sort of book the publisher wishes to be associated with)?

- What are the likely timescales involved (eg writing of drafts and reviews of chapters etc)?

- Contracts are signed outlining who is responsible for various aspects of the project and the overall output and completion date (eg between the publisher and the writer/s).

18.2.4.2 Development

We hope the project proposal is accepted by the publishers. However, this should never be taken for granted, especially in new product development where many projects 'bite the dust' at this initial stage. At this point a project manager(s) will be appointed if this has not already been done. In the case of our book example there are various levels of project management and leadership. From the editors' point of view, they are acting as project managers for the writing of the book; however, the publisher will assign a commissioning editor to liaise with the writers and to co-ordinate their activities into a bigger plan, of which the writing is only one (though important) part. Other aspects of the project involve editing, typesetting, printing and marketing of the book. If we consider, for the sake of this example, the actual research and writing of a book (as opposed to its publication) and its author as a 'project manager', then typical issues for the development stage are as follows:

- appointment of project manager and team if not decided already (eg sole author, editor, multiple authors etc)
- meeting of project team to discuss how the project will be developed (eg meeting of the writing team)
- a project plan (eg headings for the various sections and chapters, how they link together, content outline, who is doing what)
- a project schedule (eg dates for various chapters to be ready in draft and final form).

18.2.4.3 Realisation

This is the stage at which the project is carried out. Progress will be monitored against the plan. Sometimes things do not go as intended and corrective action will have to be taken. Sometimes the planner will have built in a certain amount of 'slack time' – a buffer zone – to the project. In the 'book project' example, this is the time at which the chapters are researched, written and submitted to the review process and then subsequently reviewed before final submission to the publisher.

18.2.4.4 Termination

At this stage of the project the end is in sight! However, the client still needs to accept that the work has been carried out to the agreed standard. This phase is characterised by official signing-off to accept the work and the handing over of the completed work to the client. For the authors in the book project this is initially when the final submission is accepted by the publisher, but for the publisher it is when the book is finally published and available to readers. This stage should also be one of celebration (or relief!) within the project team (Legris and Collerette 2006, p73). It also marks an opportunity for a more analytical review of the whole project and lessons learnt, and perhaps, ideas for the next project!

ACTIVITY 18.2

PROJECT PHASES

Choose a project with which you are familiar. Break it down into the four phases of conception, development, realisation and termination, and make notes.

18.3 STAKEHOLDER ANALYSIS

A project stakeholder is any individual, group or organisation that may have an interest in, an input into, or be affected by the project, either directly or indirectly. The obvious stakeholders are the client/customer for whom the project is being delivered and the project team who are the providers. Stakeholders have varying degrees of influence and the project manager needs to be aware of this. Some writers (eg Briner et al 1996, p83) divide stakeholders into 'internal', 'external' and 'customer', whereas others (eg Pinto 2007, p40) refer only to 'internal' and 'external', though Pinto places the client as an external stakeholder; in both cases 'internal' refers to those who are carrying out the project and 'external' to those outside the project manager's organisation. Both of these models reflect the traditional view of projects, for instance as carried out by a construction company for a client; for a modern change management project, the 'client' is within the organisation and is therefore an 'internal' stakeholder. There is the additional argument that the project provider should involve the customer much more within the workings of the project team, especially at the conception/design phase to align more closely with the end-user needs (Legris and Collerette 2006, p71). In some cases there will be other projects between the project organisation and the customer and a closer working relationship may be beneficial. As Rowlinson and Cheung (2008, p611) state:

> Project managers, traditionally have been seen to attempt to mollify stakeholders while focusing their attention on the details of the project management rather than to empower stakeholders to have a significant input to the project. ... This change in attitude to stakeholders marks a culture change in the real estate and construction industry, brought about by an increased emphasis on relationship management.

For these reasons the diagram shown in Figure 18.1 overleaf has placed the client/customer within the 'inner circle' of stakeholders.

Also within this inner circle are the project manager and team, the person who approves or supports the project (the project sponsor) and other senior functional managers within the organisation who are supplying staff to the project. As you would expect, the board of directors are positioned fairly close in

Figure 18.1 Project stakeholders

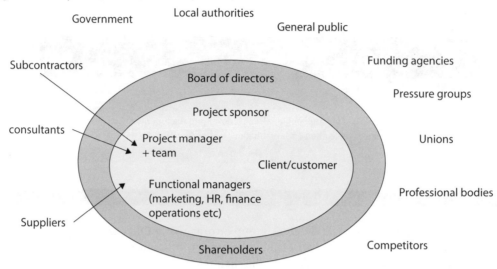

the next layer, as the management team are accountable to them. Shareholders of course own the company and have a clear interest though perhaps not always immediate influence. Consultants may provide specialist advice to project teams and subcontractors may be employed for the duration of the project to carry out certain aspects of work, so they clearly input to the success of the project. Suppliers too may be closely linked to the project, particularly if they have to deliver to quality standards set by the project team and client.

Stakeholders outside these circles, such as government, local authorities, competitors, and the general public, may be regarded as not directly related to the project (in effect the 'external stakeholders' referred to earlier) but may still have considerable influence. You should note, therefore, that the diagram is only intended to give a general indication of the stakeholder relationships and influence – particular projects may have various stakeholders who, for one reason or another, hold a lot of influence.

ACTIVITY 18.3

STAKEHOLDERS IN GGI

The following (fictional) case study may appear a little unreal but it does bring out many of the points referred to in the previous section. The characters are very much stereotypes but you may recognise characteristics which you can relate to your own work experience.

For those of you who do not know what a garden gnome is (not all cultures have them) or if you just want to browse this particular industry, please have a look at this weblink first: http://www.kimmelgnomes.com/. There are many more sites!

Read the case study and answer the question given at the end of it.

GARDEN GNOMES INTERNATIONAL: 'QUALITY 2010 AND BEYOND' PROJECT

Jemima Seagrove looked in despair out of the main boardroom window and sighed to herself, 'I just can't figure it out! Why must people always be so awkward? Surely even the dimmest idiot must see that if we don't manage to update our quality soon we'll be out of business.'

As Managing Director of Garden Gnomes International (known in the trade as GGI) Jemima knew that she had to keep up with her deadliest rival, SuperGnome Ltd, which had recently set up in the area. The process of gnome manufacture was a fairly straightforward procedure; gnomes were manufactured to the company's own design and made by casting either plaster or resin-based materials in moulds; after a suitable time for setting, the moulds were removed and the gnomes painted and stored ready for shipment to the major garden stores in the UK and overseas. In the past all of this had occurred without much fuss and everyone seemed happy with the product. However, SuperGnome was now on the scene and aggressively promoting its products with major customers. For the first time quality of production became an issue, SuperGnome boasting that its Pixie Fisherman was superior in all aspects of design and finish. Indeed several of the major buyers had not renewed contracts with GGI and had defected to SuperGnome. There was even talk that very soon Gardens Galore, one of the largest garden centres and a major customer of GGI, would be reviewing its stance towards suppliers in the light of its own efforts to achieve the recently introduced 'Certificate of Garden Centre Excellence'. What this meant in effect was that any supplier to Gardens Galore would have to have its own quality system. In theory this sounded fine, for as Jemima had thought, it was about time that the quality of both product and work systems was improved in the company. In order to continue competing in the market she had therefore decided to introduce proper

quality procedures in the company and she had called this new scheme 'Quality 2010 and Beyond'. She had tried hard to convince the board members to accept this new initiative but now it seemed she had failed. She looked at the empty coffee cups scattered around the board room table and thought back to the beginning of what should have been a successful day ...

The board meeting

Jemima had welcomed them all to the meeting: Fred Dunn, Production Director; Jeremy Luton, Sales and Marketing Director; Laura Davies, Finance Director. She explained the reasoning behind the new quality initiative and then invited comments.

Fred Dunn was the first to speak. 'Well, no one regards quality higher than me. Always telling the lads it's quality that counts. And I make sure we get it! So why waste money – which we can ill afford – on something which we've already got? It's not as though we don't know what we're doing – after all we've been knocking out quality gear now for nigh on 15 years – so don't try telling me that our quality's not up to scratch! And what about the new SuperMould machine I was promised, eh? – gone to fund this I've no doubt.' He looked menacingly around at the others. Laura nodded in approval. Jeremy glanced to one side so as not to catch his eye. Finally he looked directly at Jemima.

'Well, actually,' said Laura, 'Fred does have a valid point. Besides, there's the question of additional costs of installing these proposed quality procedures; there's the cost of a consultant for a start – and they don't come cheap. And then, Jemima, there'll be an extra managerial cost if we recruit a quality manager as you were suggesting.' At this Fred muttered something under his breath and shook his head. 'Perhaps', Laura continued, 'we should wait a while – at least until the next financial year so that our profits still look reasonably healthy for this year. We must think of our shareholders too. Let's not be hasty. Also, I'd need to be certain that we could recover the cost of the initiative within the next five years.'

Jemima had heard these arguments before. Of course Laura had a point but sooner or later the company had to grasp the nettle and improve its position in the marketplace. It wasn't just a matter of counting the pennies. She looked at Jeremy for some support.

Jeremy felt ill at ease. On the one hand anything which promoted the company had to be good for his marketing campaign – and his commission was closely linked to sales. On the other hand, installing the quality systems might initially slow down production as any teething problems were sorted out (and hence their ability to satisfy all of the potential sales he might generate) so that in the short term there might be problems.

'What's the matter, lad – didn't that fancy college of yours teach you about this sort of thing?' Fred quipped with a brief smile.

Jeremy wavered, his voice a little unsteady. 'I'm not sure, it's a tricky one this. Perhaps Laura is right. Perhaps we should wait until next year.'

Jemima sighed. This was hopeless. Jeremy, downcast turned away and fiddled with his pen.

Jemima tried one last approach. 'Look, it's our image and reputation that are at stake here. In a few more years we won't be in business if we don't do something now. That'll give SPAG (the pressure group 'Small People Against Gnomes') something to laugh about. And what about Dirty Den [she referred here to Denis Granger, Managing Director of SuperGnome] – are you going to give him the satisfaction of seeing us slowly getting picked off? Is that what you want?'

But it had all been to no avail.

Reluctantly she had drawn the meeting to a close. The board decision had been to do nothing. Now all that remained was for Jemima to think of a new strategy or possibly even to consider her own future at GGI.

> ## Question
>
> Consider the embryonic project 'Quality 2010 and Beyond' as proposed by Jemima and list all key stakeholders, making brief notes concerning their attitude towards the project and their influence.

18.4 PROJECT ORGANISATIONAL STRUCTURE(S)

Working in project teams is a different experience from working in a functional environment dedicated to one particular activity such as sales, HR, marketing, finance, or operations. In these functional environments you will work with others above, below and side-on to you but in the same discipline. For instance, a university lecturer may work in the business school's economics department of teaching staff. The same lecturer may meet with the economics department to discuss the latest developments in the field of economics and other teaching-related matters. She may be line-managed by the head of the economics department, being appraised by this person, agreeing work allocation, and reporting sickness/requesting holidays. The benefits of this arrangement relate to professionalism, research and staff development – in this case within the field of economics. However, suppose that a project group is established to consider the 'student experience' in Year 1. This project group is likely to include a range of staff, cutting across academic disciplines. Our economics lecturer might then find herself the only one from the economics department. She may well find herself making decisions with others in the group who are at different levels in the organisation's hierarchy. The project group will have its own project leader. Suddenly she finds herself with two bosses – her functional (economics department) boss and, now, her project boss. She is in a matrix organisation, though this is rarely shown on an organisational chart for ad hoc projects. The textbooks often show this form of organisational structure as the usual form for a construction company – hardly surprising as carrying out projects is what construction companies do for most of the time. Figure 18.2 shows how a construction company typically operates as a matrix structure.

Figure 18.2 Typical project management organisational structure

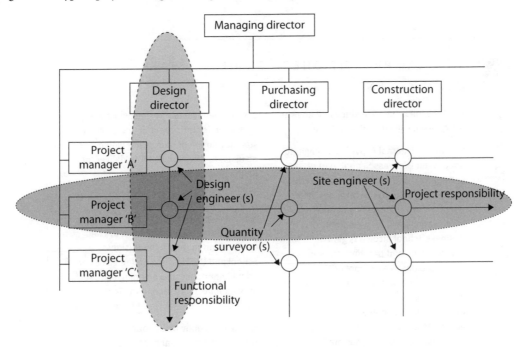

In this case the functions are those of design, purchasing, and construction (there could be more – the diagram shows only part of a possible structure). The circles represent individual members of staff. In the example shown, design engineers report to the design director, quantity surveyors report to the purchasing director and site engineers report to the construction director. However, they are also in project teams and report to the appropriate project manager. Of course a member of staff may in fact occupy two or more circles if he or she works on more than one project. Also, project managers might have more than one project.

QUESTION: IS HAVING TWO BOSSES CONFUSING?

The answer to this question is that it can be. There needs to be an agreement regarding which of the two bosses the member of staff reports to for specific purposes. There should not be direct overlap as this can lead to contrary directives to the member of staff; nor should there be any gaps where the member of staff does not know where to go for direction.

QUESTION: WHAT ABOUT POWER DIFFERENCES BETWEEN FUNCTIONAL AND PROJECT BOSSES?

This is a good question. The power relationship can actually determine whether the structure is one which has project managers as co-ordinators but where real power still lies with the functional managers (Maylor (2005, p224) calls this a 'lightweight' matrix) or as powerful project managers who draw on project team members through a process of secondment from the functional areas (Maylor (2005, p224) classifies this as a 'heavyweight' matrix).

CASE STUDY 18.2

MEDICAL PRACTITIONERS PROJECT: STAFF DEVELOPMENT

Read the following case study and answer the questions given at the end of it.

You are the External Activities Manager for Sheerwater Business School, part of Grandpool University, reporting directly to the Head of School. The Business School offers a range of degrees and other qualifications. While the majority of Business School income is generated from individual full and part-time students who attend the Business School on conventional qualification routes, your job involves you in new 'product' development for companies and government bodies. In other words, you help create and sell various staff development and educational packages unique to particular companies or industries.

You sometimes rely upon the involvement of academic tutors drawn from across the subject disciplines at the university. These academic tutors are normally specialists in their own teams (eg law, human resource management, operations management) who work in the university teaching students on degree programmes; any work they do for you is thus additional to their normal workload, although they are paid a fee by the university for the additional work. This fee would cover

development costs – ie time which they, as academic staff, spent in developing the staff development package; it would also be usual for the same staff to deliver the programme of study and receive a fee whenever they did this (this is regarded as the main incentive). However, team leaders still need to agree that their specialist tutors can work for you; team leaders tend to regard the Business School and the teaching of degrees as of prime importance and anything else, such as work for you, as secondary. Team leaders report to the Head of School.

You have recently been approached by the HR Manager of a local hospital to establish a new staff development programme for some of its senior staff (senior nursing managers and specialist 'manager's in charge of areas such as eye surgery, cancer care, the X-ray Department etc). The aim of this development programme is to deliver a mix of human resource management, law, operations management and IT skills. These are managerial and IT skills which have not traditionally been provided by the hospital's own staff development (though training has been provided for specific skills in nursing, eye surgery etc).

At the moment only the broad titles (eg

'Human Resource Management Module') have been suggested and there are no guidelines yet on possible educational content, but you do know that there will be four modules (Human Resource Management, Operations Management, Law and Computer Skills); in other words you have an 'blank page' as to what to include in the programme. However, you have been asked to somehow involve the hospital's own HR staff in the development process so as to put your Business School's managerial and IT skills into a health context. Students will be assessed throughout the programme; this is something else you need to think about.

You have six months to get the programme operational, but other than the initial contact with the hospital nothing has yet been done. Once you have established the

programme and checked that it is running properly, the project, in terms of new product development, is complete. The first thing you intend to do is create a development team for the new programme.

Questions

- Who would you include in your (new product) development team? Why?

- Draw a matrix organisational structure for the new product development team.

- How do you envisage the hospital HR staff contributing to the development of the modules/ programme?

18.5 PROJECT CONTROL

Perhaps one of the most well-known control instruments of project management is the Gantt chart. We will focus on this, although you should be aware that there are other, more advanced techniques which lie beyond the scope of this book. Named after Henry Gantt (1861–1919), one of the founding figures of the scientific management approach in the early twentieth century, the Gantt chart is now firmly established. The basic chart breaks down a project into its component activities and shows these as line bars mapped against a timescale. Its simplicity means that it is easy to understand yet is surprisingly effective at communicating, at a glance, the start and end dates of activities and, to some extent, the logical connection between dependent activities. Gantt charts can be used in various ways: to assist in the planning of a project, to allocate resources – including staff, and to monitor actual progress against the plan. The Gantt chart should be the starting point for anyone interested in project scheduling. Figure 18.3 shows a Gantt chart for the writing of a textbook by a lead author and team of authors. We will use this example to elaborate on some of the practical pointers you may encounter in your own projects.

In this example there is an initial conception phase which ends with the agreement between author and publisher for the scope of the book. The authoring team has a lead author and authors 2, 3, and 4 (normally we would give their names!). Each author has responsibility for researching a set of chapters and writing drafts. These are then submitted to the publisher who arranges for them to be reviewed anonymously and returned to the authors. The authors then

Figure 18.3 A typical Gantt chart for writing a textbook

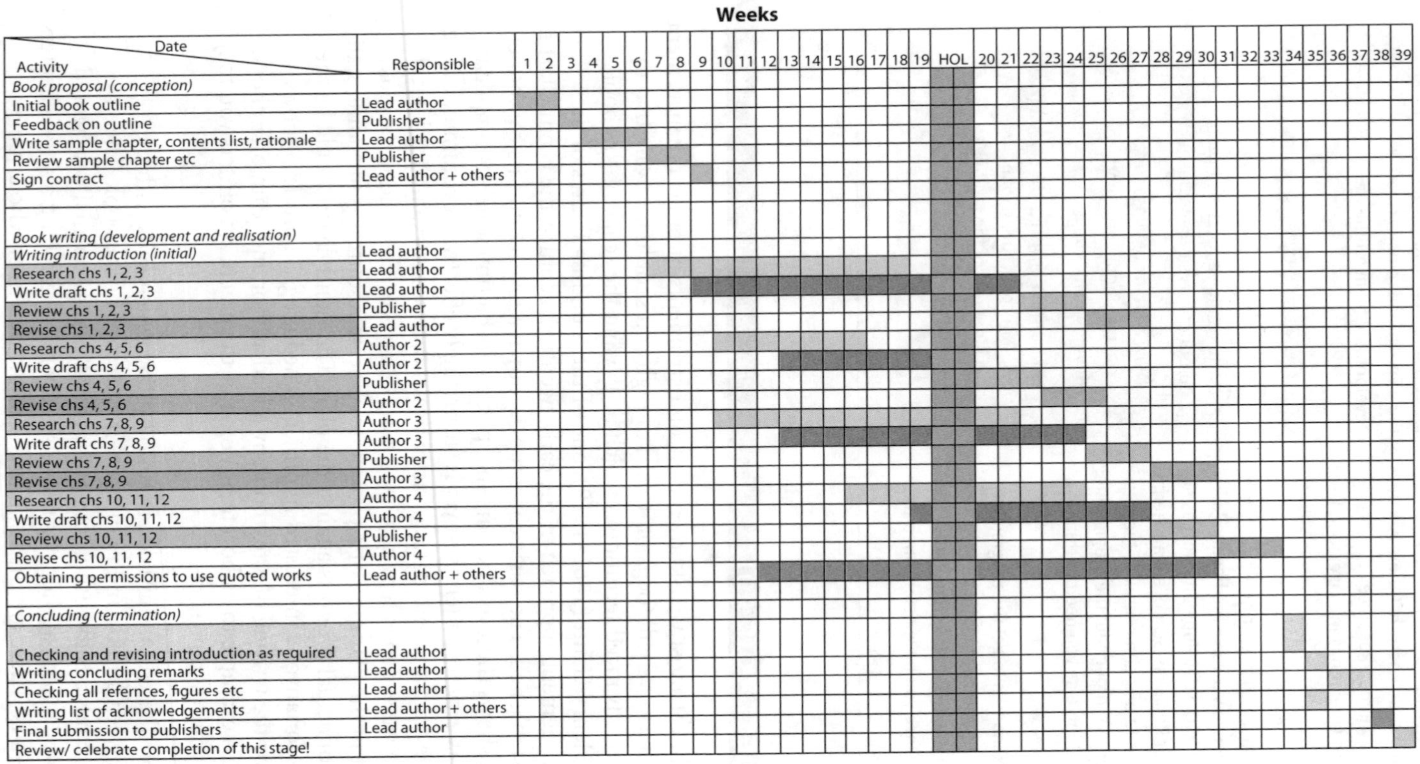

Weeks

Week columns: 1 2 3 4 5 6 7 8 9 10 11 12 13 14 15 16 17 18 19 HOL 20 21 22 23 24 25 26 27 28 29 30 31 32 33 34 35 36 37 38 39

Activity	Responsible
Book proposal (conception)	
Initial book outline	Lead author
Feedback on outline	Publisher
Write sample chapter, contents list, rationale	Lead author
Review sample chapter etc	Publisher
Sign contract	Lead author + others
Book writing (development and realisation)	
Writing introduction (initial)	Lead author
Research chs 1, 2, 3	Lead author
Write draft chs 1, 2, 3	Lead author
Review chs 1, 2, 3	Publisher
Revise chs 1, 2, 3	Lead author
Research chs 4, 5, 6	Author 2
Write draft chs 4, 5, 6	Author 2
Review chs 4, 5, 6	Publisher
Revise chs 4, 5, 6	Author 2
Research chs 7, 8, 9	Author 3
Write draft chs 7, 8, 9	Author 3
Review chs 7, 8, 9	Publisher
Revise chs 7, 8, 9	Author 3
Research chs 10, 11, 12	Author 4
Write draft chs 10, 11, 12	Author 4
Review chs 10, 11, 12	Publisher
Revise chs 10, 11, 12	Author 4
Obtaining permissions to use quoted works	Lead author + others
Concluding (termination)	
Checking and revising introduction as required	Lead author
Writing concluding remarks	Lead author
Checking all refernces, figures etc	Lead author
Writing list of acknowledgements	Lead author + others
Final submission to publishers	Lead author
Review/ celebrate completion of this stage!	Lead author

revise their chapters as appropriate, and resubmit to the publisher (for the sake of simplicity only one cycle of reviewing has been shown). Other activities need to be carried out. Note that the lead author has decided to press ahead with research on Chapters 1,2, and 3 even before signing the contract – that is his choice. However, all other authors are only asked to start by the lead author after the contract has been signed. You should note that the Gantt chart is a useful tool but it is only that – it is dependent upon the skill of the person creating it to include all activities and to give appropriate timescales. An experienced scheduler may build in some 'slack' (that is, leeway) on key tasks that lie on the 'critical path' – those activities that if delayed will result in a delay to the overall completion date of the project. There is still a place for intuition and improvisation on the part of the project manager (Sadler-Smith and Leybourne 2006).

This example has been prepared on a standard Microsoft Excel spreadsheet, although it could have easily been drawn on squared graph paper. You do not need anything more advanced than this for relatively small projects. You will see that, for the purpose of this chapter, activities have been grouped into the project phases (conception, development, realisation, and termination) described earlier. You do not need to do this, but this approach lends itself to inserting 'milestones' to indicate key points in the project (for instance, signing the contract). If you scan the whole diagram you will observe a general trend from left to right of successive activity completion; this makes it easier for you to visualise the sequential logic of activities but is not essential – placing the initial book outline at the bottom of the list of activities may look strange but the activity bar would still appear on the chart in Weeks 1 and 2 which is correct.

You will note that this 'project' has been planned from the point of view of the lead author and his team of authors. The publisher will have a more inclusive Gantt chart, viewing the project as bigger than the writing (author) stage, for instance including activities such as proofreading, typesetting, printing and marketing.

If you want to link dependent activities more obviously one another, you could add a connecting arrow from the end of one activity to the beginning point of the next one which follows logically on from it – for instance after a chapter has been reviewed by the publisher/reviewer it then needs to be revised by the author in the light of the reviewer's comments. In terms of timescale we have simply used week numbers but you could use calendar weeks. Also a two-week period has been blocked out for some sort of national holiday when it is assumed no work will be done (not always the case!).

The headings given for the Gantt chart in Figure 18.3 will suffice for simple charts. However, you may wish to add further columns to add more detail – for instance resources used, start and end dates and duration of activities. You may then have a chart with headings as laid out in Figure 18.4, which shows part of a house renovation project.

For more complex projects you may wish to use project software. A study by Ali et al (2008, p11) showed that the most commonly used project management tool

Figure 18.4 More detailed headings for a Gantt chart

Activity No.	Activity (or Task)	Resource	Start date	End date	Duration of activity	Week 1	Week 2	Week 3	Week 4 etc
23	Sand wooden floor	Sanding machine	4th May 2010	5th May 2010	2 days				

was Microsoft Project, with 75 per cent of the study's respondents using this software, 10 per cent using Primavera Project Management and the remainder using other software such as Timesheet, Excel and database applications. At present (May 2010) you can download trial versions of Microsoft Project 2010 from the website http://www.microsoft.com/project/en/us/default.aspx, which has Gantt charts as one of its features. One of the advantages of using such software is that you can now use the sort of MS drawing tools you are familiar with in, say, MS Office, and produce very professional-looking charts that you can cut and paste into your documents.

18.6 PROJECTS IN CONTEXT

This section uses the Mountech Gear case study outlined below to provide the context for further discussion on employee engagement and other important people factors within projects.

 MOUNTECH GEAR

CASE STUDY 18.3

Background information

Mountech Gear was founded in 1972 by Jeremy Burnes and Christopher Child as a company which manufactured waterproof jackets and trousers for outdoor pursuits such as walking, climbing and skiing. Operations were fairly small scale, all production being carried out in a factory unit in Northumberland. Gradually the market grew and so did the business. However in the late 1980s and 1990s competition from overseas manufacturers cut profit margins drastically, and

eventually in 2000 the decision was made to relocate manufacturing operations to Dongguan in China. This proved a successful move and recently (2009) the company has bought a new production plant, again in Dongguan, which has long had a tradition of textile manufacture and is now home to many industrial and business parks. Production centres around two lines: down products (eg sleeping bags and insulated, down jackets), and waterproofs (eg mountain jackets and trousers manufactured from high-tech fabrics). Alex Burnes, daughter of the founder Jeremy, is now the managing director of the company. Her father, Jeremy, and his business partner, Christopher Child, have now both retired from running the business but still sit on the board of directors. In 2005 the company bought out a struggling business in Stuttgart, Germany, which manufactured alpine climbing axes. Since then they have injected money into this part of the business and it is now beginning to show a profit; its main two lines are ice tools (eg ice axes) and climbing harnesses. Upon acquiring this business the company effectively consisted of two divisions; the Dongguan division was re-named MG-Wear and the Stuttgart operation given the name of MG-Climb. Head office remained in Sunderland in the UK. Currently, products from MG-Wear are sold within China and throughout Europe, while MG-Climb distributes within Europe and has a new outlet in Colorado, USA. The organisation chart is shown in Figure 18.5.

Profiles of key players at head office

Alex Burnes: Managing Director

Alex is in her mid 40s. As daughter of one of the founding partners she has been immersed in the business for most of her working life. A keen walker and skier she has a ready appreciation of the outdoor leisure market. Always on the lookout for new opportunities, attending conferences worldwide and with an eye on technical developments. Easily bored. She has a strong bond to 'her' company (she is a major shareholder). She is a professional manager who has held a variety of senior posts prior to this and has been involved in a number of company mergers. Tough. Admired and feared in equal measure by staff. By coincidence an old university acquaintance of Mr Chang (the Head of MG-Wear in Dongguan) from their time spent in Edinburgh on their MBA programme in 1996.

Figure 18.5 Organisation structure of Mountech Gear

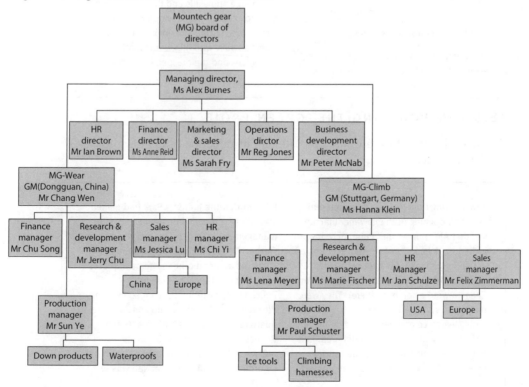

Ian Brown: HR Director

Keen to show his worth as a new director to the company. Rather fastidious about detail. Responsible for all major aspects of HR policy including health and safety, management development and selection and recruitment. Recently has spent much of his time with MG-Climb (Germany) assisting Peter McNab (see below) in overseeing the introduction of new quality assurance procedures. Previously worked within a university HR department as a senior manager. Considers this his 'big break' into industry. Not an active outdoors person as such but is an avid football supporter and coaches a local team. In his early 40s.

Sarah Fry: Marketing and Sales Director

An extrovert with an enviable list of contacts. Does not always play 'by the rules' but achieves results. Has a natural affinity for picking up on what people are looking for in a product; believes very much in promoting 'lifestyle'. Mid 50s but shows no sign of slowing down. Owns a chalet in Chamonix and is a vibrant party host.

Reg Jones: Operations Director

Previously Operations Manager for the UK manufacturing plant, now shut down.

Although ostensibly in a strategic role, tends to take on too much of a 'hands-on' approach' with operations, particularly with MG-Wear in Dongguan which replaced the UK facility. Early 50s. Tends to adopt a paternal attitude to the production manager there, Mr Sun Ye. Less close to Paul Schuster, the production manager in Stuttgart, partly because he is used to working with textiles, rather than what he calls 'ironmongery' (ice axes etc).

Peter McNab: Business Development Director

Reports directly to Alex Burnes. Does not have a department other than secretarial support. Has a strategic role in growing the business. Often involved as a project manager. Last major project was overseeing the introduction of a new quality assurance system to MG-Climb. Early retiree from project management in the petro-chemical industry, and financially secure; returned to the business world for 'one more challenge'. Now in his early 60s. An open and enquiring mind. Sees himself as a 'fixer', applying his knowledge and skills and then moving on. Keen to keep up with any new developments – technical, social, and environmental. Meets socially with Alex Burnes, other colleagues and their respective partners.

18.6.1 INTRODUCING THE 'GREEN PROJECT'

The second part of this case study provides in introduction of the way projects can be introduced.

It was during their visit to Dongguan during the 2009 opening of the new manufacturing site that Alex Burnes and Peter McNab were invited to attend a conference being hosted in the prestigious Songshan Lake Science and Technical Industry Park (a friend of Mr Chang owned a company there). They were pleasantly surprised by the mix of high-tech and research companies located within a spacious (by Chinese standards) area, laid out amongst pleasant waterways and greenery. They were even more impressed

to learn that the Industry Park had gained an award for the environmental management system ISO 14001 in 2003. Further, Dongguan City was encouraging investors and had other systems in place, including what it called 'Talent Policies'. This trip fired their imaginations. Alex felt sure that she could convince the board of directors to agree to a 'Green Project' for the company, involving MG-Wear, MG-Climb and head office in one co-ordinated push. Peter McNab was equally keen. They had noticed that the Research and Development Manager Jerry Chu was keen to emulate the practice of Songshan Lake. They were not so sure of the other MG-Wear staff as they had kept rather a low profile, other than Mr Chang, who seemed to generally be very agreeable. However, they suspected that the staff's views would be largely dictated by their departmental/team considerations. From his work with MG-Climb Peter McNab favoured inviting the HR Manager Jan Schultze as 'change manager' for the Stuttgart operation, though he would have to discuss this further with the head of the division, Hanna Klein.

18.6.2 EMPLOYEE ENGAGEMENT

This section will draw on the recent CIPD (2010) research study *Creating an engaged workforce*, drawing on its data and findings to inform the Mountech Gear case study. The data collected in the study was from 5,291 questionnaires and 180 interviews. The CIPD (2010) report measured three dimensions of engagement: emotional or affective engagement, intellectual or cognitive engagement, and social engagement, as follows:

- **Intellectual engagement**: thinking hard about the job and how to do it better.
- **Affective engagement**: feeling positively about doing a good job.
- **Social engagement**: actively taking opportunities to discuss work-related improvements with others at work.

The report also differentiated between:

- **The extent of engagement**: the strength of feeling engaged.
- **The frequency of engagement**: that is, how often individuals experience engagement.

For the purposes of this section (which relates to the previous case study) we are only considering 'the extent of engagement'. The CIPD researchers defined engagement as: 'being positively present during the performance of work by willingly contributing intellectual effort, experiencing positive emotions and meaningful connections to others' (CIPD 2010, p5). This definition has resonance with other writers (Kahn 1990, May et al 2004, Schaufeli and Bakker 2004, Truss et al 2006) as it highlights the view that engagement involves intellectual, emotional and behavioural dimensions (CIPD 2010).

Strong employee engagement in the Mountech Gear case study will be required for the 'Green Project' to be a success. Managers at Mountech Gear should bear the following questions in mind:

- How do employees add value?
- Have employees expressed optimistic and constructive views about their work?
- Can employees influence a positive outcome to the 'Green Project', for example by holding meaningful discussions with others about the task and celebrating the gains and improvements?

Table 18.1 Engaging the workforce

Types of engagement	Outcome of the study
Engagement across different organisational contexts	Comparisons across employee groups reveal a variety of interesting differences with respect to demographics and job types: • Women are more engaged than men. • Younger workers are less engaged than older workers. • Those on flexible contracts are more engaged. • Managers are more engaged than non-managers.
Strategies for engagement	• Organisations can implement a range of workplace strategies that impact upon levels of engagement. • Meaningfulness is the most important driver of engagement for all employee groups. • Two-thirds of all respondents in our study find meaning in their work. • Senior management vision and communication is a key driver of engagement, whereas senior management effectiveness is negatively related to employee engagement. • Positive perceptions of one's line manager are strongly linked with engagement.
Outcomes of engagement	• Employee engagement is associated with a range of positive outcomes at the individual and organisational levels. • Engaged employees perform better. • The majority of our respondents were rated 'good' in their last appraisal. • Engaged employees are more innovative than others. • Engaged employees are more likely to want to stay with their employer.

 ACTIVITY 18.4

ENGAGEMENT

Consider the following questions in relation to the case study:

• What does engagement mean to Alex Burnes and Peter McNab, who are tasked with overall control of the project?

• How can they mange the engagement with staff?

• What are the consequences of engagement for organisations?

• What are the consequence of success and failure for the organisation?

• How does engagement in the case relate to some of the other individual characteristics mentioned in Table 18.1?

• How is engagement related to the employee voice and representation – do they have a choice, and how will the initiative be communicated?

- How are any positive responses related to the campaign and how are these communicated to staff? (For example, if it is shown that a 'switch off' (electricity) initiative is working it will be evident by the reduction in the electricity bill the company has to pay, which would be cause for sharing the good news.)

Table 18.1 includes some of the main findings of the CIPD (2010, p2) study that may assist our analysis of the case study by offering an agenda for engaging Mountech Gear's employees.

18.6.3 PROJECT TEAMS: THEIR MULTICULTURAL NATURE AND COMMUNICATION PROBLEMS WHEN WORKING VIRTUALLY

18.6.3.1 Team groupings

As you will have realised from the Mountech Gear case study, various grouping are likely to emerge as distinct teams with each one having an individual in a change leadership role. If we take into account the executives as well as the change managers, one approach is for each team to cascade into another, as shown in Figure 18.6.

In Figure 18.6 the Managing Director (Alex Burnes) is co-ordinating an executive team (with Peter McNab as the overall Project Co-ordinator) that includes directors from the UK head office, and the German and Chinese operations. This team will oversee the project and will act as sponsors (see Section 18.3). Cascading to each of the countries (China is shown by itself in the diagram for clarity but a similar situation will exist for Germany and the UK head office) there will be other teams required to make the project work. The diagram shows someone in the Chinese operation (MG-Wear) with an overview of the whole project – this will probably be Mr Chang, head of MG-Wear. The change

Figure 18.6 Senior and next-level team configuration

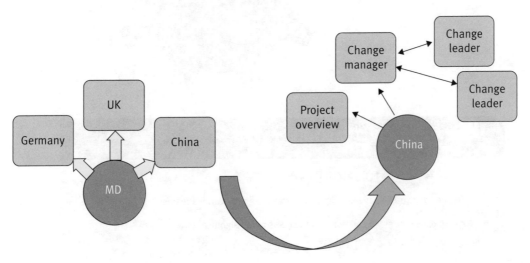

manager whose task it is to push the change through will probably be Mr Jerry Chu, who was identified in the case study as a likely, enthusiastic and able candidate to take this forward. The diagram also shows 'change leaders' – these are key individuals who wish to 'champion' the change in their particular areas of expertise or departments. Another team is also possible, and in fact desirable: a virtual team of change managers who communicate with each other at a distance (see Figure 18.7). For the purpose of the case study we may assume that in addition to Jerry Chu in China, Peter McNab will take on this role himself in the UK head office (in addition to his overall project co-ordination role), and Mr Jan Shultze (HR Manager) in the Stuttgart office.

Figure 18.7 The project and change manager team (who will be working virtually)

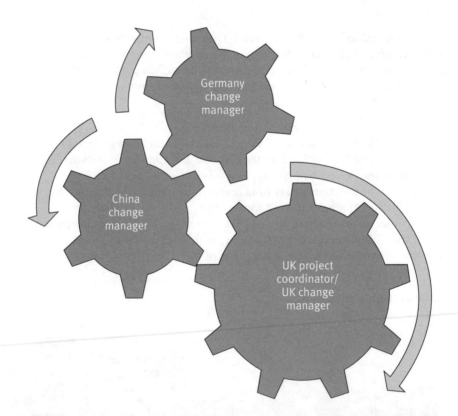

 ACTIVITY 18.5

CHALLENGES AND BARRIERS

- Describe what you see as the main challenges facing the various teams.

- What specific barriers to success do you see as being significant?

The virtual team (see Chapter 6) will have its own characteristics as well as cross-cultural and communication variables, adding to the complexities of accomplishing the task. Each country's change manager will have his or her own project team, who are not working in a virtual capacity. The challenge is to manage the external and internal interaction between and within each team or grouping and to manage the overall process of engagement.

18.6.3.2 Communication across cultures

We will assume part of your answer included concerns related to communicating across cultures. The examination of salient literature may help you analyse these issues. In our case it should be remembered that the UK head office has been working with the factories in both China and Germany for some years. However, it has not been the practice to have a combination of all three countries working together. Therefore, this spirit of co-operation is very new to all concerned, particularly the two head managers of the Chinese and German operations, who have in the recent past seen each other as rivals and have been known to disagree; indeed, on one occasion Mr Chang had walked out of an executive board meeting believing he had lost face after being challenged by Ms Klein to revisit his year end figures.

Culture and national culture are important factors as they could be barriers to co-operation. Browaeys and Price (2008) inform us that culture operates on three levels or layers: artefacts and attitudes, norms and values, and basic assumptions. The first layer can be seen in artefacts, rituals and behaviours; the second, an underlying variable, can be addressed through investigation (interviews/questions) and surveys; the third, however, is more problematic as basic assumptions can only be inferred and interpreted (Schneider and Barsoux 2003). Schein suggests these basic assumptions are 'shared solutions to universal problems of external adaption (how to survive) and internal integration (how to stay together) – which have evolved over a time and are handed down from one generation to the next' (Schein 2004, p14). Tayeb (2003, p13) refers to national culture as 'a constant thread' which runs 'through our lives which makes us distinguishable from others, especially those in other countries'.

From a Chinese perspective, relationships are valued and are seen as the channel to success, and from a business point of view so too is the building up networks of strong relationships. Drawing on connections (Luo and Chen 1997) outside the immediate family (Child 1994) is referred to as '*guanxi*' (Browaeys and Price 2008). Central to these relationships are aspects of trust and having confidence in the other person. Individuals in the *guanxi* network will grant favours, although they will expect favours in return. This, Browaeys and Price (2008) suggest, reflects village life in China. Mountech Gear is no different from many other Western companies in being affected by this well-established process operating within the business context. Chow (2004) highlights that some of the problems organisations may experience in doing business in China are a lack of understanding of these fundamental issues of culture. Chen (1995) states that *guanxi* and 'face' are intertwined in this patrimonial society (Child 1994). The preservation of face (Lockett 1988) also forms part of the four central values identified as key to understanding Chinese culture and in turn is part of

Confucian ideology. The other two are a configuration towards groups and respect for age and hierarchy, particularly male hierarchies (eg Mr Chang in the case study). 'Face' (*mianzi*), Child (1994) suggests, is a concept that relates to an individual's position, social standing and moral character. Therefore, importance is placed on how one is viewed by others, and individuals will jealously guard their public reputation as this is used to influence the decisions of others (Browaeys and Price 2008). Therefore, direct confrontation is frowned upon and can even be construed as damaging as it may result in a diminishment of prestige. Again this links to Confucianism, which distinguishes people as social beings each having their own place in the hierarchy of relationships (Michailova and Worm 2003). Consequently, doing business in China entails maintaining good relationships and being respectful of culture; Alex Burnes and Mr Chang have such a relationship, formed when they studied their MBA and MSc respectively, at a British university in 1996.

ACTIVITY 18.6

PROJECT RELATIONSHIPS

- What positive aspects of relationships within the Mountech Gear company can you detect?

- There are also some problematic elements here: do you see them as insurmountable or can you see how they can be overcome?

- Investigate how the business cultures of the UK and Germany differ from those of China. We suggest you reflect on the work of Geert Hofstede and Fons Trompenaars (eg Hofstede et al 2010, Trompenaars and Hampden-Turner, 1997).

Earley and Mosakowski (2000) proposed that if multicultural teams are used for transnational project development they can eventually out-perform monocultural teams (Ochieng and Price 2010). Weatherley (2006) contends however, that project success is difficult even when teams are co-located and this is made more problematic when geographically dispersed groups of dissimilar cultures are used. We may conclude from this that developing virtual, multicultural project teams is extremely demanding, yet if it is accomplished these teams are incredibly effective at achieving their goals. Emmitt and Gorse (2007) report that problems with communicating factual data in project teams have often been addressed by the development of higher-specification computers, better hardware and software, and better global telecommunication. Emmitt and Gorse (2007) also maintain, however, that many issues are left unaddressed in respect to teams that are both multicultural and working virtually. Examples may range from a lack of face-to-face communication that causes misunderstanding, to difficulties in developing relationships that may lead to a breakdown in trust and confidence (Weatherley 2006). This is particularly worrying for Mountech Gear as it is essential that the various project teams communicate successfully and work well together. There is no guarantee that, because communication and reporting structures have worked with head office in the past, they will do so in the future – especially with the culturally diverse make-up of the 'Green' project teams. These teams will need to establish their own versions of good practice and communications. Indeed they will need to acquire capacities that Ochieng and Price (2010, p451) suggest must be developed in such circumstances, which are: 'cultural sensitivity and the ability to manage and build future capabilities'. In their research Marquardt and Hovarth (2001) recognised that by harnessing the energy and synergy of people from various backgrounds, organisations can benefit as together these individuals stimulate creative ways of thinking in addressing the challenges and problems they encounter in project-based undertakings. Pearson and Nelson (2003) help us to summarise the implementation issues of the Green Project when they discuss, in general, the challenges facing project and change managers as: 'developing team cohesiveness; maintaining communication richness; dealing with co-ordination and control issues; handling geographical distance and dispersal of teams: and managing cultural diversity, difference and conflicts' (in Ochieng and Price 2010, p452).

The issue of communication-related risk factors (Lee-Kelley and Sankey 2008) is singled out by Reed and Knight (2010, p423); from their research, advice and comments from participants are highlighted thus:

- Particularly in large projects, communication is essential for efficient co-ordination.

- Lack of communication can lead to people 'not being on the same page' and 'working at cross purposes'.

- Lack of communication can lead to confusion that can add to costs and the time needed for projects.

- Having good communication with your client and group members is very important when working on any project.

- False starts from misunderstandings are expensive in terms of time and resources and they also create bad feeling within a team.

- Meeting overload is also a risk; projects that meet too much and work too little also suffer from poor morale.

ACTIVITY 18.7

IMPLEMENTATION ISSUES IN MOUNTECH GEAR'S 'GREEN PROJECT'

- Create a plan of how you would engage the project team as a virtual team.
- What processes or rules would you like to see in place?
- How will you deal with the cultural issues?
- Use the theory of Reed and Knight (2010, p423) as outlined above, to analyse the 'Green Project' of Mountech Gear.

18.6.4 DEVELOPING THE WORKFORCE

Learning has always been a key component of how and why Mountech Gear has prospered; whenever times have been hard, it has still encouraged training and development. This ethos was founded by Alex's father and the organisation is noted for its commitment to its employee development. Its current development strategy has been influenced by the work of Harrison (1997, 2002), who highlights the need for the whole business environment to be considered along with the business strategy and in line with the people development strategy (Figure 18.8). This has led to an increase in the organisational skills base in all three countries. Furthermore, management development has also been encouraged, as several of the existing staff have been funded to take Bachelor's or/and Master's degrees at local universities, and there is also a strong in-house training arm. However the 'Green Project' offers new challenges, as this particular initiative is about winning hearts and mind to engender change rather than training individuals in job-skill activities.

The opportunities for learning and development for many if not all the

Figure 18.8 Mountech Gear development strategy model

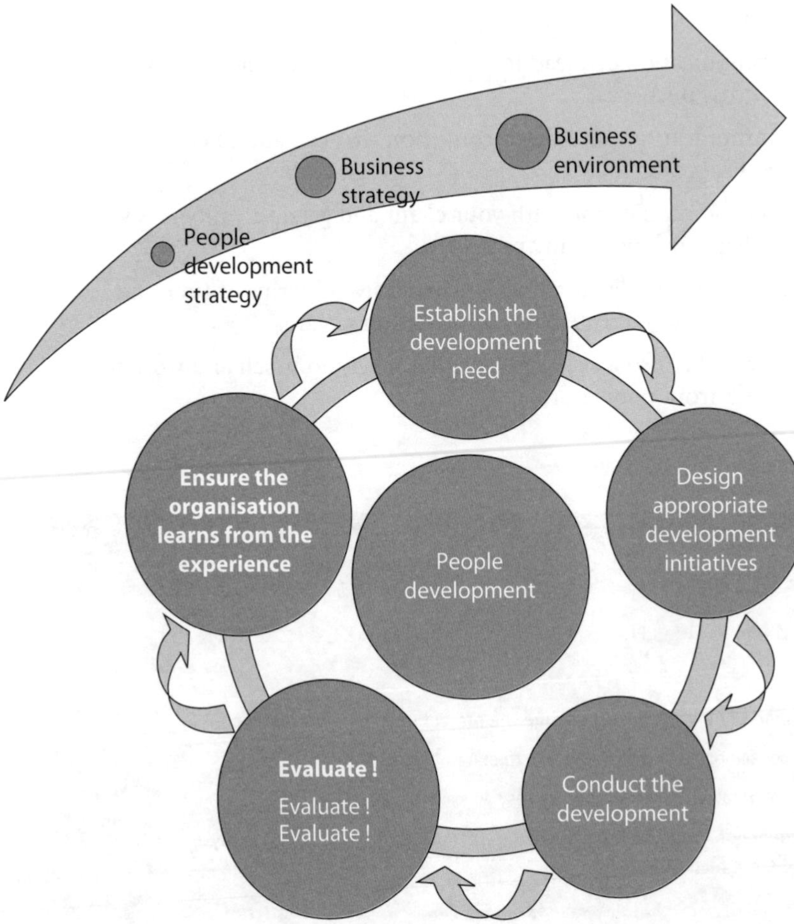

ACTIVITY 18.8

MATCHING STRENGTHS WITH OPPORTUNITIES

- Analyse the strengths, weaknesses, opportunities and threats facing Mountech Gear (Figure 18.9) with respect to:
  - its overall business strategy
  - its development strategy.

  Note: the analysis is stylised in triangular sections so that emphasis can be given to opportunities and strengths, which are placed centrally and higher up the pyramid respectively. In conducting this analysis, therefore, take the weaknesses and threats a step further by ensuring you consider how to overcome these problematic concerns. Or are they insurmountable?

Figure 18.9 Matching strengths with opportunities

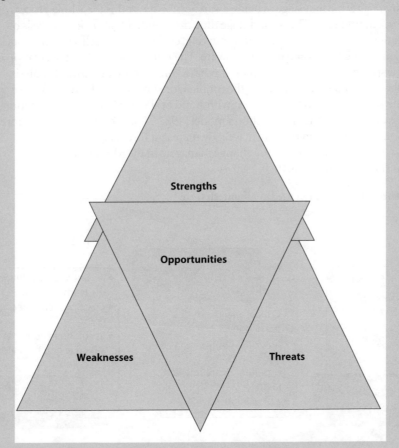

- Using the development cycle from the organisational development strategy (Figure 18.8), map out the types of activities in which various sections of staff will need to engage.
- List the resource implications for this process (you may wish to explore the scale of costs associated with such a budget).

participants in the 'Green Project' are immense. Likewise, staff in the whole organisation have the prospect of enhancing their understanding and appreciation of 'green/carbon-footprint' issues through training and then participating in the activities and initiatives the change managers will provide. The organisation as a whole will have to budget significant resources to make the project a success. The overall strategy and the development-strategy, therefore, must be calculated to recoup some of the money or/and to exploit this initiative in other ways.

18.6.5 JOURNALING

Loo (2002, p61) cites 'journaling' as a reflective learning devices for project managers (in our case we can add change managers) or indeed any management activity. He contends that reflective learning journals 'are useful tools that can help staff learn as individuals as well as members of a team' (Loo 2002, p66). The three-stage model of Scanlan and Chernomas (1997) can be adapted to help our purposes here. The model highlights the first stage as being awareness: without this the whole process of reflection cannot begin. The second stage they cite as individual critical analysis of the situation; this stage involves critical thinking, evaluation and self-examination, whilst continuing to become more self-aware. The third stage involves the creation of a new perspective or outlook that in itself is based on the previous critical analysis, the application of new knowledge to the problem or situation under the reflective gaze. The model seems to be consistent with Boud et al's (1985) model of reflection, as well as exhibiting elements of Schön's model (1987). Using elements of these three models, and journaling in particular, we may represent three stages of a reflective process which could be used by the change managers in the Mountech Gear case study, as shown in Figure 18.10.

Figure 18.10 Three-stage reflection used at Mountech Gear

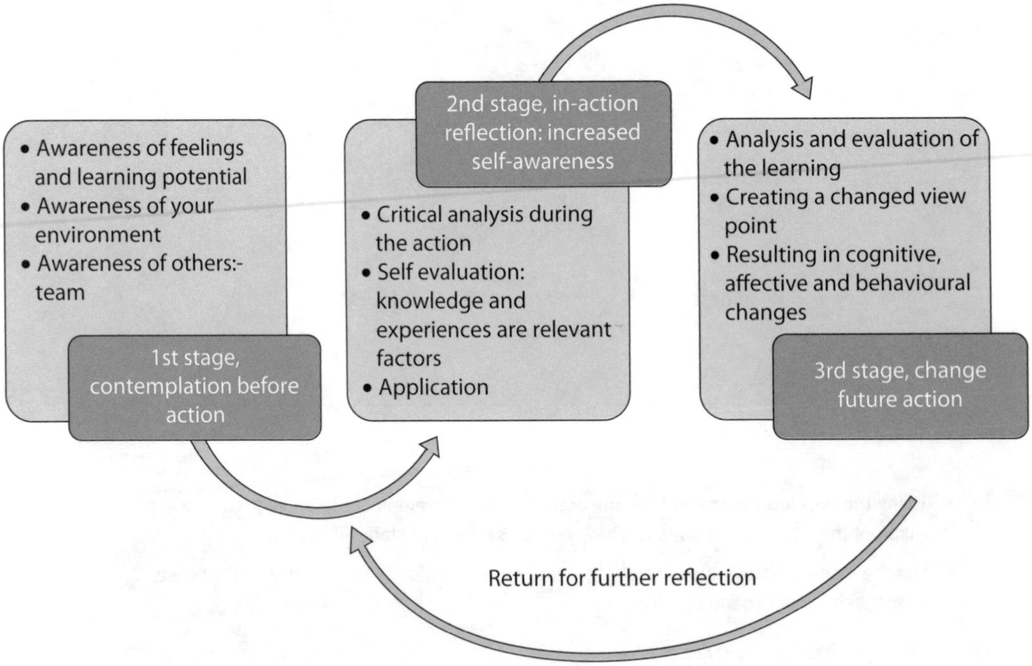

Loo (2002) contends that the expectation of individuals engaged in reflective practice is that they will become more effective in their job roles as both individuals and team members; in essence, reflective practice engenders change, and changes are adaptive. Therefore, during this adaptive process learning will have occurred. Reflective journals are part of this process.

Earlier in this book (see Chapter 1) we highlighted learning logs as relevant in assisting reflective practice and facilitating the collection of evidence of competence for portfolio or continuing professional practice purposes. Some of these previous models may be worth revisiting as they lead the reader to pose or answer certain questions. Loo's work gives a similar perspective when he poses several questions that he suggests help individuals stay focused when journaling. These questions are (Loo 2002, p62):

1. What was the learning situation or event?

2. What have I learned and how have I learned it?

3. How do I feel (good and bad feelings) about what I have learned?

4. How could I have learned more effectively/efficiently?

5. What actions can I take to learn more effectively/efficiently?

6. In what ways do I need to change my attitudes, expectations, values and the like in order to feel better about learning situations?

Keeping a log, as we have stated previously, is a tool to aid reflection: journaling takes the process to a deeper stage as it expects the writer to create an articulated narrative that is born out of the critical thinking and reflection on a specific learning event or a learning experience occurring over a period of time.

ACTIVITY 18.9

JOURNALING

- Considering the case study, how can keeping a learning journal help the change managers and the change leaders?

- Why would the company encourage such activity?

18.6.6 LEARNING AND TRAINING IN THE 'GREEN PROJECT' CASE STUDY

There is a significant amount of work for project/change managers and change leaders to do. They need to decide on a focused model for their development process, a training model and a vehicle whereby they can communicate with their colleagues. Review of the project at various stages is essential and this will form part of the course of action any project would take (highlighted in Section 18.2.3 above). However, they will need to be mindful of budgetary constraints, cultural differences and similarities, consider the relevant literature for change and conduct a development process that adds value to the organisation.

The CIPD (2009) document on *Promoting the value of learning* suggests a critical framework for assuring learning and development is best positioned, and its implications thought through to offer maximum sustainable value. The model shown in Figure 18.11 highlights the testing issues those who seek to develop staff must contemplate.

Figure 18.11 Levels of learning, training and development (LTD) provision

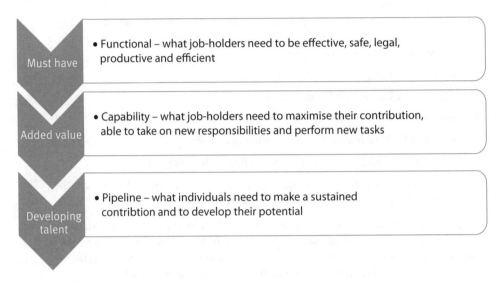

Must have
- Functional – what job-holders need to be effective, safe, legal, productive and efficient

Added value
- Capability – what job-holders need to maximise their contribution, able to take on new responsibilities and perform new tasks

Developing talent
- Pipeline – what individuals need to make a sustained contribtion and to develop their potential

Finally, we must recognise that learning is for everyone, and as far as the case study is concerned learning training and development is a key aspect which will support a successful outcome to the project.

ACTIVITY 18.10

DEVELOPING THE WORKFORCE

- Using relevant literature sources plan each stage of the development process:
    - learning needs
    - design
    - delivery
    - evaluation
    - and organisational development.
- Plan a learning process that caters for ongoing talent management of key individuals.
- Plan a presentation to senior managers to show how the workforce will be included in the development and communication process.
- How will you evaluate the success of the learning training and development aspect of the project?

18.6.7 CHANGE MANAGEMENT COMPETENCES

The case study has stated that certain staff will be designated as change managers. They are distinct from the project manager as they take on what Gareis (2010) describes as second-order change. This level of change relates to 'discontinuous, deep structural and cultural change' (Gareis 2010). According to Crawford and Nahmias (2010), second-order change requires a more insightful approach than first-order change. They cite first-order change as practised by project managers as direct and straightforward with a rational style, whereas second-order change, they suggest, requires different skills which include astuteness, sensitivity and interpersonal skills. Change managers focus on communication and engagement, encourage others to believe in the change, identify charismatic champions, train and develop staff, affect organisational culture, defuse opposition and manage the gambit of stakeholder expectation (Crawford and Nahmias 2010). Their research indicates that to be successful in this role a range of personal competences are required which are directly linked to the change activities on which change managers embark. These are: stakeholder management, leadership, team selection and development, planning, communication, decision-making and problem-solving, cultural awareness and project management skills (Crawford and Nahmias 2010).

18.7 SUMMARY OF SECTION 1

In this section we have covered a range of project-management-related topics, bringing together a wide range of skills that you will have build while studying this book. You should now be aware that projects are very widely used and you are likely to be either directly involved in carrying them through to completion, or indirectly involved by dealing with their organisational impact. You have been introduced to some of the language of project management such as 'project phases', 'stakeholders' and 'Gantt charts', and should be able to use these techniques in a basic, but nonetheless useful, manner.

You have also explored in more depth other areas introduced in previous chapters, particularly the management of change. Culture has also featured strongly in this section of the chapter, illustrated through the Mountech Gear case study which focused on the design and implementation of its 'Green Project'. Virtual teams have been discussed as part of this analysis. Much has been made of the human side of project management, with the importance of employee engagement being selected for particular emphasis. We expect that this case study will have highlighted the many skills required for the successful management of projects.

SECTION 2: THE WAY FORWARD: MANAGING YOUR TALENT AND CAREER

Section 1 above has focused on project management as an outlet in which managers and staff alike can practise and improve a wide range of skills. In

Section 2, we take a more personal approach, looking at how you can manage your talent and develop your career more effectively.

18.8 MANAGING YOUR TALENT

The concept of talent management (as highlighted in Chapter 1) was born out of an ongoing problem of skill deficiencies, shifting demographics, the increased diversity of the work force, and work–life balance initiatives (CIPD 2007), which have initiated a marked rise in the challenge organisations face to attract employees whom they believe will enhance the business. Two definitions follow:

> Talent consists of those individuals who can make a difference to organisational performance, either through their immediate contribution or in the longer term by demonstrating the highest levels of potential. (CIPD 2007, p3)

> The systematic attraction, identification, development, engagement/retention and deployment of those individuals with high potential who are of particular value to an organisation. (CIPD 2007, p3)

After appointing staff, therefore, organisations actively seek to develop and protect their investments by retaining them. They realise there must be a planned procedure for managing and challenging individuals with high potential: in other words to manage their talent. It is therefore our contention that you should do the same; manage your own talent by taking the initiative.

We can only encourage you to continue to develop or enhance your skills levels by seeking out experiences that enhance your 'human capital', even though they may be unpaid. Your motivation, however, is crucial to this endeavour, and we recommend you take a proactive attitude.

The online resources show what the Gordon Ramsay Holdings organisation did to define, identify and develop talent within their business (please access the companion website).

So, what can we learn from the Gordon Ramsay case? Table 18.2 gives suggestions for you to reflect upon.

Effective approaches to managing your talent can have substantial benefits to your overall career, your personal finances and your satisfaction, and we can only encourage you to take a strategic approach to the development of your career.

18.9 CAREER ENHANCEMENT

In the passage above we have set out certain strategic consideration regarding managing talent. The next step is to review what you can accomplish in terms of your career enhancement. You should note that the concept of 'career' is wide

Table 18.2 Talent management – learning points

Illustration	Therefore:	Outcome
Talent is specific	Give your own definition for managing your talent.	This is the start of your journey; use your definition to keep your focus.
Create a strategic plan	The plan enables you to map out what is possible and achievable.	It offers an opportunity to reflect on your aims and adjust your thinking accordingly.
Produce overarching learning outcomes	Review your learning needs: what skills do you believe you will/ should develop and enhance?	Allows for greater focus and more detailed reflection.
Gain support	This falls into three categories: • Personal: Find support from your friends, family and colleagues. • Organisational: Find out if your current employer (or one to which you have applied) has a good training and development record. • Conduct a cost–benefit analysis of your plans: can you rely on financial support from your current employer or will you be self funding?	Ensure you have the commitment and resources to develop your strategy.
Focused departmental support	Discuss your development with your line manager. Gain your line manager's commitment to act as a coach or mentor.	Act on the advice if you judge it is appropriate. Consider how you add value.
Self-help	Take the opportunities that are offered if you decide they are interesting and appropriate.	Develop an attitude that sustains you on the journey.

ranging; for instance Collin (2010, p258) asks us to conceptualise career as: 'the experience of continuity and coherence while the individual moves through time and social space'. This may sound rather like a Time Traveller/*Dr Who* definition (!) but the point is that your career is ideally coherent (ie linkages from one job to another over time) and is more than just a series of tasks – it also involves your experience with people.

Career development and enhancement is of consequence both to individuals and the organisations in which they work. To enhance your career constructively, it is useful to view its development in an organisational context. Recalling that organisations employ people to manage talent and careers, the CIPD (2003) gave this definition of career management: 'Planning and shaping the progression or movement of individuals within an organisation by aligning employee preferences and potential with organisational resourcing needs' (2003, p1).

Certainly, organisations are concerned about their 'talent-pool' whilst individuals are mindful of the job market and ensuring they gain development opportunities. Both, however, are interested in progression. It is therefore incumbent on both to think about future needs. On the one hand, the organisation must retain and build new talent through putting the right people in the right place and fostering development, thereby increasing its talent pool. On the other hand, individuals will seek an outlet for their skills and abilities as well as seeking to learn and grow with a view to future ambitions. These aspirations are necessary, even harmonious – on the surface as least, although these two perspectives can create conflicting interests. However, they can also initiate opportunity.

18.9.1 INDIVIDUAL PERFORMANCE

Individual performance systems help us focus on career enhancement by relating to individual performance in a managed way. Many of these systems are not perfect, as they are not always perceived by all to be equitable. However, most value an appraisal process as 'a well-established practice that drives decisions about pay, promotion, terminations, transfers and training needs' (CIPD 2010, p31) – in effect, the decisions that can make or break careers. Activity 18.11 is based upon a CIPD study (McMahon 2010, p31).

ACTIVITY 18.11

PERFORMANCE SYSTEMS AS THEY RELATE TO CAREER OPPORTUNITY

CIPD performance management suggestions	Your response and basis for discussion
1. Review the system It is farcical to expect performance management systems devised years ago to remain effective. Would you expect it of your IT, marketing or financial management systems? Given the current emphasis on such practices as coaching, mentoring, 360-degree feedback, competencies etc, systems should not be allowed to remain static and become ritualistic, as they will quickly fall into disrepute and be neglected. A full formal evaluation exercise is central to attaining an ongoing successful system.	Where do you and your organisation stand on this point? What influence do you have? Or, how can you influence decisions?

2. Engage the managers The support of management is crucial to a successful system. This can be secured by involving managers in the system's (re)design process and ensuring that they are reviewed on their performance management responsibilities. It also helps to secure feedback on the system's effectiveness, making sure the process and any associated training is conducive to upward feedback to identify where it is not being prioritised.	Are you or your managers involved in the system? Why/why not? Are there opportunities to give feedback?
3. Address interpersonal and interviewing skills Subjectivity, interpersonal skills and human judgments are inherent to the process of good performance management. Appropriate training, incorporating coaching and interviewing techniques, will help here. Reviews should start from jointly agreed objectives, focus on factual performance data rather than style or personality, encourage self-assessment and provide an appeal mechanism.	Does your appraisal system rest on subjectivity? Is appropriate development given to enhance your skills?
4. Define the objectives Performance management encounters difficulties when addressing a number of objectives. For example, when used for reward-related decisions, any developmental impetus it is intended to have is threatened. Playing judge and counsellor at the same time is highly problematic. It is best to opt for a combination of agreed, consistent and compatible objectives. Where this is not feasible, some organisations opt to conduct separate interviews at separate times of the year for the separate purposes. Furthermore, many organisations are now concentrating on non-financial measures and assessing key competencies.	Describe your organisation's processes. Are key objectives set and relevant competencies developed/measured?
5. Remember to follow up The manager who promises to provide additional resources or some form of personal development option is unlikely to enhance the system's reputation (or his/her own) by persistently failing to deliver. In the long run, the system is judged by the extent to which recommendations arising from review meetings actually materialise.	Is there a formalised follow-up process? Do you follow up if your manager does not?
6. Minimise paperwork Managers already feel inundated with paperwork and so resent the additional and often extensive form filling associated with performance management systems. This is exacerbated by the fact that the forms are not 'living documents', but remain stored in the archives of the HR department. So it is important to remember that the purpose of performance management is to motivate the employee for the purpose of improving organisational performance – not to generate more paperwork.	Give your analysis of this issue. Are you motivated by the current system practised in your organisation?
What can the organisation do with regard to any of the above?	What can you do in connection with any of the above?

It may be time for organisations to rethink these issues, especially in the current economic times where many companies are facing increasing pressures and struggling to survive. However, from an individual's perspective, being alert to these problems is essential because of the skills and talent people acquire; they will need a job/career where these attributes can be expressed. Otherwise the whole process may be career-demotivating rather than career enhancing.

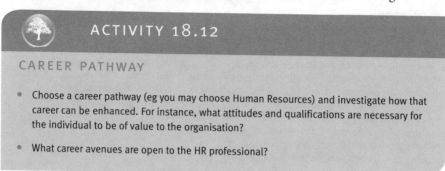

ACTIVITY 18.12

CAREER PATHWAY

- Choose a career pathway (eg you may choose Human Resources) and investigate how that career can be enhanced. For instance, what attitudes and qualifications are necessary for the individual to be of value to the organisation?

- What career avenues are open to the HR professional?

Career enhancement, we suggest, consists of four important variables: personal development, professional development, managing your performance, and progression. It is, however, important that individuals take an active role in their own career enhancement. The 'personal' element encourages us to maximise skills and abilities, while 'professional' aspects might include our general outlook and positive attitude to doing a good job; part of this may include an individual's

Figure 18.12 Career enhancement: personal, professional, performance, progression

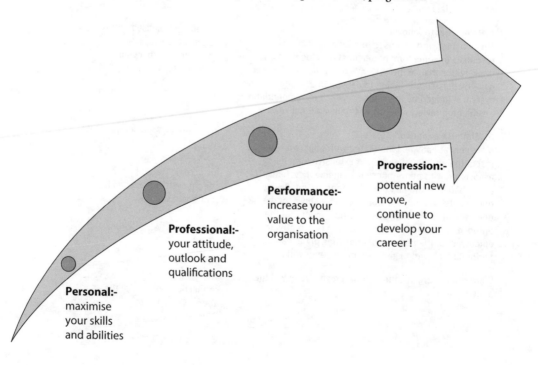

Progression:-
potential new move,
continue to develop your career !

Performance:-
increase your value to the organisation

Professional:-
your attitude, outlook and qualifications

Personal:-
maximise your skills and abilities

qualifications. The notion of adding value is prevalent in many organisational recruitment and employee engagement texts; an individual's own 'performance' therefore, can hold the key to his or her ability to progress. Last is the issue of 'progression'. Essentially this is optional, as some individuals may choose not to progress for personal reasons. However, we take the view that most people will be seeking further enhancement as well as opportunity for advancement. Therefore, progress may include actively seeking the next internal promotion, a sideways development move or a new project, or/and employment in another organisation that offers a challenge and is an all-important, enhancing step.

18.10 CONTINUOUS PROFESSIONAL DEVELOPMENT

Much has been written about CPD in Chapter 1; therefore, this section only seeks to expand and draw conclusions about some of those themes. An in-company or professional CPD programme may have many interesting and focused elements, which will differ from one organisation or professional body to another. However, we can expect that some of those more general features will remain. These general features of CPD engagement may include/require:

- Time allocated to this investment: consider this as important as any other aspect of development activity.
- The development itself should be owned and managed by you, the learner, although there may be organisational and/or professional-body support.
- It should emanate from your current situation and learning needs, such as your work role, or your forward-looking aspiration and your current learning state.
- Objectives should be set that encompass both your individual aims and those of the organisation; keep them clear and focused.
- Ensure reflective practice is emphasised particularly from a learning standpoint.
- Actively search for ways to improve performance; ensure you develop continuously.

Many professional bodies encourage individuals to be credited with formal qualifications alongside and including their CPD, although CPD is also concerned with informal and self-directed learning. Rothwell and Arnold (2005) suggest that, unfortunately, active engagement in CPD is not matched by the supposedly high value members of professional bodies (such as the CIPD) place on CPD. Nonetheless, they continue to form a clearly established characteristic of the contemporary organisation as well as the 'professional career' (Kanter 1989, p508).

18.11 SUMMARY OF SECTION 2

This section has outlined the important concept of talent management, illustrating how it might be applied through the use of case studies and encouraging you to consider your own CPD and career enhancement. It has shown how you might analyse your career enhancement, with particular reference to links with personal and professional development, personal performance and progression.

18.12 CONCLUSION

Chapter 18 has been a challenging chapter. In the first section it not only introduced the area of project management skills but also sought to integrate these with the skills developed in previous chapters. It has shown through a range of activities how leaders and managers need to develop a wide array of attributes and skills. In the Mountech Gear case study you were challenged to research certain areas of work and to think critically. In answering questions relating to this case you have had to reflect about working cross-culturally in a virtual team configuration and how to communicate with distinct groups of people: in effect you have practised a range of solution-oriented techniques to managing and leading work-based decisions and situations. The second section of Chapter 18 has picked up issues originally discussed in Chapter 1, which set out to illustrate how the use of good leadership skills can play a part in enabling you to manage your own talent and to be active in enhancing your own career. The ideas expressed have given a contemporary perspective of the rewards and challenges relating to the vital journeys of engagement and development. It is now your turn to continue to practise the skills that you have developing while studying this book and to actively manage your talent and the enhancement of your career.

KEY LEARNING POINTS

From this chapter we can conclude the following overarching points:

- Project management skills are applicable to all managers.
- Projects involve not only technical change but people-related change.
- Stakeholder analysis helps achieve success in projects.
- Scheduling of activities is a basic skill for all managers.
- Multinational teams require careful consideration of cultural factors.
- Personal and career development can be enhanced through engaging in project/change management.
- Personal and career development can be enhanced through talent management.

EXPLORE FURTHER

A rather brief but practical book for some additional tips and pointers to other sources of information specific to projects is: Deeprose, D. (2001) *Smart things to know about managing projects*, Oxford: Capstone – read the chapter on 'Power vs persuasion'.

Still regarded by technical-oriented project managers as one of the key textbooks to read is: Kerzner, H. (2009) *Project management: a systems approach to planning, scheduling, and controlling*, 10th ed. Hoboken, NJ: John Wiley and Sons. Interestingly, it devotes a whole chapter to culture – Chapter 19: 'Managing cultural differences'.

Cockburn, A (2002), *Agile software development*, Addison-Wesley ISBN 0–201–69969–9 considers incremental learning in software projects. Although unusual, this book is also interesting for its discussion of software development teams.

For cross-cultural issues we recommend you read the works by Geert Hofstede and Fons Trompenaars (eg Hofstede et al 2010, Trompenaars and Hampden-Turner, 1997) and subsequent applications.

18.13 CONCLUDING REMARKS AND RECOMMENDATIONS

These concluding remarks will serve as a conclusion to the text book as a whole. At this stage you should ask yourselves several fundamental questions:

- What have I learned?
- How will I apply what I have learned?
- Why have I engaged with this text?
- When will I feel confident to employ the techniques?

The purpose of this book has been to enhance learning using active engagement and participation throughout. In short, we have taken you through a learning process and taken a reflective stance throughout, encouraging reflective thinking when applying and experiencing the cases and activities. Many of the chapters have asked you to examine your own current practices and to self-critique and self-evaluate. The intention has been to give you a much deeper insight into what attributes you currently possess and those you may wish to enhance still further. A further point when considering yourself, is that of self-confidence. Personal experience provides a route for experimentation, allowing you to learn from your own experience as well as from the experiences of others; we hope that the activities you have experienced throughout this book have helped to raise your confidence levels and serve as an impetus for future leadership skills development.

18.14 REFERENCES

ALFES, K., TRUSS, C., SOANE, E.C., REES, C. and GATENBY, M. (2010) *Creating an engaged workforce*. January, Research Report ref.5097, 2010. London: CIPD.

ALI, A.S., ANBARI, F.T. and MONEY, W.H. (2008) Impact of organisational and project factors on acceptance and usage of project management software and perceived project success. *Project Management Journal*. Vol. 39, No.2, pp5–33.

BARRASS, R. (2002) *Study! A guide to effective learning, revision and examination techniques*. 2nd ed. London: Routledge.

BOUD, D., KEOGH, K. and WALKER, D. (eds). (1985) *Reflection: turning experience into learning*. London: Kogan Page.

BRINER, W., HASTINGS, C. and GEDDES, M. (1996) *Project leadership*. Aldershot: Gower.

BROWAEYS, M.J. and PRICE, R. (2008) *Understanding cross-cultural management*. London: Pearson Education Ltd.

BURNS, R. (1998) *Doing business in Asia*. Australia: Addison Wesley Longman.

CHEN, M. (1995) *Asian management systems: Chinese, Japanese, and Korean styles of business*. London: Thunderbird.

CHENG, J., PROVERBS, D.G, and ODUOZA, C.F. (2006) The satisfaction levels of UK construction clients based on the performance of consultants. *Engineering, Construction Architectural Management*. Vol. 13, No. 6, pp567–583.

CHILD, J. (1994) *Management in China in the age of reform*. Cambridge: Cambridge University Press.

CHOW, I.H. (2004) The impact of institutional context on human resource management in three Chinese Societies. *Employee Relations*. Vol. 26, No. 6, pp626–642.

CIPD. (2003) *Managing employee careers: issues, trends and prospects*. Survey. London. CIPD.

CIPD. (2005) *HR: where is your career heading*. London: CIPD.

CIPD. (2006) *Talent management*. Available online at: www.cipd.co.uk/researchinsights [accessed 16 April 2010].

CIPD. (2007) *Research insight: talent management*. London: CIPD.

CIPD. (2009) *Promoting the value of learning in adversity*. Available online at: http://www. cipd.co.uk/guides [accessed 21 April 2010].

CIPD. (2010) *Creating an engaged workforce*. Available online at: www.cipd.co.uk/guides (accessed 13 August 2010).

COCKBURN, A. (2006) *Agile software development*. 2nd ed. Harlow, Essex: Addison Wesley.

COLLIN, A. (2010) Learning and development. In J. Beardwell and T. Claydon (eds), *Human resource management: a contemporary approach*. 6th ed. London: Prentice Hall, pp235–282

CRAWFORD, L. and HASSANER NAHMIAS, A. (2010) Competencies for managing change. *International Journal of Project Management*. Vol. 28, No. 4, pp405–412.

EARLEY, P.C. and MOSAKOWSKI, E. (2000) Creating hybrid team cultures. *Academy of Management Journal*. Vol. 43, No. 1, pp26–49.

EMMITT, S. and GORSE, C.A. (2007) *Communication construction teams*. Oxford: Taylor and Francis.

EXECUTIVE AGENCY EDUCATION, AUDIOVISUAL and CULTURE. (2009) *Tempus*. Available online at: http://eacea.ec.europa.eu/tempus/index_en.php [accessed on 24 May 2010].

GALLAGHER, K. (2006) *The Lesotho Highlands Water Project*. CIPD Case Study Club. London: CIPD.

GAREIS, R. (2010) Designing changes of permanent organisations by process and projects. *International Journal of Project Management*. Vol. 28, No. 4, pp314–327.

HARRISON, R. (1997) *Employee development*. London: IPD.

HARRISON, R. (2002) *Learning and development*. 3rd ed. London: CIPD.

HOFSTEDE, G., HOFSTEDE, G.J. and MINKOV, M. (2010) *Cultures and organizations: software of the mind*. 3rd ed. New York/London: McGraw Hill.

HOUSE, R.J., HANGES, P.J., JAVIDAN, M., DORFMAN, P.W. and GUPTA, V. (eds). (2004) *Leadership, culture and organisations: the GLOBE study of 62 societies*. Thousand Oaks, CA: Sage.

KAHN, W.A. (1990) Psychological conditions of personal engagement and disengagement at work. *Academy of Management Journal*. Vol. 33, No. 4, pp692–724.

KANTER, R.M. (1989) Careers and the wealth of nations. In M.B. Arthur, C.T. Hall and B.S. Lawrence (eds), *Handbook of career theory*. Cambridge: Cambridge University Press, pp505–521.

LEE-KELLEY, L. and SANKEY, T. (2008) Global virtual teams for value creation and project success. *International Journal of Project Management*. Vol. 26, No. 1, pp51–62.

LEGRIS, P. and COLLERETTE, P. (2006) A roadmap for IT project implementation. *Project Management Journal*. Vol. 37, No. 5, pp64–75.

LOCKETT, M. (1988) Culture and the problems of Chinese management. *Organization Studies*. Vol. 9, No. 4, pp475–496.

LOCKYER, K. and GORDON, J. (2007) *Project management and project network techniques*. 7th ed. Harlow: Pearson.

LOO, R. (2002) Journaling: a tool for project management training and teambuilding. *Project Management Journal*. Vol. 33, No. 4, pp61–66.

LUO, Y. and CHEN, M. (1997) Does guanxi affect company performance? *Asia Pacific Journal of Management*. Vol. 14, No. 1, pp1–16.

MARQUARDT, M.J. and HOVARTH, L. (2001) *Global teams*. Palo Alto, CA: Davies-Black.

MAY, D.R., GILSON, R.L. and HARTER, L.M. (2004) The psychological conditions of meaningfulness, safety and availability and the engagement of the human spirit at work. *Journal of Occupational & Organisational Psychology*. Vol. 77, No. 1, pp11–37.

MAYLOR, H. (2005) *Project management*. 3rd ed. Harlow: Pearson.

MCMAHON, G. (2010) How to ... manage performance. *People Management Magazine*. 6 May, p31.

MICHAILOVA, E. and WORM, V. (2003) Personal networking in Russia and China: Blat and guanxi'. *European Management Journal*. Vol. 21, No. 4, pp509–519.

OCHIENG, E.G. and PRICE, A.D.F. (2010) Managing cross-cultural communication in multicultural project teams. *International Journal of Project Management*. No. 28. No. 5, pp449–460.

PEARSON, J.C. and NELSON, P.E. (2003) *Human communication*. New York: McGraw Hill.

PINTO, J.K. (2007) *Project management: achieving competitive advantage*. New Jersey: Pearson.

PROJECT MANAGEMENT INSTITUTE. (2007) *A guide to the project management body of knowledge: PMBOK guide*. 4th ed. Pennsylvania: Project Management Institute.

REED, A.H. and KNIGHT, L.V. (2010) Effect of a virtual project team environment on communication-related project risk. *International Journal of Project Management*. Vol. 28, No. 5, pp422–427.

ROTHWELL, A. and ARNOLD, J. (2005) How professionals rate 'continuing professional development'. *Human Resources Management Journal*. Vol. 15, No.3, pp18–32.

ROWLINSON, S., and CHEUNG, Y.K. (2008) Stakeholder management through empowerment. *Construction Management and Economics*. Vol. 26, No. 6, pp611–623.

SADLER-SMITH, E. and LEYBOURNE, S. (2006) The role of intuition and improvisation in project management. *International Journal of Project Management*. Vol. 24, No. 6, pp483–492.

SCANLAN, J.M. and CHERNOMAS, W.M. (1997) Developing the reflective teacher. *Journal of Advanced Nursing*. Vol. 25, No. 6, pp1138–1143.

SCHAUFELI, W.B. and BAKKER, A.B. (2004) Job demands, job resources, and their relationship with burnout and engagement: a multi-sample study. *Journal of Organisational Behaviour*. Vol. 25, No. 3, pp293–315.

SCHNEIDER, S.C. and BARSOUX, J.L. (2003) *Managing across cultures*. 2nd ed. Harlow: FT Prentice Hall.

SCHEIN, E.H. (2004) *Organisation cultural and leadership*. 3rd ed. San Francisco, CA: Jossey-Bass.

SCHÖN, D.A. (1987) *Educating the reflective practitioner*. San Francisco, CA: Jossey-Bass.

TAYEB, M. (2003) *International management*. Harlow: Pearson.

TROMPENAARS, F. and HAMPDEN-TURNER, C. (1997) *Riding the waves of culture: understanding cultural diversity in business*. 2nd ed. New York/London: McGraw Hill.

TRUSS, K., SOANE, E.C. and EDWARDS, C. (2006) *Working life: employee attitudes and engagement 2006*. London: CIPD.

WEATHERLEY, S. (2006) *Managing multicultural project teams*. Available online from GDS Infocentre at: www.gdsinternational.com/infocentre/artsum.asp?lang=en&mag=182&iss=149&art=25863 [Accessed 4 July 2010].

Name index

Note: this index contains the names of individuals and organisations discussed in the book, but not of authors of references cited in brackets and not discussed. Where there are three or fewer authors of a work, all are listed (even when their name does not appear in the text); for four or more authors, only the first is given. Names of fictitious or fictionalized individuals and organisations are not listed.

Subject index